MIDRASH UNBOUND

THE LITTMAN LIBRARY OF
JEWISH CIVILIZATION

Dedicated to the memory of
LOUIS THOMAS SIDNEY LITTMAN
*who founded the Littman Library for the love of God
and as an act of charity in memory of his father*
JOSEPH AARON LITTMAN
and to the memory of
ROBERT JOSEPH LITTMAN
who continued what his father Louis had begun
יהא זכרם ברוך

'*Get wisdom, get understanding:
Forsake her not and she shall preserve thee*'

PROV. 4: 5

*The Littman Library of Jewish Civilization is a registered UK charity
Registered charity no. 1000784*

MIDRASH UNBOUND
Transformations and Innovations

◆

EDITED BY
MICHAEL FISHBANE
AND
JOANNA WEINBERG

London
The Littman Library of Jewish Civilization
in association with Liverpool University Press

The Littman Library of Jewish Civilization
Registered office: 4th floor, 7–10 Chandos Street, London W1G 9DQ

in association with Liverpool University Press
4 Cambridge Street, Liverpool L69 7ZU, UK
www.liverpooluniversitypress.co.uk/littman

Managing Editor: Connie Webber

Distributed in North America by
Oxford University Press Inc., 198 Madison Avenue
New York, NY 10016, USA

First published in hardback 2013
First published in paperback 2016

© The Littman Library of Jewish Civilization 2013

All rights reserved.
No part of this publication may be reproduced,
stored in a retrieval system, or transmitted, in any form or by
any means, without the prior permission in writing of
The Littman Library of Jewish Civilization

This book is sold subject to the condition that it shall not, by way
of trade or otherwise, be lent, re-sold, hired out or otherwise circulated
without the publisher's prior consent in any form of binding or cover
other than that in which it is published and without a similar condition
including this condition being imposed on the subsequent purchaser

Catalogue records for this book are available from the
British Library and the Library of Congress
ISBN 978–1–906764–9–13

Publishing co-ordinator: Janet Moth
Copy-editing: Lindsey Taylor-Guthartz and Philippa Claiden
Proof-reading: Agnes Erdos
Index: Caroline Diepeveen
Designed and typeset by Pete Russell, Faringdon, Oxon.

CONTENTS

List of Contributors — vii

Note on Transliteration — viii

Introduction — 1
MICHAEL FISHBANE AND JOANNA WEINBERG

PART I
ORIGINS AND SUBSURFACE TRADITIONS

1. Midrash and the Meaning of Scripture — 13
   MICHAEL FISHBANE

2. The Hand upon the Lord's Throne: Targumic and Midrashic Perceptions of Exodus 17: 14–16 — 25
   ROBERT HAYWARD

3. Unwashed Hands: A Midrashic Controversy in the Gospel of Matthew — 41
   PIET VAN BOXEL

4. 'Tradunt Hebraei': The Problem of the Function and Reception of Jewish Midrash in Jerome — 57
   ALISON SALVESEN

5. Midrash in Syriac — 83
   SEBASTIAN BROCK

PART II
LATER MIDRASHIC FORMS

6. *Piyut* and Midrash: Between Poetic Invention and Rabbinic Convention — 99
   MICHAEL FISHBANE

7. The Mourners for Zion and the Suffering Messiah: *Pesikta rabati* 34 — Structure, Theology, and Context — 137
   PHILIP ALEXANDER

8. The *Toledot yeshu* as Midrash — 159
   WILLIAM HORBURY

9. Storytelling as Midrashic Discourse in the Middle Ages 169
ELI YASSIF

10. Performative Midrash in the Memory of Ashkenazi Martyrs 197
IVAN G. MARCUS

PART III
MEDIEVAL TRANSFORMATIONS

11. Midrash in a Lexical Key: Nathan ben Yehiel's *Arukh* 213
JOANNA WEINBERG

12. Rashi's Choice: The Pentateuch Commentary as Rewritten Midrash 233
IVAN G. MARCUS

13. The Pendulum of Exegetical Methodology: From *Peshat* to *Derash* and Back 249
SARA JAPHET

14. Midrashic Texts and Methods in Tosafist Torah Commentaries 267
EPHRAIM KANARFOGEL

15. Zoharic Literature and Midrashic Temporality 321
ELLIOT WOLFSON

PART IV
EARLY MODERN AND MODERN TRADITIONS

16. The Ingathering of *Midrash Rabbah*: A Moment of Creativity and Innovation 347
BENJAMIN WILLIAMS

17. Midrash in Medieval and Early Modern Sermons 371
MARC SAPERSTEIN

18. Rabbi Judah Loew of Prague and his Attitude to the Aggadah 389
JACOB ELBAUM

19. The Destruction of the Temple: A Yiddish Booklet for the Ninth of Av 407
JACOB ELBAUM AND CHAVA TURNIANSKY

20. Midrash in Habad Hasidism 429
NAFTALI LOEWENTHAL

Index 457

CONTRIBUTORS

PHILIP ALEXANDER
Emeritus Professor of Post-Biblical Jewish Studies, University of Manchester

PIET VAN BOXEL
Emeritus Curator of Hebraica Collections, Bodleian Library, University of Oxford, and Emeritus Fellow/Librarian, Oxford Centre for Hebrew and Jewish Studies

SEBASTIAN BROCK
Emeritus Reader in Syriac Studies and Professorial Fellow of Wolfson College, Oxford

JACOB ELBAUM
Professor Emeritus of Hebrew Literature, The Hebrew University of Jerusalem

MICHAEL FISHBANE
Nathan Cummings Professor of Jewish Studies, University of Chicago

ROBERT HAYWARD
Professor in the Department of Theology and Religion, University of Durham

WILLIAM HORBURY
Emeritus Professor of Jewish and Early Christian Studies, University of Cambridge

SARA JAPHET
Professor of Bible, The Hebrew University of Jerusalem

EPHRAIM KANARFOGEL
E. Billi Ivry Professor of Jewish History, Bernard Revel Graduate School of Jewish Studies, Yeshiva University

NAFTALI LOEWENTHAL
Lecturer in Jewish Spirituality, Department of Hebrew and Jewish Studies, University College London

IVAN MARCUS
Frederick P. Rose Professor of Jewish History, Yale University

ALISON SALVESEN
University Research Lecturer, Oxford University, and Polonsky Fellow in Jewish Bible Versions, Oxford Centre for Hebrew and Jewish Studies

MARC SAPERSTEIN
Professor of Jewish History and Homiletics, Leo Baeck College, London

CHAVA TURNIANSKY
Professor Emerita, Department of Yiddish, The Hebrew University of Jerusalem

JOANNA WEINBERG
Reader in Hebrew and Jewish Studies, University of Oxford, and Catherine Lewis Fellow in Rabbinics, Oxford Centre for Hebrew and Jewish Studies

BENJAMIN WILLIAMS
Faculty of Oriental Studies, University of Oxford

ELLIOT WOLFSON
Abraham Leberman Professor of Hebrew and Judaic Studies, New York University

ELI YASSIF
Zvi Berger Professor of Jewish Folk-Culture, Jewish Studies School, Tel Aviv University

NOTE ON TRANSLITERATION

The transliteration of Hebrew in this book reflects consideration of the type of book it is, in terms of its content, purpose, and readership. The system adopted therefore reflects a broad approach to transcription, rather than the narrower approaches found in the *Encyclopaedia Judaica* or other systems developed for text-based or linguistic studies. The aim has been to reflect the pronunciation prescribed for modern Hebrew, rather than the spelling or Hebrew word structure, and to do so using conventions that are generally familiar to the English-speaking reader.

In accordance with this approach, no attempt is made to indicate the distinctions between *alef* and *ayin*, *tet* and *taf*, *kaf* and *kuf*, *sin* and *samekh*, since these are not relevant to pronunciation; likewise, the *dagesh* is not indicated except where it affects pronunciation. Following the principle of using conventions familiar to the majority of readers, however, transcriptions that are well established have been retained even when they are not fully consistent with the transliteration system adopted. On similar grounds, the *tsadi* is rendered by 'tz' in such familiar words as barmitzvah. Likewise, the distinction between *ḥet* and *khaf* has been retained, using *ḥ* for the former and *kh* for the latter; the associated forms are generally familiar to readers, even if the distinction is not actually borne out in pronunciation, and for the same reason the final *heh* is indicated too. As in Hebrew, no capital letters are used, except that an initial capital has been retained in transliterating titles of published works (for example, *Shulḥan arukh*).

Since no distinction is made between *alef* and *ayin*, they are indicated by an apostrophe only in intervocalic positions where a failure to do so could lead an English-speaking reader to pronounce the vowel-cluster as a diphthong—as, for example, in *ha'ir*—or otherwise mispronounce the word.

The *sheva na* is indicated by an *e*—*perikat ol*, *reshut*—except, again, when established convention dictates otherwise.

The *yod* is represented by *i* when it occurs as a vowel (*bereshit*), by *y* when it occurs as a consonant (*yesodot*), and by *yi* when it occurs as both (*yisra'el*).

Names have generally been left in their familiar forms, even when this is inconsistent with the overall system.

INTRODUCTION

MICHAEL FISHBANE AND JOANNA WEINBERG

THE PURPOSE of the present volume is to enlarge the perspective on Midrash and midrashic creativity—marking its arcs and turns across the vast breadth of Jewish literature, through close studies of its varieties and transformations—and also to trace various offshoots from the tree of rabbinic Midrash now embedded in non-Jewish literatures, as well as seeds that may have been strewn abroad to yield similar if not related produce. It is our considered opinion that Midrash is a fundamental form of Jewish culture, and maintains an identifiable coherence and integrity in all its expressions over the course of two millennia. To bring this vision to a wider public, we have solicited this scholarly anthology.

In this vast enterprise, there was no possibility of exemplifying every kind of expansion or revision that exists, so we have aimed rather to provide typical cases across a multi-millennial spectrum; correspondingly, the guiding focus precluded a full complement of comparisons to non-Jewish literatures, but rather we chose to indicate some key cases in point along the way. In all, the rich diachronic spread shows a vibrancy inherent in a fundamental Jewish exegetical genre, and the selected parallels outside this cultural canon suggest new avenues for comparative study. If new research deepens and expands the many topics treated here, the goal we have envisioned will be happily realized.

*

In what follows, we wish to guide the reader to an overview of the scope of this book and to indicate its structure. There will be no attempt to summarize in advance and in general terms what must be studied in detail and sequentially, nor any attempt to relate each case to any fixed set of definitions about Midrash—as an exegetical practice and a literary genre. These latter have been subject to numerous variations over time, and in an anthology covering two full millennia and dealing with diverse topics and cultural concerns, this would have constrained the topics and impeded the studies represented here. Within the framework of general guidelines concerning the matrix of Midrash overall, each author was encouraged to develop his or her topic as case-specific expositions of the phenomenon, with the result that textual hermeneutics and literary forms play themselves out in a host of ways. As the reader will discover, that matrix includes a core attitude towards Scripture as an authoritative cultural source, explained and re-applied to new periods and situations; it expands to include a relationship of authority to other sources of tradition (including Midrash itself) that needed explanation or adaptation to contemporary life—but always, somehow, remains connected to Scripture at the core. From one point of view, horizontal in nature, this cultural creativity expands from its scriptural centre like a wide-winged accordion, with numerous harmonics put in play; from a more vertical perspective, Midrash in its fullest sense is layered like archaeological strata upon its scriptural bedrock, so that its study involves soundings into its fathomable depths. Each image has its own authenticity.

Overall, the book is subdivided into four parts, indicative of four fundamental historical periods of development. Part I treats 'Origins and Sub-Surface Traditions', and roughly covers the first to fifth centuries CE. Here certain foundational elements of literary genre, translation, displacement, and diffusion are considered, covering several cultures and expanding outwards from the ancient Palestinian core. Part II takes up 'Later Midrashic Forms', and covers roughly the fifth to eleventh centuries. The studies here focus on a deepening and thickening of the midrashic enterprise as it expands into liturgy, theological polemics, narrative elaborations, and cultural performance. Gradually, the centre shifts westwards towards Europe in the early Middle Ages. In Part III assorted 'Medieval Transformations' are taken up, including the development of intense lexical annotation of midrashic texts and traditions, their acute scholastic examination, assorted uses of midrashic teachings for cultural pedagogy, and creative uses of Midrash to deepen the sense of history and time—in a word, to actualize the immediacy of Scripture and its events and teachings. More or less, this part covers the high Middle Ages of Franco-Germany and Spain during the twelfth and thirteenth centuries. Part IV considers some of the 'Early Modern and Modern Traditions' of Midrash, and its transformations. In major ways Midrash re-enters culture through the event of printing and the collection and annotation of texts and traditions; it also returns to the synagogue through diverse philosophical filters in sermons or other compositions, or through a variety of popular texts in the vernacular or spiritual sermons delivered in native languages. This period covers (mostly) the sixteenth to twentieth centuries in central and western Europe, and eventually also in North America. Most notable in this part is the gradual return of Midrash to its popular base in the community, and the concern to adapt midrashic materials to diverse cultural mentalities. This does not mean that all the expressions are of a 'popular' nature, in the thinnest sense of the term. For the textual density of Jewish culture was always a considerable factor, even where there is an appeal to non-scholastic audiences. Just how this cultural pedagogy expressed itself will be seen repeatedly and in diverse manifestation in the following pages.

But first, we offer a slightly closer look at the contents of the volume.

Part I opens with an essay on Midrash as such, taking up the subject from a wide-ranging perspective, and considering basic phenomenological, stylistic, and exegetical features of the subject (Michael Fishbane, Chapter 1). The concern is to set the stage for the fundamental importance of Midrash in Jewish literature and culture. For rabbinic interpreters, a major moment is the closure of the scriptural canon, which establishes the principal authoritative textual source for all subsequent developments. This closure established a fixed source, so that all interpretation was to unfold through an examination of its topics and contents, a correlation of its verbal and literary features, and a filling in of legal, theological, and narrative gaps (real or perceived). This is not to say that the motivations for exegesis always arose from the text itself (contemporary circumstances were also crucial); but it is to say that the solutions and adaptations had to be correlated with the source in one way or another. Here is the beginning of Judaism as a textual culture of interpretation, built around citations and discussions of citations, and an ongoing tradition of discourse and debate. The primary setting for this was the study house, guided by sages and their disciples, and the synagogue, through preaching on various scriptural lections (for the sabbath, the festivals, and other notable occasions). Much of this material was sifted and condensed and ordered in various collections. These anthologies are primary resources for our knowledge of the play of Scripture in antiquity.

But there were other venues and avenues of cultural production. Subsequent chapters in this part take up such matters. Thus the simultaneous translation of scriptural lections (recited in the synagogue) into the Aramaic vernacular, variously infused by midrashic sources (legal and theological traditions) that enter its warp and woof (Robert Hayward, Chapter 2), was another way in which the populace was presented with the fund of learning deriving from the study hall, or heard their own legends and concerns integrated into the scriptural sources. Indeed, from the notable variety of these translations (Targumim) we can witness the play of Midrash in different settings, and its oral mediation and diverse emphases. Comparison with the classical genres of midrashic material provides us with a striking glimpse into how the latter was filtered and re-presented in the synagogue.

The reception of this material (Midrash and Targum) and its rhetorical uses beyond the synagogue are a matter of much cultural and historical significance. Such diffusion accounts for the infiltration and penetration of midrashic forms and content into a host of New Testament texts—the adaptations of which, in such new settings, attest to the ongoing and conditioning power of Midrash, as well as its capacity to undergird transformed legal and theological content—in particular those fascinating instances where the recognition of midrashic argumentation and practice clarifies the New Testament source itself and even provides a witness to rabbinic topics before their midrashic redaction (Piet van Boxel, Chapter 3). And more: there were other pedagogical streams and tributaries that carried this content further afield, preserving fragmentary but precious Jewish teachings in the various corpora of the Church Fathers. Thus it was through assorted sub-surface channels and teachers that the narrative materials of the Jews (*iudaicae fabulae*) and exegetical points found their way to Jerome, who is, paradoxically, a valued tradent of these materials—whether he received them simply to support his literal exegesis, or also maligned them to support his sense of their 'corporeal' character or emphases (Alison Salvesen, Chapter 4).

And so, by hook or by crook, midrashic content finds its way into Latin, forming invaluable deposits of Jewish scriptural exegesis. But whether such diverse factors as diffusion or conversion were involved or not, Christian Syriac church sermons and poems also reflect and refract Jewish themes on scriptural topics. Indeed, just how similar terms and topics and styles made their way to the preachers of the eastern Church is not always clear or certain, but the range of similarities is most striking and significant (Sebastian Brock, Chapter 5). In this regard, one may wonder whether certain dialogue forms recorded there derive from older (compressed) dialogues in the midrashic corpus, and even, in due course, influenced Jewish synagogue poetry, which gradually expanded these midrashic discourses in a similar poetic way (in *piyut*, see below). Such comparative matters need further research, and suggest paths of diffusion and reintegration as Jews and Christians (including those in the Byzantine Church, as evidenced by Romanos the Melodist) variously incorporated theological elements and doctrines into their liturgical prayers. Above ground or below it, and through various mouths and tradents, old midrashic procedures were preserved and invigorated. Scriptural thinking was conducted in midrashic ways by Jews and Christians east and west; and their various anthologies are all part of the unfolding literary history of the midrashic genre(s) in late antiquity.

When we turn, in Part II, to midrashic features in early medieval sources, we see several striking modes of consolidation, adaptation, and transformation, showing the ongoing and deep impact of Midrash on Jewish religious and cultural life. Seen anew, the genre was revised accordingly—'re-vision' in its twofold sense.

Just above, we mentioned the phenomenon of Jewish synagogue poetry (*piyut*) as a venue for the reuse of Midrash. Indeed the reception and transformation of midrashic materials there are extraordinary, with a classical *floruit* between the fifth and eleventh centuries. Here we see a new form of midrashic pedagogy: not through the study hall or sermon, but via the forms of the liturgy. Week by week and festival by festival, rabbinic traditions were sung in the synagogue by the cantors (*ḥazanim*), who now became the authoritative tradents and teachers of this polymorphic material, which they presented without reference to the originators or disciples of this exegesis. The variety of content and forms is astounding, as is the stylistic architecture and exegetical virtuosity of these poems. Now, in the sacred-service, all the traditions of law and theology were funnelled and promulgated, so that the open canon of Midrash was transmitted to the populace as a whole in a great act of cultural pedagogy (Michael Fishbane, Chapter 6). But this did not spell the end of Midrash itself and its vibrant creativity, for indeed, in this period, a kind of second classicism occurs, wherein older sermons were expanded and thickened, new forms were added and integrated, and, especially in the context of festival occasions, any number of theological issues were highlighted. In such ways, new attitudes were formed and formulated with regard to challenging questions of divine providence, suffering, and messianism—indeed, these materials were also gathered into new wholes as mini-clusters and anthologies within anthologies for new times and purposes (Philip Alexander, Chapter 7). Even, on occasion, the tensions of theology (beyond all intra-Jewish sectarianism) bubbled up into a new and frothing boil, with the challenges of Christianity and its messianic claims (even the life-history of Jesus himself) taken up and lambasted by midrashic pyrotechnics (William Horbury, Chapter 8). In this way Midrash, theology, and quasi-narrative forms constitute a new whole.

However, in materials more suited to Jewish pathos and sensibility, beginning with the Crusades and the ensuing martyrdoms, we begin to see other forms of Midrash. For example, types of storytelling emerge as a new midrashic genre (a kind of 'midrashic discourse'), with old legends and memories (derived from Hellenistic antiquity and the midrashic imagination) rather than scriptural lemmata serving as the fulcrum of creative adaptations to new historical conditions and the challenges of medieval life and its trials (Eli Yassif, Chapter 9). Indeed, it is only through this lens that one can adequately appreciate the nuances and values that accrue, the new ideals that are promulgated, and the overall flow of the topics. And here one must add that one of the ways in which historical memory and cultural values were reformulated was through chronicles (about the Crusade martyrs especially) that are cases of 'performative midrash', particularly where these martyrs cry out liturgical phrases in the course of a sacred and sanctified death (Ivan Marcus, Chapter 10). In such cases, the culture adapted older midrashic models of martyrological death (such as that of Rabbi Akiva) and produced texts in which these precedents were portrayed as enacted—both to sanctify and justify such acts of self-sacrifice and to establish further performative models for the culture. The line between historical fact and theological-midrashic model thus collapses: it is a midrashic death that is both enacted and memorialized in the chronicles and sacred poetry (infused in the chronicles and recited in the synagogue). Now Midrash is not something for the mind and spirit alone, but provides ideals for ritual action—alive in their performance and the portrayals of that performance. Not just recited or believed, in the medieval period Midrash is also alive as lived, lived because alive; narratives of the body, embodied in narrative acts.

This brings us to the third part of this collection, and to what we broadly dub 'medieval transformations' between the twelfth and thirteenth centuries. The cases offered are to be considered types of a vast wellspring of cultural activity. We choose to begin here once again with the issue of diffusion and diversity and ingathering. The variety of written and oral sources that underlie all the previous genres and expressions gave a typically medieval expression of near-encyclopaedic synthesis in the great compendium and dictionary of Nathan ben Yehiel in Italy in the early twelfth century. Streams of tradition well up in this reservoir of rabbinic culture, culled from all manner of materials. Sifting and listing, adducing and explaining—the great rabbinic corpora (fluid and congealed) were variously accounted for and interpreted under the headings of words and terms. Now the tradition is 'spread out' as it were, for teaching, studying, and analysis (Joanna Weinberg, Chapter 11). Who could deny the importance of the study hall and rabbinic study in Italy then, and who could think it a mere way-station of traditions on their way from the east to the west of Franco-Germany? It is more than a bridge to Ashkenaz; it is indeed a veritable cultural link as well, perhaps part of the channel of modes of study and meanings of traditions.

But if the modes of alphabetical listing and lexical explanation are among the salient virtues of Nathan's classic *Arukh*, midrashic traditions were put to quite another cultural service further to the north—principally in the context of Bible study, and especially as other methods such as *peshat* (plain or contextual sense) gained a new vibrancy and dominance. Several models are evident. For example, the integration of midrashic content into the flow of the meaning of the biblical text to yield its lexical sense and cultural significance was achieved in a landmark manner by Rashi (Ivan Marcus, Chapter 12). Indeed, we find a bold attempt to sift matrials from the Midrash that would not merely work in tandem with the received biblical text but actually fill out its 'straightforward' or even historical sense. Here, again, Midrash provides new modes of cultural pedagogy and actualization of meaning in the service of the scriptural sense, for if we pay careful attention we may discern how Midrash was used in the transmission and emphasis of certain religious values and ideals. The instruction of Scripture, its *peshat*, thus often involved passing this sense through the prism of the (selected) *derash*—as much for edification as for education.

It is thus of major cultural moment to consider how the *peshat* could be correlated or reconciled with the *derash*, or midrashic meaning, and to see how the two could be integrated and presented in coherent ways. Different teachers show how diverse oscillations might be employed to structure a solution, as sometimes the *peshat* provides the core, fundamental armature of scriptural meaning, while on other occasions its truth was deemed either to undergird or to function together with the *derash*. In striking and significant ways this oscillation has been compared here to the swing of a pendulum—inasmuch as the *peshat* may appear now in a more dominant, now in a more recessive relationship to the *derash*, as in Rashi, or as the primary feature, as in the case of his grandson Rashbam (Sara Japhet, Chapter 13). Specific instances exemplify the point in this family history. But as the reader will see, such oscillations between *peshat* and *derash* extend to other modes of integration and mediation, whereby one or the other type (now the *derash*, now the *peshat*) was either ignored or excluded by particular commentators. Thus, at certain radical poles, the core *peshat* of the Song of Songs might shed all reference to the *derash*, just as, alternatively, some philosophical interpretations of this text eviscerated the *peshat* completely. But between these extremes a more dynamic swing of the pendulum marked a number of cultural arcs—sometimes the *peshat* is the deep (and variously perceived) ground of the *derash*, and sometimes the *derash* lives conjointly with the *peshat*, in deft exegetical conjunctions.

Throughout this vast enterprise, Midrash remains alive, now driving the interpretation and now taking a back seat. In all cases, the older source is re-presented and re-visioned.

All this is especially the case in the use of Midrash in the Bible study practised among the Tosafists of Franco-Germany. These scholars sifted the midrashic traditions in relationship to Scripture, analysed their content, and transformed their various differences and similarities into analytic prototypes that needed to be reconciled in one way or another. Earlier scholarship, which focused more on talmudic debates and comments, largely ignored the enormous production and range of midrashic analysis of these great talmudic masters of the twelfth and thirteenth centuries. It now finds its consummate scholarly redemption (Ephraim Karnarfogel, Chapter 14). Hereby we get a vibrant sense of the books available to the Tosafists (such as Rabbi Baruch ben Isaac or Rabbi Isaac ben Samuel of Dampierre, known as 'Ri Hazaken'), and their thinking on any number of cases and issues. Now we have a clearer idea of the particular midrashic sources available to them, and how they were taken up in different schools and places. Indeed, through these commentaries we are able to get a fuller sense of the channels of transmission and reception, and of the modes of biblical study and analysis, as Scripture was correlated with Midrash in these most scholastic of rabbinic schools.

The usage of Midrash in the mystical corpora is a vast topic, and its integration into the classic of Spanish kabbalah, the Zohar, has various levels of significance. Sometimes the text of a Midrash is cited in order to be transcended, giving birth to insights into the highest, supernal realms; sometimes it provides the hidden armature of equally recondite and deeply concealed truths. But in all cases Scripture is actualized anew, so that if, in rabbinic Midrash, distinct times and places are collapsed into unexpected temporal unities (typological or synchronic conjunctions), in instances of mystical Midrash the arcs of time loop in transcendental embrace, with preternatural and eternal points intersecting with human time, as humans and the divine interact and embody (or manifest) midrashic elements (Elliot Wolfson, Chapter 15). Despite all appearances, the zoharic corpus comprises another midrashic classicism—reviving older sermonic forms and textual exegesis in new patterns; transforming the mode of anthology of cases into living midrashic dialogue; and projecting the focus beyond history as such (as singular events) into temporal co-ordinates that actualize hidden truths of divinity, as embodied by events and persons on earth. In this way, Midrash fosters a mysterious hologram: whether one looks upwards or downwards, the same lineaments of supernal mystery may be discovered or discerned—for they all 'are', and all are found in, Scripture.

The final part of this collection brings us to the early modern and modern periods, and their uses of Midrash. Once again, the selection of topics is exemplary and selective, intended to provide a further intellectual sampling of this subject and stimulate further avenues of research. Just as we began Part III with a study of the impetus given to Midrash and midrashic literature by the lexical examinations and ingathering of sources by Rabbi Nathan in his *Arukh*, so we begin this part with a corresponding act of ingathering and examination. This time it is the ingathering of manuscripts and their collation to produce the enormous *Midrash Rabbah*, covering the Pentateuch and the Five Megillot.[1] The beginning of the sixteenth century saw the appearance of these great printed anthologies—an editorial and publishing enterprise that stimulated new scholarly activities, including textual annotations (varia and glosses), emendations, homiletic expositions, and commentaries (Benjamin Williams, Chapter 16). With this printing event and the related study of the sources, the *Rabbah* anthologies assumed near-canonical status and achieved new significance in the great library of Jewish thought. One might even see this multifold event as the forebear of the rebirth of midrashic studies in the nineteenth century.

Independent of this momentous development, and spreading out to the east and west, are the diverse philosophical interpretations of Midrash that span the thirteenth to seventeenth centuries. Beginning in western Europe, we find significant sermons in France, Spain, and Amsterdam by such notable homilists as Rabbi Jacob Anatoli, Rabbi Shem Tov ibn Shem Tov, and Rabbi Saul Morteira, respectively. The reception of the folk figures and anthropomorphic images portraying God and theology in the Midrash was transposed into a rational key for synagogue audiences, thus giving them new access to the older *midrashim* and educating them in their 'proper' interpretation (Marc Saperstein, Chapter 17). Of similar concern was the vigorous intellectualism and rationalism brought to bear on the same midrashic features by the great Rabbi Judah Loew (Maharal) of Prague (Jacob Elbaum, Chapter 18). Here was a bold purification of seemingly offensive figures and an attempt to redignify the Midrash as a species of philosophical rationality. But if the air of Midrash became rarefied at the summit of such activity, it thickened into a rich *mélange* at the other end of the spectrum—this being the folk and vernacular (Yiddish) rendition of the Midrash in eastern Europe, particularly for women in the synagogue (Jacob Elbaum and Chava Turniansky, Chapter 19). And if the targumic tradition thus spans two millennia, a decisive shift is notable as one moves across the centuries. In antiquity, midrashic glosses slowly invade the (translated) scriptural texts, like buds of imagination seeking light and sprouting from their folk-roots. By contrast, in the early modern arena of the Yiddish Pale (beginning in the nineteenth century), the midrashic growth of centuries overruns the old lectionary texts in profusion, and produces a new, rewritten Bible.

[1] The biblical books of Song of Songs, Ruth, Lamentations, Ecclesiastes, and Esther, which are recited in synagogue on Passover, Shavuot, Tishah Be'av, Sukkot, and Purim respectively.

A final moment, itself a reprise of older patterns, is also evident in the hasidic uses of Midrash from the early modern period onwards, specifically from the eighteenth century up to the present day. Now, again, midrashic matters enter sermons, if only as the catalysts that spiritualize them in a new mystical key—be these the ethico-psychological readings produced by some hasidic masters or the more arcane kabbalistic readings developed by others (Naftali Loewenthal, Chapter 20). Thus, whether through popular homiletic *derushim* (pneumatic sermons), or via more elite and elaborate *ma'amarim* (kabbalistic recitatives), the midrashic corpus was received anew, revised for new audiences and purposes, and used to generate currents of personal and national redemption (even messianism). It might be said that in these cases the midrashic materials were again believed to conceal new content—now mystical—and thereby again provide access to the inmost keys of Jewish thought and belief. *Dor dor vedoreshav*—each generation produced its midrashic types and prototypes, in protean abundance.

*

We are most grateful to the many authors who wrote and rewrote their essays, who gladly joined the enterprise and saw its merits, and who in many cases were very patient, as the initial project gradually expanded and new intellectual spaces had to be filled—thus delaying the final product. Most forbearing and kind overall was the gracious staff of the Littman Library, who understood that scholarship takes time and that scholarly integrity must be protected. We thank Lindsey Taylor-Guthartz and Philippa Claiden for their conscientious and meticulous copy-editing of the book. It is our hope that this volume will serve its intended purpose, and itself produce a new momentum in the study and diffusion of the genre we all love—Midrash.

PART I

ORIGINS AND SUBSURFACE TRADITIONS

ONE

MIDRASH AND THE MEANING OF SCRIPTURE

MICHAEL FISHBANE

AN OLD TRADITION found in the *midrash Sifrei Deuteronomy* (343) presents a powerful image of the giving of the Law: God's word appears as a fire that emerges from his right hand, encircles the nation, and returns; the fire is then transferred by God from his left hand to his right, whereupon it is inscribed upon the tablets of Moses.[1] In this way the sages gave mythic realism to the scriptural phrase *miyemino esh dat lamo*, 'from His right hand [there emerged] a fiery law for them [the nation]' (Deut. 33: 2). Another passage, stating that 'the voice of the Lord carves out flames of fire' (Ps. 29: 7), is expressly added to indicate the world-encompassing power of divine speech. This verse from the Psalms serves here to reinforce the main teaching that the tablets were chiselled by tongues of fire (the verse was thus presumed to say that God's 'voice . . . carves out *the Decalogue by flames of fire*'). Elsewhere, Rabbi Akiva gave just this explication as an independent account of God's fiery words at Sinai.[2] The editor of our *Sifrei* passage has chosen to subordinate this teaching to his interest in the heavenly arm as an agent of the inscription.

In our midrashic myth God's word emerges from the divine essence as visible fire and takes instructional shape as letters and words upon the tablets. The written law is thus an extension of divine speech—and not merely its inscriptional trace. This identification of God's utterance and Torah is the hermeneutical core of Judaism. Midrash works out the details.

An earlier version of this chapter was published as 'Midrash and the Nature of Scripture', in Michael Fishbane, *The Exegetical Imagination: On Jewish Thought and Theology* (Cambridge, Mass.: Harvard University Press, 1998), 9–21.

[1] *Sifre on Deuteronomy*, ed. Louis Finkelstein (New York, 1969), 399.

[2] See *Mekhilta derabi yishma'el*, 'Yitro', 9 (*Mechilta d'Rabbi Ismael*, ed. Hayim Horowitz and Israel Rabin, 2nd edn. (Jerusalem, 1960), 235). The first of the anonymous traditions in *Sifrei Deuteronomy*, dealing with the arm, is attributed to R. Shimon bar Yohai in *S. of S. Rabbah*, 1: 2, §2; in this midrashic corpus the aforenoted Akivan tradition is presented by R. Berekhiah, in the name of R. Helbo, and the fire is said to have come directly to God's right hand.

The sages were alive to this point. In a teaching joined to a version of the aforementioned myth, Rabbi Azariah and Rabbi Judah bar Simon (in the name of Rabbi Joshua ben Levi) pondered the question of how much the Israelites actually learned at Sinai (*S. of S. Rabbah* 1: 2, §2). They proposed that the people learned *all* the 613 (principal) commandments of (rabbinic) Judaism at that time. This interpretation links the Ten Commandments of the tablets to all the teachings that will emerge through Jewish discourse. Such a notion is first found explicitly in Philo;[3] but something of it can already be found in tannaitic teachings of the first two centuries CE. Thus, in a variation of the above-noted *Sifrei* teaching, we learn that the meaning of the word *yevoneneihu*—'He [God] instructed him [Israel]' in Moses' Song (Deut. 32: 10)—is that Israel learned 'how much Midrash was in it [each decalogic Word], how much halakhah was in it, how many *minori ad maius* arguments were in it, and how many textual analogies were in it'.[4] Significantly, this phrase also appears in *Song of Songs Rabbah* in connection with what the angel of the Law (according to Rabbi Yohanan), or the Word itself (according to the rabbis), addressed to each Israelite as they heard each of the Ten Commandments.[5]

The Decalogue is thus a paradigmatic text, and Sinai a paradigmatic moment, for Midrash: not only does something of the mysterious fullness of divine speech comprise the letters of the Decalogue, but its revelation is accompanied by a prolepsis or encapsulation of the future achievement of rabbinic interpretation. The written text thus mediates between the original verbal revelation of God at Sinai and the ongoing discourses of the sages in history. Paradoxically, the divine Word unfolds through human speech. As exegetical act and event, this human speech is Midrash.

And more: as a field of totality, the tablets metonymically represent the truths of the whole culture. They may therefore be compared to the shield of Achilles which was fashioned for the hero by the god Hephaestus (*Iliad*, Book XVIII). The sea-like border design indicates the boundaries of civilization, and the images on the various panels depict its achievements and values. The shield is therefore more than battle armour for a day: it rather depicts the world for which the hero fights, the entire symbolic order rescued from chaos by human industry and virtue.

Similarly, to understand the shapes on the tablets is to understand the truths of God's teachings for all generations—which are the truths of Judaism insofar as the tradition is truly founded upon a scriptural foundation. As a fixed and final formulation, the tablets are therefore a canon-before-the-canon. That is to say: just as the closing of Scripture in later times meant that 'all' was 'in it' (as an old epigram put it, Mishnah *Avot* 5: 25) and nowhere else, so too is 'everything' already on the tablets. In this sense, divine instruction was virtually complete at Sinai. Ongoing

---

[3] *De Decalogo*, §§19, and 154; also *De specialibus legibus*, I, §1.

[4] *Sifre on Deuteronomy*, ed. Finkelstein, 313.

[5] This text adds that the Israelites were also informed of the judgments, punishments, and rewards consequent on obedience to Jewish law.

interpretations (of these or other Words) do not therefore add to God's original voice, but rather give it historical and human expressions. This is an essential pre-understanding of the sages, and it is fundamental to the work of Midrash.[6]

I

Taken as a whole, biblical Scripture is a complex system of written signs whose original significations make sense through the interrelation of words in their primary context—beginning with the phrase and including the sentence, the paragraph, and so on. As an anthology of cultural materials spanning a millennium, a good many of the units were originally independent of each other, and they circulated in distinct circles of instruction and tradition (such as the priestly or wisdom schools). Because of the long period of literary development, many of the materials allude to predecessor traditions and rework them in a number of ways.[7] In these cases, a new network of intertextual relations is produced, and the context of the later of the two biblical texts is greatly expanded.

In the terms of structural linguistics, we may restate this as follows. The texts of Scripture derive from any number of conditioning linguistic factors; and these, as the set of open possibilities, constitute the potentials of biblical 'language' (*langue*). By contrast, the realizations of these possibilities in actual expressions (and by this is meant the meanings constructed from the potentials through the conjunction of specific letters, words, or syntax) is biblical 'speech' (*parole*)—though, of course, this does not mean oral speech only (even if the written text is derived from an oral expression, purports to quote it directly or indirectly, or has special status when recited aloud).[8] Naturally, as a document of great historical and cultural range, Scripture is made up of many such speeches—now collected in units and genres. The books (*ta biblia*) of these anthologies constitute the Bible.

The word *torah* is indicative of these matters. At one end of the spectrum it marks very specific, short instructions of law in the priestly sources, which are attributed to Moses as speaker of divine speech; but 'Torah' also marks, eventually, the entire book of Deuteronomy as Moses' summary instruction of divine speech through him (along with historical details); and finally, by the post-exilic period, the 'Torah of Moses' serves as an even more comprehensive designation (as in Mal. 3: 22).[9] By contrast, in wisdom circles the term *torah* originally indicated some

---

[6] A classic formulation of this paradox is Targum Onkelos' transformation of the biblical statement that God spoke only the Decalogue at Sinai 'and no more' (*velo yasaf*) (Deut. 5: 18) into the rabbinic truth that God's voice resounded 'without end' (*vela fasik*); and cf. Rashi's gloss ad loc.

[7] I have discussed such matters at length in Fishbane, *Biblical Interpretation in Ancient Israel* (Oxford, 1985).

[8] For the relationship between *langue* and *parole*, see Ferdinand de Saussure, *Cours de linguistique générale*, 3rd edn. (Paris, 1967). For these terms in the wider context of structural poetics (and such issues as relational identity and binarism), see Jonathan Culler, *Structuralist Poetics* (New York, 1975), ch. 1.

[9] The 'Book of Moses' in 2 Chr. 35: 12 refers to the traditions mentioned from the books of Exodus and Deuteronomy in v. 13. See my discussion in *Biblical Interpretation*, 134–7.

didactic instruction—grounded in experience of the natural world—which was then written down as a cultural maxim. On the surface, such instructions have nothing whatever to do with Moses' divine speech. Indeed, the task of the moral teachings is to make one worldly-wise—not holy or pure. The incorporation of gnomic and priestly *torah*s in one cultural anthology shows just how diverse Scripture is.

The closure of the scriptural canon (by the beginning of the Common Era) changes matters fundamentally. It is a transformative event, for with this closure there can be no new additions or supplementations to the biblical text from without. Indeed there is now an 'in' and an 'out'—a within and a without, so to speak. And since God's Word (*parole*) is deemed comprehensive and sufficient for human culture in all its historical diversity, it is only within the existent divine words that new meanings can arise. Accordingly, the effect of the closure is to transform the many separate units (and contexts) of biblical 'speech' into the *one* speech (and context) of Scripture. Everything must be found in it.

The result is that the extended (but bounded) speech of Scripture is reconceived as the multiform expressions of divine revelation—beginning with the individual letters of its words, and including all the phrases and sentences of Scripture. These all become the constituents of possibility in the opening of Scripture *from within*. In the process, to return to our structuralist diction, the *parole* of Scripture becomes the *langue* of each and every midrashic *parole*. In other words, Scripture becomes a closed and unified system of language with particular possibilities for linking words and phrases. Midrash is the name for the speech-acts that arise from this system. Hence, just as each *parole* of Moses is an actualization of the divine *langue* through him, so each midrashic *parole* (properly) spoken by the sages is an actualization of the divine *langue* of the scriptural canon. Thus is the midrashic word inscribed within the language of Scripture.

The opening of Scripture from within radically transforms the grammaticality of the text: the ordinary connection between the letters of a word, and between the words of a sentence, is broken. These components now become extraordinary.[10] Indeed, each letter has (virtual) anagrammatical significance; each word may encode numerous plays and possibilities; and each phrase has any number of potential correlations within Scripture. Midrash determines the sense of each component through extending the context of the component to the entirety of Scripture (thus original setting or sequence is often immaterial). Letters in one place may therefore be related to letters in another; and words or phrases from a given part of Scripture are revealed through midrashic methods to be speaking about the same thing as words and phrases found elsewhere. The emergent enchainment (*ḥarizah*) of possibilities thus dramatizes what is always the presupposition of midrashic exegesis: that all Scripture is one interconnected whole. Accordingly, the use of the word *torah* in the book of Proverbs not only means that its epigrams may be correlated

---

[10] See my discussion of Scripture as a *Sondersprache* in Fishbane, *The Garments of Torah: Essays in Biblical Hermeneutics* (Bloomington, Ind., 1989), ch. 3.

with teachings of the 'Torah of Moses', but also means that the divine elements in Moses' words are related to the wise words of Solomon. Both Solomon's Proverbs and Moses' Torah are aspects of the divine *langue*—which is Scripture. Midrash establishes these correlations or equivalences again and again.

Historically considered, Ezra is the first master of the midrashic *parole*—for he 'enquires' (*doresh*) of the 'Torah of the Lord' (Ezra 7: 10) as former generations 'enquired' of God for a living oracle (2 Kgs 22: 5, 8). His act (and those of his rabbinic heirs) thus conjures new meanings from God's *langue*.[11] No part is too small to become a whole. Come and hear.

II

The account of creation in the book of Genesis is framed by a prologue and epilogue. It opens with the words *bereshit bara*, 'in the beginning' God 'created' the heavens and the earth (Gen. 1: 1); and it concludes with the coda about the heavens and earth *behibare'am*, 'when they were created' (Gen. 2: 4a). Struck by the form of this last word, the *midrash* in *Genesis Rabbah* (12: 10) ponders the agency of the divine creation. Grammatically, *behibare'am* combines the preposition *be* (used in the temporal sense of 'when') with an infinite absolute form of the verb *bara* (in the *nifal* form) and a plural suffix. And precisely because of this grammatical form, some sages intuited a parallel with the phrase *bereshit bara* in Genesis 1: 1.

Genesis 1: 1 had long since been interpreted to suggest that God 'created' (*bara*) the world 'with' or 'for the sake of' (*be*)*reshit* (variously deduced as Torah, the throne of glory, Moses, and so on).[12] A similar anagrammatical construction (though of more esoteric import, as we shall see) was proposed for the word *behibare'am* in Genesis 2: 4a by Rabbi Abbahu in the name of Rabbi Yohanan. In his view, we may find encoded here the teaching that God 'created' (*bara*) the heavens and earth 'with' or 'by means of' (*be-*) the letter *heh*. The meaning of this reading emerges from the whole teaching. It is reported as follows.

Behibare'am. Rabbi Abbahu [interpreted] in the name of Rabbi Yohanan: 'With [the letter] *heh* He created them. Just as this *heh* is the only non-lingual letter [being merely aspirated], so did the Holy One, blessed be He, create His world merely "with the word of YHVH" [Ps. 33: 6]—and immediately "the heavens were made" [ibid.].'

Rabbi Yudan Neshiya enquired of Rabbi Samuel bar Nahman, and asked: 'Since I have heard that you are an expert in aggadah, explain the meaning of [the phrase] "Extol Him who rides the clouds; the Lord [*beyah*] is His name" [Ps. 68: 5].' He answered: 'There is no place in [all] His dominion [*biyah*; Greek *bia*][13] without an

---

[11] For the relationship between oracular inquiry and exegesis, see Fishbane, *Biblical Interpretation*, 245.

[12] Cf. *Gen. Rabbah* 1: 4; see *Midrash Bereshit Rabba*, ed. Judah Theodor and Chanoch Albeck, 3 vols. (Jerusalem, 1965), i. 6–7.

[13] See the commentary *Minḥat yehudah* in *Bereshit Rabba*, ed. Theodor and Albeck, 108. *Midrash tehilim hamekhuneh shoḥer tov*, ed. S. Buber (Vilna, 1878–92), para. 114, p. 471 (note, ad loc.) renders

appointed authority—[thus] the *ekdikos* [public prosecutor] is responsible for the dominion in his city,¹⁴ [and] the *agba bastes* [*apparitor*] is responsible for the dominion in his city.¹⁵ Similarly: Who is responsible for the dominion [*biyah*] on high? *Beyah* is His name, *biyah* is His name.' [Rabbi Yudan] answered: 'O woe for those [sages] who have died but are not forgotten!; for I had [also] enquired of Rabbi Eleazar, and he did not explain it so, but rather [interpreted the word with reference to Isa. 26: 4] "for in Yah [*beyah*] the Lord [YHVH] you have an everlasting Rock [*tsur olamim*]". [Meaning:] With these two letters [*y(od)* and *h(eh)* of His name] the Holy One, blessed be He, created [*bara*; but rendering *tsiyer*] His world.'¹⁶

Now we do not know if this world was created with [the letter] *heh* and the world to come with the *yod*; but on the basis of the way Rabbi Abbahu in the name of Rabbi Yohanan explained *behibare'am* as *beheh bera'am*, surely this world was created with the [letter] *heh*. And whereas from the [graphic] shape of this *heh*, which is closed on all [three] sides but open from below, we have an indication that all the dead descend to Sheol; [so too] from the tip on the upper side we have a hint of their resurrection; and from the spatial gap in the upper corner we may [also] learn [a lesson of hope] for penitents. [Thus we may conclude:] The world to come was created with the *yod*. And just as its stature is bent over, so [will] the stature of evildoers be bent over and their faces darkened in the world to come—as we read [in Scripture]: 'Then man's haughtiness shall be humbled' [Isa. 2: 17].¹⁷

This teaching appears as a typical midrashic construction, combining a variety of voices and opinions (let us call each of them a microform) into one integrated piece (let us call the whole a macroform). First we have Rabbi Abbahu's (received) teaching that God created the world with the letter *heh*. This point is supplemented with the linguistic comment that *heh* is an aspirant. The point is apparently indicative of the ease of God's creation; but the proof-text (from Ps. 33: 6) adduced in support of this is perplexing, since it speaks of creation by the word. But appearances are deceiving in Midrash. I am inclined to suppose that this scriptural proof was initially cited to extend the view of creation through the letter *heh*. For a close reading of that phrase (in light of the ensuing discussion) suggests that it was understood quite

---

'livelihood' or 'sustenance', following Alexander Kohut's *Aruch Completum* (Vienna, 1926), s.v. *byyh*, ii. 45*a*. William Braude, *The Midrash on Psalms* (New Haven, Conn., 1959), ii. 520 n. 7, renders 'power' (Greek *bia*), so that God is 'He who wields power' (*biastes*). Braude adduces the observation of Saul Lieberman that this term is equivalent to Latin *defensor civitatis* or *defensor loci*. This would link *bia* to other juridical functions mentioned in the text (see below). Daniel Sperber, *A Dictionary of Greek and Latin Terms in Rabbinic Literature* (Jerusalem, 1984), 68–9, has adduced evidence to render 'justice'.

[14] Greek *ekdikos*; see *Minḥat yehudah* in *Bereshit Rabba*, ed. Theodor and Albeck, 108, sub-note 2, and the lexical evidence in Sperber, *Dictionary of Greek and Latin Terms*, 32.

[15] Greek *ekbibastes* ('one who executes justice'); see Saul Lieberman, note in *Tarbiz*, 36 (1967), 401, and Sperber, *Dictionary of Greek and Latin Terms*, 31–2.

[16] For the text and variants, see *Gen. Rabbah* 12: 10 (Theodor–Albeck edn., 107–9).

[17] I have followed the edition of Theodor and Albeck, pp. 107–9. For manuscript variants and alternative suggestions concerning the names of the regents, see the *variae lectiones* and the commentary of *Minḥat yehudah* on p. 108.

concretely to mean that 'the heavens were created [by God] by means of the [letters of the] word YHVH [the Lord]'—*heh* being one of those letters. And because this citation also goes on to say that 'all the hosts [were created] by the breath of His mouth', the primary teaching was supplemented by a second one about aspirants. The proof-text now does double duty: it links Rabbi Abbahu's teaching to the discussion of the letters of God's name, and it mentions the hosts who reappear as the regents of God's dominion. As is typical, the midrashic teaching is laconic. It springs from Scripture and is reanchored in Scripture. Between these poles of authority the sage mediates his message.

The ensuing queries of Rabbi Yudan seem to be an abrupt *non sequitur* after Rabbi Abbahu's teaching—a shift which even the citation of Psalm 33: 6 (as meaning that God created the heavens with his name) only partially mitigates. Moreover, though Rabbi Samuel's teaching of *beyah* as a Greek homonym is consistent with multilingual puns in the Midrash,[18] it is certainly irrelevant to this macroform as a whole. The discussion of Psalm 68: 5 is adduced merely as a prelude to Rabbi Eleazar's exegesis. The editor then cleverly brings the discussion back to the opening teaching by reconciling Rabbi Eleazar's position (that God created the world with the letters *yod* and *heh*) with that of Rabbi Abbahu (who asserted that the world was created with the one letter *heh*). The differentiation of the letters (one for this world, the other for the world to come) leads to a bit of graphology. The letters are now viewed as iconic forms—replete with religious significance. Thus does the midrashist follow God and inscribe theological truth into the depth of existence. Axiology recapitulates ontology.

The teaching in *Genesis Rabbah* thus appears as a hierarchy of voices—beginning with Scripture itself, and descending through a chain of teachers, to the anonymous editor. Indeed, beginning with the opening lemma (the word *behibare 'am*) the string of teachings is knotted by several scriptural citations. The editor seems to direct this midrashic theatre with consummate legerdemain, introducing and resolving microforms to produce a teaching that begins with the creation and ends with eschatology. But we would hardly suspect the degree to which this editor has manipulated his traditions in the process. This editorial activity only becomes clear when we examine the homily of Rabbi Abbahu and the exegesis of Rabbi Eleazar in the Jerusalem Talmud Ḥagigah 2: 1, their original context.

In this talmudic context the teaching of Rabbi Abbahu comes after traditions about the meaning and shape of the second letter *beit*, the first letter of the creation account. He offers a new proposal. In view of what may be learned about how Midrash is formed and re(-)formed, the matter deserves closer scrutiny.

---

[18] A striking example occurs in *Gen. Rabbah* 56: 4, in connection with the phrase 'God will show him the lamb [*haseh*] for the offering' in Gen. 22: 8. Deepening the irony of the father's answer, the sages played on the Greek pronoun *se* ('you'). This pun sneaks back into the vernacular in Targum Yerushalmi II (and cf. *Pirkei derabi eli'ezer*, 31). The conceptual basis for such puns is found in the teaching that God's word at Sinai divided into 70 languages (see BT *Shab.* 88*b*).

Rabbi Abbahu [said] in the name of Rabbi Yohanan: 'With two letters were two worlds created—this world and the world to come: the one with *heh*, the other with *yod*. What is the proof? "For *beyah* [with *yod/heh*] the Lord *tsur olamim* [formed, *tsiyer*, worlds; literally, is an everlasting Rock]" [Isa. 26: 4]. And [from this verse] we do not know with which letter he created which world. But since it is [also] written, "These are the generations of the heavens and the earth *behibare'am*" [Gen. 2: 4], [we may infer that] He created them with [the letter] *heh*. Thus: this world was created with the *heh*, and the world to come was created with the *yod*. And whereas *heh* is open below, this is an indication to all creatures that they will descend to Sheol; [and] whereas *heh* has a point at its top, [this is to indicate that] from the moment they descend they [may] ascend; [and] whereas *heh* is open at [nearly] every side, so [God] opens a passage for penitents; [and] whereas *yod* is bent, so will all creatures be bent over—[as is written], "and all faces will turn pale" [Jer. 30: 6]. When David perceived this, he began to praise [God] with [the same] two letters: "Hallelu-yah [Be praised, *yod* and *heh*], O servants of the Lord, give praise; praise the name of the Lord" [Ps. 113: 1].'

Rabbi Yudan Nesiya enquired of Rabbi Samuel bar Nahman: 'What is [the meaning of] this scripture?: "Extol Him who rides on the clouds; the Lord [*beyah*] is His name. Exult in His presence" [Ps. 68: 5].' He said to him: 'There is no place without an authority appointed over its dominion [*biyah*]. And who is responsible for the dominion of them all? The Holy One, blessed be He: *Biyah* is His name, for Yah is His name.' [Rabbi Yudan] replied: 'Your master Rabbi [E]leazar did not interpret [*doresh*] so; but rather [explained it by way of a parable] of a king who built a palace in a place of sewers [*bivin*], dumps, and waste.[19] [Now] if anyone would come [by] and say that the palace is built in a place of sewers, dumps, and waste, would he not malign [both king and palace]? Just so: if one were to say that the world was originally water within water, he would surely malign the garden of the King and the roof built above it. He should therefore look and not touch.'

It is clear that we have here two separate microforms: a teaching of Rabbi Abbahu regarding the two letters of the divine name used to create this world and the next; and teachings by Rabbi Samuel and Rabbi Eleazar regarding the lower and upper worlds. All three sages develop interpretations of the word *beyah*, but they do so on the basis of different texts. Rabbi Abbahu uses Isaiah 26: 4, and divides the letters anagrammatically, while the teachings of Rabbi Samuel and Rabbi Eleazar explain Psalm 68: 5 via Greek puns (*bia*, 'dominion'; and *ouai*, 'woe').[20] In many ways the macroform in JT *Ḥagigah* is more streamlined than the one in *Genesis Rabbah*, and presents each of the microforms as a distinct exegetical unit. For example, Rabbi Abbahu's homily opens with a teaching about the letters *heh* and *yod*, and proceeds to ponder the specific employment of each (resolving the issue through reference to Genesis 2: 4). By contrast, the version in *Genesis Rabbah* has separated Rabbi Abbahu's remark regarding the letter *heh* from its use to resolve the quandary as to which letter (*heh* or *yod*) was used for the creation of which world (this one or the next).

[19] Cf. *Gen. Rabbah* 1: 5.
[20] Cf. *biya biya* in BT *Yev.* 97b, and the explanation of *Yelamedenu Leviticus* 13: 24 in *Aruch Completum*, ed. Kohut, ii. 44b–45a. There is an obvious pun as well on Hebrew *biv*.

One can see by reference to the JT Ḥagigah text that *Genesis Rabbah* presents a total transformation of the tradition. For now (in *Genesis Rabbah*) Rabbi Abbahu's teaching seems limited to a comment on Genesis 2: 4; and his interpretation of Isaiah 26: 4 (in the Jerusalem Talmud) is given to Rabbi Eleazar (whose parable is totally dropped). Moreover, the ensuing query about which letter was used in the different worlds *now* seems to be the voice of the editor, since it invokes Rabbi Abbahu's first teaching by name in order to clarify what is *now* presented as Rabbi Eleazar's exegesis. The subsequent theology of the letters also reappears as the editor's voice, and not as part of the extended homily of Rabbi Abbahu as presented in the Jerusalem Talmud.

Obviously, the editor of *Genesis Rabbah* desired to privilege Rabbi Abbahu's comment on the letter *heh* in the context of a *midrash* on Genesis; but this resulted in a total relocation of interpretations and the insinuation of his own voice into a prominent position. As distinct from the redactor of the *Ḥagigah* pericope, whose voice is absolutely absent, the anonymous editor of *Genesis Rabbah* 12: 10 speaks loud and clear as an impresario of traditions. By his division of the original homily of Rabbi Abbahu in two and the transferral of one part to the end, the teachings of Rabbi Samuel and Rabbi Eleazar are now incorporated into the discourse on the letters of the creation. In the Jerusalem Talmud text, rather than being subordinate interpretations of the word *beyah*, they are simply included for the sake of the completeness of tradition. Thus while both macroforms show midrashic tradition as complex acts of tradition-building, they do so in different ways. On the one hand, the passage in JT Ḥagigah has grouped its traditions in a static chain of authorities. This stands in stark contrast with the more dynamic process of enchainment found in *Genesis Rabbah*. Here the voice of the editor actively enters the hermeneutical fray. Little wonder that he once spoke the words of Rabbi Abbahu right out of his mouth.

III

The hierarchical chain of voices that constitute midrashic pericopes is also a chain of memory. Scripture is remembered first and foremost—and then the teachers who are remembered by the anonymous editor, in their own name and that of their teachers. Thus Midrash swings between the temporal poles of a memorialized past of instruction and the present moment of re-presentation. Indeed, as a linear process time is marked by the teaching of Scripture. Meanings accumulate as one 'other thing' (*davar aḥer*) after 'another'—and these are even edited into stylized series and structures for the sake of further instruction. From the myriad phonetic and grammatical possibilities of connection, passages throughout Scripture are combined in ever new ways: 'as it is written' here, says one teacher; or 'this is what Scripture says', notes another. Exegetical discourse thus speaks from the fullness of God's canonical *langue*, revealing ever-new iterations of its truth. Our collections of midrashic *paroles* bear witness to this messianic project.

But the rabbinic sage also works under the sign of myth. For every scriptural interpretation is a re-enactment of the revelation at Sinai—the paradigmatic time of Instruction. Indeed each midrashic *parole* participates in God's canonical *langue* and revitalizes it for new generations. The divine 'word is fire', reports the prophet Jeremiah, 'like a hammer splitting a rock'; and his rabbinic heirs understood this as the Sinaitic sparks that are released from Scripture through human interpretation.[21] Every sage is thus a disciple of Moses, and may be compared to Ben Azzai, who was once interpreting Scripture 'and a flaming fire encircled him'. His colleague Rabbi Akiva thought him to be in the heat of mystical passion, but Ben Azzai explained that he 'was rather sitting and [exegetically] enchaining [*ḥorez*] the words of Torah, Prophets, and Writings to each other—and the words rejoiced as when they were given at Sinai, and were pleasant as when they were first given' (to which tradition rejoined that they were given at Sinai in fire—when the mountain was enflamed, as Scripture states).[22] King Solomon seems to have had all this in mind, suggested an anonymous sage, when he spoke of his beloved's 'cheeks as beautiful in ringlets' (*torim*; but hinting at 'the oral and written Torahs'), and her 'neck in chains of gold' (*ḥaruzim*, but alluding to the process of linking the words of Scripture, *ḥarizah*).[23] We may even perhaps perceive here something of the eros of midrashic exegesis, whereby the bride (Torah) is adorned by her rabbinic lovers through re-citations of her very essence (the words) in endless combinations.

And to whom may Ben Azzai—the great enchainer—be compared? To Rabbi Berekhiah (in the name of Rabbi Yonatan), who linked the phrase 'To the leader: [concerning] *al mut laben*' in Psalm 9: 1 to the words of Ecclesiastes. Ecclesiastes said in 3: 11 that God created each thing for its proper time, 'and even put the world [*ha'olam*] in their hearts [*belibam*]'. Reading *ha'olam* in the second passage as *ha'elem* ('the youth'), Rabbi Berekhiah re-read Ecclesiastes to mean that God has even put fathers' 'love for their children [*olelim*] in their hearts'. He thereby hinted that one should likewise understand David's words in the Psalm (that is: he construed *al mut laben* as *alamut* [*be*]*liban*, 'youth in their hearts'). Others, however, preferred to interpret Ecclesiastes as meaning that God 'concealed [*he'elim*] the day of death [*mavet*] and judgment from His creatures'—and thus likewise the words of David. That is, Psalm 9: 1 is now midrashically interpreted to mean that 'God [the Leader] hid [*he'elim*] the time of [*al*] death [*mavet*] from the hearts [*liban*] of His creatures [*laben*; "the son", construed as a collective noun].'[24]

And to whom may Rabbi Berekhiah be compared?—to yet other teachers who

---

[21] See the interpretation of Jer. 23: 29 in BT *San.* 34*a*, and the reading of R. Samuel in the Tosafot ad loc., s.v. *mah*.

[22] S. of S. Rabbah 1: 10. According to traditions in BT *Ḥag.* 14*a* and JT *Ḥag.* 2: 1, a fire descended as R. Eleazar b. Arakh dealt with mystical matters. However, also in the last source there is an account of fire which descended while R. Eleazar and R. Joshua 'were engaged' in studying Scripture and connecting verses one to another. This tradition is stylistically similar to that in *Songs of Songs Rabbah* (but correct the formulation *ḥozerim* in the JT passage to *ḥorezim*, 'linking' or 'enchaining').

[23] S. of S. Rabbah 1: 10.   [24] *Midrash tehilim* 9: 1 (Buber edn., 79–80).

interpreted David's words to refer to how God cleanses (*melaben*) the hidden (viz. unintentional) sins (*ha'alamot*) that his sons (*ben*) commit on the Day of Atonement; or with respect to the death (*al hamavet*) decreed by God against Israel (his firstborn son, *ben*; citing Exod. 4: 24) for their sins, though God will cleanse him (*malbino*) of all iniquity when he (the son, Israel) returns in true repentance. Other sages added 'another thing' when they suggested that these words even taught how God's own heart was cleansed of retributive anger with the atoning death of his sinning sons (who failed to repent in their lifetime).[25]

Surely in all these ways and myriads more the words of Scripture are renewed through new correlations, redivision, and repointing. And surely this process also reanimates the consonants of Scripture with new sounds and senses drawn from like-minded scriptures. The enchantments thus dramatize the unity of Scripture and *reveal it as a rabbinic work*. Indeed, this is ultimately the great achievement of midrashic exegesis. For in endless variations the sages show that the Written Text is one interconnected instruction; and that all the values of rabbinic Oral Tradition (as for example here: divine providence and justice, sin and judgment, or repentance by deed or death) are present in it, explicitly or implicitly. By activating the *langue* of Scripture, rabbinic *paroles* keep the fiery speech of Sinai aflame. What is more: re-animated by human breath, the old words rejoice—and not least because they reveal the 'laughing face' of God (*Pesikta derav kahana* 12: 25).

IV

The messianic dimension inherent in the midrashic desire to reveal the fullness of the divine *langue* leads to a last question. Is there a limit before the end?

The answer is threefold, at least. First and foremost one must mention the limitations imposed by spiritual or intellectual capacity. This may be enunciated through Rabbi Akiva's reply to Rabbi Ishmael's query as to how his (Akiva's) hermeneutical techniques could help him explain the meaning of the seemingly senseless accusative particles in Genesis 1: 1 (since by his own principles and tradition such elements could be interpreted).[26] Rabbi Akiva answered by way of Deuteronomy 32: 47, 'For it [Scripture] is not something [*davar*] of little-worth [*reik*] for you [*mikem*]'—meaning, as he pointedly says, that 'if it is senseless [*reik*], it is your fault [lit. "from you"; *mikem*]—for you do not [therefore] know how to interpret'! By cleverly playing on the noun *davar* as the 'word' of Scripture, and semantically restructuring the clause, Rabbi Akiva hermeneutically rebukes his interlocutor and metacommunicates the truth that the horizon of interpretation is extended both by sufficient exegetical techniques and by the individual ability to use them. The limits of the *langue* are inscribed by the *parole*.

---

[25] Ibid. 9: 4 (Buber edn., 82).
[26] See *Gen. Rabbah* 1: 14. I have followed the sequence of interlocutors as reconstructed in *Minḥat yehudah*. See the discussion ad loc., 12.

Another limitation to Midrash lies between the poles of mean-spirited and potentially anarchic readings of Scripture. The first of these two is what the sages call *hagadot shel dofi*, midrashic interpretations which are designed to malign or mock the teachings or teachers of Scripture (BT *San.* 99b).[27] Jeroboam is the paradigmatic offender, and his like are silenced lest they use the tradition to traduce it. Quite otherwise are those who show little self-restraint for their position as teachers, or those who push theology to its public limits. One thinks here of Rabbi Pappus, whose exegeses hang on gnostic horns. Rabbi Akiva senses the danger, and issues a recurrent command of 'Enough!' (*dayekha*).[28] The fact that other times and teachers might regard the interpretations as acceptable is irrelevant. The principle of *dayekha* (like the danger of *dofi*) is always a matter for social regulation.

A final consideration may be offered here by way of conclusion—and that is the limits that sin places on faithful interpretation. Indeed, this factor subverts the very possibility of Midrash. Let us learn: when the Holy One, blessed be he, gave the tablets to Moses on Sinai, their physical weight was lightened because of the holy letters inscribed thereon. Only thus could Moses bear their heavenly weight—until the moment the people sinned before the Golden Calf. As he descended with God's Law and saw the people's apostasy, the letters flew off the tablets and ascended to their heavenly source. The stones were then too heavy for Moses to bear, and they fell from his hands to the earth, as it is written, 'And he cast the tablets from his hands, and he broke them at the base of the mountain' (Exod. 32: 19).[29]

For the sages, the fiery words of God's speech transform the world of nature—elevating it towards their supernatural source. But sin confronts this truth with earthly instinct, and the holy letters fly upward. Their loss is not only the end of revelation, but of all the traditions to come. One may suspect that this myth was told with a shudder.

[27] The opposite of such exegeses are the praiseworthy *hagadot meshubahot*; cf. *Mekhilta derabi yishma'el*, 'Vayisa' 1 (Horowitz–Rabin edn., 157).

[28] See ibid., 'Beshalah' 6 (Horowitz–Rabin edn., 112), and many other places. On this tradition, see the important manuscript evidence that Menahem Kahana has reviewed and presented in his study, 'Versions of the *Mekhilta derabi yishma'el* in the Light of Genizah Fragments' (Heb.), *Tarbiz*, 55 (1987), 499–515. His arguments are compelling.

[29] I have woven together the variously similar accounts in JT *Ta'an.* 4: 4; *Tanhuma*, 'Ki tisa' 26 and 30. Cf. also *Avot derabi natan*, version A, ed. Solomon Schechter, 3rd rev. edn. (New York, 1967), 11; and Pseudo-Philo 12: 5.

TWO

THE HAND UPON THE LORD'S THRONE
Midrashic and Targumic Perceptions of Exodus 17: 14–16

ROBERT HAYWARD

MICHAEL FISHBANE has recently drawn the attention of students of rabbinic literature to a remarkable exegesis of Exodus 17: 16 preserved in *Pesikta derav kahana* and parallels,[1] which he describes as 'a subtle and daring parsing of the passage'.[2] Such is the importance of Fishbane's observations that some further consideration of the material he handles might be useful and informative, particularly when the Aramaic Targumim of the verses which he discusses are brought into the picture. Unlike the classical *midrashim*, the Targumim offer the hearer or reader a translation of the biblical texts into another language. By its very nature, translation cannot help but transform in some measure the material with which it has to deal, however scrupulous the translator might be to provide a 'literal' rendering from the original into the target language. It is also evident that the Aramaic *meturgemanim* ('translators') took special care to represent each Hebrew word in the process of their translation. While the authors of the *midrashim* could, and did, pass over in silence individual words, phrases, or even whole sentences in expounding a given biblical passage, the *meturgemanim* could not do so. This general principle holds true even for those Targumim on the Writings best known for their complex, paraphrastic expansion of the Hebrew text, like the Targum Song of Songs.[3]

This last point is particularly telling. In his search for a definition of Targum, a task involving painstaking, detailed literary and formal analysis of key targumic passages, Alexander Samely has concluded that the nature of Targum may be encapsulated in a typological definition such as the following: 'Targum is an Aramaic

---

[1] See *Pesikta derav kahana* 3: 16; *Pesikta rabati* 12; *Tanḥuma*, 'Ki tisa' 11, all cited by Fishbane, to which we may add Rashi's commentary on Exod. 17: 16.
[2] See Michael Fishbane, *Biblical Myth and Rabbinic Mythmaking* (Oxford, 2003), 189–90.
[3] See Philip S. Alexander, *The Targum of Canticles: Translated, with a Critical Introduction, Apparatus, and Notes*, The Aramaic Bible 17A (London, 2004), 29–31.

narrative paraphrase of the biblical text in exegetical dependence on its wording.'[4] This succinct definition is itself distilled from five aspects of Targum which Samely describes as basic features, and the first of these is precisely that comprehensive aspect of Targum already noted here, which requires every biblical verse to be translated, and in biblical order. Samely secondly notes the non-appearance in Targum of alternative interpretations of the Hebrew: there is no place for 'another explanation' (*davar aḥer*), so characteristic of the *midrashim*. Alternative renderings are nonetheless to be found; but they require new, 'alternative' Targumim; as we shall see presently, Exodus 17: 14–16 has no shortage of these. We shall discern also the specifically narrative character of the Targumim, which Samely lists as the third basic feature of the genre; and the two final aspects, Targum's dependence on the wording of the Hebrew original, and Targum's exegetical character, will be specially important for our purposes.[5] All this contrasts with the *midrashim*, whose segmentation of Scripture into part-verses, individual words, or even part-words without reference to their scriptural context as the foundation for particular interpretations is more or less routine.[6] The transformation which Scripture undergoes in midrashic operations may thus turn out to be quite different from its targumic transformations, even though both Targum and Midrash preserve and make use of materials which are recognizable as common to both hermeneutical endeavours.[7]

This matter of transformation is of the greatest significance, given that we now possess clear evidence that the origins of Targum predate the time of the rabbis, and that Jews who knew little of rabbinic culture made use of it. The discovery of Aramaic translations of Leviticus and Job in the Qumran caves leaves us in little doubt that the rabbis adopted the translation of Scripture into Aramaic as an already existing institution, and made the whole business of Aramaic Bible translation their

---

[4] See Alex Samely, *The Interpretation of Speech in the Pentateuch Targums* (Tübingen, 1992), 180. For a typological description and analysis of Targum in its various manifestations, see now Alex Samely, Philip Alexander, Rocco Bernasconi, and Robert Hayward, 'Inventory of Structurally Important Literary Features in Ancient Jewish Literature (Version -355)' (Manchester: http://www.manchester.ac.uk/ancientjewishliterature/inventory/). This database represents the results of an AHRC-funded project investigating the typology of Jewish literature in antiquity.

[5] On these aspects of Targum, see further Samely, *Interpretation of Speech*, 179–181. Samely's work represents the most recent in-depth analysis of the principles operating in midrashic procedures, on which see especially his *Rabbinic Interpretation of Scripture in the Mishnah* (Oxford, 2002), 31–58. He acknowledges, for example in his *Forms of Rabbinic Literature and Thought* (Oxford, 2007), p. 76, the influence of Arnold Goldberg, whose key typological perceptions on Midrash may be found most conveniently in his essay 'Die funktionale Form Midrasch', reprinted in Margarete Schlüter and Peter Schäfer (eds.), *Rabbinische Texte als Gegenstand der Auslegung: Gesammelte Studien* II (Tübingen, 1999), 199–229.

[6] On the segmentation or fragmentation of Scripture in the midrashic process, see Samely, *Forms of Rabbinic Literature and Thought*, 64–73.

[7] The *midrashim* and the Targumim, however, often turn out to share common exegetical goals and procedures: see Madeleine Taradach, *Le Midrash: Introduction à la littérature midrashique* (Geneva, 1991), 59–62.

own.⁸ A similar picture may be traced in the earliest rabbinic references to Targum (Mishnah *Meg.* 4: 4), which place it in the setting of the regular synagogue liturgy, yet another institution which was not entirely of rabbinic origin, but in which the sages became increasingly and deeply involved as time went by, extending their influence and authority.⁹ In the Mishnah the rabbis set out rules for the delivery of Targum to a congregation during the reading of the Torah and the Prophets: these rules are neither explained nor disputed. The *meturgeman*, the one responsible for the rendering of the Hebrew Scriptures into Aramaic, is likewise introduced without explanation, and his presence taken for granted. Nor does the Mishnah explain why a *meturgeman* might be needed in the first place; his function and purpose are also assumed as being already familiar. Nonetheless, Mishnah *Megilah* 4: 10 offers a strong indicator of what the sages regarded as an important function of the Targum within the synagogue service. This *mishnah* lists passages of Scripture which are not to be translated into Aramaic, even though the Hebrew corresponding to them is publicly read.¹⁰ From this, we may reasonably deduce that Targum was intended to convey the sense of the Hebrew to a congregation whose grasp of the scriptural language might not have been secure. In short, the Targum appears to have been understood as possessing an educational or didactic purpose, a point made clearer by the talmudic sages (BT *Meg.* 3*a*), who sought the origins of Targum in the careful exposition of the Torah by the Levites 'translating it and giving the sense'¹¹ during the great assembly convened by Ezra (Neh. 8: 8).

The Aramaic Bible translations from Qumran for the most part follow the Hebrew text very closely, producing a version which is as faithful as possible to the original; yet the earliest Targumim from the rabbinic period, Targum Onkelos on the Pentateuch and its counterpart Targum Jonathan on the Prophets, present a text which is much more than translation. Translation there certainly is, and it is fairly evident even to the casual reader, inasmuch as the Aramaic follows the Hebrew base text closely, very often word for word. Often, however, the Aramaic may expand

---

⁸ For the fragments of Aramaic Leviticus and Job from Qumran Cave 4 (4QtgLev = 4Q156; 4QtgJob = 4Q157), see the *editio princeps* of József T. Milik, in Roland de Vaux and József T. Milik (eds.), *Qumrân Grotte 4.II (4Q128–4Q157)*, pt. 1: *Archéologie*, pt. 2: *Tefillin, Mezuzot et Targum*, Discoveries in the Judaean Desert VI (Oxford, 1977), 86–9, 90; for the more extensive Aramaic translation of Job found in Qumran Cave 11 (11QtgJob = 11Q10), see Jan P. M. van der Ploeg and Adam. S. van der Woude, *Le Targum de Job de la Grotte XI de Qumrân* (Leiden, 1971).

⁹ See the discussion in Lee I. Levine, *The Synagogue: The First Thousand Years* (New Haven, Conn., 2000), 440–70; Levine also gives a description of how Targum might have been delivered in the setting of an ancient synagogue (ibid. 351–3). The best English introduction to Targum and its place in Jewish religious life is that of Philip S. Alexander, 'Targum. Targumim', in David N. Freedman (ed.), *The Anchor Bible Dictionary*, vol. vi (New York, 1992), 320–31; older, but still useful, is Roger le Déaut, *Introduction à la littérature targumique* (Rome, 1988).

¹⁰ All those passages which may not be translated are in some way sensitive: see Philip S. Alexander, 'The Rabbinic Lists of Forbidden Targumim', *Journal of Jewish Studies*, 27 (1976), 177–91.

¹¹ The translation of the Hebrew מפרש ושום שכל according to Adele Berlin and Marc Z. Brettler (eds.), *The Jewish Study Bible* (Oxford, 2004), 2700.

the translated Hebrew material with single words, phrases, or even whole sentences; if the reader ignores such expansions, what is left is an Aramaic rendering of the Hebrew. Yet other aspects of Targum Onkelos and Targum Jonathan are not so obvious. Let us consider a verse at random. According to the Hebrew text of Genesis 17: 6, the Almighty assures Abraham: 'and I shall make you very exceedingly fruitful, and shall make you into nations; and kings shall go forth from you'. Targum Onkelos of this verse has: 'and I shall increase you very exceedingly, and shall make you into assemblies; and kings *who have dominion over nations* shall go forth from you'. The words in italics represent an addition in the Aramaic which, if ignored, leaves us with a translation of the Hebrew base text—in a manner of speaking. For a detailed comparison of the remaining 'translational' Aramaic with the Hebrew reveals at least that in the Targum (1) the Hebrew verb 'make fruitful' has become 'increase', and (2) the Hebrew 'nations' has become Aramaic 'assemblies'. This same state of affairs also obtains in Targum Jonathan on the Prophets; and the point to be noted carefully is this. A member of a synagogue congregation might easily discern the addition in the Aramaic translation given here, having listened attentively to the Hebrew read out just before it; but the two other changes which we have noted would be rather more difficult for a congregant to register. Their import is only properly appreciated, indeed, when the Targum is read with care and due attention; and this suggests that Targum Onkelos and Targum Jonathan need to be studied. In short, they might be as much at home in the study house, or in the private library of the individual observant Jew, as in the worship of the synagogue.[12]

Occasionally, especially in their renderings of Hebrew poetic passages, the targumic additions in Targum Onkelos and Targum Jonathan described above may be extensive, and reflect interpretations to be found also in the classical *midrashim*. This is much more commonly the case in those Targumim of the Pentateuch described as 'Palestinian Targumim' (the Fragment Targumim; Targum Neofiti and its marginal glosses; and Targum Pseudo-Jonathan), the Targumim on many of the Writings (particularly the Aramaic version of Song of Songs), and some surviving fragments of Targum on the Prophets which do not belong to Targum Jonathan. A single example must suffice. The Palestinian Targumim on Genesis 18: 1–2 report God's appearing to Abraham at the oaks of Mamre as he was sitting at his tent entrance 'in the heat of the day'. He saw three men standing, ran to meet them, and prostrated himself. Both Targum Neofiti and Targum Pseudo-Jonathan on these verses relay to us midrashic statements known from other sources, that the three men were angels in human form; that each had been sent for a particular mission,

[12] On the place of Aramaic Targum in the study house and private library as well as in synagogue, see A. D. York, 'The Dating of Targumic Literature', *Journal for the Study of Judaism*, 5 (1974), 49–62, and the evidence assembled by Philip Alexander in his *The Targum of Canticles*, 53–4. The place of Targumim of the Onkelos and Jonathan type in private or communal study stands out if, as is likely, they also functioned as 'chrestomathies' for the rabbis and their students in acquiring a knowledge of biblical, as distinct from contemporary, Hebrew: see Philip S. Alexander, 'How did the Rabbis Learn Hebrew?', in William Horbury (ed.), *Hebrew Study from Ezra to Ben Yehuda* (London, 1999), 71–89.

since no angel could be responsible for more than a single task; and that the heat of the day refers in some way to Abraham's recent circumcision. Reference to several midrashic texts confirms the place of these traditions outside the Targum.[13]

The two Targumim noted here, however, conspicuously differ in their assimilation of these midrashic statements. Neofiti presents us with a major expansion of Genesis 18: 1, beginning at once with the information that three angels were sent to Abraham when he had circumcised himself, a detail not found in the Hebrew. No angel may be entrusted with more than one duty, says Neofiti; and the duties of the three are enumerated in some detail, to the extent that the five cities of the plain, which are to be destroyed by the third angel, are listed by name. At Genesis 18: 2, Neofiti notes merely that the angels were in human likeness, and that Abraham greeted them according to custom. By contrast, Targum Pseudo-Jonathan on Genesis 18: 1 follows the Hebrew by reporting first that the Almighty, the Glory of the Lord, visited Abraham as he was suffering from the pain of circumcision; only at Genesis 18: 2 does this Targum record that the three men mentioned in the Hebrew were in fact angels in human likeness, each entrusted with a single mission which is then described succinctly. Pseudo-Jonathan's presentation involves fewer than half the words used by Neofiti.

This brief description signals the different transformations to which Neofiti and Pseudo-Jonathan have subjected material which appears outside the targumic genre. For Neofiti, what is clearly central is the matter of angels, whose identity is established as a priority, despite the fact that the 'three men' do not appear in the first verse of the Hebrew base text. The angelic missions are given in detail; the number of words is no object here, and the whole block of sentences stands as a heading to a description of events unfolding in the following verses, where angels play a key part. Pseudo-Jonathan, however, seems concerned not to lose sight of the immense significance of Abraham's circumcision, which, in this Targum's version of the Hebrew, might be taken to merit the appearance of the divine presence. Unlike Neofiti, this Targum uses the midrashic traditions at its disposal to single out and stress Abraham's piety (see Targum Pseudo-Jonathan on Gen. 18: 19). A glance at the narrative as it is developed in the Targum indicates the reason for this: Abraham's prayers of intercession for the inhabitants of the cities will be much in evidence, more elaborated than they are in Targum Neofiti.

Each of the extant Targumim, it appears, may have its own agenda; and exegetical material represented in the *midrashim* can be reworked and moulded by the Aramaic translators in quite distinctive ways. In what follows, we shall encounter some startling instances of such targumic activity, which is triggered by the difficulties to be found in the Hebrew base text itself. Exodus 17: 16, like the two preceding verses, is replete with obscurities and problems of interpretation in the Hebrew as preserved

---

[13] e.g. *Gen. Rabbah* 48: 7, 50: 2; BT *BM* 86b; and *Tanḥuma* (ed. Buber), 'Vayera' 20. For a list of other relevant midrashic sources, see Bernard Grossfeld, *Targum Neofiti 1: An Exegetical Commentary to Genesis including full Rabbinic Parallels* (New York, 2000), 153–5.

for us in the Masoretic text, which reads: ויאמר כי־יד על־כס יה מלחמה ליהוה בעמלק מדר דר.
The translator is faced with a number of options, some of which may be expressed as
follows: 'And he said: For (*or*: because, *or*: when, *or*: surely) a hand is (*or*: will be, *or*:
was) upon the throne of YH: there is (*or*: was, *or*: will be) war for the Lord with/against
Amalek from every generation.' Furthermore, we may note the peculiar form of the
divine name, restricted to the two letters *yod* and *heh*; and the apparently eccentric *kes*,
rather than the usual *kise*, doing duty for the word 'throne'.[14] Out of these possibilities, *Pesikta derav kahana* presents Rabbi Levi in the name of Rabbi Huna ben Rabbi
Hanina as offering an interpretation which seeks to explain why the divine name and
throne appear as incomplete in this scriptural verse, and how that state of affairs will
be put to rights:

All the time that the descendants of Amalek endure in the world, the divine name is not
complete, nor is the throne complete. When the descendants of Amalek are destroyed
from the world, the divine name will be complete and the throne complete. And what is
the proof? 'The enemy are finished, they are ruins for ever': and 'You have abandoned
their cities, their memorial is destroyed' [Ps. 9: 7]. What is written after it? 'And YHVH
shall sit for ever, establishing His throne for judgment' [Ps. 9: 8].[15]

Here, as Fishbane explains, the temporary domination of Amalek in the world
reflects a situation in which the divine name and throne themselves are somehow
impaired; but Psalm 9: 7–8 is adduced to prove that the destruction of the 'memorial' (זכר, *zekher*) of God's enemies, the very noun used in Exodus 17: 14 where God
vows to blot out Amalek's memorial, will ensure both the 'restoration' of the complete name YHVH and that God will be seated for everlasting on his complete
throne. Completeness and incompleteness; the expectation that future divine activity will put to right past and present wrongs; and the sense that Amalek represents
something much more sinister than the average evildoer,[16] are evidently concerns
which this *midrash* and its parallels are concerned to address.

This essay will explore these themes as they are represented in the two verses
preceding the reference to the hand on the throne, and in midrashic and targumic
expositions of Exodus 17: 14–16, where the themes of completeness and incompleteness and so on are approached from standpoints differing somewhat from the

---

[14] The Samaritan Pentateuch actually reads כסא without, however, the divine name יה following at
this point, and some manuscripts of the Masoretic text read כסיה as one word: for a good summary of
modern, critical discussion of the text, see William H. C. Propp, *Exodus 1–18*, The Anchor Bible, 2 (New
York, 1998), 615, 620. Note also that the owner of the 'hand' is unspecified in the Hebrew, which is also
unclear about whether the 'war' against Amalek is envisaged as a perpetual conflict or one which manifests itself at certain particular times in Israel's history.

[15] My translation of the text in *Pesikta de Rav Kahana*, ed. Bernard Mandelbaum, 2 vols. (New York,
1962), i. 53.

[16] This is suggested by the fact that the Psalm verse adduced as proof-text speaks of 'the enemy', an
archetypal foe, as it were, understood by the *midrash* to be represented by Amalek. In those *midrashim*
where 'empirical' Amalek is under discussion, the question arises just when the annihilation of Amalek
will be complete, and what it will entail. See below.

striking interpretation of *Pesikta derav kahana*. First to claim our attention will be the efforts of individual midrashic traditions to insist that the matter of Amalek is addressed by every constituent part of the written Torah, a concern with completeness whose ramifications I shall attempt to explore. Representative of this strategy is the *Mekhilta derabi yishma'el*'s comment on Exodus 17: 14:

And the Lord said to Moses: Write this as a reminder [*zikaron*] in the book, and set it in Joshua's ears, for/because/when I shall utterly wipe out the memorial [*zekher*] of Amalek from beneath heaven.

The divine command to 'write this as a reminder in the book' is anonymously explained by *Mekhilta derabi yishma'el*, 'Amalek' 2 as follows:

This refers to what is written in this book [i.e. Exodus]; *as a reminder* refers to what is written in the prophets; *in the book*, to what is written in the Megillah.[17]

Thus the whole written divine revelation in its completeness includes mention of Amalek: the Torah, in this passage which concerns us; the Prophets, a reference to 1 Samuel 15 with its account of Saul's battle against Agag, king of Amalek; and the Writings, the book of Esther recording that the wicked Haman was an Agagite (Esther 3: 1).[18] The parallel to this in the *Mekhilta derabi shimon bar yoḥai*[19] attributes the words to Rabbi Joshua, while Rabbi Eleazar of Modin offers a variant interpretation, whereby the word 'memorial' (*zekher*) refers to the book of Esther, and the phrase 'in a book' to the Prophets. It may be significant that Rabbi Joshua (ben Hananiah) was active in the period immediately preceding the Second Revolt against Rome led by Simon bar Kokhba, while Rabbi Eleazar lived during that war. The latter, indeed, may well have been a supporter of its leader, for tradition records that he was Simon's uncle (BT *Git.* 57a; *Lam. Rab.* 2: 5), and coins from the time of the revolt bearing the legend 'Eleazar the priest' may, just possibly, refer to him.[20]

---

[17] My translation of the text as edited by Jacob Z. Lauterbach, *Mekilta de-Rabbi Ishmael*, 3 vols. (Philadelphia, Pa., 1933–5), ii. 149.

[18] The identification of Haman as an Amalekite is well known: see e.g. BT *San.* 99a; *Pirkei derabi eli'ezer*, 49.

[19] Cited from the edition of Jacob N. Epstein and Ezra Z. Melamed, *Mekhilta d'Rabbi Sim'on b. Jochai* (Jerusalem, 1955), 123–4.

[20] On the Second Revolt, see Elizabeth M. Smallwood, *The Jews under Roman Rule: From Pompey to Diocletian: A Study in Political Relations*, Studies in Judaism in Late Antiquity, 20 (Leiden, 1981), 428–66; Emil Schürer, *The History of the Jewish People in the Age of Jesus Christ*, rev. and ed. G. Vermes, M. Black, and F. Millar, vol. i (Edinburgh, 1973), 534–57, and on the traditions about Bar Kokhba preserved in rabbinic texts, see Richard S. Marks, *The Image of Bar Kokhba in Traditional Jewish Literature: False Messiah and National Hero* (University Park, Pa., 1994), 13–56. An excellent critical overview of this difficult topic is provided by Hanan Eshel, 'The Bar Kochba Revolt, 132–135', in S. T. Katz (ed.), *The Cambridge History of Judaism*, vol. iv (Cambridge, 2006), 105–27; see p. 110 for discussion of the coinage of the period. There is some evidence that the *Mekhilta* and other tannaitic *midrashim* sought to discourage hopes, which some Jews may have entertained, of direct military victory over Israel's enemies: see Gerald J. Blidstein, 'Prayer Rescue and Redemption in the Mekilta', *Journal for the Study of Judaism*, 39 (2008), 68–87.

Simon bar Kokhba was accepted by many as the messiah, and tradition presents Rabbi Eleazar as in close association with him. The understanding of the Amalek passage attributed to him may, therefore, carry with it a particular sense of completeness, a sense that Amalek's defeat in the days of the messiah is indicated in those verses. That said, we should be careful not to confine and restrict explanations and understanding of these items in the *Mekhilta*s to particular historical events *as such*. It is sufficient to recall that those who transmitted to us the final forms of the midrashic texts which are now in our hands themselves associated (rightly or wrongly from a 'historical' perspective—it makes little difference) the sages they name as authorities here with direct involvement in the Jewish bid for freedom at the time of Hadrian. Inevitably, then, that association would colour the final presentation of the various midrashic units, particularly when the scriptural verses on which they comment speak of some definitive conflict between the Almighty and foreigners bent on Israel's destruction.

With this in mind, we may note that the *Mekhilta derabi yishma'el* reports that the two sages differed in their interpretation of Exodus 17: 14, where God promises 'I shall surely wipe out' (*maḥoh emḥeh*) Amalek's memorial (*zekher*). Rabbi Joshua took the infinitive absolute form *maḥoh* to refer to Amalek and all his 'offspring', while the verb *emḥeh* he referred to Amalek and all his clans or family. Rabbi Eleazar's interpretation of these two words runs:

Wiping out [the infinitive absolute, *maḥoh*] refers to him and to all his generations; *I shall wipe out* [*emḥeh*] refers to him and to all that generation.

While Rabbi Joshua appears to restrict the verse's significance to Amalek and his immediate familial relations, Rabbi Eleazar's reference to 'all that generation' might suggest a complete, utter destruction and annihilation of all the wicked, as in the days of Noah and the great flood; just as the wicked in the days of Noah were to be blotted out (*umaḥiti*, Gen. 7: 4) from under the heavens (Gen. 6: 17), so the Almighty had determined to blot out Amalek's generation from under the heavens. This suspicion is confirmed by words ascribed a few sentences later to Rabbi Eleazar, as he comments on that very phrase in Exodus 17: 14 'from under the heavens':

When will the name of these persons be destroyed? In the hour that idolatry, it and its servants, be rooted out; then the Omnipresent shall be unique in the world and His kingdom shall exist for ever and ever. In that hour, 'the Lord shall go forth and He shall fight', etc. [Zech. 14: 3], 'and the Lord shall be King', etc. [Zech. 14: 9].[21]

In this interpretation, Rabbi Eleazar begins to look in the direction of what we found in *Pesikta derav kahana*: the destruction of Amalek is seen in terms of the complete annihilation of all idolatry and all its adherents, with concomitant repercussions for God's holy name and his kingship. While Rabbi Eleazar's language differs

---

[21] *Mekhilta de rabi yishma'el*, 'Amalek' 2 (Lauterbach edn., ll. 152–9).

from the formulations in *Pesikta derav kahana*, the underlying sentiments could be construed as similar, and the hearer or reader might feel invited to ponder further the mysterious affinity between the oneness of the name prophesied by Zechariah, and the effects of continuing idolatry on perceptions of that name in this world.

That said, when *Mekhilta derabi yishma'el* comes to expound the difficult phrase 'for a hand is upon the throne of YH',[22] it attributes to Rabbi Eleazar an explanation which suggests that both the divine name and throne are already 'complete', as it were, and that such 'completeness' guarantees and assures the future destruction of Amalek, and is indeed a prerequisite for that destruction:

Rabbi Eleazar of Modin says: The Holy One, blessed be He, swore by the throne of His glory: I will not leave posterity and descendant[s] of Amalek under the whole heaven, so that the nations may not say, 'This camel is Amalek's, this ewe is Amalek's.'

As we shall see presently, this exegesis has affinities with the Targumim, which also interpreted the 'hand on the Lord's throne' as signifying a divine oath, unlike the midrashic interpretations that Fishbane highlights. Here we must note that it is absolutely essential for Rabbi Eleazar's interpretation for the throne to be complete, since an oath sworn on or by something which is impaired, partial, or incomplete would be worthless. We note also how he imports into his interpretation the words 'under the whole heaven', clearly recalling Exodus 17: 14, to give his interpretation a sense of wholeness and completeness. By contrast, the explanation of the 'hand upon the Lord's throne' ascribed to Rabbi Joshua, which immediately precedes these words of Rabbi Eleazar, is patient of a very different sense. Taking *ki* as meaning 'when' in this context, Rabbi Joshua remarks:

When the Holy One, blessed be He, shall sit upon the throne of His kingdom and when His dominion shall exist, at that time the Lord shall have war with Amalek.[23]

In this interpretation, the Lord is the one whose hand will be upon the throne, but his conflict with Amalek is transferred to a possibly quite distant future, when the final establishment of God's dominion becomes a reality: then 'the hand upon the throne', interpreted as the Almighty's solemn inauguration of his everlasting dominion, will be the signal for the battle against Amalek to begin. It is not clear from this statement whether Rabbi Joshua believed that, before the Almighty was to sit upon the throne of his kingdom, it might be Amalek's hand that was upon the throne. His comment *could* imply as much, and he does not interpret the hand with reference to a divine oath.

The two rabbis neatly set out the conundrum. Both agree that God's sovereign

---

[22] Ibid. (Lauterbach edn., ll. 174–9). The phrase is difficult since it might suggest that it is Amalek's 'hand', that is, his power, which is 'upon' or 'against' the Almighty's throne, and this is the sense accorded to the phrase by *Pesikta derav kahana* 3: 16, and other *midrashim* cited by Fishbane, who notes precisely this point in *Biblical Myth*, 189.   [23] *Mekhilta de rabi yishma'el*, 'Amalek' 2 (Lauterbach edn., ll. 171–4).

and complete dominion is a prerequisite for the destruction of Amalek. But is that complete dominion in operation throughout history, defeating Amalek at various stages within the historical process (so Rabbi Eleazar); or is it a dominion whose completeness needs to be awaited, for a future yet to be experienced, when a final war will annihilate Amalek (so Rabbi Joshua)?

How might this affect our understanding of the divine name in this verse? It is, perhaps, significant that neither the *Mekhilta derabi yishma'el*, the *Mekhilta derabi shimon bar yoḥai*, nor later *midrashim* offering parallels to the material in the two *Mekhilta*s offer any direct comment on the name YH in Exodus 17: 16.[24] But the Aramaic Targumim, as we have already observed, are obliged to deal with it; and their exegeses are instructive for a number of reasons.

Seven different Targumim on Exodus 17: 16 are extant:[25] they include the Targumim of Onkelos, Pseudo-Jonathan, and Neofiti; two Fragment Targumim of Paris MS 110 and of Vatican MS 440; and two fragments of Targum from the Cairo Genizah, Cambridge University Library MS Or 1080 and Jewish Theological Seminary MS 605. All of them interpret the 'hand' on the throne as referring to an oath sworn by the Almighty (see Deut. 32: 40), in the manner of Rabbi Eleazar of Modin and Rabbi Eliezer as represented in *Mekhilta derabi yishma'el*; all interpret the phrase *kes yah* in the first instance as signifying the throne of glory, in the same manner as the two sages reported in *Mekhilta*; and all introduce the notion, not explicitly enunciated in the Hebrew of Exodus 17: 16, of the destruction of Amalek or of Amalek's memorial, deriving it from Exodus 17: 14. Furthermore, five of these Targumim (the exceptions are Onkelos and Pseudo-Jonathan) agree in two other important respects: they specify that *yah* is a title signifying the one who exercises complete dominion in the universe here and now; and they offer a second interpretation of *kes yah* as signifying the throne of Saul, the first of Israel's kings. The Targum fragment Cambridge University MS Or 1080 may serve as a representative of this group of Targumim:

And he said: The oath has gone forth from beneath the throne of glory of the master of all the worlds, the Lord: the first king who is destined to arise from those of the house of Israel will be Saul, the son of Kish. He shall set battle arrays against those of the house of Amalek, and of them he shall slaughter kings and rulers. And as for what is left over of them, Mordechai and Esther shall destroy them. And the Lord has said in His Word (*memra*) to destroy the memorial of Amalek for/to all generations.[26]

---

[24] *Lam. Rabbah* 3: 6; *Esther Rabbah* 10: 13; and *Ruth Rabbah* 4: 5.

[25] The following editions have been used: Targum Onkelos (TO), Alexander Sperber, *The Bible in Aramaic*, vol. i: *The Pentateuch According to Targum Onkelos* (Leiden, 1959); Pseudo-Jonathan (PJ), Ernest G. Clarke et al., *Targum Pseudo-Jonathan of the Pentateuch: Text and Concordance* (Hoboken, NJ, 1984); Targum Neofiti (TN), Alejandro Díez Macho, *MS Neophyti 1*, vol. ii: *Exodo* (Madrid, 1970); Fragment Targum (FT), Michael L. Klein, *The Fragment-Targums of the Pentateuch*, 2 vols. (Rome, 1980); and for Genizah materials, Michael L. Klein, *Genizah Manuscripts of Palestinian Targum to the Pentateuch*, 2 vols. (Cincinnati, Ohio, 1986). Translations are mine.

[26] The individual Targumim present us with some variations from this representative text, of which

It would seem that these Targumim have made a concerted effort to ensure that there should be no doubt about the identity of *yah*. He is the master of all that exists, and, should any uncertainty remain, he is the Lord revealed in the Hebrew Scriptures. These Aramaic versions also make it clear that this verse must be understood in light of Exodus 17: 14, since they employ the language of the destruction of Amalek's memorial, reasserting it in this verse and creating a parallel: in verse 14, the Lord will destroy the memorial of Amalek 'from under the heaven', while in verse 16 he will destroy this memorial 'for/to all generations' without exception, no doubt including the generation of the world to come. Here the Targumim depart from the Hebrew, which speaks of this destruction as being '*from* eternal generations', with the Masoretic text reading *midor dor*. More will need to be said of this presently. Between these two targumic mentions of Amalek's memorial stand the victory of Saul, Israel's first king, who fought the Amalekites, and the exploits of Mordechai and Esther, who outwitted the wicked Haman, a descendant of Amalek. Amalek is thus set to be destroyed both in this world and in the world to come: both history and Israel's hope for God's intervention in the future will see Amalek overcome and destroyed.

The two remaining Targumim, Onkelos and Pseudo-Jonathan, further illuminate the exegesis. Thus Pseudo-Jonathan is explicit that the Lord has sworn by the throne of his glory to wage war against Amalek and to destroy that nation '*for* three generations: *from* the generation of this world, and *from* the generation of the messiah, and *from* the generation of the world to come'. Note how, in this interpretation, the Hebrew Bible's '*from* eternal generations' is retained, along with the Palestinian Targum's 'to' or 'for' those generations. This Targum envisages a continuing battle throughout history, which will, like everything else, be finally wound up in the world to come. Its exegesis calls to mind the difficult matters addressed by Rabbi Joshua and Rabbi Eleazar of Modin in *Mekhilta*; the likelihood is that Pseudo-Jonathan represents a very particular and individual attempt to offer a resolution of their debate, since the notion that Amalek will be destroyed from three generations is expressed in the *Mekhilta derabi yishma'el* by another sage, Rabbi Eliezer, in what is most likely itself an attempt to have the last word on the meaning of the Lord's war with Amalek 'from every generation'.[27] Thus whereas Rabbi Joshua had explained the repeated word *dor* of this phrase with reference to Amalek's removal from the life of this world and of the world to come, and Rabbi Eleazar of Modin had taken it to

the following should be noted. Interpreting *yah*, TN and FT in the Paris manuscript have simply 'the Master of all the World', omitting the Tetragrammaton, which in Jewish Theological Seminary MS 605 is indicated by the substitute designation *adonai*; TN presents the first king as arising 'from the tribe of Benjamin' rather than 'from the house of Israel', while MS 605 combines both these interpretations; and the marginal gloss of TN speaks of the first king 'to sit upon the throne of the kingdom of the sons of Israel' expounding *kes yah*, doubtless under the influence of 1 Chron. 29: 23 with its note that Solomon sat upon the throne of the Lord in place of his father David.

[27] 'Amalek' 2 (Lauterbach edn., ll. 188–92).

signify Amalek's abolition from the generation of Moses and the generation of Samuel, Rabbi Eliezer had interpreted it as signifying Amalek's annihilation from the generation of the messiah, which, he says, consists of three generations, proof for this being offered from Psalm 72: 5. Pseudo-Jonathan appears to represent all these views in a kind of potpourri, settling the matter to the *meturgeman*'s own satisfaction!

Targum Onkelos, by contrast, seems to concentrate on the matter of the divine name in an exegesis which is both subtle and allusive, conveying a good deal in few words:

And he said in an oath: This has been uttered from before the Revered One whose Shekhinah is upon the throne of glory, that war before the Lord is destined to be waged against those of the house of Amalek, to destroy them from the generations of the world.

Onkelos seems to have chosen the title 'the Revered One' or 'the Feared One' (Aramaic *dehila*), deliberately in order to recall here the only other occasion on which the divine designation YH is used in the books of Moses, namely, in the Song at the Sea in Exodus 15: 2. In that verse Onkelos, faced with the Hebrew 'YH is my strength and my song', translated 'The Revered One, the Lord, is my might and my praise.' Targum Neofiti and Fragment Targum (Vatican) of this verse are very similar, speaking of 'the Revered One of all the ages/worlds, the Lord', while Pseudo-Jonathan has 'the Revered One over all the ages/worlds, the Lord'. At this point we should also record, most significantly, the rendering of Fragment Targum (Paris), which understood YH in Exodus 15: 2 as 'the master of all the world, the Lord', which is almost identical to the divine title adopted as a translation of YH at Exodus 17: 16 by all extant Targumim other than Onkelos and Pseudo-Jonathan.

In other words, the Aramaic Targumim, with the possible exception of Pseudo-Jonathan, appear to have interpreted YH in Exodus 17: 16 with an eye to the earlier appearance of that name in Exodus 15: 2, with reference either (Onkelos) to 'the Revered One' or (other Targumim apart from Pseudo-Jonathan) to the master of all the world, the Lord. In Exodus 15: 2, YH is the title of the one who has redeemed his people from Egypt, definitively and gloriously; yet, as is well known, this name YH is introduced by the rubric of Exodus 15: 1, 'Then Moses and the sons of Israel will sing (*yashir*) this song', the verb *yashir* being a future form which ancient exegetes were ready to represent as 'shall sing'—that is, the Song is one which will be sung in the future, when the final redemption, modelled on that of the going forth from Egypt, is celebrated in the age to come.[28] The divine title YH was thus perceived by the *meturgemanim* as one which specifically highlights not only God's dominion in this world, since he is master of every age or world, but also as portending his mighty victory in the world to come. As regards Amalek, therefore,

---

[28] See *Mekhilta derabi yishma'el*, 'Shirata' 1: 8–10, which states: 'Rabbi [Judah Hanasi] says: "Then Moses sang", *shar* is not written here, but rather "Then Moses shall sing" *yashir*. We find that we can derive the resurrection of the dead from the Torah.' This represents a well-known interpretation of the verse, famously represented in BT *San.* 91*b* (R. Meir).

the Targumim appear to have understood that the title YH suggests a victory achieved, and at the same time one yet to be accomplished, just as YH was the subject of Israel's praises after the definitive redemption from Egypt, while remaining as the title of the one who will be praised when the final redemption is brought about.

Careful reading of Onkelos, however, reveals a certain subtlety of interpretation which will take us back to where we started, with consideration of *Pesikta derav kahana*. According to Onkelos, the divine war against Amalek is destined to be waged 'to destroy them from the generations of the world, age, universe'. Unlike the other Targumim, which have spoken of Amalek's destruction in the time of Samuel or Mordechai and Esther, this Targum leaves matters open, perhaps deliberately so. For in the Masoretic text of the Hebrew Bible the phrase 'from eternal generations' (*midor dor*) is written defectively, without the letter *vav* in each word, an orthography which an anonymous *darshan* in *Pesikta derav kahana* 3: 16 was able to use creatively by reading the two words as one, as if it were a participle of the verb *dardar*, giving the sense that the Almighty was 'rolling after' or 'tracking' Amalek from one generation to another.[29] Once this reading was out in the open, so to speak, the sages could debate which generations might be involved, Rabbi Eliezer proposing those from Moses to Samuel; Rabbi Joshua those from Samuel to Mordechai and Esther; and Rabbi Jose those from Mordechai and Esther to the generation of king messiah, which is three generations, Psalm 72: 5 once more serving as proof for this.[30]

Before I attempt to draw together the many threads which compose these observations, and venture to offer some tentative conclusions about ancient approaches to these verses, I must take a brief look at Exodus 17: 15, which has so far not figured in the discussion. This verse relates that Moses built an altar, and that he called its name *adonai nisi*, which may be translated as 'the Lord is my miracle', or 'the Lord is my banner, ensign'. Of the many comments which could be offered on this verse,[31] one in particular is especially important for my purposes, and it is this: the Hebrew preserved in the Masoretic text is not clear about who precisely

---

[29] See William G. Braude and Israel J. Kapstein, *Pesikta de-Rab Kahana: R. Kahana's Compilation of Discourses for Sabbaths and Festal Days* (London, 1975), 55, where the text is translated as 'The Holy One said: I keep tracking Amalek from generation to generation.'

[30] *Pesikta derav kahana*, 3: 16 (Mandelbaum edn., 53).

[31] Thus the question already indicated in our translation of the verse is an important one: whether *nes* is to be understood in its general biblical Hebrew sense of 'banner, flag, ensign', or whether the extended meaning of the word as 'wonder, providential event, miracle', common in rabbinic Hebrew, is appropriate here. Then there is the question whether Moses offered sacrifice on this altar: several of the Targumim suggest that he did so, by stating that at it he 'worshipped', Aramaic *pelaḥ*, a term very frequently employed with reference to sacrifice: see TO, marginal gloss of TN, and Targumim preserved in Cambridge University Library MS Or 1080, and probably in Jewish Theological Seminary MS 605 (the text is not entirely certain). Such a view is attested already in Second Temple times by Philo, *De vita Mosis*, i. 219, and Josephus, *Antiquities of the Jews*, iii. 60.

gave the name to the altar. Was it Moses, or was it the Almighty himself? The question is already apparent in the *Mekhilta derabi yishma'el*, dealing with the words of Exodus 17: 15, 'and he called its name "The Lord is my ensign"'. Rabbi Joshua asserts that *Moses* is the subject of 'he called the altar *nisi*', while Rabbi Eleazar of Modin states that God called it by this name, making it clear that he has understood YHVH as the subject of the verb.[32] Now this uncertainty about who the speaker might be spills over, as it were, into the following verse which speaks about the 'hand upon the Lord's throne' and his war with Amalek: is it Moses who is uttering these almost oracular sentiments, or is it the Lord? While the *Mekhilta derabi yishma'el* and the Targumim presented the words in this verse as having the force of a divine oath, the *midrash* quoted by Michael Fishbane from *Pesikta derav kahana* and parallels permit the reader to surmise that it may be Moses who is speaking of the 'hand upon the Lord's throne', that is, an alien authority or power directed against the Lord's dominion, against which the Almighty will have to contend in future generations. Some ancient evidence confirms that such an interpretation was possible from as early as Second Temple times; for the fragmentary biblical manuscript 4QpaleoExod[m] states that the Lord will have war against Amalek *ad dor dor*, 'until eternal generations', a reading which makes perfect sense if Moses is envisaged as the speaker of these words.[33]

This brief survey of three very difficult verses allows us to make some tentative observations on their interpretation in antiquity. First, it is fairly clear that the Hebrew of Exodus 17: 14–16 presented to interpreters a mass of uncertainties; indeed, the more closely the Hebrew is scrutinized in the various forms which have survived from antiquity, the more exegetical possibilities inherent in the texts present themselves. Second, the matter of Amalek was perceived as a 'global' concern: it is referred to in all constituent parts of the Written Torah, and thus acquires an urgency in divine and human affairs, the notion of the completeness of God's plan for the universe being bound up with it. Finally, given the exegetical possibilities afforded by Exodus 17: 14–16, two broad approaches to the verses seem to have emerged in antiquity. One interpreted the difficult phrase about the hand on the Lord's throne as a divine oath guaranteeing the eventual destruction of Amalek, which allowed, and even encouraged, the view that God is even now in complete control of events, particularly in the perplexing matter of Amalek. The Targumim seem to have grasped at this interpretation, and to have refined it considerably by defining the divine name YH, very rare in the books of Moses, with reference to the YH of Exodus 15: 2 as either 'the Revered One' or the 'Lord of all the ages', the

---

[32] See *Mekhilta de rabi yishma'el*, 'Amalek' 2 (Lauterbach edn., p. 159, ll. 163–5).

[33] See Propp, *Exodus 1–18*, 615, 620. On the question who is the speaker in this verse, see also Nahum Sarna, *The JPS Torah Commentary: Exodus* (Philadelphia, Pa., 1991), 96. For 4QpaleoExod[m], see Patrick W. Skehan, Eugene Ulrich, and Judith Sanderson, *Qumran Cave 4.IV: Palaeo-Hebrew and Greek Manuscripts*, Discoveries in the Judaean Desert IX (Oxford, 1992), 53–130, and the bibliography cited in Florentino García Martínez, *The Dead Sea Scrolls Study Edition*, vol. i: *1Q1–4Q273* (Leiden, 1997), 248.

Lord who overthrew Pharaoh's authority and brought Israel triumphant out of Egypt. The 'uncertainties' in the verses are thus reduced, and may be more or less accommodated in questions about when, in the future, Amalek and what that nation represents will be finally destroyed; or whether Amalek will be destroyed 'in one go', as it were, or in a series of engagements throughout the generations. For the YH who is celebrated in Exodus 15: 2 is being extolled in a poem that Moses and Israel not only sang at the Red Sea, but that will be sung in the future, when the dead are raised. In short, the transformation of traditional exegesis of these verses at the hands of the *meturgemanim* is designed to reassure Israel by insisting that God is the universal sovereign, whose ultimate victory over all enemies, however powerful, is assured.

The other exegetical approach is represented by the extraordinary statements of *Pesikta derav kahana* and parallels to which Fishbane has drawn our attention. The survey undertaken here underscores just how extraordinary the words reported by Rabbi Levi in that *midrash* turn out to be, with their frank, unqualified assertions about the incompleteness of the divine name and throne while Amalek's descendants endure. We have seen that the *Mekhilta derabi yishma'el* attributed to Rabbi Eleazar of Modin the view that when idolatry and its practitioners were rooted out, then and only then might the Lord's name be truly one, and his kingly dominion eternally established. But the *Mekhilta* did not pursue this line of thought: it left it hanging, as it were, and seemingly unrelated to anything else in the commentary on these verses. Taken further, however, such thinking about the name might well have led to the insights expressed by Rabbi Levi that while Amalek endures, the Lord's throne and kingship are incomplete; this, however, remained a 'minority' interpretation of the Hebrew, and therefore all the more striking and unusual.

Given that *Mekhilta derabi yishma'el* certainly hints that more could be said about Amalek, the unity of the divine name, and God's kingship, might it be the case that the rabbinic authorities were concerned at some point to avoid the dangerous and controversial debates which might be engendered by these verses? In other words, is it possible to see the general drift of the *Mekhilta*'s exegesis as aimed at further transforming the Scripture and directing the reader to a 'safe' understanding of the Hebrew, merely hinting at the implications which Rabbi Eleazar's interpretation might have for understandings of God's name and kingship? And should not the Targumim also, perhaps, be regarded as part of a similar exegetical endeavour, not unlike that of the *Mekhilta* passages, intended in some manner to sanitize these verses, and make them safe for an unlearned audience in particular? A generally affirmative answer might be returned to these questions were it not for Targum Onkelos on Exodus 17: 16, which, as we have seen, might invite further consideration of what exactly the destruction of Amalek 'from the generations of the world/age/universe' might mean. The imagery of the Almighty 'tracking' Amalek from one generation to another might without difficulty be accommodated in Onkelos' translation, and with it the implication that, while that 'tracking' continues, the authority of the Almighty is 'incomplete'.

The question of the relative and absolute dates of the documents and traditions examined here cannot be addressed in this short paper, and its conclusions must be correspondingly modest. But the evidence we have surveyed suggests that the dramatic *midrash* noted by Fishbane, which surfaces with explosive effect in *Pesikta derav kahana* and parallels, represents the most unqualified expression of an exegesis that other documents and authorities might well have known, and have known for a long time, but were chary of articulating too publicly.

THREE

UNWASHED HANDS
A Midrashic Controversy in the Gospel of Matthew

PIET VAN BOXEL

OVER THE LAST FEW DECADES scholars interested in the Jewish context of early Christianity have turned to rabbinic literature for treatment of motif and genre in New Testament narratives. Underlying this literary choice is the idea that Christianity originated within early Judaism and developed as one of its branches.[1] Such an approach puts paid to reading the New Testament as a competitive confrontation of the historical Jesus and his followers with the rabbinic establishment in an effort to prove the pre-eminence and superiority of the Christian message, the hallmark of Strack-Billerbeck's impressive compilation of rabbinic parallels to the New Testament.[2]

---

[1] Groundbreaking work has been done by, among others, William D. Davies, *Paul and Rabbinic Judaism* (s.l., 1948); David Daube, *The New Testament and Rabbinic Judaism* (London, 1956); Geza Vermes, *Jesus the Jew: A Historian's Reading of the Gospels* (London, 1973); E. P. Sanders, *Paul and Palestinian Judaism* (London, 1977); id., *Jesus and Judaism* (London, 1985). Recent works on the subject are Reimund Bieringer et al. (eds.), *The New Testament and Rabbinic Literature* (Leiden, 2010); Dan Jaffé (ed.), *Studies in Rabbinic Judaism and Early Christianity: Text and Context* (Leiden, 2010). For a cumulative bibliography see Bieringer, *The New Testament*, 471–508. For a historical overview of the use of early Jewish literature by Christians see William Horbury, 'The New Testament and Rabbinic Study—An Historical Sketch', in Bieringer, *The New Testament*, 1–42. For recent revisionist discussions of the subject see Adam H. Becker and Annette Yoshiko Reed (eds.), *The Ways That Never Parted: Jews and Christians in Late Antiquity and the Early Middle Ages* (Tübingen, 2003).

[2] Herman L. Strack and Paul Billerbeck, *Kommentar zum Neuen Testament aus Talmud und Midrasch*, 4 vols. (Munich, 1922–8). Two years after publication the claim of Christianity's moral superiority over Judaism was heavily criticized by Herbert Loewe, see Claude G. Montefiore, *Rabbinic Literature and Gospel Teachings*, Appendix II (London, 1930), 380–9. For recent detailed analysis and criticism see Berndt Schaller, 'Paul Billerbecks "Kommentar zum Neuen Testament aus Talmud und Midrasch": Wege und Abwege, Leistung und Fehlleistung christlicher Judaistik', in Christfried Böttrich, Mudith Thomanek, and Thomas Willi (eds.), *Zwischen Zensur und Selbstbesinnung: christliche Rezeptionen des Judentums: Beiträge des von der Alfried Krupp von Bohlen und Halbach-Stiftung geförderten interdisziplinären Symposiums am 15.—16. Februar 2007 im Alfried Krupp Wissenschaftskolleg Greifswald: Julia Männchen zum 70. Geburtstag gewidmet* (Frankfurt am Main, 2009), 149–73; Andreas Bedenbender, 'Billerbecks Kommentar im Lichte von neueren Alternativansätzen', ibid. 175–214.

One of the literary devices figuring prominently in the discussion of the interdependence or intertextuality between rabbinic literature and the New Testament is the genre of Midrash. In their search for the Jewish roots of Jesus and early Christianity, New Testament scholars are tempted to discover a midrashic background in narratives such as the infancy stories and the parables in the Synoptic Gospels. Occasionally a whole gospel is regarded as a *midrash*.[3]

This chapter does not intend to give a detailed overview of the various shapes and forms of Midrash in all its complexity and, by doing so, to show the inaccurate ways in which this rabbinic genre is often applied to New Testament writings, when classifying the creative interpretation of biblical motifs and the *mise en scène* of Old Testament texts in a christological guise as early Christian Midrash.[4] Here it will suffice to refer to the essence of Midrash and an all-inclusive definition, that 'midrash springs from Scripture and is reanchored in Scripture. Between those poles of authority the sage mediates his message.'[5] It is this fundamental structure of 'biblical text—interpretation—biblical proof-text', which through intertextual association, often regulated by hermeneutical rules, gives the biblical text a renewed or altered meaning. According to this definition the reproductions of Old Testament motifs and scenes in the New Testament, creative though they may be, are to be excluded from the genre Midrash. New Testament writings are jam-packed with motifs and vocabulary derived from the Hebrew Bible. However, the occurrence of such source material without an explicit interaction between biblical text and proof-text, which legitimizes its particular, new meaning, is an insufficient criterion for applying the term Midrash to a New Testament text. Retracing in the Hebrew Bible and in post-biblical literature the development of concepts, words, and motifs used in the New Testament belongs to one of the classical disciplines of biblical exegesis, the historical-critical method of *Motivgeschichte*. This exegetical tool, however, cannot qualify as a means of establishing the use of Midrash in the New Testament.[6]

---

[3] Dale Miller and Patricia Miller, *The Gospel of Mark as Midrash on Earlier Jewish and New Testament Literature* (Lewiston, NY, 1990).

[4] For an extensive analysis of rabbinic Midrash both as form and as method see Philip Alexander, 'Midrash and the Gospels', in Christopher M. Tuckett (ed.), *Synoptic Studies: The Ampleforth Conferences of 1982 and 1983*, Journal for the Study of the New Testament, Supplement Series 7 (Sheffield, 1984), 1–18. See further Lieve Teugels, 'Midrash in the Bible or Midrash on the Bible? Critical Remarks about the Uncritical Use of a Term', in Gerhard Bodendorfer and Matthias Millard (eds.), *Bibel und Midrasch*, Forschungen zum alten Testament 22 (Tübingen, 1998), 43–63; Lieve Teugels, *Bible and Midrash: The Story of 'The Wooing of Rebekah' (Gen. 24)* (Leuven, 2004), 145–69.

[5] Michael Fishbane, *The Exegetical Imagination: On Jewish Thought and Theology* (Cambridge, Mass., 1998), 15. See further Fishbane's exposition 'Midrash and the Nature of Scripture', ibid. 9–21. See also Alexander, 'Midrash and the Gospels', 3 ff.

[6] See e.g. the detailed analysis of the curse of the fig tree in Mark 11: 14, 20–4 by Miguel Pérez Fernández, 'Midrash and the New Testament: A Methodology for the Study of Gospel Midrash', in Bieringer, *The New Testament*, 367–84. The approach is an example of improper use of the term Midrash and falls under the categories characterized by Philip Alexander as 'New Testament stories loosely modelled on Old Testament' and 'imaginative borrowings from the Old Testament, which cannot be

RITUAL PURITY IN MARK 7: 1–23

Following our definition, the identification of Midrash or elements thereof within the New Testament is inevitably narrowed down and limited to single, clearly demarcated passages, which explicitly interact with a biblical quotation. The narrative discussed in this contribution is that recorded in Mark 7: 1–23 and its parallel Matthew 15: 1–20. New Testament scholars, when discussing ritual purity, focus almost exclusively on the Gospel of Mark. With a notable interest in the historical Jesus and therefore for the most part disregarding the parallel story in the Gospel of Matthew,[7] they have taken somewhat opposite positions when interpreting the earliest recording of Jesus' attitude to ritual purity: 'one is not defiled by what goes into the body but by what comes out' (Mark 7: 13).

Since the discussion about defilement in Mark is preceded by the debate between Jesus and the Pharisees concerning the washing of hands before eating, it could be argued that defilement is to be understood as caused by food. In that case the statement reflects a tradition within early Judaism, from which it could be concluded that the saying possibly preserves an *ipsissimum verbum* of Jesus. According to archaeological evidence the washing of hands before eating is first attested in the Herodian period,[8] and could therefore be questioned or even rejected by Jesus. His position would comply with a statement in the Mishnah that impurity of hands is second-degree impurity, which can induce only third-degree impurity in other objects, from which ordinary food is excluded.[9] That moral impurity supersedes ritual impurity, as stated at the end of the narrative, is equally not an uncommon position in early Judaism and could easily have been shared by the historical Jesus.[10]

On the other hand, one could focus on Mark's explanatory notes—meant for his audience—which describe Jewish customs with a sharp oppositional edge:

---

called midrash'; see Alexander, 'Midrash and the Gospels', 10 ff. For a convincing comparison between a New Testament and a rabbinic text see Menahem Kister, 'Romans 5: 12–21 Against the Background of Torah-Theology and Hebrew Usage', *Harvard Theological Review*, 100 (2007), 391–424. A valuable contribution to the study of Midrash in the New Testament is Birger Gerhardsson, *The Testing of God's Son (Matthew 4: 1–11 & Par): An Analysis of an Early Christian Midrash* (Lund, 1966).

[7] A classic example of such an approach is Roger P. Booth, *Jesus and the Laws of Purity: Tradition, History and Legal History in Mark 7*, Journal for the Study of the New Testament, Supplement Series 13 (Sheffield, 1986). See further Thomas Kazen, *Jesus and Purity Halakhah: Was Jesus Indifferent to Impurity?* (Stockholm, 2002), 60–7.

[8] See Friedrich Avemarie, 'Jesus and Purity', in Bieringer, *The New Testament*, 255–80, esp. 264 ff.

[9] See Mishnah *Yad.* 3: 1. See further Avemarie, 'Jesus and Purity', 256 ff. For a full discussion of the subject with reference to other issues of impurity see ibid. 255–80 and the response by Thomas Kazen, 'Jesus, Scripture and Paradosis', in Bieringer, *The New Testament*, 281–8.

[10] See Avemarie, 'Jesus and Purity', 269–71. Sanders, however, considers the discussions between Jesus and the Pharisees slightly artificial and doubts that there were any substantial points of opposition between them; see Sanders, *Jesus and Judaism*, 264 ff.

They saw that some of his disciples ate with hands defiled, that is, unwashed. For the Pharisees, and all the Jews, do not eat unless they wash their hands, observing the tradition of the elders; and when they come from the market place, they do not eat unless they purify themselves; and there are many other traditions which they observe, the washing of cups and pots and vessels of bronze. (Mark 7: 2–4)

Furthermore, taking into account that not Jesus but his disciples ate with unwashed hands, it could be argued that the whole scene most likely reflects the position of the gentile church vis-à-vis contemporary Judaism and not the teaching of the historical Jesus.[11] From this point of view the statement that one is not defiled by what goes into the body does not need to be limited to eating ordinary food with unwashed hands. It may be simply understood as a statement, which declares without any exception all foods clean.[12]

Important as these discussions may be for the understanding of the relationship between New Testament texts and early rabbinic literature, this exclusive focus on the Gospel of Mark runs the risk of overlooking specific features in the parallel text, which shed light both on the historical roots of the story and on its development and redaction. When commentators do take the parallels into account, they often use them solely as explanation of the Markan narrative. The subordinate role of the Matthean version is particularly evident when scholars discuss the relationship between the two parts of the narrative (washing of hands and ritual purity) in the Gospel of Mark. The solution is often sought by pointing out the differences between Matthew's and Mark's articulation of Jesus' position vis-à-vis ritual purity. Instead of Mark's 'there is nothing outside a man which by going into him can defile him; but the things which come out of a man are what defile him' (Mark 7: 15), Matthew transmits the saying as follows: 'not what goes into the mouth defiles a man, but what comes out of the mouth, this defiles a man' (Matt. 15: 11).[13] The variant in Matthew's version 'into the mouth' is then used as a clarification of the Markan phrase 'going into him'. By placing the emphasis on food, the variant makes the connection with the first part of the pericope, which deals with the washing of hands.[14] When, however, as will be suggested, the variant 'into the mouth' is dealt with from Matthew's point of view, it will shed light on the Matthean composition in its own right and no longer be considered a reading aid for the Gospel of Mark. Equally important is the fact that Matthew omits the redactional statement in Mark 7: 18 'declaring all foods clean'. Instead, at the very end of his version he adds: 'but to eat with unwashed hands does not defile a man' (Matt. 15: 20). With this redactional intervention Matthew may have intended to transform the Markan Jesus into a Torah-observant Jew, as is often claimed.[15] But reading Matthew's redaction only as a correction of the story in the Gospel of Mark is reductive. It overlooks the

---

[11] Sanders, *Jesus and Judaism*, 265.　　[12] See Avemarie, 'Jesus and Purity', 256.
[13] The same difference occurs in Mark 7: 18 and its parallel Matt. 15: 16, and Mark 7: 20 and its parallel Matt. 15: 18.
[14] See Avemarie, 'Jesus and Purity', 266 ff.　　[15] See e.g. ibid. 272.

significance of this final sentence of the narrative in the Gospel of Matthew within the Matthean composition as a whole.

In the following it will be argued that the narrative about eating bread with unwashed hands and the question as to whether this causes ritual impurity as told in the Gospel of Matthew (15: 1–20) reflects a midrashic mode found in early rabbinic Judaism, which enables us to explain the differences in composition and redaction between the Matthean and the probably earlier version of the story in the Gospel of Mark (7: 1–23).

A SYNOPTIC COMPARISON OF MATTHEW 15: 1–20 WITH MARK 7: 1–23

The narrative about eating bread with unwashed hands (Matt. 15: 1–9 and Mark 7: 1–13) belongs to the genre of polemical discourse, typically held between Jesus and the Pharisees in Gospel tradition. The two versions of the polemic are usually treated as units in their own right.[16] In both Gospels the dispute is followed by a *paranesis*, first addressed to the people (Matt. 15: 10–11 and Mark 7: 14–16) and subsequently to the disciples (Matt. 15: 12–20 and Mark 7: 17–23).[17] Both narratives are clearly demarcated in virtually the same way, thus creating an *inclusio* that provides us with expanded text units—Matthew 15: 1–20 and Mark 7: 1–23. If we consider Mark 7: 1–23 to be the earliest version of the narrative, the various elements of the story may reflect the rejection of early rabbinic practices or principles by certain streams in the early church. Mark used these elements, which may have been articulated on different occasions, as building blocks for his narrative of the confrontation between Jesus and the Pharisees, distinguishing and liaising the textual units through inclusions. Matthew clearly used the same building blocks, but, as will be shown, created his own text units within the narrative. They share only one *inclusio*—the beginning and the conclusion of their composition. These features deserve attention when we consider midrashic elements in the stories.

Matthew	*Mark*
Why do your disciples transgress the tradition of the elders? For they don't wash hands when they eat bread. (15: 2)	They saw that some of his disciples ate with hands defiled, that is, unwashed. (7: 1–2)

---

[16] See Klaus Berger, *Die Gesetzesauslegung Jesu. Ihr historischer Hintergrund im Judentum und im alten Testament, Teil I: Markus und Paralellen*, Wissenschaftliche Monographien zum Alten und Neuen Testament hrs. von Günter Bornkamm und Gerhard von Rad 40 (Neukirchen, 1972), 487; Joachim Gnilka, *Das Matthäusevangelium II. Teil* (Freiburg, 1988), 18 ff.; Ulrich Luz, *Das Evangelium nach Matthäus. 2. Teilband Mt 8–17* (Neukirchen, 1990), 415.

[17] For the composed character of the pericope see Jan Lambrechts, 'Jesus and the Law: An Investigation of Mk 7, 1–23', *Ephemerides Theologicae Lovanienses*, 53 (1977), 24–79, esp. 29 ff.

For out of the heart come evil thoughts, murder, adultery, fornication, theft, false witness, slander. These are what defile a man; but to eat with unwashed hands does not defile a man. (15: 19–20)	For from within, out of the heart of man, come evil thoughts, fornication, theft, murder, adultery, coveting, wickedness, deceit, licentiousness, envy, slander, pride, foolishness. All these evil things come from within, and they defile a man. (7: 21–2)

When compared with the Markan narrative, Matthew's rearrangement of the text units and redactional interventions appears to have resulted in a separate story of its own. These differences, both in terms of the actual text and in the composition of corresponding material, shed light on their own specific relationship to contemporary Judaism and on the literary devices the two Gospel writers considered suitable for their community.

The most apparent difference is the fact that when Mark introduces the matter of washing hands, he indirectly addresses an audience that is not familiar with this Jewish tradition: 'they [the Pharisees] saw that some of his disciples ate with hands defiled, that is, unwashed. For the Pharisees, and all the Jews, do not eat unless they wash their hands, observing the tradition of the elders' (Mark 7: 2). The introduction to the discussion between Jesus and the Pharisees as told in the Gospel of Matthew, on the other hand, presupposes familiarity with an established custom and remains therefore an internal Jewish affair: 'Why do your disciples transgress the tradition of the elders? For they don't wash hands when they eat bread' (Matt. 15: 2). That Mark after explaining the tradition of washing hands mentions the Jewish customs of the washing of cups and pots and vessels of bronze—an exaggeration of the practice—illustrates that he did not expect that his audience had even a nodding acquaintance with contemporary Judaism. Therefore, the use of a midrashic method would not be a viable means of communicating the message.

A noteworthy second difference between the two narratives is the arrangement of the elements of the shared tradition—Jesus' counterattack that (the) Pharisees transgress the commandment to honour one's father and mother and the quotation from Isaiah 29. In Matthew's composition the accusation first provokes a counterattack, Jesus blaming his opponents for transgressing the commandment of God to honour one's father and mother for the sake of their tradition, followed by the quotation from Isaiah. In Mark's version Jesus confronts his adversaries immediately with Isaiah's harsh judgment on the Jewish people: 'this people honours me with their lips, but their heart is far from me; in vain do they worship me, teaching as doctrines the precepts of men'.[18] It is only after this quotation that Mark brings the accusation of transgressing the commandment to honour one's father and mother.

---

[18] The quotation is close to the Septuagint version.

The position of the quotation from Isaiah 29 before and after this commandment in Mark and Matthew respectively creates a different emphasis in each narrative, which discloses the specific intentions of the two authors and the literary devices in which they are conveyed to their readers, as will be shown.

ISAIAH 29 IN THE GOSPEL OF MARK: 'TEACHING AS DOCTRINES THE PRECEPTS OF MEN'

The controversy about the washing of hands and the dispute about the way one's parents should be honoured may originally have taken place on different occasions. Brought together by means of Isaiah 29, with 'the traditions of the fathers or the precepts of men' as a common denominator,[19] Mark 7: 1–13 is a well-composed unit, in which the reference to the tradition of the elders is of structural importance. Referred to both in the introduction (v. 3) and in the question put to Jesus by the Pharisees (v. 5), it forms an inclusion with 'your tradition' (v. 13) right at the end of the polemic between Jesus and the Pharisees. The quotation from Isaiah 29: 13 connects the question put to Jesus by the Pharisees and his answer, in which the tradition of men (i.e. of the Pharisees) is put on a par with the precepts of men that are rejected by God:

v. 3: For the Pharisees, and all the Jews, do not eat unless they wash their hands, observing the tradition of the elders;

v. 5: And the Pharisees and the scribes asked him, 'Why do your disciples not live according to the tradition of the elders?'

v. 7: 'in vain do they [this people] worship me, teaching as doctrines the precepts of men' [Isa. 29: 13]

v. 8: You leave the commandment of God, and hold fast the tradition of men.

v. 13: [you] making void the word of God through your tradition

The Isaiah quotation is crucial for what Mark intends to convey to his audience. By connecting the 'precepts of men' and the 'tradition of men' in parallel he explicitly defines the tradition of the elders as a plural concept by which the washing of hands and the rejection of supporting one's parents become only two examples of pharisaic tradition. It is the entire tradition —in conclusion alluded to as 'and many such things you do' (v. 13)—which according to Mark's narrative Jesus has abolished.

---

[19] See Hans Hübner, *Das Gesetz in der synoptischen Tradition. Studien zur These einer progressiven Qumranisierung und Judaisierung innerhalb der synoptischen Tradition* (Witten, 1973), 142–7. The Isaiah quotation fits Christian polemics with contemporary Judaism well and is echoed in early Christian texts such as Rom. 11: 8, 1 Cor. 1: 19, and Col. 2: 22; see Kazen, 'Jesus, Scripture and Paradosis', 287 n. 25. Not surprisingly it is not used in early rabbinic writings.

ISAIAH 29 IN THE GOSPEL OF MATTHEW: 'THIS PEOPLE HONOURS ME WITH THEIR LIPS'

Placed at the end of the polemic the Isaiah quotation in the Gospel of Matthew plays a different role. The Matthean Jesus immediately counters the criticism uttered by the Pharisees that his disciples transgress the tradition of the elders by accusing them of transgressing the commandment of God for the sake of their tradition (v. 3). Proof of the pharisaic transgression is their interpretation of the commandment 'Honour your father and your mother' in Exodus 20: 12, namely that he who has dedicated his means to God is absolved from the obligation to honour his parents. Matthew shares this tradition with Mark, who may have been his source, but has phrased the tradition differently for the sake of his uninformed audience by explaining that honouring one's parents consists in action: 'If a man tells his father or his mother, "What you would have gained from me is Korban" (that is, given to God), then you no longer permit him to do anything for his father or mother' (Mark 7: 11–12). Matthew, however, expects his audience to know this interpretation and simply keeps to the unspecified verb 'to honour'. This presupposed understanding of Exodus 20: 12 reflects a predominant understanding of the commandment in early rabbinic literature, the earliest literary witness of which is found in the tannaitic *midrash* on the book of Exodus, the *Mekhilta derabi yishma'el*. There, the exposition of the commandment starts with a typical rhetorical question: 'Should I understand it [to mean only] with words?'. Phrased in this form, the suggested interpretation is always immediately rejected as untenable, a rejection based upon another biblical text introduced by 'Scripture teaches', which discloses the right understanding of the text. The biblical key provided in the *Mekhilta* for the interpretation of Exodus 20: 12 is Proverbs 3: 9 'Honour the Lord with your substance'. Using the hermeneutical rule *gezerah shavah*, which connects biblical texts by means of identical vocabulary—here the verb 'to honour'—the author specifies the way in which the verb in Exodus 20: 12 is to be understood, namely 'with your substance'. He then spells out how his general rule is to be implemented: 'with food, and drink, and with clean garments'.[20] It is exactly this understanding of the commandment that is presupposed in the Gospel of Matthew and which according to certain pharisaic circles does not need to be upheld if one has dedicated his means to God.

The knowledge of this exegetical discussion among Matthew's readers seems to be confirmed by the position of the Isaiah quotation in the Matthean composition. That Pharisees are accused of undermining the obligation to support one's parents seems to imply that in their view it could suffice to honour parents with words as initially suggested, but this is renounced in the tradition transmitted by the *Mekhilta*. It is this interpretation that is rejected by Jesus, a rejection authorized with an appeal

---

[20] 'Baḥodesh' 8, *Mekhilta de-Rabbi Ishmael*, trans. and ed. Jacob Lauterbach, 3 vols. (Philadelphia, Pa., 1976), ii. 257.

to Scripture. Using the same hermeneutical rule Matthew expands the *midrash* by creating a contrast between 'Honour the Lord with your substance' (Prov. 3: 9) and 'This people honours me [God] with their lips' (Isa. 29: 13).[21]

THE MEANING OF HONOURING IN RABBINIC LITERATURE

The narrative in Matthew 15 is the earliest source known of the midrashic reading of Exodus 20: 12 that understands 'honour' as implying action, which became a well-established interpretation in rabbinic Judaism. One example is the *baraita* in the Babylonian Talmud: 'Our rabbis taught: What is "fear" and what is "honour"? "Fear" means that he [the son] must neither stand in his [the father's] place nor sit in his place, nor contradict his words, nor tip the scales against him. "Honour" means that he must give him food and drink, clothe and cover him, lead him in and out.'[22]

As in the *Mekhilta derabi yishma'el*, Proverbs 3: 9 is used as a biblical hermeneutical key for the interpretation of Exodus 20: 12. The *baraita* continues: 'It is said: "Honour your father and your mother." And it is also said: "Honour the Lord with your substance." Just as the latter means at personal cost, so, too, the former.'[23] In the same passage the old tradition as preserved in the *baraita* is challenged by the question of at whose expense the father should be honoured: the son's or the father's, to which the sages gave the answer that it should be at the father's expense, the personal cost of the son consisting in loss of time. It is this ruling that was brought to Palestine by Rabbi Jeremiah in the first half of the fourth century, thus changing the Palestinian halakhah that parents should be honoured at the son's expense. The Jerusalem Talmud preserves this ruling in the following discussion:

Rabbi Jonathan and Rabbi Yannai were sitting together. A man came and kissed Rabbi Jonathan's feet. Rabbi Yannai said to him: 'Which favour is he paying you back?' He said to him: 'Once he came complaining about his son, that he should provide for him. I said to him: "Go and gather the community against him and put him to shame."' He [Rabbi Yannai] said to him: 'And why did you not compel him?' He said to him: 'But can one

---

[21] With his redactional activity Matthew has no intention to transform the Markan story into a *midrash*, see Philip Alexander's critique of Michael Goulder's *Midrash and Lection in Matthew* (London, 1974) in 'Midrash and the Gospels', 14. Led by the midrashic traces preserved in the traditions transmitted by Mark, Matthew creates his *midrash* in order to convey his own message in a literary device that suits his community. These midrashic remains were either not noticed or ignored by Mark, whose community had no familiarity with the genre. Though meant for his community, Matthew's version may well come close to early, pre-Markan tradition.

[22] BT *Kid.* 31b. See further Piet W. van Boxel, 'Isaiah 29: 13 in the New Testament and Early Rabbinic Judaism', in Pieter W. van der Horst (ed.), *Aspects of Religious Contact and Conflict in the Ancient World*, Utrechtse Theologische Reeks 31 (Utrecht, 1995), 81–90, esp. 84 ff.

[23] BT *Kid.* 31a. For the eclectic use of Prov. 3: 9 as a proof-text for the interpretation of Exod. 20: 12 see van Boxel, 'Isaiah 29: 13', 85.

compel him?' He said to him: 'Is that still a question for you?' Thereupon Jonathan changed [his opinion] and established the tradition in his [Yannai's] name. Rabbi Jacob bar Aha came [and said]: 'Rabbi Samuel bar Nahman [said] in the name of Rabbi Jonathan that one may compel the son to provide for the father.'[24]

The encounter between Rabbi Jonathan and Rabbi Yannai seems to imply that Yannai, the prominent halakhist and pupil of Rabbi Judah Hanasi, made the final decision concerning the interpretation of Exodus 20: 12, and that until then the understanding of this commandment was not undisputed in Palestine. One could suggest that the text reflects a later version of the controversy embedded in Matthew's Gospel.

KORBAN AND HONOURING ONE'S FATHER AND MOTHER

The technical rabbinic term for the practice referred to by the Pharisees that enables the avoidance of the material support of one's parents is *korban*. The word is used in Mark's version, whereas Matthew uses the Greek word 'gift' (*doron*). *Korban* means either a sacrifice or is the term used to introduce a vow to abstain from something or to forbid another person to make use of one's belongings.[25] It is the latter meaning that applies to our narrative, which may well reflect a certain practice in first-century Judaea. Such a vow, however, was not necessarily binding under all circumstances. In the Mishnah it is recorded that, according to Rabbi Eliezer, 'one may grant dispensation from a vow by reason of the honour due to father and mother … and the rabbis agree with Rabbi Eliezer that in a matter between a man and his father and mother dispensation may be granted to him by reason of the honour due to his father and mother.'[26] In the Matthean controversy, however, the Pharisees make no reference to such a tradition and state that one who has given his means to God will certainly not honour his father. The precise attitude of the Pharisees to the annulment of such a vow in Mark's presentation depends on whether one translates the pharisaic injunction as a straightforward prohibition: 'you no longer allow him to do anything', or as a possibility offered to the son: 'you allow him to do nothing in future'.[27] Matthew seems to opt for a prohibition on the part of the Pharisees, which implies that they themselves transgress the commandment, a transgression that supersedes the alleged violation by the disciples of the tradition of the elders. In Jesus' answer to the pharisaic accusation a sharp contrast is made between tradition and the commandment to honour one's father and mother. By introducing the commandment with 'For God said' Matthew—in contrast to Mark, who presents honouring one's father and mother as a Mosaic

---

[24] JT *Pe'ah* 1: 1 (15*d*).
[25] See Ze'ev W. Falk, 'On Talmudic Vows', *Harvard Theological Review*, 59 (1966), 309–12, esp. 310.
[26] Mishnah *Ned.* 11: 1. See further van Boxel, 'Isaiah 29: 13', 86 ff.
[27] See Avemarie, 'Jesus and Purity', 265 n. 48.

obligation—underlines the divine origin of this commandment. That the pharisaic, traditional interpretation of Exodus 20: 12 that follows, 'but you say', is qualified as making void the word of God brings the opposition between human tradition and divine commandment clearly to the fore:

Then Pharisees and scribes came to Jesus from Jerusalem and said, 'Why do your disciples transgress the tradition of the elders? For they do not wash their hands when they eat.' He answered them, 'And why do you transgress the commandment of God for the sake of your tradition? For God commanded, "Honour your father and your mother," and "He who speaks evil of his father or mother, let him surely die." But you say, "If any one tells his father or his mother, 'What you would have gained from me is given to God,' he need not honour his father." So, for the sake of your tradition, you have made void the word of God.'

Attention should be called, however, to the fact that the content of the divine commandment is not limited to the biblical text—the *torah shebikhtav*—but includes the oral tradition—the *torah shebe'al peh*, here the midrashic interpretation as crystallized two centuries later in the *Mekhilta derabi yishma'el*.[28] Contrary to Jesus in the Gospel of Mark, the Matthean Jesus does not argue with the tradition as such, but rejects—as will be argued in the following instruction to the disciples—the tradition which is not authorized by Scripture, thus making the midrashic method an essential tool in the development of the theology of the Matthean church.[29]

ISAIAH 29: 13 AND THE *PARANESIS*

Since pharisaic/rabbinic tradition had been declared altogether obsolete, the tradition of washing hands before eating did not need further discussion in Mark's narrative. Though also dealing with defilement or impurity and therefore not completely out of place, the instruction following the controversy addresses the issue in a broader perspective that surpasses pharisaic rulings. No further mention is made of the washing of hands, and the instruction of the people is phrased in general terms: 'There is nothing outside a man which by going into him can defile him; but the things which come out of a man are what defile him' (Mark 7: 15).[30] In the

---

[28] See Alexander, 'Midrash and the Gospels', 5.

[29] *Korban* also could be understood in terms of worship, which would suggest a link between this Pharisaic teaching and the Isaiah quotation: 'in vain do they [this people] worship me, teaching as doctrines the precepts of men'. But the precepts of men remain here, in contradistinction with the Markan narrative, within the perimeter of the discussion concerning one single interpretation, namely that of Exod. 20: 13.

[30] Discussing the pre-Markan version Kazen opts for ritual hand-washing, raised by the Pharisees in the first half of the story, as the context of the saying, which then is to be understood in a relative sense; see Kazen, *Jesus and Purity Halakhah*, 65. Such a historical reconstruction, however, does not affect a synoptic comparison of the two versions of the Gospels of Mark and Matthew, and the interpretation of redactional differences as a result of their use of specific literary devices, see n. 21.

instruction of the disciples further clarification is given: 'Do you not see that whatever goes into a man from outside cannot defile him, since it enters not his heart but his stomach, and so passes on?' The redactional comment 'Thus he declared all foods clean' (7: 18–19) does not leave any doubt about the meaning of this statement. By declaring all foods clean Mark distances himself and his gentile-Christian community from biblical instruction concerning clean and unclean foods as formulated in Leviticus 11: 1–23. In light of the many studies on the Jewishness of Jesus no further proof is needed that such a statement cannot belong to Jesus' *ipsissima verba*.

In the Gospel of Matthew, however, the pharisaic accusation that the disciples did not wash their hands before eating still remains an issue, which only finds a conclusive answer, after a confrontation between ritual and moral purity, at the very end of the pericope: 'to eat with unwashed hands does not defile a man' (v. 20). Besides this explicit reference to the polemical exchange in the first half of the narrative, which is lacking in Mark's version, other small but significant redactional changes and additions refer to the discussion between the Pharisees and Jesus. After quoting Isaiah, Matthew opens his instruction of the people by changing Mark's 'there is nothing outside a man which by going into him can defile him; but the things which come out of a man are what defile him' into 'not what goes into the mouth defiles a man, but what comes out of the mouth, this defiles a man' (v. 11). The saying is repeated, using the same wording, in the instruction of the disciples, here with the explanation that 'what comes out of the mouth proceeds from the heart, and this defiles a man' (v. 18).

According to Matthew, the disciples told Jesus that the Pharisees were offended when they heard this saying. In other words, Matthew implies that they were among the people when Jesus instructed them.

A final observation concerns the evil that comes out of the heart. In Mark's version infractions of the commandments as listed on the second tablet of the Decalogue are combined with internal evil dispositions, together constituting a vice catalogue, popular in the Graeco-Roman world, but not unknown in Palestinian Judaism.[31] Mark's catalogue bears a striking resemblance to the vice list in the Community Rule of Qumran and the catalogue of sins in the *Didache*:

Mark 7: 21–2

For from within, out of the heart of man, come evil thoughts, fornication, theft, murder, adultery, coveting, wickedness, deceit, licentiousness, envy, slander, pride, foolishness.

1QS 4: 9–11

But the ways of the Spirit of Falsehood are these: greed and slackness in the search for

---

[31] See Joel Marcus, *Mark 1–8: A New Translation with Introduction and Commentary*, The Anchor Bible 27 (New Haven, Conn., 2000), 459 ff.

righteousness, wickedness and lies, haughtiness and pride, falseness and deceit, cruelty and abundant evil, ill-temper and much folly and brazen insolence, abominable deeds in a spirit of lust, and ways of lewdness in the service of uncleanness, a blaspheming tongue, blindness of eye and dullness of ear, stiffness of neck and heaviness of heart, so that man walks in all the ways of darkness and guile.

Didache 5: 1
But this is the way of death: first of all, it is evil and full of curses, murders, adulteries, lusts, fornications, thefts, idolatries, fortune-tellings, sorceries, robberies; false testimony, hypocrisy, duplicity, deception, arrogance, malice, stubbornness, greed, filthy-talking, jealousy, audacity, pride, boastfulness.

The sin catalogue in Matthew on the other hand—introduced by the general classification 'evil thoughts'—only contains murder, adultery, theft, and false witness, which are exclusively transgressions of the biblical commandments in the Decalogue.[32]

These redactional interventions should not, as is sometimes suggested,[33] be read as explanatory notes to the Markan narrative, but as literary devices connecting the instruction to the people and the disciples with the preceding polemic, whereby the position of Isaiah 29: 13 as a *trait d'union* between the two parts of the narrative plays a central role. In the discussion about the commandment to honour one's father and mother, the pharisaic halakhah that the honouring of parents with words would be sufficient was rejected by Jesus with reference to Isaiah 29: 13 as a biblical proof-text: 'This people honour me with their lips.' By creating a sharp contrast between mouth and heart in the *paranesis* Matthew undoubtedly alludes to the rest of the Isaiah quotation: 'this people draw near with their mouth ... while their hearts are far from me'. Thus through the Isaiah quotation the polemical discourse and the *paranesis* are interrelated. By reducing his sin catalogue to transgressions of the Decalogue, Matthew connects it with the preceding polemic about the biblical commandment 'Honour your father and your mother.' Even when shaped by interpretation, the commandments of the Decalogue are the words of God (*de'oraita*) as opposed to words of tradition (*derabanan*).[34] Just as the rabbinic halakhah that one may honour parents with one's lips is rejected by the Matthean Jesus with reference to Isaiah 29: 13, so in his final answer the *derabanan* tradition of washing hands before eating is annulled on the grounds of the same biblical proof-text.

---

[32] The duplications 'adultery/fornication' and 'false witness/slander' may well be caused by Matthew's use of Mark as his source.
[33] See n. 14.
[34] I would like to thank Michael Fishbane for drawing my attention to this connection between the polemic and the *paranesis*.

Matthew	Mark
|8| 'This people honours me with their lips, but their _**heart**_ is far from me;	
|10| And he called the people to him and said to them, 'Hear and understand:	|14| And he called the people to him again, and said to them, 'Hear me, all of you, and understand:
|11| _not_ what goes _into the mouth_ defiles a man, but what comes _out of the mouth_, this defiles a man.'	|15| there is _**nothing**_ outside a man which by _going into him_ can defile him; but the things which come _out of a man_ are what defile him.'
|12| Then the disciples came and said to him, 'Do you know that the Pharisees were offended when they heard this saying?' |13| He answered, 'Every plant which my heavenly Father has not planted will be rooted up. |14| Let them alone; they are blind guides. And if a blind man leads a blind man, both will fall into a pit.'	
|15| But Peter said to him, 'Explain the parable to us.'	|17| And when he had entered the house, and left the people, his disciples asked him about the parable.
|16| And he said, 'Are you also still without understanding? |17| Do you not see that whatever goes _into the mouth_ passes into the stomach, and so passes on?	|18| And he said to them, 'Then are you also without understanding? Do you not see that whatever goes _into a man_ from outside cannot defile him, |19| since it enters, not his heart but his stomach, and so passes on?' (_Thus he declared **all foods clean**._)
|18| But what comes _out of the mouth_ proceeds from the heart, and this defiles a man.	|20| And he said, 'What comes _out of a man_ is what defiles a man.
|19| For **out of the heart** come evil thoughts, murder, adultery, fornication, theft, false witness, slander.	_For from within, out of the heart_ of man, come evil thoughts, fornication, theft, murder, adultery, |22| coveting, wickedness, deceit, licentiousness, envy, slander, pride, foolishness.
|20| These are what defile a man; _but to eat with unwashed hands does not defile a man._'	|23| All these evil things come from within, and they defile a man.'

CONCLUSION

By connecting the instructions of the people and the disciples with Isaiah 29: 13 Matthew created a single narrative, which restricted the polemic to one pharisaic tradition: the washing of hands before eating. Using the building blocks of the tradition preserved in the Gospel of Mark, Jesus' answer to the Pharisees is couched in a literary device that Matthew considered suitable for his Jewish–Christian community: Midrash. This *midrash* takes its starting point in the commandment to honour one's father and mother (Exod. 20: 12), which in the *Mekhilta* is interpreted in terms of material support by quoting Proverbs 3: 9—'Honour the Lord with your substance'. The rejected interpretation—honour by means of words—provides the 'historical' portrayal of the Pharisees, who consider the material support of parents not binding under all circumstances. In order to show that they are transgressing a commandment by adopting this attitude, Isaiah 29: 13 is used as a proof-text: 'This people draw near with their mouth and honour me with their lips'.

Allusions in the *paranesis* to the whole Isaiah quotation—including 'while their hearts are far from me'—draw the instructions of the people and the disciples into the *midrash*. In this way the Isaiah quotation becomes part of a chain of explicit and implicit scriptural quotations and proof-texts that constitutes Jesus' counterattack, provoked by the Pharisees' accusation that his disciples did not wash their hands before eating.

Clearly reflecting a midrashic interpretation of Exodus 20: 12, preserved exclusively in the third-century *Mekhilta derabi yishma'el* and extended through redactional activity, the narrative in the Gospel of Matthew is a prime example of the role that New Testament compositions can play in the reconstruction of the development of early rabbinic traditions and literature.

FOUR

'TRADUNT HEBRAEI'
The Problem of the Function and Reception of Jewish Midrash in Jerome

ALISON SALVESEN

Two CONTRASTING PASSAGES from the period of Late Antiquity discuss the significance of Genesis 27: 15. The first is by St Jerome (*c*.347–420 CE), from his *Hebrew Questions on Genesis*, written around 392 CE:

'And Rebecca took with her in the house the garments of Esau her elder son, which were most desirable.' Now in respect of this verse the Hebrews have a tradition that firstborn sons performed the duty of the priests and possessed the priestly raiment, in which they were clothed as they were offering the victims to God, in the time before Aaron was chosen for the priestly office.[1]

The second passage is from *Midrash tanḥuma*:

'And God made tunics of skin for the man and his wife and clothed them' [Gen. 3: 21]. What are 'tunics of skin'? The garments of the high priesthood with which the Holy One, blessed be He, clothed them, because [Adam] was the glory of the world. Furthermore, our teachers passed on to us the tradition that before the Tabernacle was set up, the high places were permitted and sacrificial worship was attached to the rights of the firstborn. Therefore the Holy One, blessed be He, clothed Adam, the firstborn of the world, in the garments of high priesthood. Noah came and passed them on to

---

This study is dedicated to the memory of Isaac Meyers (1979–2008): 'In memoria sempiterna erit iustus; ab auditu malo non timebit. Paratum cor eius confidens in Domino' (IH Ps. 111: 7). I am grateful to Michael Graves and to the editors for their helpful comments on earlier drafts of this essay.

[1] Jerome, *Hebrew Questions on Genesis*. Translation in C. T. R. Hayward, *Jerome's Hebrew Questions on Genesis* (Oxford, 1995), 63. Jerome, *Liber Quaestionum Hebraicarum in Genesim*, ed. Pierre de Lagarde, Corpus Christianorum Series Latina (CCSL) 72 (Turnhout, 1959) p. 34, ll. 12–16, on Gen. 27: 15–16: 'Et sumpsit Rebecca uestimenta Esau filii sui maioris, quae erant desiderabilia apud se domi.'

Et in hoc loco tradunt Hebraei primogenitos functos officio sacerdotum et habuisse uestimentum sacerdotale, quo induti deo uictimas offerebant, antequam Aaron in sacerdotium eligeretur.

The Septuagint (LXX) speaks of a single garment, so only a translation based closely on the Hebrew can support the midrashic interpretation.

Shem, Shem gave them to Abraham, Abraham gave them to Isaac, and Isaac gave them to Esau his firstborn. Esau saw that his wives were engaged in idolatry, and entrusted [the garments] to his mother. When Jacob took the rights of the firstborn from Esau, Rebecca said, 'Since Jacob has taken the rights of the firstborn from Esau, he should wear these garments,' as Scripture says, 'Rebecca took the desirable clothes of Esau her elder son' [Gen. 27: 15]. Jacob went in to his father and [Isaac] delighted in his fragrance, as Scripture says, '[Isaac] smelled the fragrance of his garments and blessed him' [Gen. 27: 27].[2]

The clear parallel between the Hebrew tradition that Jerome briefly mentions and the one recorded in the *Tanḥuma* passage is just one example of the phenomenon that forms the subject of this article. It is typical of Jerome's exegetical approach, especially in his later years. However, first it is appropriate to give some background both to Jerome and to modern study of the man and his works.

Jerome is best known for what came to be called the Vulgate rendering of the books of the Jewish canon of the Old Testament. His own term for his version was the *Iuxta Hebraeos*, the version according to the Hebrews. He also wrote a large number of often lengthy letters, homilies, an onomasticon, various anti-heretical works, and a series of commentaries, especially on what Christians consider to be the prophetic books of the Old Testament. In many of these works, and increasingly in the later ones, he appeals to what he calls *Hebraica veritas*, the 'Hebrew Truth' (effectively the biblical text in Hebrew or according to the Hebrew), and he also refers to Hebrew knowledge and Jewish interpretations.

Though the issue of Jerome's knowledge of Hebrew is not of direct concern in this essay, it certainly has some relevance. According to Jerome himself, he started to learn Hebrew when he was living as a monk in the desert of Chalcis in Syria (*c*.375–77 CE) from a Jewish convert to Christianity, alleging much later that his motivation was to fend off lustful thoughts.[3] He continued with his Hebrew

---

[2] Hebrew text in *Midrasch Tanchuma*, ed. S. Buber (Vilna, 1885), 'Genesis', 67a. The association of the passage in Gen. 27 with the idea of high priestly office is in part due to the verbal link of ריח with the expression ריח ניחוח, 'a soothing odour', used in sacrificial contexts, e.g. Gen. 8: 21 (of Noah's sacrifice), Exod. 29: 18, etc.

The parallel between the Latin and Hebrew passages is cited in passing by Louis Ginzberg, 'Die Haggada bei den Kirchenvätern', *Monatsschrift für Geschichte und Wissenschaft des Judentums*, 43 (1899), 535.

[3] Ep. 125.12 (411 CE), *Sancti Eusebii Hieronymi Epistulae*, Pars III: *Epistulae CXXI–CLIV*, ed. Isidor Hilberg, Corpus Scriptorum Ecclesiasticorum Latinorum (CSEL) 56 (Vienna, 1918), p. 131, ll. 9–15.

Dum essem iuuenis et solitudinis me deserta uallarent, incentiua uitiorum ardoremque naturae ferre non poteram; quae cum crebris ieiuniis frangerem, mens tamen cogitationibus aestuabat. Ad quam edomandam cuidam fratri, qui ex Hebraeis crediderat, me in disciplinam dedi, ut post Quintiliani acumina Ciceronisque fluuios grauitatemque Frontonis et lenitatem Plinii alphabetum discerem, stridentia anhelantiaque uerba meditarer.

See the differing views of Jerome's motives in John N. D. Kelly, *Jerome: His Life, Writings and Controversies* (London, 1975), 49–50, and Adam Kamesar, *Jerome, Greek Scholarship, and the Hebrew Bible: A Study of the 'Quaestiones Hebraicae in Genesim'* (Oxford, 1993).

studies in Constantinople (*c*.380), Rome (*c*.382–85), and above all in Palestine (386–420), where he spent the last three decades of his life.⁴ The Hebrew biblical text became central to his thinking over the course of his life. His first explicit reference to 'Hebraica veritas' occurs in 391–2 CE, but some scholars, such as Adam Kamesar, trace the notion back even earlier than this.⁵

In spite of considerable supporting evidence, Jerome's knowledge of Hebrew was questioned from the early twentieth century up to the 1980s,⁶ on the grounds that he had access to a wealth of relevant material *in Greek* for his work on the Hebrew text. These sources included the Septuagint (LXX) and the three later Jewish revisers, Aquila, Symmachus, and Theodotion. All these texts had been conveniently collected and displayed synoptically in the Hexapla by the early third-century Christian scholar Origen. They appeared in parallel columns next to the Hebrew text and its transliteration into Greek, effectively presenting a useful crib for non-Hebraists, as well as serving as a guide to what was present in the Jewish biblical texts in comparison with the LXX text as used within the Christian tradition. How far Jerome relied on personal inspection of the Hexapla in Caesarea is difficult to judge. Since its creation Christian scholars had been making copious notes from it that were subsequently disseminated throughout the Christian world by means of comments in letters, marginal notes, and commentaries. Jerome would thus have been familiar with the later Jewish Greek versions long before he arrived in Palestine.⁷ He also drew extensively on Hebrew and Jewish traditions in Origen's own biblical commentaries, and on the work of Eusebius of Caesarea, the fourth-century exegete and historian.

Much information concerning the Hebrew language and Jewish traditions was therefore available to Jerome via the Hexapla and earlier Christian writers. For this reason certain scholars have cast doubt on the reality of the Jewish teachers and informants to whom Jerome refers in his works, and have also expressed scepticism about his independent competence in the Hebrew language. Günther Stemberger in particular is a self-confessed minimalist concerning the reality of Christian exegetical contacts with rabbinic Jews in antiquity. He argues that Jerome's contacts

---

⁴ Fergus Millar's article, 'Jerome and Palestine', *Scripta Classica Israelica*, 29 (2010), 59–79, is especially helpful for a survey of the evidence provided by Jerome for the ethnic and linguistic situation in Palestine at the end of the 4th and early 5th cents.

⁵ Kamesar, *Jerome, Greek Scholarship, and the Hebrew Bible*, 42.

⁶ See for instance the views of Estin and Nautin: Colette Estin, *Les Psautiers de Jérôme à la lumière des traductions juives antérieures*, Collectanea Biblica Latina XV (Rome, 1984); Pierre Nautin, 'Hieronymus', in Gerhard Müller, Horst Balz, and Gerhard Krause (eds.), *Theologische Realenzyklopädie*, vol. xv (Berlin, 1986), 309–10.

⁷ See Reinhart Ceulemans, 'A Critical Edition of the Hexaplaric Fragments of the Book of Canticles, with Emphasis on their Reception in Christian Exegesis', Ph.D. thesis, Katholieke Universiteit, Leuven, 2009, 39–56, and id., 'Greek Christian Access to the Three, 250–600 CE', in Timothy M. Law and Alison G. Salvesen (eds.), *Greek Scripture and the Rabbis*, Contributions to Biblical Exegesis and Theology 66 (Leuven, 2012), 165–91.

in Palestine were Jewish Christians or Judaizing Christians, since Jews were not officially allowed in Bethlehem and Jerusalem.[8]

However, recent studies, including work by Adam Kamesar, Matthew Kraus, and Michael Graves,[9] have vindicated Jerome's claims to an independent knowledge of both the Hebrew language and Jewish traditions. Jerome's competence in Hebrew has been demonstrated by examining places where he puts forward several different possible meanings of a Hebrew word provided by the various versions and teachers, and justifies his own choice. Sometimes this is facilitated by the authority of a Jewish informant, of course, but in other places he really does seem to have had a good passive knowledge of the language. (An active knowledge would suggest that he was able to converse in it, as did the rabbis; there is no convincing evidence of this, and it seems unlikely that he would have had Hebrew conversation lessons with his individual teachers.[10])

Below is an example of the difficulty scholars have in estimating the extent of Jerome's independent Hebrew knowledge. This passage, on Amos 3: 11, reveals a typical mixture of what he could pick up from Greek, what his Hebrew teacher said, and what he himself had learned:

Tyre in Hebrew is written with two letters, *tsade* and *resh*, and called Tsor. Aquila and the Septuagint translate in the same way. The Hebrew who taught me the Scriptures interpreted it as 'tribulation'. I agree with him, because Symmachus too, who does not render in a blindly literal way but follows the meaning, says 'siege and surrounding of the earth'. For 'siege', which he renders as *poliorkia*, Theodotion has 'strength': he considered it should be read not as *tsar* or *tsor* ('tribulation' or 'Tyre'), but as *tsur*, which properly refers to very hard rock, for which the Greek term is *akrotomos*, and which we can render in Latin as *silex* (flint).[11]

---

[8] Günther Stemberger, 'Exegetical Contacts between Jews and Christians', in Magne Sæbø (ed.), *Hebrew Bible/Old Testament: The History of its Interpretation*, vol. i (Göttingen, 1996), 569–86, esp. 583.

[9] Kamesar, *Jerome, Greek Scholarship, and the Hebrew Bible*; Matthew Kraus, 'Jerome's Translation of the Book of Exodus Iuxta Hebraeos in Relation to Classical, Christian, and Jewish Traditions of Interpretation', Ph.D. diss., University of Michigan, 1996; Michael Graves, *Jerome's Hebrew Philology: A Study based on his Commentary on Jeremiah*, Supplements to Vigiliae Christianae 90 (Leiden, 2007). See also John S. Cameron, 'The Rabbinic Vulgate?', in Andrew Cain and Josef Lössl (eds.), *Jerome of Stridon: Life, Writings and Legacy* (Farnham, Surrey, 2009), 117–30.

[10] Michael Graves believes that Jerome could understand spoken Hebrew but not speak it (*Jerome's Hebrew Philology*, 91 and 95).

[11] Jerome, *Commentarius in Amos*, on Amos 3: 11. Jerome's *Iuxta Hebraeos* version (henceforth IH) as given in his commentary: 'propterea haec dicit Dominus Deus tribulabitur et circumietur terra et detrahetur ex te fortitudo tua et diripientur aedes tuae.'

pro Tyro, quae in Hebraeo duabus litteris scripta est, sade et res, et appellatur Sor, quod et Aquila et Septuaginta similiter transtulerunt. Hebraeus qui me in scripturis sanctis erudiuit, tribulationem interpretatus est, nec renuimus eius sententiam, quia et Symmachus, qui non solet uerborum κακοζηλίαν, sed intellegentiae ordinem sequi, ait obsidio et circumdatio terrae. pro obsidione, quae ab eo dicitur πολιορκία, fortitudo a Theodotione posita est qui putauit non *sar* et *sor*, quod tribulatio, uel Tyrus dicitur, sed *sur* legendum, quod proprie refertur ad petram durissimam, quae graece appellatur ἀκρότομος, et quam nos latine silicem dicere possumus.' (*S. Hieronymi Presbyteri Opera*, Pars I: *Opera*

The difficulty in this verse in Amos lies in the ambiguity of the consonantal written form. Hebrew still lacked a fully written vowel system at this period, so in theory the meaning of a word spelt צר could vary, as Jerome's remarks indicate, even according to the informed vocalization traditions in circulation.[12] The transliterations provided by the LXX and the three later Jewish translators, the *recentiores*, would have given Jerome a strong hint of the different possible senses, as he himself notes. Yet he cites his Hebrew teacher's opinion. Is this because his own knowledge was deficient, or is it because, despite his own competence in the language, he suspected his readers would doubt his unsupported authority? Jerome gives at least the illusion of weighing up the possibilities and opting for the one adopted by Symmachus, whose translation he often favours. Another reason for bringing in the opinion of his Hebrew teacher may be because of the live reading tradition embodied in this informant, supported by Symmachus' version.[13] We should also consider that Jerome's textual decision may have been influenced by exegetical considerations, rather than decided on purely philological grounds. This would hardly be surprising. Like all other scriptural exegetes of the period, he believed that Scripture was coherent, inspired, and in harmony with doctrine, so he would scarcely opt for a meaning that did not fit what he considered to be the message of the passage as a whole.

In the case of traditions that Jerome attributes to the Jews, it is worth briefly recapitulating the history of modern scholarship on Jerome and Midrash in order to illustrate the *status quaestionis*. It has long been known that Jerome had access to Jewish sources, because of explicit statements in his many works. His example acted as a precedent for later medieval Christian scholars to draw on Jewish expertise themselves and to use Hebrew and Jewish references. Conversely, in the nineteenth and early twentieth centuries, there was particular interest in the influence of Jewish traditions on the Church Fathers among Jewish scholars such as Heinrich Graetz, Samuel Krauss, and Moritz Rahmer,[14] and especially Louis Ginzberg, whose work *Legends of the Jews* is still used today.[15] This is an exhaustive compilation of aggadic

Exegetica, 6 (1): *Commentarii in prophetas minores*, ed. Marcus Adriaen, Corpus Christianorum Series Latina (CCSL) 76 (Turnhout, 1969), book I, iii. 11, p. 250–1, ll. 256–66)
All subsequent citations from the *Commentaries on the Minor Prophets* are from Adriaen's edition.

[12] See James Barr, 'St Jerome and the Sounds of Hebrew', *Journal of Semitic Studies*, 12 (1967), 1–36.

[13] Targum Jonathan on Amos 3: 11 also understands the Hebrew to mean 'tribulation', in line with both Symmachus and Jerome's Hebrew teacher: 'Therefore thus says the Lord, *tribulation* [עקא] prevails in the land and your *strength* [תקפיך] shall fail from you and your fortresses shall be plundered.'

[14] Émilien Lamirande, 'Étude bibliographique sur les pères de l'église et l'aggadah', *Vigiliae Christianae*, 21 (1967), 1–11, gives a very useful list of lesser-known 19th-cent. scholarship on aggadah in the Church Fathers.

[15] Ginzberg was born in Lithuania in 1873, studied in Heidelberg, Germany, and lived in the USA from 1899 until his death in 1953. His doctoral thesis *Die Haggada bei den Kirchenvätern* was published in the periodical *Monatsschrift für Geschichte und Wissenschaft des Judentums* (1898/9). It covered several Church Fathers, not just Jerome, and focused mainly on the book of Genesis. However, Ginzberg noted many parallels between rabbinic Midrash and Jerome, especially in Jerome's book of *Hebrew Questions on Genesis*.

material and similar stories found in non-rabbinic sources, for instance in Second Temple literature or the Church Fathers.[16] It is based on Ginzberg's encyclopaedic knowledge of rabbinic works and extensive familiarity with patristic literature. Jerome is just one of many Fathers included in *Legends of the Jews*, but he emerges as a prominent exponent of Jewish 'legends'.

For modern study of the phenomenon of Christian knowledge of Jewish aggadah, however, Ginzberg's work is limited. First, he merely lists parallels without investigating by what routes they might have entered Christian literature. Furthermore, the study of the later Jewish Greek versions of Aquila, Symmachus, and Theodotion has advanced significantly since his day, and it has become clear that in many cases Jewish biblical traditions influenced Christian writing through such versions. Finally, Ginzberg did not have a sense of the chronological development of the aggadot he recorded. This was something that was not really attempted until Renée Bloch's work in the 1950s.[17]

Subsequent to the work of the great German Jewish academics, there has been a good deal of scepticism about the genuineness of Jerome's own first-hand knowledge of both the Hebrew language and Jewish traditions.[18] Perhaps influenced by the eirenic spirit of Vatican II, in 1967 the French Canadian Catholic scholar Emilien Lamirande criticized patristics experts for having ignored the many works by German Jewish scholars that were available on the subject.[19] For instance, in 1934 Gustave Bardy noted that some of the traditions Jerome cites as having been passed on to him by a 'Hebrew' had in fact appeared in earlier Christian writers, principally Origen. Bardy implied that Jerome had plagiarized Christian sources rather than depending directly on Jewish informants.[20] In contrast, Lamirande was

---

[16] Louis Ginzberg, *The Legends of the Jews*, trans. Henrietta Szold, 7 vols. (Philadelphia, Pa., 1909–38; frequently reprinted).

[17] Renée Bloch, 'Note méthodologique pour l'étude de la littérature rabbinique', *Recherche de Sciences Religieuses*, 43 (1955), 194–227, and ead., 'Midrash', in *Supplément du Dictionnaire de la Bible*, vol. v, ed. Henri Cazelles (Paris, 1957), cols. 1263–81 (trans. and rev. in William Scott Green (ed.), *Approaches to Ancient Judaism*, vol. i (Missoula, Mont., 1978) as 'Methodological Note for the Study of Rabbinic Literature' (29–50), and 'Midrash' (51–76) respectively); ead., 'Note sur l'utilisation des fragments de la Geniza du Caire pour l'étude du Targum', *Revue des études juives*, NS 14 (1955), 5–35.

[18] According to Graves (*Jerome's Hebrew Philology*, 3–6), this scepticism began with de Montfaucon in 1706, and was reiterated by Klostermann in 1897. As for questioning Jerome's competence in the Hebrew language, this was expressed by Eitan Burstein in 1975 and Neil Adkin as recently as 2004, though Pierre Nautin was the most dismissive of Jerome's abilities in *Origène: Sa vie et son œuvre* (Paris, 1977) and 'Hieronymus', 309.

[19] Lamirande, 'Étude bibliographique sur les pères de l'église et l'aggadah', 5. Lamirande's own article tries to redress the situation by citing several of these early works from 1854 to 1933 (he notes the tragic significance of the latter date, at which they seem to have stopped appearing).

[20] Gustave Bardy, 'Saint Jérôme et ses maîtres hébreux', *Revue Bénédictine*, 46 (1934), 145–64: 'Saint Jérôme se content de copier son devancier', and yet on the same page (164), Bardy concedes that Jerome's work is so extensive that it is possible to overlook other significant texts. However, it is abundantly clear that Jerome frequently used all kinds of material, including Christian and classical pagan sources, without acknowledgement: see Stefan Rebenich, 'Jerome: The "Vir Trilinguis" and the "Hebraica Veritas"',

able to access the works of the lesser known German Jewish scholars preserved in the libraries of Hebrew Union College and the Jewish Theological Seminary, and so was aware of how many examples of Jewish traditions in the Church Fathers had been overlooked by Bardy and others. Lamirande expressed the hope of being able to open up to 'Christian Hebraists' the field of research into the Christian use of Midrash that Renée Bloch had indicated in 1955 as crucial for understanding the formation of early Christian literature.

Evidently, the questioning of Jerome's first-hand acquaintance with Jewish Midrash tended to be voiced by scholars who themselves knew little about rabbinic Judaism, as well as ignoring German Jewish scholarship. The most balanced assessments of Jerome have invariably been produced by scholars well versed in the classical, patristic, and rabbinic traditions (as was Ginzberg himself). In the past thirty years these have included Pierre Jay,[21] Jay Braverman,[22] Robert Hayward,[23] Adam Kamesar,[24] and Kamesar's students Matthew Kraus and Michael Graves.[25]

In addition, there have been important developments in scholarship on Midrash, often influenced by the work of Renée Bloch, Geza Vermes, Samuel Sandmel, and others.[26] As a result, it is no longer sufficient to lump all possible aggadic parallels together, from Josephus to medieval Midrash. One needs to consider the development of tradition and the possible date, source, and lines of influence.

Thus the *status quaestionis* on Jerome's knowledge of Midrash can be summed up as follows. Some traditions undoubtedly derive from sources such as Philo, Josephus, the three *recentiores* mentioned above, or his Christian predecessors, rather than from his Jewish informants. In many cases similar traditions do occur in rabbinic Midrash or Targum. However, neither of these seems to have been committed to writing until after Jerome's death. Therefore it is very likely that Jerome's knowledge of aggadic

---

Vigiliae Christianae, 47 (1993), 50–77, esp. 54–5, who also points out that Jerome was far from unique in this respect. Michael Graves (personal communication) notes how Rufinus catches out Jerome claiming to have read the works of Pythagoras (see *Apologia contra Rufinum*, ed. Pierre Lardet, Corpus Christianorum Series Latina (CCSL) 79 (Turnhout, 1982), book III, §39, p. 107, ll. 1–9.

[21] Pierre Jay, *L'Exégèse de Saint Jérôme d'après son 'Commentaire sur Isaie'* (Paris, 1985).

[22] Jay Braverman, *Jerome's 'Commentary on Daniel': A Study of Comparative Jewish and Christian Interpretations of the Hebrew Bible* (Washington, DC, 1978).

[23] Hayward, *Jerome's Hebrew Questions on Genesis*.

[24] Kamesar, *Jerome, Greek Scholarship and the Hebrew Bible*, and also 'The Evaluation of the Narrative Aggada in Greek and Latin Patristic Literature', *Journal of Theological Studies*, 45 (1994), 37–71.

[25] See also the work of Ilona Opelt, 'S. Girolamo e suoi maestri ebrei', *Augustinianum*, 28 (1988), 327–38, and Sandro Leanza, 'Gerolamo e la tradizione ebraica', in Claudio Moreschini and G. Menestrina (eds.), *Motivi letterari ed esegetici in Gerolamo, atti del convegno tenuto a Trento il 5–7 dicembre 1995* (Brescia, 1997), 17–38.

[26] Samuel Sandmel, 'Parallelomania', *Journal of Biblical Literature*, 81 (1962), 1–13. Sandmel defined 'parallelomania' as 'that extravagance among scholars which first overdoes the supposed similarity in passages and then proceeds to describe source and derivation as if implying literary connection flowing in an inevitable or predetermined direction... it is in the detailed study rather than in the abstract statement that there can emerge persuasive bases for judgment' (p. 1).

motifs often derives from Jewish informants who conveyed them to Jerome in Greek. Jerome himself may thus be considered an important witness to late fourth-century Palestinian aggadah. At the same time, because of his reuse of the traditions in a new, Christian, context, it is essential to examine the function of each motif within its new setting in order to determine whether Jerome has moulded or manipulated it for his own purposes.

As noted by Hartmann and Graves, in later life Jerome alludes, in a letter to Pammachius and Oceanus designed for public consumption, to the three exegetical approaches he takes in his scriptural commentaries.[27] These approaches are represented by the three very different teachers with whom he studied in three regions: Didymus the Blind in Alexandria, Apollinaris of Laodicea in Antioch, and Baranina in Jerusalem and Bethlehem—in other words, an Antiochene, an Alexandrian, and a Jew. Jerome states that he was proud to be the student of each of these distinguished men, even though the methods of the first two are diametrically opposed and he is a bitter enemy of the 'circumcised'.

The wider context in which he makes this statement in Epistle 84 is in defending himself against the charge of the heresy of Origenism, raised by those who objected to his literal translation of Origen's *First Principles*. He implies that he is able to use his sources selectively, admiring the good and rejecting the bad. He is thus untainted by dubious theological opinions, whether Origenist, Apollinarian, or Jewish. The three teachers do not just represent different schools of thought but also symbolize the most extreme positions of Jerome's exegetical triangle.[28]

Yet it is the extensive use of Hebrew, mediated through largely Jewish sources, that is the main 'novelty' of Jerome's exegetical work, just as his recourse to the *Hebraica veritas* in his revision of the Latin biblical text marked a striking new approach. Much of what Jerome produced in his commentaries is otherwise squarely within the tradition of Greek and Latin commentary, if rather eclectic. Even his use of Jewish traditions is hardly unprecedented, since, as he himself argues, they appear in Origen, Eusebius, Clement, and others, regardless of whether the Christian author agrees with them. The main task of this essay is to look at some examples of aggadic Midrash in the exegetical works of Jerome, identify possible sources, and examine their function within his interpretative scheme.

As stated above, it seems unlikely that Midrash or Targum existed extensively in written form during Jerome's lifetime, and it is even less likely that either would

---

[27] Louis N. Hartmann, 'St Jerome as an Exegete', in F. X. Murphy (ed.), *A Monument to St Jerome: Essays on Some Aspects of His Life, Works, and Influence* (New York, 1952), 47–9; Graves, *Jerome's Hebrew Philology*, 13. The letter is Ep. 84.3, written c.400 CE.

[28] Most recently Williams has stated, 'Jerome grounded his entire exegetical edifice on the disturbing figure of the learned Jew' (Megan Hale Williams, *The Monk and the Book: Jerome and the Making of Christian Scholarship* (Chicago, Ill., 2006), 222). Against this one could argue that the foundation of Jerome's later exegesis is in fact the *Hebraica veritas*, a rather more scientific and objective concept that Williams rightly argues is an elastic and inclusive one (ibid. 89; and see also Jay, *L'Exégèse de Saint Jérôme*, 145, for the relationship between Hebrew text and Hebrew tradition).

have been available to Jerome if it had been.[29] Although, as Graves observes, Jerome sometimes mentions having seen other written works, such as Jubilees or a Nazarean Gospel of Matthew,[30] he does not speak of having seen Hebrew traditions or Jewish 'fables' in writing, even though they would arguably have been more authoritative to him and his Christian readers in such a form. All such references as *tradunt Hebraei* imply oral transmission, and it seems that they were reported in Greek; when Jerome cites the meaning of a Hebrew word in his Latin commentaries, the definition is usually in Greek which he then renders into Latin.[31]

Parallels to Jerome's Jewish traditions in rabbinic sources redacted at a much later date can be included, since it is highly unlikely that Jerome invented them and that they entered Jewish tradition from his works. It is not uncommon to find traditions in Josephus or Symmachus which subsequently appear in later rabbinic Midrash. Presumably such traditions were in oral circulation but emerged in different written sources at various points over the centuries. On the whole, what is sought is attestation in rabbinic Midrash of any period that Jerome is reporting an authentic aggadic tradition that he is likely to have gleaned from contemporary Jewish sources, and not via a Christian intermediary, from Josephus, Philo, the three *recentiores*, or what Jerome would have regarded as the Apocrypha.[32] In cases where there is no parallel at all, in rabbinic sources or elsewhere, the Jewish tradition that he reports may or may not be genuine. We may have to examine the function that it plays in its particular context, in order to see whether Jerome invented or embellished it for his own purposes.

The central issue is what Jerome actually does with the Midrash and how it functions in its new setting. What was Jerome trying to achieve by including such material?[33]

---

[29] Those who argue that Jerome had access to written Midrash on occasion refer to the passage in his Ep. 36, 'cum subito Hebraeus interuenit deferens non pauca uolumina, quae de synagoga quasi lecturus acceperat. Et ilico "habes", inquit, "quod postulaueras" meque dubius et, quid facerem, nescientem ita festinus exterruit, ut omnibus praetermissis ad scribendum transuolarem; quod quidem usque ad praesens facio'; Ep. 36 (to Pope Damasus), in *Sancti Eusebii Hieronymi Epistulae, Pars I: Epistulae I–LXX*, ed. Isidor Hilberg, CSEL 54 (Vienna, 1910), p. 268, ll. 5–13. Braverman (*Jerome's 'Commentary on Daniel'*, 8), believes that these scrolls were 'midrashim'. Graves (*Jerome's Hebrew Philology*, 92 n. 62), agrees with Vaccari that Ep. 36.4 refers to a non-biblical aggadic text and Ep. 36.1 is a non-biblical Hebrew work. Millar ('Jerome and Palestine', 64), presumes that they were biblical scrolls. Yet this letter was written in Rome, before Jerome achieved his later competence in Hebrew, and so it seems rather unlikely that he (or his amanuenses) would have been able to read and transcribe Hebrew or Aramaic scrolls.

Hayward suggested that Jerome may have consulted written Targum (C. T. R. Hayward, 'Jewish Traditions in Jerome's Commentary on Jeremiah and the Targum of Jeremiah', *Proceedings of the Irish Biblical Association*, 9 (1985), 100–120, esp. 113–14), but in a later article he is more cautious: 'Saint Jerome and the Aramaic Targumim', *Journal of Semitic Studies*, 32 (1987), 105–23.

[30] See Graves, *Jerome's Hebrew Philology*, 91–2.

[31] Of course one must exclude cases where he may be citing the Greek versions of Aquila, Symmachus, or Theodotion without acknowledgement.   [32] See Graves, *Jerome's Hebrew Philology*, 97–8.

[33] From a rabbinic point of view, Midrash includes both halakah—legal interpretation—and

There are a number of different views regarding the function of Midrash in Jerome. In Adam Kamesar's review of previous scholarship on rabbinic material in Jerome's *Hebrew Questions on Genesis*,[34] he remarks that Ferdinand Cavallera[35] regarded the *Hebrew Questions* as a 'hybrid' work, and that Angelo Penna[36] regarded the functions of the Jewish traditions it contained as 'ornamental'. As for the French scholar Bardy, mentioned above, he believed that Jerome collected rabbinic traditions without accepting them himself, and so presumably recorded them out of curiosity. However, given the hostility displayed by Christians such as Rufinus and Augustine to Hebrew as well as to Jews, collecting *midrashim* as curiosities would be a strange thing to do if Jerome himself thought they had no value at all. Jerome was prepared to court controversy in his works, but not without cause.

Kamesar admits that the criticisms of Bardy and others are to an extent true, and gives some examples. He believes that Jerome's inclusion of rabbinic material was 'not devoid of ethnographic and antiquarian considerations ... he was quite interested in Jewish lore for its own sake'.[37] In the case of the *Hebrew Questions*, which is more unusual in genre, Kamesar argues that 'this [rabbinic] material was an essential element in the study of the Bible'.[38] He also points to the *Prologue of the Commentary on Jeremiah*, where Jerome says he wants to give to Latin speakers the learning of the Hebrews and the Greeks.[39] Illustrative of Jerome's attitude to Jewish traditions is the remark in his *Commentary on Zechariah*, where he speaks of the *arcana eruditionis Hebraicae*, 'the secrets of Hebrew learning'.[40] Certainly this refers as much to Hebrew philology as to Midrash. Kamesar regards Jerome as employing the same principle concerning Jewish exegesis as he does with the works of Christian theologians who were regarded with great suspicion in Jerome's day. Jerome thus defends his use of Origen and Apollinaris, citing St Paul's words in 1 Thessalonians 5: 21: *omnia legentes, quae bona sunt, retinentes* 'reading everything, holding on to what is good' (Ep. 61.1). In other words, he is wide-ranging but selective, according to purpose and context. Ultimately, according to Kamesar, Jerome uses rabbinic traditions for his literal exegesis and not for Christological prophecy.[41]

aggadah—interpretation of narrative. However, since Jerome had little time for Jewish law in any form, what he repeats is largely aggadic.

[34] See references in Kamesar, *Jerome, Greek Scholarship, and the Hebrew Bible*, 176.

[35] 'cet ouvrage hybride': F. Cavallera, *Saint Jérôme: Sa vie et son œuvre*, 2 vols., Spicilegium Sacrum Lovaniense (Louvain, 1922), part I, tome i, p. 146.   [36] A. Penna, *S. Gerolamo* (Turin, 1949), 155.

[37] Kamesar, *Jerome, Greek Scholarship, and the Hebrew Bible*, 176–7.   [38] Ibid. 177.   [39] Ibid.

[40] Jerome, *Commentarius in Zachariam prophetam* (S. Hieronymi Commentarii in prophetas minores, ed. Marcus Adriaen, Corpus Christianorum Series Latina 76A (Turnhout, 1970)), book II, vi. 9–15, p. 796, ll. 172–5 (on Zech. 6: 9–15): 'Semel proposui arcana eruditionis hebraicae, et magistrorum synagogae reconditam disciplinam, eam dumtaxat, quae scripturis sanctis conuenit, latinis auribus prodere.' ('A long time ago I resolved to pass on to Latin speakers the secrets of Hebrew learning and the hidden teaching of the synagogue teachers, as far as it is appropriate to sacred Scripture.')

[41] Ibid. viii. 18–19, p. 820, ll. 526–30 (on Zech. 8: 18–19): 'Cogimur igitur ad Hebraeos recurrere, et scientiae ueritatem de fonte magis quam de riuulis quaerere, praesertim cum non prophetia aliqua de Christo, ubi tergiuersari solent, sed historiae ex praecedentibus et consequentibus ordo texatur' (cited

How far do Kamesar's findings for Jerome's earlier work *Hebrew Questions* hold true for later works such as the *Commentary on the Minor Prophets*? There are various possible explanations for Jerome's use of Midrash in the commentary, including a desire to demonstrate the inferiority of Jewish exegesis compared to its Christian counterpart, or a wish to show off his own supposedly 'inside line' to Jewish exegesis. Yet in his *Apology* against his erstwhile friend Rufinus, Jerome defends himself against criticism for using Jewish informants by citing the precedent of Origen, who was Rufinus' hero. Jerome also says there that Origen and others appealed to the authority of a 'Hebrew' concerning details in the biblical text.[42] Though this might suggest recourse to Hebrew philology rather than a justification for using Jewish Midrash, precedent in Christian tradition provides another potential reason for employing Jewish tradition.

At the outset it should be observed that Jerome's commentaries are as much an attack on other types of interpretation as a presentation of his own explanations. So 'Jewish' and heretical (often Jewish-Christian) exegesis is criticized, yet Jerome uses and justifies 'Hebrew' interpretations—not merely ones based on Hebrew philology but also effectively *midrashim*.

by Kamesar, *Jerome, Greek Scholarship, and the Hebrew Bible*, 178). But see also Graves, *Jerome's Hebrew Philology* (158 n. 85), where the Hebrew gives a Trinitarian meaning not present in LXX. Graves (personal communication) notes that it is surprising that Jerome does not do this more often, since part of his defence for using the Hebrew text is the argument that the Septuagint translators deliberately hid Trinitarian mysteries in their pre-Christian translation.

[42] Jerome, *Apologia contra Rufinum*, ed. Lardet, book I, §13, pp. 12–13, ll. 1–27:

Audio praeterea te ... plautino in me sale ludere, eo quod Barabban Iudaeum dixerim praeceptorem meum. Nec mirum si pro 'Baranina', ubi est uocabulorum similitudo, scripseris 'Barabban', cum tantam habeas licentiam nominum mutandorum, ut de Eusebio Pamphilum, de haeretico martyrem feceris ... ego non illum magistrum dixi, sed meum in Scripturas sanctas studium uolui conprobare, ut ostenderem me sic Origenem legisse quomodo et illum audieram. Neque enim hebraeas litteras a te discere debui.... Ipse Origenes et Eusebius et Clemens aliique conplures, quando de Scripturis aliqua disputant et uolunt approbare quod dicunt, sic solent scribere: 'Referebat mihi Hebraeus'; et: 'Audiui ab Hebraeo'; et: 'Hebraeorum ista sententia est'. Certe Origenes etiam patriarchem Hiullum, qui temporibus eius fuit, nominat.

I am told, further, that you ... make sport of me with a wit worthy of Plautus, for having said that I had a Jew named Barabbas for my teacher. I do not wonder at your writing Barabbas for Baranina, the letters of the names being somewhat similar, when you allow yourself such a license in changing the names themselves, as to turn Eusebius into Pamphilus, and a heretic into a martyr. ... I never spoke of him as my master; I merely wished to illustrate my method of studying the Holy Scriptures by saying that I had read Origen just in the same way as I had taken lessons from this Jew. [For I should not learn Hebrew from you!] ... Origen himself, and Clement and Eusebius, and many others, when they are discussing scriptural points, and wish to have Jewish authority for what they say, write: 'A Hebrew stated this to me', or 'I heard from a Hebrew', or, 'That is the opinion of the Hebrews.' Origen certainly speaks of the Patriarch Huillus who was his contemporary....' (trans. W. H. Freemantle, in Philip Schaff and Henry Wace (eds.), *A Select Library of Nicene and Post-Nicene Fathers of the Christian Church*, 2nd series, vol. iii: *Theodoret, Jerome, Gennadius, Rufinus* (Oxford, 1892), 489–90).

See Rebenich, 'Jerome: The "Vir Trilinguis" and the "Hebraica Veritas"', 61–2, who uses this interchange to corroborate Jerome's resort to real Hebrew teachers.

The examples chosen here are drawn largely from Jerome's *Commentaries on the Minor Prophets*, since the Hebrew text is often challenging for the exegete. In addition, apart from the *Commentary on Jonah* and the *Commentary on Amos*, they have not received much attention.[43] Most examples below are drawn from the commentaries on Amos, Zephaniah, and Habakkuk. Sometimes it has been possible to trace possible sources of certain Jewish traditions that Jerome cites, but often an aggadic motif known to Jerome only surfaces on the Jewish side in a later rabbinic source, such as the Babylonian Talmud. I will then examine the uses to which Jerome puts Midrash in its new, Christian context.

First of all, one group of references to Jewish interpretation which could be categorized as *millenarianist-messianic* should be excluded. In a number of places in his commentaries on the Prophets, Jerome mentions that the 'Jewish' interpretation of a particular passage states that the promises given through the prophets have yet to be fulfilled, in a future messianic age, and in material form. This is actually borne out by the exegesis of Targum Jonathan in many places, though much more in the Targum of Isaiah than in the Targum of the Minor Prophets.[44] In certain cases Jerome says that such materialistic, millenarian eschatology is shared by Jews and 'Judaizing' Christians.[45] Then he continues to what he considers to be the superior, fully Christian, spiritual understanding of the passage in question, namely that the ancient prophecies have already been fulfilled, and that the blessings described in the text of Scripture are to be understood, metaphorically and spiritually, as those that Christ has already bestowed on the Church.

An example of this kind is found in Jerome's *Commentary on Amos* 9: 11–12:

Both in this prophetic book and in others, whatever prophecies there are concerning the rebuilding of Jerusalem and the Temple and general blessing, the Jews promise themselves these things in the last time in futile expectation, and speak of their material fulfilment. However, we who 'do not follow the letter that kills but the spirit that brings life'

---

[43] Yves-Marie Duval, *Le Livre de Jonas dans la littérature chrétienne grecque et latine; Sources et influence du Commentaire sur Jonas de saint Jérôme*, 2 vols. (Paris, 1973); Jennifer M. Dines, 'Jerome's Methodology in his Commentary on Amos', in Alison Salvesen (ed.), *Origen's Hexapla and Fragments: Papers Presented at the Rich Seminar on the Hexapla, Oxford Centre for Hebrew and Jewish Studies, 25th July–3rd August 1994*, Texts and Studies in Ancient Judaism 58 (Tübingen, 1998), 421–36. Braverman, Jay, and Graves have already produced illuminating studies of Jerome's commentaries on Daniel, Isaiah, and Jeremiah respectively.

[44] e.g. Targum Isaiah, chs. 61–3, and see Bruce Chilton, *The Glory of Israel: The Theology and Provenience of the Isaiah Targum*, Journal for the Study of the Old Testament, Supplement Series 23 (Sheffield, 1983), 86–96, 112–17, and Kevin J. Cathcart and Robert P. Gordon, *The Targum of the Minor Prophets*, The Aramaic Bible 14 (Edinburgh, 1989), 6–7. Messianic interpretations are found, however, in the Targum on some of the Minor Prophets, e.g. at Hos. 3: 5, 14: 8; Mic. 4: 8, 5: 1; Hab. 3: 18; Zech. 3: 8, 4: 7, 6: 12, 10: 4.

[45] See the excellent article by Michael Graves, '"Judaizing" Christian Interpretations of the Prophets as Seen by Saint Jerome', *Vigiliae Christianae*, 61 (2007), 142–56. Graves focuses on Jerome's criticisms of the *Iudaizantes*, who, as Graves demonstrates, are Christians with a literalist millenarian theology, whereas the present writer is more interested in the degree to which this tendency was also found among Jerome's Jewish contemporaries.

[2 Cor. 3: 6] demonstrate that such things have already been accomplished in the Church and fulfilled every day in individuals. Those who are ruined through sin are rebuilt through penitence.[46]

In one sense the function of such passages describing 'Jewish' views of the biblical text in question appears little different from those where Jerome is presenting the often Jewish or Hebrew-based *littera* and *historia* as the foundation for the more advanced spiritual sense (*tropologia*) to which Christians must progress. Yet while he usually accepts this first, literal sense as a necessary and acceptable preliminary, concerning these prophetic passages which apparently present a future Golden Age he rejects a material interpretation outright.[47] (One suspects that this was not just because of his adherence to a realized eschatology, shared with many other Christians of his time, but that it was also due to his ascetic nature; he personally scorned splendour and wealth, and preferred to dwell on intangible spiritual blessings.)

As for the reality behind such charges of focusing on the material blessings, it is indeed the case that the Targums, especially Targum Jonathan of Isaiah, do apparently depict future earthly bliss, under either God's own rule or that of his messiah. However, Jerome's frequent references to 'Jewish', 'corporeal', readings of the text may be as much to a line of theology found among certain Christians (not necessarily 'Jewish' Christians), as to a specific Jewish exegesis of a passage. One should therefore be alert to the function that this alleged feature of Jewish exegesis can also play in Jerome's interpretative scheme. His comments may primarily function as an attack on a Christian line of interpretation to which he objects. Calling such Christian exegesis 'Jewish' is meant to show that he considers it in fact inadequately Christian.

Turning to individual traditions rather than broader theological tendencies, there are a number of interesting examples.

In the difficult verse Zephaniah 3: 1, an oracle of woe is pronounced against *ha'ir hayonah*, which could be understood as 'the city, the dove' (contrast modern translations: 'O, oppressing city!'). The Hebrew consonants *yod-vav-nun-heh* can

---

[46] Jerome, *Commentarius in Amos*, book III, ix. 11–12, p. 345, ll. 380–7 (on Amos 9: 11–12):

et in hoc propheta, et in ceteris quaecumque de aedificatione Hierusalem et templi, et rerum omnium beatitudine praedicantur, *Iudaei in ultimo tempore uana sibi exspectatione promittunt, et carnaliter implenda commemorant. Nos autem qui non occidentem litteram, sed spiritum sequimur uiuificantem*, iam in Ecclesia expleta conuincimus, et cotidie impleri in singulis, qui ruentes per peccatum, reaedificantur per paenitentiam.

Cf. *Commentarius in Ieremiam prophetam*, ed. Siegfried Reiter, CSEL 59 (Vienna, 1913), book VI, prologue §1, p. 367, ll. 14–16 (cited by Graves, '"Judaizing" Christian Interpretations', 149 n. 21): 'Qui igitur Christum uenisse iam credimus, necesse est, ut ea, quae sub Christo futura dicuntur, expleta doceamus.' ('Since we believe Christ has already come, we must teach that those future things which are said to pertain to Christ have been fulfilled.') See also Fergus Millar, 'Jews of the Graeco-Roman Diaspora', in Judith Lieu, John North, and Tessa Rajak (eds.), *The Jews among Pagans and Christians in the Roman Empire* (London, 1992), 97–123, esp. 113–14.

[47] Graves, '"Judaizing" Christian Interpretations', 155.

be vocalized or rearranged to form the words *yonah* 'dove', *yavan(ah)* 'Greece', or *Nineveh*. In his commentary Jerome writes that he is aware that 'many' connect the city with Nineveh, mentioned in the preceding passage (LXX 2: 13). He raises the objection that Nineveh is nowhere called a 'dove' (*columba* in Latin, following LXX *peristera*). He says that others understand the word *yonah* to mean Greece, Hebrew *Yavan* (compare 'Ionia'). Jerome says that 'thus' the whole passage is a speech against Jerusalem, the city that was once a dove (i.e. innocent?), constantly sinning, and exiled. His use of the similar phrase found in Jeremiah 46: 16 and 50: 16, 'from the edge of the sword of Iona/Greece', indicates the sacking of a city by non-Jews. He therefore identifies the city with Jerusalem.[48]

Jerome does not claim to be passing on a Hebrew or Jewish tradition here. However, all three interpretations, Nineveh, dove, and Greece, are explicitly mentioned in Petiḥta 31 in *Lamentations Rabbah*.[49] Jerome's treatment of the various options differs in matters of detail from that of *Lamentations Rabbah*. However, the three different possibilities for the word *yonah* are found both in Jerome and in the undoubtedly later rabbinic Midrash. It is likely that Jerome was aware of a number of possible interpretations of *yonah* in this verse that were circulating orally in his time.

On Zephaniah 1: 1, where the prophet's forebears are listed, Jerome mentions a Hebrew tradition that when a prophet's father or grandfather are mentioned in a book's title, this indicates that they themselves had also been prophets.[50] The Babylonian Talmud, *Megilah* 15a, concerning the same introductory formula in Zephaniah 1: 1, has the vaguer statement that where mention is made of a righteous

---

[48] The LXX version of Zeph. 3: 1, according to Jerome's Latin rendering of the Septuagint (ILXX): 'O illustris et redempta ciuitas Columba.' The Hebrew of Zeph. 3: 1, according to Jerome (IH): 'uae prouocatrix et redempta ciuitas, columba.' Jerome, *Commentarius in Sophoniam prophetam* [Zeph.], iii. 1–7, CCSL 76A, pp. 694–5, ll. 36–44, 45–8:

Sed numquam scriptura Niniuen columbam uocaret, licet in Hieremia a facie gladii columbae de Nabuchodonosor dictum quidam putent. Sed sciendum quod alii econtrario asserant, pro columba, ibi posse intelligi Ἑλλάδα, id est Graeciam, ut sit sensus: A facie gladii Iona, id est a facie gladii Graeciae. Iona enim tam columbam quam Graeciam significat. Vnde et usque hodie Graeci Iones, et mare appellatur Ionium, et apud Hebraeos permanet eorum uetus uocabulum ... omnis itaque contra Hierusalem sermo est: uae ciuitas quondam columba, semper peccans, et captiuitatibus tradita, et rursum redempta a domino.

[49] Petiḥta 31, *Lam. Rabbah* (citing Zeph. 3: 1):

What is the meaning of 'woe to her that is rebellious'? The nation that I distinguished through religious duties and good deeds like a dove.... Said R. Reuben, 'In the Greek language, they call a foolish woman "mora" [fem.] ... Should she not have learned from the city of Jonah which is Nineveh? One prophet did I send to Nineveh and the city repented, but to the Israelites in Jerusalem how many prophets did I send.' (trans. based on Jacob Neusner, *Lamentations Rabbah: An Analytical Translation*, Brown Judaic Studies 193 (Atlanta, Ga., 1989), 92–3).

The *petiḥata* to *Lamentations Rabbah* are not securely dated: see Günter Stemberger, *Introduction to the Talmud and Midrash*, 2nd edn. (Edinburgh, 1996), 286–7.

[50] Jerome, *Commentarius in Sophoniam*, i. 1, p. 656, ll. 4–6, on Zeph. 1: 1: 'Tradunt Hebraei cuiuscumque prophetae pater aut auus ponatur in titulo, ipsos quoque prophetas fuisse.'

man's ancestors, they too were of good character ('a righteous man, son of a righteous man'). However, the context of the talmudic passage does mention the twenty-two prophets and seven prophetesses of Scripture, so Jerome's comment may well reflect the same Jewish tradition that later took written form in Babylonia.

Why does Jerome mention this Hebrew tradition? At first it appears to serve merely to provide more information on the 'historical' level of the text. But Jerome soon proceeds to an extended allegorical reading of the verse, based on supposed etymologies of the names of Zephaniah's forebears, especially that of 'Chusi'. The latter's name is interpreted as meaning 'my Ethiopian' (Hebrew *kushi*) and Jerome then connects it with various Ethiopians mentioned in Scripture, leading to the Ethiopian eunuch of Acts 8: 27–38 who was baptized by Philip, and whom Jerome regards as having made himself a eunuch for the sake of the kingdom of heaven. Rightly, therefore, says Jerome, did Zephaniah son of Chusi, the 'Ethiopian', write 'Across the rivers of Ethiopia, from there shall they bring offerings to me' (Zeph. 3: 10). Jerome develops the Jewish tradition concerning the reason for Scripture mentioning a prophet's forefathers, in order to argue that the names of Zephaniah's ancestors are not merely significant in their own right but also point prophetically to a fulfilment in the New Testament.

On Zephaniah 3: 9 Jerome renders the 'Hebrew' lemma as 'because then I will bring back to the peoples a chosen tongue, so that they may all call on the name of the Lord and serve him with one shoulder'.[51] He justifies his translation of *berurah* as 'chosen' on the basis of Aquila's and Theodotion's rendering, *electum*. He cites a Jewish interpretation of the Hebrew lemma that relates verses 8–9 to the future coming of the messiah. At this time all the nations will be gathered and the Lord will pour out his wrath upon them. All who convert will speak one language, Hebrew, just as before the Tower of Babel was built.

Unsurprisingly Jerome dismisses the Jewish interpretation as 'Jewish fables' in favour of a more Christian sense favourable to non-Jews. He may have cited it in order to point out the contrast in focus between the Jewish expectation of the messiah and of judgment for the non-Jews in verses 8b–9, and his own preference for verse 8a, 'wait for me, says the Lord, in the day of my resurrection in testimony'. He follows the LXX lemma in understanding the rulers of the non-Jews to be the recipients of God's wrath, not the nations in general as in the 'Hebrew'. The reference to language he takes as having been fulfilled in the days of the apostles, who spoke in every tongue at Pentecost (*universis linguis*), but he also speaks of the restoration of a single language of confession.

---

[51] Zeph. 3: 9, IH: 'quia tunc reddam populis labium electum, ut invocent omnes nomen Domini, et serviant ei humero uno'. Jerome, *Commentarius in Sophoniam*, iii. 8–9, p. 700, ll. 253–61:

> Haec Iudaei interpretantur in aduentu Christi, quem sperant uenturum esse, et dicunt uniuersis gentibus congregatis, et effuso super eas furore Domini, in igne zeli eius terram deuorandam; et sicut ante aedificationem turris fuit, quando una lingua omnes populi loquebantur, ita conuersis omnibus ad cultum ueri dei, locuturos Hebraice et totum orbem domino seruiturum. Nos autem qui non sequimur occidentem litteram, sed spiritum uiuificantem, nec Iudaicas fabulas.

The rabbinic source that comes closest to the Jewish tradition that Jerome reports is *Midrash tanḥuma*, in its discussion of Genesis 11 and the division of languages.[52] The holy language, Hebrew, is described as the language in which the world was created and which was spoken by everyone. Zephaniah 3: 9 is then cited as a prophecy that one day God will make the whole world of one accord, calling on his name and serving him. The *midrash* does not actually state that all will speak Hebrew at that time, but that is implied.

Jerome had every reason to draw attention to the identity of the 'chosen' language, even in the rejected Jewish interpretation, and to connect it with the original language of mankind, because of his championing of the *Hebraica veritas*. Remarkably, he prefers to think in terms of the Resurrection and Pentecost, and so presents the Jewish interpretation only in order to reject it.

For the previous verse, Zephaniah 3: 8, Jerome says that his Hebrew Scripture teacher told him that *la'ed* in this verse meant εἰς ἔτι (*in futurum*) rather than *in testimonium* (= LXX εἰς μαρτύριον). Jerome explains that the word spelt *ayin-dalet* can mean both 'future' and 'witness'.[53] Targum Jonathan renders this as 'judgment', reading the Hebrew word in a similar sense to LXX. It is unclear from Jerome's remarks which of the interpretations he favours, and he may have preferred to keep his options open.

In Habakkuk 3: 5 Jerome renders Resheph in the 'Hebrew' lemma as *diabolus*. He justifies this translation on the basis of a Hebrew tradition. This is that Resheph is the name of the demon who holds sway among the others, just as Beelzebub is named prince of the demons in the gospel. He is called a bird or winged creature because of his swift flight, and is the same being who spoke to the woman in the form of a serpent. He was given the name Resheph by God, since it means 'crawling on the belly'.[54]

---

[52] *Midrash tanḥuma*, 'No'aḥ' 19.

[53] Jerome, *Commentarius in Sophoniam*, iii. 8–9, p. 702, ll. 327–35, on Zeph. 3: 8:

Hebraeus qui me in scripturis instituit, asserebat *laed* in praesenti loco magis εἰς ἔτι id est in futurum, debere intellegi, quam in testimonium. *Ed* enim, quod scribitur per litteras ain et daleth, ἔτι, et μαρτύριον, id est et futurum et testimonium, intellegi. Possumus hunc locum et de primo Christi aduentu exponere, quando, omni errore sublato, daemonibus que calcatis, et terrenis operibus destructis, apostoli uniuersis linguis locuti sunt, et ueteri errore sublato, unum confessionis redditum est labium.

In the later Masoretic tradition there is a difference in vocalization (*la'ad* for 'in the future', *la'ed* meaning 'as a witness').

[54] Hab. 3: 5, IH 'ante faciem eius ibit mors et egredietur diabolus ante pedes eius.' Jerome, *Commentarius in Abacuc*, book II, iii.5, CCSL 76A, pp. 626–7, ll. 322–9, on Hab. 3: 5:

Tradunt autem Hebraei, quomodo in euangelio princeps daemonum dicitur esse Beelzebub, ita Reseph daemonis esse nomen, qui principatum teneat inter alios, et propter nimiam uelocitatem atque in diuersa discursum, auis et uolatile nuncupetur, ipsumque esse qui in paradiso sub figura serpentis mulieri sit locutus, et ex maledictione, qua a deo condemnatus est accepisse nomen, siquidem Reseph reptans uentre interpretatur.

Some of this does accord with rabbinic tradition: Babylonian Talmud *Berakhot* 5*a* states, 'Resheph refers only to demons', in a passage on reciting the Shema on one's bed in order to drive away demons.[55] However, there appears to be no identification of Resheph with Sammael or Satan or the serpent in rabbinic literature. Moreover, the verb *resh-shin-peh* is unattested in Jewish Aramaic or Hebrew in the sense of 'crawl'.[56] On the other hand, the verb *resh-shin-peh* occurs in Syriac, where it does mean 'to crawl on the belly', and it is used of the serpent in Eden.[57] Either Jerome picked this detail up from a Syrian Christian source rather than a Jewish one, or Jerome and the Syriac sources preserve a Jewish tradition that has not survived in rabbinic sources.

The reason for Jerome's identification of the demon Resheph with the devil of Christian teaching lies in his spiritual interpretation of the passage. Here he describes the devil meeting Christ as the latter leaves the waters of baptism, and death standing before his feet, as well as the ancient serpent who tempted him for forty days in the wilderness. Jerome bases this explicitly on the Greek lemma 'the word shall go before his face, and go out in the fields after his feet', but his interpretation tacitly takes in the Hebrew lemma 'Death shall go before his face and the Devil shall go out before his feet'. The 'Hebrew' tradition of identifying Resheph with the devil has been used to support a Christian reading of Habakkuk 3: 5.

Another place where Christian theology may have been read into the Hebrew text is in Jerome's comments on Habakkuk 3: 3.[58] Here he claims that he himself

> The Hebrews have a tradition that, just as in the gospel the prince of demons is called Beelzebub, so Resheph is the name of a demon who holds sway among the others. Because he is very swift and ranges widely, he is regarded as a bird and a winged creature, and as the one who spoke to the woman in Paradise in the guise of a serpent. It was through the curse that he received from God that he received the name, since Resheph means 'crawling on the belly'.

[55] BT *Ber.* 5*a*, 'Resheph refers only to demons'.

[56] Targum Habakkuk on Hab. 3: 5 demythologises the name and renders as 'flame of fire'. See also Deut. 32: 24; Pss. 76: 4, 78: 48; Job 5: 7; and S. of S. 8: 6. *Num. Rabbah* 12: 3 also discusses Resheph in the context of demons. For the ancient origins of Resheph, see Paolo Xella, 'Resheph', in Karel van der Toorn, Bob Becking, and Piet van der Horst (eds.), *Dictionary of Deities and Demons in the Bible*, 2nd edn. (Leiden, 1999).

[57] I am grateful to David Taylor for bringing this Syriac meaning to my attention. See A. Levene, *The Early Syrian Fathers on Genesis. From a Syriac MS. on the Pentateuch in the Mingana Collection* (London, 1951), ch. 2, p. 60, l. 16, and p. 78. Aphrahat also uses the verb of the devil appearing to the Sons of the Covenant in the guise of a serpent, though not in the context of Eden (Demonstration VI. 2; *Aphraatis sapientis persae demonstrationes*, ed. Jean Parisot, Patrologia Syriaca 1 (Paris, 1894), col. 256, l. 5).

[58] Jerome, *Commentarius in Abacuc*, book II, iii. 3, p. 623, ll. 194–201:

> Audiui ego Hebraeum istum locum ita disserere: Quod Bethleem sita sit ad austrum, in qua natus est Dominus atque Saluator, et ipsum esse de quo nunc dicatur: *Dominus ab austro ueniet*, hoc est nascetur in Bethleem, et inde consurget. Et quia ipse qui natus est in Bethleem, legem quondam dedit in monte Sinai, ipse est sanctus qui uenit de monte Pharan. Pharan quippe uicinus est locus monti Sina.

> I myself heard a Hebrew explain this passage thus: Because Bethlehem (where our Lord and Saviour was born) lies to the south, he is the one of whom it is now said, 'The Lord shall come from the south,' that is, he shall be born in Bethlehem, and come forth from there. And because the one who was born

heard a 'Hebrew' explain the passage 'The Lord shall come from the south (and the Holy One from the mountain of Paran)' as meaning that the messiah will be born in Bethlehem. The opinion of the Hebrew seems to shade into Jerome's own argument that the one born in Bethlehem is the same God who gave the Law at Sinai, and thus he is also the one who came from nearby Paran (cf. Deut. 33: 2, where Sinai and Paran are treated as synonymous).

Rather later, the Babylonian Talmud (*BK* 38*a* and *AZ* 2*b*) connects Habakkuk 3: 3 and Deuteronomy 33: 2, in the context of the giving of the Law at Sinai and the rejection of Torah by the nations. *Exodus Rabbah* 5: 9 also links Habakkuk 3: 3 with Deuteronomy 33: 2, discussing from which direction the Lord comes, but the answer is that Israel cannot tell: the divine voice at Sinai reverberates throughout the world. It may even be that the Midrash found in these later Jewish works developed in order to counter the kind of Christological geography we find in Jerome.

A further category involves Midrash that is completely rejected by Jerome but still performs a function within his schema.

The first example occurs in the commentary on Habakkuk 2: 15–16. Jerome's extended discussion of these difficult verses demonstrates how he weaves several renderings and concepts together. He commences with the lemmata in Latin: the 'Hebrew' 'Woe to him who gives a drink to his friend, sending his poison and making him drunk, so that he can see his nakedness', and 'LXX' 'Woe to him who makes his neighbour drink of his own violent destruction, and makes him drunk, so that he can look in his caves.'[59] First Jerome discusses the widely differing renderings of the *recentiores*. Then he suggests a metaphorical reading, involving the devastation caused in the region by the cup of Nebuchadnezzar's wrath. Next he reports a tradition told him by a respected Hebrew *tana* (teacher) of Lydda.[60] The story goes that Nebuchadnezzar gave the captive Zedekiah a drink containing laxatives, in order to humiliate him in front of the guests at a feast because he would be unable to control his bowels. Jerome rejects this story with the remark, 'I don't have to tell you how ridiculous this story is!'[61] This is ostensibly because Jerome considers such an interpretation, involving an actual drink, incompatible with what he interprets as the metaphorical cup of calamities that God will make Nebuchadnezzar drink as punishment for his treatment of Zedekiah.

in Bethlehem once gave the law on Mount Sinai, he is the holy one who came from Mount Paran. For Paran is next to Mount Sinai.

Cf. *Mekhilta de-Rabbi Ishmael*, trans. and ed. Jacob Z. Lauterbach, 3 vols. (Philadelphia, Pa., 1933–5), ii. 198–200.

[59] Hab. 2: 15–16, ILXX: 'Vae qui propinat proximo suo subuersione turbida, et inebrians, ut aspiciat in speluncis eorum ... circumdedit te calix dexterae Domini'. IH: 'vae qui potum dat amico suo, mittens fel suum et inebrians, ut aspiciat nuditatem eius ... circumdabit te calix dexterae Domini'. The entire passage can be found in Jerome, *Commentarius in Abacuc*, book I, ii. 15–17, pp. 609–12, ll. 524–651.

[60] 'Audiui Liddae quemdam de Hebraeis, qui sapiens apud illos et δευτερώτης uocabatur, narrantem huiuscemodi fabulam' (*Commentarius in Abacuc*, book I, ii. 15–17, p. 610, ll. 578–80).

[61] Ibid., p. 610, ll. 592–3, 'Hoc quam ridiculum sit, me tacente, cognoscitis.'

There are two possible parallels to this story recorded in rabbinic literature. The first is in Babylonian Talmud *Shabat* 149b, where Habakkuk 2: 16 is interpreted as a reference to Nebuchadnezzar wishing to subject Zedekiah to sexual abuse. However, although the protagonists are the same, and the physical humiliation extreme in both cases, it is not particularly close to the *fabula* that Jerome reports. (It is the sort of *midrash* that Jerome probably had in mind when he says in his letter to Algasia that some Jewish legends are too coarse to repeat![62])

A much better parallel to Jerome's version occurs in *Esther Rabbah* 3: 1, interpreting Habakkuk 2: 15, where Nebuchadnezzar is said to have given Zedekiah warm barley bread and new wine, in order to loosen his bowels and thus reveal his nakedness.[63]

In spite of Jerome's dismissal of this *midrash* in favour of the Christian, spiritual interpretation, he nevertheless employs some of its imagery. The 'woe' is addressed to the Antichrist or the 'perverse teaching of heretics', who cause spiritual inebriation with a murky draught (*potione turbida . . . poculo turbido*). This of course relates partly to the 'Hebrew' meaning of the verse that he gives ('woe to him who makes his neighbour drink'), as well as to the Jewish *fabula*. In the following section referring to heretics, Jerome links together several images involving caves or dens where heretical rites take place, based on the LXX reading of the verse which has 'caves' rather than 'nakedness'.

He crowns this section with the statement,

Therefore we will not enter the caves of the heretics, nor hide where impious Saul was accustomed to evacuating the filth of his doctrines, but rather, we ascend to the high cave of Mount Sinai, where Elijah saw the Lord, and Moses saw his back. Isaiah proclaims, 'Here he dwells in a high cave.'[64]

---

[62] Jerome, Ep. 121.10 (to Algasia, *c*.406), ed. Hilberg, CSEL 56, p. 48, ll. 15–18:

Quantae traditiones Pharisaeorum sint, quas hodie *deuterôseis* uocant, et quam aniles fabulae, reuoluere nequeo. neque enim libri patitur magnitudo et pleraque tam turpia sunt, ut erubescam dicere.

I am unable to recount how many traditions of the Pharisees there are, that nowadays they call *deuteroseis*, and what old wives' tales they are! They are too many to be set down, and many are so improper that I would be ashamed to relate them.

[63] *Midrash ester* 3: 1: '"The one who makes to drink" is Nebuchadnezzar, "his neighbour" is Zedekiah . . . What did that wicked man [Nebuchadnezzar] do to him? He made [Zedekiah] eat hot barley bread and gave him new wine fresh from the vat. Why did he do this? In order that his bowels should be loosened. This is what is written: "In order to look on their nakedness".' The older section of *Esther Rabbah*, to which this passage belongs, dates from around 500 CE. Ginzberg comments, 'the coarse form of this legend in Jerome is to be ascribed to his own account, and not to the learned Hebrew' (*Legends of the Jews*, vi. 384). However, the rabbinic form of the legend is no less 'coarse' than Jerome's Latin account of the *fabula*. Ginzberg also refers to *Tanḥuma* B (*Yelamedenu*) II. 33 (first printed edn. Constantinople, 1523), but there the allusion is to Belshazzar and his feast in Dan. 5: 1–6, and there is no humiliation of another figure.

[64] Jerome, *Commentarius in Abacuc*, book I, ii. 15–17, p. 612, ll. 640–5: 'Non ingrediamur ergo in speluncas haereticorum, nec abscondamur ibi, ubi impius Saul stercora doctrinarum suarum egerere consueuit, sed magis ascendamus ad speluncam excelsam montis Sina, ubi et Helias uidit Dominum, et Moyses posteriora eius ante conspexit. Et Esaias de domino clamitans: *hic habitabit*, ait, *in spelunca excelsa*.'

The use of the term 'filth', *stercora*, here, may allude not only to Saul in the cave but also to the midrashic motif of a king voiding his bowels, despite Jerome's explicit rejection of the story.

Thus Jerome has woven together elements and images of several understandings of Habakkuk 2: 15–16 to suit his 'spiritual' interpretation of the passage. He frames his commentary on the passage with the image of defecating kings, one a righteous monarch forced to humiliate himself in public by his captors, and the other an impious ruler relieving himself in private during his quest to capture David. He apparently cites the *midrash* only to mock it. Yet if he had not brought it to the reader's attention, the imagery of the drugged cup and the reference to Saul in the cave (no doubt both drawn from Jerome's Latin rendering of the Septuagint, the ILXX *in speluncis* and IH *potum . . . fel*) would have been less powerful in his *tropologia*. Moreover, the very earthy, historical approach of the *midrash* functions at a literary level as a sharp contrast to Jerome's extended interweaving of Scripture and allegory, while theologically it would serve to highlight Jerome's well-worn distinction between the 'Jewish' corporeal exegesis of Scripture and the higher Christian spiritual sense.

Such use of aggadic traditions as a kind of 'frame' is also found in Jerome's *Commentary on Amos* 2: 1–3:

> The Hebrews have the tradition that the bones are those of the king of Edom, who had gone up with Joram king of Israel and Jehoshaphat king of Judah against Moab. He was buried, but his bones were subsequently torn up and set on fire by the Moabites to indulge their animosity.[65] This is the reason, they say, why God said he would send fire on Moab . . . But just as it is wrong to move the 'perfect captivity', i.e. of Solomon,[66] and shut it up in Edom, so as to make high and lofty things low and earthly, in the same way we must not 'burn the bones of the king of Edom and reduce them to dust and ashes'. The Jews shift the spiritual understanding onto Edomite flesh, and the significance of the kings, which is changed into the literal reading . . . They are not the only ones who do this, all the heretics do likewise . . .[67]

---

[65] The Targum says that Moab burned the bones of the king to plaster his house.

[66] Michael Graves (personal communication) suggests that the 'perfect captivity' is inspired by a Hebrew etymology of the name Solomon.

[67] Amos 2: 1; IH: 'haec dicit Dominus: super tribus sceleribus Moab et super quattuor non conuertam eum, eo quod incenderit ossa regis Idumaeae usque ad cinerem.' Jerome, *Commentarius in Amos*, book I, ii. 1–3, CCSL 76, pp. 229–30, ll. 20–4, 33–5, 36–45:

> Tradunt Hebraei, ossa, regis Idumaeae iam sepulti, qui cum Ioram rege Israel et Iosaphat rege Iuda ascenderat aduersum Moab, in ultionem doloris a Moabitis postea conuulsa atque succensa. Ob hanc ergo, inquiunt, causam Deus missurum se esse dicit ignem in Moab . . . Quomodo autem non oportet transferre captiuitatem perfectam, siue Salomonis, et concludere eam in Idumaeia, ut de excelsis atque caelestibus humiles faciat atque terrenos . . . sic ossa regis Idumaeae comburere non debemus, et in cinerem fauillam que dissoluere. Iudaei transferunt intellegentiam spiritalem in carnes Idumaeas, sensum que regium, qui uersatur in littera, et est solidissimus atque firmissimus, genealogiis quibusdam et traditionibus superfluis eneruant atque comminuunt, et in puluerem redigunt; et non solum illi hoc

Whoever reads that Judah went in to Tamar the prostitute and begot from her two sons, if he follows the impropriety of the literal understanding, and does not rise above to the seemliness of the spiritual sense, he 'burns the bones of the king of Edom'. Whoever thinks that Hosea took a whorish wife and sees no more in the account than the plain sense of the words, 'burns the bones of the king of Edom'.[68]

Here Jerome does not object to the *midrash* per se, as it gives a good historical sense which he appreciated,[69] as well as supporting his IH rendering (*eo quod incenderit ossa regis Idumaeae usque ad cinerem*). His criticism is that to understand Scripture properly, one must go beyond this historical, literal sense: Scripture must embrace a higher meaning than mere historical references. Why would the unsavoury episode of Tamar and Judah be included in the Bible unless it pointed to something spiritual? Just as he registers disgust over the *stercora*, the excrement in the *midrash* on Habakkuk 2: 15, he argues that sticking to the 'letter' of Scripture alone is tantamount to committing the outrage of burning the bones of a dead king.[70]

CONCLUSIONS

Though Jerome sometimes derives midrashic material from sources such as Origen, Josephus, the *recentiores*, and the Apocrypha, he also received genuine midrashic (aggadic) traditions from his 'Hebrew' informants, principally in oral form. This is hardly a new finding, merely a restatement of the most recent scholarly position, which in the main supports Jerome's claims to have access to such knowledge.[71]

---

faciunt, sed omnes haeretici, qui uolunt in modum humanae similitudinis sedere deum in solio excelso et eleuato, et pedes ponere super terram, ne scilicet pendeant.

[68] Ibid., p. 230, ll. 48–54: 'Qui legit introisse Iudam ad Thamar meretricem et ex ea duos filios procreasse, si turpitudinem sequatur litterae, et non ascendat ad decorem intellegentiae spiritalis, comburit ossa regis Idumaeae. Qui putat Osee accepisse uxorem fornicariam, et nihil plus sentit in dicto, quam uerbis simplicibus continetur, ossa comburit regis Idumaeae.' The theme of burning bones also recurs in the same commentary, in book I, ii. 4–5, on p. 231, l. 86.

[69] For the use of Midrash in patristic literature to establish the *historia*, see the important article of Kamesar, 'The Evaluation of the Narrative Aggada in Greek and Latin Patristic Literature'.

[70] Cf. on Amos 1: 6–8, *Commentarius in Amos*, book I, i. 6–8, p. 223, ll. 354–7, 'Hos ego arbitror Iudaeorum magistros, et omnes qui occidentem sequuntur litteram, noluntque recipere spiritum uiuificantem, sed quaecumque interpretantur et sapiunt, uolunt esse terrena.'

[71] Meanings of names in the *Commentaries on the Minor Prophets* are rarely credible etymologies from a modern standpoint: e.g. *Commentarius in Sophoniam*, ii. 3–4, p. 680, ll. 116–17, on Ashdod as 'ignis generationis'; ibid. ii. 8–11, p. 687, ll. 420–1, 'Damascus sanguinem bibens, aut sanguis sacci'; *Commentarius in Aggaeum*, i. 1, CCSL 76A, p. 714, ll. 12–13, Darius means 'generationes factae'; and then with greater accuracy, ibid., p. 715, l. 56, Haggai 'festiuus'; ibid., p. 717, ll. 122–4, Zerrubabbel/Zorobabel 'iste magister de Babylone' (using the rabbinic technique of word segmentation, zo + rob + Babel); and p. 717, ll. 142–3, Jehozadak/Iosedec as 'Iao iustus'. However, the rabbis themselves indulged both in similar etymologizing and in wordplays: see for instance, Howard Eilberg-Schwartz, 'Who's Kidding Whom? A Serious Reading of Rabbinic Word Plays', *Journal of the American Academy of Religion*, 55 (1987), 765–88.

The *function* of the Midrash he cites, both in terms of its theological role and its stylistic, compositional role, has been less discussed. Individual midrashic traditions always appear in the context of the *littera* and *historia*, the literal/historical/Antiochene-type basic interpretation, where historical setting, narrative coherence, and identity of the protagonists are established. Jerome uses the *littera* as a basis before he goes into the spiritual, moral *tropologia*. Sometimes the Midrash can play a part in the *tropologia*, but usually only in a transfigured form.[72] However, another value of Midrash for Jerome was that it could also reinforce the meaning of the Hebrew text.

The midrashic traditions that Jerome broadly approves of are normally flagged up with the formula *tradunt Hebraei*, 'the Hebrews have the tradition'. Those traditions that he rejects as unsuitable and erroneous are indicated by different formulae, such as 'the Jews interpret' or *Iudaicae fabulae*, 'Jewish stories' (it should be noted that Jerome is equally rude about pagan fables).[73]

Naturally these *Hebraei* and *Iudaei* are probably the very same Jews in each case, transmitting what to them would have seemed very similar traditions. But those *midrashim* that are useful to Jerome are therefore for him part of the authentic ancient tradition of the Hebrews, who are effectively the 'Good Jews', custodians of the mysteries of Scripture. Jerome often refers to *Hebraei* with apparently genuine respect,[74] even when complaining of having to pay them handsomely for their knowledge.[75] This financial motif could be interpreted in a number of different ways, not all mutually exclusive: that Jews (even *Hebraei*) are mercenary; that the knowledge they have is valuable and therefore represents an investment (ultimately,

---

[72] See Graves, '"Judaizing" Christian Interpretations', 146–9, for some other examples.

[73] e.g. *Commentarius in Amos*, book II, v. 7–9, p. 280, ll. 274–9, on Orion and Arcturus, quoting Virgil, *Aeneid* III: 516–17: 'Quando autem audimus Arcturum et Oriona, non debemus sequi fabulas poetarum, et ridicula ac portentosa mendacia, quibis etiam caelum infamare conantur' ('When we hear Arcturus and Orion, we should not follow the poets' tales, the ridiculous and revolting lies, by which they try to defame the very heavens').

[74] e.g. 'Hebraeus ... qui nos in Scripturis sanctis erudivit', *Commentarius in Amos*, book II, v, 7–9, p. 280, l. 272; 'Hebraeus qui me in scripturis erudiuit, ita legi posse asseruit' *Commentarius in Naum*, iii. 8–12, p. 562, ll. 274–5.

[75] e.g. 'quo pretio Baraninam nocturnum habui praeceptorem' (Ep. 84.3 [to Pammachius and Oceanus], *Sancti Eusebii Hieronymi Epistulae*, Pars II: *Epistulae LXXI–CXX*, ed. Isidor Hilberg, CSEL 55 (Vienna, 1912), p. 123, ll. 7–8, 'non parvis redemisse nummis' (*Prologus in libro Iob*, in *Biblia Sacra iuxta Vulgatam*, ed. Robert Weber, vol. i (rev. edn. Stuttgart, 1975), p. 731, l. 21). Williams, *The Monk and the Book*, 226, sees the financial motif as symbolizing the role that Jewish informants played in Jerome's literary economy (as opposed to his unpaid Christian teachers). Jay, *L'Exégèse de Saint Jérôme*, interprets it as demonstrating Jerome's lack of personal attachment to his Jewish teachers—it was a merely mercenary arrangement. One suspects, however, that the reality was as complex as Jerome himself. Note that the theme of buying knowledge occurs again in Ep. 84, but this time regarding Jerome's acquisition of Origen's writings: 'legi, inquam, legi Origenem et, si in legendo crimen est, fateor—et nostrum marsuppium alexandrinae chartae euacuarunt' (p. 124, ll. 10–11). Jerome also reminds Rufinus (*Apologia contra Rufinum*, ed. Lardet, book II, §34, p. 71, ll. 8–10) that the latter had acquired copies of the *recentiores* at great expense. From such examples it seems more likely that Jerome is calling attention to the value that the buyer places on what is purchased, rather than to the relationship between buyer and seller.

it was Jerome's patrons who footed the bill); that if a Jew offered help gratis, one would suspect he had a hidden agenda. Jerome attempts to avoid criticism for his use of the Hebrew text, Hebrew language, and Hebrew teachers by separating these three from the beliefs and practice of Judaism. Megan Hale Williams's recent assessment of Jerome's attitude describes it as 'paradoxical'.[76] However, Jerome's contrasting comments concerning Jewish traditions, at times respectful and at others derogatory, are surely meant to deflect possible criticism for using such sources by indicating to the reader that Jerome evaluates each individual interpretation and accepts nothing blindly.[77]

Those *midrashim* that are not of use to Christians are part of Jewish self-delusion, especially concerning their alleged eschatological expectations, shared with 'Judaizing' Christians. Alternatively the aggadah reflects what Jerome writes off as the typical Jewish (*Iudaice*) fleshly (*carnaliter*) approach to Scripture.[78] In such cases it is cited to demonstrate the superiority of Christian, spiritual, exegesis over both Jewish and Jewish-Christian interpretation.

Another function of Jerome's use of Midrash is to show his detractors that, for all his use of Jewish and Hebrew learning and traditions, he is not uncritical of what he has learned from Jews and is capable of distinguishing between what is useful to Christians and what is not. So he selects examples of Midrash to disparage, such as the example where *stercora* alludes to the coarseness of some Jewish interpretations. Even the useful historical tradition about the burning of the Edomite king's bones is used by Jerome to suggest that Jewish exegesis, being confined to the 'historical', is essentially obsolescent and even destructive. This disparagement is almost as important to him as citing Midrash that plays a positive exegetical role in his commentaries.

A further clue to the function of Midrash in Jerome's work is the context in which we tend to find it. Midrash appears rather rarely in his *Iuxta Hebraeos* version, as he generally favoured a reasonably close rendering of the text which could then receive a theological going-over in his exegetical works.[79] There is also very little

---

[76] Williams, *The Monk and the Book*, 221–5.

[77] Kamesar points out that Jerome's judicious use of aggadah needs to be seen in the context of the complaint by some classical authors that *historia* was in danger of becoming *supervacuus labor* (essentially, mere pedantry) or mythology: 'Evaluation of the Narrative Aggada', esp. 42–4.

[78] e.g. 'Haec Iudaice dicta sint', *Commentarius in Sophoniam*, ii. 12–15, p. 690, l. 517, also 'Iudaicas fabulas', ibid. iii. 8–9, p. 700, ll. 260–1; 'neque enim putandum est secundum Iudaicas fabulas et inepta figmenta', *Commentarius in Aggaeum*, ii. 16–18, p. 740, ll. 534–5.

[79] However, there are traces of Midrash in the IH: see on the book of Exodus, Matthew A. Kraus, 'Jerome, the Book of Exodus, and the World of Late Antiquity', in Lieve M. Teugels and Rivka Ulmer (eds.), *Midrash and Context: Proceedings of the 2004 and 2005 SBL Consultation on Midrash*, Judaism in Context 5 (Piscataway, NJ, 2007), 17–37. John Cameron's study of the IH Psalms found rather fewer examples of midrashic interpretation, but concludes that this is because Jerome preferred to follow a literal rendering in his translation of the Hebrew of that book: the exegesis was supplied instead in his commentaries on Psalms ('The Vir Tricultus: An Investigation of the Classical, Jewish, and Christian Influences on Jerome's Translation of the Psalter Iuxta Hebraeos', DPhil. thesis, University of Oxford, 2007, esp. 173–5).

aggadah in his homilies, because in them he was mostly promoting the *tropologia* or moral message.[80] Midrashic traditions appear most often in works such as the *Hebrew Questions on Genesis*, the *Onomasticon*, and in his commentaries on the Prophets, where he is expounding the sense of the Hebrew text.[81]

In fact Adam Kamesar argues that one cannot really separate the use of rabbinic traditions from Jerome's quest for the meaning of the Hebrew text, and that Midrash is sometimes necessary even to understand the *recentiores*.[82] By this Kamesar means that the reason for a particular rendering of the *recentiores* was not always obvious unless one knew the Hebrew philological explanation or the midrashic background to the passage. This is particularly the case with Symmachus, whose readings are often like the tip of a midrashic iceberg. Midrash is thus the key to interpreting even the Jewish Greek revisions.

Kamesar also maintains that Jerome's criterion for choosing a rendering or *midrash* was the sense of the passage.[83] He cites Jerome's remark in the *Apology against Rufinus* that 'everyone selects whatever among the uncertain senses seems to him to be the most coherent [*consequentius*]'.[84]

However, it is worth considering the criticism of Jerome's contemporary, Julian of Eclanum. Julian was a follower of the Antiochene exegete Theodore of Mopsuestia, and was also trying to recommend his own commentary on some Minor Prophets, so he is hardly an unbiased critic. But Julian does say that the problem with Jerome's commentaries on the Prophets was that not only did he waver between allegory and Midrash, he was also no good at sustaining the *perquirenda consequentia*, the *akolouthia* or logical coherence of the wording of

---

[80] There is a passing reference in *Tractatus de Psalmo CIII* on Ps. 103 (104 in the Masoretic text): 26 to Jewish views of Leviathan (p. 187, ll. 181–3), and in *Tractatus de Psalmo XV* on Ps. 15 (16): 1, on the meaning of מכתם (p. 364, ll. 1–14). In *Tractatus de Psalmo LXXVI* on Ps. 76 (77): 19, Jerome denies the possibility of a literal interpretation with the words, *Hic quid facis, Iudaee?* (p. 59, ll. 148–9), and in *Tractatus de Psalmo XCV* on Ps. 95 (96): 1 he rejects the Jewish interpretation of the title and its context in favour of a mystical and universal message (p. 149, ll. 5–14) (*Tractatus sive homiliae in Psalmos*, ed. Germain Morin, CCSL 78 (Turnhout, 1958)).

[81] For the Christian exegesis of Jerome's *Commentary on Isaiah*, see Jay, *L'Exégèse de Saint Jérôme*, who gives full explanations and examples of Jerome's use of terms such as *littera, historia, figura, tropologia*, and *spiritus*. For the Jewish elements used in his *Commentary on Jeremiah*, see Michael Graves's *Jerome's Hebrew Philology*.

[82] Kamesar, *Jerome, Greek Scholarship, and the Hebrew Bible*, 181.   [83] Ibid.

[84] Jerome, *Apologia contra Rufinum*, ed. Lardet, book I, §20, p. 476, ll. 12–16:

Et uideres quanta silua sit apud Hebraeos ambiguorum nominum atque uerborum. Quae res diuersae interpretationi materiam praebuit, dum unusquisque inter dubia quod sibi *consequentius* videtur, hoc transfert.

See also Graves, '"Judaizing" Interpretations', 1 and n. 1.

Tu verrais tout ce maquis de noms et de verbes ambigus qu'il y a chez les Hébreux! C'est ce qui fournit matière à la divergence des traductions, tandis que chacun, entre des sens incertains, choisit celui qui lui paraît le plus cohérent. (trans. Pierre Lardet, *Saint Jérôme, Apologie contre Rufin*, Sources chrétiennes 303 (Paris, 1983), 57)

Scripture.⁸⁵ Despite Jerome's own claim in the *Apology against Rufinus* about offering different possibilities so that the reader could choose what seemed most coherent in sense (*consequentius*), his weighing up of all the options in such detail and complexity (as in the long passage on Habakkuk 2: 15–16) may have overloaded some readers, who may well have felt that both they and Jerome had 'lost the plot'.

Clearly Christian doctrine played a major role in Jerome's decision whether a particular rabbinic interpretation was a 'Hebrew tradition' or a 'Jewish fable'. Both could be of value to Jerome, either for a better understanding of the meaning of the Hebrew text, or in promoting a specifically Christian reading of it in contradistinction to the alleged Jewish interpretation.

---

⁸⁵ Julian of Eclanum, prologue to *Tractate on Hosea, Joel, and Amos* (*Iuliani Aeclanensis Expositio libri Iob; tractatus prophetarum Osee, Iohel et Amos*, ed. Lucas de Coninck and Maria Josepha d'Hont, CCSL 88 (Turnhout, 1977), p. 116, ll. 48–53). The context is Julian's recommendation of his own commentary and comparison of it with those of Origen, John Chrysostom, and Jerome:

> Hieronymus porro, et ingenii capacis uir et studii pertinacis, in prophetarum quidem libros commenta digessit, sed quasi inter geminas traditiones ire contentus, de perquirenda consequentia nihil aut uoluit aut potuit sustinare curarum. Ita uel per allegorias Origenis uel per fabulosas Iudaeorum traditiones tota eius defluxit oratio.

> Jerome is a man of great ability and steadfast application who has produced commentaries on the Prophets. However, as if he were content to move between twin traditions, he was neither willing nor able to sustain the necessary coherence [i.e. the *akolouthia*]. Thus his whole discourse drifts about, either through Origen's allegories or the fictitious traditions of the Jews.

The passage is discussed by Kamesar, 'Evaluation of the Narrative Aggada', 50–2, but from a different point of view, namely the attitude to the *fabulosae Iudaeorum traditiones*.

FIVE

MIDRASH IN SYRIAC

SEBASTIAN BROCK

THE PERIOD OF Middle Aramaic (c.300 BCE–300 CE) gave birth to three literary dialects of Aramaic: Jewish Aramaic, Syriac (the local dialect of Edessa), and Mandaic. Of these Syriac was to provide by far the largest literature, and to prove to be the longest-lived in active use (it still remains productive today). As far as the exegesis of Scripture is concerned, two periods are of primary importance for their productivity, the first covering from the fourth to the seventh centuries, and the second from the seventh to the thirteenth centuries. During the course of the first of these periods one can witness a progressive Hellenization of Syriac literary culture in general that extends to virtually all areas of literary productivity.[1] Whereas earlier writers, of the fourth and fifth centuries, though by no means untouched by the Greek culture of their day, still retain an independence of their own, and write more in the style of the authors of the Hebrew Bible than in that of Greek models, their successors from the late fifth century onwards increasingly took over Greek literary models and literary style, so great was the prestige of Greek culture at the time. Thus ironically, just at the time when the Arab invasions cut Syriac Christianity off from the Greek world, philohellenism was reaching the height of its influence on Syriac authors. This meant that, by the beginning of the second period, the Syriac exegetical tradition had already become profoundly Hellenized; it could be said that in many ways it was only in the matter of language that it differed from the contemporary approach to exegesis in the Greek-speaking Christian tradition.

Given this situation, if one is looking to discover Midrash outside Judaism, an obvious place to start one's search would be the earlier Syriac literature, especially among writers of the fourth and fifth centuries, since many Jewish exegetical traditions are to be found here alone among early Christian writings.[2] First, however, a word needs to be said about the actual biblical text available to early Syriac Christianity. It is now clear, thanks largely to the work of Michael Weitzman, that the Syriac translation of the Hebrew Bible was made directly from Hebrew, and

---

[1] For this process, see Sebastian P. Brock, 'From Antagonism to Assimilation: Syriac Attitudes to Greek Learning', in id., *Syriac Perspectives on Late Antiquity* (London, 1984), ch. 5.

[2] Several examples can be found in Sebastian P. Brock, 'Jewish Traditions in Syriac Sources', *Journal of Jewish Studies*, 30 (1979), 212–32.

that this was done over the course of the second century CE, with different translators working on different books, not all at the same time.³ Having been translated at the stage in the history of the Hebrew text known as proto-Masoretic, the Peshitta (as it later came to be called) has a Hebrew textual basis far closer to that of Rabbinic Judaism than was the case with the Septuagint, several of whose books (such as Jeremiah and Job) were translated nearly half a millennium earlier from a Hebrew text that was at considerable variance with what became the Masoretic text. Whether or not one accepts Weitzman's view that Jews from a non-rabbinic background were involved in the translation,⁴ it is clear that the common heritage shared between early Syriac Christianity and subsequent Rabbinic Judaism was far greater than was the case with Greek-speaking Christianity, based on the earlier translation of the Septuagint.

The close nature of this shared heritage can readily be seen from a number of distinctive features found both in early Syriac tradition and in certain strands within Rabbinic Judaism. Two examples will illustrate this, one already embedded in the Peshitta, the other concerning exegetical terminology.

In common with the Targumim, the Peshitta frequently seeks to avoid the anthropomorphism 'and God was seen' of the Hebrew original, replacing it by 'and God was revealed to'. This is the regular rendering in Targum Onkelos, and of the Peshitta, for instance at Exodus 6: 3. Much more frequently, however, the Peshitta provides a different preposition, 'God was revealed *over*', which is a characteristic feature of the Palestinian Targum tradition.⁵

Both Jewish Palestinian Aramaic and early Syriac provide examples of a striking exegetical usage whereby instead of the form 'A (in the biblical text) signifies B', non-literal interpretations are sometimes introduced by the reverse, employing passive forms, 'B is signified by A (of the biblical text)' (*B mtil b-A/B etmtel b-A*), thus giving precedence, as it were, to the 'true', or 'higher' sense over the literal wording of the biblical text. Thus, for example, Ephrem (d. 373 CE) speaks of 'the world which is symbolized by the sea' ('*alma da-mtil b-yamma*),⁶ or (in his commentary on Gen. 49: 13) of 'sin, which is signified by Sidon' (*mtilat b-Saydon*). Once again, the origin of this usage would seem to lie in the milieu from which the Palestinian Targum emerged, seeing that the distinctive phrase features a number of times in Targum Neofiti.⁷

---

³ Michael Weitzman, *The Syriac Version of the Old Testament: An Introduction* (Cambridge, 1999). Even if some books may have been translated by Christians, these must have been recent converts from Judaism, for otherwise their good knowledge of Hebrew would be inexplicable.

⁴ Ibid. 246, and id., 'From Judaism to Christianity: The Syriac Version of the Hebrew Bible', in Ada Rapoport-Albert and Gillian Greenberg (eds.), *From Judaism to Christianity: Studies in the Hebrew and Syriac Bibles*, Journal of Semitic Studies, Supplement 8 (Manchester, 1999), 3–29.

⁵ See further Sebastian Brock, 'A Palestinian Targum Feature in Syriac', *Journal of Jewish Studies*, 46 (1995), 271–82.

⁶ Thus *Madrashe* against Heresies, XXV: 10 and *Commentary on the Diatessaron*, V. 18.

⁷ Thus Gen. 15: 17, 'Gehinnom which is signified by the furnace' (*di-mtilah b-atunah*); similarly at Gen. 40: 23; Lev. 26: 6; Num. 21: 14, 23: 9; Deut. 32: 24, and 33: 15. Later usage, such as that found in

Other examples of shared phraseology can be adduced,[8] and significantly they too point to the roots of the Syriac usage in the background that lies behind the extant Palestinian Targum tradition.

WHAT IS UNDERSTOOD HERE BY 'MIDRASH'

Before proceeding further, however, it is essential to specify more exactly what is understood here by the term 'Midrash', since a great variety of different definitions is to be found in modern literature on the subject.[9] If 'Midrash' is just understood as the term for specifically Jewish exegesis, then of course it is simply meaningless even to start to look for Midrash outside Judaism. This reductionist sense, however, is not very helpful, and for present purposes a convenient definition might be 'the discovery of meanings other than literal in the Bible'.[10]

There are, however, two essential premises underlying rabbinic Midrash which need to be stated at the outset: firstly, the biblical text is regarded as a unitary whole which represents the revealed word of God, containing all truth. As a consequence everything in the biblical text is significant, even though the significance in any one case may not at first be at all obvious; difficulties and obscurities thus serve as challenges that need, indeed demand, to be met. A corollary of this is that difficulties that arise in one place may often be resolved by consulting some other passage within the body of Scripture. Secondly, Scripture is polyvalent: many different interpretations of the same passage can happily coexist. Both these premises equally underlie all early Syriac (and other early Christian) writers, though of course they run completely contrary to any modern historical approach. It is these two underlying presuppositions, shared by both Jewish and Syriac exegetes, which provide an identical starting point for both traditions and which govern the ways in which each carries out the midrashic process.

---

the Targum on Psalms, employs the preposition *l-*, instead of *b-* (e.g. Tg. Ps. 80: 9, *bet yisra'el di-mtilin l-guphna*). The corresponding Hebrew form, *mashul b-*, occurs in late *midrashim*, e.g. *Midrash hagadol* on Gen. 37: 9, 'the just are symbolized by the stars' (*meshulim bekokhavim*). Nothing similar is to be found in Greek (where indeed no corresponding verb *parabolizo* is ever recorded).

[8] Thus the specialized use of *aggen* 'to tabernacle over/in', in sacral contexts, phraseology such as *ashri shkinteh 'al*, '(God) caused his Shekhinah to reside on', the combination *malka mshiha*, 'King Messiah', etc. For these, see Sebastian Brock, *Fire from Heaven: Studies in Syriac Theology and Liturgy* (Aldershot, 2006), chs. 10–13, and id., 'Syria and Mesopotamia: The Shared Term *Malka Mshiha*', in Markus Bockmuehl and James Carleton Paget (eds.), *Redemption and Resistance: The Messianic Hopes of Jews and Christians in Antiquity* (London, 2007), 171–82.

[9] See e.g. Irving Jacobs, 'What is Midrash?', in id., *The Midrashic Process* (Cambridge, 1995), 1–20, and Gary A. Porton, 'Midrash, definitions of', in Jacob Neusner and Alan J. Avery Peck (eds.), *Encyclopedia of Midrash*, vol. i (Leiden, 2005), 520–34; also Carol Bakhos, 'Method(ological) Matters in the Study of Midrash', in C. Bakhos (ed.), *Current Trends in the Study of Midrash*, Supplements to the Journal for the Study of Judaism 106 (Leiden, 2006), 161–87, esp. 162–7.

[10] Thus the entry on Midrash in Raphael J. Zvi Werblowsky and Geoffrey Wigoder (eds.), *The Oxford Dictionary of the Jewish Religion* (New York, 1997), 463.

In order to point to the polyvalency of the biblical text, Philo (20 BCE–50 CE) described it as an inexhaustible fountain;[11] Ephrem, who certainly did not know Philo's writings, used the same image to make the same point:

> Who is capable of comprehending the extent of what is to be discovered in a single utterance [sc. of Scripture]? For we leave behind in it far more than we take from it, like people drinking from a fountain.... God has hidden within his words all sorts of treasures, so that each of us can be enriched by them, from whatever aspect he meditates on.[12]

Midrash could thus be described as the art of discovering truths that are latent in Scripture. In this sense it has nothing to do with literary genre, but rather represents a journey of interpretation which sets out from a fixed starting point—the biblical text—and proceeds with a specific purpose in mind, namely the discovery of meaning.

Terms and Genres

As far as the technical term *midrash* is concerned, it should be noted at once that Syriac has no equivalent. It is true that the word *midrash* occurs twice in the Hebrew Bible (2 Chr. 13: 22 and 24: 27) and that the Syriac translation (the Peshitta) represents this by the cognate *madrasha* ('written in the *madrashe* of Iddo the prophet'), but Syriac readers would understand this to refer to stanzaic poems.[13] Nor is Ezra 7: 10, where in Hebrew Ezra is said to have 'begun to study [*lidrosh*] the Law of Moses', of assistance since the Peshitta renders this as 'to perform/carry out the Law of Moses'.[14] The avoidance here of the Syriac cognate verb *drash* is readily explicable in that it normally has a different sense of 'to lay a track', 'tread out a path' (thus e.g. Peshitta Isa. 62: 10, Jer. 18: 15).[15] Closer to Hebrew usage is the noun *darosha*, 'investigator'. This is the term that Aphrahat, writing in the first half of the fourth century, uses on several occasions, in his address to an imagined Jewish reader: 'O wise investigator of the [Jewish] people'.[16] (A further noun from the same root, *drasha*, will be encountered briefly below.)

It should likewise be pointed out that Syriac literature has no real equivalents

---

[11] *De posteritate Caini*, 136; cf. also 127, 153 (Loeb edn., vol. ii); *Quis rerum divinarum heres*, 31, and *De congressu quaerendae eruditionis gratia*, 120 (Loeb edn., vol. iv).

[12] *Commentary on the Diatessaron*, I. 18.

[13] The term is already used in this sense in connection with Bardaisan (154–222 CE); most of Ephrem's poetic output is in the form of *madrashe*.

[14] Since the verb *'bad* is repeated later in the verse, one wonders whether the original Syriac translation might have had *lm'qb* ('to trace out') instead of *lm'bd*.

[15] Closer in sense to the Hebrew cognate is the usage of the poet Jacob of Serugh (d. 521) in his Homily 127 (*Homiliae Selectae Mar-Jacobi Sarugensis*, ed. Paul Bedjan, vol. iv (Paris, 1908; repr. Piscataway, NJ, 2006), 627), though there the verb carries the negative overtones of making a disputatious enquiry into the biblical text.

[16] *Demonstrations* XII. 3, XV. 5, and XVIII. 4; at XVIII. 2 and XIX. 2, as a variation, he uses 'investigator of Israel'. The exact nuance intended is not clear, and the translations 'debater' or 'disputer' may be unduly negative, though such negative overtones are certainly present in later writers: thus Jacob of Serugh tells his imagined Jewish *darosha*, 'hold your tongue!' (Homily 53, ed. P. Bedjan, II, 590).

to the end products of the midrashic method in Rabbinic Judaism, namely the existing Midrash compilations. Examples of what can legitimately be described as Syriac forms of the midrashic process are to be found in a great many different literary genres. In prose there are two main forms. The first is the commentary, where the biblical text is explicated in sequence, although the treatment is often uneven; here the prime example would be the *Commentary on Genesis* by Ephrem, writing in north Mesopotamia within the Roman empire.[17] The other prose form, often written in artistic prose, concentrates on a particular episode; this can be found in various passages of Aphrahat's *Demonstrations*, composed between 337 and 345 CE within the Persian empire. Later on, this developed into the homily. On the surface, at least, there is thus a counterpart to the two types of rabbinic Midrash compilations, the exegetical and the homiletic *midrashim*. In the words of Adam Kamesar, both these Syriac writers 'may be legitimately termed "midrashists"'.[18]

What distinguishes the Syriac use of the midrashic method from the norm in Rabbinic Judaism is the frequency with which it employs verse form. Here again there are two main types: narrative and dialogue. Several long narrative poems expanding on biblical episodes are to be found in Syriac. The earlier ones, mostly anonymous works probably of the fourth and fifth centuries, provide imaginative retellings of the biblical text with little or no specifically Christian elements;[19] these narrative poems in fact fit very well into Kamesar's category of 'narrative aggada'.[20] Subsequently, however, these verse narratives developed into the distinctively Syriac genre of the verse homily (*memra*), whose two great practitioners were Narsai (d. *c*.500) and Jacob of Serugh (d. 521), though (especially in the case of Jacob) many features characteristic of narrative aggadah were preserved.[21]

---

[17] There is an English translation of Ephrem's *Commentary* in E. Mathews and J. Amar, *St Ephrem the Syrian: Selected Prose Works* (Washington, DC, 1994), 67–213.

[18] Adam Kamesar, 'The Church Fathers and Rabbinic Midrash', in Neusner and Peck (eds.), *Encyclopedia of Midrash*, i. 20–40, here 26.

[19] Particularly interesting, because of various exegetical features in common with rabbinic treatments of the Akedah, are two related poems on Genesis 22, edited and translated in Sebastian P. Brock, 'Two Syriac Verse Homilies on the Binding of Isaac', *Le Muséon*, 99 (1986), 61–129.

[20] Adam Kamesar, 'The Evaluation of the Narrative Aggada in Greek and Latin Patristic Literature', *Journal of Theological Studies*, NS 45 (1994), 37–71; he gives as his definition the 'expansion and elaboration of the biblical text in narrative form' (p. 38). Also relevant here is his 'The Narrative Aggada as Seen from the Graeco-Roman Perspective', *Journal of Jewish Studies*, 45 (1994), 52–70. See further the 'Conclusion' to Sebastian P. Brock, 'Dramatic Narrative Poems on Biblical Topics in Syriac', in *Studia Patristica*, 45 (2010), 183–96.

[21] Although the Hebrew poetry of the early *paytanim* has sometimes been adduced as being similar in character to the Syriac *memra*, they would seem to me to be very different in character: in the words of E. Fleischer, 'the hermeneutic character of *piyyut* and of the sermon is very different': 'Piyyut', in Shemuel Safrai et al. (eds.), *The Literature of the Sages* (Assen, 2006), 366. Early *piyut* has much more in common with the learned Greek poetry of Palestinian authors such as Sophronios (early 7th cent.). Much closer in spirit to the Syriac materials are some of the Aramaic poems in Joseph Yahalom and Michael Sokoloff, *Shirat benei ma'arava: Jewish Palestinian Aramaic Poetry from Late Antiquity* [Shirat benei ma'arava: shirim aramiyim shel yehudei erets-yisra'el batekufah habizantit] (Jerusalem, 1999), 82–6.

Dialogue features in poetry in several different forms, but the most distinctive is the formal dialogue poem, in which two protagonists conduct an argument in alternating verses. Here the starting point is a moment of tension between two characters in the biblical text; the implications latent in the text are drawn out by means of dialogue, often in the form of a dispute. Interestingly, one of several terms used for these arguments is *drasha*, though with the sense of 'dispute', and not with any idea of drawing out the meaning of the biblical episode in question. These Syriac dialogue poems represent an adaptation of the ancient Mesopotamian literary genre of the precedence dispute, and the theme of precedence is still present in some of the earlier Syriac poems of this sort, the earliest of which is a series of disputes between Death and Satan, by Ephrem.[22] The genre is also found in Judaism, with several (mostly prose) examples preserved in the Palestinian Targum tradition, though often in an apocopated form;[23] a particularly interesting one, since it has also turned up on papyrus in Egypt, is the dispute between Moses and the Red Sea.[24]

SOME SPECIFIC EXAMPLES

In order to explore whether one can identify Midrash in early Syriac writers, it will be helpful to examine some examples from each of three different situations: (1) places where the silence of the biblical text leaves certain questions unanswered; (2) where biblical language about God is problematic; and (3) where an entire episode in the biblical text appears on the surface to be shocking.

1. Unanswered Questions

The Sacrifices of Abel and Cain (Genesis 4)

The biblical narrative of Genesis 4 gives no indication of *how* the two brothers knew that Abel's offering had been accepted and Cain's rejected, nor of the reason *why* this had happened. In response, both rabbinic and Syriac exegetical traditions offer a wide variety of different explanations.[25] As a means of providing an answer to the second question, some sources in both traditions took as a clue for their starting point the statement in verse 8 that Cain spoke to Abel. In the Hebrew text there is no indication of what he said, though both the Septuagint and the Peshitta provide

---

[22] Nisibene *Madrashe*, 52–4. For the genre in general, see the contributions in G. J. Reinink and H. L. J. Vanstiphout (eds.), *Dispute Poems and Dialogues in the Ancient and Mediaeval Near East*, Orientalia Lovaniensia Analecta, 42 (Louvain, 1991); a listing of the known Syriac poems is given on pp. 117–19.

[23] See especially Robert Murray, 'Aramaic and Syriac Dispute Poems and their Connections', in Mark J. Geller, Jonas C. Greenfield, and Michael Weitzman (eds.), *Studia Aramaica*, Journal of Semitic Studies, Supplement 4 (Oxford, 1995), 157–87. A convenient list of them can be found in Willem F. Smelik, *The Targum of Judges* (Leiden, 1995), 415–18.

[24] Yahalom and Sokoloff, *Shirat benei ma'arava* (Heb.), 82–6.

[25] A very helpful analysis of the early Christian (Greek and Syriac) exegetical traditions can be found in Johannes Glenthøj, *Cain and Abel in Syriac and Greek Writers (4th–6th centuries)*, Corpus Scriptorum Christianorum Orientalium 567, Subsidia 95 (Leuven, 1997).

'Let us travel to the valley' (thus Peshitta; Septuagint, 'to the field'). The aposiopesis of the Hebrew served as an invitation to provide a dialogue between the two brothers that would indicate the reason for the rejection of Cain's sacrifice. This gave rise to the verbalized disputes to be found, not only in the Palestinian Targum tradition and *Genesis Rabbah*, but also in Syriac tradition,[26] most prominently in two anonymous dispute poems, the older of which probably belongs to about the fifth century. What is of interest here are the ways in which answers to exegetical questions are drawn out by means of an imagined dispute between the two brothers. In the various witnesses to the Palestinian Targum tradition the dispute is evidently a theological one: according to Abel the world is governed by providence, whereas according to Cain it is just chance.[27] By contrast, in *Genesis Rabbah* (22: 7) the argument, according to one explanation, was over possessions:

What did they quarrel about? 'Come, let us divide up the world.' One took the land, and the other the movables. The former said 'The land you stand on is mine,' while the latter retorted, 'What you are wearing is mine.' One said 'Strip [off what you are wearing],' the other retorted 'Fly [off the ground].'

In the earlier of the two Syriac dialogue poems on Cain and Abel,[28] Cain, concerned that his sacrifice has been rejected, is basically accusing God of favouritism, a theme which probably ultimately derives from the Palestinian Targum tradition; but at the same time it is interesting to find that, beside primogeniture, the possession of land is also an important concern of Cain's, as is the case in *Genesis Rabbah*. Abel, by contrast, is not interested in ownership, but is concerned primarily to point out that the matter of intention was the underlying factor behind God's choice:

CAIN: I am the eldest, and so it is right
that God should accept me, rather than you;
but He has preferred your sacrifice, and mine He has abhorred:
He has rejected mine, and chosen yours.

ABEL: In all offerings that are made
it is love that He wants to see,
and if good intention is not mingled in,
then the sacrifice is ugly, and so gets rejected.

[26] The use of imagined speeches or dialogue in rabbinic Jewish and Syriac Christian literature has a common root, in the rhetorical exercises that were part of the educational system of the Graeco-Roman world. For this aspect, see Burton Visotzky, 'Midrash, Christian Exegesis and Hellenistic Hermeneutics', in C. Bakhos (ed.), *Current Trends in the Study of Midrash*, 111–31, esp. 117–26.

[27] The different witnesses to the Palestinian Targum tradition offer slightly different texts, which in turn lend a different character to the topic of their dispute: see Geza Vermes, *Scripture and Tradition* (Leiden, 1975), ch. 7; cf. also John W. Bowker, *The Targums and Rabbinic Literature* (Cambridge, 1969), 132–41.

[28] Edited with translation, Sebastian P. Brock, 'Two Syriac Dialogue Poems on Abel and Cain', *Le Muséon*, 113 (2000), 333–75.

CAIN: I will deprive you of your 'Friend',
for the earth will not hold us both;
then He will have to accept sacrifice from me,
when there is no one else besides me!

ABEL: Grant me as a favour some small corner
in the world, and do not kill me.
The whole world shall be yours,
then you can offer up sacrifice just as you like.

(stanzas 15–18)

As Ephrem had earlier stressed in his prose *Commentary*, what was important in God's eyes was the quality of the intention, not the quantity of the offering:[29]

Even if Cain's offering had been smaller than that of his brother, it would have been accepted, but for the fact that he made his offering in a negligent way.

Interior disposition had likewise provided the explanation for Aphrahat, writing in the Persian empire a generation or so before Ephrem:

It was through Abel's purity of heart that his offering was acceptable before God, while that of Cain was rejected.[30]

The Identity of the Location of the Akedah (Genesis 22)

Key events in any sacred history have a strong tendency to become associated with sites that have a sacral character. The identification of the site of the Akedah as that of the future Temple is already hinted at in the Hebrew Bible through the occurrence, common to both Genesis 22 and 2 Chronicles 3: 1, of the toponym Moriah. Although in the Septuagint the common identity of location is no longer evident, in that Moriah is rendered in different ways in the two passages, for Syriac readers of the Peshitta their identity is still hinted at, albeit in a more oblique manner, both passages having 'in the land of the Amorites'. In the Hellenistic and early Roman periods the link is made much more explicitly in both Jubilees 18: 13[31] and Josephus, *Antiquities* i. 226. Early Christian writers generally prefer to shift the site of the

---

[29] Ephrem, *Commentary on Genesis*, III. 2.

[30] *Demonstration* IV. 2. Aphrahat also explains how they knew: fire descended on Abel's sacrifice, a tradition first attested in the Jewish Greek Bible translator Theodotion, who evidently linked the Hebrew verb *vayisha* (verse 4) with *esh*, 'fire', perhaps also having in mind the descent of fire on David's and Solomon's sacrifices (1 Chron. 21: 6 and 2 Chron. 7: 1); this also features in Ephrem's *Commentary* (III. 3). (For a further exploration of the Syriac tradition, see Sebastian P. Brock, 'Fire from Heaven: From Abel's Sacrifice to the Eucharist: A Theme in Syriac Christianity', *Studia Patristica*, 25 (1993), 229–43, reprinted in id., *Fire from Heaven*, ch. 5).

[31] It is intriguing to note that Jubilees mentions this in connection with verse 14, which is precisely the verse where the Palestinian Targum has a long expansion in the course of which mention is made of the Temple.

Akedah to Golgotha, which makes the occasional retention of the Temple in a few Syriac writings all the more interesting.[32]

The identification of Moriah was one thing, but the ancient reader also wished to know how Abraham recognized it when 'on the third day he lifted up his eyes and saw the place' (Gen. 22: 4). Just as *Genesis Rabbah* 56: 1 sought to explore the significance of the 'third' day by adducing other passages mentioning important events that took place on the third day, so too do several Syriac writers, though their attention is diverted to the resurrection of Jesus on the third day and his three days in the tomb. The poet Jacob of Serugh[33] adds that, for Abraham, Isaac was metaphorically killed during this three-day period. A different line is taken by Ephrem (*Comm.* XX.1), in common with Rabbi Akiva (*Gen. Rab.* 55: 6), in order to show that Abraham had time to think it over.

For both Syriac and Jewish *darshanim*, the specification of the 'third' day is also seen as a pointer to some sort of revelation being made to Abraham, enabling him to recognize the site. For *Genesis Rabbah* it is 'a cloud' that he sees above the mountain,[34] while in a Palestinian Targum fragment it is 'a pillar of cloud';[35] a similar tradition, that it was 'a pillar of light', was known to the ninth-century Syriac commentators Isho'dad of Merv and Isho'barnun,[36] while for the *Sefer hayashar* (eleventh–twelfth centuries?) it is 'a pillar of fire' that Abraham saw. The earlier Syriac poets, Narsai and Jacob, are somewhat more reticent, in that they simply speak of a 'revelation'.

In the Palestinian Targum (Gen. 22: 10) it is Isaac who is the recipient of a vision later on in the narrative, at the very moment when Abraham has taken the knife in his hand. Jacob likewise has Isaac say at the same point, 'I behold a picture of life set before me' (p. 98). Unusually for Christian writers, Jacob also emphasizes that Abraham was acting as a priest (p. 84), that Isaac was a willing sacrificial victim (pp. 85–90),[37] and that 'as though in very truth (Abraham) shed the blood of his only-begotten' (p. 99).

Although the details are different,[38] what is of significance here is the shared concerns in their approach to dealing with questions arising from the biblical text.

---

[32] Notably Aphrahat, *Demonstration* XXI. 5.

[33] Homily 109 (ed. P. Bedjan, IV, 77).

[34] In *Midrash hagadol* (*Sefer hagadol al hamishah humshei torah*, 1: *Sefer bereshit*, ed. M. Margulies, 2nd edn. [Jerusalem, 1967], 352) it is the 'glory of the Shekhinah'; the Shekhinah also features in Jacob of Serugh (ed. Bedjan, IV, 89), but there Abraham only sees it when they reach the mountain.

[35] Michael L. Klein, *Genizah Manuscripts of the Palestinian Targum to the Pentateuch*, 2 vols. (Cincinnati, Ohio, 1986), i. 34–5.

[36] Another opinion cited by Isho'dad held that it was in the shape of a cross, thus linking more closely with this verse Jesus's statement in John 8: 56 concerning how 'Abraham saw my day'. (For these commentators on Gen. 22 see Sebastian P. Brock, 'Genesis 22 in Syriac Tradition', in Pierre Casetti, Othmar Keel, and Adrian Schenker (eds.), *Mélanges Dominique Barthélemy*, Orbis Biblicus et Orientalis 38 (Fribourg, Switzerland, 1981), 1–30.)

[37] Isaac's awareness that he is to be the sacrificial victim is, however, quite widely indicated in the Syriac writers.

[38] One notable contrast should be noticed, namely the absence of interest, on the part of the Syriac authors, in verse 14 (for the Palestinian Targum's long expansion, with Abraham's prayer, see above, n. 31).

The Young Joseph's Dream (Genesis 37: 9–11)

Joseph's second dream, in which he saw that 'the sun, moon, and eleven stars are going to prostrate to me', elicits his father's rebuke, 'Will I and your mother and your brothers really come to prostrate to the ground to you?' An immediate exegetical problem is posed by the fact that Rachel is already dead (Gen. 35: 19). Jewish exegetical sources offer a variety of different explanations: thus, for example, Jacob's 'rebuke' is explained as being based precisely on the fact that his mother, no longer alive, is mentioned; or, the passage illustrates the fact that dreams are never fully fulfilled (BT *Ber.* 55a–b); or the reference is not to Rachel but to Bilhah, who brought Joseph up (*Midrash hagadol*), to mention just a few. Ephrem offers yet another explanation, which happens to provide a good example of the 'midrashic' way in which he proceeds:[39]

> [The brothers] hated him because of his dreams. Now they ridiculed his dreams, saying, 'How will Rachel, who is dead, come and prostrate to him?' Because it is said, 'A man and his wife are one body' [Gen. 2: 24]. Jacob, symbolized by the sun [*mtil b-shemsha*], bowed down on the head of his staff [Gen. 47: 31], and in him there bent down Rachel, symbolized by the moon [*mtilat b-sahra*], although she did not [in fact] bow down.

What according to one Jewish interpretation was the rationale for Jacob's rebuke has now been allocated to the brothers; this not only exonerates the father, but at the same time it heightens the negative image of the brothers, seeing that the altered wording has changed the rebuke into mockery. More important, from our present perspective, is the way in which Ephrem resolves the problem: like the rabbis, he simply adduces another biblical passage, in his case Genesis 2: 24, in order to explain how Rachel can be included with Jacob, and then another passage that indicates the occasion when the dream was fulfilled. What is only of secondary concern here is the fact that the first passage is quoted with slightly altered wording so as to introduce associations with two New Testament passages.[40] Likewise, the Peshitta's rendering of the ambiguous *hmth* of Genesis 47: 31 as 'staff' (*mateh*, so already LXX), and not 'bed' (*mitah*, so MT, and already Aquila), gives his exegesis Christian resonances.

2. Problematic Statements about God

Statements in the biblical text using anthropomorphic language, such as that God 'was angry', or that he 'repented', cried out for explanation. Just as in the Talmud it is stated that 'the Torah speaks in human language',[41] so too Ephrem frequently

---

[39] *Commentary on Genesis*, XXXIII. 1.

[40] 'One flesh' of Genesis is altered to 'one body', in accordance with the quotation of Gen. 2: 24 in 1 Cor. 6: 16 (similarly the quotation of Matt. 19: 6 in the Peshitta). [41] BT *Ber.* 31b.

describes God as having 'put on names' or 'terms' (*shmahe*), that is, language that is familiar to human beings:

> Let us give thanks to God, who clothed Himself in the names of the
>   body's various parts:
> Scripture refers to His 'ears'—to teach us that He listens to us;
> it speaks of His 'eyes'—to show that He sees us.
> It was just the terms [*shmahe*] of such things that He put on,
> and although in His true Being there is no wrath or regret,
> yet He put on these terms too, because of our weakness.
>
> (*Madrashe* on Faith, XXXI.1)

Furthermore, to take these metaphors, or 'borrowed terms', literally is an abuse of the biblical text:

> If someone goes astray by focusing
> on the terms borrowed [to describe God's] majesty,
> he misrepresents and dishonours that majesty
> by means of those same borrowed terms
> which [God] has put on for man's benefit,
> and he shows ingratitude to that Grace which has bent down
> its lofty stature to the level of man's childishness.
>
> (*Madrashe* on Paradise, XI.6)

Elsewhere Ephrem explains that the presence of such problematic terms used of God in the biblical text has a pedagogical function: it is to induce repentance. Thus referring to Genesis 6: 6, he writes:

The Nature which does not feel regret lowered Itself to say 'I regret', so that the rebellious generation might hear and quake in fear; and so that remorse might be sown in those whose hearts rebelled against remorse. (*Commentary on Genesis*, VI.7)

Here, as frequently elsewhere, Ephrem depicts what he sees as a regular pattern of divine action in the face of human wrongdoing: in the first place Grace (*taybuta*) intervenes, in order to encourage repentance; only when repentance is not forthcoming does Justice (*ke'nuta*) intervene. It would seem highly probable that Ephrem's Grace and Justice have their ultimate roots in the two rabbinic *midot* of Mercy (*rahamim*) and of Judgement (*din*); in any case, they function in exactly the same way.

Another frequently used means of dealing with anthropomorphic language is to interiorize, and thus spiritualize, it. Thus commenting on God's 'smelling' the fragrance of Noah's sacrifice (Gen. 8: 21), Ephrem states:

The Lord smelled—not the smell of the flesh of animals or the smoke of the wood, but he looked out and saw the simplicity of heart with which Noah offered the sacrifice from all and on behalf of all. (*Commentary on Genesis*, VI.13, 2)

3. Problematic Episodes: Genesis 38

Among passages where a surface reading of the biblical text presents a patriarch engaging in an immoral action, none is more shocking than the episode of Judah and Tamar in Genesis 38, where Tamar dresses up as a prostitute and successfully seduces her father-in-law. According to Leviticus 20: 2, both parties should have been put to death. However, the fact that the biblical text does not reproach either Judah or Tamar is seen by both Jewish and Syriac Christian writers as a specific indication that there is some deeper meaning to be found in the narrative. The biblical text's silence on this point is thus seen as an invitation to explore the episode and draw out this deeper meaning.[42] One of the most remarkable Syriac treatments of the problematic chapter is to be found in the verse homily by Jacob of Serugh devoted to the subject.[43] Jacob explains how one needs to approach the topic:

> Moses the scribe set the narrative of Tamar
> like a jewel in his Book so that its beauty might shine out among the readings.
> Why would he have written of a woman who sat like a prostitute
> by the crossroads if she had not been filled with some mystery?
> Why did Moses, who drove away all prostitutes from his people,
> extol this one who had adorned herself like a prostitute?
> Her action would have been wrong if there had not been some mystery there,
> and it would not have been successful if it had been something hateful to God.
> Her action was [indeed] ugly, but her faith made it beautiful,
> and it was resplendent and dear because of the mystery that was performed in her.
> Moses, who was the mediator of the Law,
> laid reproof and a curse on the man who was the cause of fornication,
> whereas in the case of Judah he did not reprove or lay a curse on him,
> nor did he reproach him, for he knew that there was some mystery there.
>
> (lines 147–60)

The clue pointing to the deeper meaning of the passage was the same for both Jewish and Christian interpreters: the presence of Tamar's name in the Davidic genealogy in 1 Chronicles 2: 4 (brought out further, for Christian writers, by her inclusion in the messianic genealogy of Matthew 1: 3). As *Bereshit rabati* (180) pointed out: Tamar 'was privileged to become an ancestor of the messiah'. The only difference between Jewish and Christian interpreters lay in the identification of the messiah: still to come, or identified as Jesus. As was often the case, Jacob probably took as his inspiration a passage in Ephrem's poetry:

---

[42] For the Jewish exegetical tradition see Esther M. Menn, *Judah and Tamar (Genesis 38) in Ancient Jewish Exegesis* (Leiden, 1997), which is based on the Testament of Judah, Targum Neofiti, and *Genesis Rabbah*; a much wider collection of sources can be found in Avigdor Shinan and Yair Zakovitch, *The Story of Judah and Tamar: Genesis 38 in the Bible, the Old Versions, and Ancient Jewish Literature* [Ma'aseh yehudah vetamar] (Jerusalem, 1992).

[43] Edition and translation in Sebastian P. Brock, 'Jacob of Serugh's Verse Homily on Tamar (Gen. 38)', *Le Muséon*, 115 (2002), 279–315.

Since the king [i.e. the messiah] was hidden in Judah, Tamar stole him from his loins; today there has shone forth the splendour of the beauty whose hidden form Tamar had loved. (*Madrashe* on the Nativity, 1: 12)

DOES MIDRASH EXIST IN SYRIAC?

If one understands Midrash as a process that moves from a fixed starting point, namely, the assumption that the biblical text represents the word of God, and proceeds with the aim of drawing out a deeper meaning, or meanings, then it would seem reasonable to describe many Syriac (and indeed other Christian) exegetical texts of late antiquity as a form of Midrash. What distinguishes them from their Jewish counterparts are:

1. The outward forms and end products of this process; that is, the literary artefacts that come down to us are for the most part considerably different in character; and above all:
2. The introduction of a new hermeneutical key to the understanding of salvation history, namely, a messiah who has already appeared.

Provided that one is talking about the process of exploring meanings deeper than the surface meaning, then the Syriac authors and the *darshanim* have much in common, in their basic presuppositions that Scripture is a unitary source of truth and that it is polyvalent, in their general approach, and in their concerns and aims; furthermore, this also applies to many of their exegetical traditions and specific exegetical techniques, topics which largely lie beyond the scope of the present contribution. That this should be so is hardly surprising given that a prominent strand in early Syriac Christianity evidently had its roots deeply embedded in one of the various forms of the first-century CE Judaisms out of which Rabbinic Judaism also emerged.

Just as midrashic exegesis can produce two (or more) seemingly completely different interpretations of the same biblical text, so too one might conclude with a paradox: it would seem legitimate to speak of Midrash in Syriac—provided one is referring to the process; but it is not legitimate, and simply confusing, if one is referring to the end product of that process, the artefacts of rabbinic Midrash.

PART II

LATER MIDRASHIC FORMS

SIX

PIYUT AND MIDRASH
Between Poetic Invention and Rabbinic Convention

MICHAEL FISHBANE

1. INTRODUCTION: THE REGISTERS OF TRADITION

The phenomenon of *piyut*, one of the comprehensive designations of Jewish liturgical poetry, whose major classical and early post-classical creativity spans the fifth–eleventh centuries CE, originating in the Land of Israel and spreading east and west, is quintessentially an archaeology of rabbinic tradition. It thus calls to mind the work of Michel Foucault, *L'Archéologie du savoir*,[1] and its methodological reflections on the complex relationships between the 'things said' in culture and the way their selection or re-combination organizes 'knowledge' from a vast fund of data—the so-called cultural archive. Not all the data is privileged; and not all persons make the selections. Tracking these processes is thus a matter for cultural hermeneutics. In what follows, I shall allow Foucault's insights to clear some paths of approach to *piyut*. In so doing, I intend this discussion to be a companion piece to an earlier effort inspired by his thought. In that work, I focused on some of the ruptures and transformations of biblical and midrashic literature in the creation of liturgical epics in classical and early medieval *piyut*.[2] In the present one, I should like to focus more on creative continuities between Midrash and *piyut*. And just as *piyut* is the third stratum of an archaeology of classical Jewish culture, built upon biblical and rabbinic foundations, every instance of its production plumbs these prior depths, and every instance of its analysis must sift through this stratigraphy to recover both the core deposits and their metamorphosed amalgam. I begin therefore with a brief characterization of these three layers and their essential characteristics.

The stratum of the Hebrew Bible comes first. Each one of its major divisions—Torah (Pentateuch), Nevi'im (Prophets), and Ketuvim (Writings)—is comprised of numerous forms of discourse (some named, some not), all complexly woven into

[1] Paris, 1969.
[2] 'From Midrash to Epic: The Re-Shaping of Rabbinic Discourse in *Piyyut*'; presented in January 2010 as part of the celebration of the 50th anniversary of the Israel Academy of Science and Humanities, and to be published in the conference proceedings.

more or less coherent strings of cultural data. The overarching temporal framework of this vast collection, from beginning to end, spans the creation of the world to the return of the people of Israel from exile; and thus its major historical sequences focus primarily on the emergence and establishment of the nation, through a covenant with God, and therefore on the derivative issues of its social-political destiny. Accordingly, the major religious discourses focus principally on the divine instructions delivered to the people (the laws of the Torah delivered by Moses), the speeches bearing on the people's obedience to these instructions (the various exhortations, judgements, and consolations of the Prophets), and an assortment of discourses whose subjects ponder matters like sin, justice, love, and right living (in the Writings of psalmists and masters of speculative wisdom). Through this ensemble, a diverse cultural archive is organized and presented, culled from traditions stored in numerous circles of priests, prophets, and teachers. In its sweeping scope and fund of data, the Hebrew Bible is thus, itself, an expression of traditions accumulated over centuries. But beyond the overall anthology, even its component parts reflect numerous deposits of selected and newly ordered traditions—evident through parallel and duplicating versions of material; through many anachronistic and proleptic phrases; through intertextual cross-references and summaries of topics; and through assorted revisions and explications of earlier topics.[3] Indeed, Moses himself, the archetypal Speaker of divine instructions, is also cast as the first Teacher of Tradition in the book of Deuteronomy, where he reformulates, explains, and revises the older legal and historical record for a new generation. Similar evidence of the culling and ordering of older traditions can be found in various psalms, where diverse historical events are assembled to give specific gravity to renditions of national sin and divine beneficence; and yet further expressions of this mode of liturgical historiography recur in topic summaries gathered by Ezra and Nehemiah —now also reinterpreting or splicing earlier memories concerning the covenant past and national destiny.[4]

In the hands of the emerging national-religious canon in the early post-exilic period, this multiform anthology of discourses and narratives gradually became an authoritative whole—a sacred archive of memory and instruction, in fact, interlocking in all its parts. The result was the transformation of an 'open treasury of topics', of diverse pedigree and authority, into a 'closed canon of traditions', increasingly harmonious and unified. Thus, even where the older materials manifestly attest different degrees of textual authority (from the direct, divine authority of the Law; to the inspired, divine authority of the Prophets; and the creative, human authority of the Writings), the new status of the archive gradually infused all its parts with religious authority (including the Writings). The evidence of later debates sug-

[3] For many of these matters, see Michael Fishbane, *Biblical Interpretation in Ancient Israel* (Oxford, 1985); in that context I first employed the terms *traditum* and *traditio*.

[4] Regarding all these topics, see ibid., and for the psalms in particular, cf. I. L. Seeligmann, 'Cultic Tradition and Historiosophical Creativity in the Bible' (Heb.), in Anon., *Religion and Society* [Dat vehevrah] (Jerusalem, 1964), 41–61.

gests that the canonic authority of the national archive came first, and only later were there selective discussions regarding the inspired status of some of the seemingly secular writings, and the need to ascertain whether they too, like the Torah, were 'holy' (divine) teachings that would also 'defile the hands' because of their inherent sanctity.[5] The bold attribution of such works as Proverbs, Ecclesiastes, and the Song of Songs to the Holy Spirit were among the ways these concerns were answered for all time.[6]

The stratum of rabbinic Midrash comes second. For the rabbinic heirs of Scripture, this corpus is its fundamental archive—a vast and variously integrated ensemble of interconnecting discourses. Through a complex network of textual correlations and strategies, the primary words of Torah were connected with the discourses of the Prophets and the Writings, and also explained with reference to them. Citation and reinterpretation is thus the signal mark of this reception of scriptural tradition, and the sages who produced these new discourses made sure to render them in a new linguistic key, utterly different from Scripture;[7] to index them as the teachings of named sages, utterly distinct from the biblical heroes; and to highlight the oral nature of their teachings, utterly subordinate to the Written Torah and its authority.[8] Any number of rhetorical tropes and arguments could be used to interpret 'Scripture by Scripture'. For example, the Creation narrative in Genesis could be filled out on the basis of data and allusions discovered in the books of Psalms or Proverbs; the meaning of certain patriarchal episodes could be dramatically and religiously deepened by reinterpreting a verbal expression found there on the basis of vastly different uses of the term elsewhere; and the civil or ritual laws could be correlated and explicated through various analytical or synthetical strategies of traditional authority (for one could hardly read the sacred texts with an impromptu, idiosyncratic, or natural logic). These exegetical techniques could be alternatively playful and surprising, turning common words into clever riddles needing decoding; or they could be legally sober and precise, making ambiguous rules clear and differentiating apparently similar formulations through subtle syllogisms cultivated in the scholastic repertoire.[9] Pure study of the weekly sabbath Torah readings was one motivation for such exegesis; another was the practical need to resolve complex theological and legal matters that emerged over time; and still another was the

---

[5] See the discussion and sources in Shamma Friedman, 'The Holy Scriptures Defile the Hands: The Transformation of a Biblical Concept in Rabbinic Theology', in M. Brettler and M. Fishbane (eds.), *Minḥah le-Naḥum: Biblical and Other Studies Presented to Nahum M. Sarna* (Sheffield, 1993), 117–32.

[6] Cf. the *petiḥta*s to these books in *Midrash Rabbah*.

[7] The linguistic registers are markedly different. Cf. A. Bendavid, *The Language of Scripture and the Language of the Sages* [Leshon mikra uleshon ḥakhamim], 2 vols. (Tel Aviv, 1967).

[8] For useful discussions of these matters, see Arnold Goldberg, 'Form-Analysis of Midrashic Literature as a Method of Description', *Journal of Jewish Studies*, 36 (1985), 159–74, and A. Samely, 'Between Scripture and its Rewording: Towards a Classification of Rabbinic Exegesis', *Journal of Jewish Studies*, 42 (1991), 39–67.

[9] For a richly annotated conspectus, see Yonah Fraenkel, *The Modes of Aggadah and Midrash* [Darkhei ha'agadah vehamidrash], 2 vols. (Givatayim, 1991).

attempt to connect or justify an oral practice with the written Scripture. In searching through these texts, and turning them every which way, no jot or tittle in Scripture was deemed extraneous; indeed, an 'impoverished' or problematic expression in one place could be 'enriched' and resolved through another—all depending on one's hermeneutic proclivity and presumption regarding the particular character of scriptural language (i.e. whether it resembles human discourse for the most part, or whether its graphemes were also believed to bear hyper-signification).

Through these intentional interventions and inventions, there accumulated traditions of rabbinic meanings for all the parts of the Torah—meanings that transformed biblical Scripture into a rabbinic teaching; and there also developed numerous rhetorical forms or tropes for the explication of passages—explications that could remain in the study hall or also be performed as sermons in the synagogue (the midrashic collections include both, and the locus of origination is not always certain given their present reformulations). Significantly, all alternative possibilities (for explicated theology and law) are routinely preserved in the collections, such that rabbinic anthologies of interpretations all derive from Scripture: its sentences are broken down into smaller lemmatic units (or citations), and the exegetical discourses connected with them in the name of a given sage are listed with others on the same passage as a series of expansions or variations. The lemma that sponsors or triggers these discourses thus provides the heading for each anthological subunit. The tradition thus agglutinates taxonomically around specific phrases and is multivocal in every sense (i.e. a diverse accumulation of voices of the sages recorded, stylized, and revocalized by unnamed anthologists). And when it became customary to recite certain prophetic lections on special sabbaths (in addition to Torah passages); or to recite scrolls like the Song of Songs or Lamentations on specific festivals or fast days, these Writings were similarly subjected to intense exegetical investigations and anthologized. Thus, as with the sabbath day, the stations of the liturgical year provide the scriptural selections for sacred study, with the result that ever-new correlations among the three parts of Scripture were produced by new types of exegetical discourse—in content and rhetorical form. Midrashic tradition is this vast weft of correlations and determinations; and each anthology is a synchronic canon of diachronic strings of tradition. As we have them, these discourses are now traditions for the eye; but they first emerged and were continuously circulated for the ear alone—as an open canon, orally performed by the sages in the study hall and by preachers in the synagogue.

The liturgical poems of piyut *come third*. This stratum of Jewish religious culture cannot be understood independently of the prior two. In *piyut*, however, they assume an entirely new and distinctive integration. The biblical stratum is engaged, since the liturgical poems follow the lectionary cycles of Torah readings—for the sabbaths, major holidays and intermediate days, and other special occasions (minor feast and fast days, new moon celebrations, or the four special sabbaths in the month of Adar); but they also include references to weekly prophetic lections and special prophetic cycles (of judgement and consolation). The midrashic stratum is also engaged,[10] inasmuch as all the foregoing biblical narratives, teachings, and laws are presented together with their rabbinic interpretations—be this explicitly, through use of its content in fragmentary or also more elaborate expositions; or more implicitly, through use of allusions, oblique hints, or even by simply adducing the scriptural proof-texts appended to certain midrashic teachings. And yet this hardly says it all; for if the primary cycle is the biblical lectionary, it is even more specifically the liturgical cycle of prayers for these days, and their sequences of blessings, as established in the rabbinic synagogue tradition, that sets the themes and the styles of the *piyutim* (plural). Thus, for example, the small cycle of prayers that follow the call to worship (Barekhu) and precede the proclamation of faith (Shema) include blessings for the heavenly lights and God's love of Israel, and these provide thematic topics that are also marked by references (biblical and midrashic) to the specific Torah reading for that sabbath or festival. Or, in a similar fashion, the central Amidah ('standing prayer') is also marked by thematic references to a particular lectionary for each of the eighteen prayers recited in a weekday service (*kerovah*) celebrating a festival or fast day (such as Purim or Tishah Be'av); or the first three (of the seven) statutory benedictions of the Amidah recited during the sabbath service (*shivata*), with a special emphasis on the recitation of the *trisagion* (Kedushah) recited in the third slot. Between the second and third benedictions there were also six (or more) poetic units, some of which, in the middle of this sequence, became quite long (especially the epical cycles beginning with the Creation and climaxing on the specific event celebrated on that holiday—such as the sacrificial service celebrated on Yom Kippur); or the grand epical recitations on the specific historical topic of that day (such as the exodus from Egypt), found in the final (ninth) poetic unit.[11] Add to this thematic mix the decisive fact that these materials are presented in unique verse forms (lines and stanzas), with complex and dense syntactic structures (elliptical and enigmatic), and even using special linguistic features (neologisms—deverbal nouns or denominative verbs—rooted in scriptural or rabbinic vocabularies), and one can readily appreciate the independent and complex character of this cultural stratum.[12]

But this is not all; more must be added. First, each *piyut*-unit is a distinctive collocation of traditions. That is, the older midrashic anthologies are culled and collated by the *ḥazan*, or precentor, who recites these poetic additions before the

---

[10] For overall comments, see Ezra Fleisher, *Hebrew Liturgical Poetry in the Middle Ages* [Shirat hakodesh ha'ivrit biyemei habeinayim] (Jerusalem, 1975), 266–9, and the earlier foundational study of the influence of midrashic rhetoric by Aaron Mirsky, *The Origins of Forms of Early Hebrew Poetry* [Yesodei tsurot hapiyut] (Jerusalem, 1969).

[11] On these liturgical forms, cf. Fleisher, *Hebrew Liturgical Poetry* (Heb.); also Leon Weinberger, *Jewish Hymnography: A Literary History* (London, 1995).

[12] All this effects another distinct linguistic register. Cf. the contributions of Shalom Spiegel, 'On the Language of the Paytanim' (Heb.), a fascicle reprint from *Hado'ar*, 42 (no. 23) (1962–3), 397–400, and Joseph Yahalom, *Poetic Language in Early Palestinian Liturgical Poetry* [Sefat hashir shel piyut ha'erets yisra'eli hakadum] (Jerusalem, 1985).

standard blessings. It is his poetic talent that draws from the fund of tradition and determines its formulation (even when older tropes or terms are used), so that we do not have in any instance multiple traditions on a subject (though different exegetical voices from the past may occur in different places in the liturgy where the lectionary is alluded to). Nor are the original tradents cited by name (as against hoary rabbinic precedent); only their teachings are re-cited by the *ḥazan* in his own voice. Indeed, just this precentor is the 'voice of tradition' at any given point—its latter-day channel and formulator; only he determines, in any given instance, which rhetorical devices are taken over and adapted, and what is of thematic and theological significance. The result is that all the various cultural strata are interfused for the most part, though it became customary to transcribe the biblical citations used or alluded to in the first and second blessings of the Amidah at their conclusions (hence they were not a part of the original, prayer recitation); and, in one or another of the *piyutim*, the practised ear can discern certain of the standard rhetorical forms of midrashic exegesis (as I shall examine). The *ḥazan* is thus the teacher of tradition in each *piyut*, and the prayer service becomes a place of its instruction.[13]

The fact that these teachings occur *within* the prayers themselves introduces the second point to be noted here—which is that *piyut* is a kind of *poetic theology*. As noted, each of the sub-units of the service (the theme of light, for example, at the outset of the morning service, or the references to God as the shield or protector of Abraham, in the first blessing of the Amidah) is presented together with topics derived from the particular scriptural lectionary in play for that sabbath or special day; and thus the various liturgical themes of light and love, or protection and salvation, become prisms for the theological refraction of assorted biblical and rabbinic topics. And in this overall regard, one must not discount how the forms of versification involved, with their assorted allusions and intertextual associations, create a thick texture of passages and yield the kinds of meta-semantic meanings only possible through poetic language. This matter cannot be stressed enough: the intersection of biblical and midrashic selections through new poetic collocations creates the distinctive oral theology of *piyut*. In this liturgical setting, in the course of sacred prayer, the community hears anew (in the voice of the *ḥazan*) the ancient oral tradition of the written Torah. Perceptively and imperceptively, the two become one.

Since I have presented the several cultural strata of Judaism in linguistic terms, let me resume these cultural registers in this formal mode. Taking my cue from Ferdinand de Saussure,[14] I shall describe the diverse vocal expressions of Scripture (both the named or anonymous narrative units) as distinct *paroles* of the deep *langue* (or linguistic resource) of ancient Israel (itself being variable and historically complex); and then add that as these various *paroles* coalesce into larger anthologies or

---

[13] Discussed in Fishbane, 'From Midrash to Epic', with further considerations below.

[14] *Cours de linguistique générale*, 4th edn. (Paris, 1949); regarding *langue*, see esp. 124: 'la langue est un système dont tous les parties peuvent et doivent être considérés dans leur solidarité synchronique'.

units of tradition, they themselves become the *langue* for all the later strata of the biblical tradition. Thus, with the closing of the scriptural canon, this diverse complex of *paroles* becomes, in effect, the vast *langue* of rabbinic culture.[15] Let us call this register one. Its use in interpretative acts by the sages results in distinctive exegetical *paroles* (and this holds both for the specific, biblically *based* interpretations, called Midrash, and for all the biblically *informed* or *inspired* derivations, known as Mishnah). Just this received 'textual' complex, which variously comprises the 'mind' of the sages and underlies their discourse and thinking and knowledge, is, in effect, their cultural *langue*. Let us call this register two. In turn, the collocation of these two canonical strata comprises the *basis of* and *inspiration for* the poetic *paroles* of *piyut*. I shall call this register three; and although it is clearly distinctive in language, form, and instruction, the strong impact of the biblical and midrashic heritage is evident throughout (in its linguistic bases, in its rhetorical structures, and in its theological content). It is to this complex phenomenon, and especially its creative midrashic inflections, that I now turn.

II. THE FORMS OF MIDRASH IN *PIYUT*: TYPES AND TRANSFORMATIONS

In the ensuing discussion, I shall present a variety of instances of the use and reuse of Midrash in *piyut*. These cover many different techniques, genres, and rhetorical types. Each is intended to be exemplary of a new moment in Jewish cultural creativity, and was chosen for that purpose out of numerous (and in some cases myriads) of cases. The examples were also selected to demonstrate the broad geographical and temporal spread of classical *piyut*. Hence they cut across several spatial regions (the land of Israel; Byzantium; and Ashkenaz); across a broad historical arc (fifth to eleventh centuries); and include multiple *ḥazanim* (Yose ben Yose; Yannai; Rabbi Elazar ben Killir; Rabbi Pinhas Hakohen ben Jacob; Rabbi Shimon bar Isaac Hagadol; and Rabbi Benjamin ben Samuel). This said, they are not presented in terms of historical or regional groupings, but by form or type. In exploring these cases, I shall go more deeply into topics mentioned in the initial discussion.

1. The Use and Transformation of Exegetical Anthologies into Paytanic Epic

In the *Mekhilta derabi yishma'el* ('Yitro', 9),[16] we find the following collection of rabbinic comments on the scriptural account of the Sinai revelation:

All the nation saw the thunder [*kolot*] [*and lightning*] [Exod. 20: 15]. They saw what appeared and was heard, according to Rabbi Ishmael. Rabbi Akiva said, 'They saw and

---

[15] I first used these terms for these anthologies in my *The Exegetical Imagination: On Jewish Thought and Theology* (Cambridge, Mass., 1998), 11–13.

[16] *Mechilta d'Rabbi Ismael*, ed. Hayim S. Horowitz and Israel A. Rabin (Jerusalem, 1960), 235.

heard what appeared; they saw the word of fire that went forth from the mouth of God [lit. the Power] and was chiselled [*neḥtsav*] upon the tablets, as [Scripture] says, *The voice of the Lord ignited* [*ḥotsev*] *flames of fire* [Ps. 29: 6]. *And all the nation saw* <*the* kolot: *a voice* [*kol*]> *of many voices* [*kolei kolot*], and a torch of many torches. And how many voices and torches were there? This means that [the many voices] caused each person to hear according to their capacity [*koḥo*]; as [Scripture] says, *The voice* [*kol*] *of the Lord in strength* [*ko'aḥ*] [v. 4].'

Rabbi said [that 'This phrase] proclaims the praise of Israel, for when they all stood before Mount Sinai to receive the Torah, they heard each word [viz. each commandment of the Decalogue] and interpreted [*mefarshim*] it; as [Scripture] says, *He/It encircled them* [the nation] *and they* [the nation] *understood it* [Deut. 32: 10].'

As is evident, this passage presents a series of exegetical explications on the puzzling phrase, '*All* the nation *saw* the thunder and lightning.' For what could Scripture have meant by this oxymoron of 'seeing thunder'? Surely, one naturally sees lightning but hears thunder. Two of the leading sages from the formative rabbinic generations (early second century CE), Rabbi Ishmael and Rabbi Akiva, interpret according to their proclivities. Ishmael, who understood Scripture as formulated in a comprehensible, human manner, presumed that the text is written elliptically and that one should fill in the gaps; accordingly, one should supplement an unsaid hearing of the thunder (alongside the specified seeing of the lightning) in order to render the passage sensible. By contrast, Akiva, who believed that Scripture is not bound by human convention and speaks in its own unique way, interpreted the passage as referring to a visualization of the (ten) 'voices' (or commandments) of God—which were initially intoned and therewith transformed into a fire that visibly chiselled the contents upon the tablets (an interpretation supported by a reading of a fire-chiselling *kol* in Psalm 29: 6 in terms of the same event). Clearly, the *kolot* were literally the thunderclaps for Ishmael, but the sounds or commandments of God according to his colleague. The Midrash does not resolve this issue directly; but insofar as it has added an interpretation of the *kolot* as meaning the 'voice' of God (mythically split into multiple voices), it is evident that the editor, who anonymously introduces this matter, sides with Akiva. But if he seems to suggest ten voices for this miracle of the divine revelation, another teacher poses the question of number in a far more pointed manner—and puts forward the striking view that there were as many voices as auditors at Sinai, for he adduces yet another verse (v. 4) from Psalm 29 to indicate that the *kol* mentioned there was not (literally) a sound (or thunderclap) of awesome 'power' (*ko'aḥ*), but rather that each voice was heard according to the intellectual 'potential' or capacity (*ko'aḥ*) of each individual present. This bold new reading is effected by supplanting the biblical linguistic register with its rabbinic resonance.

It is thus clear that whoever edited this collection of teachings *already* had an exegetical interpretation of Psalm 29 in terms of the Sinai revelation in mind—and it is probably he who adds this point to Akiva's own explanation. Hence, while presenting a received catena of exegeses, the editor tips his hand and shows preference for the view that at Sinai each commandment was heard and understood differently by each person. Several generations later, Rabbi (Judah the Prince) weighed in with his view, which now appears as the more normative rendition of this comment —namely, that at Sinai 'all' the people 'heard' the ten 'voices' (each 'word') and also 'interpreted' them (i.e. both the commandments *and* their explication were of Sinaitic origin). This view (by Rabbi Judah or the editor) is linked to a reading of Deuteronomy 32: 10, now taken to mean that not God himself but each one of God's words 'encircled' the people—who 'understood' them. Such a view shifts decisively away from Ishmael's opening position that the people 'heard' the divine words and accords with the one found in the contemporaneous *midrash Sifrei Deuteronomy* (313), which follows Rabbi Akiva's view that the people 'saw' the words,[17] and also specifies that they even succeeded in deducing all the *halakhot* and midrashic expositions that were latent in them (i.e. the entire corpus of rabbinic oral tradition!).[18] The theological leap from the potential of the auditors to the potential of divine language is huge.

We have here an instance of exegetical theology at its boldest—one that offers a variety of interpretations on different aspects of the same verse over the span of a century and collects them into an integrated anthology. It is a parade example of such midrashic scholasticism. There is no question that Rabbi Shimon Hagadol, one of the great sages in the Rhineland during the tenth–eleventh centuries,[19] knew this *Mekhilta* passage, since he uses it explicitly in a *siluk* (concluding poem) recited just before the Kedushah on the festival of Shavuot,[20] when Exodus 19–20 were recited in celebration of the revelation at Sinai. But now the exegetical list is entirely in verse, rendered as an epical account of ancient events and their interpretation, with no mention of the sages whose teachings inform his *piyut*. Here is the beginning of this epos:

And all the nation saw what appeared and was heard
And heard what was heard and appeared,
When the word [commandment] went forth from the mouth of God [the Power] /
    and was chiselled upon the tablets in splendour—
A voice of many voices and a storm wind; / and a torch of many fiery torches blazing:

---

[17] *Sifre on Deuteronomy*, ed. L. Finkelstein (New York, 1969), 355.

[18] Instead of the word *mefarshim* ('interpreted') this source states *hayu . . . maskilim bo veyode'im* ('they would intellectually perceive and understand each word'). Clearly this is a more developed and normative version of the tradition.

[19] See Abraham Grossman, *The Early Sages of Ashkenaz* [Ḥakhmei ashkenaz harishonim] (Jerusalem, 1988), 86–105.

[20] See the rendition of it in *Maḥzor liregalim: shavuot*, ed. Y. Fraenkel (Jerusalem, 2000), 267. In light of R. Shimon's distinguished pedigree and provenance (see above, n. 19), it is of more than passing interest to read in the *Sefer hapardes lerashi*, ed. Hayim J. Ehrenreich (Budapest, 1924), 228 (end), that the first *piyutim* that were incorporated into the prayer service as an alternative to the public sermon were *azharot* for the festival of Shavuot, and *kerovot* and *yotserot* dealing with the 'Giving of the Torah' (*matan torah*).

The voice of the Lord in strength, and the voice of the Lord in its glory /
    interpreting the word to explain it;
He/It encircled them [the nation] *and let them understand* secrets of the Torah.

One can readily observe (from the italics marking the scriptural citations, and the content) that the *ḥazan* had our *Mekhilta* passage in mind. It is the formative template for his *piyut*. But in this poetic rendition there are no strata of interpretation and no diversity of opinions—only the harmonious teaching of Rabbi Shimon, in whom all the prior voices of tradition are integrated. But for all that, the *paytan* (liturgical poet) did not hesitate to add his special input, and one feature in particular stands out against the background of earlier traditions. In this poetic version it is distinctively the voice of God in *its* strength that informs the people of the proper interpretations of the Words and guides them into an understanding of the 'secrets' of the Torah—presumably meaning here the oral tradition rather than mystical hints. Thus, according to Rabbi Shimon's theology, God gives the words along with their right meaning simultaneously, such that the entire nation is the first bearer of a revealed oral Torah, which occurs together with the revealed Decalogue (whose words are understood to encode the whole tradition, as already evidenced in a Shavuot poem by Rabbi Sa'adyah Gaon).

In presenting this account, Rabbi Shimon has transformed the older midrashic anthology into poetic verse: the catenae of discrete interpretations are concatenated into bi-cola (compare the case of Ishmael's and Akiva's views); single phrases are intensified ('strength' is paralleled by 'glory'); and ambiguities are explicated in normative terms (it is not the nation ['it'] but God himself ['He'] who gives understanding to the words). All this pertains to the specific elements. But viewed overall, special note must be taken of the new epical flow, which binds the received exegetical content into a running sequence that fills out the gaps in the scriptural text. Listening, the people in Rabbi Shimon's synagogue will now understand the meaning of the complex scriptural passage through the guidance of rabbinic interpreters. Perhaps even anticipating Rashi's vaunted technique, our *paytan* presents a plain-sense rendition of the historical events through the prism of tradition, embedding midrashic exegesis into the old scriptural narrative.[21] In this *piyut*, the interplay of Scripture and Midrash are crafted into one voice and one happening.

2. The Use and Development of Halakhic Sermons in Paytanic Instructions

Among the greatest *ḥazanim* was Rabbi Elazar ben Killir, who lived somewhere in the Byzantine empire in the sixth–seventh centuries CE; he was a grand master of

---

[21] The classic formulation of Rashi's hermeneutic paradigm occurs in his comment on Gen. 3: 8. If valid, we have here a striking forerunner of his distinctive integration of *peshat* and Midrash among the sages of Ashkenaz.

both the rabbinic tradition and of its poetic exposition.[22] Though often the subject of medieval ridicule (most famously by Abraham ibn Ezra) for his often arcane and riddling verse,[23] a more sympathetic appraisal would note how he could also weave textures of teachings that brought their complexities to light and extended older sermons in striking ways; indeed, some portions of his *piyutim* clearly function as versified *derashot*, or exegetical sermons. His verses on the ancient red heifer ritual (Num. 19) provide striking examples of this extraordinary virtuosity, and thus of the way liturgical form—formal recitation—provided the setting for sermonic formulations—recitatives sung *viva voce* during the synagogue service.

The Torah lection of the red heifer (*parah adumah*) was recited twice a year—on the regular sabbath called 'Ḥukat' (named from the first verse, where God instructs Moses and Aaron about the 'law' of this sacrifice, called *ḥukat hatorah*; Num. 19: 2); and again on the special sabbath called 'Parah' (occurring in the month of Adar, named for the designation of the heifer itself, required to be absolutely unblemished). According to Scripture, both the priest who burned this cow, and the pure person who deposited its ashes outside the camp, were rendered impure (until nightfall), as were their garments (which required immediate cleansing). More notably, the ashes of this heifer were part of a ritual that could decontaminate a person made impure by contact with a corpse, so that the individual would become pure after a week (vv. 3–15). This paradoxical process (whereby the pure were made impure, and vice versa) was pondered by the sages, and they distinguished between the agency of the heifer and those engaged with its ritual in the following ruling found in Mishnah *Parah* 4: 4: 'All that deal with the heifer, from start to finish, render garments impure' (cf. 8: 8). A sermonic exposition transmitted by Rabbi Joshua of Sikhnin (in the name of Rabbi Levi), based on the opening designation of the rite as a *ḥukat hatorah* ('a statute of law'; v. 2), considered it among the other (three) laws designated as *ḥukah* in Scripture. After citing this *mishnah*, it adds: 'but she [the heifer] herself purifies the impure' (*Pesikta derav kahana* 4: 6).[24] In the other cases, the ruling designated *ḥukah* requires a person to do something forbidden elsewhere. But not so in this instance, where it is precisely the paradoxical dynamic that is singled out for special attention: the heifer that renders the officiant impure, purifies the impure.

Thus it was proclaimed that a *ḥukah* involved some inscrutable and contradictory ruling. This became its standard rabbinic explanation, and established a class of laws different from those called *mishpatim*, whose meaning seemed more comprehensible. But this did not stop all speculation about the strange rite of the red heifer. In a celebrated episode, a non-Jew challenged Rabban Yohanan ben Zakkai,

---

[22] For a recent evaluation of the dating of this master, see Ezra Fleischer, 'Towards a Solution to the Question of the Time and Place in which R. Elazar Son of R. Killir was Active' (Heb.), *Tarbiz*, 74 (1985), 383–427. More precise specifications date him *c.*570–*c.*640 CE.

[23] See Ibn Ezra's introduction to his Torah commentary.

[24] *Pesikta derav kahana*, ed. Bernard Mandelbaum, 2 vols. (New York, 1962), i. 71 ff.

claiming that this rite looked for all the world like an act of 'sorcery' similar to pagan purification ceremonies. With a cagey move the sage initially deflected this contention by suggesting that the biblical ritual serves to rid a person of the malign 'spirit' that has invaded him through the corpse—just like similar processes familiar to the pagan. But though this calmed the contentious outsider, the disciples of the rabbi asked for an answer that would satisfy them, who had no truck with such matters! And forthwith the sage defanged the clear sense of Scripture, stating that neither does the corpse defile nor does the heifer purify—but that the entire ruling is a 'divine decree' which may not be transgressed, which is why Scripture says: 'This is a *ḥukah* of the Torah' (*Parah* 4: 7). That is, Rabban Yohanan interprets the word *ḥukah* to mean an intractable, irrevocable decree, and takes the phrase *ḥukat hatorah* to mean that it is one of the special decrees found in the Torah (i.e. a *ḥukah* of the Torah), requiring faithful acceptance.

But even this did not prevent all further interpretation. Sages hunted for the tiniest clues for further meaning. For example, probably in response to the tradition that none of the red heifers which antedated the exile existed any longer,[25] Rabbi Yosi ben Haninah suggested that the very first one, prepared by Moses, nevertheless had survived. He did so by focusing on what he saw as an oddity in the opening command. Initially, we are informed that God spoke to both Moses and Aaron (Num. 19: 1); but the ensuing verse reports the divine commandment in the singular: 'Speak [*daber*] to the Israelites and *they shall take for you* a red heifer' (v. 2). What could this shift mean? Some rabbinic interpreters understood it to signify that Moses was to function here as the high priest who performed the rite. But Rabbi Yosi suggested that these words 'hinted [*ramzu*] that all the heifers shall be null but yours shall remain' (*Pesikta derav kahana* 4: 7).[26] That is, the occurrence of a future verb plus a singular pronoun was taken as a hint that in the world to come Moses' heifer would somehow be brought forth for his use (in viable condition). Now obviously such a reading disconnects this directive from the actual rite to be performed, and may even have been offered as a homiletical supplement, but its very proposal suggests that this opaque ritual was believed to encode hidden meanings. Only this belief could have sponsored such an exegetical solution.

A more exoteric approach occurs in response to an ensuing query by one of the students of the sages: 'Why are all the sacrificial animals male and this [one] female?' In response, Rabbi Aibo offered a coarse parable about 'a son of a handmaid who defecated in the king's palace. [Whereupon] the king said, "Let his mother come [*tavo imo*] and [*ve-*] clean up the excrement." Similarly [*kakh*] the Holy One said: "Let the heifer come [*tavo parah*] and [*ve-*] atone for the making of the [golden] calf [*egel*]"' (*Pesikta derav kahana* 4: 8).[27] Evidently, the exegetical problem here is the type of animal chosen for the rite—not the rites themselves; and the solution turns on an analogy about a child that befouls the palace and the need for its mother to

---

[25] Cf. Tosefta *Parah* 3: 5 (R. Judah's view), ed. M. S. Zuckermandel (new edn. Jerusalem, 1970), 632.
[26] *Pesikta derav kahana*, ed. Mandelbaum, i. 72 ff.   [27] Ibid. 74.

clean up the mess. What was the unstated rhetorical point? Most certainly that the baby calf which desecrates the divine domain of Sinai requires a (mother) cow to repair the damage. That is, the problem facing the sages was only ostensibly the use of a *parah* in the rite. Far more puzzling was the meaning and function of its occurrence. Of concern to them was thus the very purpose of the red heifer rite at this juncture in the Torah; and using the exegetical question to resolve the theological issue, they understood the *parah* to provide a rite of atonement for the sin (*ḥet*) of the calf (hence it is also referred to as a *ḥatat* offering; v. 9). On this understanding, the red heifer ritual was a 'measure for measure' (analogical) expiation for the sin of idolatry at Mount Sinai, whereas its future enactment would decontaminate persons who contracted the impurity of corpses (vv. 10–13). In this way, the old rite retained its paradigmatic effectiveness.

Rabbi Elazar ben Killir was heir to this entire complex of concerns: the centrality and inscrutability of the rite, recited twice annually; the paradoxes of purity and defilement; and the parable which sets forth an analogical explanation in terms of sin and atonement. But his poetic treatments of these midrashic matters are not a series of exegetical sermons on fragments of biblical verse. They are instead a liturgical tour de force that incorporates all these matters (scriptural citations and rabbinic explications) and reformulates and conjoins them in new and expansive ways. In the following, I shall focus on selected parts of two *piyut* cycles for Shabat Parah, 'Aḥat sha'alti' (AS)[28] and 'Atsulat omen') (AO).[29]

One must begin with the mystery of the *ḥukah*, since Rabbi Elazar has it both ways: he holds that the rite is imponderable and opaque, surpassing understanding, and nevertheless offers exegetical solutions and hints of its secret import. In this respect, he walks a complicated line. On the one hand, he follows rabbinic convention as to the opacity of the rite's content, as one can see in his versification of the old *derashah* of Rabbi Joshua regarding the four biblical cases of *ḥukah*. Coming to the final topic, he recites:

> The command[ment] of *parah*:—
> The heifer by which the pure are rendered impure [*metame'im*];
> A balm—how was it able to purify the impure [*teme'im*]?
> The limits of its arcana from all are sealed [*atumim*],
> Even to the End-time its meanings [*te'amim*] congealed.
>
> (AS, ll. 358–62)

This stanza occurs near the climax of the *siluk*, and evidently renders older midrashic discourses in verse—without scriptural proofs or reference to the sages, but with a reformulation of the core paradox in poetic lines, followed by echoing puns of its opacity that explicate the word *ḥukah*. The density of the end-rhymes hammers home the point, and thereby emphasizes the imponderable sense of the ancient laws

---

[28] Critical edition by S. Elitzur, in *Kovets al yad*, NS 10 (1982), 11–55.
[29] In the prayer book *Seder avodat yisra'el*, ed. Y. Baer (Rödelheim, 1868), 688–93.

of purity.[30] For a rabbinic audience, the noun *te'amim* is a multifaceted reference to exegetical 'senses'—both exoteric and esoteric, which are hereby 'dumb' (*atumim*). At most, as Rabbi Elazar states elsewhere, the law's arcana were explicated by Moses and Aaron, the two original recipients of the statute; for he says that the statute of the heifer was 'interpreted [*derushah*] from the outset by two [*beyad shenayim*]' (AS, l. 132). Arguably, this is a deft allusion to the rabbinic ruling that 'One may not interpret [*dorshin*] laws of consanguinity in threes, but one may do so in pairs [*lishnayim*]' (Mishnah Ḥagigah 2: 1 with Tosefta).[31] If so, it would seem that Rabbi Elazar has classified the red heifer as one of the restricted subjects of exegesis—though he does apparently allow its explication by qualified persons (like the first high priests). But if this is correct, Rabbi Elazar transgresses this restriction when he interprets both the *te'amim* and the *remazim* (hints) of this *ḥukah*—and not just for a restricted circle, but in the context and course of the public prayer service.

3. The Transformation of Aggadic Sermons and Rhetoric into Paytanic Teachings

The modern study of *piyut* entered a new phase with the discovery of the prayer poems of Yannai, nearly a century ago. Since the initial publication by Israel Davidson,[32] and the subsequent fuller editions of Menahem Zulay[33] and Tsvi Rabinovitz,[34] we now have a remarkable *maḥzor* (festival prayer-book) from the Land of Israel in the early Byzantine period (*c.* sixth century CE), presenting compositions and cycles for the entire liturgical year. Yannai's creative dexterity, his relatively unencumbered stylistics, and his masterful familiarity with rabbinic traditions provide another window into the living oral Torah of his time. In the example offered below, we have a certain paradigmatic instance of the adaptation and revision of sermons and exegesis—seemingly clear and focused, but dependent upon hidden allusions and a thick web of citations. At one level, Yannai provides a new species of Midrash in poetic form; at another, the capacities of poetry give his theology unprecedented prismatic possibilities. And while we cannot ascertain the precise versions of midrashic tradition at his disposal, an inspection of the forms that have been preserved (in early and late collections) provides a measure for the angle of inflection introduced by this master.

One of the recurrent theological topics for exposition was the theme of the building of the Tabernacle in the desert, at divine command. Moses is instructed to

---

[30] Other internal rhymes further create a meta-semantic effect. Cf. in the last two lines: *kitsvei* || *retsufim . . . kets* (dominated by the phonemes *k/ts* and the bilabials *b–v/p–f*).

[31] Cf. Tosefta, ed. Zuckermandel, 233. AO deems the *ḥukah* a *sod* (esoteric mystery).

[32] *Maḥzor yanai*, ed. Israel Davidson (New York, 1919), with notes by L. Ginzberg.

[33] *Piyutei yanai*, ed. Menahem Zulay (Berlin, 1938); and Zulay's earlier, foundational study, 'Yannai Studies' (Heb.), *Yediot hamakhon leḥeker hashirah ha'ivrit*, 2 (1925), 213–391, as well as his 'Matters of Language in the Poetry of Yannai' (Heb.), in *Studies of the Research Institute for Hebrew Poetry in Jerusalem*, vol. vi (Jerusalem: Schocken, 1945), 165–247.

[34] *Maḥzor piyutei rabi yanai latorah velamo'adim*, ed. Tsvi M. Rabinovitz, 2 vols. (Jerusalem, 1985).

summon donations from the people, and have them 'Make Me a sanctuary that I may dwell among them' (Exod. 25: 8). Now when Solomon built his Temple, he asked outright, in his dedication prayer: 'But will God truly dwell on earth? Surely the heavens to their uttermost heights cannot contain You, how much less this House that I have built!' (1 Kings 8: 27). This act of rhetorical astonishment is even echoed by God himself at the desire of the people to rebuild the Temple following the exile, for he said, 'The heaven is My throne, and the earth My footstool—where could you build a house for Me, what place could serve as My abode?' (Isa. 66: 1). And so, how could God dwell in a tent, and how could Moses have not been equally aghast? Pondering on this paradox, the sages sought an answer. Here is one instance, preserved in *Exodus Rabbah* 34: 1, but integrating many earlier prototypes:[35]

They shall make an ark of acacia wood [Exod. 25: 10], as it says: *Shaddai—we can't attain Him; He is so great in power!* [Job 37: 23].[36] When the Holy One, blessed be He, said to Moses, 'Make Me a tabernacle,'[37] he began to ponder, saying, 'The glory of the Holy One fills the heights and depths, and He says "Make Me a tabernacle"??!' And he also envisioned that Solomon would arise and build a Temple, much larger than the Tabernacle, and say before the Holy One, *But will God truly dwell on earth?* [1 Kgs. 8: 27] Whereupon Moses deduced: 'If then, with regard to the Temple, whose size exceeds the Tabernacle, Solomon said this, how much more does this pertain to the Tabernacle [itself]? . . .'.[38] Then the Holy One answered [Moses]: 'It is not according to your reckoning, but Mine; hence [I have commanded]: twenty planks in the north, twenty in the south, and eight in the east.[39] And moreover, I shall descend and contract My Shekhinah between [the staves of the ark, within a space] one cubit by one cubit.'

This old sermon attempts to resolve the mysterious relationship between God's cosmic sovereignty and His presence at a specific site on earth. The anonymous *darshan* (preacher) begins with a scriptural passage about constructing the ark. This verse derives from the weekly Torah lection being considered. The second text, taken from the book of Job, counterpoints the first and establishes the apparent problem: God, being awesome in might, is unattainable, so how could one 'find' a proper place for him? The two texts, from distinct parts of Scripture, are then duly unpacked by the expositor: the first one representing the divine command, the second anticipating the deliberations of Moses (a striking move, since according to an ancient rabbinic tradition, Moses was himself the author of the book of Job!).[40]

---

[35] See also in *Pesikta derav kahana*, 2: 10 and 3: 6 (Mandelbaum edn., i. 33 and 121, respectively). These traditions are attributed to R. Judah bar Simon (4th-generation *amora*), in the name of R. Yohanan (2nd-generation *amora*). The *Exodus Rabbah* passage has been adduced because of the co-text from Job 37: 23 (regarding Yannai, see below).

[36] This citation breaks with the masoretic cantillation, and serves (and reflects) rabbinic theology.

[37] A pseudo-citation; the teachings in *Pesikta derav kahana* properly cite Exod. 25: 8 ('make me a sanctuary'). *Tanḥuma*, 'Naso' 11, incorporates a condensed variant, adding Isa. 66: 1 to the list. The latter refers to divine 'power' (*ko'aḥ*) and thus may have the Job text in the background.

[38] An interpolation (in the name of R. Judah bar Simon) has Moses cite Ps. 91: 1 to mean that Shaddai, who is supreme, nevertheless dwells in the *tsel* ('shade', understood as the Tabernacle). We shall advert to this metaphor below.   [39] Alluding to Exod. 26: 18, 20, 22.   [40] Cf. BT *BB* 14*b*.

As the first part unfolds, Moses deliberates through natural reason, prophetic vision, and rabbinic logic, but is left in a quandary. The turn comes in the second part, where God responds that his reckoning is unlike Moses'; for he has not commanded the impossible, but specified details for a quite feasible structure—to which he will even accommodate his worldly immanence (the Shekhinah). This unexpected conclusion firmly resolves the theological puzzle voiced by Moses; and, with it, there is a virtual reversal of the sense of the co-text. As a trigger for the exposition, it seemingly counterpoints the opening lemma. But with the ending one may perceive that this elusive citation (introduced by the formula 'as it says') is actually a statement of praise whose true import will yet unfold. For in light of the resolution, this quote is revealed as a rhetorical question, not one that opens up a theological problem, and as a rhetorical query, it asserts that no one can comprehend God's great power, this being his incomprehensible desire to dwell on earth and equally inestimable capacity to contract his almighty being between the narrow staves of the ark. Had an auditor the initial sense that this co-text was the solution, the unfolding discourse would still capture attention as the disclosure of its concealed correlation with the lemma. In both cases, the *darshan* trades on ambiguity, questions, and explicit citations. These turns allow for the expository clarity necessary for public comprehension in a synagogue sermon. By contrast, the *paytan* evokes a thick density of multifaceted resonances of brief but evocative scriptural allusions.

The passage from Yannai to which I turn comprises section 4 of the *shivata* for the sabbath *seder* (lectionary portion) beginning with Exodus 26: 1, which opens, 'And you shall build the Tabernacle'.[41] This paytanic section arguably functions as an expository closure to the first half of the *piyut*, and thus parallels the longer *siluk* that concludes the entire recitative cycle and is, similarly, without alphabetic components and more prosodic then the other units.[42] It reads:

> So great in power, we cannot attain You, Shaddai / who fills all and
>   lies between my breasts;
> And who has established for me the work of my hands / the Tabernacle
> of my labour, beloved of my beloved ones;
> Palanquin of my wedding / and love of my espousals; / place of my
>   testimonies, my curtains of protection;
> Room of my begetting / shade of my rafter; / inlaid with my love, /
>   where my love finds favour, / my place of peace—
> [All this] have You done for me, most awesome and holy [One].

On the face of it, this section is a brief poetic coda comprised of five lines: the first two have two strophes each and are relatively prosodic in form—the opening paean is followed by two descriptive clauses (each marked by 'who'), that demarcate two

---

[41] In *Maḥzor piyutei r. yanai*, ed. Rabinovitz, i. 329 ff., ll. 27–31.

[42] See Zulay, Yannai Studies', 254, and Ezra Fleisher, 'Studies in the Prosodic Character of Several Components of the *Kedushta*' (Heb.), *Hasifrut*, 3 (1971–2), 568–85, and esp. 568 ff. and 580 ff. regarding §4.

special qualities of Shaddai (his omnipresence and his guidance in the construction of the Tabernacle). The third and fourth lines have three and five strophes, respectively, and are a series of evocative descriptors of the just-mentioned Tabernacle, to which they stand in apposition; and the final, fifth line, with only one strophe, is divided between a phrase of divine acknowledgement and another of praise. The final epithet ('holy', *kadosh*) is a trace of the older function of this section, which served as a transition to the Kedushah—a function now assumed by the grand *siluk* at the recitative climax of the cycle. The sole voice of the stanza is that of the precentor, who addresses God on behalf of the people Israel ('we' and 'me'), past and present. So viewed, there is nothing midrashic in this extended doxology; it appears to be straightforward praise, without exegetical exposition.

But upon closer inspection, a quite different assessment emerges. This is evident from the outset. The opening phrase—the initial paean—whose content dominates the entire stanza (both the relative clauses and the subordinate appositions) is nothing other than the co-text of the preceding *midrash* from *Exodus Rabbah* 34: 1;[43] just as it functioned earlier as the explicit trigger of the exposition, it now provides the implicit generator of the various praises that follow. Standing at the head of the stanza, it serves as its lemmatic catalyst. And further, just as in the *midrash* this citation evokes biblical citations that consider God's omnipresence relative to his desire for a sacral dwelling, so does Yannai move from the initial words of praise to phrases that indicate these two traits—the first, 'who fills all' (*melo kol*), being an abbreviated allusion to the angelic doxology of God, 'whose glory fills all [*melo kol*] the earth' (Isa. 6: 3), and the second, 'lies between my breasts [*bein shadai yalin*]', being an explicit citation from Song of Songs 1: 13. Significantly different is the fact that in the *midrash* the co-text elicits a theological puzzle, so that the two textual references are initially regarded as mutually exclusive, whereas now, in the *piyut*, the phrase from Job 37: 23 *from the outset* signals the exceptional power of God, who is *both* omnipresent and local. The theological struggle that is resolved at the end of the *midrash* is the very starting point of the paytanic praise. All we have now are three biblical citations: the first being an assertion of positive praise, the other two being a hendiadys for this great wonder of God's manifestations. No co-text or (counterpointing) proof-texts occur here; there is only a condensed patchwork of scriptural passages.

More may be added. For it will be noticed that the opening scriptural phrase transfers the name Shaddai to the end of the line, to provide a ballast for the second half, which depicts God's wondrous worldly indwelling with the phrase '[He] lies between my breasts [*shadai*]', taken from Song of Songs 1: 13. The rhyme is stunning, since it gives a strong erotic valence to God's presence within Israel. But why

---

[43] Rabinovitz, in *Maḥzor piyutei r. yanai*, already called attention to this passage, and to others as well, in his brief annotations; Shulamit Elitzur, *Poetry of the Lectionary Cycle* [Shirah shel parashah] (Jerusalem, 1999), 137–41, has followed his lead (cf. Rabinovitz, *Maḥzor*, 370), and developed some points. My ensuing discussion goes further.

this textual citation? Because it was not just God's worldly indwelling in general that was at issue, but his presence in the desert Tabernacle (proclaimed in this sabbath's lection); and particularly because our phrase was used as a proof-text in rabbinic teachings about the staves of the ark upon which the Shekhinah rested. Consider BT *Yoma* 54a, which takes up an earlier query about how the staves in Solomon's Temple could be seen and not seen simultaneously (1 Kgs 8: 8), and suggests that they 'pressed' against the *parokhet* (curtain) 'and protruded like the two breasts of a woman'! The proof-text about the 'beloved . . . that lies between my breasts' can only refer to the Shekhinah that alights on the ark. And we may assume that the phrase conveyed a similar nuance for Yannai as well. In our poem, this reference serves the same function as the midrashic reference to the indwelling of God in a space 'four cubits by four cubits'. Only now it does so by allusion.

The use of scriptural proofs to evoke midrashic teachings has an older history in *piyut*.[44] Yannai frequently employs this mode of allusion, and he does so repeatedly in our stanza. The second line gives two more instances. The first strophe, 'And He established for me the work of my hands', is not simply a reference to Psalm 90: 17, inverting the original phrase which invokes God to 'Let the work of our hands be established'. It is, in fact, the scriptural phrase adduced in a midrashic teaching about Moses' blessing of the people at the completion of the Tabernacle. On the verse, 'And Moses blessed them' (Exod. 39: 43), a homilist asked:

With what blessing did he bless them? He said to them: 'May the Shekhinah settle upon the work of your hands'; and they responded: 'May the favour of the Lord, our God, be upon us; let the work of our hands be established, yea the work of our hands, establish [Thou] it'.[45]

Yannai thus has a strategic reason for bringing this citation; and it serves to thicken the intertextual allusions to the Tabernacle—only mentioned explicitly in the second strophe. But if the words 'the Tabernacle of my labour' are precise and direct, the synonym 'beloved' (*yedidut*) for this building is less so, and the reference to the people as 'my beloved ones' (*yedidai*) even less so. But the fact is that, once again, these words are abbreviated scriptural citations from another *midrash* that alludes to the building of the Temple for God, both called *yedid*. It is a splendid example of a classical type of rabbinic rhetoric which plays on a string of eponymous terms derived from Scripture. Viewing this form in full allows us to appreciate the condensation and transformation in Yannai's *piyut*.

Six are called 'beloved' [in Scripture]. The Holy One, blessed be He, is called 'beloved', as it says, 'I shall see to my Beloved [*yedidi*]' [Isa. 5: 1]; Abraham is called 'beloved', as it says, 'What is My beloved [*yedidi*] in My house' [Jer. 11: 15]; Benjamin is called

---

[44] See Aaron Mirsky, *Piyutei yose ben yose* (Jerusalem, 1977), 38–42; S. Elitzur tracks this phenomenon with three *topoi* from pre-classical to medieval times in 'Midrash and its Scriptural Citations as Reflected in Paytanic Compositions' (Heb.), *Sinai*, 89 (1986), 99–109.

[45] *Sifrei debei rav*, ed. H. S. Horovitz (Jerusalem, 1966), *piska* 143 (p. 191).

'beloved', as it says, 'Beloved [*yedid*] of the Lord' [Deut. 33: 12]; Solomon is called 'beloved', as it says, 'And He [God] sent a message through the prophet Nathan, and he [Solomon] was called "Beloved of God" [*yedidyah*]' [2 Sam. 12: 25]; Israel are called 'beloved ones' [*yedidim*], as it says, 'I [God] have given over My dearly beloved' [Jer. 12: 7]; [and] the Temple is called 'beloved', as it says, 'How beloved [*yedidut*] are Your dwellings' [Ps. 84: 2]. Let the 'beloved' son of the 'beloved' come and build the 'beloved House' for the 'Beloved One'; [that is:] let Israel, called *yedidim*, descendants of Abraham, called *yedid*, come and build the Temple, called *yedid*, in the territory of Benjamin, called *yedid*, for the Holy One, blessed be He, Who is called *yedid*.[46]

It is thus evident that the construct form *yedidut yedidai* ('beloved of my beloved ones') melds two proof-texts—the first derives from Psalm 84: 2, understood as a metonym for the Temple, and the second from Jeremiah 12: 7, taken as an allusion to the people Israel. It thus parallels the prior stich: the 'work' finds its synonym in the 'beloved' place; and 'my hands' (*yadai*) is reinforced by 'my beloved ones' (*yedidai*). Such poetic features may give the audience some access to the meaning of the final phrase;[47] but this should not be taken to mean that they caught the midrashic allusions, which are a scholastic conceit effected by the *ḥazan*—a kind of midrashic *jouissance* that extends throughout the succeeding construct forms lauding the significance of the Tabernacle for the nation.[48] And this brings us to an important observation: namely, that our unit is a catena of biblical phrases, nearly all of which allude to midrashic teachings about the Tabernacle or Temple, and serving as proof-texts or pretexts for such discussions. Accordingly, this rabbinic exercise is veiled by scriptural wording—a rendering apparently direct and comprehensible on the surface, but replete with hidden allusions and indirect hints. Yannai employs this feature in a masterful way.[49] For him, here, Midrash is present in its evocative absence.

---

[46] Cited from *Sifre on Deuteronomy*, ed. Finkelstein, *piska* 352 (p. 409). This rhetorical structure is classified as *ma'al* (or paronomasia) by Mirsky; see his *The Origins of Forms of Early Hebrew Poetry* (Heb.), ch. 3. He adduces this passage (and the stylistic variants found in BT *Men.* 53a and *Yalkut shimoni*, 'Berakhah', para. 955) on pp. 47 and 55 ff. Z. Yavetz, 'The Earliest *Piyutim*' (Heb.) in S. Eppenstein, M. Hildesheimer, and J. Wohlgemuth (eds.), *Sefer ledavid tsevi* [*Festschrift . . . David Hoffmann*] [Berlin, 1914], 60), already noted this rhetorical feature in the Talmud and called it *melitsat haremez* (stylistic allusions). The *siluk* by Killir for Shabat Parah (adduced by Mirsky on p. 62) follows the full rhetorical form, though in six poetic quatrains.

[47] Cf. J. Schirmann, 'Yannai the *Paytan*, his Poetry and World-View' (Heb.), *Keshet*, 23 (1964), esp. 51–4.

[48] For example, the phrase 'room of my begetting' (*ḥeder horati*) is based on S. of S. 3: 4, identified with the 'tent of meeting' in *Lev. Rabbah* 1: 10 (also noted by Elitzur, *Poetry of the Lectionary Cycle*, 141); and the phrase 'shadow of my beams' (*tsel korati*) is a double allusion: *tsel* alludes to Ps. 91: 1, identified with the Tabernacle in a *midrash* by R. Judah interpolated into the *Exod. Rabbah* 34: 1 pericope cited above; and *korati* alludes to S. of S. 1: 17, identified with the Temple in *S. of S. Rabbah*, ad loc. (end).

[49] This use of allusion is akin to the phenomenon of *kinuyim* (epithets), also derived from biblical phrases or proof-texts linked to a *midrash*. Regarding Yannai's technique, cf. A. Beitner, 'Figurative Substitutions in the Poetry of Yannai and their Relations to Midrash' (Heb.), *Sinai*, 86 (1985), 29–56.

4. Homiletic Explanations Given to Biblical and Rabbinic Commandments

From earliest times in the academy, sages pondered the details of a scriptural rule and, on occasion, their queries could also parlay into a homily. Such is the case with Rabbi Aibo's opening question in *Pesikta derav kahana* 4: 8. Apparently a rhetorical set-up to a parable about why the red heifer may 'come [*tavo*] to atone for the making of the calf', he asks: 'Why [*mipnei mah*] are male animals used for all other [communal] sacrifices, whereas a female is used for this?' But, in fact, Aibo's opening gambit is generated by a contradiction between the written and oral laws; for Mishnah *Temurah* 2: 1 categorically states that 'Individual sacrifices can be male and female, whereas communal sacrifices are only male.' Now he might have countered that the ashes of the heifer serve impure individuals in the community, not the populace at large, and that this rite has no fixed time, as is the case with communal sacrifices. But this is all beside his point, since the sage wished to teach the 'reason' for this sacrifice, revealed after the laws of Sinai—and he proposed that it was, in fact, an atonement rite for the (female) calf worshipped in the desert. His homily is compact; but noticing the formulaic similarity of the concluding phrase '[let the heifer] come' with the above-cited rhetoric about the 'beloved ones', we see that Aibo must have expatiated on his topic at greater length, and that we have but a minuscule version of the original whole.

In other cases, the question of textual sense is posed by the simple interrogatives *mah* ('what?') and *lamah* ('why'; 'for what [reason]'?), or by the phrase *mah hata'am* ('what is the meaning?').[50] This latter term, *ta'am*, had an interesting and active afterlife in *piyut*, and helps found the genre later known as *ta'amei hamitsvot* ('the meaning of the commandments'). In this development, striking reuses of midrashic themes and techniques are employed. I shall adduce samples from three masters, Rabbi Elazar ben Killir, Rabbi Pinhas Hakohen ben Jacob, and Rabbi Benjamin ben Samuel.[51] They reflect an interesting stream of learned, exegetical discourses, with clarifying expositions of laws and practices—matters that served as pedagogical aids for the congregations that received their compositions.

Towards the end of section 7 of the above-mentioned *piyut* 'Aḥat sha'alti'

---

[50] Cf. *Sifra devei rav*, 'Behar', 4: 7 (on Lev. 25: 28), which reflects an early tannaitic usage (by R. Shimon bar Yohai); the Talmud transmits this as 'R. Shimon bar Yohai interpreted *ta'ameih dikera*' (BT *San.* 21a). Subsequently, this usage changes. The use of *mah* is also found in the early strata, and even in the expanded form *mipnei mah amerah torah* ('Why did the Torah say . . .') to introduce explanations for festival practices; on this latter, see BT *RH* 16a.

[51] On the period of Killir see above, n. 22. R. Pinhas's *floruit* was near Tiberias in the Galilee at the end of the 8th cent.; see full discussion in Shulamit Elitzur, *The Piyutim of Rabbi Pinhas Hakohen* [Piyutei r. pinḥas hakohen] (Jerusalem, 2004), 4–9. With regard to the talmudist and *ḥazan* R. Benjamin, E. Fleisher has devoted an exhaustive reappraisal of the complex evidence, concluding that his provenance was northern Europe (Franco-German) around the 11th cent. On this, see his '*Azharot* by the *Paytan* Rabbi Benjamin (ben Samuel)' (Heb.), *Kovets al yad*, NS 11 (1985), esp. 8–28.

dealing with the red heifer, Killir picks up on Rabbi Aibo's sermonic query, with both stylistic and thematic variations. He asks:

Mah ta'am—For what reason is this [sacrificial] gift alone a female [*nekevah*], and for a guilt-offering and its purification with a name specified [*nekuvah*]?—
[Because] it corresponds [*kemo*] to the mother of all life who was female [*nekevah*] and because of punishment for the sin of the crouching one repaid [*ne'ekvah*].

With these lines (ll. 213–16) Killir begins a long exposition that extends over multiple stanzas (to l. 276) and explains the red heifer sacrifice as an atoning reparation for the sin of Eve, the mother of all life (Gen. 3: 20). The end-lines drive this point home, but the internal terms do so as well. For the poet characterizes the offering and its effects as *ḥatat* ('sin-offering') and *ḥitui* ('purification'), respectively, and counterpoints these to the ever-present proclivity to sin indicated by the phrase *ḥatat rovets* ('sin of the crouching one', Gen. 4: 7), which had long since become an epithet for temptation and the evil inclination. And on this basis Killir offers an explanation that shifts from the sin of the calf to the primordial sin of sins, the disobedience in Eden: it is the archetype for which the idolatry at Sinai is an exemplar; and the incitement by the crouching serpent, whose enmity was forecast into the future (through the phrase 'you will continuously strike at its heel [*ekev*]', Gen. 3: 15), is now squashed and repaid (by a verb derived from the noun *ekev*, used as a reward for obedience in Ps. 19: 12). The result is a deft instance of poetic theology that sees in this atonement rite the sacrificial end of the primordial spirit of sin.

Killir continues with many other correlations between the red heifer and its sacrifice and Eve. For example, the heifer was born 'without blemish' just as Eve was born without blemish, although she became blemished through the serpent who was blemished by leprosy (one of the curses recorded in Gen. 3: 14–16, according to the Midrash)[52]—hence the pure heifer would rectify this ancient stain; or also that the heifer was specified as never to have borne a 'yoke' (*ol*), since this would ritually rectify the sin of she who had overthrown the 'yoke' of God's commandments, after having been seduced by the serpent 'to infringe' (*limol*) upon divine property. Killir performs this homiletic magic over a dozen times, and then shifts to a series of ritual questions beginning with *velamah* ('and why', ll. 277–92). What is particularly striking in this series is that the theme of Eve's sin is replaced by attempts to interpret aspects of the ritual in terms of 'hints' of topics pointing to salvation or martyrdom (among other topics). For example, asking 'why' Scripture specifies the 'hide and flesh and blood and dung' of the heifer (cf. Num. 19: 4), Killir's answer is that it provides a *remez* ('hint') of the future eschatological feast, when the people will be sated with victory (the poem alludes to Ezek. 39: 18); and similarly, the reason 'why' three types of material (cedar, hyssop, and crimson)

---

[52] See *Gen. Rabbah* 20: 4 (*Midrash Bereshit Rabba*, ed. J. Theodor and Ch. Albeck, 3 vols. (Jerusalem, 1965), 184); l. 235 in the *piyut*.

were consumed in the fire (Num. 19: 6) was to 'hint' at the three Jewish youths (Hananiah, Mishael, and Azariah) cast into the flames in martyrdom (the *piyut* alludes to Dan. 3: 21–30).

What is most striking in all these cases is not the midrashic identifications as such, since many occur in the traditions known to Killir,[53] but the fact that he has culled a group of specific materials from a larger corpus and transformed a series of diverse identifications (*zeh*, 'this [*x*-phrase refers to *y*]') into a catena of hints regarding future events and actions. In the process, the ritual of the red heifer not only rectifies a prior ritual fault, but forecasts a number of exemplary eschatological acts. Rabbi Elazar thus brings his *piyut* to an intensified conclusion, and transforms a seemingly inscrutable law into a dense code containing hints of things to come. And just as midrashic redactors often concluded their topical collections with messianic themes of hope (as notably the entire section in *Pesikta derav kahana* that deals with the red heifer), so does our *paytan* shift towards topics of consolation at the end of his poem—weaving a series of evocative phrases on the purificatory effects of fire into ecstatic dithyrambs that rise to a mystical vision of the divine throne engulfed by angelic flames (ll. 293–336).

*

A quite different form is given to asking and explaining ritual matters in a *kedushta* for the fifth intermediate day of Passover by Rabbi Pinhas Hakohen.[54] Like Rabbi Elazar ben Killir, Rabbi Pinhas also raises ritual queries in the selection just prior to the heavenly and earthly *trisagion*; but he does not isolate the form as a special series, with one bi-colon given to the *lamah*-query and a second given to the *remez*-answer. Instead, the questions and the hints explaining them are woven into one complex stanza taking up one specific topic, here the theme of 'five', since this poem was recited within the Amidah for the fifth weekday (*ḥol hamo'ed*) between the initial and final feast days of the festival. Here then are the opening lines, just prior to the invocation to the Kedushah:

Seven days you shall celebrate together / as inscribed on the Law of tradition; and it is mentioned on five occasions / in the recitation of the Five Books. And *lamah* ['why'] on five occasions? / [Since] they went forth on the fifth day, on the basis of five things / therefore one reads [about it] on five occasions and mentions five [types of] vegetables. / And since it is one of three and six when He recalls the covenant with three: / Eitan, Only One, and Pure are three—therefore are they hinted at by three things: / roast [lamb], *matsot*, and bitter [herb]s make this threesome. (ll. 37–43)

As noted, the dominant exegetical motif for this paytanic instruction is 'five', and the poet explains that five references to Passover (occurring in the Pentateuch) are recited on the five intermediate days of the festival to mark the fact that the people left Egypt on the fifth day after taking a sheep for the sacrifice (on the tenth of the

---

[53] See especially in *Pesikta derav kahana*, 4: 9–10 (Mandelbaum edn., i. 75 ff.).
[54] *Piyutim of Rabbi Pinhas Hakohen*, ed. Elitzur, 292 ff.

month; they departed on the fifteenth) on the basis of five distinct reasons, which are not specified. The form is expository. The opening two lines refer to the rabbinic practice of reading scriptural references for the festival on the intermediate days of the festival, and do so in a straightforward (poetic) manner. The *ḥazan* functions like a *darshan* and asks 'why' (*lamah*) these are mentioned in five places, and cites his own words as the lemma. The answer adapts two midrashic passages verbatim: in the first case, he cites a passage from the *Mekhilta derabi yishma'el* which states that 'they went forth . . . on the fifth day' of the week;[55] in the second, he alludes to reasons specified similarly as 'on the basis of (*mitokh*) five things' in the Jerusalem Talmud (*Ta'anit* 1. 1, 63*d*).[56] At the conclusion of this part of the explication for the practice, Rabbi Pinhas repeats his lemma (with the term 'therefore'); but then adds one further practice marking 'fives' on Passover: the reference in Mishnah *Pesaḥim* 2: 6 to five kinds of greens by which a person may fulfil the ritual requirement of eating 'bitter herbs' (*maror*) on the holiday. Thus, all the explanations that answer the query are found in explicit rabbinic traditions.

The next section turns to another symbolic practice. Rabbi Pinhas refers to Passover as one of the three pilgrimage festivals.[57] These three festival days remind God of the three covenants made with the three patriarchs: Abraham (denoted by the epithet 'Eitan'), Isaac (called 'my only one' by his father), and Jacob (called a 'simple' or 'pure' person by the biblical narrator). All three individuals are also 'hinted at' (*remuzim*) by the 'three things' which, according to Rabban Gamliel, must be specified during the ritual meal in order 'to fulfil one's ritual obligation': the paschal offering, the unleavened wafers, and the bitter herbs (Mishnah *Pes.* 10: 5). This case is a striking and apparently novel explication of the 'threes', and adds a concluding flourish to the dominant expository theme of 'fives'.[58] Once again, Rabbi Pinhas has specified his 'reasons' on the basis of explicitly referenced sources. Creatively adapting a series of teachings, he has conjoined them into one homiletical stanza, which, despite its concision, was undoubtedly intended for the congregation at prayer. As also with the prior instances authored by Elazar ben Killir, we have some precious evidence for public pedagogy in *piyut*.

*

[55] 'Beshalaḥ', 'Vayasa' 1 (Horovitz–Rabin edn. 159 l. 9). The deduction is presumably this: since Israel departed Egypt on 15 Nisan (the first month), five days after taking the paschal lambs (on 10 Nisan), the Exodus occurred on the fifth day of the week (the schema is based on the assumption that the first Nisan inaugurated the first day of the week of Creation, i.e. Sunday).

[56] Similarly, Elitzur, *Piyutim of Rabbi Pinhas Hakohen*, 293 nn. 39–40; however, she does not note the formal structure of the key terms of darshanic exposition.

[57] The phrase is difficult: it refers to 'one of three and six'. The first number (three) alludes to the pilgrimage festivals; the second (six) is puzzling. It may refer to the six times when messengers were dispersed to inform the people that a new moon had been sighted (since festivals occurred during those months); cf. Mishnah *RH* 1: 3. See, similarly, Elitzur, *Piyutim of Rabbi Pinhas Hakohen*, 293 n. 41.

[58] Elitzur adduces an alternative tradition, found in *Exod. Rabbah* 15: 12, which links these ritual objects to Abraham, Sarah, and Jacob (with reasons).

A final example in which a *ḥazan* teaches 'reasons' for certain rituals occurs within a Passover *piyut* by Rabbi Benjamin ben Samuel, 'Az kegilgel'.[59] Eight queries about practices for the Seder ceremony are brought under the rubric *mah ta'am* ('for what reason?'). Of these, six answers state that the act is done 'in remembrance of' (*zekher le-*) of some event, while two begin with the explanatory terms 'so that' (*kedei she-*) and 'because' (*ki*). All these clusters are formulated as concise bi-cola, with one line apiece for the question and answer. Here are several examples whose sources derive from discussion in the Babylonian Talmud, *Pesaḥim* 115b–117b:

> For what reason does one dip and seep the *ḥaroset* [chopped fruit]?
> In remembrance of the clay on which they laboured.
>
> For what reason does one remove the table from its place?
> So that the youths will ask: 'Why is this night different?'
>
> For what reason does one break the [matzah] wafer into pieces?
> Because the poor and destitute have no full loaf in their tin.

These (and other) questions derive from talmudic deliberations and provide a particular adaptation of them. Their prominence as a unit in various festival prayer books (the so-called *Maḥzorei italiyah*, *romaniyah*, and *benei romi*) and their recitation on the sabbath before Passover suggest that the topics were part of the communal practices of the region and not just theoretical issues.[60] Hence they undoubtedly had a pedagogical function for these communities. But what makes this collection of special interest for the present discussion is that various halakhic discussions were sifted to produce the specific formulations herein cited. The couplets thus also demonstrate living midrashic creativity by Rabbi Benjamin, who adapted these traditions and streamlined them for his own ends. For example, the first case is derived from a long discussion which ends with 'the Talmud' asking: 'What is [the meaning of] the commandment [*mai mitsvah*] to use *ḥaroset*?' Of the two answers, Rabbi Yoḥanan's is adopted, for he says, 'It is in remembrance of the clay' (BT *Pes.* 116a). Manifestly, the question was translated from the talmudic Aramaic into Hebrew, whereas the answer was kept verbatim in Hebrew. Similarly with respect to the next unit, which asks the reason for removing or raising the table (later the plate) from its place near the outset of the ritual recital. Here too a long discussion by the sages is concluded with 'the Talmud' now asking: 'Why [*lamah*] does one raise the table?' And the answer given follows the school of Rabbi Yannai, 'So that young children will note [this] and ask [its meaning]' (BT *Pes.* 115b). Once again the original question has been reformulated by the *paytan*, while the answer has been basically cited from the source. However, in this instance, the concern is

---

[59] This *piyut* is discussed and printed by Fleisher in '*Azharot* by the *Paytan* Rabbi Benjamin' (Heb.), 15, 30–2, and earlier by L. Weinberger, 'On the Provenance of Benjamin B. Samuel Kuštani', *Jewish Quarterly Review*, 68 (1977), 48.

[60] Cf. Fleisher, '*Azharot* by the *Paytan* Rabbi Benjamin' (Heb.), 15 ff.

not to remember a historical event but to mark the ritual process and note its strangeness, thus occasioning questions and discussions (about the servitude and Exodus).

Altogether different is the query about the broken matzah, for here the answer derives from a talmudic discussion about the 'meaning' of the phrase *leḥem oni* (Deut. 16: 3). Two midrashic possibilities are offered. According to Samuel, this bread is 'read' *oni* since one may 'answer' (*onin*) many things with regard to it (namely, the matzah). But this interpretation is rejected by Rabbi Benjamin in favour of the alternative opinion, which states that the word is 'written' without vowel letters to denote that it is a poor man's (*ani*) bread; and just as such a person is sated with a piece, so does one use just a piece of bread at the ritual meal—thereby recalling the poverty of servitude (BT *Pes.* 115*b*–116*a*). In this instance the question is not found in the rabbinic discussion, though the topic is indicated; but by contrast, the answer is explicitly based on the midrashic play offered there. Our *paytan* offers it as *the* reason for the ritual practice of breaking the unleavened bread and reciting the blessing only over a piece (and not the whole matzah).

Clearly Rabbi Benjamin is not just culling older materials, but teaching them in a certain set form—a question-and-answer format that had canonical precedence in rabbinic literature, but had been stylized for ritual and pedagogical ends in accordance with the received paytanic tradition.[61] These events of 'living Midrash' gave the *ḥazan* his various voices: reciter of prayers, teacher of tradition, and homilist *par excellence*. One thus sees how multifaceted traditional prayer had become, as well as its role in public pedagogy. Significantly, this included offering homiletical reasons for the commandments and practices for appropriate liturgical occasions.

5. The Reuse and Transformation of Midrashic Dialogues in *Piyut*

I turn now to another aspect of the precentor's voice; specifically, his being the multi-role mouthpiece of midrashic dialogues—be these between personifications of nature, human beings, or a biblical hero and God. In all cases, the *mise en scène* derives from rabbinic revisions of scriptural passages, now dramatically transformed by the liturgical orator. Tracing the process offers another window onto paytanic creativity in the mirror of Midrash. The first case is part of the larger genre of 'contest literature', whose origins extend backwards into ancient Near Eastern

---

[61] It may be added that, in some cases, the explanatory pedagogy omits the question and only provides the interpretation. An interesting early instance is the way Yannai explains a mishnaic elaboration of a scriptural term. The Torah refers to a woman's menstrual flow with the term *dam*, 'blood' (Lev. 15: 25), but Mishnah *Nid.* 2: 6 discusses the five different hues that would render a woman impure. Yannai links all this (using the concept of 'measure for measure') to the primal sin of Eve through a series of explanations, beginning: 'Red blood [*dam adom*]—because she sinned with regard to Adam [*adam*] and caused his face to turn red [*he'edimah panav*] [in shame].' All the types are taken up in this exegetical form (mishnaic topic + *ki*-clause + ethical explanation). For the passage, see *Maḥzor piyutei rabi yanai*, ed. Rabinovitz, i. 434.

literature, and forwards into Greek and Syriac literature, both overlapping with rabbinic types.[62]

Scholars have often been puzzled by Psalm 68, whose phrases seem to be discontinuous and fragmentary.[63] Rabbinic commentators were less diffident and found in these verses various references to the Exodus from Egypt and the revelation at Sinai. Of particular support in this regard was the sequence beginning at vv. 8–10 (presumptively alluding to the divine advent in the desert, the trembling of the mountain called Sinai, and the tumult of nature), and resuming with vv. 16–19 (referring to the mountain desired by God, the advent of the angelic host to Sinai, and the ascension of Moses to wrest divine gifts from on high). This exegetical tradition is early, and is evident in old tannaitic sources. A typical instance occurs in the *Mekhilta derabi yishma'el*,[64] and provides a good opening to our topic:

And the whole mountain trembled. And was it [Sinai] not included among all the mountains? For it is said, 'The mountains quaked before the Lord, [even] that Sinai' (Judg. 5: 5)? And it [also] says, 'Why are you distressed [*teratsdun*],[65] O jagged [*gavnunim*] mountains?' [Ps. 68: 17]; [meaning,] He said to them, 'You are all crook-backed [*gibnim*]', as it says, 'Neither a crook-back or a dwarf' (Lev. 21: 20) . . . [a unit about God's choice of the territory of Benjamin for the Temple] . . . But, nevertheless, it [Sinai] was 'the mountain God desired for His dwelling' [Ps. 68: 17].

This passage explicates the trembling of Sinai in Exodus 19: 18 via the co-texts of Judges 5: 5 and Psalm 68: 17—both of which treat the theme of a quaking or distraught Sinai. The second passage includes this mountain among all the other crook-backed ones. They are all similar, and no one has any advantage in appearance. In this homiletic account there is no contest between them, just a common shaking at the divine advent and the inexplicable choice of Mount Sinai by God. The opening and concluding parts of Psalm 68: 17 set up and support this two-part interpretation. The interpolated unit about God's choice of the territory of Benjamin for his later dwelling is, in fact, explained in moral terms (Benjamin did not participate in the sale of Joseph); and it was probably added as the historical double of God's choice of Sinai as the first divine dwelling place.

---

[62] For the 'debate' genre in Hebrew literature, see the overview of Moritz Steinschneider, 'Rangstreit-Literatur: Ein Beitrag zur vergleichlichen Literatur- und Kulturgeschichte', in *Sitzenberichte der Philosophisch-Historisch Klasse der Kaiserlichen Akademie der Wissenschaften*, 155 (Vienna, 1908), IV. Abhandlung, 1–87. An excellent exemplar of the *piyut* genre in light of ancient literature is given by Shalom Spiegel, 'Milḥemet ha'evarim' [The Debate between the Limbs], in id., *Fathers of Piyut* [Avot hapiyut] (New York, 1997), 387–426; see also the survey by Sebastian Brock, 'The Dispute Poem: From Sumer to Syriac', *Bayn al-Nahrayn*, 7 (28) (1979), 426–17 (*sic*: English section at end of Arabic numbering).

[63] Cf. William F. Albright, 'A Catalogue of Early Hebrew Lyric Poems: Psalm 68', *Hebrew Union College Annual*, 23 (1950), 1–39.   [64] 'Yitro' 4 (Horovitz–Rabin edn., 216).

[65] In context, this question evokes the query in Ps. 114: 5–6, as to why the mountains 'dance' or 'cavort' (*tirkedu*), evoking the likelihood that *teratsdun* is a corruption or variant of *tirakdun* or *tir'adun* (tremble)—the phonemes *ts/k/'* being related in some Semitic languages (cf. Hebrew *erets* and Aramaic *arka/ar'a*).

But this was not the only version of this movement of the mountains among *tana'im* (sages of the mishnaic period), as we know from a sermon by Rabbi Yosi Hagelili preserved in *Genesis Rabbah*.[66] Here the motif of quaking is obscured by another motif, which uses Psalm 68: 17 to introduce the theme of contestation among the high places. Here is Rabbi Yosi's homily:

Why are you teratsdun, *O crook-backed mountains?* [Ps. 68: 17]. Rabbi Yosi Hagelili explicated this biblical passage in terms of 'the mountains' [thus]: When the Holy One, blessed be He, came to give the Torah on Sinai, the [other] mountains were running [about] and disputing with each other—this one saying, 'The Torah should be given on me [*alai*]!' and that one saying, 'The Torah should be given on me [*alai*]!' [Mount] Tabor came from Beit Elim and M[ount] Carmel from Aspamia, as it says, 'As I live—declares the Lord . . . Surely Tabor among the mountains [and Carmel by the sea shall come]."' [Jer. 46: 18]. This one says, 'I was called!' and this one says, 'I was called!' [Thereupon] the Holy One, blessed be He, answered: 'Why are you arguing, O mountains? You are both high mountains—but "crook-backed", as it says, "Neither a crook-back nor a dwarf" [Lev. 21: 20]. Each one of you has had idolatry performed upon you; but Sinai has not, [hence: this is] "the mountain God has desired for His dwelling" [Ps. 68: 17]. [As it is written,] "Then the Lord descended upon Mount Sinai" [Exod. 19: 20]; but this notwithstanding, "truly the Lord will dwell forever" [Ps. 68: 17]—in the Eternal Temple.'

This is a first-class homiletic disquisition, giving a rich sense of how living Midrash could unfold through co-texts and dialogues and a mythic scene that fills in the dramatic events around the advent of God on Sinai. It is clearly related to the tradition reported in the *Mekhilta*—in terms of being centred on Psalm 68: 17, which inaugurates and concludes the issue of divine choice; in terms of God citing Scripture to support the depiction of the mountains; and in terms of a divine discourse with the mountains. But if that text focused on a silent similarity among the mountains, the present homily presents a vocal debate mediated by God. The teaching opens with a contentious *mise-en-scène* at the occasion of the giving of the Torah. In one great hubbub several mountains contend for the privilege of being the place upon which God would descend. Building off the opening lemma and the word *teratsdun*, the passage states that the mountains came 'running and disputing' (*ratsim umedayenim*). By cleverly reinterpreting the opening divine query as two verbs (i.e. *teratsdun* is taken to imply two actions: (*te-*) *rats* + *dun*—'run' and 'contend') the question is transformed: God does not ask why the mountains are shaking but why they are rushing about with legal claims! Faced with this challenge, the mountains quote Scripture, invoking Jeremiah 46: 18 for their claims. But God ignores this interpretation of his words and counters with another passage that rejects them as ritually disqualified, having been the site of idolatry. As distinct from the *Mekhilta* version, a reason is given for the mountains' rejection; and this explanation also

---

[66] *Gen. Rabbah* 99: 1 (on Gen. 49: 27); Theodor–Albeck edn., 1271 ff.

serves as the basis for the choice of Sinai. Since only this place has not been defiled, only it is worthy of being the site for God's holy presence.

But then comes the surprise twist. God's choice of Sinai is temporary: he only comes to 'dwell' there—but will not reside there permanently. This point is made through a striking transformation of the concluding phrase of Psalm 68: 17. In context, the words '*af* the Lord will dwell forever' serve to re-enforce the statement that God has desired Sinai for his dwelling—where the particle *af* means 'truly' or 'indeed' (God will dwell in that place forever). But later history has intervened, and the homilist wants to valorize the shift to Jerusalem. He does so by taking the same term to introduce the qualification: *af* [*al pi khen*], meaning 'even though' God has now chosen Sinai, he will 'nevertheless' not dwell there forever.[67] And just where shall he dwell forever?—in the Temple of Jerusalem!

It is thus striking that the very source of this midrashic contest is deemed encoded in the language of Scripture itself (*teratsdun* as 'running and *disputing*'). And it is also notable that in the ensuing drama Sinai remains silent and is not engaged in the rivalry between the mountains before God. But, significantly, it is neither for physical traits nor for particular achievements that Sinai is distinguished—solely for it being unsullied among the high places. Quite different, then, is the portrayal of this mountain in a *kedushta* for Shavuot by Rabbi Solomon Suleiman al-Sanjari, an eastern *paytan* of the ninth century.[68] We pick up the recitation (in the sixth section) just after a reference to the sound of the lightning and a scriptural citation about the imminent advent of God upon the mountain, 'And it was on the third day, when morning came' (Exod. 19: 16)—taken from the Torah portion read on that day. Its biblical usages are italicized below, to give an immediate visual sense of the verbal texture; the revision of earlier midrashic features will be taken up in the ensuing discussion.

The *mountains shook and heaved* from their places and said: 'Where is He *Who weighs the mountains on a balance?*' Tabor spoke: 'I am *the highest of all the mountains*'; and it is meet that *the maker of mountains* rest upon me.'

Carmel raised its voice, *and came down into the sea*, and said: 'Upon me shall rest He *Who is greatly feared in the holy council.*' But he was *spurned for his pride* and not told: '*Blessed is he who comes.*'

Sinai shuddered and spoke naught, but mused: 'How could He *Who dwells on high* rest upon me?' The *Living One* answered him: 'Upon you *I shall make precedence*; because you have *humbled* yourself, I shall *raise you high*.'

---

[67] The *midrash* in the *Mekhilta* may be the source of this usage, but with different intent.

[68] The *piyut* was published as an anonymous composition by A. M. Haberman, *A Selection of Seventy Poems* [Mivḥar hashivim] (Tel Aviv, 1948), 40 ff., and then with an attribution and a full critical apparatus by E. HaCohen, 'The *Kedushtaot* of R. Solomon Suleiman al-Sanjary for the Festivals' [Kedushtaotav shel r. shelomoh suleiman alsanjari lemo'adei hashanah] (Ph.D. diss., Hebrew University of Jerusalem, 2003), ii. 80 ff.; for period and place, see vol. i, ch. 10.

To appreciate the techniques of poetic theology at play here, it is first of all striking that the descriptors of the mountains, the divine epithets, and the discourses are all variously derived from biblical phrases.[69] This provides a thick scriptural texture for the language of the prayer. But if the wording is biblical, the ideas and theology are rabbinic and derive from a host of older traditions. In light of the midrashic materials adduced above, one will note, first, that the speech of Carmel coming to the sea picks up the citation from Jeremiah used by the mountains to claim that they have been called by God (in the *Genesis Rabbah* passage); and second, that the reference to Sinai shuddering (*za sinai*) is a deft allusion to the deictic reference to 'that' Sinai (*zeh sinai*) in the citation from Judges used in the context of the distraught and shaking mountains at the divine advent (in the *Mekhilta* passage). But, as noted, the quaking in the latter source was due to divine awe, and not clarified any further; whereas the disturbance in the former one produced a contest, though the scriptural proof offered there was ignored by God because all of these mountains had served as sites for idolatry. The dialogue in Rabbi Solomon's *piyut* offers a different view of the controversy and the mountains' claims, through allusions to other aggadic traditions on this theme. He not only hints at the aggadic passages reviewed earlier, but alludes to other rabbinic materials referring to the disputation of the mountains.[70] In this process, our *ḥazan* is no mere collector of traditions, but a creative midrashist in a dramatic, poetic mode.

Let us begin with the very 'call to contest,' which occurs immediately after the opening stanzas set the scene with the introit, 'The foundations of the earth cracked asunder / when the Dweller Above appeared from the heavens.' At the outset, then, the mountains shake and heave and then invoke God's presence as a judge. Accordingly, this movement of the mountains is not only their response to the divine advent, but their commotion as they seek to advocate, each one on its own terms, just why the divine presence should alight upon them. It is thus that the older theme of the mountains rushing about and contending underlies this passage, though not stated in just these terms. But contend they do, and call upon God to weigh their claims on the scale of justice—thus invoking and transforming an old epithet of divine cosmic majesty (God is now appealed to as the one who can adjudicate the weight of the different arguments, not just hold these mountainous entities in His might). But what is the basis of the arguments? Tabor speaks first and simply states that its superior physical height (*gavo'ah*) makes it worthy (*na'eh*) to be the one upon whom (*alai*) God should rightly descend. This plea by the first plaintiff was not answered—though the claim to be the highest of mountains does recall the version of the episode found in *Genesis Rabbah* (by Rabbi Yosi Hagelili). In that account, the two mountains contend but make no specific case beyond the claim that they were

---

[69] Cf. Ps. 18: 8; Amos 4: 14; Isa. 40: 12; Gen. 7: 19; Jer. 46: 18; Ps. 89: 8; Prov. 16: 5; Ps. 118: 26; Isa. 33: 5; Ps. 42: 3; Micah 6: 6 (*etkademah* is used here with the multiple senses of 'approach', 'greet', 'give precedence', 'acknowledge'), and 1 Sam. 2: 7 respectively. The usages are variously citations, adaptations, and allusions. [70] For the phrase 'upon me' (*alai*), see below, n. 72.

the ones called. But this notwithstanding, when God rebuts their appeal, he first calls them 'high mountains' (*harim gevohim*)—and then also *gavnunim* ('crook-backed' ones), and therefore unqualified for sacred service. Was this reference to their height originally part of their claim? And is there some allusion to this by Rabbi Solomon when he refers to their height with a phrase alluding to Genesis 7: 19, and its reference to the highest mountain peaks at the time of the flood?

And what about Carmel's contention about coming 'into' the sea? What kind of claim is this and why is it rejected for being haughty? One might have expected that the claim (by Tabor) of being highest (*gavo'ah*) would have evoked the charge of haughtiness (*gavhut*)—a kind of rebuttal measure for measure. But this matter is not taken up, though in context it serves to set up the ascendance of Sinai for being both lowly and humble of mien. With this point, Rabbi Solomon asserts the special virtue of humility. Is this his own invention? And is there more to say about the terse assertions of Mounts Tabor and Carmel? To fill in the traditions that were in one way or another known to the *hazan* we may turn to another homily on our topic by Rabbi Nathan, who lived two generations after Rabbi Yosi.[71] According to tradition,

> Rabbi Nathan taught: When the Holy One, blessed be He, wished to give the Torah to Israel, Carmel came from Aspamia and Tabor from Beit Elim; as it is written in Scripture, 'As I live—declares the ... Lord of Hosts, surely, Tabor among the mountains and Carmel by the sea shall come!' [Jer. 46: 18]. This one said, 'I am called Mount Tabor, and upon me it is fitting [*alai na'eh*] that the Shekhinah dwell, since I am the highest of all the mountains and the flood waters did not cover me'; and this one said, 'I am called Mount Carmel, and upon me it is fitting [*alai na'eh*] that the Shekhinah dwell,[72] for I extended myself into [the sea] and [the people] crossed it over me.' The Holy One responded, 'You are both disqualified for being haughty [*gavhut*].'

Thereupon, the mountains accuse God of a miscarriage of justice and of not rewarding each one for its merits: Tabor, for some virtue that enabled it to survive the flood; Carmel, for making a land bridge so that the Israelites could survive the sea waters at the Exodus. Withal something of their claims is acknowledged, since God rewards each one with a future role in the redemption. But presumably Sinai was selected prior to this accusation of injustice—since, despite their mollification,

all the mountains began complaining and scuffling, as it says, 'The mountains quaked before the Lord' [Judg. 5: 5]. [Whereupon] the Holy One said: 'Why do you *teratsdun*? Why do you wish to contend [*tirtsu ladun*] with Sinai? For you are all crook-backed

---

[71] R. Yosi was a 2nd-generation *tana* from the Galilee, R. Nathan a 4th-generation *tana* from Babylon who flourished in the court of Simeon ben Gamliel II. The teaching is found in *Midrash tehilim*, at Ps. 68: 9; see S. Buber's edn. (Vilna, 1891), 318.

[72] In this version we have *alai na'eh*; in *Gen. Rabbah* 99: 1 only *alai*. This phrasing may be part of the rhetoric for midrashic contestations. In a snippet of an undoubtedly longer debate-type passage preserved in the Talmud, the various stones at Luz 'gathered together' to compete for the privilege of being the head-rest for the 'righteous' patriarch Jacob—each one saying that he should 'rest [his head] *alai*'. See BT *Ḥul.* 91b. It is a tradition of R. Isaac (Nappaha).

mountains [and disqualified]; but I only want [*retsoni*] Sinai, who is more humble [*shafel*] than all of you; as it says, 'I who dwell on high, in holiness, shall be with the contrite and humble of spirit' [Isa. 57: 15].

The dialogues in this homily clarify the language and innuendoes of Rabbi Solomon's *piyut*. In Rabbi Nathan's teaching, the mountains come to Sinai in response to a divine prophecy that they 'will come'—which they each interpret in terms of a divine invitation based on their special merits: presumably Mount Tabor hears the epithet 'among the mountains' as meaning that it is the exemplar among them all, and thus recalls the days of the flood; whereas Mount Carmel hears the designation 'by the sea' as recalling its extension into the Red Sea for the sake of the Israelites. But both claims are rejected for being haughty. The mountains' desire that the Shekhinah should rest *alai*, 'upon me', is quashed; and only then, *after their dismissal*, do they begin to contend with Sinai (this being less a contest then a ranting and railing—*mitra'amim umitmotetim*—for having been chosen). It is at this later point that the old tradition of controversy is introduced, and God's choice is justified. When the mountains are now called *gavnunim*, and this is again explained via the biblical law about disqualified priests, one may suppose that the proof-text is given a twist. Rather than the phrase *o giben o dak* (literally) marking a pair of ritual infirmities, it may rather set up an exegetical contrast between being 'crookbacked' (*given*) and therefore rejected (as high or haughty—*gavo'ah*), or 'thin' (*dak*) and thus favoured (as meek and lowly)—for when God justifies his choice of Sinai, he does so on the basis of the scriptural passage that the most exalted Lord dwells with the 'contrite' (*daka*) and 'humble' (*shefal ruaḥ*).

Rabbi Solomon alludes to these various topics—obliquely, with regard to Tabor's superior height; more precisely, with respect to Carmel's coming 'into' the sea (not just being by it); and strategically, with respect to Sinai's self-deprecating silence and the divine justification.[73] Given this presentation, it may be inferred that the *paytan* counted on some knowledge of these traditions by his congregation, though the overall effect would still work on its own—since comprehension is deftly guided by the patterned contentions, by the double (and marked) speeches in each stanza, and by the contrast between initiated and vocal boasts (rejected for pride) of the mountains, and the passive and quiet reserve (acknowledged with praise) of Sinai.[74] There is thus an incremental build-up of meaning for the attentive listener.

---

[73] The poet presents the contention as occurring immediately after the beginning of the divine manifestation, thus showing his own creative adaptation of this varied motif.

[74] There is good reason to suppose earlier paytanic links between the midrashic versions and their liturgical rendition. Evidence in this direction can be found in a papyrus most recently published by Pieter A. H. De Boer, 'Notes on an Oxyrynchus Papyrus in Hebrew: Brit. Mus. Or. 9180 A', *Vetus Testamentum*, 1 (1951), 49–57. My examination of the photograph of the obverse shows a tradition when certain entities *ragzu* ('gathered'; l. 6), including a *sod rivevot kodesh* ('council of myriads of angels'; l. 8), and *retsed gavnunim* ('turmoil of the ridged mountains'; l. 11)—all before there 'broke forth' (*pats*) the word *anokhi* ('I am'; l. 11). All this certainly points to a *piyut* celebrating the revelation at Sinai, and this likelihood would be further confirmed by l. 14 of the reverse, where there is apparently a reference to

Internal poetics reinforce these features. Thus, as the dialogues unfold in balanced quatrains, with strategic and purposeful end-rhymes,[75] a series of ironic contrasts further accentuates the presentation. For example, Tabor states that it is the highest of mountains before the maker of mountains; Carmel is said to come (*ba*) to the sea but is not invited (by God) to come further; and Sinai's exaltation of the divine Lord who dwells on high is counterpointed by it being raised high for its lowly comportment. Clearly, the theme of humility is central for the *ḥazan*, and follows the lead of earlier tradition as he reformulated his sources. And so, beyond the 'events' being presented, the *piyut* provides a forceful homily on humility. The older midrashic dialogues are thus sharpened into a series of dramatic scenes, with heightened verbal contrasts of proper and improper comportment; and thereby the precentor teaches the congregation about the proper traits for those who would receive God's word. Other homilists took up the moral aspects of this theme over the centuries.[76]

But perhaps it was not only the midrashic tradition that rang in Rabbi Solomon's ears as he composed this piece. For as a *ḥazan*—and quite likely one who served before Rabbi Sa'adyah Gaon himself[77]—our master had other models at hand. For indeed, when he speaks of God as he who dwells on high (*rumah*), and as a Living One (*ḥai*) who raises (*aromemah*) those who humble themselves (*hishpalta*) and judges the haughty (*gavhuto*), one may certainly hear the echo of the liturgical phrases, occurring just prior to the Amidah, that praise God as 'the Living [*ḥai*] God ... High [*ram*] and Exalted ... Who casts down [*mashpil*] the haughty ... and raises up the humble to the heights [*magbiah shefalim ad marom*]'. How significant that these phrases already appear in the Babylonian prayer-book of Rabbi Sa'adyah, the great *gaon* in the days of al-Sanjari.[78]

CONCLUSION: THE REGISTERS OF TRADITION — AGAIN

Having explored a broad range of topics that set forth the uses and transformations of earlier tradition (both biblical and midrashic) in *piyut*, a concluding reprise of the

---

ḥarutim ḥatsuvim—the words 'chiselled and incised' upon the tablets! (R. Solomon uses *ḥakukim*.) M. Beit-Arié dates the transcription to 'circa 300–400'; see his 'The Munich Palimpsest: A Hebrew Scroll Written before the Eighth Century (with Four Facsimiles)' (Heb.), *Kiryat sefer*, 43 (1978), 173.

[75] Take the second quatrain presented above: the end-rhymes of *ba*, *raba*, *tiavah*, and *haba*, refer successively to Carmels, that 'comes' to the sea, to God who is 'greatly' feared, to the claim that is 'despised' (rejected), and the refusal to receive the mountain with the greeting 'blessed is the one who comes'. The syntax of the lines thus separately and collectively effects a second-order significance. On these and related matters, cf. the classic work of Yuri Tynianov, *The Problem of Verse Language [Problema stikhotvornogo iazyka]* (Leningrad, 1924); English trans. and ed. by M. Sosa and B. Harvey (Ann Arbor, Mich., 1981).

[76] Cf. the striking moral homily on pride and humility in *Pesikta rabati* 7, where the contrast in Prov. 29: 23 is developed and applied to the choice of Sinai. See *Pesiqta Rabbati: Midrasch für den Fest-Cyclus und die ausgezeichneten Sabbathe*, ed. M. Friedmann (Vienna, 1880), 27a.

[77] See HaCohen, 'The *Kedushtaot* of R. Solomon Suleiman al-Sanjary', i. 227–49 for a full discussion.

[78] See the *Sidur rav sa'adyah gaon*, ed. I. Davidson, S. Asaf, and I. Yoel (Jerusalem, 1985), 16.

subject is in order. It allows a final sounding of the strata involved, after the artefactual evidence has been sorted and studied in some detail. We may rethink the issue as follows.

Scripture is the *primary level* and *source* of rabbinic tradition. It is the quintessential foundation text of Jewish culture, and its reading and study is foundational for its statutory public recitation on sabbaths and festivals—and thus also for its exegetical explication in Midrash and liturgical presentation in *piyut*. The words and phrases of Scripture are evident throughout this poetry—as materials woven into the liturgical recitations, as proof-texts cited and collected at various points, as direct and indirect ways of alluding to midrashic expositions, and as the basis of any number of epithets for God, humans, and places. Through this texture of citations, and a host of neologisms serving the new ends of poetry, *piyut* expresses a kind of neo-classicism—a regeneration of the creative role of Scripture that anticipates a similar revival in the subsequent Hebrew poetry of the Spanish 'Golden Age'.

If Scripture is the primary source of language and theme for ancient Judaism, Midrash is its *secondary stratum* and *secondary resource* for ideas and beliefs—even as it constitutes its *primary method* of exposition and *primary mode* of instruction. Whether in the study house or the synagogue, and thus whether in the terse exchanges of scholastic exegesis or their freer and more imaginary expression in public homilies, Midrash produced the rabbinic mind and its many religious topics. It is everywhere in evidence in the *piyut*—as snippets of interpretations woven into the poetry, as the explication and elaboration of the biblical topics recited from Scripture (its laws, narratives, and prophecies), as the theme hinted at through the allusion of proof-texts (and thus as obliquely encoded in Scripture), and through the use and revision of rhetorical forms or structures (whether elaborated or condensed). In various ways, *piyut* took over the midrashic homily (or *derashah*) and gave it new pedagogical possibilities (through sharpened formulas or structures of juxtaposition, enchaining, and repetitive variation). Through Midrash, Scripture was filtered and reformulated as the archetypal prism of its cultural possibilities. And through *piyut*, Midrash reasserted its oral character—a revival of the orality of rabbinic culture and tradition at a time when vast tracts were also being written down, stylistically condensed, and anthologized in diverse ways. And thus we are attuned to a living Midrash, offered to the ear in the form that it was known and recited by select individuals.

Piyut thus gathers all these strata of Scripture and Midrash (both language and ideas and forms) and constitutes a new *primary condition* for their public presentation in the sacred context of statutory worship. Now the new teacher of tradition is the *ḥazan*, who creatively collates and reformulates the prior traditions and sings them before a congregation in prayer—in poetic lines and stanzas; with end rhymes and internal echoes; through deft riddles or dramatic dialogues; and via strategic refrains, complex syntax, and verbal conjunctions that enchain words and ideas in tonal and rhythmic patterns. Everything depended on the virtuosity of the *paytan* and his reception and revision of older forms or productions. Indeed his voice is primary—his voice alone. The authoritative voice of Scripture is melded with the authentic teachings of the sages (strikingly unacknowledged, against rabbinic precedent), and rearticulated in the particular poetic manner of the precentor. Hence the congregation receives the wisdom of the past from this living source—and thereby the cantor is, in a vital and dramatic way, the *primary source and resource of the rabbinic tradition*. We are thus witness to a new moment of cultural pedagogy—a new moment for Scripture and tradition both, produced in the sacred domain of rabbinic life: the synagogue. Hereby, the oral tradition becomes song and prayer; and learning and prayer are integrated, all in a manner constitutive of and singular to Judaism.

In the introductory comments, the linguistic dynamic of *langue–parole* was proposed in order to shed structural light on the processes of creative speech-acts in a literary culture that plumbed the resources of Scripture for untold and unexpressed possibilities. At this point, further benefit may accrue from another linguistic dynamic: the relationship between the signifier and the signified in the several strata under review.[79]

Briefly put, the compositional level of Scripture purports to be 'straightforward', with the words and terms signifying a certain reality (the signified). That is, the world *of* the text points to a world *beyond* it—and such references create the realm of public discourse of Scripture. Texts variously refer to the created world (as a matter of fact or poetic figure), to historical events (as occurrences and as memories), and to experiences (as national or personal). Various means are used to this end, and it may require some careful interpretation to assess the purport of the words (lexically or figuratively)—but the point is that the language of Scripture is pointed outward, and the task of reading is to determine just what the signifiers signify. The question of what is meant translates into the issue of what is being referred to. The resources of a passage are 'used up', so to say, in this exegetical assessment and evaluation (*even if* one could re-read it differently).

With Midrash, matters are different. There is now presumed to be a 'surplus of sense' or a deeper resonance to the compositional language of Scripture. The world of the text is believed to encode something further, something quite different—be it supplementary, or tangential, or in a different key altogether (thus words can be read pleonastically, and add something; allusively, and refer to something; or allegorically, and thus transfer sense to another plane of reference). In such cases, there is now a disjunction between the signifier and the signified, but the correlation must be retained and these markers are essential: word x means or signifies y, via a whole series of hermeneutic procedures. Midrash cannot allow these levels to collapse or disappear from view, for then the distinction between the written and oral registers would be lost or obscured. And because written Scripture is of a divine

---

[79] This well-known pair, formulated by de Saussure with the rubrics *signifiant–signifié*, is also known by the terms *signans–signatum* and *sêmainon–sêmainomenon*.

origin (in one inspirational way or another), it is not ordinary speech but can 'mean' again and again—each additional exposition of the surplus or superfluity of sense is 'another matter' of scriptural largesse. Hence the meaning of Scripture cannot be used up, as it were (even if it can be misused), and the great collections of tradition display the authoritative possibilities of signification that any given element may have. The tradition lives off these scriptural significations, but it is founded upon the primary signifiers of Scripture. The collections string the possibilities together, and have a simultaneity as the corpus of tradition—even though they are only actualized as separate acts of interpretation (for value, belief, or action).

But *piyut* is different still. The signifiers of Scripture are everywhere in evidence and variously employed, but their signification is paramount in this rabbinic liturgy. And this means that the scriptural signifiers may be submerged into the poetry, and only discernible via allusions in this signified matter—the midrashic content of the liturgy; and this also points to a significant reversal, insofar as the latter is now the primary signification. Similarly, the old scriptural signifiers may also only allude to the midrashic materials, being adduced for the purpose of an indirect signification; and this points to a different kind of reversal, insofar as the new signifiers are the older proofs of midrashic signification, which now assume a primary function. Thus, there is a one-way interrelationship between a signifier and its signified in Scripture—marked by the codes of ordinary understanding and convention; there is a striking transformation of this relationship in Midrash—under the signs of exegetical correlation and convention; and the poetry of *piyut* introduces a vibrant two-way interrelationship between these linguistic markers—whereby one can allude to the other, back and forth, with this interchange thickening the texture of associations and resonances.[80] There is thus no obvious sense in which meaning is exhausted, but rather a bounty of features is displayed and presented. This is tradition in the actuality of its massive re-significations, whereby elements are interconnected and blended into one whole. It is not the list-anthology of Midrash, but an eclectic ensemble of rhetoric and significance. In the process, tradition becomes a dramatic, vocal 'Now'—a collocation of voices reformulated in the mouth of a *ḥazan*. He is the human encyclopaedia of an endlessly signifying Scripture.

*

With all this in mind, I shall conclude with a proof-text—a coda that draws together the content of the foregoing paragraphs and the preceding examples. A concise and characteristic case in point returns us to a *midrash* on the scriptural law of the red heifer cited earlier, and in turn to a bi-colon based on it in the *piyut* 'Atsulat omen' by Rabbi Elazar ben Killir.[81] The biblical phrase at issue is *veyikḥu eleikha parah adumah*, 'And they shall bring to you a red heifer' (Num. 19: 2). The ostensible topic is God's command to Moses to have the Israelites bring a red heifer to Moses,

---

[80] Cf. Gian Bagio Conte, *The Rhetoric of Imitation: Genre and Poetic Memory in Virgil and Other Latin Poets* (Ithaca, NY, 1986), 75.   [81] In *Seder avodat yisra'el* (above, n. 29), 690 (end of §5).

whereas the exegetical issue concerns the full or implied import of this directive, formulated in the future tense. After the *midrash* cites the key lemma, it quotes this interpretative tradition: 'Rabbi Yosi ben Rabbi Haninah taught: [The words of Scripture] hinted [*ramzu*] that all the heifers would become null [*shekol haparot beteilot*], but yours [alone] would remain [*veshelekha kayamet*].' As discussed above, this teaching is apparently based on a tradition about the enduring viability and validity of the ashes of Moses' heifer in the world to come;[82] and as also noted, the term *remez* is used to mark a putative hint in Scripture—referring to something believed to be encoded in the manifest words of the text. We thus have a clearly signifying verse in Scripture which is taken to signify something else—a hint at the surface for a deeper content. Rabbi Yosi serves as the agent of this new signification.

Centuries later, Rabbi Elazar ben Killir has these matters in mind, but renders the prose of Midrash into the poetry of *piyut*, and in so doing also provides a clearer pedagogical explication. He sings:

> *rumaz biveyikḥu eleikha heyot parato mutmedet*
> *shekol haparot kalot veshelekha la'ad omedet*
>
> It was hinted in *And they shall take to you*, since his heifer was eternal,
> that all the heifers shall waste away, but yours shall endure forever.

Once again, the contrast is between the enduring viability of (the ashes of) Moses' heifer, as against all others. But note Rabbi Elazar's version, and how it accords with the paytanic stratum of rabbinic culture. First and foremost, the biblical lemma is incorporated into the first line of the bi-colon, and does not stand separate from its midrashic explication. The 'hint' of Scripture is thus primary, and the drama of an alternative signification is enunciated from the outset. Second, the poet does not adduce the sage Rabbi Yosi, but presents the teaching without attribution, as if it were his own. Just he is the voice of new significations; just he is the mediator of meaning. His revision affects the pedagogy, as well; for the old *midrash* does not explain what induced Moses to draw a hint from the words of the divine command. Presumably, it was the unexpected future form of the verb (*veyikḥu*) that stimulated him to reflection and inference on this matter. But that does not explain why Moses took the verbal form to hint at the future viability of the heifer. Rabbi Elazar resolves the conundrum by inserting an epexegetical phrase that explains this issue to the audience: Moses understood the hint 'because *his* heifer' was of an enduring kind. Note that the *ḥazan* introduces his clarification parenthetically—after adducing the reference to the hints of Scripture, but before he recites a version of what Moses 'heard' in the words spoken to him; and note also that his explanation refers obliquely to Moses' heifer ('*his* heifer')—which highlights the fact that the remark is directed to the congregation. According to the *ḥazan*, then, Moses drew the infer-

---

[82] The main text used by Mandelbaum (*Pesikta de Rav Kahana*, i. 72 ff.) has *kayamot*; I have corrected it in accordance with the grammar and various manuscripts adduced in the apparatus; the verb *batel* connotes wasting away or ceasing to exist (cf. Mishnah *Avot* 5: 21).

ence he did precisely because he knew about the special nature of his heifer. Like Rabbi Yosi, Rabbi Elazar ben Killir depicts the words of the hint as a direct address to Moses; but the poet clarifies the significance of what was signified in secondary referential terms.

What also distinguishes Rabbi Elazar's version is his poetic technique. This is first evident in the preceding comment, which he introduces with the term *heyot* ('since'). In so doing, he uses a word that alludes to the idea of 'existence'[83]—which is precisely the issue stressed by the verb *mutmedet* ('continuously existing') at the end of the line. Other poetic features occur in the next colon, as well. For example, the adverb *kol* ('all', inherited from the original *midrash*) now sets up a phonetic counterpoint to the new verb *kalot* ('waste away'), which replaces Rabbi Yosi's somewhat ambiguous *beteilot* ('shall be null'); and in the same vein, the *paytan* replaces the term *kayemet* ('endure') with the more explicit legal phrase *la'ad omedet* ('remain forever')[84]—which also rhymes with its thematic ballast *mutmedet*. Thus, Rabbi Elazar poeticizes and explains the midrashic teaching at one and the same time, even as his larger purpose is to explain the biblical text in terms of its implied or hidden significance.

This example shows, succinctly and richly, how Rabbi Elazar has integrated the prior strata of the tradition and rendered them in a new poetic form. He teaches a 'hint' of 'Scripture' taught in the '*midrash*' by Rabbi Yosi in a poetically accessible way, taking his audience into account as a master pedagogue. In two short colons, this great *hazan* shows himself to be a skilled poet (who uses rhyme, metre, and assonance), with precise recall of the tradition (citing Scripture and Midrash), and able to proclaim it with exemplary clarity (through technical terms, parenthetical comments, and verbal substitutions). But the overriding point is that all this is expressed in one voice—his. Being a voice of voices, the synagogue *hazan* is the new spokesman of rabbinic culture; and his liturgical teachings are the new setting for public education. His formulations authorize national memory, and declaim, in conjunction with the language of prayer, the new–old possibilities of midrashic instruction. He becomes the new arbiter of significance and signification before God.

[83] The etymology of *heyot* is unclear; if it is related to the existential verb 'to be', *hayah*, the derived sense is 'being as'; if it is related to the interrogative *heh* ('where?'), it would then connote something like 'whereas' (cf. *hainu*, 'that is'). Withal, the allusion-pun is palpable.

[84] I find that Menahem Schmelzer has already observed this change in language; see his 'Some Examples of Poetic Reformulations of Biblical and Midrashic Passages in Liturgy and Piyyut', in B. Safran and E. Safran (eds.), *Porat Yosef: Studies Presented to Rabbi Dr Joseph Safran* (Hoboken, NJ, 1992), 219 ff. He notes that the shift is from rabbinic to biblical language—which complements my point.

SEVEN

THE MOURNERS FOR ZION AND THE SUFFERING MESSIAH
Pesikta rabati 34—Structure, Theology, and Context

PHILIP ALEXANDER

AN UNUSUAL HOMILY

Pesikta rabati 34, on the eschatological vindication of the Mourners for Zion, is one of the most remarkable homilies in one of the most remarkable of the rabbinic *midrashim*.[1] It belongs to a series of *piskaot*, or 'chapters', composed for the seven 'Sabbaths of Consolation' following the Ninth of Av. This liturgical setting is important and gives the *piska* a polemical edge: its rhetoric is strong, challenging the congregation to identify with the Mourners so as to be sure of sharing in their end-time reward. Within the homilies in *Pesikta rabati* associated with the Ninth of Av (26–37), Piskaot 34–37 have long been regarded as forming a distinctive group. Certainly 34 and 36–37 hang together thematically in a notably coherent way, but, as Goldberg has argued, we should probably detach 35.[2] Yet we should be careful not to harmonize the three related *piskaot* too systematically together: despite their

---

[1] *A Synoptic Edition of Pesiqta Rabbati Based upon All Extant Manuscripts and the Editio Princeps*, ed. Rivka Ulmer, 3 vols. (Lanham, Md., 2009) is now the standard edition, but being synoptic, it does not make editorial decisions. The older edition by M. Friedmann, *Pesiqta Rabbati: Midrasch für den Fest-Cyclus und die ausgezeichneten Sabbathe* (Vienna, 1880; repr. Tel Aviv, 1963) remains useful in this regard, and for its notes. *Pesikta Rabbati: Discourses for Feasts, Fasts, and Special Sabbaths*, trans. W. Braude, 2 vols. (New Haven, Conn., 1968), is the standard English translation. It is a tour de force, offering a fine reading of a very difficult text, but it should be used with caution in close exegesis, because it is so paraphrastic. Arnold Goldberg, *Erlösung durch Leiden: Drei rabbinische Homilien über die Trauernden Zions und den leidenden Messias Efraim (PesR 34. 36. 37)* (Frankfurt am Main, 1978) provides an edition specifically of Piska 34 (based on MS Parma 3122 and the Prague *editio princeps*) with a valuable German translation and commentary. Goldberg earlier devoted a study to Piska 35: *Ich komme und wohne in deiner Mitte: Eine rabbinische Homilie zu Sacharja 2,14 (PesR 35)* (Frankfurt am Main, 1977). Translations in this essay generally follow Braude, but with modifications. For a further bibliography on *Pesikta rabati* see Günter Stemberger, *Introduction to Talmud and Midrash*, 2nd edn. (Edinburgh, 1996), 296–302.

[2] Note, inter alia, how Piska 35 seems to offer an alternative homily for the fifth Sabbath of Consolation, based on an alternative *haftarah* (Zech. 2: 14): *Pesiqta Rabbati*, ed. Ulmer, vol. i, p. xxii.

striking agreements it is not at all obvious that they are by the same *darshan* (homilist). Significant differences include the fact that while 36 adopts an astonishingly universalistic stance—its messiah bears the sins of *the world*—34 focuses in more traditional fashion on the redemption of *Israel*. These *piskaot* have received a lot of scholarly comment, from Dalman, Bamberger, Goldberg, Fishbane, and others, and in particular their doctrine of the suffering and atoning messiah has engendered sharp debate.[3] While we would no longer be as confident as Scholem in identifying political messianism as normative for Judaism, there can be little point in denying that the ideas adumbrated here are not mainstream: one has only to compare them with the messianism of a core text like the Amidah to make the point.[4]

CHRISTOLOGY

The parallels with Christology are obvious, and the question of Christian influence inevitably arises. Christianity may be somewhere in the background, but I am inclined to agree with Fishbane that the doctrine advocated here can just as easily be seen as an inner-Jewish development. We must not allow apologetics to lull us into thinking that Judaism after 70 CE became uninterested in theology or theologically impoverished: the theological richness and creativity of later Judaism remained undimmed.[5] After all, as Christians have always argued, the Christian doctrine of the atonement can be rooted in Jewish tradition. Our homilists could easily have tapped into the sources on which Christianity drew. Much of their doctrine is grounded in exegesis. One has only to acknowledge Isaiah 53 as messianic in order to derive their key ideas straight from Scripture. That said, however, it

---

[3] Gustaf Dalman, *Der leidende und der sterbende Messias der Synagogue* (Berlin, 1888); Bernard Bamberger, 'A Messianic Document of the Seventh Century', *Hebrew Union College Annual*, 15 (1940), 425–31; Arnold Goldberg, *Erlösung durch Leiden*; Michael Fishbane, *The Exegetical Imagination: On Jewish Thought and Theology* (Cambridge, Mass., 1998), 73–85. Most recently see the perceptive study by Peter Schäfer, *The Jewish Jesus: How Judaism and Christianity Shaped Each Other* (Princeton, NJ, 2012), 236–72. I saw this too late to take account of it in the present essay, which was prepared some time ago. I hope in the future to return to this subject and engage with some of the important points Schäfer makes.

[4] Gershom Scholem, *The Messianic Idea in Judaism* (New York, 1972), particularly the lead essay in the volume, from which it takes its name. Scholem's sharp contrast between the political messiah of Judaism and the spiritual messiah of Christianity has been as influential as it has been misleading. For a comprehensive critique see Moshe Idel, *Messianic Mystics* (New Haven, Conn., 1998), though Idel concentrates on medieval and post-medieval sources and does not discuss our text. Idel comments on the influence of Zionism on Scholem's view, but there is more to it, surely, than that. There seems to be a kind of 'blindness' on the part of Jewish scholars to the Jewish doctrine of the suffering messiah, because it looks so Christian, and therefore, by implication, is inauthentically Jewish—a blindness not helped by Christian apologists and missionaries seizing on it as the true messianic teaching of Judaism, a claim equally untenable. I offer some remarks on typologies of Jewish messianism in 'The Rabbis and Messianism', in Markus Bockmuehl and James Carleton Paget (eds.), *Redemption and Resistance: The Messianic Hopes of Jews and Christians* (London, 2007), 227–44.

[5] Fishbane, *Exegetical Imagination*, 208 n. 48.

would be foolish to neglect Christian theology as a hermeneutical tool for analysing our texts. Seen in Christian terms, they seem to advocate a form of substitutionary atonement, or even more precisely of penal substitution. That position has been exhaustively debated and analysed within Christian thought, and its strengths and weaknesses are well known.[6] Knowledge of these Christian debates can help us explore our texts theologically and assess how well our homilists have articulated their position. From this perspective it is obvious that some aspects of their exposition remain rudimentary. Thus our *darshanim* are vague on the person of the messiah. They sense that if the messiah is to perform the mighty work of redemption assigned to him, then he must be someone special. That is why, I would suggest, Piska 34 claims that his merit is equal to that of the entire household in heaven. Yet the messiah is not an angel; he is a human soul, like all the other souls who are waiting to be born. But is he 'sinless'? Our homilists skirt round the point. The other souls are seen as (potential) sinners, and, foreseeing that they will sin, God can only allow them to be born if the messiah *in advance* undertakes to atone for their sins; but is the messiah, then, different, and if so, how and why? Is he himself sinless, and would it matter theologically if he wasn't? Key questions are left hanging in the air. One senses that our homilists, like Paul in Romans, are struggling to expound ideas that are new to them, ideas that they have not yet fully thought through; but what they offer is serious theological reflection, and it demands a serious theological response.

Incidentally, it is only when we classify their views in Christian terms that we can see how problematic direct Christian influence on them would be. If they are indeed advocating some form of penal substitution, then, assuming they lived in the East,[7] that was hardly the standard Christian doctrine of the atonement there; the *Christus victor* position was much more prevalent. Penal substitution is strongly associated with Western Latin theology (the influence on it of Roman jurisprudence has long been recognized). One of its earliest advocates was the Roman lawyer Tertullian, but even in the Latin West it was nowhere near fully developed till Anselm's *Cur Deus Homo*, and it arguably did not become a widely held Christian view till the Reformation. There is no single Christian understanding of the atoning death of Christ, and when making comparisons we should not assume

---

[6] The literature is vast, but for a preliminary orientation the following are helpful: Laurence W. Grensted, *A Short History of the Doctrine of the Atonement* (Manchester, 1920); Henry E. W. Turner, *The Patristic Doctrine of Redemption: A Study of the Development of the Doctrine in the First Five Centuries* (London, 1952); Gustaf Aulén, *Christus Victor: An Historical Study of the Three Main Types of the Idea of the Atonement* (London, 1970).

[7] Jacob Mann's idea that the *darshan* of Piska 34 was an 'Italian Agadist who settled in Jerusalem in the first half of the ninth century, where he "joined the mourners for Zion"' (*The Jews in Egypt and Palestine under the Fatimid Caliphs*, 2 vols. (Oxford, 1969), i. 47–8) is speculative. If it were true, then it might open the possibility that he could have been influenced specifically by western Latin theology, but the point remains that he would have had to have been singularly well versed in Christian thought to have picked up the doctrine of penal substitution in Italy in the 9th cent.

that there is.[8] In theological analysis nuance is all; identifying vague similarities will simply not do.

STRUCTURE

Piska 34 is an extraordinarily rich text, which certainly deserves another close reading. But first, a few words about its structure, integrity, and exegetical method. It falls into five unequal sections:

1. The first comprises the homiletic base-text, viz. Zechariah 9: 9, a verse long held to be messianic. Friedmann suggested this may have been the *haftarah* to Deuteronomy 21: 10–25: 19, the *parashah* for the fifth of the seven Sabbaths of Consolation.

2. The second brings the base-text abruptly into relationship with Isaiah 61: 9. This intersecting verse is linked only perfunctorily to the base-verse by the formula 'this is that which was said in the holy spirit by Isaiah' (*zo hi shene'emerah beruah hakodesh al yedei yeshayah*). This old exegetical formula (already found in the New Testament),[9] was originally used to assert that some event known to the speaker and his audience (*zo*) was the fulfilment of a particular prophecy (*shene'emerah beruah hakodesh*). Here, however, it serves merely to assert a link between two verses of Scripture,[10] or to claim a connection between the events they predict, the nature of which is far from clear. It is typical of late Midrash to use classic hermeneutical formulae in this vague way. The key biblical phrase in this section is 'Mourners for Zion' (*avelei tsiyon*), derived from Isaiah 61: 3.[11] This verse is not directly quoted, to

---

[8] On the face of it, there is one very major difference between the Jewish and the Christian doctrine: on the Christian side the messiah dies, whereas on the Jewish neither the messiah's, nor the Mourners' deaths figure in the work of atonement. But the difference may not be quite as clear-cut as it first seems. On the Jewish side it would have been possible in principle to have constructed a doctrine around atoning death: the Akedah or a theology of martyrdom could have pointed the way. For the former, see Shalom Spiegel, *The Last Trial: On the Legends and Lore of the Command to Abraham to Offer Isaac as a Sacrifice: The Akedah* (New York, 1967); Leroy A. Huizenga, *The New Isaac: Tradition and Intertextuality in the Gospel of Matthew* (Leiden, 2009); for the latter, see Jan Willem van Henten, *The Maccabean Martyrs as Saviours of the Jewish People: A Study of 2 and 4 Maccabees* (Leiden, 1997); Daniel Boyarin, *Dying for God: Martyrdom and the Making of Christianity and Judaism* (Stanford, Calif., 1999). And on the Christian side some have argued that the sacrificial aspect of the atonement should not be overstressed. C. F. D. Moule, for example, suggested that 'the actual death of Christ was not necessary to atonement; "if (*per impossibile*) Christ's obedience could have been total and absolute without his dying, this would have constituted atonement"' (quoted by Willam Horbury, 'Charles Francis Digby Moule', in Ron Johnston (ed.), *Proceedings of the British Academy*, vol. 161: *Biographical Memoirs of Fellows, VIII* (Oxford, 2009), 293–4, with the references to Moule's works there cited). The comment is all the more astonishing given that Moule was a noted evangelical.

[9] Acts 2: 16. The formula is actually not common in rabbinic literature and of the ten attested examples half are found in *Pesikta rabati*.

[10] Note Braude's paraphrase: 'This verse [Zech. 9: 9] is to be considered in the light of what Isaiah was inspired by the holy spirit to say [in Isa. 61: 9]' (*Pesikta Rabbati*, trans. Braude, ii. 668).

[11] The genitive could grammatically be either objective ('Mourners *for* Zion'), or locative ('Mourners

be sure, but it is implicit in the quotation of Isaiah 61: 9. It is vital to realize that our *darshan* expects his audience to have *the whole* of Isaiah 61 in mind; our homily relates intertextually to *the whole* of this chapter, not just atomistically to the one verse quoted. The second section is brought to a formal close by restating the intersecting verse: *lakhen ne'emar venoda bagoyim zaram* (Braude: 'All the foregoing commentary is derived by meditation upon the verse "And their arm shall be known among the nations"').

3. The third section is demarcated from the second by the formula *davar aḥer* ('another interpretation'). This reintroduces the base-text in the form of an abbreviated lemma, one aspect of which, the meaning of the word 'king', attracts a brief comment. Having thus reminded the audience of the base-text, the *darshan* abruptly brings in a second intersecting verse—Zephaniah 3: 8, a phrase from which the divine injunction to 'wait for me [*ḥaku li*]' is used to generate another substantial development. Waiting for God is interpreted in an idiosyncratic way as a call to a life of penitence, prayer, and eager expectation for the coming of the messiah—like the Mourners for Zion. 'Waiting for God' had apparently a special meaning for the Mourners: it was part of their sectarian idiolect. This third section is brought to a close by quoting a dictum of Rabbi Yannai in the name of Rav, though this may be a secondary addition (see below).

4. The relationship between the second and third sections, on the one hand, and the base-text, on the other, remains tantalisingly vague until we come to the fourth. This opens abruptly by re-lemmatizing the base-text and expounding it at length. It is only in the course of this exposition that the base-verse's relevance to the two intersecting verses finally becomes clear.

5. In the fifth and final section Psalm 132: 18 is slipped in as a coda to the whole: 'His enemies will I [God] clothe with shame, but upon himself shall his crown shine.' Psalm 132: 18–19 is an explicitly messianic text in which God promises that he will raise up in Jerusalem 'a horn ... unto David' and order a lamp for his 'anointed' (*mashiaḥ*). The reference to the *messiah's* enemies echoes the reference to the *Mourners'* enemies at the beginning of the homily, and forges a parallelism between them and the messiah which is, as we shall see, of fundamental importance to the theology of our *darshan*.

The composition cleverly exploits the same rhetorical dynamics as the classic *petiḥta*, though it lacks the typical *petiḥta* formulae.[12] A first subject is introduced briefly, in a major key, so to speak, only to be immediately dismissed and a second subject brought in, in a minor key, and developed at length. The question of how

---

in Zion'). The former is the correct translation, even in Isa. 61: 3. The latter, additional sense, however, came in when the phrase was used for the Karaite community in Jerusalem, on which see below.

[12] On homiletic structure, see Doris Lenhard, *Die rabbinische Homilie: Ein formanalytischer Index* (Frankfurt am Main, 1998), and the bibliography cited there.

this second subject relates to the first grows in the listener's mind as the development proceeds. The question becomes even more persistent when, having been abruptly reminded of the first subject, the listener is plunged into a third subject, also in a minor key, the relevance of which to the first subject is equally unclear. The question is finally resolved in a concluding passage in which, returning to the home key, the composer recapitulates and finally develops the first subject, in the process demonstrating the connection with the other two. An elegant little coda, echoing a motif at the opening of the piece, rounds the composition off satisfactorily with a sense of *inclusio*. Our homilist thus exploits with admirable skill the aesthetics of juxtaposition, delay, tension, and resolution to create a highly artful work.

TEXTUAL INTEGRITY

Though there are some significant variants between the major manuscripts, there is little to cause concern as to the textual integrity of Piska 34. There are, to be sure, tensions within it. Section 2 sets the vindication of the Mourners for Zion during the seven years before the messiah's manifestation. It is actual events, above all the fact that the Mourners for Zion walk unharmed, 'as a man with his friend', among the angels of destruction whom God will unleash in increasing numbers to wreak havoc on the world, that will bring Israel to her senses, and convince her that the Mourners were right. In section 3, however, the vindication takes place at the last Great Assize: God himself dramatically enters the court, not as a judge but as a witness on the Mourners' behalf, to convict their fellow Jews of their error. There is also some tension between section 4, which categorically states that the merit of the messiah covers the 'wicked', and sections 2 and 3, which, taken on their own, seem to envisage only 'the righteous' as enjoying the rewards of the messianic age. It is not impossible that this problem has arisen through a secondary attempt to appease the Torah scholars (= 'the righteous'; see below). One might also wonder whether the short passage in section 3 quoting a dictum of Rav in the name of Rabbi Yannai is original, since it does not quite fit the context, though it currently does serve a function, namely to round off the third section (see above). But these are minor problems. If different sources have been used, they have, as we have seen, been blended into an effective, well-rounded homily.

THE *DARSHAN*'S METHOD

The *darshan* develops his views exegetically. He uses the exegetical technique of *al tikrei* (literally: 'do not read') at two crucial junctures in his argument: in Isaiah 61: 9 he rereads *zaram* ('their seed' = offspring) as *zero'am* ('their arm'), the arm being the arm of God stretched out to defend them; and in Isaiah 57: 15 he rereads *et daka* as *iti daka*, to yield the sense: 'he that is of a contrite [and humble spirit] [= the Mourners] is with Me [God]', in solidarity with God's grief for the destruction of the Temple. He implicitly uses the technique of *ribui* ('inclusion') to argue from Psalm 132: 18 that just as the Mourners suffered with the messiah, so they will reign with him.[13] In a piece of allegorical exegesis worthy of Philo, he seems to take the ass in Zechariah 9: 9 that the king messiah will ride as allegorically symbolizing the wicked, whom he will steer into the straight path.[14] An apparently redundant *hu* ('he') in the same text (*tsadik venosha hu*) proves to him that there will only be one messiah. But for the most part his exegesis is straightforward, and involves no hermeneutical gymnastics.

Two biblical texts were particularly important to him. The first was Isaiah 61. As I have already noted, though only one verse of this is explicitly quoted the whole of the chapter is implied. It is from here that he gets his phrase 'Mourners for Zion'. It is vital to grasp how exactly our homilist understands this text. He is not using it simply expressively, that is to say as a convenient quarry for words and phrases. He actually believes that the 'Mourners for Zion' mentioned in the biblical text are his own group. Isaiah is not talking of his own times but, in the power of the spirit, addressing the homilist's community across the centuries. This surely reveals a sectarian mentality. As the Qumran covenanters, the early Christians, and many similar groups show, sects have a tendency to write themselves into the *Heilsgeschichte*, and the more directly the better. The second biblical text which has had an immense influence on his thought is Isaiah 53. That this forms the biblical basis for his doctrine of the suffering messiah is strongly supported by a parallel passage in Piska 37. Isaiah 53 is nowhere directly quoted but there are unmistakeable allusions to it. The homilist is almost certainly reading the description of the messiah in Zechariah 9: 9 as *oni* ('afflicted') in the light of the use of the same root to describe the sufferings of the Servant (Isa. 53: 4, *me'uneh*, 'subjected to affliction'). There is also a possibility that Isaiah 53 has played a part in his understanding of the description of the messiah in Zechariah 9: 9 as *tsadik* ('righteous'). Braude, with typical acuteness, has sensed that our homilist probably took *tsadik venosha* in Zechariah 9: 9 in a very particular sense, but his rendering, 'he is submissive and yet he promises salvation' is problematic.[15] Our homilist may have understood *tsadik* here in the light of its use in Isaiah 53: 11 for the Servant. There it is commonly understood to describe the Servant as vindicated by God against his enemies. *Nosha* in parallel to *tsadik* could easily be understood in a similar way: hence, 'vindicated and delivered'. The phrase could lie behind our homilist's reference to God's eschatological vindication of the messiah, and his delivery from prison.

---

[13] This is how Braude understands the passage, probably correctly: '*And upon himself shall his crown shine* [Ps. 132: 18]—the *And* at the beginning of this clause indicates that the crown will shine upon himself, and also on those who are one with him.' (*Pesikta Rabbati*, trans. Braude, ii. 668). All that the Hebrew actually says is: 'And *upon him shall his crown shine*—upon him and upon those who are like him.'

[14] The text is very difficult: see below.

[15] Braude reads this sense back into the phrase from his understanding of the *darshan*'s comment on it, but one despairs of making clear sense of the comment. See below.

THE MOURNERS FOR ZION OF PISKA 34

The Life of Mourning

Though his homily is all about the Mourners for Zion, our *darshan* does not formally tell us who they are; he assumes we know. However, some things can be deduced about them from what he says. The Mourners live in a *perpetual* state of mourning for the destruction of the Temple, the aim of which is to bring the redemption—the reversal of the condition that caused the mourning. Mourning for the loss of the Temple is inextricably bound up with praying for its restoration; the Mourners are, therefore, a messianic movement, but their weapons are spiritual—not swords but prayer and self-denial. All Israel may rise each morning to beseech God's mercy, but the Mourners for Zion pray for Israel's deliverance 'morning, evening, and noon'. I see no reason not to take this in a literal sense as implying a distinctive liturgy of mourning which the Mourners prayed three times a day, at the statutory times of service.

There is a hint that mourning also manifested itself in asceticism: the Mourners put the need for mourning 'before the gratifying of any other desires they had'. The implication is that they denied themselves a normal life, the fulfilment of the normal desires of the flesh—food, sleep, and sexual intercourse. That abstention from sex was involved is suggested by an allusion to the Fall of the Watchers: Israel tries to justify herself before God by arguing that if Azza and Azza'el, 'whose bodies were fire, sinned when they came down to earth, would not we of flesh and blood sin all the more?'. God retorts that the Mourners for Zion managed to deny themselves! The sin *par excellence* of the fallen Watchers was, of course, sexual: they allowed themselves to be seduced by the beauty of the mortal women (Gen. 6: 1–4). The apparent implication that sexual intercourse is equivalent to sin is startling. It might not be out of place in some areas of the Christian ascetic tradition, but such negative attitudes towards the body and procreation are rarer in Judaism before the Middle Ages.

Opponents I: 'Israel'

In a typically sectarian way, the Mourners see themselves as a beleaguered minority—a little flock facing a hostile world. Their opponents in Israel are described first as their 'enemies', over whom they will eventually triumph, but more often simply as 'the children of Israel', that is to say, the generality of the Jewish people. The persecution they face takes the form not of physical but of psychological abuse: it involves not martyrdom but 'mocking and scorning', 'making sport', and 'despising'. In other words, it is largely in the mind, and this makes it difficult to decide how objectively real it was. The fact that the Mourners feel it so deeply, and indeed regard bearing meekly such reproach as their contribution to the redemption of Israel, reveals the underlying shame-culture in which they lived. It would be wrong to dismiss the mockery as totally imaginary. The Mourners may have indulged in exaggerated behaviour which set them apart and made them the ready butt of ridicule.

Opponents II: 'The Righteous'

The opponents of the Mourners are also referred to, unexpectedly, as 'the righteous'. This term is defined as applying to those who are Torah-observant, or, perhaps, more precisely, Torah scholars. These at the end of time will acknowledge their failure to follow the example of the Mourners for Zion and to look for the coming of the messiah. They will weep and repent, but God will accept their repentance and reward them for their devotion to Torah. Implicit here seems to be a division of the opponents of the Mourners into those who are 'righteous' and those who are not. The righteous will repent and, because of the merit of their Torah, be allowed to enjoy the messianic kingdom. The unrighteous presumably will not, and so, according to this scenario of the end, as at Qumran, not all Israel will be saved. However, as noted earlier, this seems to conflict with the claim made later in the homily that the messiah's merit covers the wicked.

The key passage on the relationship of the Mourners to the 'righteous' is found at the beginning of the third section of the homily:

Another comment: "Rejoice greatly, O daughter of Zion, behold, your king comes", etc. [Zech. 9: 9]. He who is called 'king' is the one who will rule over the first generations and over the last generations. And the Holy One, blessed be He, proclaims to all the righteous men of every generation, and says to them: O righteous men of the world, even though the words of My Torah are pleasing to Me, yet you wait only for My Torah—you do not wait for My Kingdom.[16] Hence I made an oath with regard to anyone who waits for My Kingdom, that I Myself shall bear witness on his behalf, as it is said, "Therefore wait for me, says the Lord, until the day I rise up to bear witness" [Zeph. 3: 8].

The end-time is in view: the king messiah has come to exercise his universal rule, in accordance with Zechariah 9: 9. The dead have been raised, both the earlier and later generations. The final assize is convened, but paradoxically God enters it not as judge but as witness, to vindicate the Mourners for Zion and rebuke the 'righteous' for not having lived a life of 'waiting' for God's kingdom, that is to say, of longing and praying for the coming of God's king. Torah study is good, but mourning for Zion is better. This and the paragraphs that follow dramatically report the 'controversy' that will take place between God and the righteous on the day of judgment, in which God will finally convince the righteous that the only sure path to redemption was through mourning and self-affliction, through entreating God to send his messiah. The language is accommodating, even eirenic—there is no explicit denigration of Torah study and Torah observance; they make a man

---

[16] The reading *ḥ(y)kytm* (*ḥikitem*, 'you have waited') is surely superior to *ḥybytm* (*ḥibitem*, 'you have loved'), since it picks up the following *ḥikah*, which in turn picks up the *ḥakeh* of the proof-text.

righteous, and ensure that he will be raised from the dead and enjoy the world to come—but it is not Torah observance but 'mourning' that brings the redemption.

Who are the 'righteous' here? The most obvious candidates are the rabbis of the rabbinic movement. It would be hard to exaggerate how problematic the doctrine propounded here is from the standpoint of rabbinic theology. The contrast between 'waiting for Torah' and 'waiting for God's kingdom' would make no sense whatsoever to the rabbis, because they held that it is precisely through waiting for Torah that God's kingdom would come. To take upon oneself the 'yoke of Torah' is precisely to take the 'yoke of God's kingship'.[17] The nature of rabbinic messianism is complicated, and I cannot go into it in detail here; however, a few points need to be made to put our passage into context. As I have argued elsewhere, the rabbinic movement after 70 CE played down its eschatological inheritance from Second Temple Judaism, partly in reaction to a series of disastrous wars in which messianism may well have played a baleful role, partly in reaction to the rise of Christianity, an ever more successful messianic movement with its roots in Second Temple Judaism, from which Rabbinic Judaism constantly strove to distance itself.[18] The emphasis in rabbinic sources of the second and third centuries is on the observance of the Torah here and now, the realization of God's kingdom through the scrupulous fulfilment of the *mitsvot*. When, in later amoraic times, the rabbinic movement, for reasons that need not detain us here, began to re-engage with traditional messianism, it did so on its own terms: the only way in which Israel could merit the messiah was by studying and observing Torah.

This rabbinic form of messianism is clearly articulated in a document of roughly the same date as our homily—the mini-apocalypse at the end of Targum Song of Songs (7: 13–8: 10). The rabbinic credentials of this late Targum can be in no doubt: it is effectively a paean of praise for the rabbinic academy at Tiberias.[19] The link it forges between study of Torah and the bringing of the messiah could not be clearer. Israel in exile says: 'Let us rise early in the morning and let us go to the House of Assembly and the House of Study. Let us search in the scroll of the Torah and see whether the time of redemption has come for the people of the House of Israel (who are compared to the vine), when they will be redeemed from their exile. Let us ask the sages whether the merit of the righteous, who are as full of precepts as pomegranates, is revealed before the Lord, and whether the time has come to go up to Jerusalem, there to give praise to the God of heaven, and to offer burnt offerings and holy sacrifices' (Tg. S. of S. 7: 13). The following verse makes the same point with even greater clarity: 'When it shall be the good pleasure of the Lord to redeem His

---

[17] See Friederich Avemarie, *Tora und Leben: Untersuchungen zur Heilsbedeutung der Tora in der frühen rabbinischen Literatur* (Tübingen, 1996); Philip S. Alexander, 'Torah and Salvation in Tannaitic Literature', in D. A. Carson, Peter T. O'Brien, and Mark A. Seifrid (eds.), *Justification and Variegated Nomism*, vol. i: *The Complexities of Second Temple Judaism* (Grand Rapids, Mich., 2001), 261–302.

[18] Alexander, 'The Rabbis and Messianism'.

[19] See Philip S. Alexander, *The Targum of Canticles: Translated, with a Critical Introduction, Apparatus and Notes* (Collegeville, Minn., 2003).

people from exile, He will say to the king messiah: "The term of the exile is already completed, and the merit of the righteous has become as fragrant before Me as the scent of balsam. The sages of the generation are in constant attendance at the doors of the schools, diligently studying the words of the scribes and the words of the Torah. Arise now, and receive the kingdom that I have stored up for you'" (Tg. S. of S. 7: 14). Even if Israel should be poor in precepts, 'the merit of the Torah which the children study' will plead for her (Tg. S. of S. 8: 9; cf. 8: 10). And when the messiah comes he will be a mighty Torah scholar himself and will conduct in Jerusalem a great *shiur* (study session) in which hidden depths of Torah will be revealed (Tg. S. of S. 8: 1). This text resonates in an uncanny way with our *piska*. Note how the latter seems to pick up, almost ironically, the term 'righteous' in the Targum, as if to say: Yes, we agree that those who study and keep the Torah are righteous, but such righteousness on its own will not bring the messiah; the agents of the redemption are not the sages and their schools, but the Mourners for Zion and their ascetic way of life.[20]

REDEMPTIVE SUFFERING

The Suffering of the Mourners

What, then, is our homilist's theology of redemption? As I have already indicated it is not fully worked out, but certain elements of it are clear. The redemption will come not through Torah study but suffering. There are three main agents of redemption—the Mourners, God, and the messiah—and all three suffer: it is through the interaction and interconnection of their suffering that the process of redemption will be achieved. The Mourners suffer in the obvious sense that they pursue a life of asceticism and self-denial, though this is not what our homilist foregrounds but rather the distress they suffer because their fellow Israelites reject and mock them: 'The Mourners for Zion suffer great distress because it is the Children of Israel who both mock and scorn them.' To be publicly derided and not retaliate is to lose all social standing, and yet this is precisely what the Mourners did: 'they humbled their spirits, listened meekly to the abuse of their persons, keeping silent the while, and yet did not consider themselves particularly virtuous therefore.' There is a profound irony here: the mockers do not know that their own salvation depends on the Mourners not giving up. If the Mourners do not turn the other cheek, the redemption will fail.

The Suffering of God

But how exactly does the Mourners' suffering bring the messiah? An obvious answer would be that it moves God to pity: it convinces him that Israel's repentance is sincere and complete. Only if Israel longs for the redemption will she merit the

---

[20] The 'merit of the righteous' in bringing the redemption is a major theme of the Targum: see Alexander, *Targum of Canticles*.

redemption, and the sincerity of that longing can only be proved by a way of life that costs. This may be implied: why should God send the messiah, if Israel does not show any desire for him? But the actual reason that is highlighted is much more subtle—the Mourners' mourning shows solidarity with God, who, far from being a stony-hearted tyrant needing to be moved by the cries of his people, is himself already in mourning: 'Those who have waited for Me are the Mourners for Zion who grieved with Me because of My House which is destroyed and because of My Temple which is desolate. Now I bear witness for them, each of whom Scripture describes in the verse "With one that is of a contrite and humble spirit" [Isa. 57: 15]. Do not read "with one that is of a contrite . . . spirit": read rather "he that is of a contrite . . . spirit is with me".' In mourning for Zion, the Mourners are engaged in *imitatio Dei*. There is surely here an implicit contrast with the rabbinic trope of Torah study as *imitatio Dei*: God sits in heaven studying Torah, just as the scholars do on earth, and this makes Torah study the highest activity in which a Jew can engage.[21] No, suggests our homilist, God does not sit in the celestial yeshiva studying Torah with the souls of the sages; rather, he sits and mourns the destruction of his earthly House, and longs for Israel to mourn with him. God suffers in the same way as the Mourners suffer, from the indifference of Israel towards the loss of his Temple. He yearns for the sympathy of his people, and until he gets it he can see no point in restoring his earthly House.

The theme of the pathos of God is not unknown to rabbinic thought. It can be found, for example, in the astonishing Proem 24 of *Lamentations Rabbah*:

> The Holy One, blessed be He, said to the ministering angels, 'Come, let us go together and see what the enemy has done to my House.' Forthwith the Holy One, blessed be He, and the ministering angels went, Jeremiah leading the way. When the Holy One, blessed be He, saw the Temple, He said, 'Certainly this is My House and this is My resting-place into which My enemies have come, and they have done with it whatever they wished.' At that time the Holy One, blessed be He, wept and said, 'Woe is Me for My House! My children, where are you? My priests, where are you? My lovers, where are you? What shall I do with you, seeing that I warned you, but you did not repent?' The Holy One, blessed be He, said to Jeremiah, 'I am now like a man who had an only son, for whom he prepared a marriage-canopy, but he died under it. Do you feel no anguish for me and my children? Go, summon Abraham, Isaac, Jacob, and Moses from their sepulchres, for they know how to weep.'[22]

---

[21] Note, again, the Targum of Song of Songs:

> Then Israel began to speak in praise of the Sovereign of the World, and thus she said: 'My pleasure is to worship that God Who, wrapped by day in a robe white as snow, engages in [the study of] the Twenty Four Books [comprising] the Torah, the words of the Prophets, and the Writings, and [Who] by night engages in [the study of] the Six Orders of the Mishnah, and the radiance of the glory of Whose face shines like fire on account of the greatness of the wisdom and reasoning with which He discloses new meanings all day long, and He will publish them to His people on the great day.' (Tg. S. of S. 5: 10; see Alexander, *Targum of Canticles*, 155–6)

[22] Translated by A. Cohen, *Midrash Rabbah: Lamentations* (London, 1983), 41–2. For a discussion see

The idea of God's pathos here and in parallel rabbinic texts has certain similarities to what we find in our homily,[23] but I detect subtly different theological emphases. In many of the other passages the idea has been 'spun' in a way that makes it more compatible with rabbinic theology. There is a recognition of sin as the cause of the disaster, of the need for repentance, and hence, implicitly, of a return to the Torah as the basis of restoration—all of which are missing from our text, which, as we have seen, seems to rule out Torah observance as being sufficient on its own to rectify the situation. The stress in our homily appears, on the face of it, to be on inwardness of attitude rather than externality of action, a notion that comes closer to *metanoia* than *teshuvah*, and, correspondingly, puts the stress more on pure divine compassion. Suffering in and of itself appears to be redemptive.

The Suffering of the Messiah

The agent through whom God will bring salvation is the messiah, but he too suffers:

"Submissive, and yet he promises salvation" [Zech. 9: 9] describes the messiah, for when they laughed at him while he sat in prison, he submitted for the sake of Israel to the judgment imposed on him, and is therefore properly called submissive.

Why is he spoken of as "yet he promises salvation"? Because after submitting to the judgment for their sake, he said: All of you deserve extermination; nevertheless you will be saved, every one of you, by the mercy of the Holy One, blessed be He.[24]

"Afflicted, and he is riding upon an ass" describes the messiah. And why is he called afflicted? Because he was afflicted during all his years in prison while transgressors in Israel laughed at him.

Just as there is a parallelism between the Mourners and God, so there is a parallelism between the Mourners and the messiah. They suffered rejection by their fellow Israelites, but persevered because what they were doing was necessary to bring the redeemer. The messiah also endures rejection at the hands of Israel, because only thus can he atone for their sins. Where does the notion here of a suffering messiah come from? The echoes of Isaiah 53 are surely unmistakable: the messiah is the

Alan Mintz, *Hurban: Responses to Catastrophe in Hebrew Literature* (New York, 1996), 48–83; Alexander, *The Targum of Lamentations*, 34–7.

[23] Peter Kuhn, *Gottes Trauer und Klage in der rabbinischen Überlieferung (Talmud und Midrasch)* (Leiden, 1978), collects and comments on the main passages.

[24] I have simply given here Braude's translation, out of despair at producing anything that makes better sense of the text. More literally the passage could be rendered: 'Righteous [*tsadik*] and delivered [*nosha*]: this is the messiah who justifies [*matsdik*] his [God's] judgment for the sake of [*al*] Israel, and [hence] he is called "righteous" [*tsadik*]. Why is he called "delivered" [*nosha*]? Only because he justifies on their behalf [*matsdik aleihem*] the judgment. He says: "All of you are children [worthy] of extinction [*benei kela'ah*], but all of you will be delivered through the mercy of the Holy One, blessed be He!"' *Tsadik* seems to be related to the idea of *tsiduk hadin* (the justification/acceptance of divine judgment). For an alternative way of understanding of *tsadik venosha*, see above.

Suffering Servant who was despised and afflicted, but remained silent, who was taken from detention and judgment, yet bore it all for the sake of the people (see especially Isa. 53: 3–4, 7–8). There is another significant allusion to Isaiah 53 a little earlier in the homily. When the righteous at the end of days confess their sins, their language echoes Isaiah 53: 6: 'Master of the Universe, we have not acted rightly all these years—"like sheep have we gone astray [*katson ta'inu*]". And the Holy One, blessed be He, will say: "You are forgiven!"' Isaiah 53: 6 of course ends, 'And the Lord visited upon him [the Suffering Servant] the iniquity of us all'—a fact which the reader is surely meant to recall, because it suggests the basis on which the forgiveness rests.

Piskaot 36 and 37 of *Pesikta rabati*, both of which, as I have suggested, also emanated from the circles of the Mourners for Zion, confirm that this interpretation is on the right lines. In Piska 37 the patriarchs address the messiah:

'Ephraim, our true messiah, even though we are your forebears, you are greater than we because you suffered for the iniquities of our children, and terrible ordeals befell you, such ordeals as did not befall earlier generations or later ones; for the sake of Israel you became a laughing-stock and a derision among the nations of the earth; and you sat in darkness, in thick darkness, and your eyes saw no light, and your skin cleaved to your bones, and your body was as dry as a piece of wood; and your eyes grew dim from fasting, and your strength dried up like a potsherd—all these afflictions on account of the iniquities of our children, all these because of your desire to have our children benefit by that goodness which the Holy One, blessed be He, will bestow in abundance upon Israel. Yet, perhaps because of the anguish which you have suffered on their account—for your enemies put you in prison—you are displeased with them!'

He will reply: 'O patriarchs, all that I have done, I have done only for your sake and for the sake of your children, for your glory and the glory of your children, that they may benefit from the goodness which the Holy One, blessed be He, will bestow in abundance upon them—upon Israel.'

The patriarchs will say to him: 'Ephraim, our true messiah, be content with what you have done, for you have made content the mind of your maker and our minds also'.[25]

Here allusions to the Suffering Servant come thick and fast. Here we have an unambiguous statement of the doctrine of substitutionary atonement. Piska 36 expresses a similar thought: 'The Holy One, blessed be He, contemplated the messiah and his works before the world was created, and then under His throne of glory He put away His messiah until the time of the generation in which he will appear.' Also stored beneath the throne are the other souls who will one day be born in human bodies, but God foresees that they will sin. He tells the messiah that he cannot let these 'sinful souls' be born unless the messiah promises to take their sins upon himself and through suffering atone for them. The messiah agrees: 'Master of the Universe,' he says, 'with joy in my soul and gladness in my heart I take this suffering upon myself, provided that not one person in Israel perish.'

---

[25] *Pesikta Rabbati*, trans. Braude, ii. 685–6.

Piskaot 36 and 37 illuminate a number of cryptic passages in Piska 34. The references to 'Ephraim, the true messiah' in Piskaot 36 and 37 show that the quotation in Piska 34 of Jeremiah 31: 9, 'for I [the Lord] am become a father to Israel, and Ephraim is My first-born', discloses the name of the messiah. It is at once tempting to link the messiah called Ephraim with the doctrine of the messiah son of Joseph or the messiah of Ephraim, who, according to a widespread Jewish eschatological scenario, will come before the messiah son of David, and fall in battle fighting against the enemies of Israel.[26] He is the forerunner of the real messiah, who, of course, is not from Ephraim, but from Judah. However, Piska 36 makes it clear that Ephraim *is* the messiah son of David![27] There is no doctrine here of a dual messiahship, and indeed our homily categorically rejects it: 'What is implied by the seemingly unnecessary "he" in the words "righteous and delivered is he" [Zech. 9: 9]? That what he is in the days of the messiah, he will be in the world to come, and there will never be another beside him.' This is surely a categorical rejection of the doctrine of a slain messiah son of Joseph. Why the Davidic, Judahite messiah should be called Ephraim remains, however, a puzzle. The name is explicitly derived from Jeremiah 31: 9–10, but whether anything other than straightforward exegesis is involved is unclear.

Piska 36 also throws light on the statement in Piska 34 that the messiah's 'merit is equal to that of the entire household of heaven'. This comes as somewhat of a surprise: one might have expected the *darshan* to say that the messiah's merit equals that of God's whole household *on earth*, i.e. Israel. The concept of attributed merit is central to our homilist's doctrine of atonement. I shall return to this point in a moment. Suffice it to say here that if the merit of the messiah is equal to that of all Israel put together, then one can begin to understand how his vicarious suffering can atone for all Israel. Piska 36 provides a possible background to the statement: it claims that the messiah was created before the creation of the world. He originated in heaven, and indeed held an exalted position there; he rides on a throne of glory borne by four *ḥayot* ('living creatures'), like Ezekiel's chariot (*merkavah*), and he is set in opposition to the angelic princes of kingdoms. However, it would be wrong to suppose that he is other than human; he is not, like the heavenly redeemer Melchizedek at Qumran, an angelic figure. His origin in heaven is no different from that of other human souls, who start life in the treasury of souls beneath the throne of glory. There are echoes in our texts of the motif of the rivalry between angels and humans.[28] The messiah, like Metatron in 3 Enoch, is the celestial representative of

---

[26] Joseph Heinemann, 'The Messiah of Ephraim and the Premature Exodus of the Tribe of Ephraim', *Harvard Theological Review*, 68 (1975), 1–16 surveys the evidence.

[27] 'During the seven-year period preceding the coming of the son of David, iron beams will be brought and loaded upon his neck until the Messiah's body is bent low.... It was because of the ordeal of the son of David that David wept, saying, *My strength is dried up like a potsherd* [Ps. 22: 16]. During the ordeal of the son of David, the Holy One, blessed be He, will say to him, "Ephraim, My true Messiah."' (*Pesikta Rabbati*, trans. Braude, ii. 680).

[28] Peter Schäfer, *Rivalität zwischen Engeln und Menschen: Untersuchungen zur rabbinischen Engelvorstellung* (Berlin, 1975).

glorified humanity. Through its heavenly messianic representative, humanity is worth in God's esteem all his angelic household put together.

The idea of merit is central to our homilist's theology, as indeed it should be, because without it a doctrine of substitutionary atonement will not work. The redeemer has to possess superordinate merit, otherwise he cannot perform the work of redemption. If he is just like everyone else, then who will redeem him? He has to earn merit through his vicarious suffering, but this he can only do if he accepts the suffering voluntarily, if it was not something he already deserved. And there has to be a way to transfer his acquired merit to sinners to cover their sins. Our homilist senses these problems, though he does not always answer them convincingly. But there is another acute theological problem, which he feels he has to tackle head-on: how does the messiah's merit relate to the widespread doctrine of the merit of the fathers? Are not the merits of Abraham and Isaac and the other patriarchs sufficient to cover the sins of Israel? Our homilist addresses this question towards the end of his homily:

Why does Scripture say 'riding upon an ass' [Zech. 9: 9]? The ass represents the wicked who have no merit of their own and can only get along by resorting to the merit of their fathers. But through the merit of the messiah, the Holy One, blessed be He, shields them <and guides them> in a straight way and redeems them,[29] as it is said, 'They shall come with weeping, and with supplications will I lead them to walk by rivers of waters, in a straight way wherein they shall not stumble: for I am become a father to Israel, and Ephraim is My first-born' [Jer. 31: 9].

Though the passage is garbled, its basic point seems clear: the merit of the messiah is greater than the merit of the patriarchs. The merit of the patriarchs lessens the divine punishment, but the merit of the messiah somehow (how precisely is not explained) leads to spiritual transformation. Piska 37 has the patriarchs acknowledge the superiority of the messiah: 'You are greater than we,' they say, 'because you suffer for the iniquities of our children, and terrible ordeals befell you, such as did not befall earlier generations or later ones.'

Who are the beneficiaries of the messiah's merit? Clearly, and logically, in the passage just quoted, it is the wicked. But what about 'the righteous' mentioned earlier? Their guilt may be less a matter of commission than omission, in particular their failure to 'wait' on God and 'mourn for Zion', but they too are sinners, even if of a lesser kind; they too have gone astray, and so their iniquities also have to be

---

[29] Again I have used Braude's translation because I can see little way of improving on it. It is impossible to avoid conjectural emendation here. To begin with we should focus on what appears to be the basic point: the messiah riding upon the ass is a symbol of the fact that he will direct the wicked in a straight path. I would suggest we should emend the text to read as follows: *rokhev al ḥamor: mipenei haresha'im she'ein lahem zekhut; haholekh holekh umazkir avot. Bizekhut shel mashiaḥ hakadosh barukh hu memagen umolikh derekh yesharah vego'el otam* ('Riding on an ass: on account of the wicked who have no merit; he who goes goes and makes mention of the Fathers. Through the merit of the messiah, however, the Holy One, blessed be He, shields, directs in a straight path, and redeems them.')

laid upon the messiah. Piska 34 seems to focus on redemption for Israel, but in an extraordinary passage Piska 36 envisages the messiah as atoning for all humanity—all those who died from the days of Adam to the time of redemption, including abortions, and those whom God intended to create but never created. Here is a universalism worthy of the most ardent Arminian!

Piska 36 helps to elucidate one final passage in Piska 34. Piska 34 speaks of a seven-year period preceding the messiah's appearance in which God will inflict ever more terrible disasters on Israel. There is an aspect of 'measure for measure' at work here: Israel made the Mourners suffer, so God will make her suffer, while at the same time conspicuously protecting the Mourners. These sufferings of Israel, however, unlike the Mourners' sufferings, are not in themselves redemptive because they were richly deserved, though their providential aspect is stressed in that they will bring Israel to her senses, and force her to see that the Mourners were right. Our homilist here exploits the widespread doctrine of the birth-pangs of the messiah—the idea that the messiah will come at a time of unparalleled trouble in the world. Israel recognizes that these unprecedented afflictions are a sign that the end is near. The earlier in the seven-year period that one grasps the meaning of the events, the greater will one's reward eventually be. Piska 36 also speaks of a seven-year period just before the end, during which the messiah will suffer for sin. This must coincide with the seven years of disaster. Putting the two passages together we get the following scenario: during the seven years prior to his manifestation the messiah is incognito. Israel, including the Mourners, fail to recognize him (this idea of the incognito messiah is well attested in early Judaism): he is imprisoned, ridiculed, and set at nought. But he carries on with his atoning work, and it is only when this is completed that he is revealed. But as his work comes to completion, so the afflictions which God heaps upon Israel reach a crescendo, preparing her to acknowledge both the Mourners and the messiah, whom the Mourners' prayers and sufferings have finally brought.

The homily ends with a coda in which the homilist cleverly weaves together his two major themes—the suffering and vindication of the Mourners, on the one hand, and the suffering and vindication of the messiah, on the other: '"And his enemies"—those who dispute with him [the Messiah]—"will I [God] clothe with shame" [Ps. 132: 18]. "And upon him shall his crown shine" [Ps. 132: 18]—upon him and those who are like him.' Having suffered with the messiah, the Mourners for Zion expected to reign with him.

HISTORICAL AND LITERARY CONTEXT

Turning to the wider context of our homily, two questions arise. The first is, who were these Mourners for Zion? One thing is abundantly clear: they were a non-rabbinic group. But do we have any evidence for their existence elsewhere? Some have identified them with the Karaites in Jerusalem in the tenth century who called themselves, among other things, 'the Mourners for Zion'.[30] The suggestion has much to commend it. We clearly have here an anti-rabbinic community who gave prominence in their liturgies to praying and fasting for the restoration of Zion. This would date the Mourners for Zion *piskaot* rather late, and those who espouse this view are inclined, then, to see them as an addition to *Pesikta rabati*. However, for a number of reasons we should be careful about settling too quickly and definitively on this identification. Though there may be some relationship between the Mourners of Piska 34 and the Karaites in Jerusalem, it may be more complicated and oblique than straightforward identification implies.

1. First, it is clearly unwarranted to suppose that the phrase 'Mourners for Zion' could only have been used by Karaites. It is not a Karaite coinage, but derived, as we have seen, from Isaiah 61. It might have been adopted already in Second Temple times by the Qumran community.[31] It was certainly appropriated in the twelfth century by a group in the Yemen who, according to Benjamin of Tudela, ate no meat and drank no wine, wore black clothing, lived in caves and secluded cells, and prayed constantly for the end of exile.[32] There is no good reason to assume that these Yemenite ascetics were Karaites. And when we carefully examine the literature of the Jerusalem Karaites in the tenth century, the self-designation 'Mourners for Zion', though found, is by no means as prominent or exclusive as the modern scholarly literature might lead one to assume.

2. Second, there is good evidence for the existence, within the rabbinic milieu, of ascetic groups mourning for Zion well before the establishment of the medieval Karaite community in Jerusalem. I have discussed this question at length elsewhere

---

[30] So M. Zucker, 'Reactions to the Karaite Mourners for Zion in Rabbinic Literature' (Heb.), in *Jubilee Volume for Rabbi Chanoch Albeck* [Sefer hayovel lerabi ḥanokh albek] (Jerusalem, 1963), 379–90. For an overview of the Karaite Mourners for Zion see: Moshe Gil, *A History of Palestine 634–1099* (Cambridge, 1992), 617–22; Daniel Frank, 'The Mourners for Zion ca. 950–1000', in Magne Sæbø (ed.), *Hebrew Bible/Old Testament: The History of Its Interpretation*, I/2: *The Middle Ages* (Göttingen, 2000), 119–23; Yoram Erder, 'The Mourners for Zion: The Karaites in Jerusalem in the Tenth and Eleventh Centuries', in Meira Polliack (ed.), *Karaite Judaism: A Guide to its History and Literary Sources* (Leiden, 2003), 213–35.

[31] It has plausibly been restored in 11QMelch II 17 and 20. Isa. 61: 2 is clearly quoted at the beginning of II 20, and, as we have already noted, Isaiah 61 hangs together as a chapter: see P. J. Kobelski, *Melchizedek and Melchiresha'* (Washington, DC, 1981), 6, 8–9, 20, 22. It is surely intriguing that the Qumran sect may have identified themselves with Isaiah's Mourners for Zion in a text which seems to speak of their eschatological deliverance at the hands of a heavenly, priestly messiah, called Melchizedek—a deliverance not so much from external as from internal enemies, wicked Jews who, in concert with Belial, have seized power in Israel; a deliverance, in other words, that will mark their ultimate, divine vindication. On parallels between the Dead Sea Sect and the medieval Karaites, see Yoram Erder, *The Karaite Mourners of Zion and the Qumran Scrolls* [Avelei tsiyon hakara'im umegilot kumran] (Tel Aviv, 2004).

[32] Marcus N. Adler (ed.), *The Itinerary of Benjamin of Tudela* (London, 1907), Hebrew text, 46–7.

and need not repeat myself here.³³ A few points will suffice for our present purposes. Hardly surprisingly, there is a cluster of attestations to such groups relating to the period following the destruction of the Temple in 70 CE. The key text is 2 Baruch. We have the rabbis' negative reaction in Tosefta *Sotah* 15: 10–15. The absence of the designation 'Mourners for Zion' from these texts does not materially affect the case; the evidence is sparse, and this may be a matter of chance. The obvious question is whether there is continuity between these early groups and the Mourners for Zion centuries later. It is hard to be sure, but I think a case can be made. I have argued that mourning for Zion may represent a priestly spirituality belonging to a distinctively priestly tradition that continued to flourish and develop largely independently of the rabbinic movement after 70, and which was ultimately taken up into Karaism. It is intriguing to note how aggadic traditions first attested in 2 Baruch 1–12 and 77 resurface strongly in *Pesikta rabati* 26.³⁴ Was the doctrine of a suffering messiah always integral to the theology of these Mourners for Zion? It is very hard to say. The doctrine of the suffering messiah is certainly old within Judaism. It is interesting to note how easily Trypho in Justin's *Dialogue* accepts it in principle, though he denies that Jesus fits the description of Isaiah's Suffering Servant.³⁵ We also find it in *piyut*. But although the Mourners for Zion who composed Piskaot 34 and 36–37 have embraced the doctrine, it is hard to see it as integral to their core theology. It is easy to conceive of mourning for Zion that does not entail belief in a *suffering* messiah. The possibility cannot be ruled out that, although the doctrine can be seen as a natural and organic development (in other words it need not be a borrowing from outside), the development may have occurred only relatively late in the history of the movement.

3. Third, the identification of the Mourners for Zion of *Pesikta rabati* 34 and 36–37 with the tenth-century Karaites would be more convincing if the theological agreement between the two groups were closer, particularly with regard to the doctrine of the suffering messiah. Detailed work on this question remains to be done, and until it is, the jury is out.³⁶ My own preliminary impressions suggest that, although there are significant similarities, there are also important differences. And even if the parallels turn out to be stronger than seems to be the case, this does not end the matter, because it begs the question as to whether these Karaites inherited their doctrine from earlier circles.

³³ Alexander, *Targum of Lamentations*, 78–86; id., 'What Happened to the Jewish Priesthood after 70?', in Zuleika Rodgers, Margaret Daly-Denton, and Anne Fitzpatrick McKinley (eds.), *A Wandering Galilean: Essays in Honour of Seán Freyne* (Leiden, 2009), 21–5.

³⁴ Pierre Bogaert, *Apocalypse de Baruch: introduction, traduction du syriaque et commentaire*, 2 vols. (Paris, 1969), i. 222–41.

³⁵ Justin Martyr, *Dialogue with Trypho*, 36. 1; 68. 9; 99. 1.

³⁶ See Naphtali Wieder, 'The Doctrine of the Two Messiahs among the Karaites', *Journal of Jewish Studies*, 6 (1955), 14–23; Yoram Erder, 'The Negation of the Exile in the Messianic Doctrine of the Karaite Mourners for Zion', *Hebrew Union College Annual*, 68 (1997), 109–40; Erder, *The Karaite Mourners of Zion* (Heb.), 317–418.

A final question: what is such 'anti-rabbinic' material doing in a rabbinic *midrash*?[37] To some this question will make little sense. Anything that smacks of essentialism is suspect in academia, and for many the simple fact that Piska 34 is found in a 'rabbinic' text makes it 'rabbinic'.[38] But in this case the problem is particularly acute. It is not just a matter of a rather subjective judgement as to what is 'normative' rabbinism and what is not. The text itself appears to challenge openly a cardinal doctrine of Rabbinic Judaism—the absolute centrality of Torah to salvation. There is no clear answer to this question, but some points can be made. Piskaot 34 and 36–37 are arguably not the only examples of unusual material in *Pesikta rabati*: it contains mystical, gnostic, apocalyptic, and even halakhic traditions which are also surprising from the standpoint of classic Rabbinic Judaism.[39] Nor is this the only text passed down to us as 'rabbinic' that sits somewhat awkwardly with mainline rabbinism. *Pirkei derabi eli'ezer*, which dates from roughly the same period as *Pesikta rabati*, has long been recognized as containing quantities of aggadah unknown to earlier rabbinic Midrash, but paralleled in old Jewish sources from the Second Temple period. The Heikhalot literature, again from roughly the same period as our *midrash*, propounds ideas disturbing from a normative rabbinic perspective. Nevertheless, in the forms in which we now have it, it is attributed to some of the heroes of the rabbinic movement—Rabbi Akiva and Rabbi Ishmael.

The acceptance of Piskaot 34 and 36–37 into a rabbinic compilation should be set in the context of the apocalyptic revival in Judaism of the sixth to ninth centuries.[40] As I noted earlier, having in late tannaitic and early amoraic times suppressed their messianic inheritance, the rabbinic movement re-engaged with messianism in the later amoraic period. Commemorating the loss of the Temple and observing the Ninth of Av were integral to messianism, because mourning for destruction was inevitably transmuted into prayer for restoration. Indicative of this

---

[37] How can one tell what is a rabbinic *midrash*? Without resorting to essentialism, several external criteria can be used. (1) The most important is the frequent citation of rabbinic authorities. *Pesikta rabati* certainly passes this test, though the distribution of these citations may be significant. There are only two rabbinic authorities cited in Piska 34, Yosi b. Haninah and Yannai in the name of Rav, and in the latter case the passage may be secondary. (2) The use of rabbinic Hebrew. Again *Pesikta rabati* seems to pass the test, though with two caveats: (*a*) its language has never been investigated on its own, and one cannot fail to note as one reads it that it contains some linguistic peculiarities; and (*b*) we should be careful not to assume that only the rabbinic movement used Hebrew in late antiquity. Is *Sefer yetsirah* a rabbinic text? (3) Extensive sharing of aggadot and exegetical techniques with core rabbinic texts. (4) Transmission within circles that accept the authority of the manifesto texts of rabbinic Judaism, the Mishnah and the Talmuds. Again, *Pesikta rabati* qualifies under (3) and (4).

[38] Note how Goldberg (*Erlösung durch Leiden*), despite demonstrating how problematically rabbinic they are, classifies *Pesikta rabati*, Piskaot 34, 36, and 37 as 'drei rabbinische Homilien'. In Alexander, 'What Happened to the Jewish Priesthood after 70?', I discuss the problem of separating 'rabbinic' and 'non-rabbinic' strands of post-70 CE Palestinian Judaism.

[39] See the literature cited in *Pesiqta Rabbati*, ed. Ulmer, vol. i, p. xiv.

[40] For a survey, see John C. Reeves, *Trajectories in Near Eastern Apocalyptic: A Postrabbinic Jewish Apocalyptic Reader* (Atlanta, Ga., 2005).

profound new rabbinic interest in eschatology is one of the richest of the rabbinic *midrashim*, *Lamentations Rabbah*, and a fine Targum on Lamentations.[41]

The Ninth of Av lies at the heart of one of the most elaborately structured periods of the Jewish liturgical year, preceded as it is by the three Sabbaths of Rebuke and followed by the seven Sabbaths of Consolation—a structure which seems to have crystallized at the beginning of the apocalyptic revival.[42] That the Mourners for Zion would have strongly influenced the rituals, the *kinot* (elegies), and the homilies needed to sustain this large liturgical structure is more than likely. The rabbinic movement simply could not ignore the new enthusiasm for commemorating the Ninth of Av, but in addressing this, it found itself inevitably engaging at the same time with the ideas of the Mourners for Zion. It was probably in this setting that some of these ideas passed over into rabbinic tradition. But the willingness of the rabbis to consider them, despite their novelty and problematic theology, remains remarkable and may be a sign of deep, tectonic shifts within the rabbinic movement itself—its emergence from a fundamentally sectarian stance into a new openness and inclusivism that in many ways points forwards to the Middle Ages. Arguably it is only from gaonic times onwards that rabbinism can be seen in any meaningful sense as 'normative Judaism'; the challenge of Karaism is, in itself, evidence of its new-found status. But it became 'orthodoxy' only by making compromises—by becoming an inclusive 'big tent'. In *Pesikta rabati*, *Pirkei derabi eli'ezer*, and other such late rabbinic texts we can see the beginning of this process at a literary level.

[41] Alexander, *Targum Lamentations*, and further, Alexander, 'The Cultural History of the Ancient Bible Versions: The Case of Lamentations', in N. de Lange, J. G. Krivoruchko, and C. Boyd-Taylor (eds.), *Jewish Reception of Greek Bible Versions: Studies in their Use in Late Antiquity and the Middle Ages* (Tübingen, 2009), 78–102.

[42] Lewis M. Barth, 'The "Three of Rebuke and Seven of Consolation": Sermons in the "Pesikta de Rav Kahana"', *Journal of Jewish Studies*, 33 (1982), 503–16. Barth is inclined to place the emergence of this liturgical structure in 5th-cent. Palestine. I would put it a little later.

EIGHT

THE *TOLEDOT YESHU* AS MIDRASH

WILLIAM HORBURY

I

The narrative of the *Toledot yeshu* retells the story of Jesus and the rise of Christianity. Lively and memorable in its fabulous elements, it offers alternatives to Christian claims about the birth, way of life, and miracles of Jesus, his resurrection, and the subsequent apostolic preaching. It circulated in Hebrew, Aramaic, and other languages of the medieval and later Jewish community, but in content it is closer to the Gospels and the Acts of the Apostles than to Hebrew Scripture. It is thus sometimes aligned with New Testament apocrypha, as a hostile counterpart of such works as the *Acts of Pilate* or the *Narration of Joseph of Arimathaea*, similarly apologetic and imaginative compositions which envisage objections like those which it puts forward.[1] It seems accordingly to be removed from the links with exposition of the Hebrew biblical texts that are central in classical Midrash.[2]

Yet this narrative has in fact been intertwined with allusions to Hebrew Scripture (as is also true in a different way of the Gospels and Acts), and it also has kinship with the tales or *ma'asiyot* included by copyists and editors among the smaller *midrashim*.[3] In the course of transmission it has sometimes correspondingly been associated with Midrash, but it has also been treated as polemic and as a kind of history.

Thus, in the first half of the twentieth century, J. D. Eisenstein published treasuries of both Midrash and controversy, and presented texts from the *Toledot yeshu* in both.[4] With regard to Midrash he was following one of the fathers of

---

[1] Examples are Sabine Baring-Gould, *The Lost and Hostile Gospels* (London, 1874); Hugh J. Schonfield, *According to the Hebrews* (London, 1937).

[2] Thus scriptural exposition is determinative for the answer to the question 'What is Midrash?' outlined by Günther Stemberger, *Midrasch: Vom Umgang der Rabbinen mit der Bibel* (Munich, 1989), 21–6.

[3] A list with references to printed collections was published by John T. Townsend, 'Minor Midrashim', in Yosef H. Yerushalmi et al., *Bibliographical Essays in Medieval Jewish Studies*, The Study of Judaism 2 (New York, 1976), 333–92.

[4] Judah D. Eisenstein, *Otsar Midrashim: A Library of Two Hundred Minor Midrashim* (Heb.), 2 vols. (New York, 1915), ii. 557–9 (repr. from Jellinek, as cited in the following footnote); id., *Otsar Vikuḥim: A Collection of Polemics and Disputations* (Heb.) (New York, 1928), 226–35.

modern midrashic study, Adolph Jellinek, for Eisenstein reprinted extracts from the *Toledot yeshu* that had been published under the heading 'Petrus-Legende' in Jellinek's *Bet ha-Midrasch*.[5] In this editorial decision Jellinek himself had followed copyists of manuscripts who associated the *Toledot yeshu* with narrative Midrash—a link which can be suggested by the alternative and at least equally common title of the text in the manuscript tradition, *Ma'aseh yeshu*.[6] A century after Jellinek, Joseph Dan accordingly reprinted the text again in a collection of medieval Hebrew tales, including many minor *midrashim*; he stressed that in Jewish transmission it had become 'a real romance', despite its apologetic and polemical purposes.[7] Outside the Jewish setting and in modern times, something of the same kind of union of romance with polemic in the development of this text can be seen in Thomas Hardy's poem 'Panthera'; here the tale has its own fresh imaginative literary treatment, but gets some of its zest and melancholy from the polemical overtones transmitted by a freethinking author to whom the Church still means a great deal.[8]

The currency of the narrative in Muslim lands has sometimes been taken as a further pointer to its Midrash-like rather than polemical function.[9] In this environment too, however, Jewish views of Christianity could be important, as the quranic rebuke of Jewish statements about Jesus (4: 156–7) already suggests, and a polemical aspect of transmission cannot be ruled out. Eisenstein's further decision to reprint a complete text in his 'collection of polemics and disputations' indeed once more followed copyists of manuscripts, this time those who reproduced the *Toledot yeshu* together with polemical works against Christianity.[10]

---

[5] Adolph Jellinek, *Bet ha-Midrasch: Sammlung kleiner Midraschim und gemischter Abhandlungen aus der ältern jüdischen Literatur*, 6 vols. (Leipzig, 1853–77), vol. v, pp. xxvi–xxviii, 60–2; vol. vi, pp. ix–xiii, 9–14, 153–6; repr. in 2 vols. (Jerusalem, 1967), vol. ii.

[6] Examples from the Yemen where the text stands among miscellanea, including tales, added at the end of a prayer book or a *divan* (collection of poetry), are the 17th-cent. Jerusalem MS Ben-Zvi Institute 1219 (at the end of a prayer-book), the 19th-cent. Jerusalem MS Jewish National and University Library 4to 15 (at the end of a *divan*), and the Cambridge MS ULC Or. 557, copied in 1876 (at the end of a prayer-book); see, respectively, Joseph Tobi, *Yemenite Jewish Manuscripts in the Ben-Zvi Institute* (Jerusalem, 1982), 82–5, no. 153.35; B. I. Joel, *Catalogue of Hebrew Manuscripts in the Jewish National and University Library, Jerusalem* (Jerusalem, 1934), 34, no. 326; and Stefan C. Reif, *Hebrew Manuscripts in Cambridge University Library: A Description and Introduction* (Cambridge, 1997), 245–6, no. SCR 399, item 7.

[7] Joseph Dan, *The Hebrew Story in the Middle Ages* [Hasipur ha'ivri biyemei habeinayim] (Jerusalem, 1974), 122–4.

[8] Thomas Hardy, 'Panthera', first issued in his *Time's Laughingstocks* (1909), repr. in id., *Collected Poems*, 4th edn. (London, 1930; repr. London, 1970), 262–8. Professor Ralph Pite kindly drew my attention to this poem.

[9] So e.g. Riccardo Di Segni, *Il Vangelo del Ghetto* (Rome, 1985), 220, following Walther J. Fischel (who, however, also noted defence against Christian mission as a possible motive).

[10] Examples include the Bodleian MS Opp. 749, written 'in great haste and the utmost secrecy' in Prague, 1630 (*Toledot yeshu* following Isaac Troki's *Ḥizuk emunah*) and the British Library MS Or. 3660, from Italy in the late 18th or early 19th cent. (*Toledot yeshu* followed by Jonah Rappa's polemical *Pilpul*, and the dialogue *Derekh emunah*); see Adolf Neubauer (and Arthur E. Cowley), *Catalogue of the Hebrew*

An approach related to polemic as well as Midrash, but evident mainly from the texts themselves rather than their association in transmission with other works, has treated the story as a kind of chronicle or history in the style of Josippon. Thus in various forms the narrative includes a reference to Josippon, or is woven together with talmudic material on Christianity, or names known figures of Jewish and Roman history. To some extent this approximation to historical treatment can be linked with the Hebrew title that became standard, used in the first examples of the work to be mentioned in print: *Sefer toledot yeshu*, 'book of the generations of Jesus' or 'book of the history of Jesus'. The phrase no doubt hints polemically at Matthew 1: 1, 'book of the generation of Jesus' (cf. Gen. 5: 1, 'book of the generations of Adam'), but it also suggests a kind of historical narrative. This classification is true to the features just noted; the story touches love, adventure, and the marvellous in the manner of romance, but presents itself as fundamentally genuine, and so of apologetic or polemical value.

The narrative, then, could indeed be brought under the heading of Midrash, at least narrative Midrash, without undue force, by some of those who copied and developed it in medieval and later times; but its classification varied in this period. The text was on the verge of both Midrash and history, and its aspect of romance as well as polemic goes back into the period of origins, as comparison with New Testament apocrypha suggests. The essential character of the *Toledot yeshu* narrative perhaps belongs to the old literature uniting romance and historical propaganda, which was circulated under Greek and Roman rule by Jews, Greeks, and then Christians, and is exemplified in different ways by pagan Greek accounts of the Exodus and the *Acts of the Alexandrians*, Greek Jewish accounts of Moses, Christian martyr-acts and narrative apocrypha, and rabbinic anecdotes of martyrdom and wonder-working in a Roman setting.[11]

Yet this literature has indeed left traces in the Midrash; and here I should like to suggest that, despite the differences just noted, the *Toledot yeshu* verges on Midrash in more than one way, and that the label 'Midrash' should not be contrasted too sharply with the label 'polemic'. These texts are Midrash-like in their development of aggadah, as has often been noted, but this development is carried out in the service of apologetic and polemic—and the same is true of a less-noticed midrashic element in the texts, the scriptural interpretation which likewise links them with polemic and disputation.

Manuscripts in the Bodleian Library, 2 vols. (Oxford, 1886, 1906; repr. Oxford, 1994), vol. i, col. 751, no. 2172; Malachi Beit-Arié, Ronald A. May (eds.), *Catalogue of Hebrew Manuscripts in the Bodleian Library: Supplement of Addenda and Corrigenda to Vol. I* (Oxford, 1994), col. 405; George Margoliouth (and Jacob Leveen), *Catalogue of the Hebrew and Samaritan Manuscripts in the British Museum*, 4 vols. (London, 1899–1935; repr. London, 1965), iii. 533–4, no. 1105.

[11] See especially Raphael Loewe, 'A Jewish Counterpart to the Acts of the Alexandrians', *Journal of Jewish Studies*, 12 (1961), 105–22 (on the anecdote of Trajan and the Jews ascribed to Shimon bar Yohai in JT *Suk*. 5: 1 (55*b*)).

II

For Jellinek the link between these texts and others that he issued in his collection was their attestation of aggadah.[12] The connection of the *Toledot yeshu* with Midrash has been pursued accordingly with regard not only to midrashic literature in particular but also to more broadly attested legend and motifs of folklore.[13] A pervasive theme of *Toledot yeshu* texts that has lent itself to such enquiry is that of the aerial flight of Jesus, achieved by sorcery or through the power of the *shem hameforash* (Tetragrammaton), and his pursuit through the air by the faithful Judah, also empowered by the *shem hameforash*. For the present argument just two well-known aspects need re-emphasis. First, this theme is close to pentateuchal exegesis as found in classical Midrash, for the flight in the *Toledot yeshu* matches the aerial flight of Balaam, brought down to earth by the faithful pursuer Pinhas.[14] Secondly, use of this theme ties the *Toledot yeshu* together with the anti-Christian polemic that forms part of the midrashic interpretation of biblical passages on Balaam.

In the Pentateuch, when Moses is commanded to take vengeance on Midian (Num. 31: 2), he sends an army of a thousand from each tribe, and Pinhas with the holy vessels and the trumpets of alarm (Num. 31: 3–6); the Midianite males and the five kings of Midian are slain, and it is added, without explanation, that Balaam was slain with the sword (Num. 31: 7–8). In the aggadah, however, Balaam tries to help the kings of Midian to escape by enabling them to fly, and then takes to the air himself; but they are brought down by Pinhas when he shows them the divine name on the diadem of the high priestly mitre.

Balaam's end is told along these lines in the Jerusalem Talmud (*San.* 10: 2, 29a). In the Midrash this story is related in connection with Numbers 31: 2 and the sequel, especially verse 8: 'they slew the kings of Midian beside [or, upon (Hebrew *al*)] their slain ... Balaam also they slew with the sword'. It helps *inter alia* to explain why Pinhas in particular was chosen for this service by Moses, and it shows how, since those to be slain fall down from the air, *al* can be taken in its more usual sense of 'upon' or 'above'. The story is also mentioned, however, in connection with Numbers 23: 24, where Balaam himself foretells that Israel like a lion 'shall drink the blood of the slain'; this verse and 31: 8 were linked as prophecy and fulfilment, the prominence of 'the slain' in each being further enhanced by the near-repetition of 31: 8 in Joshua 13: 22, on the slaying of Balaam 'the diviner', 'with the sword beside [or, upon] their slain'.[15]

---

[12] Jellinek, *Bet ha-Midrasch*, forward to pt. 5.

[13] Samuel Krauss, *Das Leben Jesu nach jüdischen Quellen* (Berlin, 1902; repr. Hildesheim, 1977), 211–26; Bernard Heller, 'Über Judas Ischariotes in der jüdischen Legende', *Monatsschrift für Geschichte und Wissenschaft des Judentums*, 76 (1932), 33–42.

[14] For attestations of this narrative of Balaam see Louis Ginzberg, *The Legends of the Jews*, 7 vols. (Philadelphia, Pa., 1911–38; repr. 1968), vi. 144–5, nn. 853, 855; J. Maier, *Jesus von Nazareth in der talmudischen Überlieferung* (Darmstadt, 1978), 286 n. 155.

[15] See *Num. Rabbah* 20: 20 on Num. 23: 24, and 22: 5 on Num. 31: 2, 'Avenge the children of Israel'; *Tanhuma*, 'Balak' 14 (end), and 'Matot' 4, on the same passages in Numbers; *Tanhuma*, ed. Buber, 'Balak' 23 (end, on Num. 31: 2).

This story appears in Rashi's comment on Numbers 31: 6, on the sending of Pinhas with the holy vessels. A form close to the *Toledot yeshu* version, however, appears in *Midrash yelamedenu* as quoted in the *Yalkut*, and in Targum Pseudo-Jonathan on Numbers 31: 8 (though not in Neofiti, the Fragment Targum, or Onkelos).[16] Here Balaam flies by means of sorcery (the Targum) or the *shem hameforash* (the *midrash*), followed by Pinhas, relying on the *shem hameforash*. When Balaam is cast down, in the *midrash* he is brought before Moses, judged by a court (*sanhedrin*),[17] and then executed by the sword; in the Targum he asks mercy from Pinhas, but Pinhas states his crimes and then puts him to death. Here the sequence of flight, arrest, judgment by the court, and then execution resembles that found also in the *Toledot yeshu*, where Jesus is condemned but escapes into the air, is recaptured, brought again before the judge, and put to death.[18]

An explicit association with Balaam appears in the relatively early version of the *Toledot yeshu* cited in the previous footnote; here Jesus under questioning initially pretends that his magical writings are from Balaam son of Beor, but then admits that they are quite new, given him by his teacher John the Baptist.[19] The emphasis of the *midrash* quoted in *Yalkut shimoni* on lawful judgment by the court also recalls traditions about Jesus in the Babylonian Talmud (*San.* 43a), where he is likewise put to death judicially after the execution of his five disciples (a sequence itself resembling the slaying of the five Midianite kings before Balaam), and the charges against him (sorcery and false prophecy) are close to those incurred by Balaam.[20]

Just as Balaam is thought in the Midrash to give a true prophecy of his own

---

[16] *Yalkut shimoni*, pt. 1, §769, on Num. 23: 24 (Moses warns Pinhas that through spells Balaam will make the five kings fly in the air), and §785, on Num. 31: 2 (Balaam flies away, Pinhas flies after him) (*Yalkut shimoni*, 2 pts. in 1 vol. (Vilna, 1909), fo. 266, col. c, and fo. 277, col. b); Targum Pseudo-Jonathan on Num. 31: 8, in David Rieder (ed.), *Pseudo-Jonathan: Targum Jonathan ben Uziel on the Pentateuch copied from the London MS (British Museum Add. 27031)* (Jerusalem, 1974), 242–3; no rendering of Num. 31: 8 is recorded in Michael L. Klein, *The Fragment-Targums of the Pentateuch*, 2 vols., Analecta Biblica 76 (Rome, 1980).

[17] Compare the teaching ascribed to R. Nathan (*Sifrei Numbers* 157, on Num. 31: 8) that he was judged by the *beit din* (court), as the judicial description *kosem* ('diviner') in Josh. 13: 22 implies, cf. Deut. 18: 10.

[18] So in a relatively early version (probably known by the 9th cent.) attested in Genizah Aramaic texts, compared with newly discovered Hebrew texts on the same lines by Yaacov Deutsch, 'New Evidence of Early Versions of *Toledot yeshu*' (Heb.), *Tarbiz*, 69 (2000), 93–4; similarly in the text translated in the late 13th cent. by Raymund Martini, *Pugio Fidei* (Paris, 1651), 290–1, and in that published from a copy of MS Strasbourg 3974 (Hébr. 48) and translated by Samuel Krauss, *Das Leben Jesu nach jüdischen Quellen*, 43, 55–6. The incipit of the Strasbourg text seems to be that rendered into Latin as *inicium creacionis ihesu nazareni* in a Christian talmudic anthology made in the years following the Paris Disputation of 1240; see Ch. Merchavia, *The Church versus Talmudic and Midrashic Literature 500–1248* [Hatalmud bire'i hanatsrut] (Jerusalem, 1970), 328–30.

[19] Deutsch, 'New Evidence of Early Versions of *Toledot yeshu*' (Heb.), 185.

[20] On these charges against Balaam as emerging clearly from the biblical text itself see Edward Noort, 'Balaam the Villain', in George H. van Kooten and Jacques van Ruiten (eds.), *The Prestige of the Pagan Prophet Balaam in Judaism, Early Christianity and Islam*, Themes in Biblical Narrative 11 (Leiden, 2008), 3–23.

death (Num. 23: 24, discussed above), so he was envisaged as prophesying the false claims and the death of Jesus. This emerges especially in the interpretation of Numbers 23: 19 attributed to Abbahu (Caesarea, end of the third century). Balaam here says, 'God is not a man, that He should lie; neither the son of man, that He should repent: has He said, and shall He not do it? or has He spoken, and shall He not make it good?' The interpretation runs, 'If a man says to you, *I am God*, he is a liar; *I am the son of man*, he will regret it; *I am going up to the heavens*, has he said? but he shall not make it good.'[21]

Balaam in the Midrash was probably not simply a cover-name for Jesus, as was held by Geiger, Strack, and others; but on the other hand there was clearly a polemical association between the presentations of the two figures.[22] This association also underlies the *Toledot yeshu*, where a legend familiar in the Midrash on Balaam shapes the story of Jesus' death. The resulting narrative is thoroughly midrashic, in the sense of using material known from the Midrash, and at the same time, like some talmudic and midrashic treatment of Balaam, thoroughly polemical.

III

A second but less-studied midrashic element of the *Toledot yeshu* is formed by the biblical interpretations attributed in the narrative to Jesus and his disciples on the one side, and to their critics in the Jewish community on the other. These recall the biblical focus of classical Midrash, and are particularly close to the *teshuvot haminim* ('answers to heretics/schismatics') found in both Talmud and Midrash, in which a proof-text put forward by the *min* is answered, often by quotation of a further text; an example is formed by a series of responses credited to the third-century Rabbi

---

[21] JT *Ta'an.* 2: 1 (65b), discussed by Johann Maier, *Jesus von Nazareth in der talmudischen Überlieferung* (Darmstadt, 1978), 76–82 (the saying was a protest against the imperial cult, and was later misunderstood as anti-Christian); but the Christian reference is more likely to be original, as shown by Peter Schäfer, *Jesus in the Talmud* (Princeton, NJ, 2007), 107–9. On this passage in the context of other rabbinic statements on Christianity see William Horbury, 'Rabbinic Perceptions of Christianity and the History of Roman Palestine', in Philip S. Alexander and Martin D. Goodman (eds.), *Rabbinic Texts and the History of Late-Roman Palestine* (Oxford, 2010), 353–76.

[22] The cover-name suggestion was made by Abraham Geiger, 'Bileam und Jesus', *Jüdische Zeitschrift für Wissenschaft und Leben*, 6 (1868), 31–7, and followed by others including Hermann L. Strack, *Jesus, die Häretiker und die Christen nach den ältesten jüdischen Angaben*, Schriften des Institutum Judaicum in Berlin 37 (Leipzig, 1910), 18–19, 42*–43*. It is rejected by Louis Ginzberg, *The Legends of the Jews*, vi. 123–4 n. 722, 144 n. 855 (who still affirms resemblances between legends of the death of each figure); Ephraim E. Urbach, 'Homilies of the Rabbis on the Prophets of the Nations and the Balaam Stories' (Heb.), *Tarbiz*, 25 (1955/6), 281–9, repr. in Ephraim E. Urbach, *The World of the Sages: Collected Studies* [Me'olamam shel ḥakhamim], 2nd edn. (Jerusalem, 2002), 546–54 (but with a full recognition of anti-Christian polemic in aggadah on Balaam); Johann Maier, *Jesus von Nazareth in der talmudischen Überlieferung*, 68–103 (ruling out anti-Christian polemic, not always convincingly; see above, n. 21); and Ronit Nikolsky, 'Interpret Him as Much as You Want: Balaam in the Babylonian Talmud', in van Kooten and van Ruiten (eds.), *The Prestige of the Pagan Prophet Balaam in Judaism, Early Christianity and Islam*, 233–4 (recognizing anti-Christian polemic, without discussion of Maier, but stressing that Balaam can represent any 'other').

Simlai, presented in part in the *Midrash Rabbah* as well as the Jerusalem Talmud.[23] This element in the Midrash and the *Toledot yeshu* also recalls the argument from biblical evidence which was central in ancient and medieval Christian literature, from the gospels themselves to dialogues and other polemical writings against the Jews.

In the *Toledot yeshu* this argument from testimonia is reflected in different ways. In the relatively early version of the *Toledot yeshu* cited above it is chiefly represented by the debate over proof-texts between the five disciples of Jesus and their judges, which also appears in the Babylonian Talmud (*San.* 43*a*). Here the disciples seek to be spared their impending execution, and the texts which they choose for their argument suit their names. The debate was incorporated into this form of the *Toledot yeshu*.[24] It has been conjectured that it was originally focused not on five disciples but on Jesus himself.[25] At any rate, the debate on this series of texts is indeed conducted simply between Jesus and his judges in the Strasbourg *Toledot yeshu* text cited above, no doubt influenced in including the episode by the early text-form also cited, but going its own way in giving one side of the debate to Jesus: when questioned, Jesus now evasively offers several different names, those given elsewhere to various disciples, and quotes the texts associated with them.[26]

In a typical exchange of proof-texts from the more usual disciple-oriented form of this debate in the Talmud and *Toledot yeshu*, the disciple Buni quotes the text 'my son [*beni*], my first-born is Israel', messianically and on the Christian side, from Exodus 4: 22; but this is then capped ominously on the Jewish side by words from the following verse, Exodus 4: 23, 'I will slay thy son, thy first-born.' Here the response follows Rabbi Simlai's rule that whenever a biblical passage appears to support the *minim*, an answer to them is found by its side (*Gen. Rab.* 8: 9, cited above). Indeed, for medieval readers it would have seemed that the follower of Jesus maladroitly attempts to quote on his own side a text (Exod. 4: 22) which was held to form such an answer, and to invalidate Christian claims for a Trinitarian sense of the term 'son of God'.[27]

In the Strasbourg *Toledot yeshu*, and the often similar text translated by Raymund

---

[23] JT *Ber.* 9: 1–2 (12*d*—13*a*), partly paralleled in *Gen. Rabbah* 8: 9 on Gen. 1: 26, 'let us make man in our image'. Discussed by Burton L. Visotzky, 'Trinitarian Testimonies', *Union Seminary Quarterly Review*, 42 (1988), 73–85; repr. in id., *Fathers of the World: Essays in Rabbinic and Patristic Literatures*, Wissenschaftliche Untersuchungen zum Neuen Testament 80 (Tübingen, 1995), 61–74.

[24] St Petersburg and Cambridge MSS printed in parallel by Deutsch, 'New Evidence of Early Versions of *Toledot yeshu*' (Heb.), 187–8.

[25] Ernst Bammel, 'What is thy Name?', *Novum Testamentum*, 12 (1970), 223–8, repr. in id., *Judaica: Kleine Schriften I* (Tübingen, 1986), 210–15, basing himself on the implications of the proof-texts and on the Strasbourg *Toledot yeshu* cited in n. 18 above; Schäfer, *Jesus in the Talmud*, 75–81, arguing simply from the content of the proof-texts without mention of the *Toledot yeshu* or Bammel's argument.

[26] Krauss, *Das Leben Jesu nach jüdischen Quellen*, 45, 57.

[27] For its use in rebuttal of Christian claims see Daniel J. Lasker and Sarah Stroumsa, *The Polemic of Nestor the Priest*, 2 vols. (Jerusalem, 1996), i. 100, 102–3; ii. 113–14, 116 (Hebrew text, §§11 and 27); *The First Book of the Psalms According to the Text of the Cambridge MS Bible Add. 465: With the Longer Commentary of R. David Qimchi*, ed. Salomon M. Schiller-Szinessy (Cambridge, 1883), 12; *The Commentary of Rabbi David Kimhi on The Book of Psalms, I–VIII*, trans. from the Hebrew by Albert W. Greenup (London, 1918), 25.

Martini in the late thirteenth century, Jesus uses further testimonia, exemplified by two short series, quoted first when he is resisting charges about his birth and later when he is first accused of sorcery and false prophecy. Once again he sounds like a Christian testimony-book, or, rather, the whole narrative sounds like Christian argument from testimonies as it is reproduced and rebutted in medieval Jewish polemic.

In the first series Jesus shows that he is the messiah and born of a virgin by quoting the famous texts from Isaiah 7: 14, 'a virgin shall conceive' (Matt. 2: 22–3), and from his forefather David in Psalm 2: 7, 'this day have I begotten thee' (Acts 13: 33, Heb. 1: 5). He notes, as happens also in Acts (4: 24–8), that the opposition to the messiah is likewise foretold in the same psalm (Ps. 2: 12); it is indeed his Jewish opponents rather than he who are 'children of whoredoms', as a prophet again foretold (Hos. 2: 6 [4]). No counter-text is quoted by his critics, but they demand a miracle.[28]

The second series begins when Jesus has performed miracles and been arrested by the sages. Brought before Queen Helen and accused of sorcery and false prophecy, he declares once more that the prophets of old prophesied concerning him. Isaiah said, 'There shall come forth a rod out of the stem of Jesse' (Isa. 11: 1), and David spoke of his accusers in the words 'Blessed is the man who has not walked in the counsel of the ungodly' (Ps. 1: 1). The queen asks the sages if these things are indeed written in their law. They answer that the prophecies are indeed there, but that they do not refer to Jesus; what does apply to him is the commandment concerning the false prophet, 'That prophet shall die' (Deut. 18: 20). They add the argument that the messiah is to bring greater and more palpable deliverance than Jesus has done, and they quote to this effect either Jeremiah 23: 6, 'in his days Judah shall be saved' (so Raymund Martini's version) or Isaiah 11: 4, 'he shall smite the earth with the rod of his mouth' (so the Strasbourg Hebrew text).[29]

The many layers of biblical interpretation reproduced in the *Toledot yeshu* here can be illustrated simply from Psalm 2, quoted in the first series, viewed together with Psalm 1, in the second series. Earlier layers belong to Jewish exegesis irrespective of Christian claims. Thus the application of Psalms 1–2 to God's chosen and his or their opponents is already reflected in the Qumran *Florilegium* (4Q174, i, ll. 14–18), which explains successively Psalm 1: 1 and Psalm 2: 1–2 in terms of the rejection of the counsel of the wicked by the elect, and the attack upon them by the nations at the end of days. Here Psalms 1–2 are probably considered as one psalm, as in other ancient Jewish and Christian sources, and as in the exegesis ascribed to Jesus in the *Toledot yeshu*; the wicked, sinners, and scornful of Psalm 1 can thereby be associated with the raging heathen, the peoples (taken in Acts 4: 27 to be Israelites), and the kings who oppose the messiah in Psalm 2, as seems to be assumed when Psalm 1 is quoted in the *Toledot yeshu*. A messianic version of the same interpretation of Psalm 2 appears in the rabbinic application of this psalm to the messiah and his enemies, Gog and

---

[28] Krauss, *Das Leben Jesu nach jüdischen Quellen*, 41, 53; Raymund Martini, *Pugio Fidei*, 290–1.
[29] Krauss, *Das Leben Jesu nach jüdischen Quellen*, 41, 54; Raymund Martini, *Pugio Fidei*, 290–1.

Magog, in the time to come; this application is assumed in an interpretation attributed to the third-century aggadist Rabbi Levi,[30] and in the designation of the psalm as 'the chapter of Gog and Magog' in the Babylonian Talmud.[31]

The Christian use of Psalm 2 in the New Testament as cited above, referring to both Christ and his opponents, is an earlier special instance of this messianic application later found in the Midrash. In second-century Christianity it is attested in Justin Martyr's exposition of Psalms 1–2, quoted in full as a single psalm, to exemplify an exhortation to a good life and a prediction of conspiracy against Christ given by the prophetic spirit through David.[32] The Christian application is then, in a later layer of interpretation, regularly rebutted in medieval Jewish exegesis, perhaps most famously in David Kimhi's commentary on Psalm 2, but also in expressly polemical works.[33] The *Toledot yeshu* is close both to earlier layers of interpretation, as noted already, and also to this tradition of rebuttal, which itself of course has ample ancient antecedent in the *teshuvot haminim* of the Midrash.

IV

The *Toledot yeshu* is, then, a text that is close to Midrash in a number of ways. Although it is not linked with Scripture in the manner of classical Midrash, it is comparable with the short narrative *midrashim*, with which it has in fact often been associated in copying and printing. Perhaps its most obvious midrashic feature is its development of aggadah, illustrated above by the theme of aerial flight, capture, trial, and execution, which also marks Midrash on the pentateuchal narrative of the death of Balaam. A somewhat less studied midrashic aspect is presented by the importance of disputation over biblical testimonia in the *Toledot yeshu*.

Both these examples, however, lead to a renewed emphasis on the polemical character of the text. Despite attempts to contrast Midrash and polemic, it is sometimes precisely through its midrashic features that the text makes a polemical point. The *Toledot yeshu* narrative of love, adventure, and marvels often recalls the Midrash, but it cannot be fully defined simply as Midrash. It is also close to Josippon or the story of Alexander, but in its combination of romance, history, and polemic it is perhaps closest to the propaganda literature from the ancient world described above, which survives mainly in Greek but will also have been represented in Aramaic, and did indeed leave a deposit in the Midrash.

---

[30] Found at *Lev. Rab.* 27: 11 (on Lev. 22: 28); *Pesikta derav kahana* 9: 11; and *Midrash tehilim* 2: 4 (on Ps. 2: 2).

[31] BT *Ber.* 10a, in the name of another 3rd-cent. teacher, R. Yohanan, who settled in Tiberias.

[32] Justin Martyr, *I Apologia* XL. 5–19.

[33] *The First Book of the Psalms*, ed. Schiller-Szinessy, 11–12 (a rebuttal of the Christian interpretation of Ps. 2: 7 added at the conclusion of the commentary on Ps. 2); *The Commentary of Rabbi David Kimhi*, trans. Greenup, 23–6; Lasker and Stroumsa, *The Polemic of Nestor the Priest*, i. 101, ii. 110 (Hebrew text, §59) (David never thought he was saying this about Jesus); Jacob b. Reuben, *Milḥamot hashem*, ed. Judah Rosenthal (Jerusalem, 1963), 63–5 (the Christian quotes Ps. 2: 7, and Jacob gives four rebuttals).

NINE

STORYTELLING AS MIDRASHIC DISCOURSE IN THE MIDDLE AGES

ELI YASSIF

MIDRASH is virtually unique in Jewish culture for its unbroken continuity from antiquity to the Middle Ages. Indeed, in its transition from the rabbinic period to later times the genre was reinvigorated and developed in new and fascinating directions.

Much has been written about the term Midrash, regarding definitions, periodic distinctions, and generic divisions. It is not my task to go into these questions.[1] However, it is impossible to describe the phenomenon of storytelling as midrashic discourse in the Middle Ages without a basic working definition. Definitions that connect Midrash to biblical exegesis, expositions of verses, and public study are well known and have been accepted in one version or other since the beginning of the scholarly study of Midrash. But the work that touches the heart of midrashic study, not only on the theoretical level but also practically, is Isaac Heinemann's book, *Darkhei ha'agadah*.[2] In this seminal work Heinemann borrows the anthropological model of 'organic thinking', which in his view characterizes rabbinic interpretative mentality. This model provides convincing explanations of the fundamental questions that have occupied midrashic scholars since the nineteenth century, such as the explanation of the major changes made by the creators of aggadah to biblical verses and stories, the characteristics of interpretative techniques, and whether the expositors and their audiences sought to view them as authoritative texts, i.e. as having authority with regard to the Bible.

Heinemann's model of 'creative philology' and 'creative historiography' claims that, as in any indigenous society and culture, the sages interpreted the Bible, adapting it in the only way that was important to them—namely, to the reality of their life

---

[1] For a discussion of Midrash see Ch. 1 in this volume, by Michael Fishbane. For some recent discussions relevant to this chapter whose importance has not yet been sufficiently acknowledged, see for example David Stern, *Midrash and Theory: Ancient Jewish Exegesis and Contemporary Literary Studies* (Evanston, Ill., 1996); Joshua Levinson, *The Twice Told Tale: A Poetics of the Exegetical Narrative in Rabbinic Midrash* [Hasipur shelo supar] (Jerusalem, 2005).

[2] Isaac Heinemann, *The Methods of the Aggadah* [Darkhei ha'agadah] (Jerusalem, 1954).

and the meaning that the Bible could provide for it. According to this concept, Midrash is a creative reading of the biblical text that accords it meaning and a role in the reality of the creators of Midrash and of the society to which they belonged. This is a rhetorical technique that adapts the sacred text to the present in order to interpret it, endow it with meaning, and accord the appropriation process a dimension of sacredness and authority. It seems that this is the secret of the power of Midrash to exist almost un-interrupted along a historical continuum from the biblical period to the twenty-first century. It adapts itself naturally and creatively to every period, as each community uses its idiom for its own purposes and to reinforce its connection with its past.

The working definition which emerges from Heinemann's model has two components. Whereas the second component, which Heinemann dubbed 'organic' and others called 'appropriation', has been extensively discussed by recent midrashic scholars,[3] it is the first component that requires consideration, namely, the affinity to earlier texts. For the characteristics of 'search', 'preaching', 'exegesis', and 'enquiry' that are embedded in the essence of the term 'Midrash'[4] cannot but address an earlier textual entity that lies at its foundations. Without this condition imprinted on the definition, any narrative from the numerous existing genres might be called 'Midrash', which would result in its unique characteristics becoming blurred. If any literary expression may be called Midrash, its uniqueness as a rhetorical and literary genre will disappear. If everything is Midrash—the allegory and the magical story, the erotic rhymed prose, and the historical tale—one can well wonder what it is that differentiates Midrash from other cultural phenomena.

A two-dimensional working definition of Midrash such as the foregoing is particularly appropriate in the case of medieval writers. On the one hand, they were sufficiently removed from the historical context of the authors of classical Midrash that their spheres of interest and forms of expression were, in the main, irrelevant. On the other, it was just this historical distance that accorded the classic Midrash of the Land of Israel a dimension of antiquity, sanctity, and authority. Our definition also unties the Gordian knot binding the Midrash to the Bible and offers a connection to a text that is not necessarily biblical.[5] The text in question may derive from

---

[3] I wish to acknowledge the pioneering approach of Robert Bonfil for his description of the connection between medieval Hebrew storytelling and Midrash, to which the present article owes much. Robert Bonfil, 'Can Medieval Storytelling Help Understanding Midrash? The Story of Paltiel: A Preliminary Study on History and Midrash', in Michael Fishbane (ed.), *The Midrashic Imagination: Jewish Exegesis, Thought and History* (Albany, NY, 1993), 228–54. Bonfil, like other new midrashic scholars, emphasized the element of appropriation in the midrashic technique. See also Ithamar Gruenwald, 'Midrash and the Midrashic Condition: Preliminary Considerations', in Michael Fishbane (ed.), *The Midrashic Imagination*, 6–22.

[4] The essential concepts were analysed by Isaac Heinemann, 'The Development of Technical Terminology for the Interpretation of the Bible' (Heb.), *Leshonenu*, 14 (1946), 182–9; 15 (1947), 108–115; 16 (1948), 20–8. I find especially helpful the guidelines for reading Midrash suggested by Gerald Bruns, 'The Hermeneutics of Midrash', in Regina Schwartz (ed.), *The Book and the Text: The Bible and Literary Theory* (Oxford, 1990), 189–213.

[5] Bonfil has already emphasized that 'the application of the term Midrash should not be restricted to

the Talmuds and *midrashim*; but it may also be any observation of tangible or spiritual reality, such as historical memories, customs connected with birth and death, personal experiences, or visions of heaven and hell. This is the concept propounded by Clifford Geertz in his *Interpretation of Cultures*. In this work, he perceived the events of reality—either tangible or mental—as texts whose 'signs' are interpreted and deciphered by society by adapting them to its world, and thus creating culture.

In the following pages I shall demonstrate how midrashic creativity in the Middle Ages departs from the paradigm set by that of the rabbinic period. The description focuses mainly on the most independent and interesting expression of this period's midrashic writing, that of narrative Midrash. The rabbinic *midrashim* made intensive use of the tale, integrating it in various ways for a wide range of objectives.[6] As I will attempt to show, the main difference between the two periods in this respect is between the use of the tale as one of the components in a given *midrash* and the tale as carrying the main thrust of the midrashic expression. This literary process is without doubt connected to another, more comprehensive one, namely, the aspiration of the medieval Hebrew story towards literary independence. No longer is it constrained by exegesis, written law, or moral instruction. As a manifestation of independent literary work, its importance is self-contained, and does not lie in the contextual fabric of which it is a part.[7]

The process described in the following discussion of the conversion of the story to the new means of midrashic expression can also be explained by means of another typical phenomenon in medieval culture, designated 'exemplary mentality'. This is moral learning through 'real life' examples, articulated by means of a story. The *midrash* as a story no longer relies solely on the authority of an ancient sacred text, such as the Bible, but on remembrance of events (i.e. narratives) from the past or present, by means of which it is possible both to understand and investigate phenomena

biblical inquiry and exposition' (Bonfil, 'Can Medieval Storytelling Help Understanding Midrash?', 243). Joseph Dan showed that as early as the 6th cent. a mystical *midrash* disconnected itself from the biblical verses and exposed a different concept of midrashic creativity: Joseph Dan, '*Otiyot derabi akiva* and the New Concept of Language' (Heb.), *Da'at*, 55 (2005), 5–30.

[6] Ofra Meir, *The Darshanic Story in Genesis Rabbah* [Hasipur hadarshani bivereshit rabah] (Tel Aviv, 1987); Levinson, *The Twice Told Tale* (Heb.), and the vast body of research noted.

[7] The first to note this important cultural development was Joseph Dan. See his *The Hebrew Story in the Middle Ages* [Hasipur ha'ivri biyemei habeinayim: iyunim betoledotav] (Jerusalem, 1974), and Eli Yassif, *The Hebrew Collection of Tales in the Middle Ages* [Kovets hasipurim ha'ivri biyemei habeinayim] (Tel Aviv, 2004), 9–30. The history of research is described in Eli Yassif, 'The Study of Hebrew Literature of the Middle Ages: Major Trends and Goals', in Martin Goodman (ed.), *The Oxford Handbook of Jewish Studies* (Oxford, 2002), 270–94. On the theoretical level, my present approach finds much support from that of Paul Ricoeur. He coined the literary term 'interpretative narrative', which he defines as follows: 'These are narratives in which the ideological interpretation these narratives wish to convey is not superimposed on the narrative by the narrator but is, instead, incorporated into the very strategy of the narrative . . . this interpretation results directly from the narrative configuration . . . *it functions like a midrash*; that is, simply as a narrative it exercises an interpretative function' (Paul Ricoeur, 'Interpretative Narrative', in Schwartz (ed.), *The Book and the Text*, 237; emphasis added).

of importance to society (i.e. to 'expound' them), but also to present them ('relate' them) as an example of desirable conduct.[8]

A consideration of the independence of the story in the Hebrew literature of the period in relation to the exemplary mentality of the Middle Ages in general might assist us in understanding how the rhetorical–hermeneutical discourse of the rabbinic period was transformed into the narrative expression of the Middle Ages.

My purpose is not to describe the transition from the classic Midrash to the independent tale presented here as a linear process along a fixed time continuum. These new midrashic models appeared sometime between the ninth and fourteenth centuries, but do not usually indicate their historical origins. I present them here in relation to the classic models of rabbinic *midrashim* in order to highlight the formal and thematic changes they underwent. They thus do not indicate a demonstrable process or development.

EPIGONES OF CLASSICAL MIDRASH

In addition to the classical *midrashim*, the Middle Ages saw the appearance of *midrashim* that in the majority of their characteristics were similar to the ancient *midrashim*. Like the earlier *midrashim*, these works retain a close connection with the biblical verse order or portions of the Law, and expand or adapt them using linguistic, narrative, rhetorical, and other means. Thus, medieval *midrashim* such as *Midrash tanhuma*, *Pirkei derabi eli'ezer*, *Bereshit rabati*, *Midrash agadah*, and *Midrash hagadol* borrow the ancient midrashic format both in their textual structure and rhetorical connection to the sacred text, but are not identical to them. The following main characteristics emerge from the study of these later texts. In contrast to the mixture of Aramaic and Hebrew of rabbinic Midrash, Hebrew dominates; they possess an ideological uniformity that derives from omission of the names of the expositors; they highlight the cyclical structure of the homily (opening and closing with the same verse); and they create a literary unity of the whole *midrash* by combining subjects from different chapters.[9]

Despite the differences between these collections and classical *midrashim*, they

---

[8] On the exemplary phenomena in the literature and culture of the Middle Ages, compare the vast literature in Jacques Berlioz and Marie Anne Polo de Beaulieu (eds.), *Les Exempla médiévaux: Introduction à la recherche* (Carcassonne, 1992); and in Jewish culture: Yassif, *The Hebrew Collection of Tales* (Heb.), 166–213.

[9] e.g. Leopold Zunz, *Jewish Sermons and Their Historic Evolution* [Haderashot beyisra'el vehishtalshelutan hahistorit] (Jerusalem, 1954), 65–70; Jacob Elbaum, 'Characteristics of the Late Midrashic Literature' (Heb.), *Proceedings of the Ninth World Congress of Jewish Studies* [Divrei hakongres ha'olami hateshi'i lemada'ei hayahadut] (Jerusalem, 1986), iii. 57–62; Rina Drory, *The Emergence of Jewish-Arabic Contacts at the Beginning of the Tenth Century* [Reshit hamaga'im shel hasifrut hayehudit im hasifrut ha'aravit bame'ah ha'asirit] (Tel Aviv, 1988), 65–7; Ulrich Berzbach, 'The Varieties of Literal Devices in a Medieval Midrash', in Judit Targarona Borras and Angel Saenz-Badillos (eds.), *Jewish Studies at the Turn of the Twentieth Century* (Leiden, 1999), 384–91; and *Aggadat Bereshit*, trans. and ed. Lieve Teugels (Leiden, 2001), pp. xvii–xix, xxxi.

should be viewed as representing a dimension of continuity and cultural conservatism. Written in the Middles Ages, these works hardly betray any historical fingerprints. By contrast, there are scores of 'little *midrashim*', which were collected by Adolph Jellinek in his monumental *Bet ha-Midrasch* (1853–77).[10] These treatises differ from the classical *midrashim* in both literary form and thematic *Weltanschauung*. Together they constitute one of the branches of midrashic creativity in the Middle Ages, and have not yet merited the historical or literary study they deserve. As the vast majority of these *midrashim* are not of a narrative character, they are not the subject of the present study. However, in order to present the importance of this collection, and also its links with narrative Midrash, I shall describe one such treatise that bears on our subject.

Midrash tadshe (or *Baraita derabi pinḥas ben ya'ir*) is mentioned for the first time in the early medieval *midrash Bereshit rabati* and was apparently written around the ninth or tenth century CE.[11] It opens with the standard formula: 'It is written: "And God said: Let the earth bring forth grass" [Gen. 1: 11]. Rabbi Pinhas ben Ya'ir said: "Why on the third day did God decree the bringing forth of grass, seed-bearing plants, etc.?"'[12]

But from this point on the verse loses its place as the organizing element of the midrashic exposition. The second chapter opens thus:

The Temple was built in accordance with the creation of the world. In parallel with the two holy names [of God] were the two angels on the Ark of Testimony. The sky and the earth and the sea are the houses with their bolts. Corresponding to the high skies was created the Holy of Holies, corresponding to the earth the outer sacred house, corresponding to the sea was created the court, and corresponding to the high skies the twelve Temple curtains were created.[13]

And in the third chapter: 'Corresponding to the sky and the earth and the sea the three patriarchs were created—Abraham, Isaac, and Jacob: "I will make thy seed to multiply as the stars of heaven" [Gen. 26: 4].'[14] The *midrash* continues in this manner over twenty-two chapters and indicates parallels between the macrocosm of the structure of the world and human history, and the microcosm of the structure of the Temple and the contents of the Torah. The feature that connects the various chapters of the *midrash* is no longer the verses of the sacred text, but a subject, a mental structure. Thus, whereas the use of biblical verses and the way in which they connect to interpretative units are not dissimilar to the techniques used in classical

---

[10] Adolph Jellinek (ed.), *Bet ha-Midrasch: Sammlung kleinen Midraschim und gemischter Abhandlungen aus der ältern jüdischen Literatur*, 6 vols. (Leipzig, 1853–77). On Jellinek and his work, see Maren Niehoff, 'Jellinek's Approach to Aggadah' (Heb.), *Mada'ei hayahadut*, 38 (1998), 119–28.

[11] Zunz, *Jewish Sermons* (Heb.), 141, 157; Jellinek (ed.), *Bet ha-Midrasch*, vol. iii, pp. xxxiii–xxxvi. A new edition of this *midrash*, published in Orthodox schools' circles, adds a long and helpful introduction encompassing the earlier sources used by this *midrash*, as well as later authorities that mentioned and cited it: Idan Deshe Halevy (ed.), *Sefer yalkut midrashim*, 4 vols. (Safed, 2003), ii. 13–36.

[12] Jellinek (ed.), *Bet ha-Midrasch*, iii. 164.   [13] Ibid. 165.   [14] Ibid. 167.

Midrash, the concept of the uniformity of the treatise is different, reinforced not by an external text but by an internal theme that develops within the treatise and connects its various units.

The mythical character of the treatise should also be noted. It deals with the structure of the universe, and the ways in which it was formed, the structure of the human body, and the structure of human and Jewish history. According to the creative interpretation of this *midrash*, all of the above run parallel to what is written in the Bible and derive their meaning from it. Thus, the world and history that comprise thousands of details, which seem quite incomprehensible, are actually the parts of an infinite scheme built in accordance with the deep logic and meaning of the Torah. The beginnings of such ideas can be found in earlier rabbinic texts, but now entire treatises develop them in detail. These works, such as the *Pirkei derabi eli'ezer*,[15] *Midrash konen*, *Midrash temurah*, *Midrash aseret melakhim*, and *Midrash tadshe*, are characteristic of medieval Midrash that aspired to detach itself from the ancient Midrash and express the period's modes of thinking and mentality.[16] A feeling of chaotic reality with no clear, authoritative centre characterized the medieval world-view,[17] and perhaps even more so the Jewish mentality, whose perception of exile, lack of permanence, and absence of a political centre only reinforced and intensified it. Thus a treatise like *Midrash tadshe* that describes in detail the chaotic proliferation of the world and seeks to investigate it (*lidrosh*—to expound it), and prove its unity through its parallel to the Bible, not only presents a new literary form, but is also an innovative and significant statement on the Jewish mentality of the time.

HEROIC EPIC

I shall now begin my description of medieval narrative Midrash *per se* with the work called *Divrei hayamim shel mosheh*. This *midrash* is presumed to have been written in the tenth–eleventh centuries; it circulated widely and was extremely popular, as demonstrated by the many extant manuscripts and early printings of the work.[18] The *midrash* relates in great detail and with notable literary skill the mythical biography of Moses, from his birth to death. The story's raw material is derived from both rabbinic and medieval homiletic *midrashim* on the Torah. The treatise relates Moses' life story from his parents' pondering on whether to have another child under conditions of slavery, continuing with his miraculous birth, education in

---

[15] Along similar lines see: Jacob Elbaum, 'Messianism in *Pirkei derabi eli'ezer*: Apocalypse and Midrash' (Heb.), *Te'udah*, 11 (1996), 245–66.

[16] Cf. Peter Dronke, *Fabula: Explorations into Uses of Myth in Medieval Platonism* (Leiden, 1974); Dina Stein, *Maxims, Magic, Myth: A Folkloristic Perspective on Pirkei derabi eli'ezer* [Memrah, magyah, mitos: pirkei derabi eli'ezer le'or meḥkar hasifrut ha'amamit] (Jerusalem, 2004), 268–88.

[17] Aron Gurevich, 'Macrocosm and Microcosm', in id., *Categories of Medieval Culture*, trans. George Campbell (London, 1985), 41–92.

[18] For an edition and study of this text, see Avigdor Shinan, 'Divrei hayamim shel mosheh rabenu' (Heb.), *Hasifrut*, 24 (1977), 100–16.

Pharaoh's palace, his adventures in the wilderness after fleeing Egypt, his return, his leadership, the Exodus and the wanderings in the wilderness, and the narrative concludes with his death. As noted, all the details of the biography are based upon the rich homiletic literature on the subject. But while every such textual-midrashic unit in the Talmuds and *midrashim* is verse-based—each verse followed by its exegetical retelling, with references to the name of the expositor and the ways in which meaning was derived from the verse (linguistic proximity, reference to verses from other places, and so on),[19] *Divrei hayamim shel mosheh* takes a different course. It uses only the narrative part of the homily—for example, how Moses was taken from the water by Pharaoh's daughter—while omitting the verses underlying the interpretation or the names of the *darshanim* who created it, and connects it to the previous plot link. Thus a continuous story is formed, and anything that disrupts this continuity (such as citations of biblical verses or the names of sages and expositors who debated the verse's meaning) is omitted.

In sum, the details of Moses' mythical biography, which are fragmentarily spread over dozens of aggadic works, become a complete and consolidated heroic epic that uninterruptedly narrates the life story of the father of the prophets and leader of the nation. The fragmentariness becomes narrative continuity, and the learned creativeness of the exposition of the verses is now focused on the character and exploits of the hero. The overall absence of such tales of heroes in medieval Jewish literature, as compared with their plenitude in European and Arabic literature,[20] could be one of the reasons for this creative transformation of midrashic sources.

The most convincing evidence of this literary transformation is the longest and most innovative chapter of *Divrei hayamim shel mosheh*, known as 'Mosheh bekush' (Moses in the Land of the Kushites). Here, the long and convoluted tale is told of the king of the Kushites who was engaged in a long war, during which time Balaam (the sorcerer) and his sons took control of his kingdom. On his return, he found the city gates locked and launched a war against those besieged in it. Moses, in flight from Egypt, came to the city, took part in the siege as a soldier, and also advised the king on how to overcome the spells of the besieged and retake the city. Upon the death of the king his subjects married the (black) queen to Moses and crowned him king, but some time later the queen informed her ministers that Moses was not performing his conjugal duties and consequently would not produce an heir. They allowed him to leave the kingdom unharmed and he eventually came to Midian and to Zipporah, his future bride. This story is of course connected with the biblical episode (Num. 12: 1) in which Miriam and Aaron gossip about Moses' black wife (for which they were subsequently punished with leprosy), and its later expansion

---

[19] Techniques described in detail by Heinemann, *The Methods of the Aggadah* (Heb.).

[20] For some of the vast body of literature on this subject, see Norman Burns and Christopher Reagan (eds.), *Concepts of the Hero in the Middle Ages and the Renaissance* (Albany, NY, 1975); Malcolm Lyons (ed.), *The Arabian Epic: Heroic and Oral Story-Telling*, 3 vols. (Cambridge, 1995).

by both the Hellenistic Jewish writer Artapanos and Flavius Josephus, in *Antiquities of the Jews*.[21] Though this story has, since Josephus, disappeared from Jewish literature (except for a brief allusion in one of the Aramaic translations of the Torah), it returns with a flourish in *Divrei hayamim shel mosheh*. On the one hand, this appears to represent the significant return of apocryphal works to Jewish culture of the Middle Ages.[22] But any comparative reading of this version of the story with that in Josephus shows that Josephus highlights the historical–strategic aspects of the events: the political situation in Egypt and Pharaoh's fears regarding Moses, and a precise description of the besieged city. Josephus' Moses is a brilliant military strategist. In the medieval version, by contrast, Moses possesses all the qualities of a courtly hero: bravery, loyalty, control over magical powers, a high moral ethos (exemplified by his sexual restraint in lying by the queen but not touching her), and the ability to move alone over large and dangerous spaces.[23] The version of the tale of 'Mosheh bekush' in the *midrash Divrei hayamim shel mosheh* is that of a medieval hero, virtually a knight of the period.

The sacred text is not only the Bible but the rich world of rabbinic aggadah. By merging the biblical biography of Moses with its supplements and additions in aggadic literature, the medieval *midrash* is read in a new, revolutionary manner. For it does not place at its centre the historical–religious events of the Exodus and the Giving of the Law, but rather the figure of the hero, the leader who acts alone, with his great might and moral resolve, to achieve his aims. Thus Jewish culture of the Middle Ages 'expounds' the ancient text while appropriating it to its literary norms and worldview.

THE COLLECTION OF TALES AS MIDRASH

One of the most important phenomena in medieval Jewish culture is collections of tales, which first appeared in Hebrew in the ninth and tenth centuries.[24] The dominant structural feature of Eastern collections of tales such as *Kalila and Dimna*, *Tales of Sendebar* (*The Seven Sages of Rome*), or *The Arabian Nights* is the framework story. This form co-ordinates a collection of numerous stories, thus reducing the sense of their random nature and reinforcing a sense of narrative uniformity. In early Hebrew literature we know of only one example comparable to this Eastern phenomenon: *Tales of Ben-Sira*, which, using a frame story, presents the wondrous birth

---

[21] Studies on this tale: Avigdor Shinan, 'Moses and the Ethiopian Woman: Sources of a Story in The Chronicles of Moses', *Scripta Hierosolymitana*, 27 (1978), 66–78; Daniel Silver, 'Moses and the Hungry Birds', *Jewish Quarterly Review*, 64 (1973), 123–53; Tessa Rajak, 'Moses in Ethiopia: Legend and Literature', *Journal of Jewish Studies*, 29 (1978), 111–22.

[22] On this phenomenon, see Eli Yassif, *The Book of Memory, or The Chronicles of Jerahme'el* [Sefer hazikhronot—hu divrei hayamim liyerahme'el] (Tel Aviv, 2001), 31–40.

[23] On hero types, compare Burns and Reagan (eds.), *Concepts of the Hero*, and the classic study by Erich Auerbach, *Mimesis: The Representation of Reality in Western Literature* (Princeton, NJ, 1953), 123–42.

[24] See Yassif, *The Hebrew Collection of Tales* (Heb.), esp. 9–30.

of the child prodigy Ben-Sira, and his presentation to King Nebuchadnezzar. When the latter poses twenty-two questions, Ben-Sira answers him with a series of corresponding stories.[25]

Medieval Hebrew literature provides us with another framework model in treatises like *Midrash aseret hadibrot* (*Midrash of the Ten Commandments*) and the *Alphabet of Ben-Sira* (to be distinguished from the *Tales of Ben-Sira* just mentioned). In these two works it is not a narrative that creates the framework for the stories comprising them, but biblical verses or proverbs quoted in a particular order; indeed, the stories interpret them or corroborate their credibility. Significantly, this format (of a verse or proverb at the beginning of the textual unit, followed by its interpretation or a moral homily, then by a story or stories that illustrate it or develop its interpretation, with the unit concluding by citing the initial verse or proverb) is in fact the classic format of ancient rabbinic Midrash.[26]

There can be no question that framework collections of this type follow the midrashic literary tradition. But whereas the *Midrash of the Ten Commandments* follows the classical *midrashim*, insofar as its point of departure is the biblical Ten Commandments, the *Alphabet of Ben-Sira* departs from this norm. In contrast, it organizes the text in the alphabetical order of Aramaic proverbs attributed to the poet and moralist Joshua Ben-Sira of the Second Temple period, while these proverbs perform the same role as the biblical verses in midrashic tradition. In this shift from the norms of classical rabbinic Midrash, the *Alphabet of Ben-Sira* thus takes an additional, important step in the medieval transformation of the genre.[27]

It is important to add that this revolution in the concept of medieval Midrash begins with the more conservative approach taken in the *Midrash of the Ten Commandments*. For if both its structure and use of the biblical verses do not differ greatly from rabbinic *midrashim*, this is not the case with regard to its content and composition. Close textual examination shows that the balance between its moral-interpretative and narrative parts leans heavily towards the latter—in striking contrast with the aggadic *midrashim* of the classical rabbinic period.[28]

Another *midrash* on the Ten Commandments is integrated into *Pesikta rabati* (chapters 21–4). Comparison of the medieval *Midrash of the Ten Commandments* with this earlier, rabbinic instance will conclusively demonstrate the great difference between them. The earlier *midrash* in *Pesikta rabati* is a typical rabbinic composition: it plays freely with the rich meanings of the biblical verses, presents debates between rabbinic authorities, concentrates on minute hermeneutical differences

---

[25] Eli Yassif, 'Pseudo Ben-Sira and the Medieval Tradition of the "Wisdom Questions"', *Fabula*, 23 (1983), 48–63.

[26] See e.g. Joseph Heinemann, *Public Sermons in the Talmudic Period* [Derashot betsibur bitekufat hatalmud] (Jerusalem, 1970), 7–28.

[27] Eli Yassif, *Tales of Ben-Sira in the Middle Ages* [Sipurei ben sira biyemei habeinayim] (Jerusalem, 1984), 145–73.

[28] Some of these conclusions are summarized in Anat Shapira, *Midrash of the Ten Commandments: Text, Sources, and Interpretation* [Midrash aseret hadiberot: tekst, mekorot uferush] (Jerusalem, 2005), 119–58.

between words and phrases, and fascinates with its brilliant intellectual debates. It also includes some stories, but their function is to illustrate and add to the main midrashic discourse.[29]

In contrast, the homiletic part of the *Midrash of the Ten Commandments* is perfunctory and fragmentary, and moves hastily from its initial interpretative statements to the main feature: the tales. The importance accorded to the tales in contrast to the homiletical parts is also underscored by the fact that while the latter are borrowed from rabbinic sources dealing with the Ten Commandments, and contain no original material, the majority of the tales are new compositions found here for the first time in Hebrew literature.

Thus the *Midrash of the Ten Commandments* diverts attention from the homiletical and learned discourse to the story itself. As already noted, classical midrashic traditions still existed and these new trends did not efface them; rather, they created forms that are notably fresh and very often innovative.

To illustrate this transformation, I shall focus on the chapter that deals with the Fifth Commandment—'Honour thy father and thy mother' (Exod. 20: 12).[30] Immediately after the citation of the verse, the *midrash* states, 'The Holy One, blessed be He, said, "The father who begot you, honour him! The house in whose midst you slept, honour it as you would honour Me—for it is enough that they nurtured you! Support them in old age."'[31] This brief homily is taken virtually verbatim from older *midrashim*,[32] and thus contains nothing new in either content or form. But after this moralistic introduction, the text continues: 'A tale is told of a certain man who commanded his son in his hour of death, saying to him, "All of your days, cast your bread upon the waters, and do not eat of it by yourself."' There ensues a long story about the son who fulfilled his father's commandment and every day threw a loaf of bread into the water, until it was eaten by a fish, who was brought before the whale, the inquisitive king of the waters. Because the son obeyed his father's last will he was taught the languages of the animals, found a great treasure, and was thus saved from great travails because of his knowledge.[33] At the end of the story, the *midrash* continues: 'A tale is told of a pious man who was seventy years old but had no son', and after its conclusion, 'A tale is told of Rabbi Joshua ben Ulam, who was told in his dream, Be happy for you and the midget butcher will be neigh-

---

[29] On the basic model of the Ten Commandments as organizing tales, see B. Wachinger, 'Der Dekalog als Ordnungsschema für Exempelsammlungen', in W. Haug and B. Wachinger (eds.), *Exempel und Exempelsammlungen* (Tübingen, 1991), 239–63. Cf. Philip Alexander's discussion of this *midrash* above in Ch. 7.

[30] Shapira, *Midrash of the Ten Commandments* (Heb.), 63–72.

[31] The translation is from David Stern and Mark J. Mirsky (eds.), *Rabbinic Fantasies: Imaginative Narratives from Classical Hebrew Literature* (New Haven, Conn., 1990), 103.

[32] Shapira, *Midrash of the Ten Commandments* (Heb.), 64 nn. 120, 122.

[33] An important monograph on this story was written by Dov Noy, who emphasized its midrashic character: 'The Jewish Versions of the Animal Languages Folktale (AT 670)—A Typological-Structural Study', *Scripta Hierosolymitana*, 22 (1971), 171–208.

bours in Heaven.' Significantly, this is one of the first versions of the well-known medieval tale found in numerous versions in medieval literature, entitled 'The Neighbour in Paradise'.[34] At the conclusion of the three stories the moral is reiterated: 'Thus all of Israel is warned about the honour of father and mother ... All this shall the living take to their hearts, and fear God, and honour their father and mother in order that their lives will be good, and they will have many long days on the earth that God gave them.'[35]

This chapter thus displays the principal characteristics of narrative *midrash* I am seeking to highlight: an expository structure, a moral taken from known rabbinic sources, and the centrality of the place given to the stories. The contribution of *Midrash of the Ten Commandments* to Jewish culture of the Middle Ages is not in its homiletical–moral opening and conclusion (which contain nothing new), but in the previously unknown stories (though it may be assumed that it attests to oral traditions of Jewish communities of the time which were then written down).[36]

If, then, the story stands at the centre of the midrashic structure of *Midrash of the Ten Commandments*, the question must be asked: how did the story become one of the central midrashic expressions of the period? To answer this query, let us return to the second story included in the Fifth Commandment, the tale of 'The Child and the Book of Genesis'. A pious, rich, and childless man, after much prayer and pleading, was given a son in his old age. He used to carry his son to school every day on his shoulders. He asked the teacher with which book of the Torah he should start teaching his son, and was told: 'With Leviticus.' But the boy's father said to him: 'Start my son with the book of Genesis, which declares the praises and honour of the Holy One, blessed be He.'[37] One day, when the boy refused to be carried to school and went there alone, he was kidnapped by a knight from a faraway kingdom, with the book of Genesis in his hand. After many days, the king of that land became ill, and asked that a book be read to him. At random, Genesis was chosen from his library, and as no one could read it, one of his ministers recalled that there was a Jewish child-slave in his house. The boy was brought, and read and translated for the king, who was fascinated with the wonders and greatness of God. When the monarch recovered he sent the boy back home with great honour and riches. And the story concludes thus:

At that time our sages declared: Consider: this child had learned nothing more than the book of Genesis, yet the Holy One, blessed be He, gave him so much; how much more

---

[34] For a bibliography see Micha Bin Gorion and Dan Ben-Amos (eds.), *Mimekor Yisrael: Classical Jewish Folktales* (Bloomington, Ind., 1990), 177–8; Tamar Alexander-Frizer, *The Pious Sinner: Ethics and Aesthetics in the Medieval Hasidic Narrative* (Tübingen, 1991), 87–122.

[35] Shapira, *Midrash of the Ten Commandments* (Heb.), 72.

[36] Dov Noy, 'International and Jewish Tale-Types in "Midrash of the Ten Commandments"' (Heb.), in Avigdor Shinan (ed.), *Proceedings of the Fourth World Congress of Jewish Studies* [Divrei hakongres ha'olami harevi'i lemada'ei hayahadut] (Jerusalem, 1969), 352–5.

[37] Bin Gorion and Ben-Amos (eds.), *Mimekor Yisrael*, 162.

will be received by those who study Torah and Mishnah?! And furthermore, to this child who honoured his father by saying on only one occasion: 'Do not carry me on your shoulders and do not tire yourself for I can walk by myself,' the Holy One, blessed be He, gave all this money; how much greater shall be the reward received by one who honours his father *and* his mother![38]

The story of 'The Child and the Book of Genesis' told in *Midrash of the Ten Commandments* is preserved in numerous versions, which probably date back to the ninth century.[39] The assumption that the majority of the stories in *Midrash of the Ten Commandments* originated in independent folktales that were integrated by an editor who sought a normative framework for the oral traditions is reinforced by the fact that the connection between the Fifth Commandment and our story is tenuous in the extreme. The child did not refuse to go to the rabbi's house carried on his father's shoulders because of honouring his father, but because he did not want to be shamed before his friends. Even the coda of the tale opens with the story's original moral: the merit of studying the Torah, to which a further moral is added—as if the editor has remembered to connect the story, however tenuously, with honouring one's father and mother. Clearly, then, the story did not develop from within the original literary discussion of this commandment.

A close reading of the story further reveals that the narrative focal point lies in the father's instruction that the teacher begin his son's study with Genesis. This episode is usually regarded as the turning point of the plot, since immediately following it there is a reversal of direction: the child is kidnapped and the story shifts to a different geographical region and time. The father's behaviour raises two questions. First, how does a Jew of this period dare challenge the explicit precept: 'Rabbi Assi said: Why do young children commence with [the book of] the Law of the Priests [Leviticus] and not with [the book of] Genesis?—surely it is because young children are pure, and the sacrifices are pure; so let the pure come and engage in the study of the pure'?[40] And second, how would the story have changed had the teacher taught the child Leviticus and he had been kidnapped with this book in his hand?

The story testifies to a dispute over didactic issues that took place between different communities and possibly within the communities themselves. We know that several communities, in opposition to rabbinic tradition, decreed that teachers of

---

[38] Shapira, *Midrash of the Ten Commandments* (Heb.), 164.

[39] Cf. ibid. 67–9; Bin Gorion and Ben-Amos (eds.), *Mimekor Yisrael*, 163–5; Dina Levin, 'The Tale of the Book of Genesis' (Heb.), in Yoav Elstein, Avidov Lipsker, and Rella Kushelevsky (eds.), *Encyclopedia of the Jewish Story* [Entsiklopediyah shel hasipur hayehudi] (Ramat Gan, 2004), 333–49.

[40] *Lev. Rabbah* 8: 3 (*Midrash Wayyikra Rabbah*, ed. Mordechai Margulies, 2 vols. (New York, 1993), i. 156). On this see Ivan Marcus, *Rituals of Childhood: Jewish Acculturation in Medieval Europe* (London, 1996), 38–41, 95–101, who suggests a slightly different interpretation than the one I suggest following, namely that the children themselves are brought to school as a kind of sacrificial offering to God.

small children should begin their instruction with Genesis.⁴¹ The story explicitly accounts for the reasoning behind such an enactment: a child should first and foremost be acquainted with the Creator and his deeds—the Creation and the beginning of all had to be given priority over Leviticus and the sacrificial cult.

The story alludes to another, possibly more fundamental and problematic issue: imagine that the kidnapped child had in his hand Leviticus rather than Genesis, which he would have read and interpreted for the king. What would the king and his court know of Judaism—that its rituals are filled with blood frequently shed in the House of God? All this stands in starkest contrast with the universal message of Genesis, which describes the creation of a world that belongs to all human beings. Hence, the choice of Genesis as opposed to Leviticus is not a purely didactic issue, but one of *Weltanschauung*: between particularism and introversion in the case of Leviticus, as opposed to an openness to the nations of the world and an attempt to present the universality of Judaism. In the Middle Ages these were not merely theoretical issues, but existential questions that were common to Jewish culture both in Muslim countries and Christian Europe.

According to this interpretation, the story 'The Child and the Book of Genesis' constitutes an answer to a fundamental existential question of Jewish society in the Middle Ages. Jews are faced here with two books of the Torah: Genesis and Leviticus. Study of both books strengthens the connection to the Jewish past and to the sacred literature that expresses their identity. The question as to which book they should choose cannot be answered simply with: 'They will choose both,' since the choice is symbolic and expresses two different worldviews. By setting Genesis against Leviticus, the story defines the character and meaning of each of the books. The contrast thus apparently opens a window on Jewish reality in the medieval world, and a concern for its perception by the non-Jewish other.

Our reading of the story indicates that it maintains the first component of the definition of Midrash presented above, that of a connection with earlier texts (here both the Bible and Midrash). The continuation of the story, following the father's choice of Genesis, is a description of the younger generation's struggle with the harsh reality of the time, and the question is what support 'the Book' placed in its

---

⁴¹ Yassif, *The Hebrew Collection of Tales* (Heb.), 18–19; Levin, 'The Tale of the Book of Genesis' (Heb.), 346 n. 1. Outstanding evidence, from early 11th-cent. Kairouan (al-Qayrawan in today's Tunisia), is given in R. Nissim b. Jacob of Kairouan's collection of tales: *An Elegant Compositon Concerning Relief After Adversity*. After the telling of this story (in Arabic, as are all the tales narrated here), he informs the reader, 'When I was young I asked the Chief Elder, my father, the Chief Rabbi, as I was reciting before him the section beginning "And God called unto Moses" [Lev. 1: 1], "Master, why is it our custom for a child to begin recitation of Torah with Leviticus, skipping Genesis, which is the first book of the Torah? Is it right for one who wishes to read a book to begin reading it from its middle, skipping its beginning?"' His father explained that after the destruction of the Temple, as there are no more sacrifices, the reading of the sacred words of Leviticus is the atonement for our sins in their absence. This first-hand evidence presents the mainstream attitudes which were held in the Jewish communities. See Nissim ben Jacob ibn Shahin, *An Elegant Composition Concerning Relief After Adversity*, trans. William Brinner (New Haven, Conn., 1977), 88–9.

hands by the preceding generation (the father) provides as a weapon in this struggle. Indeed, the son endures, albeit symbolically, the cycle of suffering that typified the Jews of the Middle Ages: violence, separation, exile, servitude, and humiliation. It is only the book given to him by his father that enables him to rediscover and protect his identity even in distant exile, as well as to gain the respect and recognition of the nations of the world. In other words, it was the midrashic reading of the ancient text that provided medieval Jewry with the tools to contend with their harsh reality. According to our definition, by means of the midrashic story the ancient text was adapted to issues of the present and accorded an essential role in this reality.

The two other stories included in the Fifth Commandment section, as well as others included in the other nine commandments, can be examined in a similar way. What emerges is a fundamental change in perception of Midrash in the Middle Ages. It is no longer merely the homilies that interpret biblical verses that are of paramount importance, but the stories that give a new immediacy to older traditions. Thus whereas the connection with the sacred text accords the innovations authority and credence, the appropriation to the present grants them both meaning and function.

NARRATIVE MIDRASH AS INTERPRETATION OF RABBINIC AGGADAH

We do not know under what circumstances the vast majority of the midrashic works in the Middle Ages was created. But we may assume, for example, that some of the stories included in the *Midrash of the Ten Commandments* were related orally: during conversations about children's education, observing the sabbath, honouring one's parents, or gossip about an incident of adultery in the community. Nor do we know how the *Midrash of the Ten Commandments* itself was actually used once these tales were incorporated into it. How was it read as a book and who read it? Were its tales extracted from it and told separately? It may be assumed that all of these possibilities and others existed. But it is also quite plausible that in medieval schools study of Torah included considerable amounts of talmudic aggadah. Here is one well-known example:

Rabbi Ammi said: Rain falls only for the sake of men of faith ... Come and see how great the men of faith are, as is demonstrated from the tale [*ma'aseh*] of the weasel and the pit. If this is the case with one who trusts in the weasel and the pit, how much more so if one trusts [lit. believes] in the Holy One, blessed be He! [BT *Ta'anit* 8a].

On the question of who and what are 'the faithful' for whose sake the rain falls, Rabbi Ammi answers: they are the believers in the Almighty. But what sets the 'faithful' apart from other believers? According to Rabbi Ammi they believe in the Almighty at least to the same degree as those who believe in 'a weasel and a pit'. From what he says it is unclear whether the believers in 'a weasel and a pit' are also called 'the faithful' or only those who believe in the Almighty. But surely this question does not seem as important as that of the identity of the 'weasel and pit' that is the object of faith.

These and related questions have been posed for as long as tractate *Ta'anit* has been studied. Significant evidence to this effect has survived in Rashi's commentary on the passage:

> 'Truth will sprout from the earth [Ps. 85: 12]': When there is trustworthiness [lit. faith] in negotiation, then 'righteousness [*tsedek*] looks on from the heavens' [ibid.]. This means that the rains are charity [*tsedakah*]. 'From a weasel and a pit', who killed two people, is [found] in a story [*agadah*]. It is told of a young man who plighted his troth to a maiden. She said, 'Who will be a witness between us?' And there was a pit and a weasel there. The young man said, 'The pit and the weasel will witness it.' He later broke his vows and married another woman and had two children. One fell into a pit and died, and another was bitten by a weasel and died. His wife said to him, 'What have you done that our sons have died a bizarre death?' And he told her the things that had happened. [Correspondingly,] if 'one trusts in the Holy One, blessed be He'—putting Him as witness between himself and his friend—'how much the more so' [will he be cared for].

Rashi interprets the concept of 'faith', which is the leading word in this discussion, as an agreement or contract between people. When they are in need of witnesses, there are some who call on a weasel and a pit and believe in them, but the more scrupulous call the Almighty as a witness, and they are the truly 'faithful'. The great significance of this, according to Rashi (interpreting the Psalm verse), is that maintaining trust between people is a condition for attaining divine favour. (It is possible that Rashi's engagement in commerce is what focused his interpretation on trust between negotiators.)[42]

Yet it is clear that at the centre of Rashi's interpretation stands the folk story. His argument that 'it is in the aggadah' and not in *sefer agadah* (i.e. a book) apparently shows that this was a story he heard from oral tradition. Rashi's grandchildren and disciples, the Tosafists (annotators of the Talmud), tell a fuller and more comprehensible story:

> *The pit and weasel . . . one who believes in a pit and weasel.* It happened that a young maiden wanted to go to her father's house and there was a pit along the way and she fell into it.

---

[42] It is clear in any event that this is not the only possible interpretation. The immediate possibility, when the discussion deals with belief in the Almighty and divine grace, is belief in the intervention of divine power in this world to grant life to its inhabitants, and not in commercial negotiation as Rashi has it. Thus the 'believer in a weasel and a pit', as R. Ammi puts it, is not a one-time occurrence (by chance they saw before them a pit and a weasel passing by it), as the story Rashi tells implies, but constant belief in natural objects (a well, water) and animals (a weasel). In other words, R. Ammi compares belief in the Almighty with the belief of pagans, who with their worship of nature succeed in bringing rain. And if they are so 'great', that is they do succeed, how great would the success of the worshippers of the Almighty be?! This interpretation is reinforced by the discussion that comes before these words of R. Ammi, which deals with questions of incantations, prayers, loyalty to the Almighty, and their success in influencing reality.

A young man came and said, 'If I lift you out will you marry me?' She said, 'Yes.' And they swore that he would not marry another woman and she would not marry another man. And they said, 'Who will be a witness between us?' A weasel ran by the pit and they said, 'This weasel and this pit will be witnesses,' and they went on their way. The girl kept her vow, and the man married another woman and she bore him a son. A weasel came and bit him and he died. And she bore him another son and he fell into a pit and died. His wife said to him, 'What is this that we are destined to a different destiny than other people?' He remembered his vow and told the story to his wife. She said to him: 'Go and marry her,' and he gave her a divorce and married the young maiden. That is why people say: Those that believe in a weasel and a pit, which bore witness.

The tosafist version is actually the same story told by Rashi, but fuller and expanded. If the Tosafists had only known the version in Rashi's commentary, they would not have been able to present the story as they do. A more extensive account, slightly earlier or contemporary with Rashi's, is found in the responsa of the ge'onim and the *Arukh* of Nathan ben Yehiel, who apparently extracted it from the geonic version.[43] This tale, which exemplifies the cultural shift from Babylon via Italy to France and Ashkenaz, was apparently known to the Tosafists and influenced the version cited here.

The 'Weasel and the Pit' tale demonstrates several important things about the functions of the tale as Midrash during the Middle Ages. The first of these is the filling of the enigmatic gaps in the talmudic text. Just as the rabbinic Midrash viewed itself first and foremost as an interpretation and exegesis of informational gaps in the biblical text, so the story in the Middle Ages serves to fill such gaps in the talmudic text. There are many other examples that I have discussed elsewhere.[44] This literary phenomenon should apparently be linked to a wider phenomenon: the interpretation of rabbinic aggadah, whose development began precisely during this period, and, like the medieval interpretation of the Bible, became almost a profession in its own right.[45]

The stories sometimes interpret and develop concepts or names that were familiar in the rabbinic period, reflect on a proverb or aphorism, and on occasion simply allude to the *incipit* of a story. It is difficult to know whether these tales originated in the rabbinic period and came into the domain of the medieval Jewish interpreters and storytellers through oral tradition, or whether they are medieval tales presented by their tellers as originally belonging to rabbinic literature. Both possibilities can be presented and therefore each case must be examined individually. In the tale of the 'Weasel and the Pit' there seems to be no doubt that there is

---

[43] On the variants of this tale, see Bin Gorion and Ben-Amos (eds.), *Mimekor Yisrael*, 170–2; Tamar Alexander-Frizer, *The Beloved Friend-And-A-Half: Studies in Sephardi Folk Literature* [Ma'aseh ahuv vahetsi: hasipur ha'amami shel yehudei sefarad] (Jerusalem, 1999), 60–76.

[44] Eli Yassif, *The Hebrew Folktale: History, Genre, Meaning* (Bloomington, Ind., 1999), 250–65.

[45] Barry Walfish, *Esther in Medieval Garb: Jewish Interpretation of the Book of Esther in the Middle Ages* (Albany, NY, 1993), 33–6.

no connection between the story with its romantic overtones that passed through the hands of medieval exegetes—the *ge'onim*, Nathan ben Yehiel, Rashi, the Tosafists—and the words of Rabbi Ammi about the faithful. All this attests to the open, free style used by the medieval storytellers, and in this context at least they are no different from the *ba'alei ha'agadah* (storytellers) of the rabbinic period and their 'organic' use of the tale as part of their expository worldview.

The connection of the 'Weasel and the Pit' tale to an ancient text is only one component of what we referred to earlier as a 'midrashic condition'. The second and more complex part is the text's meaning in the new context of medieval Jewish reality. Rashi, as observed, focuses its meaning on the contractual trust between two parties. To a businessman or religious arbiter there is no difference between a commercial and a marriage contract, and he views the former with the same degree of gravity as he does the latter. However, the tale as he tells it contradicts this approach. For the tale is not about the breaking of a commercial contract but the life of real people: a woman abandoned to her plight, but who still keeps her vows; and an unfortunate marriage that results in the death of children and acknowledgement of the consequences of betrayal and abandonment. At the centre of all these versions of the tale in the Middle Ages stands a human tragedy based on a gender distinction: the man betrays his commitment and the women realize its significance and maintain it to the letter.

The surfeit of meaning in Rashi's tale compared with his interpretation is of great importance and highlights the difference between Midrash and exegesis. Whereas the exegesis offers one meaning, the Midrash opens up numerous possibilities. The tale can be read as the breaking of a contract, or as a story of human tragedy (i.e. as a story of male insensitivity in contrast to the profundity of female emotions). It can also be read independently of the talmudic context as a revelation of the forces of nature whose symbols here are the pit (water) and the weasel (animals), and whose loyalty and wisdom surpass those of humans. This may be viewed as a remnant of mythical-pagan beliefs that persisted throughout the medieval world, and with which the monotheistic religions attempted to compete. It seems that it is the latter interpretation that is closer to the initial talmudic meaning of the faithful who believed in a weasel and a pit.

Either way, although the narrative *midrash* of the enigmatic talmudic text presents itself as its interpretation, it opens to the reader or listener a range of meanings, each of which was explicable to the audience to which it was recounted.

FROM AGGADIC FRAGMENTS TO THE NEW MIDRASH

One of the most significant works that has constructed Jewish identity since the early Middle Ages is *Aseret harugei malkhut* (The Ten Martyrs), also known as *Midrash eleh ezkerah*. This is the story of the ten sages who were cruelly put to death after the Bar Kokhba revolt, including Rabbi Akiva, Rabbi Ishmael, Rabbi Hanina ben Teradion, and others. The treatise, known since geonic times, became a model of Jewish martyrdom (together with the ancient story of the mother and her seven sons).[46] The dispute over the event's historical authenticity, undocumented in rabbinic literature, is not our concern here. Like the *Midrash of the Ten Commandments*, *Aseret harugei malkhut* also belongs to the framework story genre. It appears that Jewish writers in the Middle Ages preferred this genre because it could bind together diverse materials (see above). But while the *Midrash of the Ten Commandments* and the *Alphabet of Ben Sira* chose a rhetorical framework—either biblical verses or Aramaic proverbs—*Aseret harugei malkhut* created a *narrative* framework. 'The emperor of Rome decided to study the Law of Moses with sages and elders,' and he, like the king in the tale of the child and the book of Genesis, began with Genesis. But when he reached the weekly portion 'Ve'eleh hamishpatim', and read the verse 'And he that stealeth a man, and selleth him . . . he shall surely be put to death' (Exod. 21: 16), he recalled the story of Joseph and his brothers. Thereupon, the emperor filled his palace with shoes and summoned the ten most prominent Jewish sages of the time. When he asked them the verdict, according to the halakhah, concerning a man who steals one of his Jewish brothers and sells him, they answered that the Torah specifies that 'he shall surely be put to death'. The emperor then informed them that they were to be put to death because they were the representatives of the ten tribes in their time. The sages requested a three-day postponement of the verdict and asked Rabbi Ishmael (the high priest) to ascend to heaven and see if their fate had been sealed there. At this point, the story reverts to the birth of Rabbi Ishmael, whose mother did not give birth until she was quite old (or according to another version, whose children died after their birth). Her husband cautions her against uncleanness after the ritual immersion, and she immerses herself eighty times, since after each immersion she is touched by a different unclean animal. The angel Gabriel awaits her at the door of the bathhouse in the guise of Rabbi Yose, her husband, 'and he held her and brought her to her home. And that same night she was impregnated with Rabbi Ishmael, who became as beautiful as the image of [the angel] Gabriel, and that is why Gabriel met him when he ascended to heaven.'[47] In heaven, at the behest of his colleagues, Rabbi Ishmael discovers that the verdict has been signed and sealed by the Almighty. The remainder of the composition relates the successive executions of the ten sages, following traditions recorded in earlier rabbinic sources.

At the centre of the frame story is the punishment meted out to the ten sages by the emperor (in the generation after the destruction of the Temple and the Bar

---

[46] On this work, see Bin Gorion and Ben-Amos (eds.), *Mimekor Yisrael*, 156–62. A critical edition was published by Gottfried Reeg (ed.), *Die Geschichte von den Zehn Märtiren: Synoptische Edition* (Tübingen, 1985). On the mother and her seven sons, see Galit Hasan-Rokem, *Web of Life: Folklore and Midrash in Rabbinic Literature* (Stanford, Calif., 2000), 115–25; Elisheva Baumgarten and Rella Kushelevsky, 'From "The Mother and Her Sons" to "Mother and Her Sons" in Ashkenaz in the Middle Ages' (Heb.), *Zion*, 71 (2006), 301–42.   [47] Jellinek (ed.), *Bet ha-Midrasch*, ii. 65.

Kokhba revolt) for the kidnapping and sale of Joseph. The dramatic act of filling the palace with shoes is designed to remind the sages of the words of the prophet Amos, 'For they sold the righteous for silver, and the poor for a pair of shoes' (Amos 2: 6). This visual cue is reinforced by textual interpretation—intertextual discussions, a basic feature of rabbinic Midrash.[48] In our case, this is the connection made by the emperor between the biblical law and the stealing of Joseph, and the words of the prophet. Such a striking connection with the biblical text highlights the story's first component of the midrashic phenomenon.

But the picture becomes more complex if we ask, as we did with the story of the child and the book of Genesis, what would have happened if the child had read Leviticus to the king? What would have happened if the sages had *not* volunteered to teach the emperor Torah? He probably would not have known about the events and their meaning, he could not have accused the rabbis of what they were not guilty of, and the entire brutal event would never have happened. Thus we return, by a different route, to the same issue inherent in the story about the child and the book of Genesis. Once again, teaching the Torah to non-Jews provides them with a weapon with which they may destroy Jews.

This view of the danger of teaching Torah to non-Jews characterizes the supporters of introversion and isolationism, and was a widely accepted position among medieval Jewry.[49] The frame story of *Aseret harugei malkhut* thus sides with this position and gives it special prominence. It argues that one of the terrible disasters that befell the Jewish people during the rabbinic period was the result of opening sacred Jewish texts to non-Jews, who only sought to harm Jews—a position that has almost no connection with the historical reality of late antiquity, but does relate to the socio-historical reality of medieval life.

Another question occurs between the lines of the frame story: should later generations pay for the sins of their forefathers? Is it possible that the afflictions that beset the Jews of the Middle Ages—exile, wandering, pogroms, and humiliation—somehow constitute a recompense for the sins of their forefathers? This question occupied Jewish consciousness of the period, and *Aseret harugei malkhut* brings it to the fore.[50] Here it seems that the martyrdom of the ten sages is not punishment for their own sins but, on the contrary, is proof of the greatness accorded to them by the Almighty, who found them worthy of bearing the punishment for the sins of earlier generations. The *midrash* of *Aseret harugei malkhut* translates the theoretical argument into narrative language, thus bringing about its resolution, not by logical or theological inference, but through collective memory and emotion. The wide

---

[48] Daniel Boyarin, *Intertextuality and the Reading of the Midrash* (Bloomington, Ind., 1990).

[49] For the prohibition on teaching Torah and Hebrew to non-Jews, see Hirsch Zimmels, *Ashkenazim and Sephardim* (London, 1958), 276–7.

[50] e.g. Hayim H. Ben-Sasson, *On Jewish History in the Middle Ages* [Toledot yisra'el biyemei habeinayim] (Tel Aviv, 1969), 255–64; Simha Goldin, *Ways of Jewish Martyrdom* [Alamot ahevukha, al-mot ahevukha] (Lod, 2002), 268–316.

dissemination of *Aseret harugei malkhut* from the early Middle Ages onwards, giving it a central role in Jewish collective memory, testifies to its effectiveness and continuing relevance for succeeding generations.

Since Leopold Zunz, scholars have stated that this *midrash* is a masterpiece of compilation, modification, and adaptation of individual martyrdom stories of sages in rabbinic literature.[51] Apart from the desire to intensify the stories of the rabbis' martyrdom by joining them into one narrative, there might be other topical motives which lie beyond our ken. Nevertheless, the public and collaborative character of the event is notable: the sages observe the heroic acts and sacrifice of their companions, answer the claims of the emperor and his people, and thus, from a series of short accounts about the individual death of each sage, the event becomes a public event—almost a communal ritual. The similarity between this tale and the story of the mother and her seven sons on the one hand, and the martyrdom memories of the Crusade period on the other is significant. It shows that medieval Jews viewed martyrdom as an event whose power lay in its public character.[52] If such an event were to take place privately, its educational and theological effect would be dissipated. The sacrifice, torture, and anguish, the blood that flowed, and the licking flames all play an educational role *only* when they are publicly dramatized. Accordingly, the disparate stories of the deaths of sages in rabbinic literature were adapted to the medieval mentality, and the new narrative *midrash* thus created expressed the attitude of the people of the period towards martyrdom, its historical significance, and its social consequence.

THE MEDIEVAL ROMANCE AS MIDRASH

The genre which seems at first glance furthest from that of Midrash is the Hebrew romance, a narrative combining epic adventure with a love story recounted in the spirit of courtly love. The Hebrew romances, which were decisively influenced by European romance,[53] have not yet been studied in depth, with the exception of the *Toledot alexandros* (History of Alexander of Macedon). This tale was originally related and written by Greek scribes in Alexandria of the second and third centuries CE, and underwent revisions and adaptations in numerous languages and cultures.[54]

---

[51] Cf. the studies mentioned in Bin Gorion and Ben-Amos (eds.), *Mimekor Yisrael*, and especially Samuel Krauss, 'The Ten Martyrs' (Heb.), *Hashiloaḥ*, 44 (1925), 10–22, 106–17, 221–33.

[52] Cf. Goldin, *Ways of Jewish Martyrdom* (Heb.), 99–129; Susan Einbinder, *Beautiful Death: Jewish Poetry and Martyrdom in Medieval France* (Princeton, NJ, 2002); Jeremy Cohen, *Sanctifying the Name of God: Jewish Martyrs and Jewish Memories of the First Crusade* (Philadelphia, Pa., 2004).

[53] On this genre, its history and variants, see William Jackson, *The Literature of the Middle Ages* (New York, 1960), 160–75. Roberta Krueger (ed.), *The Cambridge Companion to Medieval Romance* (Cambridge, 2000). For an introduction to the study of these Hebrew romances, see Joseph Dan, 'Hebrew Versions of Medieval Prose Romances', *Hebrew University Studies in Literature*, 6 (1978), 1–9.

[54] For an initial history, versions, and studies, see Richard Stoneman, *The Greek Alexander Romance* (London, 1991); John Boyle, 'The Alexander Romance in the East and West', *Bulletin of the John Rylands University Library of Manchester*, 60 (1977), 13–27; Margaret Bridges and J. Christoph Bürgel (eds.), *The Problematics of Power: Eastern and Western Representations of Alexander the Great* (Bern, 1996).

We know of seven Hebrew versions of the story that were translated from Greek, Latin, Arabic, and French between the eleventh and fourteenth centuries.[55] It is hardly an exaggeration to claim that this is the narrative most often translated into Hebrew in the Middle Ages. It demonstrates the interests of the learned elite, as well as the lay public's attraction to these kinds of stories of adventure. However, the tale of Alexander of Macedon was never called a *midrash* and was never perceived as such. I contend that it constitutes one of the most fascinating examples of the ever-expanding borders of medieval Midrash, whose characteristics I have sought to present throughout this chapter.

Indeed, the two main recensions of the Hebrew versions of the *History of Alexander* are more or less precise translations of the work from Greek, Latin, Arabic, and French recensions. They underwent minor variations in style, such as the insertion of biblical verses, and theological changes, such as the omission of Christian elements, but in principle they should be viewed as faithful translations of both the Eastern and Western romances. As such they do not display any of the characteristics of medieval Jewish Midrash, as presented above. In contrast, there is the Third Recension, known to us from two surviving manuscripts, which presents an independent version of the popular romance.[56] It tells the story of the great king and military leader from birth to death, but is not dependent on the other versions and employs a mythical biography of Alexander that connects him to Jewish tradition and culture.[57]

As is well known, Alexander is no stranger to Jewish culture, and some thirteen tales about him are documented in rabbinic literature, including stories of his campaigns and encounters with kingdoms and their leaders, his ascent to the skies, his encounter with the Elders of the Negev, and his much recounted visit to Jerusalem.[58] Surprisingly, these narrative traditions are not found in the first two medieval recensions of the *History of Alexander*. Its Hebrew translators, who were undoubtedly familiar with the tales of Alexander in rabbinic literature, seem to have chosen to be faithful to the original, non-Jewish version of the romance rather than to their own cultural traditions. The author of the Third Recension did something very different. He inserted the majority of the rabbinic traditions about Alexander

---

[55] For a sample of these studies, see *The Book of the Gests of Alexander of Macedon*, ed. and trans. Israel Kazis (Cambridge, Mass., 1962), esp. 2–58; Wout Jac van Bekkum, *The Hebrew Alexander Romance According to MS London, Jews' College no. 145* (Leuven, 1992), 1–35.

[56] The importance of this outstanding version was first acknowledged by Moses Gaster in 'An Old Hebrew Romance of Alexander', *Journal of the Royal Asiatic Society* (1897), 485–549, and the edition of this version by Rosalie Reich, *Tales of Alexander the Macedonian* (New York, 1972).

[57] These and other issues regarding the Jewish traditions of Alexander in the Middle Ages are discussed in detail in Eli Yassif, 'The Hebrew Traditions of Alexander the Great: Narrative Models and their Meaning in the Jewish Culture of the Middle Ages' (Heb.), *Tarbiz*, 75 (2006), 359–407.

[58] On these tales and their distribution in rabbinic literature, see *The Book of the Gests of Alexander of Macedon*, ed. and trans. Israel Kazis, 2–25. See also Azariah de' Rossi's important discussion of the divergencies in ch. 22 of his *Me'or einayim* (Mantua, 1573–5).

into his version, and presented them as the foundations—both structural and ideational—of the original romance of Alexander, which he had revised.

The most important of the ancient Hebrew traditions regarding Alexander in Jewish culture is the tale of his visit to Jerusalem. It was first recorded by Flavius Josephus in his *Antiquities of the Jews*. Historians argue about the tale's factual veracity. This visit was not documented by any of the contemporary historians who were respected for their detailed accounts of Alexander's travels. Some versions of the tale are found in tannaitic literature (*Megilat ta'anit*) and also in the Talmuds and *midrashim*.[59] The differences between the Flavian and the rabbinic sources have been studied extensively and need not be discussed here, but what does bear comment is the transfer of the Hebrew tale from late antiquity to medieval Hebrew literature. One significant factor is that the tale is told in a wide range of versions, from those that copy rabbinic traditions verbatim to versions that differ significantly. A second factor to be noted is that the Hebrew versions in medieval Jewish literature are found in a variety of sources: historiographical texts (*Sefer yosipon, Sefer hazikhronot*), medieval collections of tales and *midrashim*, and the various versions of the Hebrew Alexander romance mentioned above.

Although it is not possible to go into detail here regarding the differences between the various sources and versions, three divergences are of paramount importance. The first is the vision or dream in which one of the protagonists of the tale sees a supernatural figure that instructs him on how to behave. In Josephus' version, the high priest Jaddus is commanded in his dream to lead the white-garbed priests in procession to meet Alexander: 'When Alexander was still far off he saw the multitude in white garments, the priests at their head clothed in linen, and the high priest in a robe of hyacinth-blue and gold, wearing on his head the mitre with the golden plate on it on which was inscribed the name of God; he approached alone and prostrated himself before the Name and first greeted the high priest.'[60] Even in the rabbinic versions, Alexander states that he saw the high priest's image whenever he was victorious in battle.[61] In the medieval versions, by contrast, on the night before the fall of Jerusalem Alexander himself 'saw a man standing at his head garbed in white linen and an unsheathed sword in his hand',[62] as a warning against harming the city and its inhabitants. When he saw the same figure before his entry into the city, he knelt before him. The difference between these two motifs is not without significance: in the ancient versions (Josephus and the sages) the high priest

---

[59] For just a sample of research on this tale see *The Book of the Gests of Alexander of Macedon*, ed. and trans. Israel Kazis, 4–11; Bin Gorion and Ben-Amos (eds.), *Mimekor Yisrael*, 90–2; Shaye Cohen, 'Alexander the Great and the High Priest Jaddus According to Josephus', *Association of Jewish Studies Review*, 7–8 (1982/3), 41–68.

[60] Flavius Josephus, *Antiquities of the Jews*, trans. Ralph Marcus (Cambridge, Mass., 1987), p. xi. 330–3, 473–5, and the important Appendix C, 'Alexander the Great and the Jews', 512–32.

[61] BT *Yoma* 69a.

[62] *Josippon* [Sefer yosipon], ed. David Flusser, 2 vols. (Jerusalem, 1978), i. 54–61; the English translation is in Bin Gorion and Ben-Amos (eds.), *Mimekor Yisrael*, 93.

is instructed as to what he must do in order to help Alexander in his wars, but there is no threat to the king. In contrast, in the medieval versions Alexander himself is threatened and acts out of fear.

A second important difference between the versions is Alexander's suggestion that his image be placed in the Temple. Josephus does not even hint at this, but relates that Alexander 'went up to the temple where he sacrificed to God under the direction of the high priest, and showed due honour to the priests and to the high priest himself'.[63] In contrast, the medieval versions present an episode that introduces a certain degree of tension: the priests decline Alexander's offer to place his gold image in the Holy of Holies,[64] and instead suggest that they name all the priests' children born that year after him, thus preserving his memory, 'when they come to perform the service of our God in this house. For in the House of our God you are not permitted to accept any statue or picture.'[65]

A third difference is that, according to Josephus and the rabbinic accounts, the Jews request Alexander to free them of taxation in the *shemitah* (sabbatical) year and to grant religious freedom to the Jews of Babylon and Medea. Requests of this type are absent from the medieval versions. On the other hand, these versions conclude with Alexander's request to the high priest 'to question God as to whether he should go to war against Darius or not', and the high priest shows him the book of Daniel that prophesies his victory.[66] While this motif appears in Josephus, it is articulated in a short sentence that also treats the course of Alexander's exploits in Jerusalem. In the medieval versions it appears in detail, with a full citation from Daniel, and ends on a triumphant note of victory and hope for the future.

Is there a connection between these three discrepancies? I would suggest that together they indicate ideational trends and contemporary tensions in medieval Jewish society. Whereas in the ancient (Josephus) version the vision was given to the Jews, not to Alexander, and the narrator is convinced that the king, on seeing the greatness of the Jewish religion, will prostrate himself in obeisance, in the medieval version such recognition is perceived as an illusion. Only fear of divine power will influence the foreign king. Thus whereas Josephus and the tradition he documents present an idyllic picture of ruler and ruled attaining a balanced, mutual respect, the medieval versions highlight their belief that only a supernatural power can compel the regime to acknowledge the Jewish minority's rights.

We may point to another, similar tendency. Whereas in Josephus the king does not threaten the basic tenets of the Jewish faith, in the medieval versions Alexander seeks to impair belief in the one God by placing his image in the Holy of Holies.

---

[63] Josephus, *Antiquities of the Jews*, trans. Marcus, xi. 336, 477.

[64] Already in the BT *Yoma* and *Genesis Rabbah* versions (above, n. 61) there is more than a hint that when he sought to enter the Holy of Holies, the Temple guard prevented him from doing so by either enticement or threat.

[65] *Josippon* (Heb.), ed. Flusser, i. 57; English translation, Bin Gorion and Ben-Amos (eds.), *Mimekor Yisrael*, 93.

[66] *Josippon* (Heb.), ed. Flusser, i. 57; English translation, Bin Gorion and Ben-Amos (eds.), *Mimekor Yisrael*, 93.

The very same threat with which the story opens (in Alexander's dream) remains active at this stage too; though here the motif of loyalty is added. Naming the children after the ruler is presented as a pledge of (almost feudal) loyalty[67] for generations; this is what the Jews can grant the regime instead of the unacceptable infringement of the foundations of their faith.

Finally, the request to waive taxation in the *shemitah* year and to support the Jews of Babylon and Medea is replaced by the prophecy of Alexander's victory. Since the *shemitah* year was no longer significant in the medieval period, the motif of Daniel's prophecy to Alexander was shifted from the margins of Josephus' story to its centre, and became its final chord. With it emerges an idea whose importance in medieval Jewish consciousness should not be underestimated: it is the divine plan and the words of the prophets that direct historical events and are omniscient. The truth attested by Scripture does not have bearing on the Jewish people alone, but on the non-Jewish nations as well. If the deeds of Alexander the Great were planned and executed in accordance with a divine plan foretold by the prophets of Israel, then all the more so would this obtain with regard to medieval rulers. They, too, were subject to the God of Israel and his sovereign rule.

From this account it appears that the medieval tale of Alexander in Jerusalem is not an enjoyable story about an event that happened in the past, but a tale told with consideration of the needs and reality of its present readers and listeners. It is, therefore, a full expression of the midrashic mentality we are attempting to consider here; specifically, a revision of older sources in order to adapt them to a later audience, and to the reality they seek to influence.

As we have seen, rabbinic sources contain numerous additional tales about Alexander, but aside from inserting the tale of Alexander in Jerusalem, the later Hebrew translators did not permit themselves to make radical changes to the structure or content of the works they received. The open, independent, and creative character of the Third Recension is reflected in the many rabbinic tales about Alexander incorporated therein. This distinctive approach effects a dynamic integration between traditional Jewish memory and the general tradition, ancient and medieval alike. We shall specify two cycles of stories that underscore the centrality of this phenomenon.

In the first cycle Alexander crosses the Mountains of Darkness,[68] helped by a pearl that lights his way. He reaches a kingdom where he sits in judgment with its king to see how they judge there, and two litigants petition the king to give a verdict as to the rightful owner of a buried treasure. The seller claims that it belongs to the person who purchased it; the buyer claims that it belongs to the seller, since he sold him the land, not the treasure buried in it.[69] Thereupon, Alexander travels to

---

[67] See the discussion by David Flusser in *Josippon* (Heb.), ii. 136–40.

[68] Bodleian Library, MS Heb. D. 11, fo. 269a, and Rosalie Reich (ed.), *Tales of Alexander the Macedonian*, 52 ff.

[69] This, of course, is the talmudic story of Alexander and the king of Katzia. For its sources and variants, see *The Book of the Gests of Alexander of Macedon*, ed. and trans. Israel Kazis, 20–3, and also the impor-

the Land of Africa, which is ruled by women (the Amazons).[70] They say to him: 'If you kill us, people will accuse you of murdering women. If we kill you, people will say: Behold a king who was overcome by women!'

Two details in this cycle are worthy of note. First, the insertion of the Alexandrian tales from rabbinic sources in almost identical order: the Mountains of Darkness, the king of Katzia, the Land of the Amazons.[71] The narrative structure of the Third Recension as a collection of independent stories enables the integration of the cycle of stories from rabbinic sources, thus reinforcing the medieval treatise's connection to Jewish tradition. Moreover, the independent and original character of this recension is manifested by virtue of the fact that it does not copy the stories from rabbinic literature verbatim—even a common name like that of the king of Katzia, which was surely familiar, is omitted here—but rather processes and adapts them to the general narrative texture of the romance.

The second cycle of stories[72] opens with the discovery of the Fountain of Life by Alexander's cook, when the slaughtered chickens he was cleaning in the river came back to life; and it includes mention of the gates of the Garden of Eden, where the king was told: 'This is the gate of the Garden of Eden and no heathen or uncircumcised male may enter.' That night Alexander was circumcised:

The next day, the king cried out to the keepers of the gate: 'Give me tribute and I will go on my way.' He was given a box in which there was something like a piece of the eye. The king stretched out his hand to lift it from the ground but was unable, and he cried out to them: 'What have you given me?' They said: 'An eye.' 'What use is it to me?', asked the king. They said: 'This is a sign that your eyes will enjoy plenty of riches. Moreover, you will not be sated by roaming over the entire world.'[73]

The gatekeepers then told him that if he covered the eye with dust he would be able to lift it, for then his greed would be sated. Later, Alexander harnessed four eagles and with them soared into the sky, but due to the heat of the clouds he lowered the lure and the eagles returned him to his camp. He reported: 'When I was between the skies and the ground I saw the entire world in the midst of the waters—the world

tant article by Luitpold Wallach, 'Alexander the Great and the Indian Gymnosophists in Hebrew Tradition', *Proceedings of the American Academy of Jewish Religion*, 11 (1941), 63–75. For the rich literature written on the story, see Bin Gorion and Ben-Amos (eds.), *Mimekor Yisrael*, 101–2.

[70] Jacob Shavit, 'The Africa of the Talmud: A Short Journey in Imaginary Geography' (Heb.), in I. Ben-Artzi, Y. Bartal, and E. Reiner (eds.), *Studies in the Geography of Erets Yisra'el Presented to Yehoshua Ben-Arieh* [Meḥkarim bage'ografiyah shel erets-yisra'el mugashim liyehoshua ben-aryeh] (Jerusalem, 1999), 75–91.

[71] Regarding this cycle Wallach, 'Alexander the Great and the Indian Gymnosophists', 54–5, has shown that the order of the tales in the Babylonian Talmud *Tamid* is also parallel to their order in the Greek Pseudo-Calisthenes.

[72] Bodleian Library MS Heb. D. 11, fo. 272b; Reich (ed.), *Tales of Alexander the Macedonian*, 80 ff. This cycle, whose climax is Alexander's arrival at the gates of the Garden of Eden, was widely disseminated in the Middle Ages as an independent treatise known as *Iter ad Paradisum*, whose author was apparently a Jew named Solomon.   [73] Translation in Reich (ed.), *Tales of Alexander the Macedonian*, 85.

and its entire population seemed to me like a cup on the ocean.' Alexander commanded that he be lowered into the depths of the sea in a glass cage. After seeing everything he wanted to see, he throttled the chicken he had taken with him. 'Since the great sea did not tolerate blood, it vomited the king upon dry land,' but he was washed up far from his army.[74] In this account, the general outline of the talmudic story is maintained up to this point. The main changes are the addition of details and folk motifs, Alexander is judaized, and dialogues that do not appear in the shorter, more condensed versions of the talmudic narratives are introduced.

The narrative's climax takes place at the entrance to the Garden of Eden, where Alexander is circumcised in the hope that he will be allowed to go through the gate. We have argued that the other Hebrew versions of the romance 'judaize' by means of citation of biblical verses, the omission of Christian elements, and the integration of the story of Alexander in Jerusalem. But these later accounts do not bear even the slightest similarity to the Third Recension. Not only is Alexander embedded into the Jewish myth as a national hero, but he actually becomes a Jew. In this creative transformation of the Third Recension, we can feel the narrator's desire to step outside the Alexander romance familiar to Jewish audiences (both in the vernacular and its Hebrew translations), and to present a version of the romance with a decidedly 'midrashic' character. The rich and imaginative plot, mainly based on ancient Jewish traditions, is developed on the basis of the familiar skeleton of the other Alexander romances. Alexander thus becomes a Jewish hero, not by virtue of the citation of a few verses, but because he is fully integrated into Jewish mythical memory.

For the Jews of the Middle Ages, the most significant of these remote places, which are ruled by the God of Israel, is the Land of the Ten Tribes. And indeed, in one of the last episodes of the Hebrew romance Alexander reaches this region as well. His ships anchor off the Land of Kush, adjacent to that of the Ten Tribes. The river roundabout casts stones except on the sabbath. Alexander crosses the river with his troops on the sabbath, and the local inhabitants tell him, 'We are Jews with our God, from whose land we came in the days of Sennacherib, king of Assyria.' The king sends them his Jewish scribe—Menahem *hasofer*—to ask if they will allow him to traverse their land with his army:

When Menahem, the king's scribe, came to them and spoke to them in the Hebrew tongue, they asked him: 'Are you Jewish?' 'Yes,' he said. When they heard that he was Jewish, they grew angry and told him: 'Had you no fear of the God of your fathers when you did evil in the eyes of God by desecrating the sabbath? Know that you are doomed.' Menahem said: 'I beg you, do not be angry with me, for I feared the crown and was compelled to cross the water on the sabbath.'

They do not accept his explanations and drive him out of their land. Menahem returns to Alexander sorrowfully and in shame, and tells him about what has

[74] Reich (ed.), *Tales of Alexander the Macedonian*, 82–8.

happened. Although Alexander tells them that he has been circumcised, the Ten Tribes refuse to permit his army to cross their land and he goes back across the river on the sabbath in sorrow and shame.[75]

In this confrontation between Menahem the Scribe and the Ten Tribes, one may perceive something of the struggle that greatly preoccupied Jewish consciousness in the Middle Ages: between strict religious observance and survival under the conditions of exile.[76] The Ten Tribes represent the Judaism of the Bible and the halakhah in all its severity, mandatory under all conditions and in any situation. Menahem the Scribe and his forefathers, who had experienced destruction and exile, knew that the wisdom of existence mandates knowingly breaking a law of the Torah, when particular exigencies prevail. Indeed, the rabbinic reformatory injunction 'the duty of saving life overrides the sabbath' was just such a necessary ruling, though the Ten Tribes would not have known it—hence their harsh retort.[77]

*

Through midrashic creativity Jews in the medieval world pondered their situation and proposed solutions. The fact that central cultural issues bearing on minority status, the role of education, or even the significance of martyrdom were considered not only through philosophical or theological reflections but also by means of the narrative: myth and legend is among the most important achievements of Jewish cultural creativity during this period. A new midrashic creativity emerged, severed from older models of classical Midrash. Complex cultural and historical factors endowed medieval Midrash with a great degree of independence and paved the way to the use of narrative—the most open and natural discourse of any culture—as one of the principal expository means of creative expression in this period.

---

[75] See Bodleian Library, MS Heb. D. 11, fos. 276b–277a, and the translation in Reich (ed.), *Tales of Alexander the Macedonian*, 108–14.

[76] As expressed in the monumental works of Jacob Katz, *Tradition and Crisis: Jewish Society at the End of the Middle Ages* [Masoret umashber: haḥevrah hayehudit bemotsa'ei yemei-habeinayim] (Jerusalem, 1985), and Israel Ta-Shma, *Early Franco-German Ritual and Custom* [Minhag ashkenaz hakadmon] (Jerusalem, 1992).

[77] In an ancient question asked by the community of Kairouan of R. Zemah Gaon regarding Eldad Hadani, who came to them and told them about the Tribes of Israel on the other side of the river Sambatyon, he told them that 'they have the whole Bible, but do not read the book of Esther, as they were not part of that miracle . . . and in their law they have no [rabbinic] sage, but only Joshua who received from Moses who received from God' (Abraham Epstein (ed.), *Eldad Hadani: His Stories and Traditions* [Eldad hadani: sipurav vehalikhotav] (Pressburg, 1891), 4).

TEN

PERFORMATIVE MIDRASH IN THE MEMORY OF ASHKENAZI MARTYRS

IVAN G. MARCUS

I

Although students of Midrash have often focused on how readers take apart and put together biblical language to create new textual meanings, less noticed is how certain narratives record and interpret what might be called 'performative Midrash': people actually acting out, sometimes even in specific historical situations, modifications of biblical and biblically related texts. Performative Midrash builds on the notion of the creation of rites based on new exegetical interpretations of ancient words.[1] I would like to explore further what Michael Fishbane has called 'the exegetical construction of ritual reality' by considering how historical actors themselves engage in behaviour that is stimulated by their own spontaneous or planned midrashic extension of earlier literary motifs and events. Others may then represent the event so constructed in a narrative or poetic form.[2]

It is often impossible to separate performative from literary aspects of a newly imagined event and its subsequent literary representation. Compare the behaviour ascribed to Joshua, in connection with the failed battle to conquer Ai (Josh. 7), and Ezra, when he is told about intermarriage between the Jerusalem community members and the peoples of the land (Ezra 9).

In the book of Joshua, when the Israelites are defeated in the first battle of Ai, Joshua goes through an elaborate set of mourning gestures (Josh. 7: 6). The act of desecrating the war booty is referred to by the Hebrew verb *ma'al* (Josh. 7: 1), and the reason supplied for the Israelites' defeat is that one Achan ben Carmi had

---

[1] See Daniel Boyarin, '"Language Inscribed by History on the Bodies of Living Beings": Midrash and Martyrdom', *Representations*, 25 (1989), 139–51, and id., *Intertextuality and the Reading of Midrash* (Bloomington, Ind., 1990), 117–29; Michael Fishbane, *The Kiss of God: Spiritual and Mystical Death in Judaism* (Seattle, Wash., 1994), 51–125; Ivan G. Marcus, *Rituals of Childhood: Jewish Acculturation in Medieval Europe* (New Haven, Conn., 1996); Michael Fishbane, *The Exegetical Imagination: On Jewish Thought and Theology* (Cambridge, Mass., 1998), 6–8, 123–84.

[2] Fishbane, *Exegetical Imagination*, 6.

misappropriated forbidden sacred war booty (*ḥerem*, Josh. 7: 1, 11–13, 15) that was to be consecrated to God alone and not diverted for human use (Josh. 7: 18–20). In the book of Ezra, an inner-biblical midrashic expansion of Joshua 7 is behind the metaphor that the people of Israel is 'the holy seed' (*zera hakodesh*, Ezra 9: 2), and is equivalent to the sacred war booty in Joshua. The sin is expressed with a form of the verb *ma'al*, as in Joshua (Ezra 9: 2, 4), and Ezra is described as going through a series of mourning gestures as had Joshua (Ezra 9: 3–4).

In the book of Ezra, it is impossible to know whether a historical Ezra consciously acted out an 'Achan typology' that the narrator of the book expanded, or whether the editor of Ezra 9 invented a narrative about 'the holy seed' with Joshua 7 in mind and with no help from any historical event contemporary with Ezra. Is Ezra 9 a case of performative Midrash, or of the exegetical construction of reality, or a combination of both? We cannot tell.[3]

If we ask these questions about a much-discussed later historical series of events that took place in medieval German Jewish history, the anti-Jewish Crusader riots and Jewish acts of active and passive martyrdom in the Rhineland in the spring and summer of 1096, we may be able to find ways of distinguishing between performative and literary midrashic construction.

By raising this issue about a case where historiography and Midrash meet, I would like to add theoretical nuance to some earlier work that has sometimes been misread to imply that a literary construction is always an invention and cannot also be a reworking of actual historical events.[4] Historical narratives can be literary embellishments of acts that midrashic associations stimulate. Thus, in the title of this chapter the phrase 'in the memory of Ashkenazi martyrs' can refer either to the martyrs' own memory of earlier motifs and events, or it can refer to later narrators' constructions of memory about the martyrs, or to a combination of both. I will try to sort this out by focusing on specific gestures that are associated with some of the Jewish martyrs in German lands in 1096. These are acts of active ritual sacrifice performed by Jews on other Jews and the use of the verse 'Hear, O Israel [*shema yisra'el*] the Lord is our God, the Lord is One' (Deut. 6: 4) as a cry Jews uttered at the moment of a martyr's death.

In the wake of a call to an armed pilgrimage to Jerusalem, later known as the First Crusade, three Hebrew narratives, several Hebrew lamentations (*kinot*), and lists of Jewish martyrs memorialize both Christian violence against German Jews

---

[3] The comparison between Ezra 9 and Joshua 7 is based on seminars that Gerson D. Cohen taught in 1969 for the Melton Research Center of the Jewish Theological Seminary. He understood Ezra as a literary elaboration of Joshua 7 and did not deal with the issue of performative Midrash. For different midrashic approaches to understanding Ezra 9, see Jacob Milgrom, *Cult and Conscience: The Asham and the Priestly Doctrine of Repentance* (Leiden, 1976), 71–3, and 18–19; Michael Fishbane, *Biblical Interpretation in Ancient Israel* (Oxford, 1985), 115–21.

[4] Ivan G. Marcus, 'From Politics to Martyrdom: Shifting Paradigms in the Hebrew Narratives of the 1096 Crusade Riots', *Prooftexts*, 2 (1982), 40–52, and Robert Chazan, *God, Humanity and History: The Hebrew First Crusade Narratives* (Berkeley, Calif., 2000), 138–9.

and also the different kinds of Jewish reactions to their situation. Some Jews yielded to baptism; others died at the hands of Christian attackers, and still others engaged in unprecedented acts of active martyrdom that involved Jews ritually sacrificing other Jews and then committing suicide.[5]

Some legal historians who have compared descriptions of Jewish active martyrdom in 1096 to the rabbinic laws of Jewish martyrdom have concluded that the behaviour does not comply with Jewish law.[6] Others have suggested that Jews in medieval Germany imitated literary or midrashic precedents that they treated with the force of law. Of special note in this regard is the representation of the homicidal and suicidal behaviour of Jews at Masada as found at the end of *Sefer yosipon*, a tenth-century Hebrew rewriting of Josephus and a book that German rabbinic circles considered to be canonical sacred history.[7]

---

[5] The three Hebrew narratives were published together for the first time by Adolph Neubauer and Moritz Stern (eds.), *Hebräische Berichte über die Judenverfolgungen während der Kreuzzüge*, with a German translation by Seligmann Baer (Berlin, 1892; repr. Hildesheim, 1997). A frequently cited Hebrew edition of the three texts is in Abraham Habermann, *The Book of Persecutions in Germany and France* [Sefer gezerot ashkenaz vetsarefat] (Jerusalem, 1945; repr. Jerusalem, 1971). A new synoptic edition is Eva Haverkamp (ed.), *Hebräische Berichte über die Judenverfolgungen während des ersten Kreuzzugs*, Monumenta Germaniae Historica (Hanover, 2005). A complete English translation is found in Shlomo Eidelberg (ed. and trans.), *The Jews and the Crusaders* (Madison, Wis., 1977; repr. Hoboken, NJ, 1996). Some of the liturgical poems are included in the second of the three Hebrew narratives: see Habermann, *The Book of Persecutions* (Heb.), 73–4, 76, 80–1, and Eidelberg, *The Jews and the Crusaders*, 80–1, 82, 84–5, and 91–2. Others are incorporated into the Ninth of Av liturgy: see *The Lamentations for the Ninth of Av* [Seder hakinot letishah be'av], ed. Daniel Goldschmidt (Jerusalem, 1972), 85–8, 93–8, 106–9, and 118–20, and the bilingual edition *The Authorised Kinot for the Ninth of Av*, ed. and trans. Abraham Rosenfeld (New York, 1979), 127–8, 132–4, 139–42, and 148–9. Most of the lamentations about 1096 are listed in Avraham Grossman, 'The Roots of Jewish Martyrdom in Early Ashkenaz' (Heb.), in Isaiah Gafni and Aviezer Ravitzky (eds.), *Sanctity of Life and Martyrdom: Studies in Memory of Amir Yekutiel* [Kedushat haḥayim veḥeruf hanefesh: kovets ma'amarim lezikhro shel amir yekuti'el] (Jerusalem, 1993), 102 n. 7. In addition to the three Hebrew narratives and the lamentations, martyrs' names are recorded in Siegmund Salfeld (ed.), *Das Martyrologium des Nürnberger Memorbuches* (Berlin, 1898), 5–12. For a survey of the primary sources about 1096, see Abraham David, 'Historical Records of the Persecutions during the First Crusade in Hebrew Printed Works and Hebrew Manuscripts' (Heb.), in Yom Tov Assis et al. (eds.), *Facing the Cross: The Persecutions of 1096 in History and Historiography* [Yehudim mul hatselav: gezerot tatnu behistoriyah uvehistoriografiyah] (Jerusalem, 2000), 193–205.

[6] See Menachem Ben-Sasson, 'Remembering and Forgetting Persecutions: On Martyrdom in Christian and Muslim Lands in the Early Middle Ages' (Heb.), in Joseph R. Hacker, Yosef Kaplan, and Benjamin Z. Kedar (eds.), *From Sages to Savants: Studies Presented to Avraham Grossman* [Rishonim ve'aḥaronim: meḥkarim betoledot yisra'el mugashim le'avraham grosman] (Jerusalem, 2010), 55, and see Grossman, 'Roots of Jewish Martyrdom' (Heb.), 99–130; Israel Ta-Shma, 'Suicide and Killing Another Person as Acts of Martyrdom: Regarding the Place of Narrative Legends in Ashkenazi Legal Decision Making' (Heb.), in Assis et al. (eds.), *Facing the Cross* (Heb.), 150–6; and Haym Soloveitchik, 'Religious Law and Change: The Medieval Ashkenazic Example', *AJS Review*, 12 (1987), 205–21.

[7] See Grossman, 'Roots of Jewish Martyrdom' (Heb.), 113–19, and Ta-Shma, 'Suicide and Killing' (Heb.), 151–2. Menachem Ben-Sasson, 'Remembering and Forgetting Persecutions' (Heb.), 52, argues that because *Sefer yosipon* was available in Muslim as well as in Christian Jewish cultures it could not have motivated only some Ashkenazi Jews to act out the Masada example and other precedents of ritual

Those who have pointed to earlier literary motifs as underlying the active martyrdom in 1096 have not considered the acts themselves as performative Midrash, as creations of newly fashioned ritual acts based on combinations and extensions of the ancient motifs. Often they have tried to attribute priority to one or another of these motifs instead of trying to work out how the actors and narrators thought of them in new combinations with new meanings. For example, some Jews are portrayed in a Temple setting and recite a blessing of ritual slaughter answered by an antiphonal response, 'Amen'. The same acts are sometimes referred to as *akedot* in the sense of actual sacrifices, and the scenes of groups of Jews gathering together to carry out ritual acts of homicide and suicide also echo the description of how the Jews planned their deaths at Masada recorded in Josippon (*Sefer yosipon*). Altogether, the Temple sacrificial cult, the sacrifice of Isaac on Mount Moriah (*akedah*), and the finale in Josippon on the Herodian mountain fortress of Masada combine into a new rite acted out on the virtual Temple Mount of Mainz in the form of actual human sacrifices. Did the actors themselves understand this as what they were doing? Or are these associations those of the narrators who supply proof-texts?[8]

In the case of the sacrificial acts, it is not easy to untangle the ancient associations the actors themselves had in mind from what the narrators later introduced. Regarding one gesture, however, it may be possible to see the actual process of performative Midrash in action. I would like to examine more closely a gesture ascribed

---

homicide. The issue, however, is not just the presence of books but of how open Ashkenazi Jews or Jews in Muslim lands were to the books that they had. Sometimes books were present but ignored. See the remarks, *mutatis mutandis*, of David Berger and Haym Soloveitchik on the resistance of Ashkenazi Jews to philosophical texts that were available to them. The same applies to the openness of Rhineland Jews to *Sefer yosipon* and the relative indifference to it of Jews in Muslim lands. See David Berger, 'Polemic, Exegesis, Philosophy, and Science: On the Tenacity of Ashkenazic Modes of Thought', *Jahrbuch des Simon-Dubnow-Instituts*, 8 (2009), 29, and Haym Soloveitchik, 'The Halakhic Isolation of the Ashkenazic Community', *Jahrbuch des Simon-Dubnow-Instituts*, 8 (2009), 41–7. It should be recalled that the first major rabbinic figure of medieval Germany, Rabbenu Gershom b. Judah, is thought to have copied his own Mishnah, Talmud, and *Sefer yosipon*, a sign that the latter had canonical status in medieval Ashkenaz; see Abraham Grossman, *The Early Sages of Ashkenaz* [Ḥakhmei ashkenaz harishonim] (Jerusalem, 1981), 159–60. Moreover, Benzion Dinur pointed out that more *piyutim* were written for Hanukah in medieval Ashkenaz than before and were influenced by episodes associated with that holiday, including martyrdom, taken from *Sefer yosipon*. See Benzion Dinur (ed.), *Israel in the Exile* [Yisra'el begolah], 2 vols. in 10 parts (Tel Aviv, 1961), vol. i, book 4, pp. 118 and 139 n. 31; *Seder avodat yisra'el* [the Jewish prayer-book], ed. S. Baer (1868; repr. Tel Aviv, 1957), 637–46, esp. 644, and Baer's notes there.

[8] For the Temple motif, see, among others, Yitshak Baer, 'The 1096 Persecutions' (Heb.), in U. Cassuto, J. Klausner, and Y. Gutman (eds.), *Sefer simḥah asaf* (Jerusalem, 1953), 126–40; repr. in id., *Studies in the History of the Jewish People* [Meḥkarim umasot betoledot am yisra'el], 2 vols. (Jerusalem, 1986), i. 147–61; Ivan G. Marcus, 'From Politics to Martyrdom: Shifting Paradigms in the Hebrew Narratives of the 1096 Crusade Riots', *Prooftexts*, 2 (1982), 43; Alan Mintz, *Ḥurban: Responses to Catastrophe in Hebrew Literature* (New York, 1984), 94–100; for the Akedah as sacrifice, see Shalom Spiegel, *The Last Trial: On the Legends and Lore of the Command to Abraham to Offer Isaac as a Sacrifice: The Akedah*, trans. Judah Goldin (Philadelphia, Pa., 1967); for *Sefer yosipon* and Masada, see *Josippon* [Sefer yosipon], ed. David Flusser, 2 vols. (Jerusalem, 1978), i. 430–1.

to some of the martyrs of 1096 in which Jews midrashically transformed earlier literary models and did not simply imitate or combine them. I refer to the attribution by chroniclers and at least one of the liturgical poets to Jewish martyrs crying out the first line of the liturgical texts known as the Shema (Deut. 6: 4–9; Deut. 11: 13–21; Num. 15: 37–41). This act was an innovation that involved making a new interpretation of ancient traditions about the death of Rabbi Akiva, associated with the recitation of the liturgical Shema.

II

It is widely assumed that since antiquity Jews have had a tradition that a martyr at the moment of imminent death should cry out the biblical verse that begins *shema yisra'el*. Thus, one scholar observes that Muslims declare God's unity by saying the *shahada* ('There is no God but God and Muhammad is His Prophet') when about to be martyred 'just as the Shema has been since Rabbi Akiva's death'.[9] Even more confidently, another writes, 'It is no surprise, of course, to find martyrs in the Hebrew chronicles [of the 1096 crusade massacres] pronouncing the Shema "with all their heart, soul, and might" (Deut. 6: 5) such as Akiva'.[10]

Despite these assertions that Jewish martyrs 'since Rabbi Akiva's death' have recited 'the Shema', the assumption that a single ancient practice continued and resurfaced in medieval Germany and frequently thereafter needs to be revisited. As we will see, the situation portrayed in Rabbi Akiva's death is different from that of the martyrs of 1096. Moreover, there are very few documented cases of this practice well into the eighteenth century. In light of this, we need to ask why scholars and others assume the practice to be ancient and continuous.

Although there has been some speculation that Hellenistic Jewish sources, especially 2 Maccabees, already describe Jewish martyrs reciting some kind of declaration of their faith in God at the moment of passive martyrdom, there is no evidence that this utterance was the first verse of the Shema.[11] The archetype of ancient Jewish martyrs, whose death is described as taking place when he insists on reciting

---

[9] Yehuda Liebes, '*De Natura Dei*: On the Development of the Jewish Myth', in id., *Studies in Jewish Myth and Jewish Messianism* (Albany, NY, 1993), 157 n. 44.

[10] Shmuel Shepkeru, *Jewish Martyrs in the Pagan and Christian Worlds* (Cambridge, 2006), 186. See, too, Boyarin, *Intertextuality*, 128: 'All through the Middle Ages, Jews went enthusiastically to a martyr's death with R. Akiva's words on their lips', which is misleading.

[11] See Jonathan A. Goldstein (ed.), *II Maccabees: A New Translation with Introduction and Commentary* (Garden City, NY, 1983), 276 (on 2 Macc. 6: 6: 'No one was allowed ... to confess he was a Jew.'), who speculates that this might refer to saying the paragraph of the Shema that begins with Deut. 6: 4. He notes that Josephus (*Antiquities of the Jews*, IV. 8, §13, l. 212) refers to the twice-daily recitation of the Shema as 'bearing witness' (*martyrein*). See, too, Albert I. Baumgarten, 'Invented Traditions of the Maccabean Era', in Hubert Cancik, Hermann Lichtenberger, and Peter Schäfer (eds.), *Geschichte—Tradition—Reflexion: Festschrift für Martin Hengel zum 70. Geburtstag*, 3 vols. (Tübingen, 1996), i. 206, and Daniel Boyarin, *Dying for God: Martyrdom and the Making of Christianity and Judaism* (Stanford, Calif., 1999), 188–9.

the liturgical Shema that the Romans have proscribed, is Rabbi Akiva. The Tosefta, in the name of Rabbi Meir, and the Mishnah and *Sifrei Deuteronomy*, both without attribution, teach that the phrase 'and you shall love the Lord your God . . . with all your soul' (Deut. 6: 5) means: 'even if He takes your soul [life]'.[12] This teaching is subsequently connected to Rabbi Akiva's death at the hands of the Romans in the Jerusalem Talmud, in a passage in *Sotah* 5 (20c) that offers a slightly earlier version than a parallel in *Berakhot* 9 (14b). Both may be compared to the version found in the Babylonian Talmud (*Ber.* 61b):

When Rabbi Akiva was taken out for execution, it was the hour for the recital of the Shema; and while they raked his flesh with iron combs, he was accepting upon himself the kingship of Heaven. His disciples said to him: 'Our master, even to this point [will you accept suffering]?' He answered them: 'My whole life I have been troubled by this verse, "with all your soul" [Deut. 6: 5], meaning "even if He takes your soul/life". I wondered if I should have the opportunity to fulfil it; and now that I do, shall I not fulfil it?' [And so] he prolonged reciting the [final] word 'One' [in Deut. 6: 4] until his soul departed with [the word] 'One'.[13]

Although narratives about the martyrs of 1096 do not refer to Rabbi Akiva reciting the Shema at the moment of his death, they do emphasize that the martyrs in Ashkenaz will share Rabbi Akiva's personal reward in the hereafter. Thus, the martyrs of Mainz are destined to share in the eternal reward of 'the saints—Rabbi Akiva and his companions, pillars of the universe, who were killed in witness to His Name'.[14]

Moreover, as Jacob Katz correctly noted, the 1096 narratives and other medieval martyrological sources do not describe the situation that is presupposed in the Akivan traditions. The rabbinic traditions about Rabbi Akiva portray him teaching his students to love God even to death, when he insists on reciting the daily liturgical Shema on time, even though it involves his death at the hands of the Romans who have proscribed it. In 1096 the martyrs say the verse beginning *shema yisra'el* at any time of day or night, and there is no reference to the liturgical Shema in any of the accounts.[15]

---

[12] Tosefta *Ber.* 7: 7, ed. Saul Lieberman (New York, 1955), 35; Mishnah *Ber.* 9: 5. *Sifrei Deuteronomy*, §32 (*Sifre on Deuteronomy*, ed. Louis Finkelstein (New York, 1955), 55); *Sifre: A Tannaitic Commentary on the Book of Deuteronomy*, trans. Reuven Hammer (New Haven, Conn., 1986), 59; and see Steven D. Fraade, *From Tradition to Commentary* (Albany, NY, 1991), 213–14, 240 and references there. For the observation that R. Akiva's crime was reciting the liturgical Shema on time, see Aaron Oppenheimer, 'Sanctity of Life and Martyrdom after the Bar Kokhba Rebellion' (Heb.), in Gafni and Ravitzky (eds.), *Sanctity of Life* (Heb.), 85–97, esp. 90. On R. Akiva's death and the Shema, see Fishbane, *Kiss of God*, 51–86; Boyarin, *Intertextuality*, 117–29; and id., *Dying for God*, 102–10.

[13] The translation is based on Fishbane, *Kiss of God*, 66–7, with slight modifications.

[14] See Habermann, *The Book of Persecutions* (Heb.), 31, Eidelberg, *The Jews and the Crusaders*, 31; Habermann, 49, Eidelberg, 56; and Habermann, 104, Eidelberg, 115.

[15] Jacob Katz, *Exclusiveness and Tolerance* (Oxford, 1961), 88 n. 4.

The situation when the verse is uttered varies in the narratives about 1096. For example, Jews in Worms who are about to be killed by other Jews say it:

Fathers fell upon their sons, being slaughtered upon one another, and they slew one another—each man his kin, his wife, and children; bridegrooms slew their betrothed, and merciful women their only children. They all accepted the divine decree wholeheartedly and, as they yielded up their souls to the Creator, cried out: 'Hear O Israel, the Lord is our God, the Lord is One.'[16]

At other times, Jews whom Christians are about to kill say it, as in Mainz: 'And when the enemy was upon them, they all cried out in a great voice, with one heart and one tongue: "Hear, O Israel: the Lord is our God, the Lord is One."'[17]

At still other times, Jews who observe other Jews killing each other say it as witnesses to their actions, as in Wevelinghoven:

There was a pious man there of ripe old age by the name of Rabbi Samuel, son of Yehiel. He had an only son, a handsome young man, whose appearance was like Lebanon. They fled together into the water, and the youth stretched out his neck to his father for slaughter as they stood in the waters. The father recited the benediction for ritual slaughter over him, and the son answered, 'Amen'. All those standing around them responded in a loud voice: 'Hear, O Israel, the Lord is our God, the Lord is One.'[18]

In one other instance, Jews are reminded of Jacob's doubts about his own righteousness, when his sons affirm their loyalty to God by reciting *shema yisra'el* at his deathbed.[19] In all of these situations, the time of day or night is irrelevant, and Jews recite only the first verse.

Apart from these episodes in the three Hebrew narratives that involve someone crying out *shema yisra'el*, one of the lamentations (*kinot*) mentions this as well. A liturgical poem written by Rabbi Kalonymus ben Judah begins, 'I said, look away from me, while I weep bitterly' (*amarti she'u mini, babekhi amarer*):

The father subdued his compassion to be able to sacrifice his children like lambs to the slaughter, indeed he prepared the slaughter-house for his own children. . . . Who can

---

[16] Habermann, *The Book of Persecutions* (Heb.), 25, Eidelberg, *The Jews and the Crusaders*, 23, with parallels in Habermann, 73, Eidelberg, 81. In another parallel, there is no mention of the Shema: Habermann, 96, Eidelberg, 103.

[17] Habermann, *The Book of Persecutions* (Heb.), 33, Eidelberg, *The Jews and the Crusaders*, 34; Habermann, 75, Eidelberg, 83.

[18] Habermann, *The Book of Persecutions* (Heb.), 77, Eidelberg, *The Jews and the Crusaders*, 86. The parallel, Habermann, 45, Eidelberg, 52, omits the reaction and calling out *shema yisra'el*. In Xanten Jews who observe a Jew committing suicide say *shema yisra'el*. See Habermann, 78, Eidelberg, 88.

[19] See *Sifrei Deuteronomy*, §31 (Finkelstein edn., 52–3, and sources listed there); *Sifre: A Tannaitic Commentary on the Book of Deuteronomy*, trans. Reuven Hammer, 57–8; BT *Pes.* 56a; and Habermann, *The Book of Persecutions* (Heb.), 100, Eidelberg, *The Jews and the Crusaders*, 108–9.

hear [*yishma*] and not weep? The son is slaughtered, and the father recites the Shema [*kore et shema*].²⁰

Here, in the learned language of *piyut*, the rabbinic author uses the idiom of the liturgy ('recites the Shema') and in so doing may be alluding to the Akivan traditions in rabbinic literature, but the act he describes is of uttering only the first verse, not actually reciting the liturgical Shema.

III

Was the utterance of *shema yisra'el* by Jewish martyrs in 1096, like the descriptions of Jews ritually killing other Jews, reciting a blessing, and answering 'Amen', innovative behaviour, performative Midrash, or the narrators interpreting events and constructing associations on their own? While one cannot take chronicles at face value, guarded caution is not the same thing as denial. Unlike the innovation of some Jews killing others, for which we have Latin corroborating evidence at least of a generic kind, no such outside evidence supports the image of some Jewish martyrs uttering *shema yisra'el* at the moment of death.²¹

My argument, therefore, is indirect. Given the factual character of unprecedented, horrific acts of ritual homicide, I think that the equally innovative gesture of some martyrs uttering *shema yisra'el* is at least probable. Most Jews did not say it, but most Jews did not kill one another either. Some did so by adapting one part of the Akivan tradition to their own situation—he said *shema yisra'el* when he died a martyr—and they thereby affirmed Judaism by reciting Deuteronomy 6: 4. This adaptation involved detaching the first verse of the liturgical Shema from the rest and then attaching it to the martyr's moment of death, regardless of the time of day or night, possibly influenced by the talmudic trope about Jacob's sons saying it to affirm their loyalty to Judaism.

Other Jews would generate meditations to be performed during the liturgical Shema as a spiritual exercise and as preparation for martyrdom in the future.²² In effect, two themes found together in the ancient Akivan archetype were separated

---

²⁰ *Lamentations for the Ninth of Av* (Heb.), ed. Goldschmidt, 107; the translation is from *Authorised Kinot*, ed. Rosenfeld, 140, with modifications.

²¹ We know from the chronicler of the First Crusade Albert of Aachen, for example, that some Jews did kill other Jews, and the Jewish narrators claim at least that they learned about some of the incidents from eyewitness accounts. See Edward Peters (ed.), *The First Crusade* (Philadelphia, Pa., 1971), 103, also quoted in Marcus, 'From Politics to Martyrdom', 40. We also have testimony from the Trier chronicler's *Gesta Treverorum* of Jewish mothers killing their children. See Julius Aronius, *Regesten zur Geschichte der Juden* (Berlin, 1902; repr. (Hildesheim, 1970), para. 189; Eva Haverkamp, '"Persecutio" und "Gezerah" in Trier während des ersten Kreuzzugs', in E. Burgard, C. Cluse, and A. Haverkamp (eds.), *Juden und Christen zur Zeit der Kreuzzüge* (Sigmaringen, 1999), 35–71; and ead., 'What Did the Christians Know? Latin Reports on the Persecutions of the Jews in 1096', *Crusades*, 7 (2008), 59–86.

²² See Fishbane, *Kiss of God*, 87–124; and Joseph Hacker, 'Was Jewish Martyrdom Spiritualized in Early Modern Times?' (Heb.), in Gafni and Ravitzky (eds.), *Sanctity of Life* (Heb.), 221–32.

and then reconnected with different innovative practices. The liturgical recitation of the Shema was spiritualized with mystical disciplines and rites, viewed as a spiritual preparation for dying as a martyr; the actual death of a martyr was to be accompanied by the cry of Deuteronomy 6: 4, now divorced from the liturgical recitation of the Shema. Both processes may be viewed as 'performative Midrash' or as 'the exegetical construction of ritual reality'.

If the narrators of 1096 wanted Jews in the future to emulate the behaviour of the active martyrs, they rarely succeeded. The martyrs of 1096 were remembered, but hardly ever imitated. A brief glance at the main subsequent incidents of Jewish martyrdom that were recorded shows that it was unusual for a Jew either to kill his family or to utter *shema yisra'el* when martyred. I will return to why the mistaken idea persists that Jewish martyrs have died with *shema yisra'el* on their lips 'since Rabbi Akiva's death'.

Variation was the norm in 1096 and remained so afterwards. In the account of the Second Crusade riots in Germany, reported by Rabbi Ephraim of Bonn in his *Sefer zekhirah* (Book of Remembrance), there are no references to either ritual homicide or anyone crying out *shema yisra'el*. However, there is a liturgical poem that mentions both, written by Rabbi Isaac ben Rabbi Shalom, 'Ein kamokha ba'ilmim', that contains the date 1147 and is about a persecution in Würzburg.[23] Neither ritual homicide nor the recitation of *shema yisra'el* is mentioned in Rabbi Eleazar of Worms' Hebrew report in 1196 about the Crusader attack in his house that killed his wife and two daughters.[24]

In medieval France, most of the reports about the murder accusation in Blois in 1171 and the burning at the stake of thirty-one or thirty-two Jews there portray the martyrs singing the liturgical prayer 'Aleinu', not *shema yisra'el*. That prayer had come to be understood in medieval Ashkenaz as having a strong anti-Christian message, even though it had originated in early medieval or ancient times as a prayer associated with Heikhalot mysticism recited only on the Jewish New Year. Some time after the riots of 1096 it was transferred to the conclusion of each of the three

---

[23] R. Ephraim of Bonn, *Sefer zekhirah*, in Habermann, *The Book of Persecutions* (Heb.), 115–23; Eidelberg, *The Jews and the Crusaders*, 121–33. Shepkeru, *Jewish Martyrs*, 222, also noted this but does not deal with the *piyut*, printed in Habermann, 113–14, that mentions both ritual homicide and saying *shema yisra'el*. Israel Jacob Yuval, *Two Nations in Your Womb: Perceptions of Jews and Christians in Late Antiquity and the Middle Ages* (Berkeley, Calif., 2006), 154–5, connects this *piyut* to the 1096 traumas, despite the date. The lament seems to be about a persecution in Würzburg, also reported in prose in Habermann, 119–20, and Eidelberg, 127–8, though the active martyrdom mentioned in the *piyut* is not mentioned in the prose report.

[24] A short prose account is found in Habermann, *The Book of Persecutions* (Heb.), 161–4. For references to manuscripts, see Ivan G. Marcus, 'A Jewish–Christian Symbiosis: The Culture of Early Ashkenaz', in David Biale (ed.), *Cultures of the Jews: A New History* (New York, 2002), 509 n. 77. R. Eleazar also wrote elegies for his slain wife and daughters; see Habermann, 165–7. For translations, see Judith Baskin, 'Dulce of Worms: The Lives and Deaths of an Exemplary Jewish Woman and Her Daughters', in Lawrence Fine (ed.), *Judaism in Practice: From the Middle Ages Through the Early Modern Period* (Princeton, NJ, 2001), 429–37; and Marcus, 'Jewish–Christian Symbiosis', 475–8.

daily services, asserting its significance as a marker of Jewish identity. Nevertheless, Rabbi Hillel ben Jacob of Bonn's *piyut* to memorialize the martyrs of Blois does mention *shema yisra'el*.[25]

From around the same time, the account of the imaginary immolation of Rabbi Amnon of Mainz refers to neither *shema yisra'el* nor 'Aleinu' at the moment of death but to the recitation of the *piyut* that begins 'Unetaneh tokef'.[26]

There is a Latin account about Jews reciting the phrase *shema yisra'el* in a completely different context. The French king Philip Augustus' court historian, Rigord, reports about the moment when the teenage king decided to expel the Jews in his domain in 1182:

The infidel Jews, perceiving that the great of the land, through whom they had been accustomed easily to bend the King's predecessors to their will, had suffered repulse, and astonished and stupefied by the strength of mind of Philip the king and his constancy in the Lord, exclaimed with a certain admiration: Shema Israel [that is, Hear O Israel] and prepared to sell all their household goods. The time was now at hand when the king had ordered them to leave France altogether, and it could not be in any way delayed.[27]

The exclamation that Rigord ascribes to 'the infidel Jews' of royal France in 1182 has nothing to do with martyrdom but may be an echo of the talmudic story about Jacob and his sons, affirming their loyalty to Judaism by reciting the first verse of the Shema when they became aware that they were powerless to avoid being deported. Rigord mistakenly thinks the expression is a sign of the Jews' admiration for the king's piety and resolve. He understands the phrase 'Hear, O Israel' to be a

---

[25] See Robert Chazan, 'The Blois Incident of 1171: A Study in Jewish Intercommunal Organization', *Proceedings of the American Academy for Jewish Research*, 36 (1968), 13–31; and Susan Einbinder, *Beautiful Death: Jewish Poetry and Martyrdom in Medieval France* (Princeton, NJ, 2002). For one of the Hebrew prose accounts, see Habermann, *The Book of Persecutions* (Heb.), 124–6; and a translation in Jacob R. Marcus (ed.), *The Jew in the Medieval World: A Source Book, 315–1791* (1938; 2nd rev. edn. with new introd. and updated bibliographies by Marc Saperstein, Cincinnati, Ohio, 1999), 142–6. Other sources are translated in Susan Einbinder, 'The Jewish Martyrs of Blois, 1171', in Thomas Head (ed.), *Medieval Hagiography: A Sourcebook* (New York, 2000), 537–60; and an excerpt is in Einbinder, *Beautiful Death*, 28. The Hebrew text of R. Hillel's *piyut* is in Habermann, 137. For 'Aleinu' and Blois, see also Yuval, *Two Nations in Your Womb*, 192–204, and the earlier literature cited there. Of related interest is Lee Patterson, '"The Living Witnesses of Our Redemption": Martyrdom and Imitation in Chaucer's Prioress's Tale', *Journal of Medieval and Early Modern Studies*, 31 (2001), 507–60.

[26] See Ivan G. Marcus, 'A Pious Community in Doubt: Qiddush ha-Shem in Ashkenaz and the Story of R. Amnon of Mainz', in Zvia Ben-Yosef Ginor (ed.), *Essays on Hebrew Literature in Honor of Avraham Holtz* (New York, 2003), 21–46; and Jeremy Cohen, *Sanctifying the Name of God: Jewish Martyrs and Jewish Memories of the First Crusade* (Philadelphia, Pa., 2004), 130–41. For the antiquity of the *piyut*, see Israel Davidson (ed.), *Thesaurus of Mediaeval Hebrew Poetry* [Otsar hashirah vehapiyut], 4 vols. (1929; repr. New York, 1970), ii. 199–200 (*vav* #451).

[27] The translation, with minor alterations, is taken from Marcus (ed.), *The Jew in the Medieval World*, 29–30, quoting James Harvey Robinson (ed.), *Readings in European History*, vol. i (Boston, Mass., 1904), 426–8. For the Latin original, see H. François Delaborde (ed.), *Œuvres de Rigord et de Guillaume le Breton*, vol. i (Paris, 1882), 29.

call by Jews to other Jews to obey the king: 'Heed [the French king], O Israel.' In fact, we can view the utterance as a 'hidden transcript', a reaction that appears to acquiesce in the French king's decision as Rigord understands it, but is intended to be a subtle act of Jewish loyalty to the King, the God of Israel, as the verse continues, 'the Lord is our God, the Lord is One'.[28]

A group of Jews at York in 1190 is reported to have killed their families and committed suicide under duress. The Hebrew prose account mentions that some of the victims were brought back to Cologne for burial, and this suggests that the Jews of York may have brought with them a German practice. There is no mention of anyone saying *shema yisra'el* at the moment of death in the prose account or in liturgical poems written about York.[29]

In the second half of the thirteenth century, Rabbi Meir of Rothenburg (d. 1293), the leading German rabbinical authority, records an often-cited case of a distraught father who reports that he thought 'Crusaders' were coming to attack his family and pre-emptively killed his wife and children. The threat was averted before he could kill himself, and this surviving husband and father wanted to know whether he required a penance or had done the right thing.

In Rabbi Meir's responsum we find an important indication of how the memory of 1096 reached him, and perhaps German Jews in general. He refers to the memory of 1096 not on the basis of the chronicles but rather of Rabbi Kalonymus ben Judah's *piyut*, quoted earlier:

For we have heard that many important people killed their sons and daughters, and Rabbenu Kalonymus did likewise [as in] the lamentation that begins 'I said, look away from me' [*amarti she'u mini*]. . . . Whoever requires a penance of such a person casts aspersions on the saints of old, especially since his intent was for the good, out of his abundant love for his Creator, may His Name be blessed, he harmed those most dear to him.[30]

The incident described in this responsum corresponds to an entry in the medieval memorial book of Jewish martyrs for 15 Nisan (2 April) 1265 in Koblenz which reports that 'the wife of Rabbi Abraham ben Moses and his children who were slaughtered', in the passive form.[31]

In 1285 in Munich a penitential poem (*seliḥah*) mentions 'ninety holy souls' who were accused of a blood libel and were to be burned alive if they did not convert. The author is an otherwise unknown Rabbi Hayim ben Makhir, and the poem was

---

[28] See James C. Scott, *Domination and the Arts of Resistance: Hidden Transcripts* (New Haven, Conn., 1990).
[29] See Habermann, *The Book of Persecutions* (Heb.), 127 for the prose account; ibid. 147–51, esp. 150, for R. Menahem b. R. Jacob's lament that also refers to active martyrdom there; and another lament, ibid. 152–4, that refers to Jews actively slaughtering their family (p. 150); see, too, Richard B. Dobson, *The Jews of Medieval York and the Massacre of March 1190* (York, 1974), 27.
[30] R. Meir b. Baruch of Rothenburg, *Sefer sha'arei teshuvot*, ed. Moses Bloch (Berlin, 1891), 346–7.
[31] Salfeld (ed.), *Das Martyrologium*, 15.

part of a local Bavarian liturgy, *minhag regensburg*, recited on the date of the persecution, 12 Heshvan (12 October), which became a local fast day. Before the gathered Jews were burned alive in the synagogue, some apparently killed their families and the author, a witness, heard the sound of *shema yisra'el*.[32]

In 1288, in Troyes, France, thirteen Jews were burnt at the stake and were memorialized in laments in Hebrew and Old French, but there is no mention in them of anyone crying out *shema yisra'el*.[33] Shortly afterwards, however, in widespread anti-Jewish riots in German lands associated with a ringleader named Rindfleisch, in 1298, there is a relatively vague mention of Jews killing other Jews and singing when they were about to die.[34]

A few years later, Latin accounts of anti-Jewish riots that accompanied the so-called Lepers and Shepherds Crusade in 1320–1 mention that Jews killed their families in France and Spain, but again there is no reference to *shema yisra'el*.[35] And a few years later, apparently during the Black Death in the middle of the fourteenth century, we have another isolated case of a ritual homicide but, again, no mention of *shema yisra'el*.[36]

The German innovation of ritual homicide sometimes affected Jews in late medieval Iberia, in part, at least, due to the influence of the migration to Toledo in 1305 of a distinguished student of Rabbi Meir of Rothenburg, Rabbi Asher ben Yehiel, who brought German customs with him. One of his descendants was a victim of the peninsula-wide anti-Jewish riots in 1391 and is reported to have killed his own family.[37] In Portugal, in 1497, groups of Jewish parents killed their children so that they would not be taken into monasteries and converted. Here, again, there is no mention of anyone calling out *shema yisra'el*.[38]

---

[32] See Habermann, *The Book of Persecutions* (Heb.), 198–201, esp. 200; Hayim Schirmann (ed.), *Lamentations on Persecutions in the Land of Israel, Africa, Spain, Germany, and France* [Kinot al hagezerot be'erets yisra'el, afrikah, sefarad, ashkenaz, vetsarefat], *Kovets al yad*, NS 3 (13) (1940), 58–62, esp. 61; and Salfeld (ed.), *Das Martyrologium*, 146–7.

[33] On the memorializing poems of this event, see Einbinder, *Beautiful Death*, 126–54; Kirsten Fudeman, 'Restoring a Vernacular Jewish Voice: The Old French Elegy of Troyes', *Jewish Studies Quarterly*, 15 (2008), 190–221; and ead., 'These Things I Will Remember: The Troyes Martyrdom and Collective Memory', *Prooftexts*, 29 (2009), 1–30.

[34] See R. Moses b. R. Eleazar's 'Meh kol hatson hazeh', in Habermann, *The Book of Persecutions* (Heb.), 220–6, esp. 224.

[35] See Malcolm Barbour, 'The Pastoureaux of 1320', *Journal of Ecclesiastical History*, 32 (1981), 147, 156; id., 'Lepers, Jews and Moslems: The Plot to Overthrow Christendom in 1321', *History*, 66 (1981), 1–17; David Nirenberg, *Communities of Violence: Persecution of Minorities in the Middle Ages* (Princeton, NJ, 1996), 43–124; H. Géraud (ed.), *Chronique Latine de Guillaume de Nangis de 1113 à 1300*, 2 vols. (Paris, 1843), ii. 35; 'Continuatio Girardi de Fracheto ad an. 1320', in Dom Bouquet, et al. (eds.), *Recueil des Historiens des Gaules et de la France*, 24 vols. (Paris, 1738–1904), xxi. 54–5.

[36] Shlomo Spitzer (ed.), *Laws and Customs of R. Shalom of Neustadt* [Hilkhot uminhagei rabenu shalom mineustadt] (Jerusalem, 1977), 137, para. 402.

[37] R. Abraham Zacuto, *Sefer yuḥasin hashalem* (1857; 3rd edn. Jerusalem, 1963), 51*b* and esp. 222*b*. He also reports a case of active martyrdom in 1497.

[38] See Joseph Hacker, '"If We Have Forgotten the Name of our God [Ps. 44: 21]": Interpretation in

From the middle of the seventeenth century, the chronicle of the Chmielnicki massacres in the Ukraine, Nathan of Hannover's *Yevein metsulah*, published in 1653, reports that in Tolchin three rabbis urged Jews to die as martyrs and not convert. At that point, the Jews signalled their agreement by calling out *shema yisra'el* before being killed. And in 1768, we find among the Hebrew accounts of an anti-Jewish riot in Uman, also in the Ukraine, a reference to a Jew who ritually killed 'his wife, his children, and then himself', but no mention of *shema yisra'el*.[39]

There may be other examples of Jews performing ritual homicide or crying out *shema yisra'el* at the moment of dying as a martyr, but this brief survey is sufficient to show that the evidence for either practice is spotty at best. The performative Midrash of Jews doing one or the other act in 1096 did not catch on even in medieval Germany, but neither gesture disappeared entirely. Despite this uneven record, Jewish memory and even scholarly memory has assumed the cry of *shema yisra'el* to be a continuous martyrological practice.

A clue to what has happened lies in the assumption that the practice of a Jewish martyr crying out *shema yisra'el* dates back to the death of Rabbi Akiva. Scholars have read back into the talmudic tale of Rabbi Akiva's death a practice that is attested there only potentially and not documented in fact until 1096 and in a few cases thereafter. They have performed a midrashic rereading of the Akivan texts. And because the texts about Rabbi Akiva's death, now read to include the 1096 performative Midrash, are canonical, the inference was then drawn that Jews must have done 'this' 'since Rabbi Akiva's death'. If scholars are convinced that a Jewish martyr in 1096 uttering *shema yisra'el* is no different from the Akiva traditions, how are ordinary Jews to make distinctions? We have here, then, an example of the 'exegetical construction of reality' in which later midrashic behaviour has been retrojected back into an earlier canonical text that is then assumed to have become a standard practice among Jewish martyrs.

Light of the Realities in Medieval Spain' (Heb.), *Zion*, 57 (1992), 253–64; Abraham Gross, 'On the German Syndrome of Martyrdom in Portugal in 1497' (Heb.), *Tarbiz*, 64 (1995), 83–114; Ram Ben-Shalom, 'Martyrdom and Martyrology in Aragon and Castile in 1391: Between Spain and Germany' (Heb.), *Tarbiz*, 70 (2001), 227–82; Abraham Gross, 'Apostasy and Acts of Martyrdom in 1391: The New Appraisal' (Heb.), *Tarbiz*, 71 (2002), 269–77; Ram Ben-Shalom, 'Jewish Martyrology and Apostasy in Spain and Germany in the Middle Ages' (Heb.), *Tarbiz*, 71 (2002), 279–300; and Abraham Gross, *Struggling with Tradition: Reservations about Active Martyrdom in the Middle Ages* (Leiden, 2004), 93–9, for a debate over the diffusionist (Gross) or independent (Ben-Shalom) explanations of Iberian active martyrdom. See, too, Ben-Sasson, 'Remembering and Forgetting Persecutions' (Heb.).

[39] Nathan of Hannover, *Yevein metsulah* (Venice, 1653), reprinted in Moshe Rosman (ed.), *Sipurei hagezerot bishenot tah vetat* (Jerusalem, 1981), 31; on Uman, see Shimon Bernfeld (ed.), *Sefer hademaot*, 3 vols. (Berlin, 1923–6), iii. 292.

PART III
MEDIEVAL TRANSFORMATIONS

ELEVEN

MIDRASH IN A LEXICAL KEY
Nathan ben Yehiel's *Arukh*

JOANNA WEINBERG

THE LEXICOGRAPHICAL impulse to order, sift, and systematize key vocabulary or terminology and to clarify and restore meaning to words that have become obscure over time manifests itself in all literate societies, and provides an essential guide to the intellectual world which sets such an impulse in motion. It often develops out of a particular community's commitment to the study of a common body of texts. This is certainly true of some of the dictionaries produced in Arabic from the ninth century onwards, the purpose of which was to offer interpretation of obscure lexemes in the Quran and prophetic tradition.[1] In the same linguistic context Jews began to produce dictionaries of their own canonical texts. Particularly significant is the recent discovery of a number of leaves of the 'lost' dictionary of Hai Gaon (939–1038), entitled *Kitab al-hawi*, which lists words belonging to the main corpora of the author's religious tradition: Scripture, Targum, Talmud, and Midrash.[2] In the dictionary, written in Judaeo-Arabic and organized anagrammatically, difficult or obscure vocabulary from *Genesis Rabbah* and *Agadat vayikra* (*Leviticus Rabbah*) is listed alongside words from the Mishnah and Talmud; all are the object of the same philological scrutiny. The evidence provided by the extant remains of Hai's book thus demonstrates that the corpus of written texts to which Hai and his scholarly community were committed included both halakhic and aggadic works.[3] The lexicographer's task was not to assess the relative authority of different traditions as transmitted in varied sources, but simply to provide a straightforward interpretation of difficult or unfamiliar words and phrases.

---

[1] See John A. Haywood, *Arabic Lexicography: Its History and its Place in the General History of Lexicography* (Leiden, 1965), and Tilman Seidensticker, 'Lexicography: Classical Arabic', in *Encyclopaedia of Arabic Language and Linguistics* (Leiden, 2008), iii. 30–7.

[2] On this text see Aharon Maman, 'The Remnants of R. Hai Gaon's Dictionary *Kitab al-hawi* in the Taylor and Taylor-Schechter Genizah Collections' (Heb.), *Tarbiz*, 69 (2000), 341–419, and id., 'Rabbinic Hebrew in Rav Hai Gaon's *Kitab al-hawi* According to the Adler and Taylor-Schechter Genizah Collections' (Heb.), *Leshonenu la'am*, 56/1 (2006), 23–33.

[3] Important to point out here is the obvious fact that the production of glossaries or lexica can only be a function or need of a textualized society. See below for development of this theme.

Not long after Hai Gaon penned his dictionary, another lexicon—Nathan ben Yehiel's *Sefer he'arukh*—was produced, in Hebrew rather than Arabic,[4] and in a Latin Western context rather than in Pumpeditha in the domain of geonic Babylonia. One feature alone links the *Arukh*, written in Rome at the beginning of the twelfth century, with Hai's dictionary—the citation of rabbinic writings, including the main works of classical Midrash. Nathan, like Hai, harvested the entries for his dictionary from all extant sources and traditions without imposing a hierarchy of reading on his readers. But here the similarity ends; as Aharon Maman has noted, the nature of Nathan's philological undertaking differed from that of his predecessors such as Ibn Janah and Hai.[5] Although, as we shall see, Nathan does attempt to provide simple meanings of rabbinic vocabulary, the scope of his dictionary goes far beyond the demands of 'scientific' philology, providing a whole range of interpretations culled from a vast store of post-talmudic sources, which do not always purport to give the literal meaning of the term or explain the word in its textual setting. This is certainly why, in his well-known report of his visit to Rome in 1165 or thereabouts, Benjamin of Tudela refers to 'Rabbi Nathan who composed the *Arukh* and its explanations' (*perushav*).[6] This is not only an accurate description of how Nathan introduces explanations of terms and texts, but it also focuses attention on the wide-ranging nature of Nathan's explanations of rabbinic vocabulary, which are conceived in a fashion that transcends the usual confines of a lexicon.[7]

THE AUTHOR OF THE *ARUKH*

Before attempting to explain Nathan's unusual conception of the lexicographer's task and examining the conspicuous presence of Midrash in his work, I must first

[4] Nathan does not appear to have known the *Arukh* attributed to Tsemah bar Paltoi Gaon, which Abraham Zacuto (1452–c.1515) cites several times in his chronicle *Sefer yuḥasin*. See H. Z. Taubes, 'The *Sefer he'arukh* of R. Nathan of Rome and the old *Arukh* of Rav Tsemah bar Paltoi Gaon' (Heb.), in Umberto Nahon (ed.), *Sefer zikaron lishelomoh me'ir: kovets letoledot yehudei italiyah* [Memorial Volume for Sally Meir: Essays on the History of the Jews of Italy] (Jerusalem, 1956), 126–41, who, on the basis of Genizah fragments, concludes that where Nathan's and Tsemah's *Arukh* cite the same interpretations the two compilers are simply deriving their information from the same geonic sources. There is also no evidence that Nathan had read the *Seder alfa-beta* of R. Makhir (brother of Rabbenu Gershom), which is no longer extant.

[5] Aharon Maman, '*Peshat* and *Derash* in Medieval Hebrew Lexicons', *Israel Oriental Studies*, 19 (1999), 343–57.

[6] Benjamin speaks with admiration of the prominent positions that Roman Jews held within the Roman Curia, referring in particular to 'R. Yehiel, the official of the Pope. He is a handsome, intelligent and erudite young man who frequents the Papal palace, for he is the steward over his house and all his possessions. He is a grandson of R. Nathan who composed the *Arukh* and its explanations/commentaries [*perushav*]' (Nathan Adler, *The Itinerary of Benjamin of Tudela: Critical Text, Translation and Commentary* (London, 1907), 6–7).

[7] Nathan uses the term *perush* to introduce all manner of explanations of words or larger sections of texts. In the introduction to his *Dictionary of Jewish Babylonian Aramaic of the Talmudic and Geonic Periods* (Baltimore, Md., 2002), Michael Sokoloff states that lexicographers of Nathan's persuasion viewed themselves as text commentators as much as lexicographers.

outline some of the relevant biographical and historical facts.[8] In his historical work *Shalshelet hakabalah* (Chain of Tradition), Gedaliah ibn Yahya refers to and cites from two poems by Nathan that appeared in 'a very old manuscript' of the *Arukh* in his possession. These appear to be the same poems that were published in the first printed edition of the work (Rome, *c.*1469–72) and subsequent editions. The verses allow the reader a fragmentary glimpse into the life of Nathan ben Yehiel.[9] Apparently he worked together with his father in communal matters in Rome; the poems proudly refer to the construction of a *mikveh* (ritual bath) and a beautiful synagogue. We are also told that, on the death of his father in 1070, Nathan assumed leadership of the community together with his two brothers, Daniel and Abraham. After the tragic deaths of four of his five sons, he composed the *Arukh* in 1102.[10]

Amid the obscure rhetoric of his verses, encumbered with pious sentiments, Nathan announces the purpose of his work, which, he alleges, is to list the abstruse words in the Oral Torah together with examples of their usage. However, as indicated before in relation to Hai's lexicon, any superficial examination of the *Arukh* reveals that the listing of abstruse words, although certainly part of his literary endeavour, is not the sole criterion according to which a particular word is inserted in the text. The entries are arranged alphabetically in an order that presupposes a biliteral conception of the consonantal roots of the Hebrew language. Chapters mark the separation between words which begin with one letter in its combination with a second letter, beginning with *alef* and proceeding alphabetically. To the modern reader, this sequence seems strange simply because it ignores the idea of the triliteral root, and finding an entry becomes, in Michael Sokoloff's words, 'a both time-consuming and daunting task'.[11] However, we should bear in mind that, at least in the West, alphabetic ordering was not always the rule. In a jocular aside Julius Pollux (second century CE) opened his encyclopaedic *Onomasticon* with words that would be anathema to a modern lexicographer: 'I shall begin, as is right, with the gods, and all the rest, I shall put just as it comes.'[12]

THE *ARUKH* IN ITS RABBINIC CONTEXT

The reader of the *Arukh* is overwhelmed by the panoply of sources that Nathan cites in relation to the lemmata. A vast number of talmudic and midrashic passages is quoted, sometimes together with explanations by major rabbinic figures of past and

---

[8] Alexander Kohut's monumental *Aruch Completum*, 8 vols. (Vienna, 1878–92), in which he listed and discussed Nathan's sources, cannot be overestimated. However, readers should beware that his constant intermingling of his own contributions and that of his 17th-cent. predecessor Benjamin Musafia to the meaning of words within the entries often introduces confusion, so that the reader cannot distinguish between Kohut and Nathan.   [9] Gedaliah ibn Yahya, *Shalshelet hakabalah* (Venice, 1587), 41*b*.
[10] In his chronicle or chain of rabbinic authorities to his own time (1467) Joseph ibn Zaddik of Arevalo states that Nathan died in 1106 (Adolf Neubauer, *Medieval Jewish Chronicles and Chronological Notes* (Oxford, 1887), 93).   [11] Sokoloff, *A Dictionary of Jewish Babylonian Aramaic*, 15.
[12] Julius Pollux, *Onomasticon*, ed. Ericus Bethe (Stuttgart, 1987), 1.

present, while sometimes the explanations are given anonymously but are actually verbatim transcriptions from sources to which he explicitly refers in other passages. It should be emphasized that we are not confronted here with plagiarism, but rather with a typically medieval method of composition, in which the compiler functions as a transmitter of traditions. It is taken for granted that the opinions expressed are derived from authoritative sources. On the other hand, it is also clear that the compiler chooses his traditions and in this respect stamps his own mould on his chosen fragments of texts.

The main schools of talmudic exegesis are represented in the *Arukh*. There is a vast number of geonic pronouncements, among which those of Hai Gaon figure prominently, and on a few occasions, reference is made to a certain Matsliah, which has led to the unproven assertion, mooted by Kohut, that Nathan studied in Sicily with Matsliah, who had himself studied in the academy of Hai.[13] The emerging schools of northern Europe and North Africa, whose authorities are near contemporaries of Nathan, figure conspicuously: Hananel ben Hushiel of Kairouan, North Africa (d. 1057) is frequently cited explicitly or implicitly,[14] as is his pupil Rabbenu Nissim (d. 1062), whose commentaries on the Talmud and *Megilat setarim* are combed by Nathan for relevant information;[15] he transcribes a long verbatim section from Rabbenu Nissim's commentary on Tohorot.[16] What should be stressed here is that Rabbenu Nissim cites extensively from both halakhic and aggadic *midrashim*. In other words, Nathan, like his immediate predecessor Nissim, does not make any distinction between talmudic and midrashic sources; rather, different types of traditions and commentaries are intertwined within the same lexical units.

From northern climes, the teachings of Rabbenu Gershom and the 'sages of Mainz' are given their place.[17] The liturgical poet and commentator Meshulam ben

---

[13] The printed text, s.v. אנפקינון, 'oil made of unripe olives', reads 'I heard from the mouth of R. Matsliah'. The earliest manuscript does not have this phrase; it is true, however, that the phrase does appear in Bodleian MS Opp. Add fo. 42, a late 13th-cent. Spanish manuscript of the *Arukh*. In other entries, e.g. מתי, he simply refers to the statement of 'R. Matsliah of blessed memory'. But due attention is needed since explanations are taken from earlier sources, e.g. the third entry for חלק cites R. Hananel, then Rabbenu Gershom, and later 'and he [i.e. Gershom] said to us'.

[14] He often uses Hai word for word, makes frequent use of the Jerusalem Talmud, and explains Arabic and Greek words. For the first detailed list of Nathan's use of Hai Gaon and Rabbenu Hananel b. Hushiel, see vol. ix of Kohut produced by Samuel Krauss, *Supplements to Aruch Completum* [Sefer tosefot he'arukh hashalem] (New York, 1892).

[15] See Shraga Abramson (ed.), *Nisim gaon* (Jerusalem 1965), 19–27. Abramson discusses, for example, how the phrase 'some interpret' in the entry for *gamzo* appears to refer to Hananel. He rejects Schorr's suggestion that Nathan read Nissim's *Mafte'aḥ*, but does think it likely that Nathan read Nissim's lost commentary on BT *Berakhot* (p. 21).

[16] According to Abramson, Nathan's citations of the Jerusalem Talmud are culled partly from Rabbenu Nissim's commentary, but are partly direct quotations, as indicated by his use of the term *yerushalmi* as opposed to *gemara divenei ma'arava* (the Gemara of the people of the West).

[17] Avraham Grossman, *The Early Sages of France: Their Lives, Leadership and Work* [Ḥakhmei tsarefat harishonim: koroteihem, darkham behanhagat hatsibur, yetsiratam haruḥanit] (Jerusalem, 1995), 99,

Kalonymus (second half of the tenth century), who died in Mainz but is said to have been born in Lucca in Italy, is given prominence in the first entry for סעד.[18] It is noteworthy that the traditions Nathan cites as issuing from 'the mouth of our teacher Moses of Narbonne' (Moses Hadarshan), which suggest that he may have studied with the master in Narbonne, all relate to halakhic matters.[19] Moses of Narbonne and his school are normally associated with Midrash, and in particular with *Genesis Rabbati*, *Midrash agadah*, and the revision of the first part of *Numbers Rabbah*. Indeed it is difficult to understand the exact nature of Nathan's relationship to this shadowy figure. It is Rashi, Nathan's contemporary, who often refers explicitly to consulting the *Yesod* of Moses Hadarshan, allegedly a text containing the latter's interpretation of Scripture.[20] Since the *Arukh* is not a dictionary of biblical vocabulary, it is difficult to establish the extent to which Moses Hadarshan's exegesis underlies Nathan's interpretations. The occurrence of the same interpretation of the word פצם in Psalm 60: 4 in Rashi and in the *Arukh*, accompanied by the same proof-text and quotation from the Palestinian Targum, may be evidence of Moses Hadarshan's presence in the lexicon, but this cannot be proven categorically.[21]

Nathan's *Arukh* 'is in large part a collection of Geonic glosses on the Talmud'—thus Louis Ginzberg.[22] That Nathan had at least one foot on the shoulders of his geonic predecessors is without doubt, but traces of his own reworking of the source or sources may be detected, since the correspondences between the geonic text and the *Arukh* are usually not exact. A prime example is the entry for *tataf* טטף, which bears an amazing similarity to an anonymous responsum published by Harkavy,[23] including the same reference to a Greek word (though not to the Arabic synonym cited in the responsum). Like his source, Nathan combines talmudic (Jerusalem and Babylonian) and midrashic sources but the phrase 'in our place' in the responsum is replaced by 'there are places'. More significant is the fact that, although Nathan includes the citations from *Agadat vayikra* and *Shir hashirim ḥazita*, he does not

241–3, has demonstrated once and for all that Nathan and his brother did not correspond with Rashi, and that 'Shelomoh Yitshaki' refers to somebody living in Italy.

[18] As we shall see, this long entry provides a complete discourse on theodicy and death, which fits in with his treatment and selection of midrashic passages.

[19] The five references are all listed by Kohut, *Aruch Completum* (vol. i, p. xv) and discussed by Hananel Mack, *The Mystery of Rabbi Moses Hadarshan* [Misodo shel mosheh hadarshan] (Jerusalem, 2010), ch. 8.

[20] Rashi appears to have been consulting a written text since he usually refers to 'finding in the words of R. Moses Hadarshan', for example, on Num. 7: 23, where he cites a long interpretation ending with the words 'thus far R. Moses Hadarshan'.

[21] Rashi on Ps. 60: 4: 'However, R. Moses Hadarshan explained the verb as referring to "tearing" and derives its interpretation from "and he cuts out windows for it" [Jer. 22: 14], which is rendered *ufatsem* in the Targum.'

[22] Louis Ginzberg, *Geonica*, vol. i (New York, 1909), 204. And see e.g. ibid., vol. ii (New York, 1909), 293–301, where he discusses Genizah fragments of geonic texts and their use in the *Arukh*, and points out variants and differences.

[23] Abraham E. Harkavy, *Geonic Responsa* [Teshuvot hage'onim] (repr. New York, 1959), 14.

include the liturgical formula at the end of the responsum, 'May it be His will to regard both you and us as meritorious enough to see His deliverance and the rebuilding of His Temple and the ingathering of His exiles—a great salvation.' Instead Nathan ends with a new source—*Midrash tehilim* (on Ps. 48: 13), a difficult text, which Buber pronounced to be corrupt, that describes the numerous natural gardens, towers, and *tatrafiliyot* (mansions?) that would adorn Jerusalem in a future age when waters would flow into 990 aqueducts.

The liturgical ending of the responsum had no place in the lexicon; instead, Nathan presents another example of the difficult lexeme from a *midrash* not cited by his source. The eschatological theme continues, though encased within the lexicographical frame. Of course it could be argued that he was actually conflating more than one source in order to deal with this problematic word, but such conjectures are riddled with uncertainty. In Carlotta Dionisotti's incisive words about the *De orthographia* of Bede (eighth century): 'If an item in Bede exactly reproduces the wording of just one extant work there is a presumption that that was his source and the presumption may become certainty if there are several items corresponding to the same text. . . . But what if, as often, Bede's item is found in several texts, or if it is not exactly like any one, but analogous to several? How can we decide what source he is using, or whether he is conflating more than one? Maybe it is no longer extant.'[24] These cautionary words seem to be eminently applicable to Nathan and highlight our limitations in attempting to reconstruct his mode of compilation with any degree of certainty.

THE *ARUKH* IN ITS NON-JEWISH CONTEXT

The *Arukh* was written by a native Roman in 1102. Any reader of the work cannot fail to notice the Italian origins of its author, for he translates more than five hundred Hebrew or Aramaic words into his own Italian vernacular (*le'azim*).[25] The presence of the vernacular in this work draws attention to its historical and cultural context. Nathan was a Roman Jew, addressing Italian Jewish readers who, like him, were not divorced from the non-Jewish environment in which they lived. Such an impression is also somewhat reinforced on reading, for example, the entry for *prokope* (to which I shall return). Nathan mentions that his brother Daniel had turned to an erudite (non-Jewish) lawyer (*dayan filosofo gramatiko*) for explanation of the word. Similarly, Hai Gaon records that he asked a Greek-speaker to enlighten him about the meaning of a talmudic word, and, according to the celebrated story

---

[24] Carlotta Dionisotti, 'On Bede, Grammars and Greek', *Revue Bénédictine*, 82 (1982), 112–13.

[25] Luisa Cuomo devoted her doctoral thesis, 'Le glosses volgari dell'Arukh di R. Nathan ben Jechiel da Roma' (Hebrew University of Jerusalem, 1974), to a linguistic analysis of these words and has also published on the subject. See Luisa Ferretti Cuomo, 'Le glosse volgari nell'Arukh di r Natan ben Yehiel da Roma. Note di lavoro a proposito del fondo germanico', *Medioevo romanzo*, 22/2 (3 of 3rd series) (1998), 232–76, and 'Le glosse volgari nell' "Arukh" di R. Natan ben Yehi'el da Roma: interferenze lessicali e semantiche', *Italia*, 13–15 (2001), 25–52.

Hai told his disciple Matsliah to discuss the meaning of a word in a psalm with the local Catholicos in Baghdad.[26] It is not unlikely, therefore, as Israel Ta-Shma also surmised,[27] that Nathan was familiar with the lexicographical scholarship of his non-Jewish neighbours.

The eleventh and twelfth centuries mark the beginning of a sustained stream of production of codes and lexicographical compilations.[28] Isidore of Seville's seventh-century *Etymologies* often formed the starting-point of medieval compilations, which were intended to satisfy curiosity about etymology and grammar, and often became 'summae' of medieval knowledge. Attention was also given to the transmission of classical texts. One might point to the Monte Cassino monastery, where under Abbot Desiderius (1057–87) there was a revival of copying and transmitting classical texts. Particularly relevant to our enquiry is a work produced about the same time as that of Nathan, which itself derived partly from a *liber glossarum*, the so-called *Glossarium ansileubi*, but clearly modified the earlier structures of compilation. The author, Papias, is inextricably linked to his dictionary, the *Elementarium doctrinae rudimentum* (Basic Introduction to Education).[29] Like Nathan, Papias constructs his dictionary according to a particular alphabetical order with divisions and subdivisions.[30] As with Nathan, there is a personal element to the dictionary. Papias writes to instruct 'his dear children' in various branches of knowledge. A patriotic sentiment is expressed in his entry for Italy, which he describes as a 'country which is extremely beautiful in every respect on account of the fertility of its soil, and which is well endowed on account of the richness of its crops'.[31] It may be that a similar sentiment can be detected in the *Arukh*, where the entry for 'Italia' is fairly lengthy, with reference to the identification of Kittim (Gen. 10: 1) in the Jerusalem Talmud and *Genesis Rabbah* (37: 1) with Italy, and to Targum Lamentations 4: 21, identifying the land of Uz with Rome (Uz is also the name for Rome in *piyutim*, and Uzi is Josippon's equivalent to Latinus in his description of the founding of Rome).[32] In his preface, Papias speaks of 'excerpting, and compiling from all the writings that I have found'. At the same time, he distinguishes his work from that of previous glossators. Difficult words and biblical names are found in his dictionary. The lemmata are either given short explanatory comments or longer discussion covering

---

[26] See Maman, 'The Remnants of R. Hai Gaon's Dictionary (Heb.), 418–19.   [27] See below, n. 29.

[28] Whether this phenomenon should be described as a renewal and amplification of cultural impulses at work in Carolingian times is discussed by Marvin B. Becker, *Medieval Italy* (Bloomington, Ind., 1981), ch. 2.

[29] Israel Ta-Shma also drew the parallel with Papias in 'The *Sefer he'arukh* of R. Nathan ben Yehiel of Rome' (Heb.), *Rassegna Mensile di Israel*, 67, 1–2 (2001), 21–6 (repr. in id., *Collected Studies* [Keneset meḥkarim], vol. iii (Jerusalem, 2005), 3–8). On Papias see Lloyd W. Daly and B. A. Daly, 'Some Techniques in Medieval Latin Lexicography', *Speculum*, 39/2 (1964), 229–39.

[30] For a recent, illuminating discussion on medieval concordances and their alphabetization, see Ann Blair, *Too Much to Know* (New Haven, Conn., 2010), 33–46.

[31] Papias, *Elementarium doctrinae rudimentum* (Venice, 1485), s.v. 'Italia' (entry 1): *terra omnibus in rebus pulcherima soli fertilitate et pabuli ubertate gratisssima*.

[32] See *Josippon* [Sefer yosipon], ed. David Flusser, vol. i (Jerusalem, 1978), 11.

grammatical, etymological, rhetorical (e.g. his entry for *argumentum*), and even historical matters. Like Nathan, Papias refers to languages (in his case, Greek, Hebrew, and Syriac, i.e. Aramaic) with which he had, in all probability, no acquaintance.[33] Cultural considerations shape even compilatory works such as those of Nathan and Papias. Under the entry for *aetas*, Papias gives a long chronological excursus from creation to his own time, or in his words, 'until the thirteenth year of Henry II, son of Conrad II', that is to say, 1041.[34] Nathan's lexicon also has its chronological axe to grind in the entry for שבע, 'seven'. The number seven gives rise to an extended excursus on the chronological calculations connected with Daniel's seventy weeks, in the midst of which he also refers to the Italian Hebrew reworking of Josephus, the *Josippon*, a work of the preceding century.[35] Chronology, in other words, has a place in medieval lexica.

Of course, there are differences between the two works, but their similarities and historical proximity allow us to view the *Arukh* as a landmark in Jewish lexicography, much in the same way as Papias' dictionary was hailed in the Latin tradition. Both dictionaries suffered the fate that usually befalls such works. Extensive tampering with their text and accretions occurred over the centuries, which becomes particularly explicit in their *editio princeps* garb. The first printers clearly felt that there was a readership for these two lexica. The *Arukh* was published in about 1469 in Rome[36] and Papias' dictionary was printed four times in the fifteenth century in Milan and Venice.[37] The fifteenth-century editor, imbued with Renaissance values, inserted important, unknown fragments of Hesiod and Theocritus into Papias' lexicon, thus lending credence to the view that Papias knew Greek. The phrase 'and I heard from the mouth of Rabbi Matsliah', absent from the oldest manuscripts that I consulted, is found in the Hebrew incunabulum, perhaps testifying to a desire to portray Nathan as a student of the students of Hai Gaon. Both dictionaries were praised and criticized, used and rejected.

ORAL AND LITERARY TRADITIONS

In the first poem appended to the text Nathan writes that his work is derived from 'what I heard, saw, and thought'. This combination of the oral and written is a notable feature of this work and, one might add, characteristic of the period in which

---

[33] Nathan's Greek, Arabic, and Persian references are often simply taken over from his sources; similarly Papias uses Greek grammatical and rhetorical terminology that can be shown to derive from Isidore or from the *Glossarium Ansileubi*.

[34] *Papiae Elementarium*, Litera A, ed. V. De Angelis, vol. ii (Milan, 1978), 111–23.

[35] The passage from *Josippon* is in the first entry for שבע.

[36] This edition (printed by Obadiah, Manasseh, and Benjamin of Rome) was less tampered with than subsequent 16th-cent. printings: Pesaro, 1517; Venice, 1531/2; Venice, 1553 (with additions by Samuel Archivolti); and Basle, 1599. There were also abbreviated versions of the work: Constantinople, 1511; Kraków, 1592; and Sebastian Münster's Latin translation of excerpts, Basle, 1517.

[37] 1476, 1485, 1491, 1496.

he was writing. The famous declaration of Meshulam bar Kalonymus at the end of the tenth century, 'We have not heard from our rabbis nor seen their commentary,'[38] similarly indicates the transformation of methods of transmission of learning, or, as Brian Stock has described the phenomenon, 'the new interdependence between the oral and the written'.[39] In other words, textuality did not drive out orality; rather, their relationship changed. Throughout the *Arukh* written traditions are put on record in great number, but interpretations 'from the mouth of' different authorities are recorded alongside them. In one case Nathan quotes his father about the meaning of the expression *ben arel* (an uncircumcised person) in Babylonian Talmud Ḥulin 134*a*: 'My father, my master, of blessed memory, read the word as *ben tadal* with the initials of each letter signifying [using the device of *notarikon*]: Give attention to what he teaches, i.e. pay attention to his words for he has a point.'[40] The written tradition does not dispense with the oral communication but provides a relative point of contact. With Brian Stock's ideas in mind, Talya Fishman confronts questions of orality and textuality in her recent book about the transmission of the Talmud.[41] According to Fishman, inevitable changes occur as texts are set down in writing—written texts command more respect than living tradents. The Talmud became authoritative once it had been put into writing. In her reconstruction of medieval Jewish culture and its receptivity to textualization, Fishman suggests that Rabbenu Nissim's Talmud commentary made the presence of a teacher unnecessary. As indicated above, Rabbenu Nissim's voice is very dominant in the *Arukh*, but it is by no means the sole authority or the only way in which rabbinic texts are heard and seen on the page. Rather, the *Arukh* serves as a conduit through which flow all the streams of rabbinic scholarship known to Nathan, providing an encyclopaedic, although selective, guide to understanding the common heritage. The *Arukh* did indeed become an authoritative teacher for the succeeding centuries, teaching the meaning not only of Talmud but also of Midrash.

THE CORPUS OF *MIDRASHIM*

There are more than sixty manuscripts and several Genizah fragments of the *Arukh*; it should be borne in mind that Alexander Kohut used only six manuscripts for his monumental edition. My analysis of the text has been partly based on the British Library twelfth-century manuscript, which was not known to Kohut, and which,

---

[38] See Israel Ta-Shma's discussion of this pronouncement in *The Exegetical Literature of the Talmud in Europe and N. Africa* [Hasifrut haparshanit latalmud be'eiropah uvetsafon afrikah], vol. i (Jerusalem, 1999).

[39] Brian Stock, *The Implications of Literacy: Written Language and Models of Interpretation in the Eleventh and Twelfth Centuries* (Princeton, NJ, 1983).

[40] By using *notarikon*, the three consonants in *tadal* are separated into three words: *ten* (give), *da'atekha* (attention), and *lomed* (teaches). The reading *ben tadal* became the standard reading of the text although different interpretations of the expression are offered. Cf. Rashi on BT Ḥul. 134*a*.

[41] Talya Fishman, *Becoming the People of the Talmud: Oral Torah as Written Tradition in Medieval Jewish Cultures* (Philadelphia, Pa., 2011).

according to Beit-Arié, is of oriental or Byzantine provenance, possibly Italian. It is the earliest extant exemplar of the text.[42]

Sacha Stern has written about the cumulative process by which rabbinic texts were edited, implying that they must remain undated. He has nevertheless acknowledged that at a certain moment redacted works began to emerge and to be treated, if only by name, as single identifiable entities.[43] This phenomenon is already attested in Hai's lexicon and it becomes even more established in Rabbenu Nissim's works and the *Arukh*. At the same time, we must heed Neil Danzig's statement that the texts or fragments of midrashic texts coming to light from the Cairo Genizah indicate that aggadists were continually innovating, building new *midrashim* on the basis of both oral traditions and written texts.[44]

The reader of the *Arukh* is struck not only by the extensive citation of a wide range of *midrashim*[45] but also by the precision with which the compiler refers to the texts. The mode of citation suggests that the classical midrashic corpora were as familiar to the students of the Roman yeshiva as were the tractates of the Talmud. Moreover, the ability of modern editors of *midrashim* to determine which manuscript or manuscript tradition Nathan may have been using furnishes eloquent proof that he was indeed quoting from written texts. Particularly compelling for this argument is his constant reference to *parashah* numbers when quoting from *Genesis Rabbah*. Indeed, on account of a slight discrepancy in number references, Judah Theodor was able to determine which manuscript of the *midrash* bore the greatest affinity to that used in the *Arukh*.[46] Similarly, Mordechai Margulies was able to prove that Nathan was generally using a text of *Leviticus Rabbah* corresponding to Munich MS 177, though he also had access to other versions of the *midrash*.[47] Nathan is the first known writer to give it the designation *Midrash vayikra rabah* rather than *Agadat vayikra*. He also refers to *Megilat eikhah*, namely *Lamentations Rabbah*, and, as I shall show, used a version identical to the Casanatense

[42] According to Malachi Beit-Arié (cited in Cuomo, 'Le glosses volgari', 34), the script is very ancient, and has particular characteristics of the Dead Sea Scrolls, where the top of the letter *gimel* ends on the right (rather than the left).

[43] Sacha Stern, *Jewish Identity in Early Rabbinic Writings* (Leiden, 1994), p. xxii.

[44] Neil Danzig, *A Catalogue of Fragments of Halakhah and Midrash from the Cairo Genizah in the Elkan Nathan Adler Collection of the Library of the Jewish Theological Seminary* (New York, 1977), 56.

[45] Statistically speaking the references to both Talmuds and the Tosefta are much more numerous, but this fact does not detract from the significance of the extensive references to halakhic and aggadic *midrashim*.

[46] See 'Der Midrasch Bereschit Rabba', *Monatsschrift für Geschichte und Wissenschaft des Judentums*, 37 (1893), 38 (1894), 39 (1895) in 12 instalments.

[47] Mordechai Margulies, *Introduction, Appendices and Indices to Midrash vayikra rabah* (Heb.) [Mavo, nispeḥim umafteḥot lemidrash vayikra rabah] (Jerusalem, 1960), pp. xxxvii–xxxix. According to Margulies, this manuscript contains errors and additions from the Babylonian Talmud. Nathan does not always give precedence to this text. Margulies demonstrates that sometimes the readings Nathan gives agree with Genizah fragments and with Bodleian MS Opp. Add. fo. 3 and MS Opp. Add. fo. 51, and MS Jerusalem Heb. 8vo 515.

manuscript used by Buber for his edition of the text. A wealth of references to *Tanḥuma* and *Yelamedenu* adorn the lexicon; it would appear that the texts are not extant, with the exception of the passages from Exodus (which correspond to those in the printed text of *Tanḥuma*).[48] Nathan's Italian or rather southern Italian Jewish legacy may be reflected in this extensive use of these particular *midrashim*, since it has often been suggested that the *Tanḥuma/Yelamedenu midrashim* were created in the Byzantine schools of Bari or Otranto.[49] Also frequently cited is *Pesikta derav kahana*, referred to as *Pesikta*, followed by the title of the *piska*. It should not be forgotten that Leopold Zunz was able to propose the very existence of this *midrash* and proceed to reconstruct its content solely on the basis of the citations in the *Arukh* and *Yalkut shimoni*.[50] The halakhic *midrashim* are represented by citations from the *Mekhilta* (*derabi yishma'el*), *Sifra*, which he calls *Torat kohanim*, and *Sifrei*, called *Sifrei debei rav* (and *Seder olam*). In this category we might also put some aggadic texts he quotes such as *Baraita derabi eli'ezer*, otherwise known as *Pirkei derabi eli'ezer*.[51] Later *midrashim* such as *Midrash tehilim*, which he calls *Hagadat tehilim* or *Agadat ḥazita*,[52] *Song of Songs Rabbah*, also called *Agadat ḥazita*, and *Ecclesiastes Rabbah* are cited by *piska* and verse.[53]

MIDRASH IN DIFFERENT GARBS IN THE *ARUKH*

There is a multiplicity of ways in which *midrashim* and aggadic traditions are transmitted through the *Arukh*. The following examples will attempt to pinpoint the focus of each lemma in respect to its source.

---

[48] The first to discuss the *Yelamedenu* entries in the *Arukh* was Ezra da Fano, the editor of the Mantua 1565 edition of *Tanḥuma*. In his edition of *Tanḥuma* (Vilna, 1885; repr. Jerusalem, 1964) Salomon Buber published lists of all the entries on *Yelamedenu* and *Tanḥuma* in the *Arukh* and established that the references to *Yelamedenu* Exodus agree with the standard text of *Tanḥuma* Exodus. For the problems of the designations of *Tanḥuma/Yelamedenu* see Buber's discussion, ibid. 87–8.
See also Louis Ginzburg (ed.), *Ginzei Schechter*: 1. *Kitei midrash vehalakhah* [Genizah Studies in Memory of Doctor Solomon Schechter, 1. Midrash and Haggadah] (New York, 1928). For a recent description of study of the development of *Tanḥuma/Yelamedenu* traditions, see Marc Bregman, *The Tanḥuma–Yelamedenu Literature: Studies in the Evolution of the Versions* [Sifrut tanḥuma yelamedenu] (Piscataway, NJ, 2003).

[49] See Adolf Neubauer, 'Le Midrasch Tanhuma et extraits du Yelamedenu et de petits Midrashim', *Revue des études juives*, 13 (1886/7), 224–38; 14 (1887), 92–113, and more recently Marc Bregman, *The Tanḥuma–Yelamedenu Literature* (Heb.), and Lieve Teugels, 'New Perspectives on the Origins of "Aggadat Bereshit"', in Judit Borrás and Angel Sáenz-Badillos (eds.), *Jewish Studies at the Turn of the Century*, vol. i (Leiden, 1999), 349–57, esp. 354–5.

[50] The entry for מסקיד mentions the Rosh Hashanah *piska* as *rosh piskaot*, i.e. 'the first of the *piskaot*', thus suggesting an order of the *midrash* which confirms Zunz's original reconstruction: see Naftali Loewenthal's discussion in this volume, Ch. 20 n. 79. (Nathan also refers to 'the first of the *piskaot*' in מסאסא but this is not attested in all manuscripts.) See also Mandelbaum's introduction to his edition of *Pesikta derav kahana* (*Pesikta de Rav Kahana, According to an Oxford Manuscript*, 2 vols. (New York, 1962), i. 7–9, 12–13).   [51] See *Midrash eikhah rabah*, ed. Salomon Buber (Vilna, 1909), 39.

[52] Rabbenu Nissim quotes it in *Megilat setarim*, as does Rashi on several occasions. See *Midrash tehilim*, ed. Salomon Buber (Vilna, 1891), 66–7.

[53] For a full listing of the midrashic sources see Kohut, *Aruch Completum*, viii. 107–26.

In his discussion of storytelling as medieval Midrash in this volume (Chapter 9), Eli Yassif selected the story of the pit and weasel as an example of the diverse ways in which an enigmatic talmudic passage was transmitted and interpreted over the centuries and 'opens to the reader or listener a range of meanings, each of which was explicable to the audience to which it was recounted'.[54] As Yassif indicated, one of the longest versions of the tale is recorded in the *Arukh* under the entry for *ḥoled*. Nathan narrates the story as an explanation (*perush*) of the talmudic statement given in the name of Hanina (Rabbi Ami): 'Come and see how great the men of faith are—this is demonstrated by the tale of the weasel and the pit. If this is the case with one who trusts in the weasel and the pit, how much more so if one trusts in the Holy One, blessed be He.'[55] Rabbi Ami's cryptic pronouncement is decoded in the *perush* by means of a moralizing folktale, thus transforming the entry into a Rashi or tosafistic type of gloss. But the gloss is both preceded and followed by other talmudic (halakhic) fragments related to weasels, true to the method employed throughout the *Arukh*; even in this most remarkable example, halakhah and aggadah are intertwined. Yet the length of the story—perhaps the longest non-halakhic entry in the dictionary—surely reveals Nathan's compilatory purpose. The story contains motifs about demons, contracts kept and broken, madness, and the wisdom of women, and has a happy ending clinched by a scriptural proof-text: 'My eyes are on those who keep faith in the world' (Ps. 101: 6), a fitting conclusion to a story that celebrates the good faith of the female protagonist and the efficacy of two unlikely witnesses —the weasel and the pit.

In this midrashic form, the tale becomes instructive by reason of the final scriptural citation, and the origins of the obscure talmudic phrase 'the weasel and pit' are located in a tale embedded in folklore.

Given the constant use of earlier interpretations it would be foolhardy to suggest that the choice of citations for any lemma demonstrates a conscious selection process on the part of the compiler. And yet there are clear signs that either Nathan or his source set out to provide the reader with a key with which to approach the midrashic creations. This may be exemplified by his entry for *atleitin*, for which he provides two parables (*meshalim*) from *Genesis Rabbah* in which the term occurs. The theme of both parables concerns God's interference in human matters. In the first, well-known *mashal* that confronts the question of theodicy in relation to Cain's murder of Abel, the two athletes (*atleitin*) fight in the presence of the emperor. In his death throes the defeated athlete raises his eyes to the emperor's box and begs, 'Let my case be pleaded before the king' (Gen. Rab. 22: 9). In the second example, the significance of the phrase 'Jacob was left alone' (Gen. 32: 25), after his struggle with the angelic adversary, is investigated by means of a parable: 'This may be compared to an athlete who was wrestling with a prince. Lifting up his eyes, he saw a king

---

[54] See above, Ch. 9.
[55] BT *Ta'an.* 8a. This version bears greatest affinity to that published by Moses Gaster in his *Exempla of the Rabbis* [Sefer ma'asiyot], 2nd edn. (Leipzig, 1929), 59–60 n. 89.

standing over him and threw himself before him' (*Gen. Rab.* 77: 3). The two parables use the same term, but the messages are contradictory. In the first example, the parable is used to accuse God of having failed to save Abel by not exerting his imperial authority. In the other case, God's providential care is emphasized through his mere presence.[56] Through these *midrashim* theological considerations are brought to the attention of the reader. It may be that Nathan did not choose these particular texts with the express purpose of conveying their theological messages; and yet one of the consequences of combining these particular texts in one lemma is that the reader has to confront the peculiarly midrashic mode of scriptural interpretation that reflects upon the complexities of the interaction between the divine and human realms in a plurality of voices.

A similar consideration for the human relation to the divine is communicated in the entry for *ḥavarbar*. Nathan quotes a lengthy passage from *Genesis Rabbah* (82: 14):

When were hybrids created? In the days of Anah, as it says: 'This is Anah who found the wild ass [in the wilderness]' [Gen. 36: 24]. What did he do? He brought a she-ass and crossed it with a horse and the result was a mule. Said the Holy One, blessed be He, 'I did not create anything harmful, while you have created something harmful. By your life, I will create something harmful.' He brought a *ḥakhinah* [a snake] and crossed it with a *ḥardon* [a species of lizard] and the result was a *ḥavarbar* [striped lizard]. Nobody has ever been bitten by a *ḥavarbar* and survived or been kicked by a mule and survived, but only provided that the mule was white.

Nathan then refers to two talmudic passages from Babylonian Talmud *Berakhot* 33*a* and cites in full the parallel passage from the Jerusalem Talmud (5: 1, 9*a*):

Woe to the person who is touched by a *ḥavarbar* and woe to the lizard who bit Rabbi Hanina ben Dosa. As regards a poisonous lizard, if the person drinks water first, the lizard dies. But if the lizard drinks water first, the person dies. His [ben Dosa's] students said to him, 'Master, didn't you feel anything [when the lizard bit you]?' He said to them, 'I swear I was concentrating on my prayer and felt nothing.' Said Rabbi Isaac bar Eleazar, 'God created a spring beneath his [ben Dosa's] feet to fulfil the verse, "He will satisfy the desire of all who fear him; He also will hear their cry" [Ps. 145: 9].'

---

[56] The *Arukh* gives a third example from the lost *Yelamedenu*, on Lev. 23: 40 'And you shall take on the first day', referring to Sukkot: 'First they blow the shofar and then the athletes enter.' The text appears to refer to Yom Kippur, which is then followed by Sukkot, and the struggle against sin. Nathan's explanation (*perush*) of the word 'those who struggle' interestingly ignores the Greek origins of the word. In the printed *Tanḥuma* a similar passage is found, but it reads: 'It is like people who come before the king for judgment... The king passes judgment on them and they do not know who has won the case. The king says: "Anyone who goes out with a garland in his hand knows that he has won." Similarly with Israel. The non-Jews enter for judgment on Yom Kippur and human beings do not know who has won. The Holy One, blessed be He, says, "Take your *lulavim* in your hands so that everybody can know that you are innocent."'

The *midrash* ends on a negative note, but the talmudic text proffers hope for the pious. God creates deadly monsters, but in response to the prayers of the saints also provides life-enhancing waters. The lemma is deliberately constructed to ensure that the dark message of the *midrash* is tempered by the more optimistic talmudic text. Again, it is not impossible that Nathan was copying from a text which presented the text on 'hybrids' in the same order. What is clear and indisputable is that the moral of the story with its proof-text pushes the 'Just So Story' about hybrids aside and sets the exemplary tale centre stage.

Under the entry for *altikhsia* אלטיכסייא Nathan transcribes an entire unit of *Genesis Rabbah*, without providing any commentary.[57] It is one of the well-known units in the long section on Genesis 1: 26, 'Let us make man', which describes the controversy engendered among the angels of kindness (*ḥesed*) and the angels of truth (*emet*) through God's suggestion that Adam should be created. Psalm 85: 11, 'Mercy and truth met together', is used in order to express this idea. In defiance, God casts *altikhsia* (i.e. *aletheia*, Greek: 'truth') to the ground. The angels react with horror, 'How can you show such contempt for your *altikhsia/aletheia*?' The response is drawn from the following verse in the psalm, 'Let truth [*emet*] spring up from the earth' (*emet me'erets titsmah*, Ps. 85: 12). Putting aside the patently mythical elements in the *midrash*, we must reflect on the ways it would have been received by Nathan's readers. The problem is, of course, that the spelling of this Greek loan-word is hardly recognizable. Instead of following his normal practice of translating the alien word, Nathan simply transcribes the entire *midrash*. The verse itself supplies explication of the word. Uncertainty about the meaning of the loan-word necessitated the transcription of the entire *midrash*. In the process, I suggest, readers would have been able to fathom the complexity of the text, and to reflect on how, according to this *midrash*, the divine seal—truth—became the stuff out of which the earth is fashioned.

Nathan does not transcribe his texts mechanically. As often as not, variant readings are recorded. For example, in discussing the word *kampon*, Nathan first quotes a passage from Mishnah *Kelim* 23: 2: 'a horse-cloth is susceptible to uncleanness for it is used for sitting upon in the *kampum*'. He asserts that *kampon* is a Greek word (like many other military and administrative words in Byzantine Greek, it is a calque from the Latin *campus*, 'plain') and then enters the vernacular term, *campo*. He then cites three midrashic passages in which this word appears. In *Pesikta derav kahana*, 'Beshalaḥ', 11: 6, the king summons everybody to the *kampum* because they had cast aspersions on his daughters. The second text, *Leviticus Rabbah* 6: 2,[58] stresses the obligation of the witness (Lev. 5: 1). Nathan quotes part of the text: 'He [the governor] issued a proclamation throughout the province saying, "Let all the people go out to the *kampus*." What did he do? He brought some weasels.' He then cites from another passage in the same *midrash* (31: 4):[59] 'It is like a king who issues a decree

---

[57] *Gen. Rabbah* 8: 3 (*Midrash Bereshit Rabba*, ed. J. Theodor and Ch. Albeck, 3 vols. (Jerusalem, 1965), 60).

[58] *Midrash vayikra rabah* (ed. M. Margulies, Jerusalem, 1974), vol. i, p. 129.   [59] Ibid. 719.

and says: "Whosoever will gather and eat the fruit of the sabbatical year will be led around the *kampon*."' Nathan then concludes his presentation of the lemma with the comment: 'There is another reading, *kanpon*.' This is the mark of a good textual critic. He first gives the reading that he deems to be correct, but does not fail to place all witnesses to the text on record. What is particularly striking is his careful choice of texts, albeit in abbreviated form, whereby the reader is given a sense of how the term *kampon* is used to denote the public domain.

Nathan uses a multiplicity of terms to denote the languages he employs. The designation *lashon gramatikah* occurs in the passage to which I alluded before, in which his brother Daniel is reported as having turned to the *dayan filosofo gramatiko* for a translation of the word *prokope*. Nathan quotes from a cluster of midrashic sources in which this term appears. In the first example, from *Genesis Rabbah* 12: 16, he gives a fairly full citation of the *midrash*, whose purpose is to explain why 'earth' is given precedence in the verse, 'In the day that the Lord made the earth and heaven' (Gen. 2: 4). 'The earth was the first to fulfil My desire. I shall therefore confer *prokope* upon her, of which she shall never be deprived, as is stated, "Who did establish the earth upon its foundation, that it shall not be moved for ever and ever" [Ps. 105: 5].' The second example, from *Genesis Rabbah* 48: 6, is less complete:[60] 'The king said, "Anyone who captures him [the robber who had rebelled against his sovereignty] will be given *prokope* by me. He [the one who caught the robber] was anxious as to what kind of *prokope* he would be given.' The third example, also from *Genesis Rabbah* (90: 2),[61] is an explanation of Pharaoh's declaration to Joseph, 'according to your mouth shall all my people be kissed [*yishak*]' (Gen. 41: 40): 'No man shall receive *prokope* without your agreement.' In the last passage from *Genesis Rabbah* (an extract from the last section, referred to as *shitah ḥadashah*, in Theodor's edition) Nathan simply quotes a snippet, 'He allocates *prokope* to them.'[62] These texts are followed by an extract from *Leviticus Rabbah* 18: 5,[63] in which the way human rulers impose exile and other punishments is compared to that of God. As the homily draws to an end, more positive analogies come to the fore: 'A human gives *prokope* and likewise the Holy One, blessed be He, as it is said, "Take the head" [Num. 1: 2], in other words, "Give prominence to the community of the children of Israel."' Finally he quotes an unidentified passage from *Yelamedenu*: 'He appoints them as governors and leaders and allocates *prokope* to them.' Once again, the lemma term acquires its inflection from the *midrashim*; at the same time, particularly in the first *Genesis Rabbah* extract and in the *Leviticus Rabbah* citation, the meaning of the *midrashim* is effectively communicated. In the first case, explication is given for the reversal of the position of the earth—after all, in Genesis 1, the heavens are mentioned first. Similarly, in the *Leviticus Rabbah* passage, the rather vague expression acquires a new connotation.

---

[60] It is a gloss on the verse Isa. 33: 14, 'The sinners in Zion are afraid.' The parable is used here to explore the nature of the fear expressed in the verse.   [61] Theodor–Albeck edn., 1100.
[62] *Gen. Rabbah* 96 (Theodor–Albeck edn., 1203). The word occurs in a long passage about Jacob blessing his sons: 'When his sons entered to receive their blessings he began to confer *prokope* upon them.'
[63] *Midrash vayikra rabah* (Margulies edn.), 411.

The designated midrashic collections were lying open on the tables in the Roman yeshiva, but what were Nathan's readers supposed to do with these titbits?

Nathan concludes his survey of the midrashic use of *prokope* with the report that the lawyer had told his brother that in the 'grammatical language' the term *prokope* meant 'honour' (*kavod*). (In classical Greek the word simply means 'progress' or 'advance', but in patristic Greek the term expresses 'preferment', as in this context.) Thus we see that Nathan is expressing a typical view in this burgeoning period of the vernacular, namely that 'grammatical language' refers to those languages which are said to obey rules of grammar, namely Latin and Greek, in contrast to the vernacular, which is not subject to grammar. Not only does this notable incident recorded in the lexicon afford us a precious insight into the learned world of Nathan and his brother[64] and suggest their limited knowledge of Greek—and it should be remembered that the greater number of the classical midrashic words under discussion are Greek words—it also indicates that on occasion the mere citation of the *midrashim* and traditional explication of the texts did not suffice, but required elucidation from other quarters.

The Italian terms in the *Arukh* cover all *realia*, which gives the impression that the work is a 'Reallexikon', to quote Vogelstein and Rieger:[65] agricultural, botanical, military, musical, military terms, and the like abound, but, as Cuomo has pointed out, there is scant use of terms related to trade and business. The vernacular is not always introduced in order to convey the meaning of the word under discussion. In the entry for *basilike*, Nathan refers to some of the rabbinic texts in which the word occurs, including the famous description of the synagogue in Alexandria in Babylonian Talmud *Sukah* 52b: 'He who has not seen the double colonnade of Alexandria has never seen the glory of Israel. It was said that it was like a huge basilica, one colonnade within the other.' Nathan explains, 'It is a large palace; *basilica* in the vernacular.' By the eleventh century, *basilica* was the word for churches, and no longer carried its classical meaning of royal building. Here, then, Nathan just points to the existence of a vernacular word that is virtually identical to the rabbinic term.

The entry for *basilike* makes no mention of churches, and yet presumably a Roman Jew, like his Christian counterpart, would associate the *basilica* with a Christian place of worship. More intriguing and equally puzzling are two entries in which Nathan cites notorious passages that contain apparently anti-Christian taunts. Under *stada*, Nathan simply refers to the *notarikon* on the name <u>stat da miba'alah</u>, 'she turned away from her husband' (BT *San.* 67a). This sentence occurs in the passage about Stada and Pendira, where Ben Stada is identified with Jesus and Stada with Mary, who in this context is being accused of adultery. Nathan does not offer the reader any of this contextual information.

---

[64] Cuomo, 'Le glosses volgari', vol. i, pp. 157–8 n. 81, discusses this incident; she suggests that they knew people linked to the *scriptorium* of the pontifical curia.

[65] Hermann Vogelstein and Paul Rieger, *The History of the Jews in Rome* (Philadelphia, Pa., 1949).

Nathan's assertion that his purpose was to provide clarification of difficult words does not adequately explain his work. The medieval lexicographer draws from his sources, but clearly has his own agenda. Like Papias, Nathan has a selection of proper names among his lemmata, but at first glance, there is no particular rationale for their inclusion in the dictionary. Abraham is entered, but Isaac and Jacob do not appear. With regard to Abraham, Nathan writes: 'In *Genesis Rabbah* 49: 7: "Abraham was still standing before the Lord" [Gen. 18: 22]. Rabbi Simon said: "This is a case of scribal emendation [*tikun soferim*]; the Shekhinah was waiting for him,"[66] and in *Leviticus Rabbah* [this appears] at the beginning of "And it was the eighth day".' Both *midrashim* refer to the notion that the verse had actually been emended to avoid the unseemly depiction of God waiting for Abraham.

There is no doubt that these passages shed light on one particular assessment of the patriarch Abraham: such was Abraham's exemplary behaviour that he merited a visit from God, who actually waited for him. The potential misuse of recording the facts as they were had led the scribes to emend the passage. The brevity of the citation suggests that readers of the *Arukh* were being subtly instructed in the pitfalls of biblical interpretation; alternatively it was simply a way of communicating one of the many midrashic treatments of Abraham.

The length of the entries varies from a brief explanation to a long, extended discourse. Clearly, the brief, pithy comment has no less significance than the lengthy, discursive entry that provides all kinds of food for thought. The long exemplary folktale of the pit and the weasel belongs to the people—it does not bear the name of an authoritative sage—but enters learned discourse at an unknown date. The story has its place in the lexicon alongside interpretations and recently composed commentaries. Meshulam bar Kalonymus' popular commentary on 'everything is prepared for the feast', the last line of the dark allegory about reward and punishment and the life to come in Mishnah *Avot* 3: 24, is entered under the lemma for סעד. It interprets all the valences of the *mishnah*, but ends with the observation: 'Why is death called "feast"? Its purpose is to teach you that everybody enters through one door, but when they sit they are seated according to their position. So, too, the moment of death happens to the righteous and wicked alike, but each one is accorded respect in accordance with his deeds.' Once again the homiletic message is driven home within the lemmatic form. Meshulam's commentary became popular and was reused in subsequent centuries and beyond the gates of Rome. It appears in a late thirteenth-century manuscript collection of *midrashim* equipped with a commentary based mainly on the *Arukh*.[67] The use

---

[66] For clarification see e.g. Rashi on Gen. 18: 22: 'But surely it was not Abraham who had gone to stand before Him, but it was the Holy One, blessed be He, who had come to see him and had said to him, "Because the cry of Sodom and Gomorrah is great". And it should therefore have written here, "And the Lord stood yet before Abraham." But it is a scribal emendation.'

[67] Bodleian MS Opp. Add. fo. 3, a late 13th-cent. compendium of *midrashim* including a commentary (fos. 445ʳ–453ᵛ) based mainly on the *Arukh*, with various extracts from Mishnah *Avot* 3: 16.

of the *Arukh* in this manuscript is not coincidental. The rich and sometimes unfathomable language of the *midrashim* required an interpreter; the *Arukh* provided such a service.

In 1983 Isadore Twersky wrote about the contribution of Italian sages to rabbinic literature.[68] Adhering to a conventional view of Italy as an intermediary between Palestine, Babylon, and Ashkenaz, he came to the conclusion that there was 'no Italian innovation, no indigenous developments; there are contributions'.[69] These contributions, he admitted, were important. Indeed, he asserts that no study of medieval Jewish literature may claim to be comprehensive without integrating the contributions, attitudes, and insights of the thirteenth-century Rabbi Isaiah di Trani the Elder (Rid). It was Isaiah di Trani's talmudic *Pesakim* that the female scribe Paola daughter of Rabbi Abraham was transcribing in 1293 when she appended the colophon referring proudly to her lineage 'from the holy stock of Rabbenu Yehiel, father of our Rabbi Nathan ben Yehiel, author of the *Arukh*'.[70] Nathan's father is presented here as a founding figure, and with him is singled out the author of the *Arukh*.

In fact, the *Arukh* was certainly used beyond the confines of Italy within a short time of its composition. Rabbi Samuel ben Meir (Rashbam, *c*.1085–*c*.1158) refers to it in his commentary on Babylonian Talmud *Bava kama*, and the Tosafists make numerous allusions to the work.[71] It was translated into Arabic.[72] Speaking of northern European Jews in the twelfth to fourteenth centuries, Talya Fishman wrote: 'It is hard to imagine that a sense of kinship could have been inculcated among much larger numbers of European Jews ... were it not for their sharing of a common library—modelling their lives on the same revered texts.'[73] A common library of texts is invoked from within the pages of the *Arukh*, a product that bears the stamp of Mainz and Baghdad but is also clad in a Western garb. Nathan contributed to the survival of a wide range of midrashic traditions in non-Italian, non-Roman contexts.

Discussing the use of learning 'aids' for societies bedevilled by information overload, Ann Blair has astutely remarked, 'The great variety of aids to learning

---

[68] Isadore Twersky, 'The Contribution of Italian Sages to Rabbinic Literature', in *Italia Judaica: Atti del 1 convegno internazionale*, Bari 18–22 May 1981 (Rome, 1983), 383–400. But note the response of Israel Ta-Shma in *Creativity and Tradition: Studies in Medieval Rabbinic Scholarship, Literature and Thought* (Cambridge, Mass., 2006), 70–1, where he challenges Twersky's definition, which was based on a perspective from the 13th-cent. Provençal scholar Menahem Meiri, partly on the grounds that Meiri could not be used as evidence for such a view, given that he was altogether unfamiliar with Italian traditions.

[69] Twersky, 'Contribution of Italian Sages', 389.

[70] I am grateful to Malachi Beit-Arié, who drew my attention to this manuscript (Bodleian Can. Or. 89, 90), which contains *Piskei harid* on BT *Zevaḥim*, *Ḥulin*, *Menaḥot*, and *Bekhorot*.

[71] Rashbam glossed *Bava batra* 52*a* with the statement, 'I also found this in the book of the *Arukh* which was brought from Rome.' As Ephraim Kanarfogel shows in Ch. 14 of this volume, the Tosafists made thorough use of a large range of *midrashim* and commentaries.

[72] Shraga Abramson, 'R. Nathan b. Yehiel's *He'arukh* in Arabic (from a Trilingual Dictionary)' (Heb.), *Leshonenu la'am*, 58/1 (1993), 59–86.   [73] Fishman, *Becoming the People of the Talmud*, 224.

devised in different contexts typically involved combination of a few basic methods of managing texts that are still central today—sorting and storing selections from and summaries of them. But the results in each case were shaped by many contextual factors.'[74] There is no doubt that Nathan performed the lexicographer's task, namely, gathering and transmitting material in lemmatic form, and that, in so doing, he provided a textual service for his co-religionists (and later also for Christian scholars). The few examples I have given show that Nathan, like Papias, attempted to put his own stamp on a traditional literary genre, thereby producing his own indigenous Roman *summa* of rabbinic culture.

[74] Blair, *Too Much to Know*, 33.

TWELVE

RASHI'S CHOICE
The Pentateuch Commentary as Rewritten Midrash

IVAN G. MARCUS

ALTHOUGH many have written supercommentaries, essays, and even books about Rashi as a biblical or talmudic exegete, until recently few have looked at him as an original medieval Jewish thinker, let alone as a historical source reflective of northern European Jewish *mentalité*. And yet, no medieval Jew shaped the collective identity of Ashkenazi and even Sephardi Jewry more than this remarkable figure, whose genealogy is obscure but who is often compared and contrasted to his Sephardi analogue, Maimonides, whose genealogy was long and distinguished. Could Rashi have been so widely accepted as 'the' interpreter of biblical-talmudic Judaism for all times had he himself not been a person of his own time as well as a refashioner of it?[1]

The master exegete Rashi of Troyes (c.1040–1105) proposed Jewish core values to his readers, especially in his Pentateuch (Humash) commentary. He did not write a treatise but wrote biblical commentaries in the form of a selective editing of

---

[1] Among the many studies that have been written on Rashi, see Eliezer Meir Lipschuetz, 'Rashi' (Heb.), in id., *Writings* [Ketavim], 2 vols. (Jerusalem, 1947), i. 9–196; Benjamin J. Gelles, *Peshat and Derash in the Exegesis of Rashi* (Leiden, 1981); Esra Shereshevsky, *Rashi: The Man and His World* (New York, 1982); Sarah Kamin, *Rashi's Exegetical Categorization in Respect to the Distinction Between Peshat and Derash* [Rashi: peshuto shel mikra umidrasho shel mikra] (Jerusalem, 1988); Dov Rappel, *Rashi: His Jewish World* [Rashi: temunat olamo hayehudit] (Jerusalem, 1995); Avraham Grossman, *The Early Sages of France* [Ḥakhmei tsarefat harishonim] (Jerusalem, 1995), chs. 4 and 6; Moshe Ahrend, 'L'Adaptation des commentaires du midrash par Rashi et ses disciples à leur exégèse biblique', *Revue des études juives*, 156 (1997), 275–88 (repr. in Gilbert Dahan, Gérard Nahon, and Elie Nicolas (eds.), *Rashi et la culture juive en France du Nord au moyen âge* (Paris and Louvain, 1997), 137–49); Avraham Grossman, *Rashi* (Heb.) (Jerusalem, 2006); Daniel Krochmalnik, Hanna Liss, and Ronen Reichman (eds.), *Raschi und sein Erbe* (Heidelberg, 2007); and Avraham Grossman, *Rashi's World-View* [Emunot vede'ot be'olamo shel rashi] (Alon Shevut, 2008). Several important studies are in Avraham Grossman and Sara Japhet (eds.), *Rashi: The Man and His Work* [Rashi: demuto viyetsirato] 2 vols. (Jerusalem, 2008). On Rashi supercommentaries, see Eric Lawee, 'From Sepharad to Ashkenaz: A Case Study in the Rashi Supercommentary Tradition', *AJS Review*, 30/2 (2006), 393–425.

rabbinic lore. Even when he did not interpret narrative biblical irregularities, he wrote what I would call 'rewritten Midrash'.²

Readers have been divided over what Rashi did as a commentator. Religious educators saw him as a master teacher who sought to inculcate specific Jewish values. Although some anthologized his comments according to their own lights, others like Eliezer Lipschuetz and the renowned Bible teacher Nehama Leibowitz taught that Rashi's values were always answers to textual difficulties and not freely offered words of his own wisdom.³

Academic Bible scholars shifted the focus to Rashi as a literal or literary exegete who should be studied as a transitional figure leading to the later northern French exegetes, such as his grandson, Rabbi Samuel ben Meir (Rashbam, c.1085–c.1158), Rabbi Eliezer of Beaugency (twelfth century), Rabbi Joseph Kara (c.1065–c.1135), and Rabbi Joseph Bekhor Shor (twelfth century), and as being more traditional and less grammatically up to date than the Sephardi commentator, Rabbi Abraham Ibn Ezra (1089–1164). Since the nineteenth century, modern scholars have been biased in favour of appreciating a strict philological style of biblical interpretation in medieval Spain and northern France, under the lure of 'the Sephardi mystique'. Consequently, they have seen Rashi as a transitional figure between ancient Midrash and literal or so-called plain-style commentaries.⁴

Precisely because Rashi's Humash commentary is an enigmatic mixture of more Midrash than philology, Bible scholars have tended to emphasize Rashi's method, including the idea that Rashi used Midrash in certain cases where he thought the ambiguous text required it, the so-called 'double' interpretations. These scholars point to Rashi's methodological aside in Genesis 3: 8 or to his introduction at the beginning of Song of Songs as warrant for this. In light of Bible scholars' legitimate concern for getting at the text of the Bible as written, it is understandable that they

---

² This notion draws on and extends to medieval figures the idea of understanding some midrashic texts as 'rewritten Bible'. See e.g. Steven Fraade, 'Rewritten Bible and Rabbinic Midrash as Commentary', in Carol Bakhos (ed.), *Current Trends in the Study of Midrash* (Leiden, 2006), 59–78.

³ See Lipschuetz, 'Rashi', 93–5. On Leibowitz, see Grossman, *Rashi* (Heb.), 88–9, where he quotes Leibowitz's reliance on Rashi's methodological dictum on Gen. 3: 8, meaning that she believes Rashi quotes a *midrash* only when commenting on textual problems, but he notes correctly that Rashi does not adhere to this. A text-centred view of Rashi is also found in Moshe Greenberg's comparison of Rashi and his grandson, Rashbam. See Moshe Greenberg, 'The Relationship between Rashi's and Rashbam's Torah Commentaries' (Heb.), in Yair Zakovitch and Alexander Rofe (eds.), *Isaac Zeligman Jubilee Volume* [Sefer yitshak zeligman] (Jerusalem, 1983), Hebr. vol., 559–67; Moshe Greenberg, 'Northern French Jewish Bible Exegetes' (Heb.), in Moshe Greenberg (ed.), *An Introduction to Jewish Biblical Exegesis* [Parshanut hamikra hayehudit: pirkei mavo] (Jerusalem, 1985), 70–5, 77–9.

⁴ On the northern French school, see Avraham Grossman, 'The School of Literal Jewish Exegesis in Northern France', in Magne Sæbø (ed.), *Hebrew Bible/Old Testament: The History of Its Interpretation*, I/2: *The Middle Ages* (Göttingen, 2000), 321–71. For two statements of 'the Sephardi mystique', see Ivan G. Marcus, 'Beyond the Sephardic Mystique', *Orim*, 1/1 (1985), 35–53, and Ismar Schorsch, 'The Myth of Sephardic Supremacy', *The Leo Baeck Yearbook*, 34 (1989), 47–66.

were concerned by the way Rashi's use of Midrash did or did not compromise his commitment to the contextual meaning of the biblical text.[5]

Neither the educators nor the Bible scholars were open to the possibility that Rashi was sometimes interested in expressing his own point of view despite the text. The third or historical approach, in contrast, takes an empirical view of what Rashi actually does in practice and is willing to ignore or play down the centrality of Rashi's own so-called methodological statements, as well as the comment his grandson offered about Rashi's preference for contextual comments (see below). All these comments reinforce the plain-sense bias of the Bible scholars, who value Rashi only to the degree that he is interested in anything, including Midrash, only because it is a way to understand the way the biblical text is written.[6]

The new historical approach to Rashi as a medieval thinker takes for granted a need to establish a methodology for distinguishing Rashi's own voice from those of his rabbinic sources. The method emphasizes that Rashi repeats a comment in different settings or edits his sources by omitting a section that differs from the words he does include. In these cases of repetition for emphasis or the editing of an earlier text, the method argues that the words of the biblical text do not require these comments, and that they thus represent Rashi's original ideas rather than his interpretation of the text (see below).

Regardless of how Rashi is understood, all agree that of the northern French commentators on the Pentateuch, Rashi's commentary became the most popular, even if he wrote originally for a select circle of students.[7] By the thirteenth century, his Humash commentary was standard even in Spanish circles, despite the local preference for a grammatically based literal reading. Soon, the ancient religious requirement of studying Humash with the Aramaic Targum could be fulfilled by studying Humash and Rashi, a practice that continues to the present day.[8]

---

[5] On 'double' comments, see Kamin, *Rashi's Exegetical Categorization* (Heb.), 158–207, and Grossman, *Rashi* (Heb.), 94–6.

[6] For a historical approach to Rashi as a medieval Jewish thinker, see Jacob Katz, *Exclusiveness and Tolerance: Jewish–Gentile Relations in Medieval and Modern Times* (1961; repr. New York, 1962), 14–18; Rappel, *Rashi* (Heb.); Elazar Touitou, *Exegesis in Perpetual Motion* [sic!] ['Hapeshatot hamithadeshim bekhol yom': iyunim beferusho shel rashbam latorah] (Ramat Gan, 2003), 34–47; Grossman, *Rashi* (Heb.); and id., *Rashi's World-View* (Heb.).

[7] See Eran Weisel, 'For Whom Was Rashi's Bible Commentary Written?' (Heb.), *Beit mikra*, 52 (2007), 139–68. I thank Ed Greenstein for the reference. See, too, Elazar Touitou, 'What Motivated Rashi to Write his Commentary on the Pentateuch?' (Heb.), in Grossman and Japhet (eds.), *Rashi* (Heb.), i. 51–62, esp. 54.

[8] On Rashi's popularity in Spain, see Abraham Gross, 'Spanish Jewry and Rashi's Commentary on the Pentateuch' (Heb.), in Zvi Arie Steinfeld (ed.), *Rashi Studies* [Rashi: iyunim biyetsirato] (Ramat Gan, 1993), 27–55; Grossman, *Rashi* (Heb.), 53–7; R. Jacob b. Asher, *Tur*, 'Orah hayim', para. 285; Grossman, *Early Sages of France* (Heb.), 175–81; and Eric Lawee, 'The Reception of Rashi's Commentary on the Torah in Spain: The Case of Adam's Mating with the Animals', *Jewish Quarterly Review*, 97/1 (2007), 33–66.

Moreover, well over 150 supercommentaries were written on Rashi's Humash commentary alone, and it is the first dated printed Hebrew book (1475). There are so many manuscripts that the text can sometimes be established only with difficulty. In contrast, the northern French Jewish literal commentaries died on the vine, often surviving in a single manuscript, and were not published until modern times, Rashbam in 1705, and the others only in the nineteenth century.[9] The Christian *ad litteram* interpreters fared no better.[10]

What, then, did Rashi do in his Humash commentary? He did not write a *midrash* on the Bible; he wrote a commentary. A commentary can be midrashic but it is not a *midrash*. The difference lies in the principle of selectivity and authorship. By adding so much rabbinic material to his own selected gloss, he made his commentary look like and sound like a *midrash*. In part this may explain his success. The authority of rabbinic Midrash augmented his own. If a writer declares that he is interpreting the Bible on its own terms, the author stands before us, as author, with nothing to screen his own interpretative work as commentator. If, as Rashi does in the Humash commentary, he produced both a florilegium or anthology of rabbinic midrashic comments and his own grammatical and other glosses, the figure/ground relationship of the two is blurred. Is Rashi adding to a collection of rabbinic comments, or are the rabbinic comments embedded in his continuous gloss? There is no right answer. By making his commentary appear to be a rabbinic anthology and, at the same time, writing his own running commentary, Rashi did both.[11]

What, then, did his grandson Rashbam mean when he quoted his grandfather as saying that had he (Rashi) had enough time he would have rewritten his commentary to emphasize the literal interpretations that were appearing every day?

The text runs as follows:

And also Rabbenu Solomon, my mother's father, enlightener of the eyes of the exile, who interpreted the Torah, Prophets, and Writings, applied himself to interpret the meaning of the text of Scripture [*peshuto shel mikra*]. And, even I, Samuel, son of Rabbi Meir, his son-in-law, may the memory of the righteous be blessed, argued with him, and he conceded to me that had he enough time he should produce other comments in accordance with the literal meanings that are being rediscovered every day [*lefi hapeshatot hamithadeshim bekhol yom*].[12]

---

[9] See Grossman, 'School of Literal Jewish Exegesis'. An earlier edition was published in Rome in *c.*1470. See A. K. Offenberg, 'The Earliest Printed Editions of Rashi's Commentary on the Pentateuch', in Gabrielle Sed-Rajna (ed.), *Rashi 1040–1990: Hommage à Ephraim E. Urbach* (Paris, 1993), 493.

[10] On literal-sense Christian scholars, see Beryl Smalley, 'The Bible in the Medieval Schools', in G. W. H. Lampe (ed.), *The Cambridge History of the Bible: The West from the Fathers to the Reformation* (Cambridge, 1969), 219.

[11] On authorship and authority in medieval Latin Bible commentaries, see A. J. Minnis, *Medieval Theory of Authorship*, 2nd edn. (Aldershot, 1988).

[12] R. Samuel b. Meir (Rashbam), *Perush hatorah*, ed. David Rosin (1882; repr. New York, 1949), 49. On Rashi's use of the phrase *peshuto shel mikra* as 'contextual' based on the meaning of the root *peh-shin-tet* ('extend'), see Menahem Banitt, *Rashi: Interpreter of the Biblical Letter* (Tel Aviv, 1985), 1 n. 6, and Kamin, *Rashi's Exegetical Categorization* (Heb.).

Maybe Rashi said it and meant it. Maybe he was flattering his grandson or just putting him off ('Can't you see I'm busy? I have no time for this!'). Maybe Rashbam misinterpreted something the old man told him. We have Rashbam's words, not Rashi's, on the matter. Maybe Rashbam made it up. Those words certainly are self-serving, if true.

One would hardly guess from this comment that Rashbam frequently (perhaps too frequently?) tended to bend over backwards to show respect for ancient midrashic comments (for instance, on Gen. 1: 1) and to credit his grandfather's approach (for instance, on Exod. 21: 1, end of Exod. 40, and just before Lev. 1: 1). At other times, without citing those with whom he disagreed except as 'prede cessors' (*rishonim*), he lashed out at their errors and foolishness.[13]

Perhaps their intergenerational relationship is a case of 'the anxiety of influence'? For as Sarah Kamin has shown, Rashbam's departure from Rashi's approach was more of a method of execution than of a new theory of exegesis. Rashi himself forged a new exegetical principle from two rarely used talmudic rules. In his introduction to the Song of Songs commentary, he referred to the principle 'Though one verse may have several meanings, it is never to be deprived of its literal meaning' (*mikra ehad yotse lekhamah te'amim vesof davar ein lekha mikra yotse midei mashmao*).[14] This new rule combined the first half of a dictum in Babylonian Talmud *Sanhedrin* 34a: 'One verse has several meanings; one meaning is not derived from several verses' (*mikra ehad yotse lekhamah te'amim; ve'ein ta'am ehad yotse mikamah mikraot*) with a slight modification of another that appears only three times in the Talmud: 'a verse is never to be deprived of its literal meaning' (*ein mikra yotse midei peshuto*; BT *Shab.* 63a, BT *Yev.* 11b and 24a).

Basing himself on Rashi's newly defined two spheres of meaning in theory, Rashbam now 'drew a clear line of demarcation between literal and non-literal, both in theory and in practice'.[15] Thus, Rashbam acknowledged his debt to Rashi but found his approach wanting, because Rashi persisted in blurring midrashic readings

---

[13] See Sarah Kamin, 'Affinities between Jewish and Christian Exegesis in Twelfth Century Northern France', in ead. (ed.), *Jews and Christians Interpret the Bible* [Bein yehudim lanotsrim befarshanut hamikra], 2nd, enlarged, edn. (Jerusalem, 2008), pp. xxv–xxvi; R. Samuel b. Meir (Rashbam), *Perush hatorah*, ed. Rosin, 3, 113, 144, and 145. On Rashbam's attacks on his unnamed predecessors, see his comments on Gen. 45: 28, *Perush hatorah*, ed. Rosin, 65: 'they are worthless' (*vehinam hevel*), and on Exod. 3: 11, ibid. 83: 'Whoever wants to reach the real meaning of the text should study my comment here because my predecessors did not understand it at all' (*mi sherotseh la'amod al ikar peshuto shel mikraot halalu yaskil beferushi zeh ki harishonim mimeni lo hevinu bo kelal ukhelal*), both cited in Samuel Poznanski, *Kommentar zu Ezechiel und den XII Kleinen Propheten von Eliezer aus Beaugency* [Perush al yehezkel uterei asar lerabi eli'ezer mibelgantsi] (Warsaw, 1913), p. xlvi. On Rashbam's attitude towards his grandfather, see too Elazar Touitou, 'Rashbam's Attitude Towards Rashi's Approach' (Heb.), in Touitou, *Exegesis* (Heb.), 68–76, who also sees Rashbam as mainly expressing independence from Rashi's approach.

[14] See Kamin, 'Affinities between Jewish and Christian Exegesis', 152, and Judah Rosenthal (ed.), 'Rashi's Commentary on Song of Songs' (Heb.), in S. Bernstein and G. A. Churgin (eds.), *Samuel K. Mirsky Jubilee Volume* [Sefer yovel likhvod shemu'el kalman mirski] (New York, 1958), 136.

[15] Kamin, 'Affinities between Jewish and Christian Exegesis', 153.

with the literal meaning of the text, even though he claimed to acknowledge their difference when juxtaposing them (Rashi on Gen. 3: 8 and introduction to Song of Songs).

Rabbi Jacob ben Meir, known as Rabbenu Tam (1100–71), offers insight into Rashbam, his older brother, who also differed from their grandfather's more conservative practice about how one should emend sacred texts:

> And Rabbenu Solomon [Rashi], when he emended a text, did so in his commentary, but he did not emend the [text in the] book itself.... And may the Lord forgive Rabbenu Samuel [Rashbam], because for every one emendation Rabbenu Solomon made, he [Rabbenu Samuel] made twenty. Moreover, he also erased [readings and emended them] in the book itself! I know that he did so only out of his great learning and analytical ability.[16]

From the backhanded compliment at the end of his comment, we see that Rabbi Jacob was critical of his older brother as being too cavalier with tradition and also too independent of their grandfather's ways. Perhaps his very dependence on Rashi's exegetical originality made Rashbam need his grandfather's approval for his own new consistency in applying the method Rashi had invented but had not applied throughout his commentaries.

Whatever Rashbam said or meant to say about his grandfather's attitude towards the newer approach to exegesis, Rashi had produced a midrashic commentary with a tendency to account for the values and words in the biblical narrative as he understood them, and he claimed that his understanding was also rabbinic Judaism's understanding, even if in a new key. He was thus insisting that the Written and Oral Torah are harmoniously unified and that he could rewrite ancient *midrashim* to explain the biblical narrative's true meaning.

That basic working principle, which Rashi scholars take for granted, is fraught with important methodological as well as ideological implications. Methodologically, it is possible to distinguish between the text of an ancient *midrash* and Rashi's rewriting of it so we can compare them. Ancient *midrashim* survive in medieval manuscripts, and when we compare Rashi's comment to the best editions or manuscript witnesses of ancient midrashic sources such as *Genesis Rabbah* or *Tanḥuma* or the Talmuds, Rashi's comments display a consistently different style, sometimes combining different elements into a seamless new whole, amounting to a rewritten text rather than to another witness to the ancient *midrash*. This stylistic consistency is apparent even when one takes into account the variations in language in different Rashi manuscripts. One way to minimize these variations in Rashi's Humash commentary is to rely on early manuscripts such as Leipzig Hebrew 1, which includes distinctly

---

[16] See R. Jacob b. Meir (Rabbenu Tam), *Sefer hayashar lerabenu tam: ḥelek haḥidushim*, ed. Shimon Schlesinger (1959; repr. Jerusalem, 1980), 9. Others commented on Rashi's practice of emending a text in his commentaries. See R. Isaac b. Moses of Vienna, *Sefer or zarua*, 2 pts. (Zhitomir, 1862), pt. 1, para. 63.

identified elements that were added by Rashi's student, Rabbi Shemayah, and that is what scholars have done. In this way, there is a high degree of probability that we can compare Rashi's Humash commentary with his sources and see how he rewrote them to illustrate his belief in the unity of rabbinic lore and the Hebrew Bible.[17]

To whom did Rashi address his rewritten midrashic commentary on the Pentateuch? What was competing with it in his world of eleventh-century Germany, where he studied, or Champagne, where he was born, lived, and died in 1105? If Rashi were writing in Baghdad or in Spain, for example, one might be tempted to think that his insistence on connecting Midrash to Bible was an anti-Karaite argument. But there were no Karaites in northern France in Rashi's day.[18]

From the earliest Christian centuries onwards, however, when Church writers reinterpreted the Hebrew Bible in Christological terms, some also tried to prevent Jewish post-biblical, midrashic teachings from immunizing Jews to exposure to Christian interpretations. They argued that the rabbis who taught or preached *deuterosis*, that is, rabbinic midrashic interpretation of the Hebrew Bible, were keeping Jews from seeing the true, Christological meaning of the Hebrew text.[19]

Rashi could not have been aware of the ancient Christian insistence that Jews should not study post-biblical rabbinic texts, a move that erupted in full force in France only in the mid-thirteenth century, although Christian thinkers were becoming increasingly familiar with post-biblical Jewish writings.[20] On the other hand, there is abundant evidence that Rashi's familiarity with and wish to resist Christian claims and assumptions about the Bible's meaning motivated him to select and weave into his commentaries carefully rewritten rabbinic sources.

---

[17] On Rashi's distinctive style, see Ephraim Hazan, 'Stylistic Features in Rashi's Commentary on the Pentateuch' (Heb.), in Steinfeld (ed.), *Rashi Studies* (Heb.), 87–95; Yonah Fraenkel, *Rashi's Commentary on the Talmud* [Darko shel rashi beferusho latalmud] (Jerusalem, 1975), 123; Grossman, *Rashi* (Heb.), 77–112. On MS Leipzig Hebrew 1, see Grossman, *Early Sages of France* (Heb.), 187–93 and the literature cited there; and Joseph Ofer, 'Maps of the Land of Israel in Rashi's Torah Commentary and MS Leipzig Hebrew 1' (Heb.), *Tarbiz*, 76 (2007), 435–43, cited in B. Z. Kedar, 'Rashi's Map of the Land of Canaan and Its Cartographic Background' (Heb.), in Joseph R. Hacker, Yosef Kaplan, and Benjamin Z. Kedar (eds.), *From Sages to Savants: Studies Presented to Avraham Grossman* [Rishonim ve'aharonim: mehkarim betoledot yisra'el mugashim le'avraham grosman] (Jerusalem, 2010), 128.

[18] On the hints about Karaites in medieval Germany and France, see Judah Rosenthal, 'Karaites and Karaism in Western Europe' (Heb.), in Judah Leib Maimon, Abraham Weiss, and Eliezer Aryeh [Louis] Finkelstein (eds.), *Jubilee Volume for Rabbi Chanoch Albeck* [Sefer hayovel lerabi hanokh albek] *Festschrift for R. Hanokh Albeck* (Jerusalem, 1963), 425–42; repr. in Judah Rosenthal (ed.), *Texts and Studies* [Mehkarim umekorot], 2 vols. (Jerusalem, 1967), i. 234–52; and Shlomo Eidelberg, 'On the Karaites and Karaism in Medieval Germany to Modern Times' (Heb.), *Hado'ar*, 78/20 (20 Aug. 1999), 8–10.

[19] For the prohibition in Emperor Justinian's legislation, Novella 146 (553), and discussion, see Amnon Linder (ed.), *The Jews in Roman Imperial Legislation* (Detroit, Mich., 1987), 402–11.

[20] It is frequently noted that Church figures do not seem to know about the Talmud until the 12th cent., but some of them were aware of other types of post-biblical Jewish writings, for example, the archbishop Agobard of Lyons knew of versions of the *Toledot yeshu*. On the Church's growing awareness of Jewish writings before the 13th cent., see Ch. Merchavia, *The Church versus Talmudic and Midrashic Literature (500–1248)* [Hatalmud bire'i hanatsrut] (Jerusalem, 1970), 71–223.

Rashi was keenly aware of his Christian surroundings. His use of thousands of French vernacular expressions (*le'azim*) about everyday life demonstrates this.[21] He also was explicit in offering some interpretations of verses in Isaiah, Psalms, and Proverbs, for example, that were to be answers to *minim* ('heretics' or 'sectarians'), whom he often identified as Christians.[22] Even if he was subtler most of the time in his Humash commentary and rarely stated that an interpretation was meant to answer an opponent, he clearly was aware of Christian readings of the Hebrew Bible. Indeed, it would seem that when Rashi was interpreting a large literary unit in an anti-Christian way, he rarely used expressions like 'an answer to sectarians' (*teshuvah laminim*); he only did so when he commented on single disjunctive verses. Thus, his extensive polemical commentaries on texts that the Church interpreted Christologically, such as Song of Songs or Isaiah 53, do not contain explicit indicators of a polemical intent. This is because the entire text is meant to be a polemic. This stylistic convention also applies to the Humash commentary.[23]

Rashi's choice of *midrashim* to rewrite constitutes a series of brush strokes forming a positive portrait of a community that appears to be rejected and insignificant, but that is actually the central actor in God's plan for humanity. In this way, he reiterates for his time the eternal validity of the biblical saga as being about God and the Jewish people, when interpreted selectively from the Midrash by a single commentary attached to the sacred text itself. In their books about Rashi's world-view as shaped by his rewritten Midrash, Rappel and Grossman in particular have offered hundreds of examples worked out in detail. I offer here a small sampling of Rashi's comments on the important subject of God's relationship to Israel and the nations.

---

[21] Arsène Darmesteter, *Les Gloses françaises de Raschi dans la Bible* (Paris, 1909); Shereshevsky, *Rashi*, 155–239.

[22] For Rashi's explicit identification of *minim* with Christians, see Judah Rosenthal, 'The Anti-Christian Polemic in Rashi on the Bible' (Heb.), in S. Federbush (ed.), *Rashi: His Teachings and Personality* (New York, 1958), 49–59, repr. in id., *Texts and Studies* [Meḥkarim umekorot] (Jerusalem, 1967), i. 101–16, especially 105; and on Rashi's polemics in general, see esp. Sarah Kamin, 'Rashi's Commentary on Song of Songs and the Jewish–Christian Debate' (Heb.), in ead., *Jews and Christians* (Heb.), 22–57; Katz, *Exclusiveness and Tolerance*; Rappel, *Rashi* (Heb.); Grossman, *Rashi* (Heb.); and Grossman, *Rashi's World-View* (Heb.).

[23] Shaye Cohen, basing himself on Rashi's use of explicit indicators of polemics elsewhere (*teshuvah laminim*), has argued that Rashi's Torah commentary lacks them and that he did not engage in polemics there. See Shaye J. D. Cohen, 'Does Rashi's Torah Commentary Respond to Christianity? A Comparison of Rashi with Rashbam and Bekhor Shor', in Hindy Najman and Judith H. Newman (eds.), *The Idea of Biblical Interpretation: Essays in Honor of James L. Kugel* (Leiden, 2004), 449–72. Rashi on Gen. 6: 6 (and Gen. 49: 10, *pace* Cohen) are exceptions to Cohen's otherwise correct stylistic observation about Rashi's polemical writings. For Rashi on Isaiah 53, see Adolf Neubauer (ed.), *The Fifty-Third Chapter of Isaiah According to the Jewish Interpreters*, 2 vols. (1876/7; repr. New York, 1969), i. 37–40. Rashi seems to be responsible for making the equation of the Servant of the Lord and the people of Israel into an accepted trope in later Jewish literature. See Rosenthal, 'Anti-Christian Polemic' (Heb.), 112.

RASHI: ON GOD AND ISRAEL AND THE NATIONS

One of the central themes that all agree Rashi features in his Humash commentary is an emphasis on both God's love of the people of Israel and his critique of non-Jews, especially as personified in such figures as Esau. One starts, of course, with the obvious point that the Hebrew Bible makes this point the centre of its message, and any commentator would have to emphasize it. Scholars who have focused on Rashi as author, however, note that Rashi is more consistent on this score than the rabbis of the Midrash. The Midrash is made up of thousands of opinions and can express many views about any theme; Rashi as an author does not reflect this midrashic variability, but instead repeats or edits sources so that a more homogeneous point of view emerges.

In his study of rabbinic legal discussions of how the laws about idolatry applied to contemporary economic situations with medieval Christians, Jacob Katz discusses Rashi as a writer who makes his case by repetition and selection. Thus Katz notes that Rashi praises Israel and faults the nations, by teaching three times that God first offered the Torah to the nations but they refused to accept it. Only Israel accepted it.[24]

The first comment, on Deuteronomy 2: 26, reads: 'Then I sent messengers from the wilderness of Kedemot [a name that implies, from ancient times, *kedem*] to King Sihon of Heshbon with an offer of peace.' Rashi comments on 'wilderness of Kedemot': 'Even though God did not command me to offer peace to Sihon, I learned it from Sinai—that is, from the Torah that existed from before [*kadmah*] the world was created. When the Holy One, blessed be He, came to give [the Torah] to Israel, he offered it first to Esau and Ishmael. Even though He knew that they would not accept it, He began "with an offer of peace".' The comment plays on the root *k-d-m* and inserts the principle that the nations, especially Esau and Ishmael, representing Christendom and Islam, refused to accept the Torah when God offered it to them; Israel, on the other hand, did so.

The second comment appears on Deuteronomy 33: 2: 'The Lord came from Sinai; He shone upon them from Seir; He appeared from Mount Paran.' On Seir, Rashi comments: 'First he spoke to the sons of Esau [who are from Seir, i.e. the Christians] and offered them the Torah but they did not want it'; on Paran, 'Then He went there and offered it to the children of Ishmael [who come from Paran according to Gen. 21: 21; that is, the Muslims] who did not want it.' Although, as Katz notes, the idea is found in the rabbinic *Sifrei Deuteronomy*, that *midrash* contains elaborate and diverse comments; Rashi reduces them to two phrases that emphasize that Christian Edom and Muslim Ishmael refused the offer of the Torah before Israel accepted it. Similarly, we find the general idea in Babylonian Talmud *Avodah zarah* 2b that God offered the Torah to 'the nations', but that text does not specify just Esau and Ishmael, as does Rashi.[25]

---

[24] Katz, *Exclusiveness and Tolerance*, 14 n. 3.

[25] See *Sifrei Deuteronomy*, §343 (*Sifre on Deuteronomy*, ed. Louis Finkelstein (1940; repr. New York, 1969), 394–8).

The third comment is on Song of Songs 2: 3: 'Like an apple tree among the trees of the forest'. Rashi notes: 'As all run away from the apple tree that does not provide shade, so all the nations ran from the Holy One, blessed be He, at the giving of the Torah. But, in contrast, "I delight to sit in its shade" [S. of S. 2: 3].'[26]

Although Katz emphasizes here that Rashi expresses his view by sheer repetition, it is also clear, even in these cases, that Rashi has selected and rewritten his midrashic sources. We also see this in examples that Dov Rappel cited in his short but very illuminating study of Rashi as thinker.[27]

For example, Rashi comments on the word 'enemy' in Psalm 9: 7: 'The enemy is no more—ruins everlasting [*netsaḥ*].' Rashi: 'The enemy whose ruins from his hatred were for us an eternity refers to [standard ed.: Amalek; ed. Maarsen: Esau], about whom Scripture says, "and his fury stormed unchecked [*netsaḥ*]" [Amos 1: 11]'.[28] The passage in Amos is about Esau ('Thus says the Lord: For three transgressions of Edom'), but Rashi transfers that specific enemy to the generic term 'enemy' in the psalm verse, moving from Edom, equated with Esau, to Christendom, the enemy *par excellence* of the Jewish people. He transfers the meaning from one verse to the other, based on the ancient rabbinic midrashic technique of *gezerah shavah*, or having terms in common, since the word *netsaḥ* is found in both verses.[29]

Rappel also points out that Ibn Ezra's comment on the verse in Amos 1: 11 refers to Edom in the past, whereas Rashi puts it in the present. Thus the verse continues, 'because his anger raged unceasing and his fury stormed unchecked'. Rashi: 'It still rages and he storms without any remorse.' Rappel offers many similar examples of Rashi's selective use of midrashic comments.[30]

Abraham Grossman, like Jacob Katz, points to Rashi's repetition as a sign of his own voice, in cases where the text does not require the comment. Thus, in order to emphasize the values of the Torah and of the Jewish people, Rashi repeats the idea that the world depends on Israel accepting and following the Torah. This can be illustrated by the following three passages:

1. Exodus 32: 16, on 'the tablets were God's work' (or 'occupation'): Rashi: 'It is like a person who tells his neighbour that his sole occupation is doing such and such; so, here, the sole occupation of the Holy One, blessed be He, is with [giving the] Torah [to Israel].' The world was created so that Israel would accept the Torah.

---

[26] See Rosenthal, 'Rashi's Commentary' (Heb.), 145. For other midrashic comments on this verse that Rashi did not adopt, see R. Shimon Hadarshan, *Yalkut shimoni*, 2 vols. (Jerusalem, 1960), i. para. 273. For other examples of Rashi engaged in rewritten Midrash, see Katz, *Exclusiveness and Tolerance*, 15–17.

[27] Rappel, *Rashi* (Heb.).

[28] Ibid. 32 n. 7. For the reading 'Esau' see *Parschandatha: The Commentary of Rashi on the Prophets and Hagiographs* (Heb.), ed. I. Maarsen, pt. 3: *Psalms* (Jerusalem, 1936), 9.

[29] On the term and its exegetical use, see Günter Stemberger, *Introduction to the Talmud and Midrash*, 2nd edn. (Minneapolis, Minn., 1996), 18–19.

[30] Rashi on Amos 1: 11 in *Parschandatha: The Commentary of Rashi on the Prophets and Hagiographs* (Heb.), ed. I. Maarsen, pt. 1: *The Minor Prophets* (Amsterdam, 1930), 34.

2. Genesis 1: 31: *'the* sixth day' (*yom ḥashishi*). Rashi: 'God added to the completion of creation the Hebrew letter *heh* [signifying the number five, that stands for the five books of Moses], to mean He made a condition with humankind: the world will continue to exist only on condition that Israel will accept the five books of the Torah.'

3. Psalm 40: 6: 'The wonders You have devised for us'. Rashi: 'You created Your world for our sake.'[31] As in the examples of Rashi's repetition noted by Jacob Katz, here too Rashi reinforces his central values by repetition, even when the text does not require reiteration in each passage.

Grossman offers another example of Rashi's own point of view, also mentioned by Dov Rappel, that involves quoting a midrashic source beyond the requirement of a particular biblical passage. The full quotation reinforces a central value addressed by Rashi—God's love for Israel.

The comment interprets Song of Songs 3: 11, 'wearing the crown that his *mother* gave him on his wedding day'. Rashi's source, *Midrash tanḥuma*, 'Pekudei' 8, includes a parable with three special relationships, not just the one between a mother and child described by the verse. Rashi includes all three loving relationships from the *midrash*:

'Rabbi Simeon bar Yohai asked Rabbi Eleazar ben Rabbi Yosi: Did you ever hear from your father the meaning of "wearing the crown his mother gave him"? He said to him: A parable of a king who had an only daughter and loved her dearly. He loved her so much he called her "my daughter", as in "Listen, daughter, and realize" [Ps. 45: 11]; he loved her so much he called her "my sister", as in "Open for me, my sister, my darling" [S. of S. 5: 2]; he loved her so much he called her "my mother", as in "Listen to me, my people [*ami*], my nation [*le'umi*]" [Isa. 51: 4]. The word *le'umi* is written as though pronounced *le'imi* [my mother]. Rabbi Simeon bar Yohai rose and kissed him on the head.'[32]

RASHI'S MIDRASHIC COMMENTARY AS AN OBJECT OF CHRISTIAN SCORN

Rashi wrote his Humash commentary to provide Jewish readers with a Jewish world-view that selectively reinforced the rabbis' understanding by rewriting it to undermine a Christian interpretation of the world. Jews appreciated the positive Jewish rewriting of ancient sources that Rashi made an integral part of the weekly reading of the Humash. In marked contrast, when the Church authorities finally learned that Jews were studying Talmud as well as Bible, they also discovered Rashi's

---

[31] The passages from the Pentateuch are in *Rashi al hatorah*, ed. Abraham Berliner (Frankfurt-am-Main, 1905; 2nd edn. Jerusalem, 1962), 197 and 4–5 respectively; the one from Psalms is in *Parschandatha* (Heb.), ed. Maarsen, pt. 3, 39. See Grossman, *Rashi* (Heb.), 166.

[32] See Rappel, *Rashi* (Heb.), 58, and Grossman, *Rashi* (Heb.), 168. The source is in *Midrash tanḥuma*, ed. Salomon Buber (Jerusalem, 1964), 'Pekudei', 67b, and see Buber's n. 72 about the form of the word *le'umi/le'imi*. The quotation from Rashi on Song of Songs is in Rosenthal, 'Rashi's Commentary' (Heb.), 154.

commentaries on both texts as being worthy of their scorn. At issue was the Church's objection to Jews adding rabbinic teachings to biblical study, thus concealing the Christian truth of the Old Testament. In addition, complaints were raised about supposed insults to the Church in the Talmud. A papal inquiry was addressed to several princes of the Church, but only the ecclesiastical authorities in France conducted an investigation and trial. This resulted in the burning of several cartloads of Talmuds and other Jewish manuscripts in 1242.[33]

A product of the investigation was the *Extractiones de Talmud*, a Latin collection of translated passages from the Talmud as well as from Rashi's talmudic commentaries. In addition, a separate section contained 160 passages from Rashi's commentaries on the Hebrew Bible.[34] This separate section of the *Extractiones* indicates how ecclesiastical authorities correctly understood Rashi as relying on rabbinic Midrash. They were unaware of or ignored all the other northern French Hebrew Bible commentators who had written after Rashi.[35]

The introduction to the selected quotations from Rashi's biblical commentary makes it clear that the Christian authorities knew about Rashi's influence on Jewish readers: 'The Jews . . . repute authority to whatsoever he said as if it had been spoken to them out of the mouth of God.'[36] How did they read Rashi? To paraphrase a question that is often used in the study of Rashi on the Humash: 'What bothered the Dominicans who read Rashi?'

The compilers did not translate the passages that dealt with classical polemical verses between Jews and Christians. We do not find Rashi, for example, on Genesis 1: 26 or 49: 10.[37] Rather, the passages were selected according to seven categories written alongside the texts themselves: foolishness (*stultitia*), error (*error*), divina-

---

[33] For the papal texts, see Solomon Grayzel (ed.), *The Church and the Jews in the XIIIth Century*, rev. edn. (New York, 1966), no. 104 (pp. 251–3) and no. 119 (pp. 275–80). On the Paris Talmud trial, see Isadore Loeb, 'La Controverse de 1240 sur le Talmud', *Revue des études juives*, 1 (1880), 247–61; 2 (1881), 248–70; 3 (1881), 39–57; Judah Rosenthal, 'The Talmud on Trial: The Disputation at Paris in the Year 1240', *Jewish Quarterly Review*, 47 (1956/7), 58–76, 145–69; Robert Chazan, *Medieval Jewry in Northern France: A Political and Social History* (Baltimore, Md., 1973), 124–33; Jeremy Cohen, *The Friars and the Jews: The Evolution of Medieval Anti-Judaism* (Ithaca, NY, 1982), 60–76; William C. Jordan, *The French Monarchy and the Jews* (Philadelphia, Pa., 1989), 137–9. For the Hebrew text of the event, *The Disputation of Rabbi Yehiel of Paris* [Vikuah r. yeḥi'el mipariz], see Cohen, *Friars and the Jews*, 66 n. 26.

[34] Part of this text has been edited by Gilbert Dahan, 'Rashi, sujet de la controverse de 1240', *Archives juives*, 14 (1978), 43–54; and see Herman Hailperin, *Rashi and the Christian Scholars* (Pittsburgh, Pa., 1963), 103–34.

[35] On the Latin list of Rashi's Bible quotations, see Merchavia, *The Church versus Talmudic and Midrashic Literature* (Heb.), 419, and for selected English translations, Hailperin, *Rashi and the Christian Scholars*, 116–28. See, too, Gilbert Dahan, 'Un dossier latin de textes de Rashi autour de la controverse de 1240', *Revue des études juives*, 151/3–4 (July–Dec. 1992), 321–36, repr. in Steinfeld (ed.), *Rashi Studies* (Heb.), pp. xv–xxiv. On Augustinian theory, see Cohen, *Friars and the Jews*; id., *Living Letters of the Law: Ideas of the Jew in Medieval Christianity* (Berkeley, Calif., 1999), 23–71; and Jeremy Cohen, 'Revisiting Augustine's Doctrine of Jewish Witness', *Journal of Religion*, 89 (2009), 564–78.

[36] Hailperin, *Rashi and the Christian Scholars*, 276 n. 48 (Latin), 117 (English).

[37] Dahan, 'Un dossier', 327.

tion (*sortilegium*), Talmud, *blasphema*, *goy*, sages (*sapientes*).[38] That is what the compiler meant when he said in the introduction: 'Of the glosses of Solomon of Troyes on the Old Testament I have translated almost nothing although there are there infinite wonders (*mirabilia infinita*); and they contain a great part of the Talmud.'[39]

What bothered the compiler was that Rashi 'left almost nothing without corruption, to the extent that he kept neither literal nor spiritual meaning or sense, but perverted the whole and turned it into fables'.[40] From the ecclesiastical point of view, Rashi was not successful at interpreting either the 'literal' or the 'spiritual' meaning of Scripture. His commentary was filled with talmudic nonsense and blasphemy.

RASHI'S 'DOUBLE POLEMICAL APPROACH' IN HIS BIBLE COMMENTARY

Although ecclesiastical authorities in the thirteenth century may have found in Rashi what they were looking for, a compiler of rabbinic tales and insults to the Church, they did not appreciate how successful he had become in replacing Christian readings with Jewish ones by his rewritten Midrash. His Jewish readers understood him as providing both some guidance about the Hebrew text itself as well as an edited rabbinic midrashic commentary on the Humash about God and Israel. Because he did this, he was more popular than any of his successors.[41]

Was a literal approach adequate to negate Christian readings of the Bible? This issue has been addressed by the late Sarah Kamin, who argues that the motivation for the Jewish literal interpretative shift in northern France cannot be explained by a need for Jews to develop anti-Christian readings of the Hebrew Bible. This is because according to Christian exegetical theory, the literal sense did not undermine the allegorical meaning of the Bible, as it could for Rashi and Rashbam and their colleagues. Since at least the time of the Church Fathers, a fourfold or threefold approach to different meanings of the Bible meant that they were not mutually exclusive. To paraphrase the Talmud, the biblical text never loses any of its senses, as Kamin notes:

> One of the reasons for ascribing an anti-Christian polemical factor to the emergence and development of the literal method of exegesis is the assumption that the literal method was an efficient weapon in repudiating the Christian allegorical sense of Scripture.[42]

But Christian interpreters, such as Hugh of St Victor, basing himself on earlier Christian multiple levels of Scripture, did not see a mutually exclusive opposition

---

[38] Ibid. 328–9, with examples of each type.
[39] Merchavia, *The Church versus Talmudic and Midrashic Literature* (Heb.), para. 46, 458 (Latin); Hailperin, *Rashi and the Christian Scholars*, 117 (English).
[40] Merchavia, *The Church versus Talmudic and Midrashic Literature* (Heb.), para. 46, 458 (Latin); Hailperin, *Rashi and the Christian Scholars*, 117 (English).   [41] Poznanski, *Kommentar* (Heb.), pp. xv–xvi.
[42] Kamin, 'Affinities between Jewish and Christian Exegesis', 155.

between the literal and the spiritual meanings of the text, as did Rashi, Rashbam, and the other northern French Jewish exegetes.[43]

Did the Jewish interpreters, then, project their own sense that there was a dichotomy between *peshuto shel mikra* and *midrash agadah* onto their Christian opponents and assume that their new literal readings *would* undermine Christological and other Christian readings of the Hebrew Bible? There is no way of knowing whether the medieval French rabbis even knew Christian exegetical methods. Besides, did the Christians whom rabbis and other Jews encountered in discussions of the meaning of the Hebrew Bible understand Christian exegesis? Some passages in Rashbam's commentary suggest that he was successful in convincing his Christian opponents with his literal interpretations.[44]

Still, even if a learned Jew could use literal interpretations to win an argument with a Christian, it left most Jews with only the literal meaning of the Bible and nothing else. Rashi, however, offered his Jewish readers much more. In addition to providing many isolated analytical, philological comments, directed at *minim*, and aimed at negating Christological interpretations, in his synthetic commentaries, such as those on the Humash or the Song of Songs or Isaiah 53, Rashi provided his Jewish readers with positive traditional Jewish readings of Jewish history and experience that replaced any putative Christian world-view. The literal interpreters did not.

I refer to these two complementary strategies in Rashi's polemical Bible exegesis as his 'double polemical approach'. By this I mean, not his methodological justification, as in Genesis 3: 8, of 'double' comments on a verse in which Rashi says that he selected a *midrash* that he thought was compatible with a more philological or contextual meaning. Rather, the extended 'double polemical approach' refers to his analytical and synthetic polemical readings of Scripture. When confronted with a verse's Christological meaning, he directed his literal interpretation as an 'answer to Christians' to undermine their Christological readings. His emphasis on the inner-biblical Hebrew meaning of those passages sought to rebut a Christological reading by restoring the Hebrew text to its contextual literary meaning.

That, however, was not sufficient. In addition, Rashi offered his Jewish readers rewritten Midrash, not, as he said in his methodological statements, because it fits the words in question, but because, even if it did not fit, his rewritten Midrash is a positive synthetic reading of large units and replaces the Christian allegorical meaning of those texts. Rightly or wrongly, Rashi thought that a literal reading of the biblical text could refute a Christological allegorical meaning, but it could not replace it. Only rewritten Midrash could do that.

By the thirteenth century, then, the Church understood well that Rashi was popular and that he had created a midrashic barrier between Jews and the attrac-

---

[43] Kamin, 'Affinities between Jewish and Christian Exegesis', 152.
[44] e.g. on Exod. 20: 13, *Perush hatorah*, ed. Rosin, 111 (on 'thou shall not murder'), or on Lev. 19: 19, ibid. 161; both are cited in Poznanski, *Kommentar* (Heb.), p. xlviii.

tiveness of Christianity. Although they dismissed him as promoting talmudic foolishness and insults, deserving of censure, they missed the real contribution Rashi had made to his Jewish readers.

Although the ecclesiastical denigration of Talmud and Midrash in the thirteenth century could not have motivated Rashi to concentrate on rabbinic lore in the first place, he did just that for his own reasons. The result was that Jews embraced him and Christian investigators proscribed him, though they could not stop Jews from reading him. Without Midrash, Jews and the Hebrew Bible were relatively defenceless against Christian attack over the alleged Christological meanings of their text. Rashi's rewritten Midrash provided the necessary defence.

THIRTEEN

THE PENDULUM OF EXEGETICAL METHODOLOGY
From *Peshat* to *Derash* and Back

SARA JAPHET

THE TERMS *PESHAT* AND *DERASH*

In the first half of the tenth century a new exegetical methodology broke into the world of Jewish learning, a methodology commonly defined as *peshat* or *peshuto shel mikra*. This methodology was first applied to the interpretation of Scripture in the eastern Jewish communities under the rule of Islam, but it soon spread to all the centres of Jewish learning: Spain, Ashkenaz (northern France and Germany), Provence, Italy, Byzantium, and their branches. After dominating the field of biblical exegesis for several centuries, the power of *peshat* methodology began to wane, until it almost disappeared from the world of Jewish learning.

It should be clarified at the outset that, although the terms *peshat* (in Aramaic) and *peshuto shel mikra* (in Hebrew) originate in talmudic literature, the meaning of these terms in different layers of Jewish literature and for practitioners of the exegetical methodology they define is far from uniform.[1] However, since these terms have been adopted by modern biblical scholarship and no alternative terms have been offered, I continue to use them, with the caveat that the modern definition of this methodology is not necessarily identical to the use of the terms *peshat* or *peshuto shel mikra* in earlier sources. A modern description of this methodology has been proposed by Sarah Kamin:

> the interpretation of the biblical text according to its language, syntactical structure, context, genre and literary structure, and in consideration of the mutual relationships between all these components. In other words, an interpretation by the *Peshat*

---

[1] See David Weiss Halivni, 'The Meaning and History of the Noun *Peshat*', in id., *Peshat and Derash: Plain and Applied Meaning in Rabbinic Exegesis* (New York, 1991), 52–88; Mordechai Z. Cohen, 'Reflections on the Conception of *Peshuto shel mikra* at the Beginning of the Twenty-First Century' (Heb.), in S. Japhet and E. Viezel (eds.), *'To Settle the Plain Meaning of the Verse': Studies in Biblical Exegesis* [Leyashev peshuto shel mikra: asupat meḥkarim befarshanut hamikra] (Jerusalem, 2011), 5–40.

methodology is an interpretation which takes into consideration all the linguistic elements in their combination, and accords a meaning to each of them by the whole.²

The English language does not offer an adequate equivalent for the term *peshat*, the most common suggestions in the scholarly literature being 'plain meaning', 'literal meaning', and 'contextual meaning'. 'Plain meaning' is a rather literal rendering of the Hebrew term, but the shortcoming of this phrase is that 'plain' might be understood as 'simple', which is certainly not the case. 'Literal meaning' is only partially correct, because when the text itself is figurative, either in its properties (such as a simile or metaphor), or in its genre (such as a parable or allegory), the *peshat* is not the literal meaning but the figurative one. The same may be said about the more recently proposed 'contextual meaning'. Although the consideration of context is indeed a major aspect of the *peshat* methodology, it is not the only one—unless we stretch the term 'context' to include linguistic, literary, historical, and scientific contexts, a stretch which is not self-evident. I have therefore decided to use the traditional term *peshat*, understood according to Kamin's definition.

A common misinterpretation of the term *peshat* is its identification with the concept of the 'right', or 'correct', meaning. Although some of the practitioners of *peshat* would adopt this identification, this is certainly not an adequate definition. An interpretation should be defined as *peshat* if it is reached by the employment of *peshat* methodology, rather than by its passing some test of right or wrong.³ Therefore, *peshat* interpretations are always temporary, never final, and very much dependent on the commentator's mastery of exegetical tools and adherence to *peshat* principles. Such interpretations were thus adequately described by Rabbi Samuel ben Meir (Rashbam, c.1085–after 1159) as 'the *peshat* interpretations that are constantly renewed'.⁴

The exegetical methodology that dominated the field of biblical interpretation prior to the appearance of *peshat* methodology was that designated as *derash* or *midrash*, which are, more precisely, umbrella terms for a variety of interpretative strategies. The most important feature of this methodology is its extremely liberal approach to the biblical text, with the waiving of almost any boundary. Isaac Heinemann defined *derash* as 'creative philology' and 'creative historiography',⁵ and we may add to this the aspect of 'creative theology', founded on an absolute

---

² Sarah Kamin, *Rashi's Exegetical Categorization in Respect to the Distinction Between Peshat and Derash* [Rashi: peshuto shel mikra umidresho shel mikra] (Jerusalem, 1986; repr. Jerusalem, 2007), 14.

³ See Sara Japhet, 'Rashbam's Commentary on Genesis 22: "Peshat" or "Derash"?' (Heb.), in ead. (ed.), *The Bible in the Light of its Interpreters: Sarah Kamin Memorial Volume* [Hamikra bire'i mefarshav: sefer zikaron lesarah kamin] (Jerusalem, 1994), 349–66 (= ead., *Collected Studies in Biblical Exegesis* [Dor dor ufarshanav: asupat meḥkarim befarshanut hamikra] (Jerusalem, 2008), 170–88.

⁴ הפשטות המתחדשים בכל יום (Rashbam on Gen 37: 2). For an English translation of Rashbam's commentary on Genesis, see *Rabbi Samuel ben Meir's Commentary on Genesis*, ed. Martin L. Lockshin (Lewiston, NY, 1989).

⁵ Isaac Heinemann, *The Methods of the Aggadah* [Darkhei ha'agadah] (Jerusalem, 1970), 4–7, and throughout the book.

independence of each and every part of the text from any other part, and from any binding system or boundaries, except those established by the commentator himself. There are some practical differences between the legal Midrash and the non-legal (homiletic) Midrash, but their basic presuppositions are the same.[6] Recent scholarship has demonstrated that the roots of this interpretative methodology may be found as early as the biblical literature itself;[7] and while some scholars are satisfied with defining this biblical stage as 'inner biblical exegesis',[8] others would regard it as already Midrash.[9]

The interpretations reached by the *derash* methodology, in a lengthy process of study and preaching, were originally transmitted orally. At a later stage, however, they were incorporated into the various forms of rabbinic literature and eventually collected into extensive anthologies; the atomistic literary units were organized into continuous compositions, their structure dictated by the order of the biblical texts. These anthologies—in both the legal and non-legal fields—had no individual authors in the strict sense of the term, but only anonymous editors who compiled the traditional homiletic material.[10]

THE PURPOSE OF THE CHAPTER

The purpose of the present chapter is to bring to light the interrelationship between the two methodologies—*peshat* and *derash*—and in particular the movement of the pendulum from one methodology to the other. I take for granted the assertion that these two approaches to Scripture have existed side by side throughout the rabbinic period. Although Midrash had been the dominating exegetical methodology for many centuries, and although some scholars tend to see it as the exclusive rabbinic approach to the biblical text, the facts of the matter are different: the *peshat* was always there, side by side with the *derash*. One may consider this assertion as self-evident: the text was always there and so also its 'plain' meaning. Even among

---

[6] In practice, the rabbis tried to articulate certain principles (*midot*) by which the two kinds of homilies might be crafted (the Thirteen Principles of Rabbi Ishmael and the Thirty-Two Principles of Rabbi Eliezer, the son of Rabbi Yosi); but the Midrash—and in particular the non-legal Midrash—is not completely governed by these principles.

[7] See Isaac Leo Seeligmann, 'Voraussetzungen der Midrasch Exegese', in *Congress Volume: Copenhagen, 1953*, Vetus Testamentum, Supplement 1 (Leiden, 1953), 150–81 (Hebrew trans. in id., *Studies in Biblical Literature* [Meḥkarim besifrut hamikra] (Jerusalem, 1992), 429–53); id., 'Beginnings of Midrash in the Book of Chronicles' (Heb.), *Tarbiz*, 49 (1980), 14–32 (= Seeligmann, *Studies in Biblical Literature* (Heb.), 454–74; German trans. 'Anfänge der Midraschexegese in der Chronik', in id., *Gesammelte Studien zur Hebräischen Bibel* (Tübingen, 2004), 31–54); Nahum M. Sarna, 'Psalm 89: A Study in Inner Biblical Exegesis', in A. Altmann (ed.), *Biblical and Other Studies* (Cambridge, Mass., 1963), 29–46. (See also the following notes.)

[8] Michael Fishbane, *Biblical Interpretation in Ancient Israel* (Oxford, 1985).

[9] Yair Zakovitch, *Inner-Biblical and Extra-Biblical Midrash and the Relationship Between Them* [Tsevat bitsevat asuyah: mah bein midrash penim mikra'i lemidrash ḥuts mikra'i] (Tel Aviv, 2009).

[10] The literature on Midrash and the midrashic corpus is extensive. For an introduction, see Jacob Neusner and J. Avery Peck (eds.), *Encyclopedia of Midrash*, 2 vols. (Leiden, 2005).

the midrashic homilies we may find quite a few individual interpretations that certainly pass the test of *peshat*. However, in the eyes of the rabbis the *peshat* was held in very low esteem, and it was very often put aside, overturned, or overwritten by the *derash*. Thus, for example, in legal discussions we find quite often that the literal meaning is suggested first and then rejected in favour of a different interpretation.[11] On some occasions the literal meaning is suggested as a question: 'Is it according to the literal meaning?' and again, the negative answer is followed by a different interpretation.[12]

This low valuation of the *peshat* may be illustrated by several explicit statements. One of them is the personal confession of Rav Kahana, a talmudic sage of the third century: 'By the time I was eighteen years old I had studied the whole Talmud, yet I did not know until today that a verse cannot depart from its plain meaning [*ein mikra yotse midei peshuto*].'[13] According to the view expressed somewhat naively by Rav Kahana, the plain meaning of the text was regarded as so insignificant and so non-binding that it could be totally disregarded. This is stated explicitly: 'Come and see: for Rabbi Yohanan said in the name of Rabbi Ishmael: in three places the halakhah crushes the scriptural text under heel.'[14] Needless to say, if the homiletic interpretation revokes the biblical verse in legal injunctions, this is all the more true for non-legal homiletic interpretations.

All these statements, and the general consensus they express, reflect the rabbis' ambivalent attitude to the plain meaning of the biblical text. On the one hand, the written text is the 'living words of God'; on the other hand, the oral tradition as expressed by the Midrash is superior to the written text as it is, and may revoke it altogether.

As noted above, in the tenth century the methodology of *peshat* broke into the world of Jewish biblical interpretation and the exegetical pendulum moved from one methodology to the other. Some commentators regarded the *peshat* as exclusive—the only legitimate methodology that would lead to the true understanding of the biblical word—while others considered it parallel to homiletic methodology, maintaining different degrees of proportion between the two. The purpose of this chapter is to illustrate the movement from one methodology to the other through an actual example, taken from the interpretation of the Song of Songs.

---

[11] See numerous examples in tractate 'Nezikin' of the *Mekhilta derabi yishma'el* (*Mekhilta de-Rabbi Ishmael*, trans. and ed. Jacob Z. Lauterbach, 2nd edn., 2 vols. (Philadelphia, Pa., 2004)).

[12] e.g. *Mekhilta*, 'Nezikin' 2, s.v. לעולם (Lauterbach edn., 366): 'What does Scripture mean by saying "and he shall serve him for ever"? This could just as well be taken literally. But Scripture says . . . Rabbi says: come and see that "for ever" here cannot mean more than fifty years.' See also the end of 'Nezikin' 7, under: אך אם יום, and more.

[13] BT *Shab.* 63*a*. The term *peshuto shel mikra* appears in the Talmud only twice more, in BT *Yev.* 11*b* and 24*a*. For an analysis of the talmudic terms see Halivni, *Peshat and Derash*.

[14] BT *Sot.* 16*a* (English trans. *The Babylonian Talmud: Tractate Sotah*, ed. I. Epstein, trans. B. D. Klein (London, 1985)).

THE SONG OF SONGS IN TRADITIONAL EXEGESIS

The Song of Songs occupies a special place in the history of biblical exegesis. From the earliest stages both Jews and Christians based their interpretations on the assumption that the Song of Songs is concerned with the divine sphere rather than with the human sphere, a view that received its epigrammatic expression in the statement of Rabbi Akiva in the second century: 'For all the scriptures are holy, but the Song of Songs is holiest of all [literally: holy of holies].'[15] The interpretative consequence of this presupposition was that the Song of Songs was regarded as an allegory, describing the relationship between God and his people in Judaism, and between Christ and his Church, or between Christ and the individual believer, in Christianity.[16] The poetic discourse of the Song of Songs was interpreted by rabbinic exegetes as carrying a national/historical meaning, applicable to the relationship between God and Israel in the past, the present, and the future. This allegorical interpretation was viewed as a *midrash* on the biblical text and greatly elaborated. In this traditional approach there was no place for the actual text of the Song of Songs; it was regarded as having no *peshat* at all![17]

The first Bible commentator who voiced the need to explain the text of the Song of Songs 'as it is', as well as its allegorical meaning, was Rashi (1040–1105); he argued that when a biblical text is figurative (a parable or allegory), the tenor of the allegory should be interpreted as well, and that this applies also to the Song of Songs. Rashi defined the two levels of interpretation as *peshat* for the tenor and *midrash* for

---

[15] Mishnah *Yad*. 3: 5 (*The Mishnah: A New Translation*, trans. J. Neusner (New Haven, Conn., 1988), 1127).

[16] For a concise review of the history of allegorical interpretation of the Song of Songs, see J. Cheryl Exum, *Song of Songs: A Commentary*, The Old Testament Library (Louisville, Ky., 2005), 73–7; Yair Zakovitch, *Das Hohelied*, Herders Theologischer Kommentar zum Alten Testament (Freiburg, 2004), 94–101. On the Christian commentaries see E. Ann Matter, *The Voice of My Beloved: The Song of Songs in Western Medieval Christianity* (Philadelphia, Pa., 1990).

[17] The fact that such an interpretation of the Song of Songs did exist, at least in the very early stages of biblical interpretation, may be learned from the rebuke of R. Akiva: 'R. Akiba says: "He who warbles the Song of Songs in a banquet-hall and makes it into a kind of a love-song has no portion in the world to come"' (Tosefta *San*. 12: 10; *The Tosefta*, trans. J. Neusner (New York, 1981)). Scholars have pointed to a few *peshat* interpretations among the midrashic homilies on the Song of Songs, but not all of these designations are convincing. See the example brought by Ephraim E. Urbach from Mishnah *Ta'an*. 4: 8 (Ephraim E. Urbach, 'The Homiletical Interpretations of the Sages and the Expositions of Origen on Canticles and the Jewish–Christian Disputation', in J. Heinemann and D. Noy (eds.), *Studies in Aggadah and Folk-Literature*, Scripta Hierosolymitana 22 (Jerusalem, 1971), 247). The essay was originally published in Hebrew in *Tarbiz*, 30/2 (1960/1), 148–79. And see also the words of R. Jonathan in *S. of S. Rabbah* 4: 24 (end), on S. of S. 5: 1. For a different view of these examples, and the general issue of *peshat* interpretations in rabbinic Midrash, see Shlomo Naeh, '"Your love is more delightful than wine": A New Look at Mishnah *Avodah zarah* 2: 5' (Heb.), in M. Bar-Asher et al. (eds.), *Studies in Talmud and Midrashic Literature in Memory of Tirzah Lifshitz* [Meḥkarim betalmud uvamidrash: sefer zikaron letirtsah lifshits] (Jerusalem, 2005), 414–15 nn. 8–9.

the allegory.[18] This revolutionary approach laid the foundation for the application of *peshat* methodology to the interpretation of the Song of Songs.[19] It is quite fitting, then, that the question of the moving pendulum should be addressed through an example from the Song of Songs.

THE POINT OF DEPARTURE: THE MIDRASH ON THE SONG OF SONGS

Among the characteristic components of the love poetry in the Song of Songs are the poems of praise, which describe at length and in detail the physical beauty of the lovers. These poems represent a particular literary genre, known in scholarly terminology as 'description poems', or by the Arabic term *wasf*.[20] The term *wasf* had been applied to these poems by the end of the nineteenth century,[21] but its adequacy has now been called into question. The interest in the genre greatly increased after it was identified as an element in ancient Near Eastern love poetry, particularly in Egypt.[22] The connections between this genre and the more general category of 'list' or 'catalogue' poetry have strengthened its position among the genres of ancient poetry.[23]

The description poems received much attention in the traditional interpretation of the Song of Songs, and their metaphors were deciphered in detail in the

---

[18] Rashi states his views in his introduction to the commentary on the Song of Songs: 'Since the prophets spoke their words in figurative language [*dugma*], one should interpret the figure in its manner and order, just as the verses are ordered one after the other. . . . I decided to capture the literal meaning of the verses, to explain them in order, and to [bring] each of the homilies of our rabbis in its place.'

[19] See in detail, Sara Japhet, 'Rashi's Commentary on the Song of Songs: The Revolution of the *Peshat* and its Aftermath' (Heb.), in A. Grossman and S. Japhet (eds.), *Rashi: The Man and His Work* [Rashi: demuto viyetsirato] (Jerusalem, 2008), 183–226 (= Japhet, *Collected Studies in Biblical Exegesis* (Heb.), 135–56).

[20] S. of S. 4: 1–5, 5: 10–16, 7: 2–7, and perhaps also 6: 5–7. Three of the poems describe the female body while one (5: 10–16) describes the male. There is no consensus among scholars regarding the precise literary boundaries of the poems, but their classification is generally accepted. For a definition of the genre and its description, see: Richard N. Soulen, 'The *wasfs* of the Song of Songs and Hermeneutic', *Journal of Biblical Literature*, 86 (1967), 183–90; J. David Bernat, 'Biblical *wasfs* beyond Song of Songs', *Journal for the Study of the Old Testament*, 28/3 (2004), 327–49 (esp. 328–34). For a more comprehensive bibliography, see Sara Japhet, 'The "Description Poems" in Ancient Jewish Sources and in the Jewish Exegesis of the Song of Songs', in David J. A. Clines and Ellen van Wolde (eds.), *A Critical Engagement: Essays on the Hebrew Bible in Honour of J. Cheryl Exum* (Sheffield, 2011), 216–29.

[21] The first to apply the term *wasf* to the poetry of the Song of Songs was Karl Budde, in his commentary on the Song of Songs, *Die fünf Megillot: Das Hohelied, das Buch Ruth, die Klagelieder, der Prediger, das Buch Esther*, ed. K. Budde, A. Bertholet, and G. Wildeboer (Freiburg, 1898). Budde viewed this genre as the key to the interpretation of the Song of Songs.

[22] See Michael V. Fox, *The Song of Songs and the Ancient Egyptian Love Songs* (Madison, Wis., 1985), 269–84; Marvin Pope, *Song of Songs: A New Translation with Introduction and Commentary*, The Anchor Bible 7c (New York, 1977), 54–85 (with extensive bibliography); Wilfred G. E. Watson, *Classical Hebrew Poetry: A Guide to its Techniques*, 2nd edn., Journal for the Study of the Old Testament, Supplement 26 (Sheffield, 1995), 353–6.

[23] See ibid. 352–3; Bernat, 'Biblical *wasfs*', 330–1, with a list of earlier literature on this topic.

framework of the allegorical interpretation of the Song.[24] The literary structure of these poems, however, received only limited attention. An exception to this lack of attention is a brief but interesting literary observation in *Song of Songs Rabbah*:[25]

> Rabbi Berekhiah said two things, one in the name of Rav Kahana.... In the name of Rav Kahana he said: She praised him and he praised her. She praised him from above downwards and he praised her from below upwards. She praised him from above downwards, because he was in the upper [spheres] and he let his presence [*shekhinah*] dwell in the lower [spheres]. And he praised her from below upwards, because she is in a low level and he is going to raise her up, as it is said: 'The Lord your God will set you high' [Deut. 28: 1].[26]

The homily is formally attached to Song 5: 16: 'His mouth is delicious and all of him is delightful'; however, it refers not to the verse itself but rather to the literary structure of two of the description poems, Song 5: 10–16 and Song 7: 2–6. The homily develops in three stages. First, there is a definition of the genre: the poems are described as 'praise poems', where 'she praises him' and 'he praises her'. Then there is a note on the literary structure of the two poems, through a comparison between them: 'she praises him from above downwards', and 'he praises her from below upwards'. And finally, the meaning of this literary structure is presented: 'she praises him ... because ...', and 'he praises her ... because'.

Underlying the homily is an apprehension of the two poems as complete literary units—an especially outstanding observation against the general atomistic approach of the Midrash. The concise remarks, which present the genre of the poems and their literary structure in a matter-of-fact manner with no detail or proof-texts, are clearly the outcome of a literary analysis of the texts, itself a characteristic feature of a *peshat* interpretation. Only in the third stage of the homily, where the meaning and message of the literary structure are presented, does the homily move from the *peshat* meaning to the allegorical one. The different directions of the body descriptions are explained within the framework of the traditional, homiletical/metaphorical approach to the Song of Songs: 'he' is God and 'she' is the people of Israel. This identification of the protagonists, however, is not explicitly stated but rather taken as self-evident.

The allegorical interpretation reveals a certain imbalance in the significance of the two different directions. While the 'bringing down' of the Lord, which signifies

---

[24] See in particular *S. of S. Rabbah* 4: 1–13, on S. of S. 4: 1–5; 5: 6–6: 4 on S. of S. 5: 10–16; 7: 3–11 on S. of S. 7: 2–6; *S. of S. Zuta* 4: 1–6; 5: 10–15; 7: 2–10.

[25] *Song of Songs Rabbah* is one of the earlier anthologies of homiletic interpretations, and is commonly regarded as having been compiled in Palestine in the 6th cent. See Tamar Kadari, 'On the Redaction of Midrash shir hashirim rabah' [Limelekhet ha'arikhah bamidrash shir hashirim rabah], Ph.D. diss., Hebrew University of Jerusalem, 2004, 1–5.

[26] *S. of S. Rabbah* 6: 4 (end). The translation is mine, since the standard translation, *Midrash Rabbah*, trans. Maurice Simon (London, 1939), 255–6, is interpretative. The same homily appears also in *Midrash tanḥuma* on Exod. 31: 18 (*Tanḥuma*, 'Ki tisa', 18) in its two versions (see below), and in *Yalkut shimoni*, §987, in the name of R. Judah b. Abba (attached to S. of S. 4: 11).

his letting his presence dwell in the midst of his people, is presented as a matter of the past, the raising up of Israel is viewed as a promise for the future. Moreover, and perhaps more importantly, while the Lord's letting his presence dwell in the midst of his people is an act of a religious and spiritual nature, the 'raising up' of Israel is primarily a realistic/political act, which will secure Israel's place among the nations of the world.

A more elaborate version of this homily is found in *Midrash tanḥuma*:[27]

'And he gave unto Moses, etc.' [Exod. 31: 18]. Scripture states elsewhere in allusion to this verse: 'Thy lips, O my bride, drip honey' [4: 11]. Rabbi Abba the son of Judah said: The community of Israel praised the Holy One, blessed be He, from on high to below, while the Holy One, blessed be He, praised Israel from below to on high. Israel praised Him from on high to below when she caused Him to descend from the upper spheres to the lower spheres, as it is said: 'that they may make Me a sanctuary' [Exod. 25: 8]. He praised them from below to on high when He said 'The Lord thy God will set them on high' [Deut. 28: 1]. 'Who is she that cometh out of the wilderness' [3: 6].

She praises Him from above to below, that is, from His head to His foot: 'His head is as the most fine gold . . . his locks . . . his eyes . . . his cheeks . . . his lips . . . his hands . . . his loins . . . his legs . . . his mouth is most sweet . . . This is my beloved' [5: 11–16]. While He praises her from below to above: 'How beautiful are thy steps . . . the roundings of thy thighs . . . thy navel is like a round goblet . . . thy belly is like a heap . . . thy two breasts . . . thy neck is as a tower . . . thy eyes . . . thy nose . . . thy head upon thee is like Carmel' [7: 2–6]. 'Thy lips drip honey' [4: 11].[28]

The homily is only superficially connected to the lemma of Exodus 31: 18 to which it is attached, and even the opening citation from Song 4: 11 serves as a jumping-off place from Exodus to the Song of Songs rather than as the textual starting-point of the homily. The homily is clearly an independent literary passage, concerned with the two description poems of the Song of Songs mentioned above: the description of the male in 5: 10–16 and of the female in 7: 2–6. It follows the lines of *Song of Songs Rabbah* in viewing the two poems as complete literary units, and describing them as poems of praise, but stands out in its extensive detail and elaboration.

The homily is clearly composed of two distinct parts, the allegorical/midrashic interpretation and the *peshat*. The midrashic interpretation starts with a general statement regarding the literary structure of the poems: 'from on high to below', and 'from below to on high'. As I pointed out above, the observation of the literary structure is in itself a *peshat* interpretation. However, in contrast to the version of *Song of Songs Rabbah*, which refers to the protagonists in the neutral 'he' and 'she', in the *Tanḥuma* version the speakers are identified at the outset in accordance with

[27] *Tanḥuma*, 'Ki tisa', 18. On the date and provenance of *Tanḥuma* see Marc Bregman, *The Tanḥuma-Yelamedenu Literature: Studies in the Evolution of the Versions* [Sifrut tanḥuma yelamedenu] (Piscataway, NJ, 2003), 3–19.

[28] English trans. by Samuel A. Berman, *Midrash Tanhuma-Yelammedenu: Genesis and Exodus* (Hoboken, NJ, 1996), 597; I have adapted his translation, where necessary, to the Hebrew original.

the traditional interpretation of the Song of Songs as 'Israel' and the 'Holy One, blessed be He'. In this way, the entire first part of the homily—including the observation of the literary structure—consists of the allegorical interpretation.

After observing the different directions of the body descriptions the homily goes on to present the meaning and message of the directions, repeating—with some changes—the views of *Song of Songs Rabbah*. The female, the community of Israel, praises the Lord 'from on high to below' because Israel 'caused Him to descend from the upper spheres to the lower spheres', and the male, the Lord, praises the community of Israel 'from below to on high' because 'The Lord thy God will set them high' (Deut. 28: 1). Both directions are illustrated by biblical verses: the Lord's descent to dwell among his people was made possible by the building of the Tabernacle (Exod. 25: 8), while the 'raising up of the community of Israel' means Israel's elevation above all the nations (Deut. 28: 1).

The same imbalance between the two directions that we observed in the version of *Song of Songs Rabbah* is illustrated here as well. The imbalance is even greater in the version of the same homily in the second version of *Tanḥuma*, the *Tanḥuma* edited by Salomon Buber. On the one hand, in this version the two acts belong to the past, with the description of the elevation of Israel presented as a historical fact: 'Because she was down and He raised her up. When she was enslaved with bricks He redeemed her.' On the other hand, the different nature of these acts is more emphatically expressed: Israel's elevation was her delivery from an acute economic, social, and political situation, while the Lord's descent was a major transition from his transcendental abode to immanent presence: 'When He was set above the seven skies she brought Him down to herself.'[29]

The second part of the homily, beginning with 'she praised Him', consists of the *peshat* interpretation of the scriptural units, the concrete depictions of the human body through metaphor. The details of the body parts as set forth in the poems of the Song of Songs are presented in full, first for the male lover, following Song 5: 10–16, and then for the female lover, following 7: 2–6. The systematic repetition of the details of the biblical texts brings to light the full *peshat* understanding that underlies the homiletic passages, although no explicit statement to this effect is provided.

This *peshat* part of the homily seems to stand on its own, as a literary unit in its own right, independent of the allegorical level. One wonders where this unexpected full-blown piece of *peshat* exegesis comes from. In another context I raised the possibility that the compiler of the *midrash* was aware of the original function of the description poems in the non-religious sphere: poems of praise for male and female lovers, extolling their beauty by mutual detailed descriptions of their bodies.[30]

---

[29] The English translation follows John T. Townsend, *Midrash Tanḥuma: Translated into English with Introduction, Indices, and Brief Notes (S. Buber Recension)*, vol. ii: *Exodus and Leviticus* (Hoboken, NJ, 1993), 153–4, with some adaptations.   [30] See Sara Japhet, 'Description Poems'.

RASHI (RABBI SOLOMON YITSHAKI)

The rabbinic homily was adopted and continued by two of the classical commentators of the French medieval school of exegesis, Rashi (1040–1105) and Rashbam (Rabbi Samuel ben Meir, c.1085 to after 1159). As already mentioned, Rashi was the first Bible commentator who voiced the need to explain the *peshat* meaning of the Song of Songs as well as the allegorical meaning, and who claimed that although the Song of Songs was an allegory, the tenor of the allegory should be interpreted as well.[31] Rashi referred to the body descriptions twice, in his comments on Song 7: 2 and 5. His comment on Song 7: 2 reads:

> The praise of the Holy One: Israel praises Him from top to bottom. They begin with 'His head is finest gold' [5: 11] and go on descending until 'His legs are like marble pillars' [5: 15], because they come to please Him and to move His dwelling down from the upper [spheres] to the lower [spheres]. And He tells her praise from bottom up, 'how lovely are your footsteps' (7: 2)—these are the feet—and goes on listing until 'the head upon you is like Carmel',[32] for He comes to draw her to Him.

Although the comment is included in one of the description poems, it refers to both of them—the female lover in 7: 2–6 and the male lover in Song 5: 10–16—as do the midrashic homilies cited above. The interpretation is dependent on the homily of *Midrash tanḥuma*—one of Rashi's favourite sources—but is presented in a more condensed form and a more concise style. Rashi's interest is clearly focused on the allegorical meaning of the passages and so he combines the two separate parts of the *Tanḥuma* homily into one comment, integrating the listing of some of the body parts in their ascending or descending order into the allegorical interpretation. Rashi also deviates from the *Tanḥuma* homily in the significance he assigns to the movement from 'bottom to top'—the direction which is the structural spine of the poem to which the comment is attached. As we saw above, the midrashic homily explained the female description 'from bottom to top' in concrete political terms, illustrated by Deuteronomy 28: 1: 'The Lord your God will set you high above all the nations of the earth', and thus created a certain imbalance between the two directions of the body descriptions. In Rashi's interpretation the imbalance disappears. The different directions assume a more similar, spiritual meaning: 'They come to please Him and move His dwelling down from the upper [spheres] to the lower [spheres] . . . and He comes to draw her to Him.' The 'drawing up', according to Rashi, implies a spiritual nearness to God, rather than a historical, political supremacy. Rashi does not dwell on the precise form of this spiritual 'drawing up' to God, but it is not too far-fetched to assume that he had in mind some kind of mystical form.[33] One may

---

[31] See above.

[32] New Jewish Publication Society translation (Philadelphia, Pa., 1979), 346: 'like crimson wool'.

[33] For Rashi's knowledge of the mystical literature and movements of his time, see Avraham Grossman, *The Early Sages of France: Their Lives, Leadership and Works* [Ḥakhmei tsarefat harishonim],

also wonder whether the improved balance between the two directions of the body parts does not reflect an original version of the homily, which was not preserved in the versions that have come down to us.

Rashi's second reference to the description poem is of a different nature altogether. In his comment on Song 7: 5 he suggests an original interpretation of the figure, 'your nose like the tower of Lebanon'. He states emphatically that the meaning of the word *af* in this verse is 'forehead', rather than the common meaning 'nose'. His arguments proceed as follows:

[a] I cannot explain it to mean 'nose', neither in the *peshat* context nor in the allegorical context, for what kind of praise of beauty is there in a big nose, upright like a tower? [b] I say that 'your nose' means 'face' and the fact that he uses the singular rather than the plural is because he speaks about the forehead, which is the true splendour of the face.... [c] You should realize that he praises her from the bottom up—'Your eyes like pools in Heshbon'—and then the forehead.

The arguments adduced by Rashi in his attempt to make sense of the simile, 'your nose like the tower of Lebanon', are all guided by principles of the *peshat* methodology: linguistic, literary, and rational. The comment as a whole is devoid of any allegorical connotation. Rashi unveils the literary principle that governs the body descriptions: praise of the lover through the regular listing of the body parts in an orderly direction. According to this literary principle, the eyes should not be followed by the nose but by the forehead.

The significance of this comment goes beyond its immediate exegetical implications. It illustrates in a most persuasive way that, while the important aspect of the Song of Songs, for Rashi as much as for his predecessors, is the Song's allegorical message, he is fully aware of the *peshat* foundation of the allegorical interpretation; he simply did not deem it necessary to bring this out in a consistent manner.

RABBI SAMUEL BEN MEIR (RASHBAM)

Rashi's interpretation of the description poems finds its continuation in the work of his grandson, Rabbi Samuel ben Meir, who elaborates on this matter and presents it from a different perspective. Rashbam dwells on the structure of the body descriptions in his comments on almost all the relevant passages, four times altogether: once on Song 4: 1–6, once on Song 5: 8–6: 3, and twice on Song 6: 11–7: 11.[34] He begins his comment on Song 4: 1–6 with the observation, 'Now he tells the praise and beauty of his beloved,' and concludes the comment with, 'Until now he told the beauty of his beloved from top to bottom: her hair and eyes and teeth and lips and

---

2nd edn. (Jerusalem, 1996), 205 and nn. 248–9, and in particular Ephraim Kanarfogel, *'Peering through the Lattices': Mystical, Magical, and Pietistic Dimensions in the Tosafist Period* (Detroit, Mich., 2000), 143–54.

[34] On Rashbam's method of composing his comments around literary units rather than verse by verse, see *The Commentary of Rabbi Samuel ben Meir (Rashbam) on the Song of Songs* [Perush r. shemu'el ben me'ir leshir hashirim], ed. Sara Japhet (Jerusalem, 2008), 113–16.

words and face and neck and stature and breasts.'[35] On the poem of 5: 8–6: 3 he comments: 'He is beautiful and glorious in all his limbs, from his head to his feet, more than any man on earth, as I will tell you from top to bottom.'[36] Then again, on the poem of 6: 11–7: 11: 'He answers her to reconcile her and to tell her praise from bottom to top,' and concludes with 'Now she is reconciled and pleased by his words, as he told the praise of all her body from the bottom up.'[37]

Rashbam's dependence on *Midrash tanḥuma* and Rashi is obvious; nevertheless, the conclusion to be drawn from his interpretations is rather the opposite of theirs! According to his view, the detailed listing of the body parts is indeed of importance, but not the direction of the listing, which has no inherent meaning in and of itself. As we saw above, the homiletic passages in the Midrash and Rashi claimed that the difference in the direction of the body parts between the praise of the male and the praise of the female carries with it a special meaning.[38] Rashbam opposes this view not by explicit polemic statements, but by demonstrating that the interpretation of his predecessors did not take into account all the relevant texts. The midrashic homilies and Rashi based their conclusion on the difference in direction between the description of the male in 5: 10–16 and the description of the female in 7: 2–6. Rashbam adds to these two texts the description poem of Song 4: 1–6, and shows that the direction of the body parts in this poem is 'from top to bottom: her hair and eyes and teeth and lips and words and face and neck and stature and breasts'. This means that the female lover herself is described in two opposite directions: 'from bottom to top' in 7: 2–6, but 'from top to bottom' in 4: 1–6, and this means in turn, that the difference in direction is not determined by the object of the description—male or female. With this conclusion the basis of the *Tanḥuma*'s homily is simply crushed. One cannot but wonder whether this is not why both the Midrash and Rashi refrain from commenting on the literary structure of Song 4: 1–6.

Another feature of Rashbam's handling of this matter is the clear distinction between the two levels of the interpretation—the text as it is and the allegory—in the specific comments on these passages. Rashbam's commentary on the Song of Songs is composed very carefully according to a systematic plan: a division of the Song into literary units, and the interpretation of each unit in two distinct sections—the text as it is, and the allegorical message, defined systematically by the term *dimyon*, that is, figurative.[39] The first section, which is generally the longer one, is devoted to the interpretation of the tenor, which then serves as the basis of the allegorical section, with the equivalence between the two sections being rather general. Only selected details of the tenor have their counterpart in the allegorical interpretation. In contrast to Rashi, Rashbam regards both sections as *peshat*; since according to his view the Song of Songs is an allegory both the tenor and its allegorical

---

[35] See *The Commentary of Rabbi Samuel ben Meir* 253 and 257 respectively.   [36] Ibid. 263–4.
[37] Ibid. 271 and 272 respectively.   [38] See above.
[39] For a detailed analysis of this method of composition see *Rashbam on the Song of Songs*, ed. Japhet, 82–5, 165–6.

meaning represent the plain meaning of the text, and the same methodological principles should be applied to both parts.[40]

Contrary to the Midrash and to Rashi, Rashbam restricts his notes concerning the listing of the body parts to the first section of each comment—the explanation of the tenor—and refrains from repeating them or even alluding to them in the allegorical section. The literary structure is presented as meaningful only at the level of the tenor: the complete and systematic listing of the body parts and the extraordinary metaphors are accordingly the ultimate literary expression of a person's beauty.

The avoidance of the element of sequence in the allegorical section is coupled with another feature of Rashbam's comments, the discussion of the metaphors themselves. As already mentioned, Rashbam tends to point to an essential bond between the two levels of meaning in the literary units,[41] and he follows this procedure in the description of the male lover in 5: 10–16, where some of the metaphors of the tenor are alluded to in the allegorical interpretation. This is not the case, however, in the two description poems that relate the beauty of the female. Here the allegorical interpretations are extremely short, and the references to the tenor are no more than general. It is quite clear that Rashbam is eager to elaborate on the Lord's saving acts on behalf of Israel, which are implied by the allegory of 5: 10–16, but is reluctant to draw any allegorical implications of the description of the female, Israel.

These features of Rashbam's unique approach—the repeated notes on the literary technique of the descriptions, the avoidance of mentioning this technique at the allegorical level of the interpretation, and the limited discussion of the metaphors—indicate that his dependence on his sources is selective. He appears to have adapted the *peshat* foundation of the interpretation, but left behind its midrashic significance.

These aspects of Rashbam's commentary seem to express not only his exegetical methodology but also his theological stance. Together with his strict adherence to the national/historical allegory, they seem to exhibit a rational, historical, and anti-mystical world-view. Rashbam does not state this goal explicitly, but it provides a plausible explanation for his exegetical endeavour.[42]

With Rashbam's commentary on the Song of Songs the pendulum of exegetical methodology made the final swing from one side to the opposite, from the

---

[40] For Rashbam's methodological approach to the Song of Songs see ibid. 79–104.

[41] Ibid. 120–2, 166–8.

[42] Explicit anti-mystical statements may be found in Rashbam's commentaries on the books of Ecclesiastes (Kohelet) and Job. See *The Commentary of Rabbi Samuel ben Meir (Rashbam) on Qoheleth*, ed. Sara Japhet and Robert B. Salters (Jerusalem, Leiden, 1985), 52–3; *The Commentary of Rabbi Samuel ben Meir (Rashbam) on the Book of Job* [Perush r. shemu'el ben me'ir lesefer iyov], ed. Sara Japhet (Jerusalem, 2000; 2nd edn. Jerusalem, 2009), 153–8. See also Sarah Kamin, 'Rashbam's Conception of the Creation in Light of the Intellectual Currents of his Time', in Sara Japhet (ed.), *Studies in Bible*, Scripta Hierosolymitana 31 (Jerusalem, 1986), 27*–68* (= Sarah Kamin, *Jews and Christians Interpret the Bible* [Bein yehudim lenotserim befarshanut hamikra], 2nd edn. (Jerusalem, 2009), pp. xxxvi–lxxiv).

midrashic methodology to the *peshat*. This move is all the more impressive in the example I have discussed. While the source of the interpretative comments is the traditional homiletic literature, the principles employed in the act of exegesis are strictly those of the *peshat*, applied with vigour and courage.

The activity of the *peshat* school of exegesis continued into the thirteenth century with, among others, several commentaries on the Song of Songs.[43] These works may be divided into two groups: (a) commentaries based on the traditional view that the Song of Songs is an allegory, their comments devoted to both the tenor and the allegory;[44] and (b) commentaries that restrict their attention to the level of the tenor and avoid the allegory altogether. Two of these—the commentary of Rabbi Isaiah of Trani (*c*.1180–1250), and the anonymous commentary in MS Oxford, Bodleian Library (Huntington 268)—pay some lip service to the allegory in the introductions to their commentaries, but restrict their actual comments to the level of the tenor.[45] Two additional anonymous commentaries—the one in the National Library of the Czech Republic (in Prague) and the other in the Oxford Bodleian Library collection[46]—avoid the allegory in principle. The first commentator states his methodological position explicitly: the Song of Song is not a religious allegory but a secular love-song, and the allegorical interpretation is therefore midrashic. The true meaning of the Song of Song is the *peshat* alone, and any kind of allegory or Midrash should be avoided.[47] The exegetical methodology employed by these commentaries

---

[43] See Sara Japhet, 'Rashi's Commentary on the Song of Songs' (Heb.). One of the greatest representatives of the *peshat* school in the 12th cent. is Abraham ibn Ezra (1089–1164), the great Sephardi commentator. Although he probably knew the work of Rashi, and perhaps also that of Rashbam, his contemporary, he did not adopt these comments in the two editions of his commentary on the Song of Songs.

[44] Among them the anonymous commentary of the Turin manuscript on S. of S. 1–3, which was published by Eppenstein and has since been lost (S. Eppenstein, 'Fragment d'un commentaire anonym du Cantique des Cantiques', *Revue des études juives*, 53 (1907), 242–54), and the anonymous commentary ascribed wrongly to Rashi in MS Florence, Biblioteca Medicea Laurenziana (acquisti e.Doni 121, fos. 16r–23r). For this commentary, still unpublished, see for the time being B. Alster, 'Human Love and Its Relationship to Spiritual Love in Jewish Exegesis on the Song of Songs' [Ahavah enoshit vezikatah le'ahavah ruḥanit bafarshanut hayehudit leshir hashirim], Ph.D. diss., Bar-Ilan University, 2006, 14–16, and *passim*.

[45] *The Commentary of Rabbi Isaiah de Trani the First on the Prophets and the Hagiographa* [Perush nevi'im ukhetuvim lerabenu yeshayahu harishon mitrani], ed. Abraham J. Wertheimer, 3 vols. (Jerusalem, 1991), iii. 271–84. The commentary in MS Oxford, Bodleian Library Huntington 268 (Uri 102), has still not been published. Sections from it have been cited by S. Salfeld, *Das Hohelied Salomo's bei den jüdischen Ereklärer des Mittelalters* (Berlin, 1879), 153–4.

[46] The first, in MS Prague, Narodni Knihovna v. Praze XVII F 6, was published by A. Hübsch in 1866. I recently republished it in a critical edition: Sara Japhet, 'The Anonymous Commentary on the Song of Songs in MS Prague: A Critical Edition and Introduction' (Heb.), in Sara Japhet and Eran Viezel (eds.), *'To Settle the Plain Meaning of the Verse'* (Heb.), 206–47. The second commentary, in MS Oxford, Bodleian Library Opp. 625 (O1.1370), fos. 223r–228r, was published by H. J. Mathews, 'Anonymous Commentary on the Song of Songs', in *Festschrift zum achtzigsten Geburtstage Moritz Steinschneider* (Leipzig, 1896), 164–85, 238–40.

[47] See Japhet, 'Anonymous Commentary', 209–13.

brings the pendulum of exegetical methodology to the most extreme end, to a 'pure *peshat*'. However, insofar as our example is concerned, none of these commentaries adopted the observation that the poems of praise in the Song of Songs are structured according to a specific literary principle; their view on this matter remains unknown.[48]

BACK AGAIN: PHILOSOPHICAL MIDRASH

The peak of the *peshat* school in the twelfth to the thirteenth centuries is also the beginning of its decline, as the field of biblical exegesis is taken over by other schools of exegesis, old and new. Among the new currents are the philosophical commentaries that follow the teaching of Maimonides,[49] and it is there that we next find, rather surprisingly, the literary observation concerning the description poems in the Song of Songs. The first to make this observation is Moses ibn Tibbon (d. 1283),[50] who refers to the order of the description poems twice, in his comments on 5: 10–16 and 7: 2–6. Ibn Tibbon draws directly on *Midrash tanḥuma*, which he quotes; but he accords to the difference in direction a meaning of his own. In the comment on the description of the male, he remarks:

She began his praises from the head and went down to his feet, because the essence of his existence is on high and his action descends down. In *Yelamedenu* 'Ki tisa', Rabbi Abun son of Judah said: The community of Israel praises the Holy One, blessed be He, from above downwards, His head, His locks, etc., because she made Him descend from the upper [spheres] to the lower [spheres], 'that they make Me a sanctuary', and the Holy One, blessed be He, praises from below upwards, 'how beautiful are thy steps', etc., because He raised her, 'and God will set you on high'.[51]

---

[48] Since all these authors were certainly familiar with the commentaries of Rashi and Rashbam, the fact that they refrained from bringing the literary observation discussed above is perhaps not accidental and should be explained. Several arguments come to mind. One is that since the source of the literary observation is a midrashic passage, these commentators regarded the observation itself as Midrash and avoided it; they did not adopt Rashbam's more refined approach, which distinguished between the literary observation itself and its alleged allegorical meaning. Another factor might be their diminished interest in the literary aspects of the text, as otherwise illustrated in their works; and one may also consider the possibility that they were influenced by the commentaries and attitudes of Ibn Ezra. All these possibilities must remain in the realm of conjecture.

[49] See, among others, the philosophical commentaries of Joseph ibn Aknin (*c.* 1150–1220), Moses ibn Tibbon (13th cent.), Joseph ibn Kaspi (1279–1340), and Levi ben Gershom (Gersonides; 1288–1344). Another new current was the mystical, which became more dominant in the following centuries. In the 12th to 13th cents. we already have the mystical commentaries of Ezra Girodi (d. *c.* 1240) and Isaac b. Moses Sahulah (b. 1244). For a full list of the commentaries and their classification, see Barry D. Walfish, 'An Annotated Bibliography of Medieval Jewish Commentaries on the Song of Songs' (Heb.), in Sara Japhet (ed.), *The Bible in the Light of its Interpreters* (Heb.), 518–71 (the classification is on p. 571).

[50] Moses Ibn Tibbon, *A Commentary on the Song of Songs*, ed. L. Silberman (Lyck, 1874), republished in *Mikraot gedolot orim gedolim* (Jerusalem, 2005), 103–46. The following citations are from this edition.

[51] On S. of S. 5: 10–16, p. 134.

The comment is clearly composed of two parts, like many of Ibn Tibbon's comments in this work. He first provides his own interpretation and then goes on to cite the traditional, midrashic one, presented here as a quotation from the Midrash. In the first part of the comment, which presents his own view, he refers only to the order of the description but not to the difference between the two directions: God is praised from on high to below 'because the essence of His existence is on high'.

Ibn Tibbon's remark on the second poem is even shorter, and includes only his own view: 'He began to praise her from her feet because the essence of her existence is on earth.'[52]

It is quite obvious that Ibn Tibbon is aware of the difference between the directions of the praises, and, following the Midrash, sees this feature as determined by the object of the praises. However, he ascribes to it a philosophical rather than a national/historical meaning and regards the matter as of a rather secondary significance.

The second author is Gersonides (Levi ben Gershon, 1288–1344).[53] For him the order of the praises is a major feature of the Song of Songs, and he refers to it five times, both in the introduction ('Proposition', in his phrasing) and in the commentary itself.

In characterizing Gersonides' philosophical commentary, Menachem Kellner points out that Gersonides' main interest here is not philosophy itself, but the right way to study it: 'we find detailed discussions of the process of learning and constantly reiterated emphasis on the importance of approaching the process of learning in a properly structural fashion'; Gersonides 'propagandizes unceasingly for the proper approach to the study of science and philosophy'.[54]

This is the context for his discussion of the function of the description poems. Gersonides emphasizes the 'changing orderings' (*hasidurim hamithalfim*) of the praises, but contrary to the Midrash, Rashi, and Ibn Tibbon, and similarly to Rashbam, he observes that the differences in order exist not merely between the praises of the male and female lovers, but within the praises of the female herself, and that therefore another explanation is indicated.

Gersonides draws attention to these differences in the introduction:

We ought to be aware of the different orderings in which the praise of this beloved woman and her beauty are described in the book. Thus, the first time he began his praises from her head and descended with them gradually to her breasts [S. of S. 4: 1–5]. The second time he began his praises from her head, the praises never left the head, that is, they never descended below her head [S. of S. 6: 4–8]. The third time he began his praises with her legs and did not cease ascending with them until he reached her head [S. of S. 7: 2–6]. This could not possibly be without significance in so perfectly structured an allegory.

[52] On S. of S. 7: 2, p. 137.
[53] *Commentary on the Song of Songs by Levi ben Gershom (Gersonides)*, ed. M. Kellner (New Haven, Conn., 1998; Hebrew edn., Ramat Gan, 2001). [54] Ibid., English edn., p. xxiv.

These introductory observations present a fine literary analysis of the praise poems, which is completely in the realm of *peshat* exegesis. The texts are even defined in this way, as 'perfectly structured'. Gersonides treats the three passages as literary units, presents their topic as praise of the beloved's beauty, and brings to light their literary structure. The only point made at this stage of the commentary concerns the purposefulness of this structure and its importance for the understanding of the Song of Songs, but nothing is said as yet about the *meaning* of the 'changing orderings'; these will be clarified in the commentary itself.

In the commentary Gersonides points to the order of the praises in all the texts that he mentioned in the introduction—as well as the description of the male in Song 5: 10–16—and connects them to the different disciplines of knowledge that are the goal of study. He emphasizes that successful acquisition of knowledge may be achieved only if this process is conducted in a proper order, and this order is determined by the specific science that is the goal of learning. Mathematical sciences, like astronomy, should be studied in one order, the physical sciences in another. The methods he presents are two: induction, which he defines as 'from the prior to the posterior', and deduction, defined as 'from posterior to the prior'.[55] Induction is represented in the Song of Songs by the descending order, while deduction is represented by the ascending order. Thus for the first method: 'He began praising her from her head and descended step by step to her breasts since in this science [that is, mathematical sciences] one always proceeds from the prior to the posterior when we judge the existence of one thing because of the existence of another thing.'[56] For the second method: 'Since with this apprehension he moves from the posterior to the prior as we explained, he moves here in the recounting of her praises from her leg to her head, as opposed to the way in which he praised her earlier, with respect to the other apprehension.'[57]

The similarity in methodological strategy between *Midrash tanḥuma* and Gersonides is striking. For both, the foundation of the interpretation is a careful observation of the literary structure of the poems of praise, stemming from a *peshat* analysis of the relevant textual units. Both, however, see the meaning of the poems as resting exclusively in the allegorical/midrashic level of interpretation; it signifies a national/historical message for the one, and a philosophical/epistemological conception for the other.

CONCLUSION

This detailed discussion of the various approaches to the description poems in the Song of Songs has demonstrated how the *peshat* 'was always there', even when the meaning and message of the text were conceived only in the midrashic sphere. This

---

[55] See ibid. 68 n. 110.

[56] On S. of S. 4: 1–6, see ibid. 56–7. See also on 5: 10–16: 'you ought to know that the step-by-step account of her beloved's praises descending by degrees from his head indicated that his apprehension went from prior to posterior' (ibid. 70).   [57] On S. of S. 7: 2, see ibid. 79.

was true not only for traditional, national/historical Midrash, but also for the philosophical interpretation. We saw how the approach to the *peshat* was radically changed when the *peshat* methodology erupted into the field of biblical exegesis. This school of exegesis spread, developed, and flourished until the thirteenth century, and then began to decline until it almost disappeared. Although even then the *peshat* meaning of the text was not lost sight of, no attempts were made to explain the biblical texts by way of this methodology. The terms *peshat* and *peshuto shel mikra* assumed various meanings, sometimes quite distant from the methodology of *peshat*.

Peshat methodology owes its modern revival to the critical approach to the Bible, initiated and developed in the European Christian milieu, conventionally dated in its inception to the seventeenth to eighteenth centuries. Differently conceptualized and defined, and unacquainted with the term *peshat* and its history, the literary historical method promoted a similar approach to Scripture. We may say indeed that critical biblical scholarship caused the pendulum of exegetical methodology to swing back towards its *peshat* end again, where it stayed (though not exclusively) for over 300 years. Some modern Hebrew-speaking scholars have in fact defined this critical approach as 'scientific *peshat*' (*hapeshat hamada'i*), thereby designating it as one of the 'seventy faces of the Torah', and by this definition providing what they have regarded as a necessary legitimization of the critical approach.[58]

This sovereignty, however, is now being shaken and weakened, not by considerations related specifically to the interpretation of Scripture, but rather by the new winds blowing through the general disciplines of language, literature, and exegesis. New theories of reading and interpretation have opened a whole set of perspectives on the interrelationship between the text and its readership, while the application of a variety of disciplines to the act of interpretation and the strong impact of comparative studies have affected the interpretation of texts in general, Scripture being one of its important components. It seems that the pendulum of exegetical methodology is now moving back to its opposite end, from the *peshat* to what may be defined as 'neo-Midrash', or more generally, 'unlimited semiosis'.[59] Will these new developments swing the pendulum all the way back so that the *peshat* is lost altogether? Or will they find their place by the side of the *peshat* methodology, but not entirely replace it? Only time will tell.

---

[58] See Uriel Simon, 'The Religious Significance of the Constantly Renewed *Peshat* Interpretations' (Heb.), in id., *The Bible and Us* [Hamikra va'anaḥnu] (Tel Aviv, 1979), 144. See also Umberto Cassuto, 'Our Role in Biblical Research' (Heb.), in Haim Beinart et al. (eds.), *Biblical and Oriental Studies* [Meḥkarim bamikra uvamizraḥ hakadmon], 2 vols. (Jerusalem, 1972; English trans., Jerusalem, 1973), i. 3–11 (Heb. edn.).   [59] See Umberto Eco, *The Limits of Interpretation* (Bloomington, Ind., 1994).

FOURTEEN

MIDRASHIC TEXTS AND METHODS IN TOSAFIST TORAH COMMENTARIES

EPHRAIM KANARFOGEL

I

The relationship between biblical and talmudic studies in medieval Ashkenaz is rather complex, and a number of trenchant questions remain.[1] From all that we know about the Tosafists, and as E. E. Urbach's thorough treatment of their extensive literary corpus (in his seminal work, *The Tosafists: Their History, Writings, and Methods*) serves to demonstrate, talmudic and halakhic studies were at the core of the tosafist enterprise. Although the Talmud obviously cites and interprets myriad biblical verses for both halakhic and aggadic purposes and Tosafot passages include a fair amount of biblical interpretation in the course of their discussions and deliberations, the talmudocentric orientation of the Tosafists remains paramount throughout.

Thus, for example, in the realm of biblical studies, we cannot be certain that the search for *peshat* in twelfth-century northern France took place within the confines of the tosafist study halls, even though some of its leading adherents were also leading talmudic Tosafists. Rashi's grandson Rashbam (Rabbi Samuel ben Meir, c.1085–c.1158), the first of the twelfth-century northern French *pashtanim* (exegetes who sought the simple meaning of Scripture) who was also a full-fledged Tosafist, produced a comprehensive commentary on the Torah dedicated to *omek peshuto shel mikra* (the simple, literary interpretation of the biblical text), as well as commentaries on many of the other books of the Bible, not all of which are extant.[2] Rabbi Joseph ben Isaac Bekhor Shor of Orléans (d. c.1200), a Tosafist student of Rabbenu

---

[1] See e.g. Kanarfogel, *Jewish Education and Society in the High Middle Ages* (Detroit, Mich., 2007), 66–99.

[2] See e.g. Sara Japhet, *The Commentary of R. Samuel ben Meir on the Book of Job* [Perush rashbam lesefer iyov] (Jerusalem, 2000), 9–11. On Rashbam as an early northern French Tosafist, see Efraim E. Urbach, *The Tosafists* [Ba'alei hatosafot], 4th edn., 2 vols. (Jerusalem, 1980), i. 48–57. Cf. Israel Ta-Shma, *The Literature of Talmudic Commentaries* [Hasifrut haparshanit latalmud], vol. i (Jerusalem, 1999), 58–66, 111–12, and Kanarfogel, 'Torah Study and Truth in Medieval Ashkenazic Rabbinic Literature and Thought', in Haim Kreisel (ed.), *Study and Knowledge in Jewish Thought* [Limud veda'at bemaḥshevet yisra'el] (Be'er Sheva, 2006), 101–19.

Tam (Rabbi Jacob ben Meir, 1100–71), authored an extensive Torah commentary that was somewhat closer to the method of Rashi's commentary in terms of its use of both *peshat* and *derash*, as well as a commentary on the book of Psalms, of which only fragments are extant.³ In another study, I demonstrate that there were several other Tosafists in this period and beyond, including two additional Tosafist students of Rabbenu Tam, Rabbi Yom Tov of Joigny and Rabbi Jacob of Orléans (both of whom died in England *c*.1190),⁴ as well as Rabbi Moses of Coucy (d. *c*.1250), who produced a significant number of comments on the Torah, broadly following the commentaries and exegetical styles of Rashi and Bekhor Shor.⁵ Nonetheless, the venue for these scriptural activities remains unclear, especially since these Tosafist exegetes do not appear to interact overtly with students (or teachers) in the course of their biblical commentaries, as they often did in the course of talmudic discussions and comments.

In similar fashion, the phrase *pashteh* (or *peshatei*) *dikera* (the simple meaning of the verse), found in a number of Tosafot comments on the Talmud, does not necessarily mean the same thing as *peshat* or *peshuto shel mikra* within the biblical commentaries of northern French *pashtanim*. Rather, in the parlance of Tosafot, this phrase typically refers to the way that most people would read or understand a biblical verse, unencumbered by the halakhic or rabbinic derivations and interpretations that are engendered by the hermeneutics of the Oral Law.⁶

³ See Yehoshafat Nevo (ed.), *Perushei r. yosef bekhor shor al hatorah* (Jerusalem, 1994), editor's introd., 1–17; S. A. Poznanski, *An Introduction to Northern French Biblical Commentators* [Mavo al ḥakhmei tsarefat mefareshei hamikra], 2nd edn. (Jerusalem, 1965), pp. lv–lvi, and Moshe Idel, 'R. Joseph Bekhor Shor's Commentary on Psalm Nineteen' (Heb.), *Alei sefer*, 9 (1981), 63–9.

⁴ R. Jacob of Orléans died as a martyr in London in 1189 (during the coronation of Richard the Lionheart), and R. Yom Tov of Joigny was killed in the pogrom at York in 1190. See Urbach, *The Tosafists* (Heb.), i. 142, 144.

⁵ See Kanarfogel, *The Intellectual History of Medieval Ashkenazic Jewry* (Detroit, Mich., 2012), chs. 2–4.

⁶ There are close to forty uses of this phrase (which appears in the Talmud itself some seven times; see e.g. *Eruv.* 23*b*, and Tosafot ad loc., s.v. *pashteh*) in the standard Tosafot on the Babylonian Talmud. For the usual connotation of this phrase as described here, see e.g. Tosafot on *Shab.* 3*a*, s.v. *ba'asotah*; *Bets.* 20*a*, s.v. *lamad*; *Ket.* 7*b*, s.v. *shene'emar*; *Yev.* 78*a*, s.v. *mitsri*; *BM* 61*a*, s.v. *kari*; *San.* 42*b*, s.v. *melamed*; *Men.* 53*b*, s.v. *ben yedid*; *Ḥul.* 24*a*, s.v. *minayin*. Tosafot on *Arakh.* 26*a*, s.v. *mai*, maintains that since the *pashteh dikera* of the verse being discussed by the Talmud supports the halakhic interpretation of the *tana* R. Eliezer, the Talmud's attempt to ascertain the reasoning behind R. Eliezer's position appears to be superfluous. In two instances in tractate *Ta'anit*, the use of this phrase in Tosafot does have the connotation of more specialized *peshat* exegesis. See Tosafot on *Ta'an.* 5*a*, s.v. *lo avo* (in reference to Hos. 11: 9, and cf. the commentaries of Rashi and R. Joseph Kara, ad loc.); *Ta'an.* 20*a*, s.v. *venatarot*; and cf. Tosafot on *Ḥag.* 5*b*, s.v. *hen* and *vayeḥi*. It is also interesting to note that use of the phrase *pashteh dikera* is almost never identified in the standard Tosafot with the name of a particular Tosafist. Cf. Tosafot on *San.* 43*b*, s.v. *amar* (Rabbenu Tam); *San.* 83*b*, s.v. *ein* (R. Jacob of Orléans); and cf. Urbach, *The Tosafists* (Heb.), i. 107 and ibid 460 (regarding R. Yehiel of Paris and his *Shitah lemo'ed katan*). On the connotation of *pashteh dikera*, see also Sarah Kamin, *Rashi's Exegetical Categorizations* [Rashi: peshuto shel mikra] (Jerusalem, 1986), 28–37; *Rashbam's Commentary on Deuteronomy*, ed. Martin Lockshin (Providence, R.I., 2004), editor's introd., 2–3; and Moshe Ahrend, *Biblical Exegesis and its Instruction* [Parshanut hamikra vehora'ato] (Jerusalem, 2006), 9–16.

As the leading rabbinic scholars in northern Europe during the twelfth and thirteenth centuries, the Tosafists also cite (not surprisingly) a wide range of midrashic collections and perspectives in their talmudic comments.[7] Indeed, the standard Tosafot on the Babylonian Talmud question and analyse talmudic *sugyot* (literary units) not only on the basis of halakhic and aggadic *midrashim* that were considered to be contemporary with the Talmud (i.e. that were thought to have been composed or edited during the talmudic period), but also in light of other *midrashim* whose origins and milieux are later and less clear.[8]

Study of the weekly Torah portion, together with the commentary of Rashi, surely provided additional opportunities for both the review and close analysis of *midrashim* (if not for the study of *peshuto shel mikra* as well).[9] Indeed, *Genesis Rabbah* seems to have been an especially important and widely studied text in this regard. An unidentified German rabbinic student of two French Tosafists of the mid-thirteenth century, Rabbi Yehiel of Paris and Rabbi Tuviah of Vienne, records his efforts at verifying a text of *Genesis Rabbah* that had been cited by Rashi in his Torah commentary, but that did not appear in full in the student's copy of *Genesis Rabbah*.

---

[7] See e.g. Peretz Tarshish, *Figures and Books in the Tosafot* [Ishim usefarim batosafot] (New York, 1942), 87–9, 93–7, for lists of the various midrashic works cited within the standard Tosafot on the Babylonian Talmud.

[8] See Urbach, *The Tosafists* (Heb.), ii. 701, 704, 713–15. Cf. Yonah Fraenkel, *The Methods of Aggadah and Midrash* [Darkhei ha'agadah vehamidrash] (Givatayim, 1991), i. 516–23.

[9] On the study of the weekly Torah portion (especially with the commentary of Rashi) as part of the curriculum of the tosafist academies, or as an individual activity undertaken by leading Tosafists and other rabbinic figures and their students, in fulfilment of the talmudic requirement of *shenayim mikra ve'ehad targum* (reciting each verse of the weekly Torah portion twice and the Aramaic Targum of the verse once) (BT *Ber.* 8a–b), see e.g. Kanarfogel, *Jewish Education and Society*, 81–2, and 182 n. 111; Y. S. Penkower, 'The Canonization of Rashi's Commentary on the Pentateuch' (Heb.), in Kreisel (ed.), *Study and Knowledge in Jewish Thought*, 123–46; R. Isaac b. Moses, *Sefer or zarua* (Zhitomir, 1862), pt. 1, 'Hilkhot keriat shema', §11; and R. Samson b. Zadok, *Sefer tashbets*, §185. The standard Tosafot on the Babylonian Talmud cite Rashi's Torah commentary (*perush ḥumash lerashi*, or *nimukei ḥumash/rashi* in Tosafot on *Ḥag.*, 6b, s.v. *r. akiva*; 12a, s.v. *misof*; and 16b, s.v. *av*) on nearly twenty-five occasions. These citations are introduced, however, mostly to confirm or to question the Talmud's interpretation or use of a particular verse or phrase. See e.g. Tosafot on *Ket.* 20b, s.v. *r. yoḥanan*; *Git.* 60a, s.v. *torah*; *BB* 115b, s.v. *melamed*; *Men.* 94a, s.v. *ukheshehu*. On occasion, however, a Tosafot passage will take the opportunity to deliver a critical review of (and even to question) Rashi's comments on the Torah. See e.g. Tosafot on *RH* 3a, s.v. *vayishma* (*verashi lo dak beferusho ḥumash*); *Yoma* 4a, s.v. *nikhnesu* (*vekhen piresh rashi peshuto beferush ḥumash*); *Yoma* 5b, s.v. *biketonet*; *Ket.* 37b, s.v. *ve'aḥar*; *BB* 117a, s.v. *umaḥazirin*; *Men.* 75a, s.v. *kemin* (*verashi piresh beferush ḥumash sheneḥleku bahen ḥakhmei yisra'el . . . velo matsinu maḥaloket zeh bashas shelanu*). Tosafot on *Arakh.* 15b, s.v. *hitavu*, presents a comment by R. Joseph Kara about the quail that the Israelites received as food, which conflicts with Rashi's comment on that verse (Num. 11: 4). Tosafot on *Men.* 65a, s.v. *aḥad asar*, points to a contradiction between Rashi's talmudic commentary and his Torah commentary (on Deut. 1: 2). Cf. Y. Fraenkel, *Methods of Aggadah and Midrash* (Heb.), i. 517. For a discussion and detailed talmudic analysis of a comment by Rashi on the Torah (Exod. 4: 19) that seems to have taken place, at least initially, within the literature of the Tosafot on the Talmud (even as Rashi's comment is not explicitly mentioned), see Tosafot on *Ned.* 7b, s.v. *aniyut*, and Tosafot on *AZ* 5a, s.v. *ela*. Cf. *Tosafot hashalem*, ed. Jacob Gellis, vol. vi (Jerusalem, 1987), 114–15, and MS Paris (Bibliothèque Nationale) Heb. 1292, fo. 49ᵛ.

The student thought that his copy was perhaps defective. When he reached France, however, he checked the *Genesis Rabbah* texts that belonged to each of his teachers and found them both to be the same as his. The student then offered his own suggestion of how to fill in the lacuna.[10]

The widespread availability and authoritative status of *Genesis Rabbah* in medieval Ashkenaz during the mid-thirteenth century is to be expected, given the esteem in which this work was held in earlier centuries. A commentary on *Genesis Rabbah* (along with a briefer commentary on *Leviticus Rabbah*) was produced in Ashkenaz during the late eleventh and early twelfth centuries. The author of this *Genesis Rabbah* commentary cites, among others, Rabbi Joseph Kara (*c*.1065–*c*.1120) and Rabbi Meshulam ben Kalonymus of Rome (*c*.1030–*c*.1090). Rabbi Joseph Kara also plays a role in the commentary printed in the standard editions of *Genesis Rabbah*, which has been erroneously attributed to Rashi.[11] It should also be recalled that Rashi himself, at the beginning of his brief methodological statement at Genesis 3: 8 (in which he first puts forward his programme of interpreting according to *peshuto shel mikra va'agadah hameyashevet divrei mikra*, the simple meaning of scripture, as well as aggadic materials that account for the specific details found in the biblical text), notes that there are 'many aggadic *midrashim* that have already been

---

[10] See MS Paris (Bibliothèque Nationale) Heb. 260 (a variant of *Moshav zekenim al hatorah*; see Y. S. Lange, '*Moshav zekenim* on the Torah: The Paris Manuscript' (Heb.), *Hama'ayan*, 12 (1972), 75–95), fos. 92 r–v (on Gen. 44: 8):

> הן כסף אשר מצאנו בפי אמתחותינו השיבונו אליך מארץ כנען ואיך נגנב מבית אדוניך כסף או זהב. פרש"י זה אחד מעשרה ק"ו שבתורה [=שבתנ"ך] והם מפורשים בבראשית רבה. א"ל תנא דבי ר' ישמעאל וכו' והנה לפי המנין שמנה בב"ר אין בהם כי אם ט' ק"ו. ואמרתי שמא חסר בב"ר שלי. וכשבאתי לצרפת ראיתי בב"ר של מורי ה"ר יחיאל וגם ב"ר של מורי ה"ר טוביה והיה כתוב כמו בשלי. ונראה לי דזה ק"ו הוא חסר בספרי[ם] הנה שני המלכים לא עמדו לפניו וכו'.

Tosafot hashalem, ed. Gellis, vol. iv (Jerusalem, 1885), 186–7, cites the published edition of *Moshav zekenim*, ed. Solomon Sassoon (Jerusalem, 1959; based on MS Sassoon Library (London) 409), 87, which contains this passage without the names of R. Yehiel and R. Tuviah (*ukheshebati letsarefat ra'iti ba'aherim vehayah katuv besheli*). The passage in the published edition of *Moshav zekenim*, however, includes the name of the uncle of its narrator: *vehigadti ledodi harabi yitshak vehayah lo kasheh kemo ken*. On the relationship between R. Yehiel and R. Tuviah (and perhaps the identity of their student as well), see Urbach, *The Tosafists* (Heb.), i. 486–7, and see also Simcha Emanuel, 'R. Yehiel of Paris: His Biography and Connection to the Land of Israel' (Heb.), *Shalem*, 8 (2009), 94–8. (The first line in Urbach, 487, is missing in some editions: בקשרים אמיצים עם ר' יחיאל מפריס עמד ר' טוביה בן אליהו מויאנה.)

[11] See Israel Ta-Shma, *Keneset meḥkarim*, vol. i (Tel Aviv, 2004), 96–112; Avraham Grossman, *The Early Sages of France* [Ḥakhmei tsarefat harishonim] (Jerusalem, 1995), 339–40; Y. Fraenkel, *Methods of Aggadah and Midrash* (Heb.), i. 512 and iii. 904. The commentaries on *Genesis Rabbah* and *Leviticus Rabbah* are found in MS Mantua (Municipal Library) 37, while related commentaries on *Mekhilta* and *Sifrei* are found in MS Mantua (Municipal Library) 36. The commentary on *Leviticus Rabbah* was published in a critical edition by M. B. Lerner, *Perush kadum levayikra rabah* (Jerusalem, 1995). Cf. Avraham Goldberg, 'Unresolved Difficulties in the Editing and Redaction of *Genesis Rabbah* and *Leviticus Rabbah*' (Heb.), in Y. Sussmann and D. Rosenthal (eds.), *Talmudic Research* [Meḥkerei talmud], vol. iii (Jerusalem, 2005), 130–52, and C. Milikowsky, '*Leviticus Rabbah* 30, Sections 1 and 2: The History of its Transmission and Publication and the Presentation of a New Edition' (Heb.), *Sefer bar ilan*, 30–1 (2006), 269–94.

organized by the rabbis in their own framework [*ukhevar sidrum raboteinu al mekhonam*]', in *Genesis Rabbah* and other midrashic collections (*uvishe'ar midrashot*), which will not be presented by Rashi in his commentary. Leaving aside the implications of this formulation for the study of *peshuto shel mikra*, Rashi is also indicating here that *Genesis Rabbah* is the most important and best-known or most available midrashic collection in his day.[12] His programmatic statement notwithstanding, Rashi cites *Genesis Rabbah* by name some thirty times in his Torah commentary, although, to be sure, Genesis is the only book of the Pentateuch that did not spawn a venerable *midrash halakhah* (such as *Mekhilta*, *Sifra*, and *Sifrei*, which were also consulted frequently by Rashi throughout his Torah commentary).[13] In a comment on Genesis 47: 2, Rashi characterizes *Genesis Rabbah* as an '*agadat erets yisra'el* [aggadic work from the Land of Israel], which offers [in this instance] a different approach to [that of] our Babylonian Talmud'.[14] Similarly, the standard Tosafot on the Babylonian Talmud cite *Genesis Rabbah* dozens of times, far more than any other named midrashic text or collection. Most of these citations, however, are intended to explain the text of the Talmud or to provide additional rabbinic materials related to the talmudic discussion, rather than being treated as an opportunity to analyse or to discuss the *Genesis Rabbah* passage cited for its own sake.[15]

[12] On the basis of manuscript evidence, Abraham Berliner, in his edition of *Rashi al hatorah*, 2nd edn. (Frankfurt am Main, 1905), 7–8, places the phrase *uvishe'ar midrashot* in parentheses, a reading which underscores Rashi's view that *Genesis Rabbah* was indeed the single most important repository of midrashic teachings.

[13] See *Perushei rashi al hatorah*, ed. C. B. Chavel (Jerusalem, 1983), 628. On Rashi's citation and use of *midrashim* that appear to be beyond the criterion of *agadah hameyashevet divrei mikra* (aggadic materials that account for the specific details found in the biblical text), for pedagogic or other broader purposes, see e.g. Grossman, *Early Sages of France* (Heb.), 193–201; id., *Rashi* (Heb.) (Jerusalem, 2006), 100–3; Nehama Leibowitz, *Studies in Shemot (Exodus)* [Iyunim besefer shemot] (Jerusalem, 1983), 500–2; Moshe Berger, 'The Torah Commentary of Rabbi Samuel ben Meir', Ph.D. diss., Harvard University, 1982, 343–5; Yonah Fraenkel, 'Piyyut and Interpretation: On the Place of Aggadah in Rashi's Biblical Commentary' (Heb.), in Samuel Vargon et al. (eds.), *Studies in the Bible and its Exegesis* [Iyunei mikra ufarshanut], vol. vii (Ramat Gan, 2005), 475–90; Moshe Ahrend, *Biblical Exegesis and Its Instruction* (Heb.), 53–7, 75–87.

[14] On Rashi's use of *Genesis Rabbah* (even on occasions where he does not cite it explicitly), see e.g. Kamin, *Rashi's Exegetical Categorizations*, 62–71, 210–17, 233–6, and Mayer Gruber, *Rashi's Commentary on Psalms* (Philadelphia, Pa., 2007), 897. Cf. Grossman, *Rashi* (Heb.), 87–94; Leibowitz, *Iyunim besefer shemot*, 505, 518; and Hananel Mack, 'The Later Midrashim' (Heb.), *Maḥanayim*, 7 (1994), 139. See also Kamin, 142–51, regarding Rashi's similar use of *Midrash tanḥuma*. On Rashbam's lesser use of *Genesis Rabbah* in his Torah commentary, see e.g. Berger, 'The Torah Commentary of Rabbi Samuel ben Meir', 334–7; Elazar Touitou, *Exegesis in Perpetual Motion* [Hapeshatot hamitḥadshim bekhol yom] (Ramat Gan, 2003), 71, 138–9, 158–9.

[15] See Tarshish, *Figures and Books in the Tosafot* (Heb., 87–9, 93–7). For Tosafot passages that cite *Genesis Rabbah* mainly in the context of *parshanut hamikra* (biblical exegesis), see e.g. Tosafot on *RH* 11a, s.v. *ela*; *Naz.* 23b, s.v. *umidyanim*. As Tarshish's lists of citations indicate, the standard Tosafot on the Babylonian Talmud mention *Leviticus Rabbah* about ten times (similar to the rate of citation for *Tanḥuma*), while the other volumes of *Midrash Rabbah* (which were composed significantly later than *Genesis Rabbah*) are barely cited at all. Cf. *Exodus Rabbah* [Midrash shemot rabah, *parashiyot* 1–14], ed. Avigdor Shinan

An indicative example of tosafist methodology in the realm of aggadic Midrash can be found in connection with the *sugya* in Babylonian Talmud *Bava metsia* 86b, where the standard Tosafot compare the talmudic view, that the angels merely appeared to be eating the food that Abraham had served them (Gen. 18: 8) in order not to deviate from the common earthly practice, but were not doing so in reality, with a passage in the *Seder eliyahu* (*rabah*) that rejects this approach, and insists that the angels actually ate in this instance (against their fundamental nature or status), out of respect for Abraham.[16]

Tosafot on *Bava metsia* concludes simply that the *Seder eliyahu* passage is at odds with the Talmud on this issue (*upliga ade-hakha*).[17] There are, however, other reverberations of this discussion within tosafist commentaries on the Torah. A Tosafot-like Torah commentary that has been associated with the study hall of Rabbenu Tam presents the talmudic approach as well as the approach of *Seder eliyahu*, and suggests that demonstrating proper respect for Abraham is an essential element of both.[18] The

(Jerusalem, 1984), editor's introd., 21–2; *Deuteronomy Rabbah* [Midrash devarim rabah], ed. Saul Lieberman (Jerusalem, 1992), editor's introd., pp. xi–xiii, for the extent to which these *midrashim* were used in medieval Ashkenaz; and I. Ta-Shma, *Keneset meḥkarim*, i. 96–112. The same pattern of midrashic citation (with *Genesis Rabbah* the most frequently cited by far, followed by *Leviticus Rabbah* and *Tanḥuma*) can be found in the extensive Ashkenazi *piyut* commentary composed by R. Abraham b. Azriel of Bohemia (c. 1230). See *Arugat habosem lerabi avraham b. azri'el*, ed. E. E. Urbach, vol. iv (Jerusalem, 1963), 168–9, 266–7, and cf. *Perushei sidur hatefilah laroke'aḥ*, ed. M. Hershler, vol. i (Jerusalem, 1992), 18–19 (introd.). It should also be noted, however, that the standard Tosafot cite a *midrash* or *midrashim*, without the particular midrashic collection or work being identified, close to ninety times. These citations require further study in order to pinpoint their origins.

[16] See Tosafot on *BM* 86b, s.v. *nirin ke'okhlin*. Cf. *Pesikta rabati*, ch. 25 (end), and R. Hezekiah b. Manoah's *Ḥizekuni* commentary on Gen. 18: 8 (end). *Seder eliyahu rabah* is also cited in Tosafot on *Ket.* 106a, s.v. *vehaynu* (together with *Seder eliyahu zuta*), and in Tosafot on *BM* 114a, s.v. *mahu*. Cf. Y. Fraenkel, *Methods of Aggadah and Midrash* (Heb.), iii. 839–41, and Mack, 'The Later Midrashim', 140.

[17] See also e.g. Tosafot on *Ber.* 48a, s.v. *veleit hilkheta*, in which a passage from *Genesis Rabbah* is cited in opposition to material found in the Babylonian Talmud ('Rabbenu Tam asserted that the halakhah is not according to this [midrashic] passage, because it disagrees with our Talmud'); Tosafot on *Shab.* 104a, s.v. *amar leh* (which notes that both *Genesis Rabbah* and the Jerusalem Talmud conflict with the passage at hand in the Babylonian Talmud); Tosafot on *Yev.* 16b, s.v. *pasuk* (in which conflicting aggadic approaches are noted); and Tosafot on *BK* 77b, s.v. *matbe'a* (in which an apparently contradictory description in *Genesis Rabbah* is reconciled with that of the Babylonian Talmud). Cf. Chaim Milikowsky, 'On the Formation and Transmission of Bereshit Rabbah and the Yerushalmi: Questions of Redaction, Text-Criticism and Literary Relationships', *Jewish Quarterly Review*, 92 (2002), 521–61. In his Torah commentary on Gen. 18: 8, Rashi follows the talmudic position that the angels merely appeared to eat, while Radak (following the approach of Maimonides in *Moreh nevukhim*, ii. 42) avoids the problem entirely by suggesting that this episode involving the angels occurred to Abraham in a prophetic dream or vision. It should be noted that the Tosafot on the *Bava metsia* passage on the angels (86b) was concerned fundamentally with talmudic interpretation, and is not necessarily taking into account or responding to Rashi's Torah commentary in this instance (even as Tosafot passages do on occasion). Cf. above, n. 9.

[18] See MS Paris (Bibliothèque Nationale) Heb. 167, fo. 94ʳ:

נראין כאוכלין מטעם כבודו של אברהם. תנא דבי אליהו רבה קאמ' שהיו אוכלין ממש משום כבודו של אברהם.

extant textual versions of *Genesis Rabbah* follow the talmudic approach, that the angels merely appeared to eat.[19] However, *Sefer hagan*, a tosafist Torah compilation (discussed more fully below) that was compiled *circa* 1240 by a northern French rabbinic figure, Rabbi Aaron ben Jose[ph] Hakohen, cites a statement of Rabbi Barukh ben Isaac[20] that *Genesis Rabbah* maintains (at least according to the version of this work available to Rabbi Barukh) that the angels actually did eat, in order not to deviate from the common earthly practice.[21] Other tosafist Torah compilations simply present the

See also *Tosafot hashalem*, ed. Gellis, vol. ii (Jerusalem, 1983), 123, §19, and the parallel passage in MS Moscow National Library (Guenzburg) 362, fo. 128ʳ. The colophon of MS Paris 167 (Byzantium, 1443) describes this commentary (fos. 51ᵛ–103ᵛ) as *tosafot shel rabenu tam*, although it is also described as a *perush hatorah lerabi shelomoh hakohen ben rabi ya'akov hakohen*. Rabbenu (Jacob) Tam of Ramerupt is mentioned by name close to fifteen times in this manuscript (as are a number of his students, from both northern France and Germany). However, the tosafist editor or compiler does not refer to Rabbenu Tam as his teacher, thereby rendering as unproven the suggestion that one of Rabbenu Tam's students, either R. Jacob of Orléans (often referred to as Rabbenu Tam of Orléans), or R. Jacob of Corbeil, edited this commentary. See Urbach, *The Tosafists* (Heb.), i. 44 n. 78, and cf. Abraham Shoshana, 'Novellae on the Torah by Rabbenu Tam' (Heb.), *Yeshurun*, 14 (2004), 15–26, for a description and publication of several passages from the Moscow manuscript. Moreover, R. Judah Hehasid is mentioned in MS Moscow 362 (fos. 129ʳ, 178ʳ), as is R. Isaac of Corbeil (d. 1280), who is referred to as *r. yitshak ba'al hahotam* (fo. 177ᵛ).

A series of responses by R. Jacob of Corbeil to Rabbenu Tam's questions and observations about Rashi's approach to the recitation of *keriat shema* in the evening (with which Rabbenu Tam disagreed), and a formulation by R. Jacob about the protective powers that are engendered by reciting the Shema, are found in MS Paris 167, fos. 92ʳ–93ᵛ (on the Torah portion 'Va'ethanan'). Only one of R. Jacob's responses is found in *Sefer or zarua*, 'Hilkhot keriat shema', §1, and R. Jacob's view on the protection provided by this recitation is otherwise cited only by others in his name. See Kanarfogel, *'Peering through the Lattices': Mystical, Magical, and Pietistic Dimensions in the Tosafist Period* (Detroit, Mich., 2000), 197–200.

On MS Moscow 362 (Candia, 1400), fos. 125ʳ–181ᵛ, whose colophon describes the work as *pesakim shel rabenu tam shehem kemo tosafot al perush rabenu shelomoh* (and whose introductory line begins, *athil hidushim shel rabenu tam al hatorah*), see also Hazoni'el Touitou, '*Minhat yehudah*: A Commentary by R. Yehudah b. Elazar' [*Minhat yehudah shel r. yehudah ben elazar*], Ph.D. diss., Bar-Ilan University, 2004, 93–4. On the nature and style of this commentary, which for the most part presents tosafist talmudic and halakhic discussions according to the order of the text of the Torah (rather than as an interpretation of the biblical text from its own perspective), see also below, nn. 48, 112.

[19] See *Midrash Bereshit Rabba*, ed. J. Theodor and Ch. Albeck (Jerusalem, 1962), 411.

[20] R. Barukh (d. 1211), ostensibly the author of *Sefer haterumah*, was a leading tosafist student of R. Isaac b. Samuel of Dampierre (Ri Hazaken, d. 1189).

[21] See *Sefer hagan*, ed. Y. M. Orlian (Jerusalem, 2009; based on MS Vienna (National Library) 19/Heb. 28), 155: וממורי רבינו ברוך בהר״ר יצחק שמעתי שיש בב״ר דודאי אכלו כדי שלא לשנות מן המנהג. (*Tosafot hashalem*, ed. Gellis, ii. 122, §16, erroneously includes this passage in the name of R. Barukh b. Isaac at the beginning of a citation from MS Oxford/Bodleian Opp. 27, a Torah commentary attributed to R. Eleazar of Worms. Cf. *Perush haroke'ah al hatorah*, ed. J. Klugmann, vol. i (Jerusalem, 1979), 152–3.) On the dating of *Sefer hagan*, and the identity and background of its compiler, see *Sefer hagan*, ed. Orlian, 24–8. R. Barukh is also cited in *Sefer hagan* on Exod. 21: 29 (ed. Orlian, 246), and on Num. 12: 14 (ed. Orlian, 301). For the Exodus passage, see also *Tosafot hashalem*, ed. Gellis, vol. viii (Jerusalem, 1990), 232, §13, and MS British Library Or. 9931 (Gaster 730), fo. 59ʳ. After recording an interpretation (*lefi hapeshat*) to explain the fate of the owner of a *shor tam* (an ox that had no prior history of goring human beings) that has killed someone, a question is presented in the name of Rabbenu Barukh that if most oxen are not so easily watched and restrained, why did the Torah not exempt the owner from full payment in *shen veregel*

two divergent talmudic and midrashic views together,[22] while some propose a resolution of the rabbinic sources under discussion by suggesting that the angels did not consume the food by eating it. Rather, they consumed the food with their fiery touch, leaving Abraham with the impression that they had actually eaten it.[23]

(damage caused by the animal walking or eating, as a means of lessening the owner's liability), as it did in the case of *keren* (goring, for which the owner pays only half). R. Barukh responds to his own question by noting that the Torah did ease the owner's burden in another way, by declaring him exempt from damages of *shen veregel* that are committed in the public domain. This is clearly a halakhic mode of interpretation, which might well have emerged from R. Barukh's halakhic writings or talmudic analysis. Although the issue of the angels eating is more aggadic, this could also easily have been discussed or addressed in the course of talmudic study and interpretation (rather than in a forum dedicated specifically to biblical study). The same may be said with respect to R. Barukh's interpretation of Num. 12: 14, found also in *Perushei hatorah lerabi hayim palti'el*, ed. Y. S. Lange (Jerusalem, 1983), 502, and in MS Oxford/Bodleian Opp. Add. 4ᵗᵒ, 103 (an enhanced manuscript version of the tosafist Torah commentary *Pa'ane'ah raza* (Jerusalem, 1998), compiled in the late 13th cent. by R. Isaac b. Judah Halevi), fo. 111ᵛ: ואמ' לי רבי' ברוך ב"ר Cf. Lange, יצחק דבשני הסגרות די ב"ג ימים והכי אמרי' אין בהסגרות יותר מי"ד יום דיום ז' עולה לכאן ולכאן ibid., n. 67, and Ta-Shma, *Keneset mehkarim*, i. 236–7, 240. (This interpretation by R. Barukh follows an interpretation in the name of Rabbenu Tam on the implied *kal vahomer* (*a fortiori* argument) associated with the leprosy contracted by Miriam, and a question about the fourteen-day waiting period for Miriam by the *peshat* exegete R. Joseph Bekhor Shor of Orléans, who was also a tosafist student of Rabbenu Tam. Rashi had cited this *kal vahomer* from the *Sifrei*, and R. Aaron Hakohen, the compiler of *Sefer hagan*, offered his own suggestion here as well.) As Lange further notes, the 14th-cent. tosafist Torah compilation, *Moshav zekenim al hatorah* (cf. below, n. 30), presents an interpretation quite similar to that of R. Barukh, in the name of R. Barukh's contemporary and fellow tosafist student of Ri, R. Isaac b. Abraham (Rizba). See Urbach, *The Tosafists* (Heb.), i. 354, for a listing of R. Barukh's Tosafot on many tractates of the Talmud (in addition to his *Sefer haterumah*), and cf. Simcha Emanuel, 'On the Biography of R. Barukh ben Isaac' (Heb.), *Tarbiz*, 69 (2000), 423–40, on R. Barukh's entirely northern French provenance. On R. Barukh's comments on the Torah, cf. Leopold Zunz, *Zur Geschichte und Literatur* (Berlin, 1845), 88, 97, and *Tosafot hashalem*, ed. Gellis, vol. i (Jerusalem, 1982), 101, §7, and 146, §8.

[22] See e.g. MS Oxford/Bodleian Opp. Add. 4ᵗᵒ, 103, fo. 23ᵛ. According to this text (and similar to the approach of R. Barukh b. Isaac in n. 21 above), actual eating was also done by the angels in this instance so as not to deviate from the prevalent earthly custom.

[23] See MS Vatican Ebr. 45 (attributed inaccurately to R. Joseph Bekhor Shor), cited in *Tosafot hashalem*, ed. Gellis, ii. 122, §17. See also MS Vatican Ebr. 123 (a German Torah commentary, composed perhaps by R. Eleazar of Worms; see Amos Geulah, 'An Introduction to and Citations of *Midrash Avkir*' [Midrash avkir: mevo'ot umuva'ot], MA thesis, Hebrew University of Jerusalem, 1998, 114–15), fo. 41ʳ: *nirin ke'okhlin veha'esh maviro* (they appeared to be eating, but the food was being consumed by fire). Indeed, the *Da'at zekenim* commentary (on Genesis, fo. 15*b*, cited also in *Tosafot hashalem*, ed. Gellis, ii. 123, §18), which will be one of the main foci of our analysis below, goes so far as to suggest that the word *vayokhelu* (ויאכלו) in Gen. 18: 8 does not mean 'and they ate'. Rather, it means 'and they consumed the food through fire', as per Exod. 3: 2, *vehaseneh einenu ukal* (אוכל), where the root אכל is clearly used by the Torah to mean that the bush did not burn (*einenu nisraf*). Cf. M. M. Kasher, *Torah shelemah*, vol. iii (Jerusalem, 1938), 754–5. R. Joseph Bekhor Shor's influence on subsequent tosafist Torah commentaries was quite significant; see e.g. Sara Japhet, 'Hizekuni's Commentary on the Pentateuch—Its Genre and Purpose' (Heb.), in Moshe Bar-Asher (ed.), *Rabbi Mordekhai Breuer Festschrift* [Sefer yovel likhvod harav mordekhai breuer], vol. i (Jerusalem, 1992), 97–8. This fact helps to explain the misattribution of the commentary in MS Vatican 45 to Bekhor Shor, among other such Torah commentaries found in manuscripts that include MS Hamburg (National and University Library) Hebr. 45, and MS Leiden University Library

In this instance, it is quite possible (and perhaps even likely, as I have indicated in some detail in the notes on the above discussion) that the various tosafist approaches and interpretations were developed initially during the course of talmudic study, and were only later gathered or placed in the context of a series of biblical comments on the verses in question. Nonetheless, the Tosafists' awareness of and affinity for midrashic literature, as a distinct area of interest, is also evident from these interpretations. Indeed, the commitment of medieval Ashkenazi rabbinic scholarship to midrashic literature as a distinct genre (which, at the same time, constituted a significant repository of rabbinic teachings and scriptural exegesis) is expressed quite clearly by the Ashkenazi commentaries authored from the eleventh to the thirteenth centuries on various halakhic and aggadic *midrashim*, several of which have only recently come to light.[24]

II

Whether in the realm of *peshuto shel mikra* or in the realm of midrashic interpretation, the comments and approaches of specific Tosafists have gone largely unnoticed, due mainly to the fact that these comments on the Torah are strewn throughout a variety of printed works and manuscript texts, and have not been systematically identified or analysed. Thus, for example, the exegetical work of the Tosafists Rabbi Yom Tov of Joigny, Rabbi Jacob of Orléans, and Rabbi Moses of Coucy (mentioned above) appears to be somewhat similar to two collections of comments produced during the same period (from the late twelfth to the middle of the thirteenth centuries), most of which have been published: Rabbi Judah Hehasid's exoteric commentary on the Torah, which he transmitted towards the end of his life (through the form of *reportatio*) to his son, Rabbi Moses Zal(t)man,[25] and the *Nimukei ḥumash* of Rabbi

(Warner) 27. See H. J. Zimmels, 'MS Hamburg Cod. Hebr. 45 and its Attribution to R. Avigdor Katz' (Heb.), in Anon., *Articles in Memory of Rabbi Tsevi Peretz Chajes* [Ma'amarim lezikhron r. tsevi perets ḥayes] (Vienna, 1931), 248–61, and Yehoshafat Nevo, 'MS Leiden 27 and its Attribution to R. Yosef Bekhor Shor' (Heb.), *Tarbiz*, 52 (1983), 651–64. On Ashkenazi attitudes towards the resolution of divergent talmudic and midrashic passages in halakhic contexts, cf. e.g. *Sefer ḥasidim* (Parma), ed. J. Wistinetski (Frankfurt am Main, 1924), 403, §1667, and A. Geulah, 'Aggadic Midrashim Known Only in Ashkenazic Lands' [Midreshei agadah avudim hayedu'im me'ashkenaz bilvad], Ph.D. diss., Hebrew University of Jerusalem, 2007, 9.

[24] See e.g. Ya'akov Sussmann, 'Rabad on Shekalim? A Bibliographical and Historical Riddle' (Heb.), in Ezra Fleischer et al. (eds.), *Me'ah She'arim: Studies in Medieval Jewish Spiritual Life in Memory of Isadore Twersky* [Me'ah she'arim: iyunim be'olamam haruḥani shel yisra'el biyemei habeinayim lezekher yitsḥak tverski] (Jerusalem, 2001), 131–70 (esp. 168–9); Ta-Shma, *Keneset meḥkarim*, i. 96–112; and R. Eleazar b. Judah of Worms' commentary on *Lamentations Rabbah*, published (from MS Oxford/Bodleian Heb. E. 80 in the final section of *Sifrei harabi ele'azar migermaiza*, ed. A. Eisenbach (Jerusalem, 2006), 1–206.

[25] *Perushei hatorah lerabi yehudah heḥasid*, ed. Y. S. Lange (Jerusalem, 1975), and see the editor's introd., 7–12. To be sure, quite a number of the comments in this edition cannot be verified as those of R. Judah, since the key manuscripts on which this edition was based (MS Moscow National Library (Guenzberg)

Isaiah di Trani (known as Rid, c.1180–c.1250), an Italian rabbinic scholar who studied with the German Tosafist Rabbi Simhah of Speyer (c. 1200). Rabbi Isaiah's commentary on the Torah deals extensively with Rashi's commentary (Rashi is typically referred to as *hamoreh*, 'the teacher'), and includes citations from a number of German and northern French rabbinic figures and exegetes.[26]

Fortunately, however, it turns out that the comments of these tosafist exegetes, and those of Rabbi Judah Hehasid as well, together with the commentaries of Rashi and Bekhor Shor (which are, not surprisingly, the most frequently cited commentaries overall),[27] form a substantial core of the so-called tosafist commentaries on the Torah (*perushei ba'alei hatosafot al hatorah*), a number of which have been published.[28] The earliest of these compilatory commentaries, the partially published *Sefer hagan*,

---

82 and MS Cambridge University Library Add. 669.2) contain comments in which the names of R. Judah and R. Moses appear, as well as those that do not mention their names. The comments of R. Judah discussed in this study appear either in his name in these manuscripts, or are cited in his name by other roughly contemporary Ashkenazi figures and collections. Cf. below, n. 83. I discuss this issue in much greater detail in *The Intellectual History of Medieval Ashkenazic Jewry*.

[26] *Nimukei ḥumash lerabi yeshayah ditrani*, ed. C. B. Chavel (Jerusalem, 1972), and see also I. Ta-Shma, 'Sefer nimukei ḥumash lerabi yeshayah di trani', *Kiryat sefer*, 64 (1992/93), 751–3. R. Isaiah subsequently composed the so-called *Tosafot rid* (in which Rashi is also cited as *hamoreh*), which contain talmudic interpretations and analyses from Rabbenu Tam. These were received by R. Isaiah from Rabbenu Tam's German students such as R. Isaac b. Mordekhai (Ribam) of Bohemia and R. Ephraim of Regensburg. See e.g. Ta-Shma, *Keneset meḥkarim*, vol. iii (Tel Aviv, 2005), 9–19, 24–62, and cf. Kanarfogel, 'Mysticism and Asceticism in Italian Rabbinic Literature of the Thirteenth Century', *Kabbalah*, 6 (2001), 135–49. There is discussion about whether the commentaries attributed to R. Isaiah di Trani on the Prophets and the Writings were authored by this R. Isaiah (b. Mali), or by his grandson, R. Isaiah b. Elijah (Riaz; R. Isaiah the Younger), although the scholarly consensus now supports the former possibility. See e.g. *Teshuvot harid*, ed. A. Y. Wertheimer (Jerusalem, 1975), editor's introd., 49–53; S. Z. Leiman, 'Late Medieval Exegetes in Spain, Provence and Italy', in *Encyclopaedia Biblica* (Heb.), vol. viii (Jerusalem, 1982), 708; E. Z. Melammed, *Studies in Scripture, its Aramaic Targumim, and Commentaries* [Meḥkarim bamikra, betargumav uvimefareshav] (Jerusalem, 1984), 420–2.

[27] See Poznanski, *Introduction to Northern French Biblical Commentators* (Heb.), pp. lxxiii, cxiv; *Sefer hagan*, ed. Orlian, 36–7, 42–8; Japhet, 'Ḥizekuni's Commentary' (Heb.), 93–7; H. Touitou, '*Minḥat yehudah*', 103–13; and Yehoshafat Nevo, 'The Exegetical Methods of *Hadar zekenim* on the Torah' (Heb.), *Sinai*, 101 (1988), 25–6. From among the northern French *pashtanim* (and as opposed to Rashi and Bekhor Shor), Rashbam is cited by the compilatory tosafist Torah commentaries (leaving aside the more *peshat*-oriented *Ḥizekuni* commentary) only from time to time, and R. Joseph Kara is generally cited even less frequently. Cf. *Sefer hagan*, ed. Orlian, 37–8, and Nevo, 23. At the same time, there are any number of instances in which an earlier exegetical approach is cited, but no names are attached. Indeed, tosafist compilations sometimes mix different types of *peshat* approaches together, with little indication of the original authors whose comments are involved. See e.g. *Tosafot hashalem*, ed. Gellis, vol. x (Jerusalem, 1995), 93–6 (on Exod. 33: 4–6).

[28] See e.g. Poznanski, *Introduction to Northern French Biblical Commentators* (Heb.), pp. xcii–cxiv (who also describes a number of important manuscript collections); *Tosafot hashalem*, ed. Gellis, editor's introd., i. 11–20; and the more extensive descriptions in *Sefer hagan*, ed. Orlian, 83–97. (As far as I can tell, the various published collections described by Orlian are arranged according to alphabetical rather than chronological order.) *Tosafot hashalem*, ed. Gellis, i. 21–38, contains brief descriptions of the large selection of manuscript collections that were consulted in producing this work. See also Deborah Abecassis,

dates from around 1240, while most were compiled in the late thirteenth and early fourteenth centuries. As opposed to his northern French contemporary, Rabbi Hezekiah ben Manoah, who merely hints poetically in the introduction to his *Ḥizekuni* commentary at the roster of medieval exegetes whose interpretations are included anonymously, Rabbi Isaac ben Judah writes explicitly in the introduction to his late-thirteenth-century compilation, *Pa'aneaḥ raza*, that he will present the interpretations of several northern French exegetes. On his list are Rabbi Jacob of Orléans, Rabbi Joseph Bekhor Shor of Orléans, and *Sefer hagan*, which was 'composed by the rabbi of France, *harav mitsarefat*'), in addition to 'some *peshat* interpretations and *gematriyot* [numerological interpretations] of Rabbi Judah Hehasid'.²⁹ These are indeed the most frequently mentioned names (and comments) within *Pa'aneaḥ raza*. Although the published edition of *Pa'aneaḥ raza* cites interpretations from Rabbi Yom Tov of Joigny on a few occasions, manuscript versions of this work preserve quite a number of additional comments from him as well.³⁰ To be sure, the tosafist Torah compilations also preserve scattered (but in some ways more expected) talmudic and midrashic interpretations from leading Tosafists, such as the passage(s) from Rabbi Barukh ben Isaac in *Sefer hagan* that have also been noted above. Indeed, these tosafist Torah compilations tend to introduce additional midrashic texts and materials, as we shall see.

A good example of the interface, or transition, from the comments of the tosafist exegetes of the mid-twelfth and early thirteenth centuries (and their presence in the

---

'Reconstructing Rashi's Commentary on Genesis from Citations in the Torah Commentaries of the Tosafists', Ph.D. diss., Concordia University, 1999, 42–8, 247–51.

²⁹ The introductory passage is found in slightly defective form at the beginning of the published edition of *Pa'aneaḥ raza* (above, n. 21), and in full at the end of MS Oxford/Bodleian Opp. Add. 4ᵗᵒ, 103, fo. 144ʳ (from which I have rendered this description). After mentioning the comments of R. Judah Hehasid, both versions also refer to comments by R. Eliezer or R. Eleazar of Worms (characterized in the published version as *peratim*, 'details') as well. R. Isaac b. Judah Halevi also indicates in this introduction that he called his compilation *Pa'aneaḥ raza* because the numerological value (*gematriyah*) of each of these words is equivalent to that of his name, *yitsḥak*. This title as a whole ('explainer of the secret'; cf. Gen. 41: 45, and Rashi ad loc.) also reflects the amalgam of *peshatim* (and other exoteric interpretations), together with the more esoteric concepts and *gematriyot* that are found throughout this work. Cf. Ta-Shma, *Keneset meḥkarim*, i. 236, who attempts to identify the figure ר"יק, whose *ḥidushim* are also noted in this introduction; Kanarfogel, *Peering through the Lattices*, 248–9; and Joy Rochwarger, 'Sefer Pa'aneah Raza and Biblical Exegesis in Medieval Ashkenaz', MA thesis, Touro College, Jerusalem, 2000, 43–51, 109–17. On *Ḥizekuni*'s poetic introduction to and use of his sources, see Japhet, 'Ḥizekuni's Commentary', 91–110.

³⁰ R. Yom Tov is often cited in these texts by the acronym תיט"ב. See esp. MS British Library Or. 9931; MS Munich (Bavarian National Library) 50, and Urbach, *The Tosafists* (Heb.), 146 n. 13. The *Moshav zekenim* collection also cites virtually all of these tosafist figures with some frequency, in addition to R. Isaiah di Trani (who is cited for the most part by name, but is sometimes cited only by the initials *resh-yod*). Cf. Yehoshafat Nevo, 'The Exegetical Methods of *Moshav zekenim* on the Torah' (Heb.), *Sinai*, 100 (1987), 587–93; id., 'The Tosafist Torah Commentary *Moshav zekenim*' (Heb.), *Sha'anan*, 1 (1995), 11–33.

compilatory works of the thirteenth century), followed by the further midrashic expansions found in these compilatory works, can be seen in connection with the story of the sale of Joseph towards the end of Genesis 37. At issue here for many medieval exegetes were the nationalities and the number of the groups that appeared to be involved in the acquisition of Joseph from his brothers and his transferral to Egypt. Reference is made by the biblical text, at various points, to *yishma'elim*, *midyanim*, and *medanim*. In addition, the sequence of the transactions is somewhat confusing. In Genesis 37: 27, for example, the brothers speak of selling Joseph to the *yishma'elim*, but in the following verse, the Torah writes that merchants from among the *midyanim* took Joseph out of the pit and sold him to the *yishma'elim*, who brought Joseph down to Egypt. At the same time, Genesis 37: 36 states that the *medanim* were the ones who sold Joseph to Egypt. Rashbam (on Gen. 37: 28), following his stated exegetical goal of presenting *omek peshuto shel mikra*, suggests that while the brothers were waiting for the *yishma'elim* to arrive, a group of *midyanim* happened upon Joseph in the pit and took him out (unbeknown to the brothers), and then sold him themselves to the *yishma'elim*, who in turn sold him to Egypt. Although the brothers thus did not actually sell Joseph into slavery in Egypt, their course of action certainly led to this consequence. Alternatively—and according to Genesis 45: 4, where Joseph specifically attributes his being sold to Egypt to his brothers—Rashbam suggests that the brothers first instructed those *midyanim* who came along to remove Joseph from the pit and then sold him to the *yishma'elim*. Rashbam (on Gen. 37: 36) further notes that the *medanim* and *midyanim* were kin, while the *medanim* (who sold him to Egypt) and the *yishma'elim* (who brought him to Egypt), according to the *peshat*, are identical. Thus, the removal of Joseph from the pit, and his sale and transfer to Egypt, were essentially accomplished through two groups of related merchants.[31]

Rabbi Joseph Bekhor Shor (on Gen. 37: 28) summarizes Rashbam's approach (in the name of 'there are those who interpret', *yesh mefarshim*), but he rejects it as a 'self-invention' (*bada'ut*) that is 'not worthwhile' (*vekhol zeh eineno shaveh li*).[32] Rather, as he had already explained (on Gen. 37: 25), Bekhor Shor holds that the three groups mentioned by the Torah represent three brothers, all of whom were sons of Hagar and Keturah, Abraham's concubines, who were therefore considered to be one nation. Thus, there was only one conglomerate of merchants involved here, that contained representatives from each of these larger families. The Torah

---

[31] See *Rabbi Samuel ben Meir's Commentary on Genesis: An Annotated Translation*, ed. Martin Lockshin (Lewiston, NY, 1989), 257–8, 260. As Lockshin notes (260 n. 3), Rashi also appears to think that there were only two groups, but he labels them differently. Rashbam is also directing his comment against Rashi's view that it was the brothers themselves who removed Joseph from the pit, a point made, without attribution, by the later *Ḥizekuni* as well (Lockshin, 258 n. 2).

[32] *Perushei r. yosef bekhor shor al hatorah*, ed. Yehoshafat Nevo, 68–9. Cf. *Rabbi Samuel ben Meir's Commentary on Genesis*, ed. Lockshin, 257 n. 3; MS Florence/Laurenziana Plut. II, 20, fo. 160ᵛ: ופי' רשב"א כי מדן ומדין וישמעאל אומה אחת היא; and below, n. 137.

is referring only to this one larger nation or group, alternately using the three individual names of its constituents.[33]

Rabbi Judah Hehasid, in his Torah commentary (on Gen. 37: 28), arrives at a similar approach to that of Rashbam, from a different direction. Rabbi Judah was troubled by Joseph's seemingly untrue statement to Pharaoh's butler (Gen. 40: 15) that he had reached Egypt 'because I had been kidnapped from the land of the Hebrews'. Rabbi Judah therefore suggests an interpretation 'according to the *peshat*, to explain what had occurred'. While eating their meal, the brothers saw a caravan of *yishma'elim* and decided to sell Joseph to them. They made Joseph swear that he would neither tell nor write to their father without their permission about this arrangement, and they enacted a *ḥerem* (ban) among themselves that they would not tell. While they were involved with the *yishma'elim* in writing up the document of sale, a group of *medanim* passed by and looked into the pit where Joseph was, in search of water. They saw Joseph in the pit and removed him. The *medanim* were fearful that they would be pursued (by whomever had put Joseph into the pit in the first place), so they quickly sold him to the *yishma'elim* for twenty pieces of silver, a relatively small sum. Leaving aside the embellishments with regard to Joseph being made to swear not to tell his father and the *ḥerem* enacted between the brothers (which are midrashic approaches representing an aspect of this story that Rabbi Judah discusses in his *Sefer ḥasidim*),[34] Rabbi Judah's *peshat* here essentially comports with the exegetical approach taken by Rashbam. Indeed, Rabbi Moses Zal(t)man asked his father how he then understands Genesis 45: 4, where Joseph identifies himself as the one whom the brothers sold to Egypt. Like Rashbam, Rabbi Judah answers that their throwing Joseph into the pit initially is what caused him to be sold to Egypt, making them responsible, in effect, for his sale.[35]

Sefer hagan seeks to reconcile Genesis 37: 36, which states that the *medanim* sold Joseph to Egypt, with a later verse (39: 1), according to which Potiphar acquired Joseph from the *yishma'elim*, who had brought him down to Egypt. The first answer presented, characterized as *lefi hapeshat*, is that the *yishma'elim* had sold him to the *medanim*, who brought him down to Egypt for sale. *Sefer hagan* then presents an

---

[33] Bekhor Shor's comment on Gen. 37: 25 is found in his name in *Moshav zekenim* (ed. Sassoon, 72), along with some other unnamed alternatives. This is also the interpretation of Ibn Ezra and Radak on Gen. 37: 28, although it is unclear whether Bekhor Shor had Ibn Ezra's Torah commentary before him. See e.g. *Perushei r. yosef bekhor shor al hatorah*, ed. Y. Nevo, editor's introd., 10; ibid., Bekhor Shor's commentary, 10 (on Gen. 2: 24), and Nevo's note; and cf. *Tosafot hashalem*, ed. Gellis, i. 115, §§9, 11; i. 277–8, §3.

[34] Cf. *Sefer ḥasidim*, ed. J. Wistinetski, §1961, and the references to *Tanḥuma* and *Pirkei derabi eli'ezer* in *Perushei hatorah lerabi yehudah heḥasid*, ed. Lange, 51 nn. 39, 40. This passage is cited in the name of R. Judah Hehasid in *Moshav zekenim* (ed. Sassoon, 72) in two parts, just before and just after R. Joseph Bekhor Shor's interpretation. See also *Tosafot hashalem*, ed. Gellis, iv. 45–6, §9.

[35] *Perushei hatorah lerabi yehudah heḥasid*, ed. Lange, 51. R. Judah adduces support for this kind of causality from the way that the Torah (in Num. 32: 5) assigns responsibility to Moses for the crossing of the Jordan river by the children of Israel.

unidentified *midrash* that appears to be a passage from *Genesis Rabbah* found (in extant versions of this work) at the later verse about Potiphar.³⁶ This *midrash* posits a kind of racial problem that the Egyptians had with the dark-skinned *yishma'elim* selling the fair-skinned Joseph to them as a slave. Although Joseph was technically in the possession of the *yishma'elim*, the Egyptians required the *medanim* to act as guarantors on behalf of the *yishma'elim* for this sale, in order to resolve this difficulty. Consequently, the Torah can credibly assign this sale to both groups. Rabbi Aaron Hakohen, the compiler of *Sefer hagan*, offers this interpretation as one that he heard from his brother Rabbi Jacob, who had himself heard it in the name of Rabbi Moses ben Shene'ur (d. c.1250).³⁷ Rabbi Moses, who, together with his brothers Rabbi Samuel and Rabbi Isaac, headed the active tosafist study hall in Evreux (Normandy), was inclined (as was his brother Rabbi Isaac, as we shall see)³⁸ to put forward midrashic interpretations of the Torah (and to expand or otherwise manipulate passages in *Genesis Rabbah*), even as this particular passage from *Genesis Rabbah* might be fairly characterized as an *agadah hameyashevet divrei mikra*. From this point on, however, the focused interpretation of *Sefer hagan* (and of Rabbi Moses of Evreux) is cited in only a few tosafist Torah compilations.³⁹ Most other tosafist Torah commentaries take this passage in *Genesis Rabbah* and link it to a different passage in the same work and to additional *midrashim*, creating a much larger midrashic picture and discussion.⁴⁰ This was done,

---

³⁶ The later *perush* (or Tosafot) compilation of R. Asher (Rosh) (see below, n. 70) on Gen. 37: 28 (fo. 16*b*, 'and they sold Joseph to the *yishma'elim* for twenty pieces of silver') cites and identifies this *midrash* as *Genesis Rabbah*. Cf. M. M. Kasher, *Torah shelemah*, vol. vi (Jerusalem, 1938), 1441. *Gen. Rabbah* 86: 3 on Gen. 39: 1 (Theodor–Albeck edn., 1055) describes how the Egyptian officer Potiphar, who acquired Joseph from the *yishma'elim*, makes a very similar point from a different perspective. Upon seeing the fair-skinned Joseph being offered for sale by the dark-skinned *yishma'elim*, Potiphar sensed that Joseph was not really a slave, and he cleverly requested a guarantor for the sale in the event that Joseph had been stolen or kidnapped, and was not rightfully in the possession of the *yishma'elim*.

³⁷ See *Sefer hagan*, ed. Orlian, 187 (on Gen. 37: 36):

ומה שכתוב והמדנים מכרו אותו [אל מצרים] לפוטיפר ובמקום אחר כתוב מיד הישמעאלים אשר הורידוהו שמה [בראשית, לט :א] לפי הפשט הא דכתב והמדנים מכרו אותו למצרים היינו לישמעאלים להוריד למצרים. ויש במדרש כי הישמעאלים היו מוחזקים ממנו והורידו למצרים למכרו. אמרו המצרים גרמוני מוכר כותי ואין כותי מוכר גרמוני, כלו' דרך הלבן למכור שחור כי הלבן הוא הבן חורין והשחור הוא העבד. אתמה אין כאן עבד תנו ערב והמדנים ערבו הדבר לכן הוא אומר והמדנים מכרו אותו. כך שמעתי מאחי ה"ר יעקב ששמע משם הר"ר משה ב"ר שניאור ז"ל.

See ibid. 179, 234, 299, for other citations of R. Moses b. Shene'ur.

³⁸ See below, section VIII. On the academy and methodology at Evreux, see Urbach, *The Tosafists* (Heb.), i. 479–85; I. Ta-Shma, *Keneset meḥkarim*, vol. ii (Tel Aviv, 2004), 110–18; Kanarfogel, *Jewish Education and Society*, 74–9, 172–80; id., *Peering through the Lattices*, 59–68; and S. Emanuel, *Shivrei luḥot* (Jerusalem, 2006), 93–7.

³⁹ *Perushei hatorah lerabi ḥayim palti'el*, ed. Lange, 124 (on Gen. 39: 1) cites R. Moses b. Shene'ur by name (based on MS Munich (Bavarian National Library) 62; cf. *Tosafot hashalem*, ed. Gellis, iv. 57, §2. *Pa'aneaḥ raza*, 168, cites this interpretation in the name of *har' ya'akov gan*, and see also MS Florence/Laurenziana Plut. II, 20, above, n. 32.

⁴⁰ See e.g. *Moshav zekenim*, ed. Sassoon, 71–2 (on Gen. 37: 25); *Tosafot hashalem*, ed. Gellis, iv. 44–6, §§6–7, 10 (on Gen. 37: 28, citing *Minḥat yehudah*, *Perush harosh*, *Hadar zekenim* and *Da'at zekenim*, and several manuscripts), and see also *Perushei hatorah lerabi ḥayim palti'el*, ed. Lange, 117–18 (on Gen. 37: 27).

in part, to explain Rashi's overall approach to this series of events,[41] but new, broader directions and midrashic solutions were also suggested, which had little to do with Rashi's commentary.

The compilers or editors of these thirteenth- and fourteenth-century collections were, for the most part, unknown rabbinic figures; they were not typically recognized as Tosafists themselves. In all likelihood, these works took on the name or genre of tosafist Torah commentaries because of the large number of genuine tosafist teachings or comments that formed their core, albeit in an unsystematic way.[42] One of the few exceptions, in terms of its editor's status, is the commentary compiled by Rabbi Hayim ben Jacob Paltiel, a student and colleague of Rabbi Meir of Rothenburg (d. 1293) and Rabbi Eliezer of Tukh, who was himself a leading redactor or compiler of Tosafot texts on the Talmud.[43]

A similar comment on this matter from MS Oxford/Bodleian Opp. Add. 4to, 127 (on Gen. 37: 36) is reproduced in *Tosafot hashalem*, iv. 57, §3. This brief commentary on the Torah portions 'Bereshit' to 'Beshalah' (entitled *peshatim latorah*, and found on fos. 1–16), was composed by an otherwise unknown R. Isaac b. Hayim, a student of R. Moses of Coucy and R. Yehiel of Paris (contemporaries of the brothers of Evreux), as indicated in three comments on fos. 16^{r–v}. There are indeed a number of *peshat*-like comments recorded, including three in the name of Rashbam (fos. 5^r, 7^{r–v}, 11^v). On fo. 3^r, an explanation for Rashi's exegetical *kal vaḥomer* regarding the punishment of the snake (Gen. 3: 14) is presented in the name of R. Moses of Evreux:

ארור אתה מכל הבהמה ומכל חית השדה. [פרש״י] אם מבהמה נתקלל מחיה לא כל
שכן. יש לשאול מהו לא כל שכן. ושמעתי בשם הרב ר' משה דאיברא אם מבהמה
שאיננה חפשית מן האדם שהיא ברשות ידו לכל עבודת פרך ואם ממנה נתקלל, מחיה
שהיא חפשית מן האדם לא כל שכן?

See also *Tosafot hashalem*, ed. Gellis, i. 134, §9. On this commentary, cf. Poznanski, *Introduction to Northern French Biblical Commentators* (Heb.), p. xciv; *Tosafot hashalem*, ed. Gellis, editor's introd., i. 21.

[41] Several compilations work to resolve the passage in *Genesis Rabbah* (84: 11) cited by Rashi (on Gen. 37: 3) as an aggadic *midrash* (that Joseph was sold four times), with Rashi's comment on 37: 28 (following *Tanḥuma*), that Joseph was sold three times. Among the named interpretations of Rashi cited by *Tosefot harosh* and *Minḥat yehudah* are those attributed to Rashbam (above, n. 31) and Rabbenu Tam, while R. Judah b. Eliezer in *Minḥat yehudah* adds another from his own immediate teacher, R. Elyakim. On R. Elyakim and his method, see H. Touitou, '*Minḥat yehudah*', 85–92. On the role of the tosafist Torah compilations as supercommentaries on Rashi, see Japhet, 'Ḥizekuni's Commentary' (Heb.), 108, and Touitou, '*Minḥat yehudah*', 3–9.

[42] Touitou (ibid. 34–65) has suggested that these works of the late 13th and early 14th cents. were designated as *perushei ba'alei hatosafot al hatorah* because the criteria for being considered as a *ba'al hatosafot* on the Torah (in terms of textual methods and goals, as well as literary orientation) were somewhat different and distinct from those criteria that were used to identify talmudic Tosafists. I am not persuaded by Touitou's arguments in this regard, but, as I shall indicate throughout this study, I fully agree with his suggestion that the so-called *perushei ba'alei hatosafot al hatorah* collections were composed and disseminated, for the most part, by members of the second-level intelligentsia or secondary elite, who wished to expose their generally less learned readers to a broader and more easily digested sampling of the teachings of the Tosafists as a whole (and to their own biblical, midrashic, and halakhic interpretations), as arrayed around the portions of the Torah. See also Kanarfogel, 'Between the Tosafist Academies and Other Study Halls in Ashkenaz during the Middle Ages' (Heb.), in I. Etkes (ed.), *Yeshivot and Batei Midrash* [Yeshivot uvatei midrashot] (Jerusalem, 2006), 85-108.

[43] On R. Hayim Paltiel's commentary and his rabbinic career (he also composed a collection of *minhagim* that became prominent in central and eastern Europe), see *Perushei hatorah lerabi ḥayim palti'el*, ed. Y. S. Lange (Jerusalem, 1981), editor's introd., 7–12; id., 'On the Identity of R. Hayim Paltiel' (Heb.),

Taken together, however, these tosafist Torah commentaries constitute a vast body of literature that remains to a large extent in manuscript, and which requires much scholarly attention and careful study.[44] Many (although certainly not all) of these manuscripts were available to Leopold Zunz, who identified and discussed their contents along with those of the commentaries that had been published by his day.[45] The present study traces the contributions made by scholars over the past century to the illumination of this genre, beginning with the groundbreaking work of Poznanski, as part of his larger introduction to biblical exegesis in northern France during the high Middle Ages.[46] It is clear that there has been some renewed interest in this genre within the last twenty-five years or so.

The so-called tosafist Torah commentaries in their most common form do not purport to be 'full-fledged' commentaries that seek to offer a range of different exegetical possibilities on a verse-by-verse basis. Rather, they are comprised of relatively brief *ḥidushim* (new insights) that add new approaches or new material, mostly in the realm of Midrash but also in the realm of *peshat*, to verses for which either of these dimensions was perceived to be needed or novel, while always remaining mindful of and interested in the sources and analysis of Rashi's commentary on the Torah as well. At the same time (and as opposed to the commentaries of Rashi and Rashbam), the tosafist Torah compilations rarely if ever offer any methodological statements or guidelines.[47]

Alei sefer, 8 (1980), 140–6; Urbach, *The Tosafists* (Heb.), ii. 582; Ta-Shma, *Keneset meḥkarim*, i. 259; Eric Zimmer, *Olam keminhago noheg* (Jerusalem, 1996), 276–7, 282–3; 292, 296–7; and Emanuel, *Shivrei luḥot*, 221–7.

[44] See e.g. Y. S. Lange, 'The Tosafist Torah Commentary in MS Paris 48' (Heb.), *Alei sefer*, 5 (1978), 74; Japhet, 'Ḥizekuni's Commentary' (Heb.), 107; ead., 'The Nature and Distribution of Compilatory Commentaries' (Heb.), in M. Bar-Asher et al. (eds.), *Biblical and Commentary Studies* [Iyunei mikra ufarshanut], vol. iii (Ramat Gan, 1993), 215; I. Ta-Shma, *The Literature of Talmudic Commentaries* [Hasifrut haparshanit latalmud], vol. ii (Jerusalem, 2000), 96; id., 'The Tosafist Academies in the Academic Milieu of France during the Twelfth and Thirteenth Centuries: Parallels that Do Not Meet' (Heb.), in I. Etkes (ed.), *Yeshivot and Batei Midrash* (Heb.), 83 n. 10; and H. Touitou, '*Minḥat yehudah*', 62 n. 74; Abba Zions, '*Pa'ane'aḥ raza* and its Author' (Heb.), *Or hamizraḥ*, 25 (1976), 71–80, and id., 'On the Author of *Pa'ane'aḥ raza*' (Heb.), *Or hamizraḥ*, 29 (1981), 210–14, sees R. Isaac b. Judah, the compiler of *Pa'ane'aḥ raza*, as a Tosafist of standing. Zions's evidence, however, is problematic. At most, R. Isaac was a descendant or relative of certain Tosafists. Cf. Yehoshafat Nevo, 'The *Pa'aneaḥ raza* Commentary on the Pentateuch' (Heb.), *Sinai*, 98 (1986), 177–84.

[45] See Zunz, *Zur Geschichte und Literatur*, 76–95.   [46] See above, n. 28.

[47] See Japhet, 'Ḥizekuni's Commentary' (Heb.), 99–101, 107–10. Cf. Y. Nevo, 'Exegetical Methods of *Hadar zekenim* on the Torah' (Heb.), 26–9; *Perush rashbam lekohelet*, ed. S. Japhet and R. Salters (Jerusalem, 1985), editors' introd., 34–5 (on the distinction between an *osef be'urim*, a collection of comments, and a *ḥibur parshani*, a cohesive exegetical work); and below, n. 149. As Japhet demonstrates, R. Hezekiah b. Manoah's *Ḥizekuni*, the subject of her study, is somewhat different in regard to these and other related compositional characteristics. At the same time, there is at least one 13th-cent. example (which perhaps took its cue from the Torah commentary that has been attributed to the study hall of Rabbenu Tam; see above, n. 18) of a collection that consists, in large measure, of talmudic Tosafot that have been placed according to the order of the verses of the Torah, rather than in accordance with the talmudic texts that anchor them. This collection (which is extant only on the weekly Torah portions

I shall now turn my attention to two of these tosafist Torah compilations, *Da'at zekenim* and *Hadar zekenim*, which were compiled anonymously in the second half of the thirteenth century in northern France.⁴⁸ Our discussion will be limited, however, to selections from the steady stream of *midrashim* and their analysis that are found on the books of Genesis and Exodus. A sampling of these passages will allow a working assessment of the presence and use of midrashic texts in these tosafist Torah compilations, the extent to which known Tosafists adhered to these same patterns, and the relationship of the midrashic methodology of the tosafist Torah compilations to Rashi's stated exegetical goal, which was to focus on *agadah hameyashevet divrei mikra*, rather than on other kinds of aggadot or *midrashim*.

III

Da'at zekenim contains an interpretative expansion of a passage in *Genesis Rabbah* (20: 7) that discusses the extent of man's domination over woman as expressed in Genesis 3: 16, 'and he will dominate you'.⁴⁹ The core midrashic passage consists

'Shofetim' and 'Ki tetse') was published by Shraga Abramson (from MS Oxford/Bodleian Heb. e. 10) as *Ba'alei hatosafot al hatorah* (Jerusalem, 1974), along with a lengthy introduction. With respect to the development of halakhic *midrashim*, most modern scholars still believe that these texts and their scriptural derivations preceded the mishnaic organization of tannaitic material in a topical way. See e.g. E. E. Urbach, 'Scriptural Derivation as the Basis for Jewish Law and the Problem of the Rabbinic Scribes' (Heb.), in id., *From the World of the Sages* [Me'olamam shel ḥakhamim] (Jerusalem, 1988), 50–66, and the discussion and studies cited in David Halivni, *Midrash, Mishnah, Gemara* (Cambridge, Mass., 1986), 18–68. In the case of the Tosafists, however, there is no doubt that the talmudic Tosafot were the original site of activity, and the placement of these materials into a kind of Torah commentary reflects a subsequent development.

⁴⁸ See Poznanski, *Introduction to Northern French Biblical Commentators* (Heb.), pp. cvii–cvix; *Sefer hagan*, ed. Orlian, 85–7 (which also contains an assessment of the influence of *Sefer hagan* on these works); and *Tosafot hashalem*, ed. Gellis, editor's introd., i. 12–13. *Hadar zekenim* appears to have been composed after *Da'at zekenim*; see below, n. 103. Japhet notes that both *Da'at zekenim* and *Hadar zekenim* were among the sources for *Ḥizekuni*, which she dates to 1275 (or perhaps a bit later). See Japhet, 'Ḥizekuni's Commentary' (Heb.), 99–100. *Da'at zekenim* was first published in Livorno in 1783. It was published under the title *Rabotenu ba'alei hatosafot al hatorah* in Warsaw in 1876 (together with *Minḥat yehudah*, composed in 1313 by R. Judah b. Eliezer (Riba), and the Torah commentary by R. Ovadyah Bartenura). This edition was reprinted several times, most recently in Jerusalem in 1967.

⁴⁹ See *Rabotenu ba'alei hatosafot al ḥamishah ḥumshei torah* (Jerusalem, 1967), 'Genesis', fo. 4a (= *Tosafot hashalem*, ed. Gellis, i. 138–9, §13):

אמרינן בב"ר [בשם ר' יוסי הגלילי] יכול ממשלה מכל צד ת"ל לא יחבול רחים ורכב. ופי' ר' יצחק יכול ממשלה מכל צד שיהא לו רשות למשכן כדדרשי' ת"ל לא יחבל ריחים ורכב. ואשתו נקראת ריחים כדכתי' ויהי טוחן בבית האסורים כדדריש בסוטה [דף י ע"א] וכתי' תטחן לאחר אשתי. ובירושלמי תרגם פסוק זה לא ממשכנין ריחיא ורכבא צרכי נפשתא אינן. ופי' לא תאסור כליין וחתנין שאם אירס אשה לא יניחנה לישב עגונה באירוסין זמן מרובה.

This passage is also found in one of the more reliable manuscript versions of *Da'at zekenim*, MS Moscow National Library (Guenzberg) 268, fo. 78ʳ, and is cited in briefer form (and without the names of either R. Yose Hagelili or R. Isaac) in *Ḥizekuni*, which, as Sara Japhet has suggested, uses *Da'at zekenim* as one of its unnamed sources. See Japhet, 'Ḥizekuni's Commentary' (Heb.), 99–101, and cf. M. M. Kasher, *Torah shelemah*, vol. ii (Jerusalem, 1929), 274.

of a statement by Rabbi Yose Hagelili that Scripture does set limits to a husband's domination of his wife. This is based on Rabbi Yose's euphemistic (and non-contextual) interpretation of Deuteronomy 24: 6 ('one may not take in pawn a lower or upper millstone'), to mean that a husband (represented by the upper millstone) may not harm his wife (the lower millstone).[50] *Da'at zekenim* then cites an expansion of Rabbi Yose's comment in the name of a Rabbi Isaac, that a husband may not use his wife as collateral for his debts, by sending her to work or to serve in the home of another man (even in theoretically permitted roles, such as cleaning the home), again on the basis of his marginally more contextual understanding of Deuteronomy 24: 6. *Da'at zekenim* concludes with a passage from the Palestinian Targum (Targum Yerushalmi), which understands the phrase in Deuteronomy 24: 6 to mean (in a vein similar to that of Rabbi Yose Hagelili) that it is inappropriate for a bridegroom to make his bride into a kind of *agunah* ('chained woman'), thus depriving her of intimacy with him, by delaying the full implementation of their marriage (*nesuin*) for an extended period of time, once the initial halakhic betrothal (*kidushin*) has been accomplished.

Establishing the identity of Rabbi Isaac in the *Da'at zekenim* passage presents something of a challenge. An instinctive reaction might be to suggest that he is the best-known Rabbi Isaac from within the tosafist period and milieu, Rabbi Isaac ben Samuel of Dampierre (Ri Hazaken, twelfth cent.). The only positive support for this suggestion, however, comes from the late thirteenth-century tosafist Torah commentary compiled by Rabbi Hayim Paltiel. This compilation cites the entire passage found in *Da'at zekenim* on Genesis 3: 16 on the phrase in Deuteronomy 24: 6. Here, Rabbi Isaac's comment is introduced by his initials (*ufiresh r"y*), which is the most common way that Tosafot texts on the Talmud refer to Ri of Dampierre.[51] Moreover, immediately preceding this passage in Rabbi Hayim Paltiel's compilation is a halakhic analysis of Deuteronomy 24: 6 (concerning the care that must be taken when confiscating items from the borrower for collateral that are vital to the borrower, the primary meaning and context of this verse) that can be found in Tosafot texts on the talmudic tractates *Bava metsia* and *Menahot*.[52]

---

[50] Deut. 24: 6 literally reads that one may not seek collateral for a debt owed that would be ruinous to the borrower, such as the impounding of a gristmill that the borrower uses for basic sustenance. R. Yose Hagelili understands the two parts of the gristmill to be a euphemism for husband and wife, a rabbinic conception for which the midrashic passage cites additional biblical verses.

[51] This passage, including the interpretation in the name of Ri, is also found (with some variation) in a sermon of R. Joshua ibn Shu'eib, the 14th-cent. Spanish *darshan*. See Shraga Abramson, 'The Epistle on Holiness Attributed to Nahmanides' (Heb.), *Sinai*, 90 (1982), 235 n. 28. On the coincidence of R. Isaac and Ri in the corpus of Tosafot, cf. e.g. Tosafot on *Ber.* 11*b*, s.v. *shekevar*: ו הש י ב ר"י ... נשאל להרב יצחק and Tosafot on *BB* 13*a*, s.v. *kofin*: ... דאין זה תקנה ... ואור"י ... ואומר ר"י דמשום מצוה ... ואומר רבינו יצחק חדא ... ואור"י דנתיני וכו'.

[52] Tosafot on *BM* 115*a*–*b*, beginning with s.v. *vehayav*; Tosafot on *Men.* 58*b*, s.v. *ein*. On the northern French dimensions of the standard Tosafot on *Bava metsia* and *Menahot*, see Urbach, *The Tosafists* (Heb.), ii. 646–58, 663–5.

The sequence of the presentation in Rabbi Hayim Paltiel's compilation perhaps suggests that the primary halakhic implications of Deuteronomy 24: 6 (concerning the confiscation of vital items as collateral) were taken up first, after which Tosafists proceeded to discuss the midrashic use of this phrase, which deals with the limits of what a husband may demand from his wife as well as the related issue of a bridegroom not placing his bride in an unfair situation.[53] Nonetheless, Ri's name does not appear in any of those Tosafot texts that discuss the primary halakhic implications. Moreover, of the dozens of times that *Genesis Rabbah* is cited in the standard Tosafot on the Babylonian Talmud, Ri's name is found in less than a handful of instances,[54] although his son and dedicated student, Rabbi Elhanan (who died as a martyr in 1184), is associated with several other such passages.[55] On balance, Ri's presence in the *Da'at zekenim* passage at hand cannot be effectively confirmed. Interestingly, one manuscript of a tosafist Torah compilation attributes the basic comment of Rabbi Isaac (and the relationship between Gen. 3: 16 and Deut. 24: 6) found in *Da'at zekenim* to Ri's uncle Rashbam.[56] No extant formulations of Rashbam's commentary on Genesis or Deuteronomy include this comment, however, and it is exceedingly difficult to imagine that Rashbam would have offered a comment or addendum to a passage in *Genesis Rabbah* as part of his *peshat* Torah commentary.[57]

In fact, however, Rabbi Isaac's addendum to the first part of the *Da'at zekenim* passage is found precisely (albeit without attribution to Rabbi Isaac) in *Bereshit rabati*, a work associated with the eleventh-century Provençal rabbinic scholar

---

[53] See *Perushei hatorah lerabi ḥayim palti'el*, ed. Lange, 604, and esp. n. 9, for the Tosafot parallels to the first part of the discussion.

[54] See e.g. Tosafot on *Pes. 3b*, s.v. *rokhevet*; Tosafot on *BK 38a–b*, s.v. *nasa*; Tosafot on *AZ 10a*, s.v. *she'ein*; and the next note.

[55] See e.g. Tosafot on *BM 86b*, s.v. *hahu*; Tosafot on *AZ 25a*, s.v. *lemosheh*. R. Elhanan is also mentioned together with Ri in Tosafot on *Bava kama* in the above note. It should also be noted that the standard Tosafot on *Avodah zarah* are based to a large extent on those edited by R. Elhanan. Cf. Urbach, *The Tosafists* (Heb.), ii. 655; *Tosafot al masekhet avodah zarah lerabenu elḥanan b. yitsḥak*, ed. David Fraenkel (Husiatyn, 1901), fos. 10b (*AZ 10a*, s.v. *she'ein*), 28 (*AZ 25a*, s.v. *lemosheh*); and *Tosefot harash mishants* in M. Y. Blau (ed.), *Shitat hakadmonim al masekhet avodah zarah* (New York, 1969), 50, 80.

[56] See MS Florence/Laurenziana Plut. II: 20, fo. 145ᵛ:

והוא ימשול בך. אמ' בב"ר יכול ממשלה מכל צד, ת"ל לא יחבל ריחים. ופי' רשב"ם יכול ממשלה מכל צד פי' שיוכל למשכנה ת"ל לא יחבל ריחים. ועל האשה כתי' כי יקח איש אשה ואשה נקראת ריחים דכתי' גבי שמשון ויהי טוחן ואמ' רז"ל שכל אחד הביאה לו אשתו וכתי' ותחן לאחר אשתי.

[57] Cf. above, n. 14. *Moshav zekenim*, ed. Sassoon, 5, records a different comment at the beginning of Gen. 3: 16 in the name of Rashbam, which is also not attested by verified manuscript evidence. On the difficulty in properly reconstructing this part of Rashbam's commentary on Genesis, see *Perush hatorah asher katav harashbam*, ed. David Rosin (Breslau, 1882), editor's introd., p. xxxix. For some recent attempts to clarify the texts of (and to find additional comments of) Rashbam on the Torah on the basis of citations found in other related published works and in manuscript, see e.g. E. Touitou, *Exegesis in Perpetual Motion* (Heb.), 189–209; Ithamar Kislev, 'The Commentary of Ḥizekuni as a Textual Witness for Rashbam's Torah Commentary' (Heb.), in M. Bar-Asher et al. (eds.), *A Gift for Sara Japhet* [Shai lesarah yefet] (Jerusalem, 2008), 173–93; and cf. Moshe Sokolow, '"Interpretations that are Discovered Anew

Rabbi Moses Hadarshan and his school.⁵⁸ Given that *Da'at zekenim* cites passages from *Bereshit rabati* on several occasions (once in the name of Rabbi Moses himself, but most often without any name and without even mentioning the name of the work),⁵⁹ it is likely that we are dealing here with a midrashic text that completely predates the tosafist period and did not have any tosafist input into its original formulation, and in which Rabbi Isaac is an unidentified figure from the talmudic period or beyond. *Da'at zekenim*, then, is simply presenting and linking a series of related midrashic and aggadic passages and observations.⁶⁰

At the same time, however, the last part of the *Da'at zekenim* passage, which cites the Palestinian Targum and relates the imagery of the millstone to a groom who withholds from his bride the full measure of marital status and married life, does have analogues within tosafist literature.⁶¹ The tosafist Torah commentary *Pa'ane'aḥ*

Each Day": New Sections from the Torah Commentary of Rashbam' (Heb.), *Alei sefer*, 11 (1984), 72–80.

⁵⁸ *Midrash bereshit rabati nosad al sifro shel r. mosheh hadarshan*, ed. Ch. Albeck (Jerusalem, 1940; repr. Jerusalem, 1984). As Albeck notes in his introduction (1–5), the work that we have is apparently an abridgement of a longer work (*Bereshit rabah gedolah*) that R. Moses composed. Cf. Mack, 'The Later Midrashim', 147; id., 'The Path of a Homily, from the Work of R. Moses Hadarshan to Rashi's Torah Commentary' (Heb.), *Tarbiz*, 65 (1996), 253, 260 n. 46. The comment under discussion here is found in the body of Albeck's edition, on p. 46: והוא ימשול בך. א״ר יוסי הגלילי יכול ממשלה מכל צד ת״ל לא יחבל רחים ורכב. ומנין שאינו רשאי למשכנה שנאמר ולא תחבול בגד אלמנה. The passage in *Bereshit rabati* then continues with the case of a woman who was being taken advantage of by her robber-husband, which is also found in the original *Genesis Rabbah* text. Albeck (46 n. 2), however, raises the possibility that this passage follows an alternative version of the original *Genesis Rabbah* text, since *Bereshit rabati* cites Deut. 24: 17 (*lo taḥavol beged almanah*) as the proof-text for the follow-up to R. Yose Hagelili's initial statement (attributed in *Genesis Rabbah* to R. Isaac), that a wife may not be used as collateral, rather than Deut. 24: 6 (*lo yaḥavol reḥayim varakhev*). Cf. *Midrash Bereshit Rabba*, ed. Theodor and Albeck, 191, for a version that also cites Deut. 24: 17 as the proof-text for R. Yose Hagelili himself. This verse perhaps conveys a bit more directly both R. Yose Hagelili's point (that a wife may not suffer at the hands of her husband) as well as the next point about her not being used as collateral. See also below, n. 65.

⁵⁹ On the role of *Bereshit rabati* as an interpretation of *Genesis Rabbah*, see Albeck's introduction, 2–4. On the use of *Bereshit rabati* by *Da'at zekenim* (which appears to have the most citations among the so-called tosafist Torah commentaries), see Albeck's introd., 31 (and the body of *Bereshit rabati*, ed. Albeck, 61 n. 24). R. Moses' name is cited in *Da'at zekenim*, 'Genesis', fo. 51a (on Gen. 49: 25). As Albeck also notes (introd., 35–6), a handful of medieval texts, including the tosafist Torah compilation *Minḥat yehudah* (and at least one other Ashkenazi work), cite explanations from *Bereshit rabati*, which they attribute to contemporary teachers. See also Albeck, 33, for a passage in Tosafot on *AZ* 10b, s.v. *amar leh*, which cites part of a lengthy passage from *Bereshit rabati*. These Tosafot were based on the Tosafot of R. Elhanan, son of Ri; see above, n. 55.

⁶⁰ For instances of the name R. Isaac appearing in tosafist Torah commentaries in which the references do not seem to be to Ri of Dampierre but rather to some other medieval Ashkenazi rabbinic figure, see e.g. *Da'at zekenim*, 'Genesis', fo. 50a (on Gen. 49: 10, and cf. *Tosafot hashalem*, ed. Gellis, v. 52, §1); *Minḥat yehudah*, 'Exodus', fo. 20a (on Exod. 16: 14, and cf. *Tosafot hashalem*, vii. 267, §3); *Moshav zekenim*, ed. Sassoon, 16 (on Gen. 12: 6); *Tosafot hashalem*, ii. 108, §2 (MS Jewish Theological Seminary 791); *Tosafot hashalem*, iv. 110, §3 (MS Verona (Municipal Library) 4); and MS Paris 1292, fo. 56ᵛ.

⁶¹ See also the so-called *perush rashi* on the standard edition of *Genesis Rabbah*, 20: 7. This commentary is characterized briefly by Ta-Shma, *Keneset meḥkarim*, i. 97.

raza presents a comment on Exodus 20: 13 (*lo tinaf*, 'do not commit adultery') in the name of a northern French Tosafist from the first half of the thirteenth century, Rabbi Samuel ben Solomon of Falaise. According to Rabbi Samuel of Falaise, the prohibition of *lo tinaf* is also meant to proscribe (as derived through a kind of *notarikon* application[62]) 'the placing of anger [*lo titen af*] between husband and wife', which will lead to the cessation of marital relations, as well as the rendering of the husband and wife impotent through some form of sorcery, 'so that they cannot have relations, which will foster enmity between them'. The passage in *Pa'ane'aḥ raza* concludes by citing the Palestinian Targum of Deuteronomy 24: 6, which forbids damaging the relationship between husband and wife, as found at the end of the *Da'at zekenim* passage.[63]

The full *Da'at zekenim* passage and the *Pa'ane'aḥ raza* passage in Exodus associated with Rabbi Samuel of Falaise have a common rabbinic theme, which is larger than the contextual interpretation of the Torah verses in question. Despite the relative dominance of the husband within marriage, the Palestinian Targum passage stresses that nothing untoward may be imposed either from within or from without that will force husband and wife to live apart, whether by a third party or even by the husband himself. The rabbinic conception is predicated on the notion that the husband's dominance is limited in this regard and in related matters. Although this conception is linked to verses in Genesis (3: 16), Exodus (20: 13), and Deuteronomy (24: 6), it is not so much about local biblical exegesis as about putting forward a rabbinic teaching on the basis of several different biblical verses that would allow this principle to become fully and repeatedly established.[64]

---

[62] *Notarikon* is a shorthand representation of a word by a single letter or letters. In this instance, *lo tinaf* is thereby expanded to connote *lo titen af*.

[63] See *Tosafot hashalem*, ed. Gellis, viii. 116, §13 (citing the published edition), and see also MS Oxford/Bodleian Opp. Add. 4ᵗᵒ, 103, fo. 62ᵛ:

לא תתן אף בין איש ואשתו מכשפים לאסור אדם ואשתו בשעת נישואין ושונאין זה
את זה ועובר על לאו דלא תחבול ריחים ורכב כמו שתרגם ירושלמי לא תאסר כלין
וחתנין ארי כל דעביד כן חייב (לממד) דריחים זה האשה ורכב זה האיש. בין איש
לאשתו כלו' לא תתן אף שבזה מטיל אף בינה ובין בעלה שאסרה עליו. אי נמי אזהרה
להקושר את האיש ואת האשה במכשפות מבלי יוכל לשמש ומטילין שנאה ביניהם.
הר"ר שמואל מפלייזא. ובתרגום ירושלמי מפרש על זה לא תחבול רחים ורכב ריחיים
זה האשה ורכב זה האיש.

R. Samuel of Falaise, a Tosafist and halakhist, studied with several of Ri's important students, including R. Judah of Paris, R. Solomon of Dreux and R. Barukh b. Isaac; see Urbach, *The Tosafists* (Heb.), i. 461–5. R. Samuel's father, R. Solomon b. Samuel, was connected to the German Pietists in terms of esoteric and magical teachings, as well as biblical exegesis, although there is no evidence that R. Samuel was similarly trained. See Kanarfogel, *Peering through the Lattices*, 94–103. The later *Moshav zekenim* collection on Exod. 20: 13 (ed. Sassoon, 168) records only the name of R. Samuel (without his locale of Falaise), which might provide at least a tangential explanation for the misattribution of the related passage in *Da'at zekenim* to R. Samuel b. Meir (Rashbam, above, n. 57). Cf. below, n. 92.

[64] See also *Ba'alei hatosafot al hatorah*, ed. S. Abramson, 57–8 (on Deut. 24: 6). This text cites the Palestinian Targum, that one should not interfere with the marriage of a man and a woman, as the interpretation of the phrase *lo yaḥavol reḥayim varekhev*, arguing also for this interpretation in light of the scriptural juxtaposition, in which this verse is preceded by the proviso (in Deut. 24: 5) that a newly married

Irrespective of the identity of Rabbi Isaac, the citation of the elongated or expanded *Genesis Rabbah* passage by *Da'at zekenim*, that a husband may not use his wife as collateral, together with the passage from the Palestinian Targum, injects a broader halakhic dimension, as well as a larger social norm or theme that moves well beyond the exegetical approach of Rashi and other medieval commentaries on Genesis 3: 16. Rashi limited this verse to a narrower interpersonal dynamic between husband and wife. He interprets the phrase *vehu yimshol bakh*, 'and he shall rule over you' (based on BT *Eruvin* 100b, and see also *Yevamot* 62b), in terms of a man's ability to ask directly for intercourse, while a woman typically does not, as well as a man's ability to accomplish sexual intercourse without the woman's arousal, while the reverse is not possible.[65]

To be sure, Rashi's much more contextual interpretation is strongly supported by the prior phrase in Genesis 3: 16, 'and your desire will be toward your husband', and this basic approach is followed and elaborated upon by Rabbi Joseph Bekhor Shor and (almost identically) by *Sefer hagan*.[66] Indeed, Rashi's interpretation also fits better with the first portion of the verse, which refers to the pain of childbirth. The entire verse, according to Rashi, relates in different ways to the effects and dynamics of marital relations. Although it is possible that *Da'at zekenim*'s interpretation here was developed initially as an alternative to Rashi's comment, it is more likely that *Da'at zekenim* proceeded from an altogether different approach, in terms of both textual interpretation and broader exegetical aims. The *Genesis Rabbah*

---

husband not serve in the army for the first year of marriage (which concludes with the phrase *vesimaḥ et ishto asher lakaḥ*, immediately before the next verse, *lo yaḥavol reḥayim varekhev*). This juxtaposition and interpretation is also found in *Moshav zekenim* on Deut. 24: 5 (ed. Sassoon, 510). Abramson (*Ba'alei hatosafot al hatorah*, 57 n. 60) refers to the tosafist Torah approach to Exod. 20: 13, as found in the collection of *Moshav zekenim* (in the name of R. Samuel; see above, n. 63). He also notes that this approach is cited similarly in the *derashot* of Ibn Shu'eib (including the notion that a man should not keep his fiancée in a state of *erusin* (halakhic betrothal) for too long, in the name of Ri; cf. above, n. 51). Abramson further refers to the comment of Ibn Ezra on Deut. 24: 6, in which Ibn Ezra sharply rejects the claim of the Karaites that the phrase *lo yaḥavol* refers to a marriage situation (which they too based in part on the juxtaposition of this verse to Deut. 24: 5). Abramson nonetheless notes some differences between the tosafist and Karaite exegesis on these verses. On Ibn Ezra's criticism of the Karaites in this instance, see Ayelet Seidler, 'Scriptural Juxtaposition of Commandments in the Bible Commentary of Ibn Ezra' (Heb.), *Shenaton leḥeker hamikra vehamizraḥ hakadum*, 17 (2007), 273–5, and cf. H. H. Ben-Sasson, *Chapters in the History of the Jews in the Middle Ages* [Perakim betoledot hayehudim biyemei habeinayim] (Tel Aviv, 1958), 164.

[65] See also *Tosafot hashalem*, ed. Gellis, i. 138, §12. For midrashic sources that may have impacted Rashi's interpretation, cf. Kasher, *Torah shelemah*, ii. 275.

[66] See *Perushei r. yosef bekhor shor al hatorah*, ed. Y. Nevo, 12; MS Vienna 28, fo. 2ᵛ (*Sefer hagan*, ed. Orlian, 130): ואל אישך תשוקתך. שתהי' מתאווה לו. וא״ת אכבוש יצרי מפני הצער לכך נאמר והוא ימשל בך בעל כרחך. MS Nuremberg (Municipal Library) 5, fo. 6ᵛ: וא״ת אכבוש יצרי מפני הצער . . . והוא ימשול בך ויקחך בעל כרחך. See also *Pa'ane'aḥ raza* (on Gen. 3: 16), 32–3. Ḥizekuni cites Rashi first (by name), but then cites most of the *Da'at zekenim* passage, beginning with the *Genesis Rabbah* passage (but without any other names), treating the passage attributed to R. Isaac as an answer, in effect, to the question raised by R. Yose Hagelili. Cf. Japhet, 'Ḥizekuni's Commentary' (Heb.), 99–101, 107–10.

passage suggests an important limitation and appreciation of the relationship between husband and wife, which deserves wider attention and conflation. The result found in *Da'at zekenim* is a kind of rabbinic *midrash*, based on *Genesis Rabbah*, that might impact the reader in a more meaningful or beneficial way on the one hand, and that could be repeated or reformulated at other points in the Torah on the other. If, for Rashi, *derash* or Midrash are mostly exegetical tools, this midrashic text and method for *Da'at zekenim* are destinations in and of themselves, on the way to a broad, popular presentation of sensitive rabbinic morals and halakhic observances.

IV

Da'at zekenim's comment on Genesis 6: 9 ('Noah was a righteous man in his generations'),[67] begins with another passage from *Genesis Rabbah* (30: 8) that is very brief and has no connection to Rashi's commentary on the Torah: people who are characterized by the Bible as *tamim* ('perfect' or 'complete') lived to an age that was marked or measured by the 'perfect' number of seven.[68] *Da'at zekenim* then cites the Tosafist Rabbi Isaac ben Abraham (Rizba or Riba of Dampierre, d. 1210), who explains that this midrashic passage means to indicate that the lifetimes of these people can be divided 'perfectly' by the number seven, without any remainder.[69] Rizba adds, as an extension of this midrashic passage, that Abraham, who is also referred to as *tamim*, in Genesis 17: 1, lived 175 years (a number which is divisible by seven). A question is then raised, however, from the case of Noah, who is called *tamim*, but who lived for a total of 950 years (which is not divisible by seven, leaving a remainder of five years). A manuscript version of *Da'at zekenim* identifies the questioner here as the Tosafist Rabbi Solomon (ben Judah) of Dreux who was, like Rizba, a student of Ri. Indeed, it was Rabbi Solomon of Dreux who asked Rizba both about the basic meaning of the word *tamim* (as reflecting divisibility by seven), as well as the specific application to Noah.[70] The answer given by Rizba to Rabbi

---

[67] *Rabotenu ba'alei hatosafot*, 'Genesis', fo. 5b:

איתא בב״ר פ׳ ל׳ סי׳ ז שכל מי שנאמר בו תמים, בידוע שנשתלמו שנותיו למדת השבוע. ופירש ח״ר יצחק ב״ר אברהם ששנותיו הולכין בשביעיות כמו שמצינו באברהם ע״ה שחי קע״ה. ונח שחי תשע מאות שנה וחמשים שנה והם ה׳ שנים יתרים על השביעיות י״ל שיש לחשוב משעה שנאמר לו תמים דהיינו כשאמר ה׳ יתברך לעשות התבה והוא מתעסק בה מאה ועשרים שנה. וש״נ שנח אחר המבול הרי לך ת״י. סלק שנת המבול שאינה נחשבת לפי שנשתנו בה סדרי בראשית והנשארים הולכים לשביעיות.

[68] *Midrash Bereshit Rabba*, ed. Theodor and Albeck, 273: תמים. בר חוטה אמר כל מי שנ׳ בו תמים השלים שנ[ות]יו למידת שבוע.

[69] Cf. below, n. 72. On the location and circumstances of Rizba's death, see S. Emanuel, 'R. Yeḥiel of Paris', 96–9.

[70] See MS Moscow 268, fo. 79r:

תמים. אמ׳ בב״ר שכל מי שנאמר בו תמים, בידוע שנשתלמו שנותיו למדת השבוע/לחשבונם. ושאל ח״ר שלמה דרויש לה״ר ריצב״א הפירוש. והשיב לו ששנותיו הולכים לו בשביעיות באברהם שחי קע״ה שנה. והקשה לו מנח וכו׳ והשיב לו וכו׳.

A similar passage is found in the so-called *Tosafot harosh al hatorah* (*sha'al r. shelomoh lariva*; see also

Solomon concerning Noah, after presenting the clear example of Abraham, is that Noah's life is to be calculated according to the factor of *tamim* (divisibility by seven) only from the point that he was actually called *tamim*. Noah was given this appellation at the beginning of the Torah portion that bears his name, when he was instructed to construct the ark. The construction of the ark took 120 years, and Noah lived for another 350 years after the flood, for a total of 470 years. The year of the flood itself, however, must be deducted from this total, because the order of Creation and normal human existence were effectively suspended during that year.[71] The remaining number, 469, is indeed perfectly divisible by seven.

Sefer hagan provides additional examples that support the core *Genesis Rabbah* passage. Division by seven is easily calculated not only for Abraham, but also for the lifespans of Job (who is referred to as *tamim* in Job 1: 1, and lived for 140 years) and for Jacob (Gen. 25: 27, *veya'akov ish tam* 'and Jacob was a mild man', who lived for 147 years). The question concerning Noah is raised by *Sefer hagan*, but a somewhat different solution from the one proposed by Rizba is suggested. In Noah's case, his lifespan as a *tamim* is to be calculated only for the period of time that he lived after the flood, which is mentioned explicitly in the Torah as a period of 350 years (Gen. 9: 28, 'And Noah lived 350 years after the flood').[72] The concern of *Sefer hagan*, like that of Rizba, seems to lie mostly with explicating the brief passage in *Genesis Rabbah*,

---

Perushei hatorah lerabi ḥayim palti'el, ed. Lange, 15), and in other manuscripts of tosafist Torah commentaries (including MS Oxford/Bodleian Opp. 27, fo. 21ʳ, which links this interpretation to a R. Mordekhai Hatsarefati and to *Midrash lekaḥ tov*, and refers to dividing the lives of Abraham and Noah into *shemitot* (seven-year sabbatical cycles)). See *Tosafot hashalem*, ed. Gellis, i. 198, §30, and cf. MS Oxford/Bodleian Hunt 569, fo. 3ʳ, and *Ḥizekuni*. All the ten or so comments found in the tosafist Torah compilations in the name of R. Solomon of Dreux are either talmudic or midrashic in nature. See Norman Golb, *The History of the Jews in Rouen during the Middle Ages* [Toledot hayehudim be'ir rouen biyemei habeinayim] (Tel Aviv, 1976), 190–2, and Urbach, *The Tosafists* (Heb.), i. 339–40. Indeed, Urbach suggests that R. Solomon's biblical interpretations were taken from his talmudic Tosafot. Regarding Rizba, see Urbach, i. 270 (citing Zunz), and ibid. 261 n. 4; above, n. 21; and below, n. 74. On the nature of *perush/tosafot harosh al hatorah*, and its attribution to R. Asher b. Yeḥiel, see e.g. A. H. Freimann, *R. Asher ben Yeḥiel and his Descendants* [R. asher b. yeḥi'el vetse'etsa'av] (Jerusalem, 1986), 129; *Tosafot hashalem*, ed. Gellis, editor's introd., i. 20; *Sefer hagan*, ed. Orlian, 95–6; *Sarei ha'elef*, ed. M. M. Kasher and Y. D. Mandelbaum, vol. i (Jerusalem, 1979), 67; and I. Ta-Shma, *Keneset meḥkarim*, ii. 163. The scholarly consensus is that the R. Asher who may have composed this work was probably not the famous halakhist R. Asher b. Yeḥiel, and it is possible that the work emanated from northern France rather than from Germany (although like *Moshav zekenim*, it also refers to a number of Spanish writings including Naḥmanides' Torah commentary).

[71] See e.g. *Gen. Rabbah*, 33: 10.

[72] See *Tosafot hashalem*, ed. Gellis, i. 198, §29 (= *Sefer hagan*, ed. Orlian, 137):

בב"ר שנינו כל מי שנא' בו תמים השלים שניו למנין שבע. וק' תניח איוב אברהם ויעקב דכת' בהו תמים מצינו בהו שהשלימו שנותיהן למנין שבע. נח דכת' ביה תמים מאי איכא למימר? והרי לא השלימו שנותיו למניין שבע דמניין שנותיו ט' מאות ונ' פשו להם ה' שנים. וי"ל דאשכחן בהו מניין שבע בשנים שחי אחר המבול דכתיב ויחי נח אחר המבול שלוש מאות וחמישים שנה.

Gellis, ibid., notes that this passage is also found in MS Oxford/Bodleian Opp. Add. 4ᵗᵒ, 127 (above, n. 40), in the name of R. Ahai (?). On *Sefer hagan*'s use of *Genesis Rabbah*, cf. ed. Orlian, 32–3.

and providing clear examples of what the midrashic passage means and how it works, before tackling the more difficult calculation for Noah.

Sefer hagan and *Da'at zekenim* also discuss a neighbouring passage in *Genesis Rabbah*. On the same verse in Genesis about Noah, *Genesis Rabbah* notes that people who are characterized in the Bible by the verb *hayah*, 'was' (as was Noah: *tamim hayah bedorotav*, 'he was perfect in his generations'), witnessed a 'new world', a kind of sea change within the period of their own existence. Noah, as indicated in the Torah, went from a world that was destroyed to a new and better world. Joseph went from being a lowly prisoner to being the viceroy of Egypt, Moses went from fleeing from Pharaoh for his life to seeing Pharaoh drown in the Red Sea, Mordechai went from the possibility of being hanged for disobeying the king to being paraded around on the king's horse, Job went from a state of abject suffering to a life of blessing. Moreover, according to this passage in *Genesis Rabbah*, those who are characterized by the term righteous (*tsadik*) are noteworthy for providing sustenance and support for others. Noah supported his family (and thus the entire world) during the period of the flood, Moses supported the Jewish people during their sojourn in the desert, Job consistently fed the poor, and Mordechai took care of babies (as the Midrash describes, on the basis of Esther 2: 7).[73]

In this second passage, *Genesis Rabbah* itself provides a full roster of named biblical examples, as opposed to the prior piece on divisibility by seven, where it does not. The *Da'at zekenim* text combines both elements of the second passage, asserting that those who are characterized by the verb *hayah* 'saw a new world and supported others'. The names of Noah, Joseph, Moses, and Job are then mentioned, with no discussion. *Da'at zekenim* concludes simply, 'in all of them you will find these two characteristics'. It was perhaps the fuller discussion within *Genesis Rabbah* itself as part of the second passage that caused the compiler of *Da'at zekenim* to treat the terms of *hayah* and *tsadik* so briefly.

The lengthier discussion in *Sefer hagan* on the terms *hayah* and *tsadik* contains no tosafist names or addenda; it simply presents the midrashic text and its examples more fully. Regarding the midrashic passage about *tamim*, however, the tosafist addenda in both *Sefer hagan* and *Da'at zekenim* are fairly significant. Indeed, both of these tosafist compilations may have taken their cue in this matter from the Midrash itself, which did present the various named examples in full in the passage dealing with the terms *hayah* and *tsadik*. Thus, with respect to *tamim*, the compiler of *Da'at zekenim* includes the names and views of the Tosafists (Rizba of Dampierre and Rabbi Solomon of Dreux) who were initially involved in the explanation and expansion of the midrashic passage, while *Sefer hagan* presents its different explanation for the view of *Genesis Rabbah* and adds the names of Jacob and Job to those whose lives were divisible by seven.

---

[73] This passage is found in both of the extant manuscripts of *Sefer hagan*, MS Vienna 28 (see *Sefer hagan*, ed. Orlian, 137), as well as MS Nuremberg 5. See also *Tosafot hashalem*, ed. Gellis, i. 197–8, §27. The piece from *Sefer hagan* cited in the above note, however, is found only in the Vienna manuscript.

From both of the two approaches to calculating Noah's years as a *tamim* put forward by *Sefer hagan* and *Da'at zekenim*, we can appreciate the substantive involvement of northern French Tosafists in the interpretation of passages in *Genesis Rabbah* that are not linked in any obvious ways to talmudic discussions, or to the comments of Rashi on the biblical verses involved. Questions were posed and solutions were offered for the midrashic text itself. The aim of these discussions was to explain and to clarify the text and approach of *Genesis Rabbah*. As with the prior example concerning the limits of a husband's domination, however, these tosafist views and passages also made their way into other venues within the corpus of tosafist Torah commentaries and compilations. As with that example, this strategy allows for suggestive rabbinic principles or issues of interpretation, that are not fixed around or within any single verse or section of the Torah, to be presented and highlighted.

A manuscript version of *Pa'ane'ah raza*, on the phrase 'and Jacob was a mild [*tam*] man' (Gen. 25: 27), cites *Sefer hagan* as linking its own solution to the problem of the *tamim* lifetime of Noah with the name of Rizba,[74] as does *Moshav zekenim* on that verse. Indeed, *Moshav zekenim*, which begins by explicitly quoting the text of *Genesis Rabbah* that *tamim* reflects a type of perfection related to the number seven, invokes the seven weeks of the *omer* period, characterized by the Torah as *temimot* ('perfect' or 'complete', in Lev. 23: 15), as a model for this concept.[75] By moving this discussion away from its original locus in Genesis 6: 9, *Moshav zekenim* and the *Pa'ane'ah raza* variant further highlight the broader appeal of this *derashah*, and position it as a midrashic discussion that can be appreciated irrespective of a particular talmudic *sugya* or passage in Rashi's Torah commentary.[76] Indeed, the larger scholarly discussion about whether a particular midrashic collection typically provides local scriptural exegesis of the verses (or Torah portions) in question, or whether the Midrash conflates the verses and essentially addresses ideological or conceptual issues that emerge from these verses in homiletical form, can be applied to the tosafist Torah compilations as well.[77] The passages from the com-

[74] See MS Oxford/Bodleian Opp. Add. 4to, 103, fo. 31r-v:

ויעקב איש תם. כתיב במדרש כל מקום שנא' בו תמים הולכים שנותיו [בגליון: הולכות שנותיו] לאחר שבוע. ופי' רבינו יצחק בן אברהם כתי' והיה תמים וחי קע"ה שהן שבועיות ויעקב איש תם וחי קמ"ז דהיינו שבועיות. ואיוב איש תם וישר חי ק"מ שנה שהם שבועיות. ואמ' רבי' יצחק ב"ר אברהם דאין למנות עיקר מנין שני נח כי אם מן המבול ואילך דכל מה שנברא קודם שנתבטל. ומשם ואילך חי ש"נ שנים והיינו שבועיות. ג"ן.

Sefer hagan could certainly have cited the northern French Tosafists mentioned in the *Da'at zekenim* passage. As noted in the index to *Sefer hagan*, ed. Orlian, 99–110, R. Isaac b. Abraham is mentioned three times in the Vienna manuscript of *Sefer hagan* (on Gen. 25: 23, Gen. 31: 33, and Lev. 19: 27), and R. Solomon of Dreux is mentioned once (on Lev. 27: 29).

[75] *Moshav zekenim*, ed. Sassoon, 39.

[76] Cf. *Perushei hatorah lerabi hayim palti'el*, ed. Lange, 69–70 (and esp. n. 70), with regard to not counting the two years that Isaac spent in *gan eden* following the Akedah (according to one midrashic approach) as part of his lifespan.

[77] See e.g. A. Geulah, 'Midreshei agadah avudim', 36–41 (and the literature cited in p. 36 n. 251), and 184 n. 1217.

pilations under discussion, like the midrashic passages that they present and expand, do not explain the essential meaning of the word *tamim* (or the terms *hayah* and *tsadik*), nor do they resolve scriptural problems or questions engendered by the use of these words. Rather, they provide a broader framework through which to link the biblical figures to whom this word is applied, and to appreciate these figures in light of the noteworthy characteristics that they shared.

V

To this point, the passages from the tosafist Torah commentaries that we have reviewed contain only the names of northern French Tosafists, even as some of the later collections that have been mentioned (most notably *Perushei rav hayim palti'el*) were compiled by scholars who lived or studied in Germany. Indeed, we have already noticed a particular affinity among French Tosafists for the study and interpretation of *Genesis Rabbah*. Nonetheless, names of German Tosafists and rabbinic figures do appear with some frequency in the so-called tosafist Torah commentaries as well, even in those collections that were compiled or composed within northern France, such as *Da'at zekenim* and *Hadar zekenim*. Indeed, no less a leading German figure than Rabbi Judah Hehasid figures fairly prominently in a number of these collections.[78] It is certainly worthwhile to see how German rabbinic scholars during the period of the Tosafists dealt with issues of aggadic and midrashic interpretation, as they related to the text of the Torah.

Towards the end of the portion of 'Ḥayei sarah', the Torah records that Abraham gave gifts to the children of his concubines, and sent them away from his son Isaac (Gen. 25: 6). Rashi on this verse cites the talmudic interpretation, found in Babylonian Talmud *Sanhedrin* 91a, in the name of Rabbi Yirmiyah bar Abba, that Abraham 'transmitted to them an impure name [*shem tumah*]'. From the exegetical standpoint, Rashi's intention is to explain that the 'gifts' that Abraham gave in this case were not physical ones that had any monetary value, since the previous verse had stated that Abraham gave 'everything that he had' to Isaac. However, the precise metaphysical or occult mechanisms being suggested by the talmudic passage that Rashi cites surely require some clarification.[79] *Ḥizekuni*, citing the talmudic passage directly rather than Rashi, first suggests that Abraham transmitted a divine name that they could make use of even when they were in a state of bodily impurity,

---

[78] See e.g. *Da'at zekenim*, 'Genesis', fos. 4a, 18a, 24a (cf. below, n. 104), 25b, 41b; 'Exodus', fo. 37a (twice); *Hadar zekenim* (Jerusalem, 1963), fos. 11a, 17b, 19b; and cf. Y. Nevo, 'Exegetical Methods of *Hadar zekenim* on the Torah' (Heb.), 23. R. Judah Hehasid is also mentioned in *Pa'ane'ah raza* (cf. above, n. 29); *Moshav zekenim*; *Perushei hatorah lerabi hayim palti'el*, ed. Lange (cf. the editor's introd., 11); and *Tosefot harosh*.

[79] Rashbam and Ibn Ezra on Gen. 25: 6 were apparently unconcerned with this contextual problem. Both of these *pashtanim* understood the word 'gifts' simply, as connoting substantial monetary payments; see also Radak, ad loc.

without suffering any harm.⁸⁰ *Ḥizekuni* also offers a second interpretation, that it would have been highly inappropriate for the totally righteous Abraham to transmit a divine (holy) name of any sort to spiritually wicked people. Rather, he gave them a formula or a name that they could adjure in order to thwart demons, who typically held sway over them.⁸¹ *Ḥizekuni* cites another passage in *Sanhedrin* 65b in order to justify the use of the phrase *shem tumah* in this way, as a demonic adjuration rather than a divine name, and he concludes with a supportive *gematriyah*. The word *matanot* (gifts) in this verse is spelled defectively, without a *vav* at the end. This spelling of the word equals the *gematriyah* equivalent of the Hebrew phrase, *limdem lehasbia hashedim* ('he taught them how to adjure demons').

Ḥizekuni appears to be functioning here as a kind of supercommentary on Rashi (if not as a commentary on the talmudic passage that Rashi had cited), a role that this commentary often plays, as Sara Japhet has noted.⁸² In fact, however, and again in accordance with Japhet's suggestions about the compilatory nature of *Ḥizekuni*, the various interpretations presented by *Ḥizekuni* on this verse reflect an earlier series of comments and discussions by both German and northern French rabbinic figures and Tosafists, and may well include passages from both *Da'at zekenim* and *Hadar zekenim*.

The first Ashkenazi figure following Rashi to discuss the talmudic assertion in *Sanhedrin* 91a about the *shem tumah* is Rabbi Judah Hehasid. In the relatively simple Torah commentary that he transmitted to his son Rabbi Moses Zal(t)man,⁸³ Rabbi Judah cites and explains the talmudic interpretation along the lines of the first

---

⁸⁰ Generally speaking, the adjuration of divine names for personal and other magical purposes requires the operator to be in a state of ritual purity. See e.g. Michael Swartz, *Scholastic Magic* (Princeton, NJ, 1996), 157–72; and Peter Schafer, *The Hidden and Manifest God* (Albany, NY, 1992), 89–91, 113–17.

⁸¹ In Rashi's commentary on *San.* 91a, s.v. *shem tumah*, this name is interpreted as *kishuf uma'aseh shedim* (sorcery and the conjuring of demons). Although there is a degree of ambiguity here as well, it would seem that Rashi means to suggest that Abraham gave them a method either to neutralize these forces, or to marshal them to do their will. Cf. Reuven Margoliot, *Margaliyot hayam al masekhet sanhedrin* (Jerusalem, 1977), 136, §18. On Rashi's familiarity with magical and occult practices and rites, see Kanarfogel, 'Rashi's Awareness of Jewish Mystical Literature and Tradition', in D. Krochmalnik et al. (eds.), *Raschi und Sein Erbe* (Heidelberg, 2007), 23–34. On the attribution to Rashi of the commentary on *Perek ḥelek* found in the standard editions of the Babylonian Talmud, see Yonah Fraenkel, *Rashi's Methods in his Commentary on the Talmud* [Darko shel rashi beferusho latalmud] (Jerusalem, 1980), 304–8, and Shamma Friedman, 'Rashi's Commentary on the Talmud, Corrections and Recensions' (Heb.), in Zvi Arie Steinfeld (ed.), *Rashi: Investigations into his Literary Corpus* [Rashi: iyunim biyetsirato] (Ramat Gan, 1993), 164–6.

⁸² See Japhet, 'Ḥizekuni's Commentary' (Heb.), 108–10. Chavel, in his edition of *Perushei rashi al hatorah* (p. 91 n. 102), notes that this comment is not found in the first edition of Rashi's Torah commentary. There are, however, a number of tosafist Torah commentaries and compilations that do ascribe this comment to Rashi. See e.g. *Moshav zekenim*, ed. Sassoon, 35, and *Tosafot hashalem*, ed. Gellis, ii. 289–90, §§7, 11.

⁸³ See Ivan Marcus, 'Exegesis for the Few and for the Many', *Jerusalem Studies in Jewish Thought*, 8 (1989), 7–8; Gershon Brin, 'Underlying Principles in the Torah Commentary of R. Judah the Pious' (Heb.), *Te'udah*, 3 (1983), 215–16; and *Perushei hatorah lerabi yehudah heḥasid*, ed. Lange (above, n. 25).

approach found in *Ḥizekuni*. According to Rabbi Judah, Abraham gave the children of his concubines a divine name that could be uttered even by those who were impure, in opposition to the many divine names that required great purity and cleanliness, which could only be used by the Jewish people. Rabbi Moses notes that his father then set out to explain what compelled Abraham to do this. Rabbi Judah suggests that since Abraham was sending these progeny away from Isaac, thereby depriving them of Isaac's spiritual companionship and guidance, he was concerned lest they encounter committed idolaters, who would use their idolatry in order to divine the future. If that effort was successful, these progeny would then become idolaters themselves, in order to continue to be able to learn about their future. To counteract this possibility, Abraham presented them with a divine name that would allow them to have an awareness of the future on their own, so that they would not need to seek out this information from idolaters.[84] Rabbi Judah's approach is also followed in some versions of the Torah commentary of his associate, Rabbi Ephraim ben Samson.[85]

In commenting on this verse, *Da'at zekenim* does not cite Rabbi Judah Hehasid by name.[86] It does begin, however, with Rabbi Judah's interpretation, that Abraham's progeny would be able to use a divine name, characterized by *Da'at zekenim* as the Tetragrammaton, the *shem hameforash*, even in a state of impurity without being harmed (which is the first interpretation in *Ḥizekuni*), adding that there are some Muslims presently who are proficient in using this name, which they invoke even in a state of impurity. *Da'at zekenim* then continues with the question raised by Rabbi Judah as to what caused the righteous Abraham to do such a thing —again the order followed by *Ḥizekuni*—attributing this question, however, to 'Rabbi Moses'. This is perhaps a reference to Rabbi Moses Zal(t)man, the son of Rabbi Judah, who had reported his father's question and response. The answer recorded in *Da'at zekenim*, however, is presented in the name of a German rabbinic figure who flourished in the second half of the thirteenth century, Rabbi Jacob ben Nahman, and is different from the answer given by Rabbi Moses in the name of Rabbi Judah. It is also the second answer listed by *Ḥizekuni*, that the name that Abraham gave these progeny was actually a name associated with demons, which could neutralize their effect. *Da'at zekenim* also refers to a book of sorcery, *Sefer*

---

[84] See ibid. 35. In this instance, the passage appears in two of the best manuscript sources for R. Judah's comments, MS Moscow 82 and MS Cambridge 669.2 (above, n. 25). R. Judah's comment is introduced by R. Judah's son, leaving little doubt that it is authentic. Although R. Judah Hehasid's subject here is the talmudic passage, his Torah commentary contains quite a bit of *peshat* and he often seeks to explain Rashi, whether Rashi's name is mentioned explicitly or not. See e.g. ibid. 214–15; Marcus, 'Exegesis for the Few and for the Many', 1–24; and Kanarfogel, *The Intellectual History of Medieval Ashkenazic Jewry*, ch. 3.

[85] See *Tosafot hashalem*, ed. Gellis, ii. 290, §11. The standard edition of *Perush rabenu efrayim al hatorah*, ed. J. Klugmann (Jerusalem, 2000), 80, notes that the *gematriyah* of *asher le'avraham* (in the phrase *velivnei hapilgashim asher le'avraham*) equals *shem tumah masar lahem*. See also Kasher, *Torah shelemah*, vol. iv (Jerusalem, 1934), 995–6.

[86] Cf. above, n. 78.

bilad,⁸⁷ explains how this kind of adjuration comports with the designation as a *shem tumah*, and presents the *gematriyah* derivation which supports this approach. The passage in the published version of *Da'at zekenim* also has a concluding attribution to 'Rabbi Moses'.⁸⁸ Understanding this as a reference to Rabbi Moses, son of Rabbi Judah Hehasid, is somewhat difficult, however, since the last answer was not part of the interpretation originally suggested by Rabbi Judah, at least as attested to by the commentary properly attributed to him. Indeed, at least two manuscript versions of the passage in *Da'at zekenim* omit any reference to Rabbi Moses in this passage.⁸⁹

It should be noted that the late thirteenth-century tosafist Torah compilation *Pa'aneaḥ raza* (also compiled in northern France) interprets Rashi to mean that Abraham gave the children of the concubines a divine name that they could use even in a state of impurity, in order to cause them to leave the idolatrous objects (*haterafim*) that had already been telling them the future, in line with the suggestion by Rabbi Judah Hehasid. This passage in *Pa'aneaḥ raza*, which presents both the question and the answer of Rabbi Judah, is attributed, however, to Rabbi Moses, ostensibly Rabbi Judah's son.⁹⁰ The published edition of *Pa'aneaḥ raza* contains a number of comments that are attributed to a Rabbi Moses, although it is often unclear to whom these references are intended. Indeed, they may well refer to a rabbinic

---

⁸⁷ The text in MS Moscow 268, fo. 80ʳ, reads ספר בוליאדר. Both these variants perhaps refer to the collection of magical recipes grouped under the term *baladur* (which is referred to in medieval Ashkenaz by *Sifrut devei rashi*). See Joshua Trachtenberg, *Jewish Magic and Superstition* (New York, 1939), 191–2, and cf. Gershom Scholem, *Demons, Spirits, and Souls* [Shedim, ruḥot uneshamot], ed. E. Liebes (Jerusalem, 2004), 9–53.

⁸⁸ *Rabotenu ba'alei hatosafot*, 'Genesis', fo. 23*b*:

נתן אברהם מתנות. אמרו בפ' חלק שמות בטומאה מסר להם פי' שיהו יכולין להזכיר שם המפורש בטומאת הגוף ולא יזיק להם. וגם היום יש ישמעאלים שבקיאין בשם ומזכירין אותו בטומאה. וקשה לה"ר משה היאך אדם חשוב וצדיק כאברהם ילמד השם לרשעים. לכן פי' ה"ר יעקב בה"ר נחמן שם טומאה שם השדים שמשביעין אותן ואדוניהם הממונים עליהם לעשות כל מה שרוצים כמו ספר בילא"ד. ושם טומאה נקרא על שם רוח הטומאה כדאמרי' במס' חגיגה הלן בבית הקברות כדי שתשרה עליו רוח טומאה רמז לזה שהרי מתנות כתי' חסר וא"ו והוא עולה בגימטריא למדם להשביע השדים. מה"ר משה.

Cf. MS Moscow 268, fos. 79ᵛ–80ʳ.

⁸⁹ See MS Jewish Theological Seminary 791, fo. 20ᵛ:

נתן אברהם מתנות. פ"ה שם בטומאה מסר להם. ד"א שיכולים להזכיר שם המפורש בטומאת הגוף ויועיל להם. ואם ישראל מזכיר, לא יועיל ומזיק לו. וק' וכי צדיק כאברהם למד שם המפורש לרשעים להזכיר בטומאה? לכ"פ ה"ר יעקב ב"ר נחמן שם בטומאה זהו שם שדים שמשביעים אותם ואדוניהם הממונים עליהם לעשות להם רצונם ונקרא שם טומאה על שם רוח הטומאה כדאיתא בחגיגה הלן בבית הקברות כדי שתשרה עליו רוח טומאה.

This manuscript also does not contain the supporting *gematriyah* found at the end of the standard *Da'at zekenim* passage. Cf. below, n. 102. MS Leiden 27, fo. 16ᵛ, retains R. Jacob b. Nahman's name without any reference to R. Moses, and also includes the *gematriyah* of *matanot* without the letter *vav*, but adduces this *gematriyah* in support of Rashi's interpretation (*veteda perush hakuntres dehakhi perusho sheharei matanot ḥaser vav*).

⁹⁰ See *Pa'aneaḥ raza*, 120. See also *Moshav zekenim*, ed. Sassoon, 35, and cf. *Perushei hatorah lerabi ḥayim palti'el*, ed. Lange, 64 (with no names other than Rashi).

scholar from the late thirteenth century named Rabbi Moses.[91] There is, however, at least one other occasion on which *Pa'ane'aḥ raza* mentions the names of Rabbi Judah Hehasid and Rabbi Moses together, where the intended reference is to a comment of Rabbi Judah that had been put forward by his son Rabbi Moses.[92]

This discussion is found in even greater detail, with additional names and observations, and some new points that require clarification, in the tosafist collection *Hadar zekenim*. One of the additional observations is that the name which Abraham gave to his progeny, which could be effective and would not cause them any harm if they used it in their state of impurity, would not work, on the other hand, if a Jew tried to use it. Moreover, such use would cause harm to the Jewish operator. The unattributed question as to why Abraham would do this is then raised, and the answer of Rabbi Jacob ben Nahman is given in full, along with his name, together with the connotation of *shem tumah* as being used for adjuring demons and the *gematriyah* support for this approach. As was the case in *Da'at zekenim*, this passage concludes with the initials מהר״ם, most likely a formalized reference to Rabbi Moses rather than a reference to the better-known Maharam of Rothenburg. An additional interpretation of *shem tumah* is then presented in the name of an otherwise unknown Rabbi Jacob of Monteux.[93] In response to the question of how Abraham could give the power of divine names to his impure progeny, Rabbi Jacob suggests that in fact what Abraham taught them was not a divine or demonic name that could be used in

---

[91] Thus, for example, the name R. Hayim, which is also mentioned in *Pa'ane'aḥ raza* with some frequency, refers in fact to R. Hayim Paltiel. See *Perushei hatorah lerabi ḥayim palti'el*, ed. Lange, editor's introd., 11, and J. Rochwarger, 'Sefer Pa'aneah Raza and Biblical Exegesis in Medieval Ashkenaz', 52–5.

[92] See *Pa'ane'aḥ raza*, 274 (on Exod. 21: 3), where the names רי״ח [=ר' יהודה החסיד] and מה״ר משה appear after this passage. See also *Moshav zekenim*, ed. Sassoon, 35, and cf. *Perushei hatorah lerabi ḥayim palti'el*, ed. Lange, 104. Lange (ibid., n. 11) suggests that the *Pa'ane'aḥ raza* passage means to suggest that the interpretation of R. Judah Hehasid was transmitted by R. Moses of Coucy, but there is no such indication here (and the reference to R. Moses Zaltman is, in any case, much more plausible). In the case at hand, the published version of *Da'at zekenim* appears to be a later version of the *Pa'ane'aḥ raza* passage. It omits the name of R. Judah Hehasid, includes the name of R. Jacob b. Nahman, and concludes with the name of R. Moses (although some related manuscripts are different in this regard, as noted above, n. 88). This pattern is then followed by *Hadar zekenim* (below, n. 94). Cf. Mordechai Friedman, *Studies and Research on Rashi's Commentary* [Sefer pores mapah: meḥkarim ve'iyunim beferush rashi] (Brooklyn, 1997), 205–17.

[93] This Hebrew form for Monteux is found in Henri Gross, *Gallia Judaica* (Paris, 1897), 321. R. Judah b. Eliezer, *Minḥat yehudah* on Gen. 25: 6 record (הר״ר יעקב) ממונטי״ל, the more common Hebrew spelling of Monteux (Gross, *Gallia Judaica*, 320–1). Other variations of these spellings are found in MS Vatican Ebr. 48 and MS British Library Add. 22,092 (see below, n. 94). ר' יעקב הגזבר ממוט׳רוייל is mentioned in an earlier passage in *Hadar zekenim* (fo. 7b), on Abraham's request to the Almighty that perhaps ten righteous people could be found in Sodom. On the basis of manuscript references, the name is found in *Tosafot hashalem*, ed. Gellis, ii. 148, as ה״ר יעקב ממונטרוייל הגזבר מנצר הגרני. In that instance, R. Jacob is responding to an explicit critique of Rashi's interpretation. Cf. Norman Golb, *The Jews in Medieval Normandy* (Cambridge, 1997), 45, 52, and I. Ta-Shma, *Keneset meḥkarim*, i. 290–2, for a Solomon b. Isaac of Monteux (מונטייל), in connection with the Ashkenazi commentary on the book of Chronicles found in MS Munich (Bavarian National Library) 5.

a state of impurity or in various impure demonic venues. Rather, perhaps as a final gesture towards ensuring their acceptance of monotheism, Abraham taught them to refer to their idolatrous gods in derisive or demeaning terms (literally, to give them impure names). Up to this point, they had been referring to these deities using the name of God.[94]

Like Rabbi Judah Hehasid and his son Rabbi Moses, Rabbi Jacob ben Nahman of Magdeburg, who suggests in these texts that the name given by Abraham was used to mobilize demons (rather than being a divine name), was a German rabbinic scholar, albeit a lesser-known figure. He flourished during the mid-thirteenth century, and is cited with some frequency in a collection of customs that was composed by the Tosafist Rabbi Hezekiah ben Jacob of Magdeburg (and also in a manual by Rabbi Moses Fuller, an eastern European halakhist, dealing with issues of ritual slaughter and inspection), although it does not seem that Rabbi Jacob ben Nahman of Magdeburg was Rabbi Hezekiah's father.[95] Rabbi Jacob of Monteux, who suggested that the names given by Abraham were meant to name their idolatry, so that they would not use God's name for this any longer, is virtually unknown. It appears that this Rabbi Jacob, and perhaps Rabbi Jacob of Magdeburg as well, were part of the secondary rabbinic elite during the thirteenth century, who did not participate in or engage with the core group of Tosafists in the development and formulation of tosafist talmudic interpretations and analysis, but who certainly admired the tosafist oeuvre.[96]

---

[94] *Hadar zekenim*, fos. 9b–10a:

פי' שיכולים להזכיר שם המפורש בטומאת הגוף ומועיל להם ולא יזיק אותם. ואם ישראל מזכירו בטומאה לא יועיל לו ויזיק אותו. וקשה וכי צדיק כאברהם למד שם המפורש לרשעים להזכירו בטומאה. לכך פי' ה"ר יעקב בן ה"ר נחמן שם טומאה כמו שם השדים שמשביעים באדוניהם הממונים עליהם לעשות רצונם ונקרא שם טומאה על שם רוח הטומאה כדאיתא בחגיגה וכו'. ותדע דה"פ שהרי מתנת חסד ועולה בגי' מת"ת הם להשב"ע אד"ם לשדי"ם יאמר לאדם להשביע לשדים. מהר"ם. וה"ר יעקב ממוט'רוייל אומר שם טומאה כלו' למדם לקרות לע"ז שלהם שם מטומאה כמו פעור ומרקוליס שנקראו ע"ש שמטמאין אותם. ומתחלה היו קוראים אותם בשם הקב"ה כדכתיב או הוחל לקרא בשם ה'.

See also MS Vatican 48, fo. 15ʳ; MS Moscow National Library (Guenzberg) 898 (*Ḥidushei tsarefat*), fo. 16ᵛ; and MS British Library Add. 22,092, fo. 19ᵛ. This is also found in later published tosafist collections as well, such as the early 14th-cent. *Minḥat yehudah lerabi yehudah b. eli'ezer* (Riba), 'Genesis', fo. 23b:

יש פירושים כתוב בהם שם טומאה מסר להם. וה"ר יעקב ממונטי"ל פי' שם טומאה זהו שלמדם לקרות שם טומאה לע"ז שלהם כמו פעור ומרקוליס ע"ש שמטמאין אותו וכו'. Both MS Florence/Laurenziana, Plut. II. 20, fo. 159ʳ, and *Moshav zekenim*, ed. Sassoon, 35, reproduce R. Jacob of Monteux's piece briefly, in the abbreviated name of Ri. Cf. *Tosafot hashalem*, ed. Gellis, ii. 289–90, §7.

[95] See S. Emanuel, *Shivrei luḥot*, 223–7. (The passage by R. Jacob b. Nahman referred to ibid. 224 n. 26, as found in *R. Israel Bruna's Glosses on the Tur Commentary on the Torah* [Sefer gilyon rabenu yisra'el mibruna leferush hatur al hatorah], ed. S. Englander (Lakewood, NJ, 2001), 20–1, is R. Jacob's comment on Gen. 25: 6.) R. Hezekiah of Magdeburg's collection of customs was used by R. Hayim Paltiel in formulating his similar collection; cf. above, n. 43. On the much better-known R. Hezekiah, see Urbach, *The Tosafists* (Heb.), ii. 561–5; Emanuel, *Shivrei luḥot*, 219–22; and Kanarfogel, 'The Appointment of *Ḥazzanim* in Medieval Ashkenaz: Communal Policy and Individual Religious Prerogatives', in B. Huss and H. Kreisel (eds.), *Spiritual Authority: Struggles Over Cultural Power in Jewish Thought* (Be'er Sheva, 2009), 7–20.

[96] See Kanarfogel, 'Between the Tosafist Academies and Other Study Halls'.

There are a number of such names recorded in the so-called tosafist Torah commentaries and, as we have noted, most of the compilers of these commentaries fall into the same category. It is possible to suggest that members of the secondary elite engaged in the compilation of the tosafist Torah commentaries as a means of providing a lay audience with selections of authentic tosafist material (on both biblical and talmudic texts, organized according to the order of the Torah portions), together with their own addenda and comments on this tosafist material. By the second half of the thirteenth century, the tosafist oeuvre was largely complete, but it was the product of small groups of elite scholars who interacted almost exclusively with each other.[97] The tosafist Torah commentaries opened this corpus to a wider audience during the middle of the thirteenth and the early fourteenth centuries, by providing a digest of tosafist materials and allowing its compilers and other participants to contribute their own insights and clarifications.

In any case, the lesser-known German and northern French rabbinic figures involved in this instance put forward a more miraculous (or supernatural) approach towards understanding what Abraham gave his progeny. Indeed, the interpretation of Rabbi Jacob of Monteux was perhaps suggested to modify this new direction. Interestingly, Nahmanides (Rabbi Moses ben Nahman, 1194–1270), whose mystical background and familiarity with the uses of divine names is well attested, does not pick up on this aspect at all. As noted, the *pashtanim* Rashbam and Rabbi Abraham ibn Ezra (1089–1164), among others, interpreted Abraham's gifts in a more literal and simple sense, as a form of compensation. Although the tosafist Torah commentaries begin here, as they often do, with a comment of Rashi (and its underlying talmudic origin), and Rashi's own awareness of the powers of divine names is clearly attested,[98] it was the comment of Rabbi Judah Hehasid and his approach that were adopted by the subsequent, lesser rabbinic figures in both France and Germany, and this is what becomes central within the tosafist commentaries here. As opposed to the rationalistic tendency of northern French *pashtanim* such as Rabbi Joseph Kara, and the Tosafists Rashbam and Rabbi Joseph Bekhor Shor, who try to minimize (even as compared to Rashi) the miraculous or supernatural nature of even those biblical events and phenomena that genuinely appeared to have such a dimension,[99] the tosafist Torah compilations typically

---

[97] On the small size of the tosafist study halls, see Kanarfogel, *Jewish Education and Society*, 65–8.

[98] See above, n. 81, and cf. M. Lockshin, *Rabbi Samuel ben Meir's Commentary on Genesis*, 128, who suggests that Rashbam's comment here is directed against Rashi's comment, which invokes the notions of sorcery and witchcraft.

[99] See e.g. S. Poznanski, *Introduction to Northern French Biblical Commentators* (Heb.), p. lxvii; *Perushei r. yosef bekhor shor al hatorah*, ed. Y. Nevo, editor's introd., 15; Grossman, *Early Sages of France*, 318–20; Berger, 'The Torah Commentary of Rabbi Samuel ben Meir', 162–4; *Rabbi Samuel ben Meir's Commentary on Genesis*, ed. Lockshin, 155 n. 5; Moshe Sokolow, *Studies in the Weekly Parashah Based on the Lessons of Nehama Leibowitz* (Jerusalem, 2008), 48–9; Judith Kogel, 'L'Utilisation du midrash dans le'exégèse de la France du nord de Rashi aux recueils des Tossafistes', in Gilbert Dahan (ed.), *Les Brûlement du Talmud à Paris* (Paris, 1999), 145–50, 156.

move in the other direction. This approach may be another indication of the more popular dimension and the intended audience of their work.

VI

At the beginning of the Torah portion 'Toledot' (Gen. 25: 20), Rashi, following *Seder olam* (traditionally attributed to the *tana* Rabbi Yose bar Halafta), notes that Rebecca was 3 when she married Isaac, who, according to this verse, was 40 at the time. In almost identical passages, *Da'at zekenim* and *Hadar zekenim* question Rashi's comment, on the basis of a passage in *Sifrei Deuteronomy* (towards the end of 'Vezot haberakhah'), according to which Rebecca and Kehat were among those pairs of biblical figures who shared the same lifespan, in their case 133 years.[100] Based on calculations and reckonings of the milestones of her life, these tosafist compilations point out that if Rebecca was married at the age of 3, her life would have ended at the age of 122. The suggestion is therefore made that Rebecca was in fact 14 at the time that she married Isaac, thus restoring the missing eleven years to her lifespan. Indeed, both compilations also point to a better, or corrected, reading in the text of the *Seder olam* (*hakhi garsinan/hakhi ita*), that in fact records this age as the year of Rebecca's marriage, and *Da'at zekenim* also cites this as an assertion (*vekhen amar*) in the name of an otherwise unidentified Rabbi Judah. Both these tosafist Torah compilations also note that the passage in *Seder olam*, which indicates that Abraham received news of the birth of Rebecca upon his return from the binding of Isaac, should be understood to mean that Abraham was made aware at that point that Rebecca had been born ten or eleven years earlier and was by now at an optimal age for marriage, rather than as an indication that Rebecca was literally born at that time.[101]

Another problem with Rashi's claim that Rebecca was 3, raised by both compilations, emerges from the Mishnah and talmudic discussion in Babylonian Talmud

---

[100] *Sifrei Deuteronomy*, 'Vezot haberakhah', §7 (*Sifre on Deuteronomy*, ed. Louis Finkelstein (New York, 1969), 429), and see also *Gen. Rabbah* 100: 10. *Sifrei* notes that Moses was one of four great sages who lived for 120 years (the others being Hillel, Raban Yohanan b. Zakkai, and R. Akiva), and also that there were six pairs of biblical and rabbinic figures who shared the same lifespan, Rebecca and Kehat, Levi and Amram, Joseph and Joshua, Samuel and Solomon, Moses and Hillel, and Raban Yohanan b. Zakkai and R. Akiva. *Sifrei* itself does not specify the ages of each pair (except for the last two, which were mentioned earlier in this section), but the numbers were derived by later rabbinic scholars on the basis of both biblical and midrashic texts. There are also some medieval textual variants on this passage. Indeed, texts of *Da'at zekenim*, as well as *Ḥizekuni*, include a third member, Ben Azzai, together with the pair of Rebecca and Kehat, who all lived for 133 years. See *Tosafot hashalem*, ed. Gellis, iv. 5, §3, found also in MS Florence/Laurenziana Plut. II. 20, fos. 159–160ʳ. Cf. MS Jewish Theological Seminary (Lutzki) 794, fo. 2ᵛ.

[101] Once again, *Ḥizekuni* follows a very similar pattern of questions and responses to those found in *Hadar zekenim* and *Da'at zekenim*, and concludes by suggesting that there was a reading in the *Seder olam* (*vekhen garsinan*) that Abraham was informed after the Akedah that Rebecca had been born eleven years before this event.

Ketubot (57a–b). The *sugya* there uses what was said about Rebecca by her family, 'let the young girl [*na'arah*] remain with us for ten or twelve months' (Gen. 24: 55), to derive the mishnaic ruling that a *na'arah* (defined as being between the ages of 12 and 12 and a half) is given a full year to remain with her family in order to make her preparations following *kidushin* (betrothal), after which she is required to come forward and enter into *nisuin* (marriage), while a *bogeret* (who is past the age of 12 and a half) is given only three months of preparation before she must accept *nisuin*. According to the view put forward by *Da'at zekenim* and *Hadar zekenim*, however, Rebecca was not herself a *na'arah* (or a pre-*na'arah*) but rather a *bogeret*, since she was 14. *Da'at zekenim* presents this question in the name of the otherwise unknown Rabbi Moses Solomon bar Abraham, 'known as Ansiman',[102] but leaves it unresolved. *Hadar zekenim* omits this name, but provides an answer; these differences perhaps serve to confirm that *Hadar zekenim* is the later of the two roughly contemporary compilations. The allowance of a year for a *na'arah* to prepare may still be derived from Rebecca, since her family referred to her as a *na'arah*. Even though Rebecca was 14, her family believed that there was no difference between the time to be given to a 12-year-old and the time to be given to a 14-year-old; both were to be given a full year. Rebecca's response according to the text of the Torah, that she was prepared to return to Isaac's homeland immediately, was her response to this technical issue as well, in terms of how it applied to her. There was, in fact, a difference between a *na'arah* (which she was not) and a *bogeret* (which she was), and she therefore replied that she would leave immediately, since she did not have such a long period to remain with her family in order to complete her preparations prior to *nisuin*.[103]

There is a lengthy tosafist literary history behind all of these various comments and nuances. Before proceeding to trace that history, however, it is important to note that the subsequent comments in this instance may have been triggered by Rashi's comment about Rebecca's age, on the verse about Isaac's age at marriage. For Rashi as well, this was not so much of a local exegetical problem in this verse as much as an appreciation of the larger picture within the biblical narrative, both at this point and in future scenes. In the hands of the Tosafists, as the comments of *Da'at zekenim* and *Hadar zekenim* suggest and as we shall soon see, the discussion is broadened even further to include not only the rectification of rabbinic texts that had already been included in this discussion, such as *Seder olam*, but a number of other talmudic and rabbinic texts as well, whose connections are somewhat less direct. I thus cannot rule out the possibility that the discussion here emerged

---

[102] אנסימאן; cf. *Da'at zekenim* on Gen. 9: 6 (fo. 9a), for a passage with respect to an episode of martyrdom that records an observation of the otherwise unknown מהר״ש בר אברהם המכונה אוכמן. On this passage, see Kanarfogel, 'Halakhah and Metziut (Realia) in Medieval Ashkenaz: Surveying the Parameters and Defining the Limits', *Jewish Law Annual*, 14 (2003), 205 n. 38, and 213 n. 59. See also the reference to a R. Zussmann (along with R. Isaac Fuller) in MS British Library Or. 9931, fo. 123ᵛ, and cf. above, n. 93.

[103] See *Da'at zekenim*, 'Genesis', fo. 24a (and cf. *Tosafot hashalem*, ed. Gellis, vol. iii (Jerusalem, 1984), 5, §3), and *Hadar zekenim*, fo. 10a.

initially from the context of talmudic or rabbinic texts, even as Rashi's biblical comment continues to hover over this discussion.

The earliest tosafist source to deal with this issue appears to be the Torah commentary (noted above) that has been associated with Rabbenu Tam's study hall. The discussion there begins with the observation found in *Seder olam*, that Abraham learned on his return from the binding of Isaac that Rebecca had been born, and waited three years (until she would be at least physically marriageable) to have Isaac marry her. This reading of *Seder olam* is then questioned, on the basis of a talmudic passage in Babylonian Talmud *Yevamot* 61b. The Talmud there connects the halakhic status of a *betulah* (virgin) with that of a *na'arah* (i.e. a *betulah* is presumed to be at least 12 years old), on the basis of a verse that describes Rebecca (Gen. 24: 16), 'the young woman [*na'arah*] was very beautiful, and she was a virgin [*betulah*]'. Accordingly Rebecca must have been substantially more than 3 when her marriage was being arranged. In order to solve this problem, the Torah commentary attributed to Rabbenu Tam's study hall then moves to suggest, on the basis of the passage in *Sifrei Deuteronomy* (that Rebecca and Kehat both lived for 133 years), that Rebecca was actually 14 when she was married (the chronology of her life is then fully calculated, in order to show how this determination squares with all of the other numbers), and the text of *Seder olam* should be, or was, emended accordingly.[104]

Moreover, this approach is confirmed on the basis of another talmudic passage in *Yevamot* 64a, which discusses the amount of time that a man should wait for his barren wife to give birth. Although the ten-year model, based on the lives of Abraham and Sarah, is the one which the Talmud favours, a twenty-year model based on the lives of Isaac and Rebecca is also discussed by the Talmud. Isaac was married at 40, and Rebecca gave birth to their twins when Isaac was 60. This model, however, does not make sense if Isaac married Rebecca when she was 3 (and he was 40), since a woman is not expected to be able to have a child until she is at least 12. Isaac would thus not have been waiting for her to give birth for twenty years, but only for a bit more than ten. If, however, Rebecca was 14 when they married, the model of a twenty-year waiting period is securely based.[105]

---

[104] Both *Da'at zekenim* and *Hadar zekenim* arrive at the fact that Jacob received the blessings from Isaac at the age of 63 by referring to Rashi on the Torah portion 'Toledot' (Gen. 28: 9), who develops this calculation at length. The present tosafist passage arrives at its numbers in a different way, based in part on a *sugya* in tractate *Megilah* (17a), to which Rashi on 'Toledot' also refers, as does Rashi on Gen. 25: 17. Indeed, the various northern French and German rabbinic figures arrived at their specific calculations in different ways; cf. *Ḥizekuni* on Gen. 25: 20. On the age of Rebecca at the time of her marriage (and her age at the Akedah) according to *Seder olam* and its variants, see C. J. Milikowsky, 'Seder 'Olam: A Rabbinic Chronography', Ph.D. diss., Yale University, 1981, 21. Ibn Ezra (on Gen. 22: 4) famously suggests (from a rationalistic perspective, *miderekh sevara*) that Isaac was around the age of 13 at the time of his binding (acknowledging that *Seder olam* places his age at 37). Although Ibn Ezra expresses other considerations, and notes that some suggested that Isaac was only 5 years old, one wonders whether the fact that Isaac is referred to in this episode as a *na'ar* ('a youth'; Gen. 22: 5) played a role in the development of these different views.

[105] See MS Paris 167, fos. 55ʳ⁻ᵛ (cited in *Tosafot hashalem*, ed. Gellis, iii. 6, §4), and the parallel MS Moscow 362, fo. 128ʳ⁻ᵛ. In the Paris manuscript, the emendation of the *Seder olam* text is not clearly

Much of the material produced in these *Da'at zekenim* and *Hadar zekenim* passages can be found in this commentary associated with the students or study hall of Rabbenu Tam, but there are other, earlier, Ashkenazi texts that must also be considered as contributing sources to the later tosafist Torah compilations. As noted, the *Da'at zekenim* passage refers to a Rabbi Judah, who explicitly states that Rebecca was 14 years old. In both the Moscow and Cambridge manuscripts of Rabbi Judah Hehasid's comments on the Torah,[106] at the end of 'Ḥayei Sarah' (Gen. 25: 17), the commentary introduces a passage very similar to *Sifrei Deuteronomy*, stating that Ishmael, Levi, and Amram lived 137 years, followed by Rebecca and Kehat, who lived 133 years. This passage arrives at the calculation that Rebecca was 14 when she was married, based on her lifespan and the lives of Jacob and Ishmael, although the details and focus differ slightly from those of the texts just analysed, and there are no explicit references to *Sifrei Deuteronomy*, *Genesis Rabbah*, or any of the talmudic *sugyot* noted thus far.[107]

Nonetheless, the material in Rabbi Judah Hehasid's Torah commentary shares common ground and even a degree of connection with the Tosafot passage on *Yevamot*, on the *sugya* which suggests that Rebecca herself was a 12-year-old *na'arah* and not a younger girl. The standard Tosafot there begin by citing *Seder olam*'s claim that Rebecca was 3, and then present the view of Rabbi Samuel Hehasid of Speyer (b. 1115), the father of Rabbi Judah Hehasid and a contemporary of Rabbenu Tam, that Rebecca was in fact 14. Rabbi Samuel bases his view on the list of the ages of various biblical couples in *Sifrei Deuteronomy* and the full accounting of Rebecca's life that flows from there, which shows that this approach was pursued in both northern France and Germany at this time, as Rabbi Judah's own comments indicate. As with the position noted above in connection with Tosafot on *Bava metsia* 86a, on the issue of whether the angels who appeared to Abraham actually ate, the standard Tosafot conclude that there are conflicting midrashic approaches at work here, and that the talmudic passage at hand and the seemingly contradictory *Seder olam* represent these two distinct and different midrashic traditions.[108] Not surprisingly, this was also the response of the standard Tosafot later in *Yevamot*,

---

indicated, since there appears to be a word missing: *vetsarikh [lomar]*. The suggested emendation is made quite clear, however, in the Moscow manuscript version. It is interesting to note that Rashbam includes here the idea that Rebecca was barren for twenty years. Rashbam apparently wants to show support for the twenty-year period found in the Talmud, especially since Rashi supported the ten-year period. See *Rabbi Samuel ben Meir's Commentary on Genesis*, ed. Lockshin, 130–1. Clearly, the nexus between *peshat* and talmudics in Rashbam's commentary on the Torah is not completely severed.

[106] MSS Moscow 82 and Cambridge 669.2 are two of the three best manuscripts in this regard, although neither contains the direct *reportatio* of R. Moses Zalman in this instance.

[107] See *Perushei hatorah lerabi yehudah heḥasid*, 35–6 (and cf. esp. n. 69). See also *Perush haroke'aḥ al hatorah*, ed. Klugmann, i. 177–8 (on the end of the Torah portion 'Vayera'), and *Perushei hatorah lerabi ḥayim palti'el*, ed. Lange, 66–7.

[108] See Tosafot on *Yev*. 61b, s.v. *vekhen*. The standard Tosafot also cite R. Judah Hehasid by name. See Tosafot on *BM* 5b, s.v. *veḥashid*, and Tosafot on *Ket*. 18b, s.v. *vekhule*. Cf. Urbach, *The Tosafists* (Heb.), i.

regarding the question of how Isaac could have waited twenty years for Rebecca to have a child (without divorcing her, according to the talmudic discussion at that point) if she had been married at the age of 3, since she would not have been expected to be able to do so for the first ten years or so after marriage. Tosafot suggests that this too is the result of conflicting midrashic traditions, or that perhaps women were capable of bearing children at a much younger age in antiquity.[109]

Variant Tosafot texts maintain, however, that the correct text of the *Seder olam* reads 13, and they cite Rabbi Samuel Hehasid as suggesting that 14 is even more accurate, or claim that Rabbi Samuel Hehasid himself emended the *Seder olam* text to read 14.[110] It should also be noted that Rabbi Isaiah di Trani, whose Ashkenazi training has been noted, begins his comment on Genesis 25: 20 with Rashi's comment, and then poses the same kind of talmudic questions found in the various Tosafot texts, albeit in a somewhat different order, to demonstrate that Rebecca was 14 when she was married. Moreover, Rabbi Isaiah takes issue with several of Rashi's exegetical details as they relate to *Seder olam*, and follows a variant reading that lists Isaac's age at the Akedah as 26 (rather than 37).[111]

All told, the later tosafist Torah compilations, at least in theory, could choose from a rather rich series of Tosafot and other tosafist sources, the products of different locales and differing exegetical strategies.[112] Indeed, the only piece of the *Da'at zekenim* and *Hadar zekenim* passages that seems to have originated after the main Tosafot era is the one regarding Rebecca leaving her home and the time given for a *na'arah* to prepare for *nisuin*. This discussion or interaction with the talmudic *sugya* is not found otherwise in biblical or talmudic comments that can be attributed directly to the Tosafists. By mustering various aspects of Tosafot interpretation around Rashi's comment on the Torah, and by adding some additional discussion

---

192–5, 410–13, and Kanarfogel, 'R. Judah *he-Hasid* and the Rabbinic Scholars of Regensburg: Interactions, Influences and Implications', *Jewish Quarterly Review*, 96 (2006), 17–37.

[109] See Tosafot on *Yev.* 64*a*, s.v. *veleilaf miyitshak*.

[110] See *Tosafot yeshanim al masekhet yevamot*, ed. Abraham Shoshana (Jerusalem, 1994), 369–70 (on *Yev.* 61*b*; the question begins with Rashi's Torah commentary, מכאן קשה לפ״ה דבפי׳ בחומש דרבקה בת היתה דגדולה משמע דהכא היתה שנים ג׳) and cf. ibid. 369 n. 41, and *Tosefot maharam verabenu perets*, ed. H. Porush (Jerusalem, 1991), 178–9: לכך הגיה הר״ר שמואל החסיד בסדר עולם בת י״ד שנים. ומייתי ראיה מסיפרי וכו׳. In light of this emendation attributed to R. Samuel Hehasid, this version of Tosafot does not need to conclude that there were *midrashim ḥalukim* (midrashic passages in disagreement). On R. Samuel Hehasid and his training, see Urbach, *The Tosafists* (Heb.), i. 192–5, and Sussmann, 'Rabad on Shekalim?'. On the provenance and development of the Tosafot collections on tractate *Yevamot*, see Urbach, *The Tosafists* (Heb.), ii. 620–5; *Tosafot yeshanim*, ed. Shoshana, editor's introd., 23–31; and *Tosefot maharam*, ed. Porush, editor's introd., 7–9.

[111] See *Nimukei ḥumash lerabenu yeshayah ditrani*, ed. C. B. Chavel, 23. On Isaac's age at the Akedah according to *Seder olam* and its variants, see Milikowsky, 'Seder Olam'.

[112] Several later compilatory texts, of both French and German provenance, record Ri as raising one of the key questions with regard to *Seder olam*. See e.g. *Tosafot hashalem*, ed. Gellis, iii. 67, §6 (based on several *Minḥat yehudah* manuscripts; on the northern French origins of this work, see H. Touitou, '*Minḥat yehudah*', 9–11), and *Perushei hatorah lerabi ḥayim palti'el*, ed. Lange (whose German affiliation is

and detail, *Da'at zekenim* and *Hadar zekenim* succeed in effectively presenting talmudic *sugyot* and midrashic analysis to their reading audiences on the larger issue of the chronology of the patriarchs, which had roots and ramifications in both biblical and rabbinic literature.

VII

The Torah writes that 'Esau returned from [hunting in] the field and he was exhausted' (Gen. 25: 29). Rashi, on the basis of *Genesis Rabbah*, explains that Esau was tired from the murders that he had committed, as per the verse in Jeremiah 4: 31, 'my soul was tired from the killings'. The presence of this language in the book of Jeremiah gives the *Genesis Rabbah* passage the quality of an *agadah hameyashevet divrei mikra* (one of Rashi's key exegetical criteria as enunciated in his comment on Genesis 3: 8), and that is how Rashi uses it here.[113]

Once again, both *Da'at zekenim* and *Hadar zekenim* pick up on Rashi's approach, but they also turn to *Genesis Rabbah*, in addition to the Talmud and other *midrashim*, in order to provide a fuller midrashic context for Esau's involvement in murder. Esau's target had been Nimrod, whom he succeeded in killing on that very day. This scenario is the result of an amalgamation of the passage in *Genesis Rabbah* towards the beginning of 'Toledot' that Rashi had cited, and another passage in *Genesis Rabbah* (65: 16) on a verse found later in this portion (Gen. 27: 15), which Rashi also cites, but only at that point.[114] According to *Da'at zekenim*, when Esau started out as a hunter, he found his main competitor to be Nimrod, who was extremely successful at hunting. Moreover, Nimrod asserted that only he could conduct hunts, and he challenged Esau to a battle. Esau consulted Jacob, who explained that as long as Nimrod was wearing his 'choice garments' (*begadav haḥamudot*), Esau would not be able to defeat him. If, however, Esau could get Nimrod to remove these garments, he could then defeat him. Esau did so and then killed Nimrod, which in turn contributed to Esau's physical and moral exhaustion, as per the verse in Jeremiah.[115]

indicated above, n. 43). It is more than likely, however, that the initials *resh-yod* refer here either to R. Judah Hehasid or to R. Isaiah di Trani (see above, nn. 107 and n. 111). Similarly, *Moshav zekenim* (ed. Sassoon, 36) records this question in the name of the French compilation *Sefer hagan* (and see also *Tosafot hashalem*, ed. Gellis, iii. 4–5, §2, and *Perushei hatorah lerabi ḥayim palti'el*, ed. Lange, 66 n. 17), although this passage does not appear in either of the two main manuscripts of that work (MS Vienna 28, or MS Nuremberg 5).

[113] See *Gen. Rabbah* 63: 12, and cf. *Rashbam's Commentary on Deuteronomy*, ed. Lockshin, editor's introd., 5.   [114] See *Midrash Bereshit Rabba*, ed. Theodor and Albeck, 727.

[115] *Da'at zekenim*, 'Genesis', fos. 25*a–b*:

שאותו היום הרג נמרוד שנלחם עמו כי כאשר התחיל עשו לצוד בשדה מצאו נמרוד
שהיה גבור ציד ואמר לו שאין שום אדם רשאי לצוד בשדות אלא הוא ולקחו יום
מלחמה ונטל עצה מיעקב ואמר כל זמן שהיה נמרוד לבוש בגדיו החמודות לא תוכל לו.
אך תאמר לו שיפשיטם אז תוכל לו וכן עשה והרג נמרוד. ולכך אמר כי עיף אנכי
כדכתיב כי עיפה נפשי להורגי'.

See also M. M. Kasher, *Torah shelemah*, iv. 1033.

Similarly, *Da'at zekenim* interprets the later verse, 'And Rebecca took her older son Esau's choice garments [*bigdei esav . . . haḥamudot*] which were with her in the house, and clothed her younger son [Jacob, Gen. 27: 15]', to mean that Esau had taken them (*ḥamdan*) from Nimrod (as per *Genesis Rabbah*). However, these garments were at the same time special (*ḥamudin*), since images of all the animals, beasts, and birds were vividly depicted on them. Other creatures were attracted to these vivid scenes, in which the various animals appeared to be alive, so that when Esau was in the field, animals and birds came to him and allowed themselves to be captured.[116] This last description comes from *Pirkei derabi eli'ezer*, chapter 24. Rashi, citing the second *Genesis Rabbah* passage, describes how Esau took Nimrod's hunting garments, but he does not refer to Esau killing Nimrod over them, nor does he cite the related description in *Pirkei derabi eli'ezer*. As opposed to *Da'at zekenim*, Rashi's comments on the portion 'Toledot' characterize Esau as a depraved and immoral individual who even engaged in murder, but he does not link Esau's murderous activities specifically to Nimrod. Interestingly, in one place in his talmudic commentary, Rashi does refer to Esau killing Nimrod over his hunting garments, which renders the absence of this detail in his Torah commentary even more telling.[117]

Hadar zekenim, after beginning with Rashi's comment on the cause of Esau's exhaustion (albeit without mentioning Rashi by name), cites a fuller version of the passage in *Genesis Rabbah*, on the multiple sins committed simultaneously by Esau, that appears in the name of Rabbi Yohanan in Babylonian Talmud *Bava batra* 16*b*. The *Genesis Rabbah* text initially lists two sins: murder and illicit relations with a betrothed woman, and then adds theft.[118] The talmudic *agadah* details five crimes or sins that Esau committed on the very same day (adding two that were essentially against God rather than against man), which occasioned his great exhaustion. These include having relations with a betrothed woman, murder, denying God, denigrating and dismissing his status as a first-born son, and theft. *Hadar zekenim* reproduces

---

[116] *Da'at zekenim*, 'Genesis', fo. 26*b*:

שחמדן מנמרוד וחמודין היו שהיו מצויירין עליהם כל החיות והעופות שבעולם ונראין כאלו הן חיין וכשהיה בשדה חיו החיות והעופות באין אצלו וניצודין מאליהן.

See also *Tosafot hashalem*, ed. Gellis, iii. 64, §3.

[117] See Rashi on *Pes.* 54*b*, s.v. *bigdo shel adam harishon*:

שהיו חקוקות בו כל מין חיה ובהמה והוא נמסר לנמרוד על כן יאמר כנמרוד גבור ציד [בראשית, י :ט]. ועשו הרגו ונטלו לפיכך היה איש ציד והן [צ״ל והוא] שכתוב בהן החמודות אשר בבית [בראשית, כז :טו]. ואני שמעתי בגדיו של אדם הראשון היינו כתנות עור שהיו לו.

It should be noted that the specific element of animal figures, which were vividly sketched (חקוקות or מצויירין) as a way of drawing his prey to Nimrod, is not found in the passage from *Pirkei derabi eli'ezer*, and may have originated with Rashi himself.

[118] Like the published edition of *Hadar zekenim*, MS Oxford/Bodleian Marsh 225 (among other manuscript texts) refers to the talmudic passage as a *midrash* (*veyesh bamidrash*), due in all likelihood to the several basic commonalities between these two rabbinic sources. See *Tosafot hashalem*, ed. Gellis, iii. 27, §5.

the talmudic derivations of all of these crimes from Genesis 25: 29, and concludes with Jacob's advice to Esau on how to defeat Nimrod. The special garments that Nimrod wore were originally the clothing worn by Adam (as per *Pirkei derabi eli'ezer*). Esau was instructed to tell Nimrod to remove them as a pre-condition to their battle. When Nimrod did so, Esau came and put them on deceitfully, and then arose and slew Nimrod (as per the second *Genesis Rabbah* passage), which was the main cause of Esau's tiredness that day. *Hadar zekenim* also includes a formulation which describes the tiredness of Esau as akin to the deep tiredness that hunters feel when 'they wander around the woods for four or five days and feel that they might die from the great hunger and thirst that envelops them'.[119]

Similarly, in commenting on Genesis 27: 15, *Hadar zekenim* initially indicates that the special clothes of Esau were the clothing that the Almighty had used to clothe Adam. These were akin to priestly vestments, since Adam was the first-born of the world, and the first-born were initially meant to perform the sacred cult (*avodah*). These vestments came to Esau from Nimrod. After noting that Eve was also clothed by the Almighty, which suggests that this clothing was not the same as the special priestly vestments of the first-born, *Hadar zekenim* turns to the *Genesis Rabbah* passage that defines the clothes as having been taken from Nimrod by Esau. Esau had undoubtedly taken them because of their special properties. The figures of the animals and birds that were drawn upon them appeared to be alive and attracted other animals to them and thus to the hunter, as described in *Pirkei derabi eli'ezer* and amplified by Rashi.

Hadar zekenim concludes by noting that, according to the first midrashic approach—that these were the vestments of the first-born—it is clear why Rebecca placed them on Jacob. In this way, Jacob could perform the appropriate *avodah* of the season through his parental service, since according to rabbinic tradition, Jacob received the blessings from Isaac on Passover. According to the second midrashic approach, however—that these garments had been taken from Nimrod by Esau and were a special aid in hunting—why did Rebecca insist that Jacob don them when serving Isaac? *Hadar zekenim* suggests that this was done in order to present Jacob to Isaac in the full and precise image of Esau, including his special hunting

---

[119] *Hadar zekenim*, fo. 10b:

והוא עיף. מן הנפשות שהרג כמו שנאמר כי עיפה נפשי להרוגים. ויש במדרש ה'
עבירות עבר אותו רשע באותו יום בא על נערה המאורסה הרג נפש כפר בעיקר בזה
הבכורה וגנב. ונפקא לה בגזירה שוה נאמ' כאן ויבא עשו ונאמר להלן אם גנבים באו
לך נאמר כאן שדה ונאמר להלן ואם בשדה ימצא האיש וכו'. הרג נפש דכתי' עיף כדפי'.
והיה עשו חלש כל כך שלא יכול להגיע ידו לפיו כדרך ציידים שתועים ביערים ד' ימים
או ה' ימים והם יגעים ומתים כמעט ברעב ובצמא וכו'. ואותו יום הרג את נמרוד
שנלחם עמו כי כשהתחיל עשו לצוד בשדות בא נמרוד וכו'. ואמר מי הרשהו לצוד
בשדות בלא רשותו. סוף דבר לקחו זמן ויום נועד להלחם יחד, בא עשו ונתייעץ עם
יעקב. א"ל יעקב כל זמן שיש לנמרוד בגדי אדם הראשון לא תוכל לו. אך תאמר לו
שיסירם מעליו ותלחם עמו וכן עשה וכשהפשיטם נמרוד בא עשו וילבשם במרמה וקם
והרג נמרוד ולפיכך היה עשו עיף כדכתיב עיפה נפשי להרוגים.

clothes.[120] Moreover, *Hadar zekenim* sees Esau's statement, 'behold I am going to die' (Gen. 25: 3), as a function of his impending battle with Nimrod, and the power of Nimrod and his garments as reflected in the various midrashic strands.[121] In short, both *Da'at zekenim* and *Hadar zekenim* join and conflate a series of *midrashim* in presenting their interpretations. Various tosafist Torah comments focus on the number and scope of Esau's sins, as enumerated by the aggadic passage in *Bava batra*.[122] This is not, however, a significant factor in the passage in *Da'at zekenim*, although *Hadar zekenim* does include this discussion before linking Esau to the killing of Nimrod over his hunting garments.

Even for *Hadar zekenim*, however, the focus is not so much on the litany of Esau's sins in the talmudic passage as about weaving this passage together with a series of *midrashim*, as well as Rashi's comments, in order to create an overarching story about Esau and Nimrod that spans much of 'Toledot'. This approach links the villainous Esau with the equally heinous Nimrod, who is characterized by Rashi on Genesis 10: 9 (towards the end of the portion 'Noah', where Nimrod is described as a 'mighty hunter', *gibor tsayid*), following *Genesis Rabbah* 37: 2, as one who 'captured the minds of other people through suasion, by which he tricked them into rebelling against the Almighty'. The only explicit scriptural cue that connects Esau to Nimrod is the fact that Nimrod is referred to as a *gibor tsayid*, while Esau is characterized as an *ish yode'a tsayid* (lit. 'a man who knows hunting', Gen. 25: 27). At first blush, however, it would seem that these two biblical figures lived several generations apart. *Da'at zekenim* and *Hadar zekenim* bring them together in both time and (negative) purpose.

Rashbam, Rabbi Joseph Bekhor Shor, and *Sefer hagan* all offered *peshat* interpretations or definitions of the nature of Esau's special clothes that reflect

---

[120] *Hadar zekenim*, fo. 11b:

והם הבגדים שהלביש הקב"ה לאדם הראשון ... ובגדי כהונה הלבישו לפי שהיה בכורו של עולם ועבודה בבכורות ובאו ליד עשו מיד נמרוד. וקשה דלחוה נמי עשה בגדים כדכתיב לאדם ולאשתו כתנות אור. א"כ משמע שמלבושיהם שוים. לכך נראה כמדרש אחר החמודות שחמדן מנמרוד, וחמודים היו לפי שהיו מצויירים בהם כל מיני חיות ועופות ודומה כאלו הן חיים והיו עופות וחיות באים אצלו מעצמן כשראו הבגדים וקשה למה הלבישו אותם יעקב בשלמא למדרש ראשון הלבישתו לעבוד עבודה בי"ט פסח. אבל למדרש שני קשה. ונראה טעמא לפי שרצתה להכירו לגמרי בדמיון עשו.

[121] *Hadar zekenim*, fos. 10b–11a:

המדרש אומר שפעם אחת הלך עשו לצוד חיות ועופות וראה צבי רץ לפניו וירץ אחריו ומצא נמרוד. וא"ל למה אתה צודה ביער שלי אני רוצה להלחם עמך ולקח זמן להלחם עם עשו. בא עשו ולקח עצה מיעקב ויעץ לו כפי' לעיל. והבגדים היה להם כח כ"כ שהחיות רעות ומסייעיות אותו שהיה לבוש הבגדים. ועל פי מדרש זה אמר עשו הנה אנכי הולך למות כי יש לי יום נועד למחר להלחם עם נמרוד ואין לי כח להלחם כנגדו. ומה אנכי חושש מהבכורה. מדרש זה אינו כמו שפי' לעיל והוא עיף לפי שהרג נמרוד אדרבה נראה שעדיין לא הרגו. עוד י"ל הנה אנכי הולך למות כלו' בכל יום ובכל שעה אני הולך במקום סכנה.

Cf. Kasher, *Torah shelemah*, iv. 1035.

[122] See MS Paris 167, cited in *Tosafot hashalem*, ed. Gellis, iii. 28, §6 (and n. 2); MS Moscow 362, fos. 128v–129r; MS Oxford/Bodleian Opp. 31, fo. 41; *Perushei hatorah lerabi hayim palti'el*, ed. Lange, 70; and *Moshav zekenim*, ed. Sassoon, 39. See also *Bereshit Rabba*, ed. Theodor and Albeck, 695; and Kasher, *Torah shelemah*, iv. 1031.

either Esau's relationship with his father Isaac (for Rashbam, '[Esau] always served his father meals in them'), or that reflect the common practice of hunters to have two sets of clothes, one set worn while hunting and another, clean and more fashionable, that was worn in the presence of other people. Both Bekhor Shor and *Sefer hagan* note that occasionally Esau wore his finer garments in the field too (or changed into them immediately upon his return), and so they carried a scent of the field as well.[123] None of these interpretations, however, refers to Nimrod's garments in the way that *Da'at zekenim* and *Hadar zekenim* do (and as Rashi had), although Rashbam's approach can also be located in *Genesis Rabbah*, alongside that of Rashi.[124]

Moreover, both Bekhor Shor and *Sefer hagan* interpret the phrase *vehu ayef* ('and he was tired,' Gen. 25: 29) according to the typical routine of hunters: 'It is the way of the hunters to become extremely tired when they pursue the animals of the wild. Sometimes they roam the forests for three or four days, until they reach the "gates of death" because of their hunger and thirst. This is what occurred to Esau.'[125] We should recall that this description of the hunter is also recorded in *Hadar zekenim*, in the midst of a section on Esau's depraved behaviour and his vendetta against Nimrod.[126] For *Hadar zekenim*, this was just a passing observation, taken from the oft-cited commentary of Bekhor Shor (or perhaps from *Sefer hagan*).[127] For Bekhor Shor and *Sefer hagan*, however, this expression of the realia of the hunters' life is the essential (*peshat*) interpretation of this verse.[128]

Against the approach of these *pashtanim*, and against even the midrashic approach of Rashi, *Da'at zekenim* and *Hadar zekenim*, no less carefully and in full accordance with their own overarching methodology, build a midrashic structure that transfers and joins midrashic sources at both ends of 'Toledot'. The result is that the midrashic theme linking Nimrod and Esau is brought to the fore, and the protracted attempt to subvert the garments (and the service) of Adam runs through both of these hunters. Esau and Nimrod were also both beneficiaries of a

---

[123] See *Tosafot hashalem*, ed. Gellis, iii. 64, §4 (Bekhor Shor), §6 (Rashbam), and §7 (*Sefer hagan*, ed. Orlian, 173).

[124] See *Rabbi Samuel ben Meir's Commentary on Genesis*, ed. Lockshin, 154 n. 2.

[125] See *Perushei r. yosef bekhor shor al hatorah*, ed. Y. Nevo, 43, 181; *Sefer hagan*, ed. Orlian, 171; and *Tosafot hashalem*, ed. Gellis, iii. 28, §8. This explanation is undoubtedly linked to the phrase in Gen. 25: 32, 'behold I am going to die' (ostensibly due to his great hunger and thirst). See also above, n. 122.

[126] See above, n. 119.

[127] See also *Perushei r. yosef bekhor shor al hatorah*, ed. Y. Nevo, 43 n. 14, who lists several other tosafist Torah commentaries, both published and in manuscript, that include this description, and see also Ḥizekuni on Gen. 25: 29. This supports the observation of Japhet, 'Ḥizekuni's Commentary' (Heb.), 107, that the tosafist Torah compilations did retain references to *peshat* as well.

[128] Rashbam does not comment on the phrase *vehu ayef*, perhaps because Esau's tiredness was perfectly understandable as a normal result of the great physical exertion demanded by hunting. He does, however, refer to the danger inherent in hunting wild animals in the forests (specifically mentioning lions and bears, if not tigers) in his comment on Gen. 25: 32, 'behold I am going to die'. Citing his father, R. Meir, Rashbam suggests that this pursuit caused Esau's life to be constantly at risk.

miraculous set of garments that augmented their earthy natures, and made them very powerful adversaries. Defining the enemies of the heroes of the Torah in very clear terms, and giving them an array of supernatural powers, further advances the goal of the tosafist Torah commentaries to appeal to a more popular readership and mindset. Nonetheless, the transference and presentation of a series of midrashic texts that are not always so obviously related, and that sometimes generate conflicts between them which must then be resolved, bespeaks rabbinic scholars who are well versed in this literature and possess a fair degree of creativity and intellectual consistency. The tosafist Torah compilations are not simply collections of *midrashim* that amass such texts irrespective of whether there is any relationship between them. On the contrary, it is precisely the deft handling of the midrashic material that allows these interpretations to be presented as worthy alternatives to those of Rashi and the earlier tosafist *pashtanim*. The broader and more complete picture that is presented, and the interesting and authentic rabbinic texts on which it is based, surely appealed to a different audience from that of the *pashtanim*, and was undoubtedly appreciated and understood by some as a positive extension or expansion of Rashi's exegetical methodology.[129]

VIII

When Joseph returned to the house of Potiphar, none of the household staff was there (*ve'ein ish me'anshei habayit sham babayit*). Seizing this opportunity, the wife of Potiphar makes her advance on Joseph (Gen. 39: 11–12). *Hadar zekenim* notes that a *peshat* approach understands the phrase 'none of the household staff was there' to mean simply that Joseph was alone in the house with Potiphar's wife. Rabbi Isaac (Ri) of Evreux interprets, however, that Joseph's 'manhood was removed'. The phrase *ein ish*, literally 'there is no man', according to this approach, connotes that Joseph was 'not a man'. As Rabbi Isaac explains, Joseph's reproductive organ became suddenly and miraculously covered or otherwise ineffective, thus preventing him from sinning with Potiphar's wife.[130] Neither the published version of *Hadar*

---

[129] On Rashi's more limited approach to Nimrod, cf. N. Leibowitz, *Iyunim besefer shemot*, 512–13, and M. Berger, 'The Torah Commentary of Rabbi Samuel ben Meir', 200–1. On Rashi's considerations in moving (or not moving) *midrashim* to verses other than where they were originally introduced, cf. Leibowitz, *Iyunim besefer shemot*, 518–22.

[130] *Hadar zekenim*, fo. 18b: ואין איש מאנשי הבית שם בבית. הפשט שלא היה בבית רק יוסף. והר״י מאיוו״רא מפרש מלמד שבדק עצמו ומצא שאינו איש שבאותה שעה נוטל זכרותו למונעו מן החטא. The beginning of the passage in *Gen. Rabbah* 87: 7 (Theodor–Albeck edn., 1072–3) reads: ואין איש. בדק את עצמו ולא מצא את עצמו איש. This *midrash* then offers three rabbinic interpretations of this somewhat enigmatic passage, each supported by verses that testify to Joseph's resolve, specifically in the terms being suggested: אמר ר׳ שמואל [בר נחמני] נמתחה הקשת וחזרה. ר׳ יצחק אמר נתפזר זרעו ויצא דרך צפורניו. ר׳ הונא אמר איקונין של אביו ראה ונצטנן דמו. R. Isaac of Evreux's interpretation matches none of these views exactly. It is either his own understanding of the initial phrase in *Genesis Rabbah*, or it is perhaps his adaptation, in more graphic and miraculous terms, of Joseph's sudden inability to function sexually, according to the first interpretation in the *midrash* (by R. Samuel). On the presentation of both *peshat* and *derash* in this pas-

zekenim, nor any identifiable manuscript source of this tosafist Torah compilation, notes the fact that Rabbi Isaac of Evreux's interpretation is an extension of a passage in *Genesis Rabbah*.[131]

This same interpretation, that Joseph checked himself and found that his manhood had become covered and rendered ineffective, headed by an attribution to an unnamed *midrash*, is found in a variant Tosafot comment on the Talmud, the so-called Tosafot Evreux on *Sotah*. These Tosafot were composed in the study hall of Rabbi Isaac of Evreux and his brothers, Rabbi Moses and Rabbi Samuel ben Shene'ur of Evreux, in the mid-thirteenth century, and this comment comes at a point where an aggadic passage in the Talmud is discussing Joseph's actions in the house of Potiphar.[132] What we have here, then, is a talmudic interpretation from Evreux that was taken into a tosafist Torah commentary, as well as yet another significant use of *Genesis Rabbah* by a Tosafot text on the Talmud. Whether or not Rabbi Isaac of Evreux had a text of *Genesis Rabbah* that actually read this way, or whether this is his own extension or explanation of the midrashic text, the commitment of this tosafist *beit midrash* to the study and interpretation of *Genesis Rabbah*, and its incorporation into both biblical and talmudic interpretation, is once again evident.[133] In this instance, it is the Tosafist Rabbi Isaac of Evreux himself who

sage in *Hadar zekenim*, cf. Japhet, 'Ḥizekuni's Commentary' (Heb.). *Sotah* 36b records these three opinions, in the name of other *amora'im*, but combines them in a different way. Tosafot on *Sot*. 36b, s.v. *be'otah*, presents R. Moses Hadarshan's interpretation of Joseph's response, which follows the psychological approach, that Joseph saw the image of his father's face before him and was unable to sin.

[131] See *Tosafot hashalem*, ed. Gellis, iv. 97, §9, and cf. Kasher, *Torah shelemah*, vi. 1501. The name of R. Isaac of Evreux is cited in full in MS Vatican 48, fo. 35ᵛ, and MS Moscow 268, fo. 81ᵛ. MS British Library Add. 22,092, fo. 40ʳ, MS Jewish Theological Seminary 791, fo. 40ʳ, and MS Moscow 898, fo. 29ᵛ, cite this passage in the name of Ri of Evreux, and MS Munich 50, fo. 82ᵛ, reads וה"ר מאייברא.

[132] See *Tosefot evreux al masekhet sotah*, ed. Ya'akov Lifshitz (Jerusalem, 1969), 100 (on *Sot*. 36b, s.v. *ve'ein ish me'anshei habayit*): יש במדרש שבדק יוסף את עצמו ולא מצא מעשה של איש, שלא היה לו מילה שמצא את עצמו טומטום.

[133] In his comments on the Tosafot Evreux passage cited in the above note, Y. Lifshitz suggests (p. 100 n. 88) that since R. Isaac of Evreux's interpretation is not found so clearly in the *midrash*, this passage should perhaps begin with the phrase *yesh lefaresh* (it should be interpreted) rather than *yesh bamidrash* (it is found in the Midrash). Such an emendation, however, aside from not being indicated on any other level, fails to take into account the strong affinity that the tosafist academy at Evreux had for *Genesis Rabbah* and its interpretation. Although the piece about Joseph and the wife of Potiphar derives from Tosafot Evreux (and R. Moses of Evreux is cited by name four times in *Sefer hagan* and had contact with the compiler of this work, R. Aaron Hakohen; see above, n. 37), this interpretation is not found in *Sefer hagan*, perhaps because of its more overtly miraculous nature (although cf. below, n. 139). Kasher (above, n. 131) presents this passage in the name of *Tosefot shants lesotah* (36b). Although R. Hayim Joseph David Azulai (Hida, d. 1806) thought that this collection of Tosafot was indeed Tosafot Sens (Hebr. *shants*), Lifshitz (*Tosefot evreux al masekhet sotah*, editor's introd., 9–14, following the approach of Y. N. Epstein and others) demonstrates that these are the later Tosafot Evreux. R. Moses of Evreux evidently studied with R. Samson of Sens and R. Samuel with Samson's brother, R. Isaac (Rizba). See Urbach, *The Tosafists* (Heb.), i. 480, and see also ibid. 291–2. Urbach suggests there that a passage from Tosafot Sens on tractate *Sotah* (which may not otherwise be extant) is cited by R. Judah b. Eliezer in his *Minḥat yehudah*, on the Torah portion dealing with the laws of the *sotah* ('Naso', fo. 3b, s.v. *ve'amrah ha'ishah, kakh piresh*

favours a more miraculous and dramatic perspective on the biblical episode, and not merely the compiler of the tosafist Torah commentary that cites this interpretation alongside the *peshat*. Indeed, in this situation, Rashi also favours the non-miraculous, psychological approach.[134]

In the Song of the Sea (Exod. 15: 8), the Torah characterizes the water as being piled up or heaped (*ne'ermu mayim*). Rashi, following Onkelos, interprets the word *ne'ermu* as a form of *armimut*, or cleverness. The cleverness of the water is understood by some to mean that it arranged itself in a way that would fool the Egyptians into entering the sea, or that it covered only the Egyptians and not the Jews.[135] In any case, Rashi also puts forward an even more *peshat*-like approach. According to 'the sense of clarity of the verse', *ne'ermu* is akin to the phrase in a verse in the Song of Songs (7: 3), 'a pile of wheat' (*aremat ḥitim*), as demonstrated also by the phrase in Exodus, *nizvu kemo ned nozlim*, that the running water stood straight as a wall. *Hadar zekenim* (without mentioning Rashi by name, as was often its wont) com-

---

hatosefot shants). Note that Tosafot Sens on *Sanhedrin* is cited by *Minḥat yehudah* (on the Torah portion 'Mishpatim', fo. 32*b*, s.v. *vegunav, veshuv matsati betosefot shants*), and R. Samson himself is cited twice (as R. Samson b. Abraham) by *Minḥat yehudah* on 'Bereshit'; see H. Touitou, '*Minḥat yehudah*', 80. *Minḥat yehudah* also cites Tosafot Touques several times, referring to it usually as שיטת תוך (see e.g. 'Yitro', fo. 24*a*, s.v. *heyu nekhonim*; 'Ki tisa', fo. 44*a*, *ki boshesh*, and fo. 45*b*, s.v. *vayashlekh*), and once as לשון ר' אליעזר מתו"ך ('Tazria', fo. 12*b*, s.v. *bekaraḥto*).

[134] See Rashi on Gen. 39: 11, and cf. above, n. 98; *Tosafot hashalem*, ed. Gellis, iv. 97, §10; and above, n. 129. Rashbam on Gen. 39: 10, followed by Bekhor Shor on Gen. 39: 11 (*Perushei r. yosef bekhor shor al hatorah*, ed. Y. Nevo, 72) suggests that Joseph remained alone one day in the house with the wife of Potiphar through happenstance, although Rashbam also cites an aggadic *midrash* (= *Genesis Rabbah*) that everyone else had gone out that day to watch as the Nile river overflowed its banks. Cf. *Rabbi Samuel ben Meir's Commentary on Genesis*, ed. Lockshin, 272 n. 3. R. Isaac of Evreux also interacted with comments by Rashi. See e.g. MS Moscow 268, fo. 82ʳ (on Exod. 4: 24):

ויהי בדרך במלון ויפגשהו ה' ויבקש המיתו. ולמה נענש [פרש"י] לפי שנתעסק במלון תחלה. [פי'] מהר"י יצחק מאייברא שנענש לפי שמל ידי שנסע ביום ראשון כבר קיים מצות המקום שאמ' לו לך וא"כ היה יכול למולו מיום ראשון שנסע [ולא עשה כך]

and cf. *Tosafot hashalem*, ed. Gellis, vi. 119, §§2–3; and MS Moscow 82, fo. 15ᵛ (on Exod. 12: 15, found also in *Hadar zekenim*, fo. 29*b*):

שבעת ימים תאכל מצות. פ"ה כתוב אחד אומר שבעת ימים תאכל מצות וכתוב אחר אומר ששת ימים תאכל מצות למדתנו על שביעי שהוא רשות. לכן פי' הר"י מאיוורא דששת ימים רשות מדכתב בערב תאכלו מצות משמע מכאן ואיל אינו מחויב לאכול ואין זה כפי' הקונטרוס. ומה"ר ל"ט [מיואני?] מקיים פי' רש"י.

See *Tosafot hashalem*, ed. Gellis, vii. 90–1, §6 (and MS Leiden 27, fos. 55ᵛ–56ʳ, לכן נראה לי דששת ימים רשות . . . ומורי הרב ש"י מקיים פי' רש"י); vii. 53, §8 (= MS Vatican 45, fo. 22ᵛ); and see also *Da'at zekenim*, 'Exodus', fo. 13*a*); and vii. 64, §7, n. 5 (citing *Da'at zekenim*). See also *Tosefot evreux al masekhet sotah*, ed. Lifshitz, editor's introd., 34–5 n. 21. For R. Moses of Evreux and Rashi, see MS Oxford/Bodleian Opp. Add. 4ᵗᵒ, 127, fo. 3ʳ. In the context of halakhic exegesis, see *Tosafot hashalem*, ed. Gellis, vii. 89, §5. Cf. Tosafot on *Bets*. 21*b*, s.v. *lakhem* (citing both R. Moses and R. Samuel of Evreux = *Tosafot hashalem*, vii. 94, §1), and MS Moscow 268, fo. 92ʳ (citing R. Hayim, the son of R. Moses of Evreux); *Tosefot evreux al masekhet sotah*, ed. Lifshitz, 27–8; *Perushei hatorah lerabi ḥayim palti'el*, ed. Lange, editor's introd., 11; and Urbach, *The Tosafists* (Heb.), i. 484.

[135] See Kasher, *Torah shelemah*, vol. xiv (New York, 1951), 125, and cf. *Perushei hatorah lerabi ḥayim palti'el*, ed. Lange, 239–40.

Midrashic Texts and Methods in Tosafist Commentaries 313

ments first that *ne'ermu* is 'like a pile of wheat'.[136] *Hadar zekenim* then proceeds to deal with the translation of Onkelos (listed first by Rashi), which *Hadar zekenim* finds somewhat difficult to explain, since cleverness is not a trait that can be easily applied to water. From *Sefer hagan*, *Hadar zekenim* presents the view of Rabbi Meir ben Shene'ur that there is a *midrash* which maintains that the water itself became intelligent and offered its own song.[137]

The original text of *Sefer hagan* corrects the source of the attribution to Rabbi Moses ben Shene'ur (of Evreux).[138] Once again, *Hadar zekenim* and *Da'at zekenim* (without attribution) have introduced an even more miraculous midrashic interpretation than the one proposed by Rashi, not to mention Rashbam and other *pashtanim*, that derives from a head of the tosafist academy at Evreux.[139]

[136] This is the interpretation given by Rashbam and Ibn Ezra, using the same proof-text and it is also found in Menahem b. Saruk's *Maḥberet*. See *Rashbam's Commentary on Exodus: An Annotated Translation*, ed. M. Lockshin (Atlanta, Ga., 1997), 156, who suggests that these commentators are thereby avoiding Onkelos' approach. This interpretation is also found in the name of R. Joseph Kara. See *Tosafot hashalem*, ed. Gellis, vii. 226, §9, and cf. the interpretation from MS Hamburg 45 found ibid., §5 (*lefi hapeshat*).

[137] *Hadar zekenim*, fo. 32*a*:

נערמו מים. כמו ערימת חטים. ועל מה שתרגם אונקלוס חכימו מיא קשה, מה חכמה שייכא במים. ואומר ה"ר מאיר ב"ר שניאור דיש במדרש שנכנסה בהם ערמימות של חכמה ואמרו שירה. ג"ן. ול"מ שהחכמה היתה כאשר נצבו כמו נד נוזלים.

Note that both of the basic interpretations given by Rashi and *Hadar zekenim* are also found in the *Mekhilta*. A later tosafist Torah compilation, *Peshatim uferushim al ḥamishah ḥumshei torah lerabi ya'akov mivinah*, ed. M. Grossman (Mainz, 1888), 68, cites anonymously the view attributed by *Hadar zekenim* to R. Meir b. Shene'ur: נערמו מים תרג' חכימא מיא ומה היא חכמתן שאמרו שירה וכן במדרש as does *Da'at zekenim* ('Exodus', fo. 18*b*). See also MS Oxford/Bodleian Opp. 31, fo. 14ᵛ; *Tosafot hashalem*, ed. Gellis, vii. 227, §11; and Poznanski, *Introduction to Northern French Biblical Commentators* (Heb.), p. xcviii.

[138] See MS Vienna 28 (on Exod. 15: 8 = *Sefer hagan*, ed. Orlian, 234):

על מה שתרגם אונקלוס חכימו מיא. נערמו לש' ערמה וחכמה. וקש' מה שחכמה שייכא במים. וא"ל הר"ר משה בן שניאור דיש במדרש בפירוש שנכנסה בהן ערמומית של חכמה ואמרו שירה.

(The other major manuscript of *Sefer hagan*, MS Nuremberg 5, does not contain comments on the book of Exodus.)

[139] In a remarkable passage, *Sefer hagan* on Gen. 31: 52 (ed. Orlian, 179, and see also Poznanski, *Introduction to Northern French Biblical Commentators* (Heb.), p. cii, and *Tosafot hashalem*, ed. Gellis, iii. 200) reports a principle put forward by the Tosafist R. Solomon b. Judah of Dreux (see above, nn. 63, 70), or by R. Solomon b. Abraham of Troyes, a brother of R. Samson of Sens (see Urbach, *The Tosafists* (Heb.), i. 344 and 340 n. 34, and cf. Poznanski, *Introduction*, pp. cii–ciii, n. 2), as is found subsequently in *Sefer hagan* on Exod. 24: 8 (see below, and in variants on Gen. 31: 52 in *Perushei hatorah lerabi ḥayim palti'el*, ed. Lange, 543; *Pa'aneaḥ raza*, 150; and *Moshav zekenim*, ed. Sassoon, 57), that any time the Torah (= the Bible as a whole) indicates that an *ed* (a sign or witness) has been established to mark the making of a covenant, one who violates that covenant will be punished by the very sign or substance that was used to establish the covenant (or testimony) in the first place. Thus, the covenant established with stones by Joshua (Josh. 24: 27), to confirm that the Jewish people would not desert the Almighty, meant that anyone who did so (through idolatry) would be punished by stoning (as per Deut. 17: 7). Upon hearing this principle, R. Moses of Evreux was greatly troubled (*me'od hukshah be'einav venitsta'er bah*), on account of the covenant of stone (*ed hagal hazeh*) that was established between Laban and Jacob as described by the verse in Genesis. According to the talmudic view (*San.* 105*a*) that Balaam and Laban were one and the

IX

The Torah opens the final section of the portion 'Beshalaḥ' with the appearance of Amalek (Exod. 17: 8), who arrived in order to engage in battle with Israel at Refidim. *Hadar zekenim* comments that it is found in the Midrash that Esau pressured his son Elifaz to swear an oath to kill Jacob for stealing the birthright, telling Elifaz that if he succeeded in killing Jacob, the status of the first-born would return to him. Elifaz consulted with his mother Timna, who told him that Jacob was a greater warrior, and that he would kill Elifaz; indeed, it was Esau's own fear of Jacob that had caused him to assign this task to someone else, since Esau surely would have preferred to kill Jacob himself if he could have. In order to keep his promise to his father nonetheless, even if minimally, Elifaz went to Jacob and took all his money, in line with the rabbinic dictum that 'a pauper is considered to be dead'. When Esau saw that Elifaz had not done as he had been instructed, he went to Elifaz's son Amalek and told him to kill Jacob. Amalek acceded to his grandfather's request, and swore to him that he would kill Jacob. When Timna heard this bad news, she warned Amalek as she had Elifaz, but Amalek did not accept her words. Timna then told him that the descendants of Abraham had a great burden upon them, as Abraham had been told 'they will serve them and they will be afflicted' in Egypt. If Amalek killed Jacob at this point, this burden would be transferred to the progeny of Esau, since they too are descended from Abraham. Thus, Timna's advice to Amalek was

---

same, Laban violated his covenant with Jacob when, as Balaam, he sought to curse Jacob's descendants. At no time, however, was Laban/Balaam punished for his violation by the stones of the original covenant. This passage then reports that R. Moses was told in a dream to go and look carefully in the *midrash Bereshit zuta* (*ad sheheru lo baḥalomo puk vedok bivereshit zuta*). R. Moses went and found this thin volume (*matsa sefer katan*), in which it was written that a sword (*ḥerev*) had been stuck into the stone, to seal the covenant between Laban and Jacob (*shena'atsu ḥerev betokh hagal le'ikar keritat berit*). Moreover, the stone fence into which Balaam's leg was rammed by his donkey (Num. 22: 25) was the very stone of the covenant, and the sword that ultimately killed Balaam (as per Num. 31: 8, *ve'et bilam ben be'or haregu beḥarev*, which further intimates that the particular sword in question was a known one, with a history) was the very sword that had been stuck into the rock. And therefore, Rashi interprets Num. 22: 24, 'a fence on this and a fence on that [side]' (*gader mizeh vegader mizeh*) with the words 'that an otherwise unidentified fence is made of stone' (*setam geder shel avanim hu*), to hint (*veramaz*) that Balaam/Laban was being punished at this point (via the stone fence) for violating his covenant with Jacob. The passage concludes: כך שמע[תי] ממה"ר משה ב"ר שניאור. (I intend, in a separate study, to treat the issue of dreams as a source of both rabbinic interpretations and halakhic rulings in medieval Ashkenaz.) *Sefer hagan* reprises this interpretation, without reference to R. Moses of Evreux, on Exod. 24: 8 (ed. Orlian, 249). The Jewish people were sprinkled with blood at Mt Sinai, to signify that one who does not keep the Torah will pay with his blood, as confirmed by both scriptural and aggadic texts. 'And from here is a significant proof of what we explained in the name of R. Solomon b. Abraham regarding *ed hagal hazeh* [Gen. 31: 52], that the one who violates the covenant will be punished by the substance used to seal the covenant.' See *Tosafot hashalem*, ed. Gellis, viii. 363, §1; and cf. *Hadar zekenim* on Exod. 24: 8 (fo. 40a, citing *Sefer hagan*), and on Num. 24: 8 (fo. 59b, citing an unidentified *midrash*). On Balaam and Lavan, see also *Tosafot hashalem*, ed. Gellis, vi. 14–15, §9.

that he should at least wait until the subjugation of the Jews in Egypt had been completed and the Jews had left Egypt. It was at that point that Amalek came upon the Jews to fulfil his oath, as the verse reads, 'And Amalek arrived'.[140]

Rashi employs a version of this *midrash* as the second interpretation in his commentary on Genesis 29: 11, to explain why Jacob cried when he met Rachel. Jacob cried because he had no money, since Elifaz had taken everything from him. In Rashi's version of this *midrash*, Elifaz was torn between his father's demand to kill Jacob and the fact that he had grown up in close proximity to Isaac. Elifaz confessed his ambivalence and his dilemma to Jacob, who advised him to take all his money so that Jacob would be 'a pauper who is considered to be dead', thereby fulfilling Esau's wishes on a technical level, while not shedding the blood of Isaac's son.[141] In his comment on 'And Amalek arrived' (Exod. 17: 8), however, Rashi does not refer to this *midrash* at all, but instead offers a comment based on a passage in *Pesikta rabati*. The arrival of Amalek and its conflict with Israel is juxtaposed with the previous section in the Torah, in which the children of Israel complained about their thirst and Moses provided water for them by hitting the rock at the instruction of the Almighty (Exod. 17: 1–7), to teach an important spiritual and behavioural lesson. Even though God always provides for the children of Israel, they often ask, nonetheless, if God is with them, failing to recognize his presence as manifested in his responsiveness. Rashi includes a parable illustrating this kind of human insensitivity, with the object lesson being that, on occasion, the Almighty may pull back from Israel when they do not remember him properly. They will then be required to pray to him and cry out for help when this new difficulty appears, causing them to appreciate him anew.

Rashi's use of the story of Elifaz and Jacob in Genesis 29, as an *agadah hamayeshvet divrei mikra*, and his failure to use it in Exodus 17 is most likely a function of scope. The midrashic encounter described, occurring directly between Elifaz and Jacob, might well explain Jacob's sadness when he met Rachel. Indeed, Rashi, towards the end of the portion 'Vayishlaḥ' (Gen. 36: 7), offers a midrashic explanation for the fact that Esau departed the land of Canaan for his own land 'because of his brother',[142] which contains another element of this much larger midrashic theme: Esau did not want to

---

[140] *Hadar zekenim*, fos. 32b–33a:

ויבא עמלק. נמצא במדרש עשו השביע את אליפז בנו להרוג את יעקב לפי שרמהו מן הבכורה וא״ל בני בכורי אם תהרגהו תשוב לך הבכורה. הלך אליפז נתייעץ עם תמנע אמו והיא מנעתו ואמרה לו בני, יעקב גבור ממך ויהרגך. ואביך הרשע אם לא היה ירא ממנו פן יהרגהו היה חפץ להורגו מידו יותר מעל ידי אחרים. מה עשה אליפז כדי לקיים מצות אביו ושבועתו הלך אל יעקב ונטל ממנו כל ממונו ועני חשוב כמת. כיון שראה עשו שלא עשה אליפז מצותו הלך לעמלק בן אליפז וא״ל שיהרג יעקב. נתרצה עמלק לדברי זקנו עשו ונשבע לו שיהרגהו. כששמעה תמנע הדבר הרע הזהירה בו כמו שעשתה לאליפז ולא קבל דבריה. אמרה לו חוב גדול מוטל על זרעו של אברהם כדכתי׳ ועבדום וענו אותם ואם תהרג יעקב הרי החוב מוטל עליך ועל זרעו של עשו כי אתם מזרע אברהם. ולכך המתין עד אחר השעבוד שנשרע החוב ויצאו ממצרים ויבא אליהם להנקם משבועתו. והיינו דכתיב ויבא עמלק.

[141] This version of the *midrash* has roots in *Deuteronomy Rabbah* and the midrashic *Sefer hayashar*, but does not appear in *Genesis Rabbah* at this point. See *Rashi al hatorah*, ed. Berliner, 59; and cf. *Tosafot hashalem*, ed. Gellis, iii. 134, §3.   [142] See *Gen. Rabbah*, ad loc. (82: 13).

receive, in any way, the obligation or decree of servitude that would be placed upon those to whom which the Land of Israel had been given, so he left that land. The fuller midrashic story of Amalek finally avenging the challenge of Esau, however, does not especially suggest itself as an appropriate, focused exegetical comment for Rashi to make on the verse 'And Amalek arrived'. Unlike Rashi, however, *Hadar zekenim* had no such qualms about opening with this larger *midrash* here, just as *Hadar zekenim* preferred this kind of broad-based *midrash* in many of the other examples discussed above.

Ḥizekuni's comment on 'And Amalek arrived' essentially reproduces the Rashi passage on Genesis 36: 7, concluding that Amalek's desire to avoid the burden of servitude in Egypt serves to explain why he waited to attack the children of Israel until after they had left Egypt and their debt of servitude was complete. At the same time, *Ḥizekuni* does not present any aspects of the more lengthy, yet related *Hadar zekenim* passage on 'And Amalek arrived', even though *Hadar zekenim* was a work to which *Ḥizekuni* had access.[143] Clearly, *Ḥizekuni* wished to employ a helpful midrashic theme for an exegetical purpose, without having to subscribe to all of the larger and more diffuse dimensions of that theme, as it was recorded and used by *Hadar zekenim*. In the same way, but with even tighter exegetical considerations and standards, Rashi was content, in his comment on Exodus 17: 8, to make an ethical or behavioural point from the juxtaposition found there, as was his wont, rather than resorting to a larger midrashic theme whose presence in this case was not so germane or so obvious.[144]

Interestingly, *Da'at zekenim*, like *Ḥizekuni*, also presents a fairly compact version of the midrashic motif surrounding Amalek's attack on the Jews that has no explicit reference to Elifaz, and that attributes the decision not to move against Jacob until the Jewish people had left Egypt to Amalek himself.[145] Nonetheless, and not surprisingly, the larger midrashic approach found in the printed edition of *Hadar zekenim* does appear in other tosafist Torah collections, and in manuscripts related to these works, with some omissions or variations to be sure, as the compilers of these works sought to conflate broad rabbinic and midrashic themes that

---

[143] See above, n. 47.

[144] On Rashi's use of *midrashim* to convey points of pedagogy and ethics, see above, n. 14. On Rashi's comment on Exod. 17: 8, cf. N. Leibowitz, *Iyunim besefer shemot*, 497–8; M. Sokolow, *Studies in the Weekly Parashah*, 99–101; and above, n. 129.

[145] *Da'at zekenim*, Exodus, fo. 21b:

ויבא עמלק. תימה למה איחר להלחם עם ישראל עד עכשו ולא בא מיד [כ]שירדו למצרים שלא היו כי אם שבעים נפש. י"ל שאמר לו הקב"ה לאברהם ועבדום וענו אותם. וכשמת אברהם הטיל החוב על יצחק. וכשמת יצחק הטיל על יעקב ובניו ועשו ובניו. ואמר עמלק הרשע בלבו אם אכרית את יעקב וזרעו יהיה החוב מוטל עלי. לכך המתין עד שיצאו ממצרים שכבר נפרע החוב ואז בא להלחם עמהן.

Moshav zekenim, ed. Sassoon, 148, offers a different, broad midrashic perspective, which seeks to explain why Amalek chose to attack Israel precisely at a time that the word was being spread of the many miracles that had been done on behalf of Israel. The *Moshav zekenim* passage concludes with an attribution to *Sefer hagan*, but that may only apply to a second midrashic passage found towards the end of the comment.

would resonate in a variety of verses and situations within the Torah, and to supply them to their readers.[146]

X

The midrashic interpretations and expansions found in *Da'at zekenim* and *Hadar zekenim* move well past simple responses to Rashi's comments, or citations from Rabbi Joseph Bekhor Shor and those of his Tosafist colleagues who worked with the exegetical categories of *peshuto shel mikra* and *agadah hameyashevet divrei mikra* in ways similar to Rashi. These compilations often presented comments from Tosafists who were inclined to read the biblical text mainly through the prism of talmudic and midrashic literature, with particular emphasis on *Genesis Rabbah* and related works. In addition to exposing their readers more effectively to this tosafist material, *Da'at zekenim* and *Hadar zekenim* (as representatives of their genre) sought to highlight more miraculous descriptions of the events that took place in the Torah, and to put forward and conflate *midrashim* that could be applied to multiple sections or episodes in the Torah. Although there is a measure of *peshat* included as well, these compilations were meant to be more popular or broad-based than those of the *pashtanim* of northern France and their successors, and were intended to attract readers who were below the level of the highest rabbinic elites.

Indeed, there are at least three examples from the mid- to late thirteenth century of extensive collections from Germany and Austria (with distinct authors) that were designed to present tosafist material primarily in the realm of halakhah, but also in Midrash and aggadah, arranged according to the verses of the Torah. It would appear that these works were also intended to reach an audience larger than the rabbinic elite who populated the most prestigious or advanced *batei midrash*. These works are *Perushim ufesakim* by Rabbi Avigdor ben Elijah Katz of Vienna,[147] the no

---

[146] See *Tosafot hashalem*, ed. Gellis, vii. 298–9, §§2–3. MS Oxford/Bodleian Opp. 31, fos. 14ᵛ–15ʳ is virtually identical to the published version of *Hadar zekenim*. Cf. e.g. MS Vatican 45, fos. 25ᵛ–26ʳ:

מה ראה עמלק להלחם בישראל בשביל צוואת אביו אליפז כשפירש יעקב מאביו ומאמו
ללכת (אל) [מ]ארץ כנען לחרן אל לבן שמע עשו וצוה לאליפז להורגו. ותמנע פלגשו
שמעה הדבר מיחה בו. אמרה אם תהרוג יעקב בניך יהיו משועבדי' תח' יד פרעה מלך
מצרים. כי הק' הבטיחו לאברהם בברית בין הבתרים כי גר יהיה זרעך בארץ לא להם.
ואליפז השיב מה אעשה לצוואת אבי והשיבה לו תצוה לעמלק בנך כשיצאו ממצרים
שיבא וילחם בהם וזהו ויבא עמלק.

and Kasher, *Torah shelemah*, xiv. 252–3.

[147] See Emanuel, *Shivrei luḥot*, 175–81, and Kanarfogel, *Peering through the Lattices*, 95–8, 225–7. This work was published under the title *Perushim ufesakim lerabenu avigdor tsarefati* [sic], ed. I. Herskovits (Jerusalem, 1996), on the basis of MSS Hamburg 45 and British Library Or. 2853. The attribution of the (as yet unpublished) *peshatim* in MS Hamburg 45 to R. Avigdor is not as certain. R. Avigdor cites a number of northern French and German Tosafists by name, most often in halakhic contexts. As listed in Hershkovits' index (pp. 536–7), Bekhor Shor's Torah commentary is cited only once, while Rashbam is cited more than ten times (although many of these citations refer to his commentary on *Bava Batra* or to comments made by Rashbam in Tosafot, rather than to his Torah commentary). Interestingly, there is a core of halakhic material on various verses contained in the 14th-cent. *Moshav zekenim* that parallels

longer extant *Kol bo* by Rabbi Shemaryah ben Simhah,[148] and *Derashot ufiskei halakhot* by Rabbi Hayim ben Isaac.[149]

Although the so-called tosafist Torah commentaries composed from the mid-thirteenth to the early fourteenth centuries were, on the whole, more committed to midrashic interpretation than to *peshuto shel mikra*, we have seen nonetheless that their use of Midrash followed certain patterns, methods, and aims, and was far from random. This was clearly the case for the earliest of these compilations, such as *Sefer hagan*,[150] but it also appears to hold true for the *Da'at zekenim* and *Hadar zekenim* collections, on which this study has focused, and even for some of the latest tosafist Torah compilations such as *Minhat yehudah*.[151]

Further study of Torah commentaries composed by full-fledged Tosafists, as well as the tosafist Torah compilations that bring together a fair amount of this material in addition to what was added by their lesser-known compilers, may serve to open additional windows into the thought and individualistic positions of the Tosafists, as well as their successors and contemporaries among the secondary elite within medieval Ashkenaz. Great care must be exercised when attempting to isolate the personal views of the Tosafists from the standard forms and features of tosafist talmudic interpretation, since the Tosafists typically followed the flow and the nuances of the talmudic corpus itself in offering interpretations and raising problematics.

To be sure, Tosafot comments on talmudic *sugyot* dedicated to themes and topics in aggadah were not automatically predicated on a commitment by the Tosafists to understand literally or uncritically the underlying biblical and rabbinic concepts. Thus, as I have demonstrated elsewhere, there are instances in which tosafist beliefs and ideological positions were shaped by or adhered to views that emerged essentially from the rubric of talmudic study, which was surely the most extensive site of the interpretational endeavours of the Tosafists.[152] Nonetheless, the somewhat

---

material found in both MS Hamburg 45 and MS British Library Or. 2853. See e.g. Emanuel, *Shivrei luhot*, 172 n. 89.

[148] See ibid. 166–74.

[149] This work was published in a critical edition by Y. S. Lange (Jerusalem, 1973) and by M. Abitan (Jerusalem, 2002). Of these three works, this one appears to have the least amount of non-halakhic exegesis and discussion. Cf. Noah Goldstein, 'R. Hayyim Eliezer b. Isaac Or Zarua: His Life and Work', D.H.L. diss., Yeshiva University, 1959, 36–7. These German and Austrian works parallel the various halakhic abridgements that appeared in northern France during the second half of the 13th cent., chief among them the *Sefer mitsvot katan* of R. Isaac b. Joseph of Corbeil, whose intended appeal to a larger and less knowledgeable audience was explicitly noted. See e.g. I. Ta-Shma, 'On *Sefer mitsvot gadol*, the Abridged *Sefer mitsvot gadol* and the Literature of Abridged Works' (Heb.), in Y. Horowitz (ed.), *The Abridged* Sefer mitsvot gadol *by Rabbi Abraham ben Ephraim* [Kitsur sefer mitsvot gadol lerabi avraham b. efrayim] (Jerusalem, 2005), 13–21; id., *Keneset mehkarim*, ii. 114 n. 9; and Urbach, *The Tosafists* (Heb.), ii. 571–4. Cf. also above, n. 47.

[150] See *Sefer hagan*, ed. Orlian, 52–67.   [151] See H. Touitou, '*Minhat yehudah*', 170–87.

[152] See e.g. Kanarfogel, 'Medieval Rabbinic Conceptions of the Messianic Age: The View of the Tosafists', in E. Fleischer et al. (eds.), *Me'ah She'arim: Studies in Medieval Jewish Spiritual Life in Memory of Isadore Twersky* (Jerusalem, 2001), 147–70.

surprising range of views among the Tosafists during the twelfth and thirteenth centuries on the question of anthropomorphism and the divine image or form were most often expressed in biblical comments or commentaries, or in otherwise separate and often multifaceted remarks devoted to this topic, in which both talmudic and non-talmudic texts and approaches were taken into account.[153] In the same vein, it is safe to say that we know much more about Rashi's proclivities in matters of thought and belief from his biblical commentaries than we do from his talmudic commentaries.[154] Further analysis of the various Ashkenazi Torah commentaries from the late twelfth to the early fourteenth centuries can shed much additional light on the intellectual and spiritual lives of the first- and second-level elites during the tosafist period and beyond.

[153] See Kanarfogel, 'Varieties of Belief in Medieval Ashkenaz: The Case of Anthropomorphism', in M. Goldish and D. Frank (eds.), *Rabbinic Culture and Its Critics* (Detroit, Mich., 2008), 117–59.

[154] Cf. above, n. 14. I am indebted to my friend and colleague Professor Moshe Sokolow of Yeshiva University for reading an earlier draft of this study and offering a number of helpful suggestions in terms of both content and style.

FIFTEEEN

ZOHARIC LITERATURE AND MIDRASHIC TEMPORALITY

ELLIOT WOLFSON

WE ARE AT A POINT in the academic study of the Zohar of great transition and uncertainty, one might even be tempted to say a moment of aporetic suspension. The dominant view for the better part of the twentieth century, spearheaded by Gershom Scholem and Isaiah Tishby,[1] that the bulk of this work, with the exclusion of the *Raya meheimna* stratum and the *Tikunim* (first published in Mantua in 1558), was composed by Moses ben Shem Tov de León, has been challenged from a number of perspectives. The model of single authorship of diverse literary strata lumped together under the rubric *guf hazohar* ('the body of the Zohar') has been replaced by the idea of a circle,[2] or perhaps a multiplicity of circles,[3] which were

---

[1] Gershom Scholem, *Major Trends in Jewish Mysticism* (New York, 1956), 156–243; Isaiah Tishby, *The Wisdom of the Zohar: An Anthology of Texts*, trans. David Goldstein, 3 vols. (Oxford, 1989), i. 1–126.

[2] Yehuda Liebes, *Studies in the Zohar*, trans. Arnold Schwartz, Stephanie Nakache, and Penina Peli (Albany, NY, 1993), 85–138; id., 'Zohar as Renaissance' (Heb.), *Da'at*, 46 (2001), 5–11; id., 'Zohar and Tikunei zohar: From Renaissance to Revolution' (Heb.), *Te'udah*, 21/22 (2007), 251–301.

[3] Ronit Meroz, 'Zoharic Narratives and Their Adaptations', *Hispania Judaica*, 3 (2000), 3–63. Meroz has elaborated and refined her thesis in a number of other studies: 'The Chariot of Ezekiel—An Unknown Zoharic Commentary' (Heb.), *Te'udah* 16/17 (2001), 567–616; ead., 'Der Aufbau des Buches Sohar', *PaRDeS: Zeitschrift der Vereinigung für Jüdische Studien*, 11 (2005), 16–36; ead., 'The Weaving of a Myth: An Analysis of Two Stories in the Zohar' (Heb.), in Howard Kreisel (ed.), *Study and Knowledge in Jewish Thought*, vol. ii (Be'er Sheva, 2006), 167–205; ead., 'The Middle Eastern Origins of Kabbalah', *Journal for the Study of Sephardic and Mizrahi Jewry* (2007), 39–56; ead., 'R. Joseph Angelet and his "Zoharic Writings"' (Heb.), *Te'udah*, 21/22 (2007), 303–404; ead., 'The Path of Silence: An Unknown Story from a Zohar Manuscript', *European Journal of Jewish Studies*, 1 (2008), 319–42; and ead., 'The Writing of the Zoharic *Sitrei torah*—R. Ya'akov Shatz and His Co-Writers' (Heb.), *Kabbalah: Journal for the Study of Jewish Mystical Texts*, 22 (2010), 253–81. See also Daniel C. Matt, *The Zohar: Pritzker Edition*, vol. i (Stanford, Calif., 2004), p. xvi: 'Within the manuscripts themselves were signs of an editorial process: revision, reformulation, and emendation. After careful analysis, I concluded that certain manuscripts of older lineage reflect an earlier recension of the *Zohar*, which was then reworked in manuscripts of later lineage.' In spite of recognizing that we cannot speak of an 'original' text or even a 'best' manuscript, Matt adopts a conventional methodology of producing an eclectic text based on what he judges to be the better readings from among the variants culled from manuscripts, the first two printed editions, the edition used by Moses Cordovero in his 16th-cent. commentary, *Or yakar*, and a series of

allegedly active in Castile and/or Aragon in the thirteenth and fourteenth centuries. It has even been argued that the contours of the text did not assume stability until the sixteenth century, at the time that kabbalists were actively engaged in preparing the material for publication.[4]

At the present stage of research, many of the philological and historical issues that a scholar would ideally be expected to know before proceeding to thematic analyses are still unresolved. In this chapter, I will nevertheless assume the relative coherence and dependability of the zoharic corpus from the standpoint of the first two printed editions (Mantua and Cremona, 1558–60) and the publications of ancillary parts not included in the aforementioned recensions, the *Midrash hane'elam* on Ruth published as *Yesod shirim* or *Tapuḥei zahav* (Thienigen, 1559, Venice, 1566, and Kraków, 1593), also published together with the section on Song of Songs (Salonika, 1597), as well as other units and fragments assembled by Abraham ben Eliezer Halevi Berukhim on the basis of manuscripts that circulated among the Safed kabbalists and printed with the title *Zohar ḥadash* (Kraków, 1603, followed by the second and third editions respectively in Venice, 1658 and Amsterdam, 1701). The justification for doing so is not to deny the advancements of the field and the heightened sensitivity with regard to the fluidity of the redactional boundaries of the collection of textual units that eventually circulated as *Sefer hazohar*. Regarding this matter, let me say that, while I accept the general drift of the current research, I do not think there is sufficient material evidence to afford the scholar the possibility of isolating and identifying 'original' strata set apart from later accretions.[5] I thus agree with the contention of Daniel Abrams regarding the 'textual instability' of the Zohar

---

other printed sources, including Menahem Recanati's *Perush al hatorah*, Joseph Angelet's *Livnat hasapir*, Abraham Galante's commentary on the Zohar in *Or haḥamah*, Simeon Lavi's *Ketem paz*, the *Derekh emet*, ed. Joseph Hamits, Shalom Buzaglo's *Mikdash melekh*, Yehudah Ashlag's *Perush hasulam* on his zoharic translation, and the marginalia in *Gershom Scholem's Annotated Zohar* [Sefer hazohar shel gershom sholem], 6 vols. (Jerusalem, 1992; see p. xvii n. 8).

[4] Boaz Huss, '"Sefer ha-Zohar" as a Canonical, Sacred and Holy Text: Changing Perspectives of the Book of Splendor between the Thirteenth and Eighteenth Centuries', *Journal of Jewish Thought and Philosophy*, 7 (1997), 257–307; id., *Like the Radiance of the Sky: Chapters in the Reception History of the Zohar and Construction of Its Symbolic Value* [Kezohar harakia: perakim betoledot hitkablut hazohar uvehavniyat erkho hasemali] (Jerusalem, 2008); Daniel Abrams, 'Critical and Post-Critical Textual Scholarship of Jewish Mystical Literature: Notes on the History and Development of Modern Editing Techniques', *Kabbalah: Journal for the Study of Jewish Mystical Texts*, 1 (1996), 17–71; id., 'The Invention of the Zohar as a Book: On the Assumptions and Expectations of the Kabbalists and Modern Scholars', *Kabbalah: Journal for the Study of Jewish Mystical Texts*, 19 (2009), 7–142; and the expanded versions of these studies in Daniel Abrams, *Kabbalistic Manuscripts and Textual Theory: Methodologies of Textual Scholarship and Editorial Practice in the Study of Jewish Mysticism*, with a foreword by David Greetham (Los Angeles, 2010), 17–117, and 224–428.

[5] In this matter I differ with Daniel Matt, for whom the printed text of Margaliot, whose format can be traced back to the Mantua edition, continues to serve as a base text whence one determines if a variant is desirable. As Matt himself states, his aim is to remove the 'accumulated layers of revision, thereby restoring a more original text', and thus he believes that it is still meaningful to speak of recovering 'the Zohar's primal texture and cryptic flavor' (*The Zohar: Pritzker Edition*, vol. i, p. xviii).

and the prudence of thinking of it as a 'family' of disparate 'literary phenomena'[6] rather than as a 'closed book' whose 'original version' can be 'recovered from a comparison of the scattered manuscripts'.[7] Thus, I accept the mandate that Abrams proposes for scholars to abandon any form of 'textual idealism', that is, the assumption that we can 'carve out' an original text from the 'surviving witnesses',[8] but I would take issue with him inasmuch as I think that it is still possible to posit a coherent textual sense with respect to the homiletical passages gathered together within the margins of this literary artefact in the course of at least three centuries. In my judgement, we can still profitably refer to these passages as expressive of a singular phenomenon classified as the zoharic kabbalah, even if this necessitates extending the boundaries of the text over several centuries to accommodate a principle of anthologizing that unifies through multiplicity.

The very metaphor of 'family' is here instructive: genetic connectivity is the characteristic that holds together the potentially indefinite and incongruent branches on any family tree, linking together individuals who may have no bond in the conventional social-anthropological sense. The conception of time underlying the kabbalistic hermeneutic, to be discussed below, is what upholds expanding the notion of textual kinship to include the dissimilar on equal footing with the similar. On this score, the discord and divergence preserved in the assortment of texts eventually published as the Zohar promoted the harmonization of voices across time. I thus do not accept that it is only the modern scholar who can speak of the 'family resemblance' between the 'multiple efforts to write about certain biblical sections' that were canonized as the book of the Zohar in the sixteenth century.[9] This resemblance was already at play in kabbalistic textual communities from the latter part of the thirteenth century, and hence it is feasible to contemplate authorial intention without succumbing to textual idealism.[10]

A full analysis of this topic lies beyond the concerns of this chapter, but I will illustrate the point by considering Meroz's hypothesis regarding the bilingual text that she has designated the 'Midrash of Rabbi Isaac' and that she traces to eleventh-century Palestine or Egypt. The dating is based, in part, on the statement that Israel would be exiled for one thousand years after the destruction of the Jerusalem Temple, which Meroz assumes would probably have been written sometime in the eleventh century but prior to 1068.[11] The text appears in both the Mantua and

---

[6] Abrams, *Kabbalistic Manuscripts*, 423-4.
[7] Ibid. 464, 466-7.
[8] Ibid. 446.
[9] Ibid. 439.
[10] See, by contrast, ibid. 526-34. Compare ibid. 13, where Abrams attempts to distinguish his own methodology from my own. While I appreciate the generosity of his tone, I have serious questions about the legitimacy of this contrast, since when it comes to any discussion of ideas embedded in Abrams's investigation of the textual culture of kabbalistic materials, I do not see a radical break with my own thinking. More importantly, not one of my phenomenological and hermeneutical studies would have to be modified by appeal to 'textual instability' or the 'fluidity of the text' (ibid. 446). Simply put, my critical interventions are not based on presuming that an *Urtext* of any document can be recovered.
[11] Meroz, 'The Middle Eastern Origins', 46-9.

Cremona editions of the Zohar, but, as Scholem has already observed, there is an interesting discrepancy with respect to a section of the text: in the Mantua version (2: 16b–17a) there is a mixture of Hebrew and Aramaic, whereas the parallel in the Cremona edition (Exodus 7c, column 27) is entirely in Hebrew.[12] At best, what Meroz has demonstrated is that there is an older midrashic microform that has been incorporated into the zoharic corpus, either in the original Hebrew or translated into Aramaic at some later phase of the editorial process. It is not clear, however, that if we isolate the microform from its redactional context—and, as far as I can tell, there is no manuscript evidence of the microform apart from collections of zoharic material[13]—it should be labelled in some 'originary' sense as part of the Zohar.[14] In my judgement, all attempts to reconstruct the redactional strata of the zoharic text are subject to this criticism and thus remain highly conjectural. This is so even when manuscripts (invariably from a later period than the presumed times of composition of the distinct textual seams) have been used to substantiate the elaborate and at times rather fanciful reconstructions, especially the effort to demarcate the sociological parameters of the zoharic circles based on variants that are essentially orthographical and philological in nature.[15] The import of my suggestion to shift the focus of the discourse from the question of pseudepigraphy to an appreciation of the literary, moral, and religious value of anonymity in medieval kabbalistic fraternities was to loosen the grip of the historiographical concern in the field to pinpoint the authors and date of composition of this text.[16]

In spite of the methodological problems currently at the centre of the scholarly agenda, I readily acknowledge the likelihood that the zoharic text accrued over an extensive period of time and that, in great measure, the taxonomy of a 'book' applied to it is a later invention.[17] We must be attentive not only to the manifold layers of this compilation and the probability of different authors, but also to the fact that many interpolations, particularly from the period of aggressive redaction in the sixteenth century, have found their way into the received text. Notwithstanding the cogency of these claims, it is still viable, in my opinion, to speak of a homogeneous vision underlying the various strata of zoharic literature. Recognition of plurivocality does not undermine the soundness of positing a uniform world-view; on the contrary,

---

[12] *Gershom Scholem's Annotated Zohar*, 1140. See also Yehuda Liebes, 'Hebrew and Aramaic Languages of the Zohar', *Aramaic Studies*, 4 (2006), 35–52, esp. 42.

[13] The manuscripts mentioned by Meroz, 'The Middle Eastern Origins', 41–2 nn. 9–10 are Zurich Heidelberg 83 (Spanish script *c*.1500), Munich 20 (Spanish script from the 16th cent.), and Moscow Guenzberg 293 (Italian script written in Pisa 1549).

[14] For an independent critique of Meroz's argument, see Abrams, *Kabbalistic Manuscripts*, 346–7.

[15] The comments of Tishby, *The Wisdom of the Zohar*, i. 100, still seem to me relevant even though today we have a better sense of the scope and diversity of the zoharic manuscripts.

[16] This shift in orientation is the gist of my argument in Elliot R. Wolfson, 'The Anonymous Chapters of the Elderly Master of Secrets—New Evidence for the Early Activity of the Zoharic Circle', *Kabbalah: Journal for the Study of Jewish Mystical Texts*, 19 (2009), 143–278.

[17] This is the thesis endorsed most vigorously by Abrams; see references above, n. 4.

heterogeneity may itself be demonstrative of a shared perspective, and repetition may be the impetus for difference.[18] It goes without saying that I no longer accept Scholem's surmise that the multiple explanations of a verse found in any given zoharic pericope bespeak 'homiletical variations on one subject' rather than 'a plurality of writers'.[19] However, one can posit several authors of a treatise—even straddling several centuries—and continue to speak of a unifying factor; indeed, one might make the case on hermeneutical grounds that it is precisely the unifying factor that allows for diversity. The weave of the textual fabric does not disrupt the possibility of an iteration that renews itself indefinitely.[20] It is from that methodological viewpoint that I proceed to discuss the midrashic element in the zoharic compilation.[21]

MIDRASH AND THE SPACING OF TIME

There have been many approaches to Midrash both as a literary genre and as an exegetical modality. For the purposes of this chapter I wish to focus on a somewhat neglected aspect of the midrashic mentality, the intersection of time and hermeneutics, or, more specifically, the discontinuity and reiteration that characterize the assumptions about time underlying the rabbinic approach to the scriptural text that

---

[18] This point is sorely missed by Idel's erroneous characterization of my work as 'monistic' or 'totalizing' and the appeal to his own alleged sense of *différence* and celebration of diversity, or what he calls polychromatism. For a specific criticism of my reading of zoharic literature, see Moshe Idel, *Kabbalah and Eros* (New Haven, Conn., 2005), 129–30, and my rejoinder in the first reference cited below, n. 20.

[19] Scholem, *Major Trends*, 172. Scholem entertained the possibility that the 'existence of a multitude of writings of apparently very different character, loosely assembled under the title of "Zohar", seems to leave no argument against the view that they do in fact belong to different writers and different periods' (p. 159). However, he reached the conclusion that the different strata 'are the work of one author. It is not true that they were written at different periods or by different authors, nor is it possible to detect different historical layers within the various parts themselves. Here and there a sentence or a few words may have been added at some later date, but in the main the distinction . . . between so-called authentic parts and subsequent interpolations does not bear serious investigation' (p. 163). The argument for the 'constructional unity' of the Zohar, based on similarity of literary style, language, and ideas, is repeated in Gershom Scholem, *Kabbalah* (Jerusalem, 1974), 220–1. The position rejected by Scholem has emerged today as the dominant paradigm of zoharic research.

[20] For a more elaborate discussion, see Elliot R. Wolfson, 'Structure, Innovation, and Diremptive Temporality: The Use of Models to Study Continuity and Discontinuity in Kabbalistic Tradition', *Journal for the Study of Religions and Ideologies*, 6 (2007), 153–6. See also id., *Language, Eros, Being: Kabbalistic Hermeneutics and Poetic Imagination* (New York, 2005), 47–8.

[21] An alternative way to approach this topic would have been to discuss the impact of midrashic collections (especially from the 11th and 12th cents.) on the zoharic authors, to show the creative appropriation and recasting of the earlier sources, which would also afford the opportunity to assess the protokabbalistic elements in the rabbinic *midrashim*. See the concise statement on this literary possibility in Gershom Scholem, *Origins of the Kabbalah*, ed. R. J. Zwi Werblowsky, trans. Allan Arkush (Princeton, NJ, 1987), p. 17. Scholem's assessment is limited to the impact of the *midrashim* edited or redacted by rabbinic circles in Languedoc on the *Bahir*, but his words could be applied to Spanish kabbalists as well, particularly those responsible for the zoharic homilies. On the midrashic sources used in the Zohar, see Scholem, *Major Trends*, 173, and compare the reference below, n. 32.

is the subject of interpretation. Critical to this strategy of reading is the spatial bridging of past and future in the irreducible present that is constituted transcendentally within the immanence of consciousness. Phenomenologically speaking, past and future have no temporal density apart from the noematic lived experience of the present, but the latter lacks any ideational content except through the noetic synthesis of the intentional acts of retention and protention, which point respectively to the past and future crisscrossing in the moment, the primordially perceptual present that cannot be represented as presence inasmuch as it always exceeds what can be presented, the now, we might say, that is perpetually not-now. As Heidegger succinctly expressed the archaic poetic wisdom, 'time goes ... in that it passes away. The passing of time is, of course, a coming, but a coming which goes, in passing away. What comes in time never comes to stay, but to go.'[22] The temporal comportment, accordingly, is occasioned by the repetition of the indeterminate and the indeterminacy of the repetitious colluding in the living instant, the *tempus discretum*, the cut that binds one synchronically to the diachronic opening of time, the rhythmic discontinuity[23] of the continuous present, the non-coincidental coincidence, the blink of the eye that is both repetitive and diremptive.

This sense of time has far-reaching implications for how we construe the proximity and distance of the present to the past and to the future, a determination that is crucial to appraise the hermeneutical presuppositions of what can be called the midrashic condition. Rather than viewing the temporal as a sequence of punctual nodules strung together in a linear fashion like beads of a necklace, or as a succession of discrete points rotating in a circular manner, time is better considered as a swerve—the linear circle or the circular line—that necessitates the constant accommodation of the recollected past to the bestowal of the future and of the anticipated future to the yielding of the past. In the givenness of the indivisible and non-representable present, every reverberation is a recurrence of what has never transpired. From the perspective of the egological narrative that shapes our perception of the normal lifespan, the duration of time is experienced as a river that flows from birth to death, but from a perspective that is not so constricted, time may be better imagined as a whirlpool, a vortex in which remembrance is as much of the future as expectation is of the past.

This calibration supplies the key to understanding the midrashic approach to Scripture. This is not to deny the current trend in the field of rabbinics to avoid generalizations, and to apply instead a type of literary analysis that rests on a form-critical approach that treats the different parts of the corpus atomistically. I would

---

[22] Martin Heidegger, *What Is Called Thinking?* trans. Fred D. Wieck and J. Glenn Gray, with an introduction by J. Glenn Gray (New York, 1968), 96.

[23] I borrow this expression from Eftichis Pirovolakis, *Reading Derrida and Ricoeur: Improbable Encounters between Deconstruction and Hermeneutics* (Albany, NY, 2010), 43–81. While many of the insights expressed in this essay repeat what I have written about time and hermeneutics in several previously published studies, the formulation here has benefited from the analysis offered by Pirovolakis.

appeal nonetheless to the philosophical truism that plurality is discernible only against the backdrop of uniformity, just as uniformity is discernible only against the backdrop of plurality; the dialectical relation of identity and difference should forestall setting them in antithetical conflict. The dialectic I envision does not involve overcoming the difference between identity and difference by affirming the identity of identity and difference, but rather the paradoxical identification of their identity in virtue of their difference.[24] In my judgement, it is still theoretically warranted and heuristically feasible to ponder the variant expressions of the midrashic sensibility in different textual settings by identifying patterns of thought and unified systems. I hasten to add that these patterns are expressive of an *infinite genetic multiple*,[25] that is, the systemic assumptions that provide the relatively stable framework through and in which the changing patterns evolve, dissolve, and revolve. We are justified, then, in presuming that sameness is precisely the criterion that engenders difference and, as such, there is no need to bifurcate the two. Echoing the words of Theodor Adorno, we could say that it is unity alone that transcends unity,[26] for the 'nonidentical' itself is the 'thing's own identity against its identifications'.[27] The cognitive ideal 'combines an appetite for incorporation with an aversion to what cannot be incorporated, to the very thing that would need to be known', the 'essence' of the individual—as opposed to the universal—about whom it can always be said that it 'is more than it is', a 'more' that 'is not imposed upon it but remains immanent to it', the 'innermost core of the object' that 'proves to be simultaneously extraneous to it, the phenomenon of its seclusion'.[28] Adorno approvingly mentions Husserl's insight that 'the universal dwells at the centre of the individual', but he adds that 'absolute individuality is a product of the very process of abstractions that is begun for universality's sake. The individual cannot be deduced from thought, yet the core of individuality would be comparable to those utterly individuated works of art which spurn all schemata and whose analysis will rediscover universal moments in their extreme individuation.'[29]

Based on this calculation, I would proffer that it is still prudent to speak collectively of the literary culture of the rabbis as long as we are mindful that the general will constantly be recovered from the extreme individuation of the particular. The notion of an indissoluble individual is as much an abstraction as that of an immutable universal. This supposition has a direct impact on the viability of thinking about a concept of temporality endemic to the midrashic imagination, predicated on

---

[24] The articulation of this logic has been central to much of my work. See e.g. Wolfson, *Language, Eros, Being*, pp. xix–xx, 64–5, 99–105. For a magisterial analysis of the history of dialectical thinking and its persistence in contemporary currents of Western philosophy, see Frederic Jameson, *Valences of the Dialectic* (London, 2009).

[25] My coinage is indebted to the 'infinite generic multiple' mentioned by Alain Badiou and Slavoj Žižek, *Philosophy in the Present*, ed. Peter Engelmann, trans. Peter Thomas and Alberto Toscano (Cambridge, 2010), 26–48.

[26] Theodor W. Adorno, *Negative Dialectics*, trans. E. B. Ashton (New York, 1979), 158.

[27] Ibid. 160. [28] Ibid. 161 [29] Ibid. 162.

configuring time in such a way that the past is appropriated and thereby determined by the present, even as the present is appropriated and thereby determined by the past. The possibility of a future arises from this reversal of the prevailing paradigm of causality. Applying this hermeneutically, we can similarly speak of the text delineated by the interpretation that is delineated by the text. Within this circle of reciprocity—a circle that is open at both termini—the timeline of exegesis, which allows for the creative recasting of biblical law and narrative in accord with the impressional exigencies of the moment, can be drawn.

ZOHARIC EXEGESIS AND THE FOURFOLD TEMPORALITY OF THE NARRATIVE

The conception of time that informed the midrashic mindset reaches a crescendo in the homilies that were eventually included in what may be called the zoharic literature.[30] In spite of the complexity of the history of the text, we can assert with relative confidence that the decisive redactional strategy was to organize the exegetical sermons as a commentary on the Pentateuch. Here it is apposite to recall Scholem's observation that the literary composition of the Zohar 'outwardly imitates the form of the Midrash. It is evident that the author had no clear perception of the difference between the old Midrash, whose tradition he tried to carry on, and the medieval homily which issued from his pen without his being aware of it.' Scholem goes on to note that 'in the old Midrash' the introductions that precede the interpretation of the relevant verse from the Pentateuch 'display a loose mosaic of authentic remarks and sayings', whereas in the 'mystical Midrash' of the Zohar they 'are really like homilies carefully built up with an eye to formal unity and coherence of thought'.[31] Not only did the zoharic authors draw freely from rabbinic *midrashim*, including, to name a few of the most important sources, the various texts that were eventually published as *Midrash Rabbah*, *Tanḥuma*, *Pesikta derav kahana*, *Pesikta rabati*, *Midrash tehilim*, and *Pirkei derabi eli'ezer*,[32] but structurally and rhetorically, the Zohar is essentially midrashic, and this extends from the earliest stratum, the *Midrash hane'elam*, which is made up of exegetical narratives closest in spirit to the aggadic *midrashim*, to the latest stratum, the *Tikunim*, which is organized around seventy different interpretations of the first word of Genesis. Rather than simply repeating the rabbinic dicta, the medieval kabbalists fabricated a more coherent narrative laid

---

[30] The locution, which has become prevalent in contemporary scholarship following the lead of Liebes, was already used by Scholem, *Major Trends*, 159.

[31] Scholem, *Major Trends*, 171. See ibid. 174, where Scholem characterized the imagination of the zoharic author in terms of a 'tendency towards dramatization, equally apparent in the architecture of whole compositions and in the manner in which brief Talmudic stories or legends are converted into lively Aggadoth on the same subject. Where an Aggadah already contains mystical elements, these are of course duly emphasized and occasionally woven into an entirely new myth.' On the mystical reinscription of myth in zoharic homilies, compare Michael Fishbane, *Biblical Myth and Rabbinic Mythmaking* (Oxford, 2003), 313–14.   [32] Tishby, *The Wisdom of the Zohar*, i. 75.

atop the biblical account,[33] one that reflects a distinctive metaphysical scheme that renders the scriptural idiom symbolically based on the identification of the Torah and God.[34] I am inclined to accept that there are traces of this idea in older sources, but it does not become explicit until the Middle Ages, whence it emerges as an axiom—one might say ground concept—of Jewish esotericism. In the specific location of the zoharic homilies, the identity of God and Torah fosters the ideal of textual embodiment,[35] which effectively narrows the gap between revelation and interpretation. To study the text is to behold the image of the divine.[36] Michael Fishbane well captured the hermeneutical stance of the zoharic kabbalists when he noted that 'there is no separation between living the truth of Scripture and living the truth of God ... Scripture suffuses all; for it is the real myth of God ... God's truth is refracted in fragments of myth bound by the syntax of Scripture.'[37]

The zoharic kabbalists creatively expanded the sense of time at play in the collections of midrashic dicta from late antiquity and the early Middle Ages. To be sure, the kabbalistic reworking of the earlier material is enhanced by two assumptions: first, as I have already noted, the belief that the Torah is the body or the image of the divine, and second, the pseudepigraphic attribution of the zoharic dicta to the ancient sages. The combination of these tenets extended the twofold nature of time operative in the rabbinic sources to a quaternal conception. Thus, in the zoharic homilies we can distinguish four temporal modalities corresponding to four identities that mould the interpretation of the scriptural narrative: (1) the divine emanations, (2) the biblical personae, (3) the rabbinic figures, and (4) the unnamed kabbalists.[38]

[33] On the zoharic exegetical creativity as an *ars poetica*, see Yehuda Liebes, 'Zohar and Eros' (Heb.), *Alpayim*, 9 (1994), 67–115.

[34] This principle has been discussed by several scholars. See Gershom Scholem, *On the Kabbalah and Its Symbolism*, trans. Ralph Manheim (New York, 1965), 37–44; id., 'The Name of God and the Linguistic Theory of the Kabbala', *Diogenes*, 79 (1972), 79–80; 80 (1972), 178–80, 193–4; Tishby, *The Wisdom of the Zohar*, iii. 1079–82; Moshe Idel, 'The Concept of Torah in Hekhalot Literature and Its Metamorphosis in Kabbalah', *Jerusalem Studies in Jewish Thought*, 1 (1981), 23–84, esp. 49–58; id., *Absorbing Perfections: Kabbalah and Interpretation*, foreword by Harold Bloom (New Haven, Conn., 2002), 69–74, 119–24, 298–9, 459–60; Wolfson, *Language, Eros, Being*, 26, 41, 124–5, 137–8, 239–40, 243–6, 248–9, 255–8.

[35] For an extensive discussion of what I call the 'textual embodiment' and 'poetic incarnation', see Wolfson, *Language, Eros, Being*, 190–260.

[36] Elliot R. Wolfson, *Through a Speculum That Shines: Vision and Imagination in Medieval Jewish Mysticism* (Princeton, NJ, 1994), 375–7.

[37] Fishbane, *Biblical Myth and Rabbinic Mythmaking*, 309. For an earlier formulation, see id., *The Garments of Torah: Essays in Biblical Hermeneutics* (Bloomington, Ind., 1989), 41–3. On the 'exegetical spirituality' and the hermeneutical process in the Zohar, see id., *The Exegetical Imagination: On Jewish Thought and Theology* (Cambridge, Mass., 1998), 105–22. Fishbane duly notes how zoharic interpretation develops 'through the exegetical transformation of biblical passages' (p. 114). See also the analysis of language, experience, and myth in Maurizio Mottolese, *Analogy in Midrash and Kabbalah: Interpretive Projections of the Sanctuary and Ritual* (Los Angeles, 2007), 336–65.

[38] Wolfson, *Language, Eros, Being*, 37–8. The relationship of temporality and narrativity in zoharic exegesis, based on my prior observations, is noted as well by Nathan Wolski, *A Journey into the Zohar: An Introduction to the Book of Radiance* (Albany, NY, 2010), 213–14, 255 n. 48 (where the author's indebtedness to me is acknowledged).

These four can be grouped under two types of temporality: the first, which stands by itself, comprises the genus of eternal time, the unfolding of the infinite darkness in the innumerable folds of light that constitute the eternality of time and the temporality of eternity; and the remaining three, which constitute the genus of temporal time, the time of temporality measured by human technology and recorded as the annals of historical epochs. The movement through these four gradations is presented at times as an exegetical journey of a linear sort, passing hierarchically from the mundane to the divine, the lower to the upper, the corporeal to the spiritual. The journey, however, is anything but linear. For the kabbalists, the line (*kav*) must always be considered in conjunction with the circle (*igul*), the two dominant geometric prisms through which the constellation of the divine pleroma, and indeed the whole concatenation of being, is constructed in the human imagination.[39] Rather than viewing the linear and circular as antinomical, the kabbalistic mindset requires the paradoxical identification of the two, epitomized, for instance, in Abraham Abulafia's arresting image of the 'circular ladder' (*sulam agol*),[40] to which he also refers as the 'spherical ladder' (*hasulam hakaduri*).[41] Time and space are arranged in the same dual pattern. Focusing on the former, I would conjecture that to be attuned to the linear circularity of the timeswerve is to traverse the commonplace threefold demarcation of the temporal: the past is the present as future, the present, the future as past, and the future, the past as present.[42]

The compresence of the three tenses of time—a notion derived by kabbalists from a longstanding understanding of what is implied by the Tetragrammaton, that God is, was, and shall be concurrently—renders simultaneity and sequentiality coterminous: what is experienced as sequential from one vantage point is in fact simultaneous from another. In this regard, the conception of time enunciated by the voices preserved in the Zohar is quintessentially poetic, since the poem entails, as Paul Celan has eloquently articulated it, the 'mystery of encounter', which takes place in the 'one unique, momentary present'—the 'here and now' that transforms 'its already-no-longer [*Schon-nicht-mehr*] into its always-still [*Immer-noch*]'.[43] This corresponds

---

[39] Ronit Meroz, 'Redemption in the Lurianic Teaching' [Hage'ulah betorat ha'ari], Ph.D. thesis, Hebrew University of Jerusalem, 1988, 232–4, 239–42; Mordecai Pachter, *Roots of Faith and Devequt: Studies in the History of Kabbalistic Ideas* (Los Angeles, 2004), 131–84.

[40] Abraham Abulafia, 'Sefer hamelits', in *Matsref hasekhel vesefer haot*, ed. Amnon Gross (Jerusalem, 2001), 30.

[41] Ibid. 31. See Moshe Idel, *The Mystical Experience in Abraham Abulafia* (Albany, NY, 1988), 109–11; Elliot R. Wolfson, *Abraham Abulafia—Kabbalist and Prophet: Hermeneutics, Theosophy and Theurgy* (Los Angeles, 2000), 128 n. 92, 135, 152 n. 157.

[42] For a more elaborate discussion of linear circularity, see Elliot R. Wolfson, *Alef, Mem, Tau: Kabbalistic Musings on Time, Truth, and Death* (Berkeley, Calif., 2006), 55–117, esp. 58–9.

[43] Paul Celan, *The Meridian: Final Version—Drafts—Materials*, ed. Bernhard Böschenstein and Heino Schmull with assistance from Michael Schwarzkopf and Christiane Wittkop, trans. and with a preface by Pierre Joris (Stanford, Calif., 2011), 8–9; German: Paul Celan, *Der Meridian: Endfassung–Entwürfe–Materialien*, ed. Bernhard Böschenstein and Heino Schmull with assistance from Michael Schwarzkopf and Christiane Wittkop (Frankfurt am Main, 1999), 8–9. I have also consulted the

exactly to the enigmatic locution in one zoharic passage, *milin ḥadetin atikin*, 'new ancient words',[44] that is, the words of Torah that are concomitantly novel and ancient.[45] Analogously, according to a second passage, the disciples of the school of Rav—probably a cipher for the Spanish kabbalists—are described as 'renewing the ancient words every day, and the Shekhinah dwells upon them and listens to their words'.[46] In zoharic kabbalah, moreover, textual interpretation is similarly akin to Celan's depiction of poetry as 'language-become-shape' (*gestaltwordene Sprache*)—to express it in terminology germane to Jewish esotericism, the *shiur komah* of the divine body, the name that is the Torah[47]—a process of poiesis that is perpetually 'underway' (*unterwegs*), a verbal gesticulation that 'wants to head toward some other', to let 'the most essential aspect of the other speak', albeit in the 'immediacy and nearness' of 'its time' (*dessen Zeit*).[48] Its time—the momentary present, 'already-no-longer' but 'always-still', indeed, always-still precisely because already-no-longer.

THE TIME OF WALKING AND THE HERMENEUTICAL PATH

It is this conception of time that underlies the centrality of the image of walking in the visionary landscape[49] of the zoharic anthology.[50] Prima facie, one might be tempted to gauge the importance of this activity from the vantage point of spatiality.[51] This is

alternative translation in *Selected Poems and Prose of Paul Celan*, trans. John Felstiner (New York, 2001), 401–13, esp. 409.

[44] Zohar iii. 166*b*.

[45] On the relationship of the old and new in zoharic exegesis, see Daniel C. Matt, '*Matnita Dilan*: A Technique of Innovation in the Zohar' (Heb.), *Jerusalem Studies in Jewish Thought*, 8 (1989), 123–45; id., '"New-Ancient Words": The Aura of Secrecy in the Zohar', in Peter Schäfer and Joseph Dan (eds.), *Gershom Scholem's 'Major Trends in Jewish Mysticism': 50 Years After* (Tübingen, 1993), 181–207. Speaking about Moses de León's pseudepigraphic activity, Matt writes that 'Ramdal liberates himself from the fetters of time, space and ego. He has surrendered his identity as author, but in the process, he has gained ancient authority' ('"New-Ancient Words", 184). Although I would not quibble with the main point, I think it is more accurate to say that de León (or any of the other historical personae whose voices are preserved in the zoharic text) enters another dimension of time and space rather than being liberated therefrom. To speak without qualification of the creative process as liberation from the confinement of space and time presupposes a monolithic understanding of these phenomena.

[46] Zohar iii. 197*b*.   [47] Ibid. ii. 87*a*, 90*b*, 124*a*; iii. 13*b*, 75*a*, 159*a*. See above, n. 34.

[48] Celan, *The Meridian*, 9; *Der Meridian*, 9–10.

[49] The phrase is appropriated from Paul Piehler, *The Visionary Landscape: A Study in Medieval Allegory* (Montreal, 1971).

[50] This motif of walking was explored extensively by my student David Greenstein, 'Aimless Pilgrimage: The Quotidian Utopia of the Zohar', Ph.D. diss., New York University, 2003. On the mystical praxis of wandering on the path or walking on the way, see also Melila Hellner-Eshed, *A River Flows From Eden: The Language of Mystical Experience in the Zohar*, trans. Nathan Wolski (Stanford, Calif., 2009), 116–20; Nathan Wolski, 'Don Quixote and Sancho Panza Were Walking on the Way: El Caballero Andante and the Book of Radiance (*Sefer ha-Zohar*)', *Shofar: An Interdisciplinary Journal of Jewish Studies*, 27 (2009), 24–47; id., *A Journey into the Zohar*, 10–12, 143.

[51] Greenstein, 'Aimless Pilgrimage', 199–323.

a reasonable assumption—the stations of the crossing are determined by the points of departure and destination—but, as it happens, in these texts the sense of expedition seems to be primarily an orientation of time. I do not mean to suggest that one can actually separate the spatial and the temporal or that the spatial is to be conceived of as an epiphenomenon of the temporal; I agree with thinkers who have argued that the two dimensions of experience cannot be disentangled,[52] an idea that finds support in kabbalistic literature as well.[53] In the jargon of quantum mechanics, objects that exist—understood either as 'solid material bodies' or as 'localized fields of energy'— are characterized by the 'spatiotemporal extensiveness of actualities and systems of actualities'.[54] We may infer, kabbalistically, that the tensiveness of the event is similarly grasped by this notion of spatiotemporal extensiveness. Insofar as the nature of being is linguistic, the actual occasion, the eventfulness of becoming, can be specularized ontically or hermeneutically. Hence, the task of reading that may be elicited from zoharic texts, as I have argued elsewhere, is a gesture of meandering in the 'imaginal time-space' wherein one finds 'oneself always in the middle, along the path, betwixt and between, conceiving the imagined as real and the real as imagined'.[55] The homiletical language of these kabbalists may be likened poetically to a mirror of temporal spaces and spatial intervals in and through which the image of the imageless is refracted.[56] Nevertheless, there is a sense in which time is granted a privileged position in a manner that is consonant with the way that in the Western philosophical tradition (noticeably since Kant) the correlation of consciousness and time has engendered an epistemological preference for the temporal,[57] an idea that culminates in the phenomenological and post-phenomenological conceptions, most notably, Husserl's specification of time as the self-temporalization of intentional consciousness, Heidegger's notion of being-toward-death as the ground of the ecstatic temporality of human existence, and Levinas's conception of diachrony as the endless continuity that proceeds from the relationship of the self with the Other, a relationship that precludes the possibility of coincidence, since the other to which the self is related always exceeds the capacity of that self to know or to experience. Without ignoring the medieval context within which the kabbalistic ideas arose, it seems to me defensible to think of the zoharic texts in light of the post-Kantian temporocentrism.

---

[52] Wolfson, *Alef, Mem, Tau*, 46–9.

[53] Ibid. 56, 86–7, 106; Elliot R. Wolfson, 'Kenotic Overflow and Temporal Transcendence: Angelic Embodiment and the Alterity of Time in Abraham Abulafia', *Kabbalah: Journal for the Study of Jewish Mystical Texts*, 18 (2008), 182–6. On the convergence of time and space in kabbalistic doctrine, see as well Haviva Pedaya, 'The Divinity as Place and Time and the Holy Place in Jewish Mysticism', in Benjamin Kedar and R. J. Zwi Werblowsky (eds.), *Sacred Space: Shrine, City, Land—Proceedings of the International Conference in Memory of Joshua Prawer* (Jerusalem, 1998), 85.

[54] Michael Epperson, *Quantum Mechanics and the Philosophy of Alfred North Whitehead* (New York, 2004), 164–5. [55] Wolfson, *Language, Eros, Being*, 37. [56] Ibid. 43.

[57] See the comment of John Sallis, cited in Wolfson, *Alef, Mem, Tau*, 17, and my own remarks on Schelling and Heidegger, ibid. 29–34. On the relationship of time and space in the later Heidegger, see ibid. 42–6.

Time, not space, is the measure of what is considered ultimate reality, the substance of that which exists in the divine, human, and cosmic planes of being.[58]

The temporal essence of walking as a hermeneutical praxis is thematized in the following passage:

> Rabbi Judah and Rabbi Yose were walking on the way. Rabbi Judah said to Rabbi Yose: Open your mouth and engage in [the study of] the Torah, since the Shekhinah is found with you. For whenever words of Torah are engaged, the Shekhinah comes and joins, and all the more so on the way, since the Shekhinah precedes and arrives, and walks before those who are worthy of the faith of the blessed Holy One.[59]

The author of this text combines two rabbinic principles, the first that the divine presence (Shekhinah) is found with those who are occupied in the study of Torah,[60] and the second that scholars who travel on the road should engage in study.[61] Note that the exposition of Scripture is not envisioned as the cause that theurgically occasions the presence of the divine, but rather it is the presence of the divine that occasions the exposition of Scripture. The Shekhinah is thus described as coming before—in both a temporal and a spatial sense—those who are worthy of the faith (*meheimanuta*) of God, a technical term in zoharic kabbalah that denotes either the last of the ten sefirotic potencies or the totality of the pleroma envisioned as the union of the masculine impulse to overflow and the feminine capacity to receive.[62]

The exegesis that immediately follows ostensibly reverses the positioning of Shekhinah on the outside:

> Rabbi Yose opened and said: 'Your wife shall be like a fruitful vine within the recesses of your house; your sons shall be like olive saplings around your table' [Ps. 128: 3]. 'Your wife shall be like a fruitful vine'—the whole time that your wife is within the recesses of the house and does not venture outside, she is chaste [*tsenuah*] and fit to produce worthy offspring. 'Like a fruitful vine'—just as a vine is planted only with its species, not with another species, so a laudable woman does not produce saplings with another man. Just as a vine cannot be grafted with another tree, so too, a laudable woman. See her reward: 'your sons shall be like olive saplings around your table'—just as the leaves of olive saplings do not fall all year round, and they are all constantly attached, so too, 'your sons, like olive saplings around your table'. What is written after it? 'So shall the man who

---

[58] With regard to this matter, my thinking is in accord with Abraham Joshua Heschel, who was influenced by many of the same sources. See my comments in *Alef, Mem, Tau*, 204–5 n. 361, and 205 n. 3.

[59] Zohar i. 115*b*.   [60] Mishnah *Avot* 3: 2; BT *Ber.* 6*a*.

[61] BT *Eruv.* 54*a* (one who travels alone should be engaged in Torah study) and *Ta'an.* 10*b* (in that case, the teaching deals with two scholars travelling together). The rabbinic sensibility is likely to have been informed by the language of Deut. 6: 7.

[62] See Jonathan Garb, 'The Secrets of Faith in the Book of the Zohar' (Heb.), in Moshe Halbertal, David Kurzweil, and Avi Sagi (eds.), *On Faith: Studies in the Concept of Faith and its History in the Jewish Tradition* [Al ha'emunah: iyunim bemusag ha'emunah uvetoledotav bimesoret hayehudit] (Jerusalem, 2005), 294–311. References to previous scholarship can be found in Garb's essay.

fears the Lord be blessed' [*hineh ki khen yevorakh gaver yere yhvh*] [Ps. 128: 4]. It should have been written *hineh khen*! [It is written *hineh ki khen*] in order to augment another matter, for we learn from this that the whole time that the Shekhinah is hidden appropriately in her place, as it were, 'your sons shall be like olive saplings', this refers to Israel when they dwell on the land. 'Around your table'—eating, drinking, offering sacrifices, and rejoicing before the blessed Holy One, and the ones above and below are blessed on account of them. After the Shekhinah departed, Israel were expelled from their father's table, and they were among the nations, crying out every day. There was no one to heed them but the blessed Holy One, as it is written, 'Yet, even then, when they are in the land of their enemies [I will not reject them or spurn them so as to destroy them, annulling my covenant with them: for I the Lord am their God]' [Lev. 26: 44].[63]

In contrast to the exteriority associated with the Shekhinah in the introductory part of the passage, which is attributed to Rabbi Judah, the acceptable code of conduct for the Jewish woman below, as it emerges from Rabbi Yose's exegesis, is for her to stay confined within domestic boundaries. The spatial constraint signifies that the chastity suitable to the feminine is linked inherently to a state of interiority, to her being sheltered on the inside[64]—the word *tsenuah* has the double connotation of modesty and concealment.[65] Another facet of this timidity and containment is that the commendable woman cohabits only with her husband—she is not out there prowling around the street—and, as a consequence, she merits producing worthy offspring. From the example of Jewish women, the zoharic author generalizes about the status of the Shekhinah: when she is hidden in her place—a reference to the Jerusalem Temple—Israel dwell joyously on the land, but when she is exiled, the nation, too, is displaced. Even though the literary conceit of the text is that the walking mentioned at the beginning of the homily supposedly takes place within the boundaries of the land of Israel, we may assume that it is, in fact, emblematic of the exilic wandering of the divine feminine when she is no longer restricted to her place. Rootlessness is a sign of alienation and dislocation, but it is also the catalyst that stimulates textual exegesis. The image of the mystic itinerants, therefore, is symbolic of the hermeneutic predilection. In the sedentary state, the feminine is the interior *par excellence*, the container that encompasses and encircles the male—metaphors that reflect the medieval kabbalistic understanding of the female genitals and, by extension, the dynamics of heterosexual eros—the sheltering that gives form to and thereby reveals that which is concealed, the opaque mirror in

---

[63] Zohar i. 115*b*–116*a*.

[64] On the depiction of the redemptive state as a sheltering of the feminine within her boundaries like the point enclosed in the centre of a circle, see Wolfson, *Language, Eros, Being*, 382–3.

[65] The image of the princess being hidden in the king's chamber appears in the bahiric anthology. See Daniel Abrams, *The Book Bahir: An Edition Based on the Earliest Manuscripts* (Los Angeles, 1994), §104, pp. 187–9. Regarding this theme, see Elliot R. Wolfson, 'Secrecy, Modesty, and the Feminine: Kabbalistic Traces in the Thought of Levinas', in Kevin Hart and Michael A. Signer (eds.), *The Exorbitant: Emmanuel Levinas Between Jews and Christians* (New York, 2010), 64–5.

which the supernal images that are invisible are seen,[66] the light that is a canopy that covers and, consequently, exposes the hidden light of Yesod, the phallic potency of the divine anthropos.[67] Here we touch on a vital nerve of the gender implication of the intertwining of esotericism and eroticism in the theosophic symbolism: the female is assigned the role of the veil or the garment, different terms that express the idea that the feminine is the agency that discloses the concealment of the masculine, albeit by concealing it—a point perhaps best illustrated by the liturgical tradition of pronouncing the name YHVH by the epithet Adonai, that is, the epithet makes the ineffable name audible even as it preserves its ineffability.[68]

The motif of the members of the fraternity studying Torah as they walk on the way recurs frequently in the zoharic corpus.[69] In one passage, which may be considered illustrative, the master of the imaginary fraternity, Shimon bar Yoḥai, is said to be travelling with his son, Rabbi Eleazar, Rabbi Yose, and Rabbi Hiya; while they are walking, his son says to him: 'The way is prepared before us; we desire to hear

---

[66] Zohar ii. 149b.

[67] Ibid. iii. 204b. This is not the context to respond in detail to the use of this passage in Hellner-Eshed, *A River Flows from Eden*, 168–70, to challenge my understanding of the gender construction of the feminine in zoharic kabbalah. Briefly, let me state that I have never denied that the feminine functions symbolically as the veil that simultaneously reveals and conceals the masculine, nor have I disavowed that the feminine is the potency with which the masculine desires to unite. As a matter of fact, if one reads my work carefully, it should be abundantly clear that a crucial part of my presentation of kabbalistic esotericism is based precisely on assigning this role to the feminine. I have touched on this theme in numerous studies, but see especially 'Occultation of the Feminine and the Body of Secrecy in Medieval Kabbalah', in Elliot R. Wolfson (ed.), *Rending the Veil: Concealment and Revelation of Secrets in the History of Religions* (New York, 1999), 113–54, slightly revised in id., *Luminal Darkness: Imaginal Gleanings From Zoharic Literature* (London, 2007), 258–94. Furthermore, I have repeatedly commented on the desire of the female to receive the overflow of the male as part of the drama that rectifies the split of the primordial androgyne. What I have argued, however, is that this desire is characteristic of the exilic state of separation, but that the consummation of that longing results in the restoration of the feminine to the masculine in accord with the kabbalists' interpretation of the creation of Adam in Genesis 1: 26–7 in light of the account in Genesis 2: 21–4. Since the first stage is one in which male and female must be reunited, heteroerotic imagery is appropriate, but in the second stage, once the split has been repaired, there is a turn to the homoerotic. See Wolfson, *Language, Eros, Being*, 109–10, 147–9, and the concise summary of my view in id., *Venturing Beyond: Law and Morality in Kabbalistic Mysticism* (Oxford, 2006), 85. Finally, I have duly noted that the feminine is the locus of the imagination and therefore crucial to kabbalistic poetics. See Wolfson, *Through a Speculum That Shines*, 306–17. Hellner-Eshed's insinuation that I one-sidedly depict the feminine in words such as 'lack and absence, ruthless penetration, negation, and submersion in the masculine' is a misleading and simplistic portrayal of my work. Even so, I would still contend that her insistence on the 'reciprocal drama of the feminine's yearning to joyfully fill her living, spacious, and desiring womb with all the variegated qualities that flow into her' falls short of providing a 'feminine erotics' that is not informed by the overarching phallocentrism. The depiction of the womb as a space craving to be filled with the overflow of the male is a rather standard expression of a phallocentric point of view.

[68] Zohar i. 39b, 145a, 232b; ii. 230b; iii. 65b, 71b. See Wolfson, *Abraham Abulafia*, 31–3; id., *Language, Eros, Being*, 71.

[69] Zohar i. 7a, 69b, 83a, 87a, 145a, 204b, 205a, 213a, 219a–b; ii. 68b, 80a, 87b, 121b, 149a; iii. 55b.

words of Torah.'⁷⁰ Significantly, the master begins by interpreting a verse that sheds light on the nature of the way:

Rabbi Shimon opened and said: 'A fool's mind⁷¹ is also wanting when he travels [and he says to everybody that he is a fool]' [Eccl. 10: 3]. When a person desires to establish his way before the blessed Holy One, prior to setting out on the way, he should confer with Him and pray to Him concerning the way, as we have learned,⁷² for it is written 'Righteousness goes before him, and he sets out on his way' [Ps. 85: 14], and, then, the Shekhinah will not depart from him. And what is written concerning one who does not trust his Lord? 'A fool's mind is also wanting when he travels.' What is 'his mind'? This is the blessed Holy One, who will not accompany him on the way. That person is lacking his escort on the way because he did not trust his Lord before he set out on the way and he did not seek His assistance. And even when he is walking on the way, he does not engage in words of Torah, and hence 'his mind is also wanting', for his Lord does not walk with him and He is not found in the way. 'And he says to everybody that he is a fool,' even when he hears a word of the faith of his Lord, he utters that it is foolish to engage in it. Like the time that someone was asked about the sign of the covenant engraved on the flesh of the person, and he said that it is not [a matter of] faith. Rabbi Yeiva the Elder heard and gazed upon him, and he turned into a heap of bones.⁷³ We, who are on the way with the support of the blessed Holy One, must speak words of Torah.⁷⁴

It is plausible to interpret this passage literally, since it is based on the two rabbinic principles previously mentioned, which purportedly presume an actual excursion. I am doubtful, however, of the validity of this tactic when assessing material in which it seems virtually impossible to distinguish the factual and the fantastic.⁷⁵ Hence, it is equally plausible to interpret the text metaphorically, so that the 'way' should be decoded as a reference to the hermeneutical path, and that walking figuratively denotes the act of textual explication. The end of the passage clearly indicates that the imaginary sojourn in the zoharic homily is meant to be understood in this fashion. Moreover, inasmuch as the kabbalists equate Torah and God, it is reasonable to depict exegesis of the text as a mode of embellishing the divine.⁷⁶ To embark on

---

⁷⁰ Zohar i. 58b.

⁷¹ The expression *libo*, which is translated as 'his mind', literally denotes 'his heart', but biblically and rabbinically the heart is the locus of cognition as well as of emotion. See Isa. 6: 10; BT *Shab.* 33b. Obviously, many more examples could have been mentioned.

⁷² The allusion is probably to the prayer for travelling on the way (*tefilat haderekh*) mentioned in BT *Ber.* 29b.

⁷³ Based on earlier rabbinic descriptions of the destructive power of the gaze of the sages; see BT *Ber.* 58a; *Shab.* 34a; *BB* 75a; *San.* 100a.

⁷⁴ Zohar i. 58b–59a.

⁷⁵ My approach has affinity with the position articulated by Daniel Boyarin, *Sparks of Logos: Essays in Rabbinic Hermeneutics* (Leiden, 2003), 89–113.

⁷⁶ Cf. Zohar i. 145b: 'All that the blessed Holy One made in the earth was in the mystery of wisdom, and everything was to manifest the supernal wisdom to human beings, so that they may learn from that action the mysteries of wisdom. And all of them are appropriate, and all of the actions are the ways of the

that path demands a preliminary act of placing one's trust in God. Only by this gesture can one be assured that the divine presence will accompany one on that path. The fool lacks this trust—indeed foolishness is innately a lack of trust—and thus when he journeys, he is alone, effectively undermining the way, even to the point that he does not discern that the covenantal sign of circumcision is a matter of faith. It is unlikely that the specific example was chosen arbitrarily. Given the correlation of circumcision and the Tetragrammaton,[77] and the further identification of the latter and the Torah,[78] this rite assumes gargantuan significance in zoharic homilies. The place of this covenant, the male organ, which corresponds to the attribute of Yesod, is the locus of secrecy *par excellence*—the name that is the Torah, which comprises the totality of the sefirotic emanations, the mystery of faith (*raza dimeheimanuta*). The fool who denies this matter—a position that is on a par with the standard Christian perspective that diminishes the spiritual worth of the physical circumcision[79]—is worthy of death. By contrast, those who get on the way properly are empowered by bearing the sign on their flesh, a prerequisite for the Shekhinah escorting them.

The midrashic prowess from the zoharic perspective is encapsulated in the dynamic of venturing along the path to gain gnosis of the words of Torah (*leminda milei de'oraita*), the very words that constitute the ontological foundation of existence.[80] Hence, it is incumbent that the way be arrayed by the exegetes, as we see, for instance, in a passage where Rabbi Hiya and Rabbi Yose were travelling; when they saw Rabbi Yeisa the Elder[81] walking behind them, they sat down, waited for him to join them, and then proclaimed, 'Now the way is rectified before us!'[82] The rectification (*tikun*) of the way is made dependent on the aggregation of three sages, who presumably correspond to the three columns of the divine pleroma or the balance of the right and the left in the centre. Be that as it may, what is critical is the presentation of walking as a trope to convey the revelatory nature of hermeneutics

Torah, for the ways of the Torah are the ways of the blessed Holy One, and there is not even a minuscule word that does not contain several ways, paths, and mysteries of the supernal wisdom.'

[77] For discussion of this theme, see Elliot R. Wolfson, 'Circumcision and the Divine Name: A Study in the Transmission of Esoteric Doctrine', *Jewish Quarterly Review*, 78 (1987), 77–112.

[78] See above, n. 34.

[79] On the motif of circumcision in the kabbalistic polemic against Christianity, accentuated in the zoharic corpus, see Elliot R. Wolfson, 'Remembering the Covenant: Memory, Forgetfulness, and the Construction of History in the Zohar', in Elisheva Carlebach, John M. Efron, and David N. Myers (eds.), *Jewish History and Jewish Memory: Essays in Honor of Yosef Hayim Yerushalmi* (Hanover, 1998), 214–46, esp. 222–4, revised version in Wolfson, *Luminal Darkness*, 185–227, esp. 196–8; id., *Venturing Beyond*, 94–6, 151–4.

[80] Zohar i. 83*a*. In that context, R. Shimon is walking on the way with R. Eleazar, R. Abba, and R. Judah, and the secret that is disclosed relates to the nocturnal ascent of the soul, which is linked to the verse 'My soul desires you in the night, the spirit within me in the morning' (Isa. 26: 9).

[81] I have here followed the reading of the Cremona edition of the Zohar, p. 338; the reading of the Mantua edition, i. 145*a*, and all subsequent editions based on it, is 'R. Yose the Elder'.

[82] Zohar i. 145*a*.

and the hermeneutical nature of revelation. Again, Rabbi Shimon, the master of the fictional circle, exemplifies the point. According to one passage, Rabbi Isaac reports that once he was walking with Rabbi Shimon and when the latter began to expound words of Torah, he saw

> a pillar of cloud fixed from above to below, and a splendour was radiating from within the pillar. I experienced great fear, and I said, 'Praiseworthy is such a man [Rabbi Shimon] that such a thing is summoned for him in this world.' What is written with respect to Moses? 'When all the people saw the pillar of cloud poised at the entrance of the Tent, all the people would rise and bow low, each at the entrance of his tent' [Exod. 33: 10]. This was appropriate for Moses, the trustworthy prophet, superior to all other prophets of the world, and that generation, which received the Torah on Mount Sinai, saw several miracles and several wonders in Egypt and on the [Reed] Sea. But the supernal merit of Rabbi Shimon facilitates miracles to be seen by this generation on his account.[83]

Much is revealed in this text about the midrashic inclination of the zoharic authors, and especially about its revelatory nature. As traditional kabbalists and critical scholars alike have noted, there is a homology between the biblical Moses and the imaginary Shimon bar Yohai. The power of the one, as the power of the other, is essentially supernatural. Just as the Israelites experienced miracles when they departed from Egypt, so the generation of Rabbi Shimon is worthy of seeing miraculous wonders. In spite of the fact that this propensity is attested in earlier sources, there is no question that it is elevated and prioritized in the zoharic material. To be engaged in midrashic activity is to undergo an ecstatic transformation on a par with being illumined by the radiance of the splendour of the pillar of cloud. The dichotomy between contemplation and action is rendered completely irrelevant. Contemplative absorption in the study of the text is the supreme form of piety, of acting in the world in such a way that the coarse materiality is transfigured into the superior form of the hyletic, the body that is composed of the letters that are contained within the Tetragrammaton.

MIDRASHIC POIESIS AND THE PARABOLIC WAY

Countless other examples could have been adduced from the zoharic collection to illustrate this seminal point. By walking the path, one merits to receive the 'hint of wisdom' (*remiza deḥokhmeta*)[84] whence one can unlock the mystery of the text that fosters an ecstatic vision of or union with the divine. The emphasis on mystery in the zoharic homilies intimates that midrashic activity consists primarily of explicating Scripture parabolically, a stance that resonates formally with the Maimonidean hermeneutic. One of the ways that this is expressed is in the remark

---

[83] Zohar ii. 149*a*.

[84] Ibid. i. 219*b*. Cf. ibid. iii. 158*b*. The Aramaic *remiza*, as its Hebrew equivalent *remez*, in the zoharic lexicon has a broader connotation than allegory. On this usage, see Tishby, *The Wisdom of the Zohar*, i. 65–6.

that the Song of Songs is the 'principle of all the Torah' (*kelala dekhol oraita*).[85] Building on an idea implicit in several rabbinic dicta, the author of this comment affirms explicitly that the Song of Songs is the one biblical book that is commensurate with the whole Torah.[86] When translated into a theosophic register, this can be explained in terms of the heteroerotic imagery of the Song, that is, the reciprocal desire of the male and female signifies the dynamic between the King and the Matrona in the sefirotic pleroma, a dynamic that is indicative of the union of the divine potencies, expressed in sundry images including the dual Torah (written and oral) of the rabbinic tradition. In this sense, the dramatic narrative of the Song portends the mystical crux of the revealed word. The secret of this pairing is encoded in the first four words of the book, *shir hashirim asher lishelomoh*, 'The Song of Songs by Solomon', which allude to the fourfold conjunction of Malkhut and the three emanations, Hesed, Gevurah, and Rahamim, the four legs of the chariot.[87]

The zoharic assertion that the Song encompasses the entire Torah can also be interpreted midrashically as indicating that this text is the one whose literal meaning is figurative. This book, accordingly, illumines the mythopoeic nature of Torah as inherently parabolic.[88] The exemplar of the kabbalistic hermeneut—the wise of heart (*hakimei liba*), to whom the 'supernal mystery' (*raza ila'ah*) is bestowed—is offered in the following passage:

It is written, 'He uttered three thousand proverbs, and his songs numbered one thousand and five' [1 Kgs. 5: 12]. This verse was established by the companions. But [the meaning of] 'he uttered three thousand proverbs' is that surely each and every word that he spoke contained three thousand proverbs, like the book of Ecclesiastes, which is in the supernal mystery, and it is in the way of the parable [*be'orah mashal*], for there is no verse in it that is not in the supernal wisdom and in the way of the parable, even the smallest verse in it. When the first Rabbi Hamnuna the Elder reached this verse, 'O youth, enjoy yourself while you are young! Let your heart lead you to enjoyment in the days of your youth' [Eccl. 11: 9], he would cry, and he would say, 'Surely, this verse is appropriate and it is in the way of parable. Who can explicate this parable homiletically [*uman yakhil lemebad derasha vemashal da*]? And if there is a homiletical meaning [*derasha*], then it is only with regard to what is seen with the eyes. And if there is wisdom [*hokhmeta*], who can know it?' Immediately, he responded and said, 'It is written, "These, then, are the generations of Jacob: Joseph at seventeen years of age [tended the flocks with his brothers]" [Gen. 37: 2]. The verse from Ecclesiastes is a parable for the wisdom of the verse of the Torah, the one is a parable for the other. ... "These are the generations of Jacob: Joseph"—Joseph was contained in Jacob. Who can know the mysteries of the secrets of the Torah [*razin desitrei torah*]? This parable extends into three thousand parables, and they are all in this parable. At the moment that Joseph was contained

---

[85] Zohar ii. 143*b*.
[86] Wolfson, *Language, Eros, Being*, 335–6, 359.
[87] Zohar ii. 144*a*. See Wolfson, *Language, Eros, Being*, 367.
[88] Wolfson, *Language, Eros, Being*, 360–1; id., 'Suffering Eros and Textual Incarnation: A Kristevan Reading of Kabbalistic Poetics', in Virginia Burrus and Catherine Keller (eds.), *Toward a Theology of Eros: Transfiguring Passion at the Limits of Discipline* (New York, 2006), 346–52.

in Jacob, three thousand are in Abraham, Isaac, and Jacob, and all of them are in this parable in the mystery of wisdom [*beraza deḥokhmeta*].'[89]

A full exposition of this text lies beyond our immediate concern. I will focus instead on the most important exegetical issues that illumine the midrashic approach in the zoharic corpus. The framework of this passage is the talmudic reading of 1 Kings 5: 12 attributed to Rabbi Hamnuna—signalled by the reference to the companions (*ḥavraya*)—that 'Solomon uttered three thousand proverbs for every single word of the Torah and one thousand and five reasons for every single word of the Scribes.'[90] According to the zoharic reworking, this maxim is invoked to explain another rabbinic tradition (transmitted in the name of Samuel bar Isaac) that raises concern about the legitimacy of canonizing Ecclesiastes, based on the seemingly heretical implication of the verse 'O youth, enjoy yourself while you are young! Let your heart lead you to enjoyment in the days of your youth' (Eccl. 11: 9).[91] Unlike the rabbinic version, in which the verse is justified by its conclusion, the zoharic author accomplished this feat by juxtaposing it with Genesis 37: 2. The juxtaposition yields the insight that the parable (*mashal*) can refer either to the homiletical sense (*derasha*) or to the esoteric wisdom (*ḥokhmeta*). The former, apparently, is what can be discerned empirically by the vision of the eyes, whereas the latter is a matter of an inner vision of the theosophic intent of the text, the mysteries of Scripture, as we see in the example of the biblical verse that informs us of the containment of Joseph (Yesod) in Jacob (Tiferet). What is worthy of underscoring here is that the literal meaning is accorded no standing apart from the parabolic, and thus there is an overlapping of the exoteric and the esoteric. For the kabbalists, whose views are conserved anonymously in the zoharic homilies, enlightenment consists of discerning that these are not in binary opposition.[92] Thus, the emphasis on the dual nature of the Torah being concealed (*setim*) and revealed (*galya*) is set alongside the tradition that the name is concealed and revealed.[93] Obviously, what undergirds this correspondence is the aforementioned identity of the name and the Torah, but an additional conceptual point is to be elicited: just as, in the case of the name, the revealed and the concealed cannot be separated performatively—one vocalizes YHVH as Adonai—so in the case of the Torah, the hidden and the manifest cannot be

---

[89] Zohar ii. 145*a*.

[90] BT *Eruv.* 21*b*.

[91] *Lev. Rabbah* 28: 1 (*Midrash Wayyikra Rabbah: A Critical Edition Based on Manuscripts and Genizah Fragments with Variants and Notes*, ed. Mordecai Margulies, 2 vols. (New York, 1993), pp. 648–9); *Pesikta derav kahana*, 8: 1 (*Pesikta de Rav Kahana According to an Oxford Manuscript with Variants from all Known Manuscripts and Genizoth Fragments and Parallel Passages with Commentary and Introduction*, ed. Bernard Mandelbaum, 2 vols. (New York, 1962), p. 135); *Pesikta rabati*, 18: 1 (*Pesiqta Rabbati: A Synoptic Edition of Pesiqta Rabbati Based upon All Extant Manuscripts and the Editio Princeps*, ed. Rivka Ulmer, 3 vols. (Atlanta, Ga., 1997), pp. 382–5); *Eccles. Rabbah* on Eccles. 1: 3, 11: 9.

[92] Elliot R. Wolfson, 'Beautiful Maiden Without Eyes: Peshat and Sod in Zoharic Hermeneutics', in Michael Fishbane (ed.), *The Midrashic Imagination: Jewish Exegesis, Thought, and History* (Albany, NY, 1993), 155–203; repr. with corrections in Wolfson, *Luminal Darkness*, 56–110.

[93] Zohar ii. 230*b*; iii. 75*a*, 159*a*.

separated exegetically—one can fathom the mystery only through the sheath of the letters.

According to one oft-cited passage, Shimon bar Yohai laments that some people think the Torah is nothing more than a storybook and hence they fall short of ascertaining that 'all the words of Torah are supernal words and supernal mysteries'.[94] The hermeneutical precept of analogical meaning[95] is supported by the doctrine of ontic parallelism, which echoes the archaic theory of correspondence expressed, perhaps most famously, in the beginning of the *Tabula Smaragdina*, a series of gnomic utterances attributed to the legendary Hermes Trimegistus, 'What is below is like that which is above, and what is above is like that which is below, to accomplish the miracles of one thing.'[96] In the zoharic language:

> Come and see: The supernal world and the lower world are weighed on one scale, Israel below and the supernal angels above. Concerning the supernal angels it is written, 'He makes his messengers spirits' [Ps. 104: 4]—when they descend below they are garbed in the garment of this world, and if they were not garbed in the garment in the likeness of this world, they could not exist in this world and the world could not endure them. And if this is so with respect to the angels, how much more so with respect to the Torah, which created them and all the worlds, and on account of which they exist. When [the Torah] descends to this world, if it were not garbed in the garments of this world, the world could not endure. Thus the stories of the Torah are the garment of the Torah. The one who thinks that this garment is the actual Torah and not another matter, let his spirit deflate, and he has no portion in the world to come. Therefore, David said, 'Open my eyes that I may perceive the wonders from your Torah' [Ps. 119: 18], from what is beneath the garment of the Torah.[97]

In this part of the homily, a twofold conception of the text is embraced: the garment, which refers to the narratives, and that which is underneath the garment. The matter is explained incarnationally: just as the angels, which are spiritual beings, must don the garment of the physical world when they descend thereto, so the immaterial essence of the Torah must be garbed in images that relate to the material of this world.[98] In the continuation of the passage, the external/internal distinction yields a fourfold delineation: the garment is correlated with the narratives, the body with the laws, the soul with the mystical meaning, and the soul of soul with the even deeper meaning that will be revealed in the messianic future. The four strata are

---

[94] Zohar iii. 152a.

[95] For an extensive discussion of this theme, see Mottolese, *Analogy in Midrash and Kabbalah*.

[96] John Read, *Prelude to Chemistry: An Outline of Alchemy, Its Literature and Relationships* (Cambridge, 1966), 54.

[97] Zohar iii. 152a. See Scholem, *On the Kabbalah and Its Symbolism*, 63–4; Liebes, *Studies in the Zohar*, 45–6; Wolfson, *Through a Speculum That Shines*, 379; id., *Language, Eros, Being*, 221–2.

[98] On the theme of the garments of Torah, see Tishby, *The Wisdom of the Zohar*, iii. 1083; Dorit Cohen-Alloro, *The Secret of the Garment in the Zohar* [Sod hamalbush umareh hamalakh besefer hazohar] (Jerusalem, 1987), 45–9; Wolfson, *Through a Speculum That Shines*, 376 n. 172.

associated, moreover, with four ontic planes in the following sequence: the garment corresponds to the heavens, the body to the tenth emanation Keneset Yisra'el, that is, the Shekhinah, the soul to the sixth emanation Tiferet Yisra'el, and the soul of soul to the first emanation Atika Kadisha. It is possible to view these vertically, ascending from the garment to the soul of the soul. On the face of it, this vantage point is substantiated by the alignment of the latter with what will be disclosed in the endtime. And yet, it is equally possible to view the levels concentrically, the one contained in the other. Just as cosmologically there are no gaps in the chain of being, so hermeneutically, each degree of meaning is contained in the one that precedes and succeeds it. The progression implied in the second model, therefore, entails the presumption that the fourth rank is comprised in the first, that the innermost soul of the text is discernible from the garment. Shifting from a vertical to a concentric model puts into relief the inadequacy of Scholem's assessment that this passage attests to a 'devaluation of the simple literal meaning'.[99] I would counter that the passage does not belittle the simple literal meaning as much as it imparts another view about its nature. The zoharic perspective sanctions a hyperliteral understanding of the literal, that is, the literal relates predominantly to the actual letters of the text. From this vantage point, the *peshat* is venerated as the only way to gain access to the secrets.[100]

The four grades of meaning are demarcated alternatively—in a manner that is closer to the well-known classification associated with the word *pardes* read acrostically as a reference to *peshat* (literal), *remez* (allegorical), *derash* (homiletical), and *sod* (mystical)[101]—in a second zoharic passage, the parable of the beautiful maiden and the castle: *remizah* (sign), *derashah* (homily), *ḥidah* (allegory) or *hagadah* (narrative), and *razin setimin* (hidden mysteries).[102] The four levels are presented sequentially

---

[99] Scholem, *On the Kabbalah and Its Symbolism*, 63.

[100] On the tendency of kabbalistic hermeneutics to 'save' the letter of the text, see the comments of Mottolese, *Analogy in Midrash and Kabbalah*, 306–8.

[101] For scholarly discussions of the kabbalistic doctrine of the fourfold sense of Scripture, see Wilhelm Bacher, 'L'Exégèse biblique dans le Zohar', *Revue des études juives*, 22 (1891), 33–46, esp. 37–40; id., 'Das Merkwort PRDS in der Jüdischen Bibelexegese', *Zeitschrift für die alttestamentliche Wissenschaft*, 13 (1893), 294–305; Scholem, *On the Kabbalah and Its Symbolism*, 53–62; Tishby, *The Wisdom of the Zohar*, iii. 1077–89; Albert van der Heide, 'Pardes: Methodological Reflections on the Theory of the Four Senses', *Journal of Jewish Studies*, 34 (1983), 147–59; Moshe Idel, 'Pardes: Some Reflections on Kabbalistic Hermeneutics', in John J. Collins and Michael Fishbane (eds.), *Death, Ecstasy, and Other Worldly Journeys* (Albany, NY, 1995), 249–68; id., 'The Zohar as Exegesis', in Steven T. Katz (ed.), *Mysticism and Sacred Scripture* (Oxford, 2000), 89–91; id., *Absorbing Perfections*, 429–37.

[102] I have discussed this zoharic text previously in several studies. See Wolfson, 'Beautiful Maiden'; id., *Through a Speculum That Shines*, 384–8; id., *Language, Eros, Being*, 222–4. This section has been discussed by several other scholars. For instance, see Michal Oron, '"Place Me As a Seal Upon Your Heart": Reflections on the Poetics of the Author of the Zohar in the Section of *Sava demishpatim*' (Heb.), in Michal Oron and Amos Goldreich (eds.), *Masuot: Studies in Kabbalistic Literature and Jewish Philosophy in Memory of Prof. Ephraim Gottlieb* [Masuot: meḥkarim besifrut hakabalah uvemaḥshevet yisra'el mukdashim lezikhro shel profesor efrayim gotlib] (Jerusalem, 1994), 1–24; Pinchas Giller, 'Love and Upheaval in the Zohar's *Sabba de-Mishpatim*', *Journal of Jewish Thought and Philosophy*, 7 (1997), 31–60;

as stages of an ever-increasing disclosure: the first offered through the barrier of a wall, the second from behind a curtain, the third through a more subtle screen, and finally, the fourth, ostensibly clearing away all obstructions, is marked as a face-to-face encounter, which idiomatically signifies union of the most intimate sort. But as the Torah exposes herself fully to her lover, he realizes that the secret was already present in the initial hint. At the moment of enlightenment he understands that *peshatei dikera*, the 'literal' text—the text in its linguistic embodiment—must be as it is, with no word added or subtracted. The linear progression from the exoteric (*peshat*) to the esoteric (*sod*) turns out, in fact, to be circular—one learns that the mystical meaning disclosed at the end is the same as (or was already contained in) the literal sense revealed at the beginning.

To detect the mystery of the original insinuation at the termination confirms the hermeneutical point that the secret, which is the light,[103] can be seen only through the cloak of the letters. The uncovering of the innermost meaning in the culminating leg of the journey is thus a recovery of the overt sense disclosed allusively in the beginning. If it is true that every translation is interpretation, it is equally true that every interpretation is translation, literally a 'crossing over', by which one gives expression to the inward sense through the outward forms. The somewhat unusual choice of the term *remizah* to denote *peshat* underscores that the literal and figurative should not be viewed in binary terms. Once again, we confront the circularity of the interpretative enterprise and the reversibility of the timeline implied thereby: the reader begins with the literal and advances to the symbolic, but the literal cannot be truly known except through the symbolic. Apprehending this truth affords us a glimpse of the midrashic process that informed the inimitable approach of the zoharic kabbalah.

id., *Reading the Zohar: The Sacred Text of Kabbalah* (Oxford, 2001), 35–68; Daniel Abrams, 'Knowing the Maiden Without Eyes: Reading the Sexual Reconstruction of the Jewish Mystic in a Zoharic Parable', *Da'at*, 50–2 (2003), pp. lix–lxxxiii; Oded Yisraeli, *The Interpretation of Secrets and the Secret of Interpretation: Midrashic and Hermeneutic Strategies in 'Sava demishpatim' of the Zohar* [Parshanut hasod vesod haparshanut: megamot midrashiyot vehermene'utiyot besaba demishpatim shebazohar] (Los Angeles, 2005), 191–266; Hellner-Eshed, *A River Flows From Eden*, 68–9, 160–2.

[103] The identification of the secret and the light is substantiated by kabbalists through the numerical equation of the words *raz* and *or*, that is, the sum of the numerical values of their Hebrew letters both equal 207. See Scholem, *On the Kabbalah and Its Symbolism*, 63, and other sources cited in Wolfson, *Through a Speculum That Shines*, 375 n. 170.

PART IV

EARLY MODERN AND MODERN TRADITIONS

SIXTEEN

THE INGATHERING OF *MIDRASH RABBAH*
A Moment of Creativity and Innovation

BENJAMIN WILLIAMS

WHEN *Midrash Rabbah* was first printed in the sixteenth century, ten *midrashim* of diverse chronological and geographical provenance were gathered together for the first time. Although these *midrashim* had circulated individually and in various combinations long before, there are no extant manuscripts of '*Midrash Rabbah*' as a tenfold 'anthology of *midrashim*'[1] on the Pentateuch and the Five Megillot. Rather, this composite volume was the product of two intense waves of publication of books of Midrash and aggadah that took place in the sixteenth century. These found focus first in Constantinople and then in Venice. The *midrashim* of *Midrash Rabbah* were published in both these cities, and were later reprinted in Kraków and Salonica.

The successive sixteenth-century editions of *Midrash Rabbah* provoked outbursts of scholarly creativity. These early printed volumes allowed scholars to expound established and widely disseminated books of *midrashim*. Their expositions could relate directly to the details of the text in the hands of their readers. Scholars even rose to the challenge suggested by the tenfold nature of the newly printed *Midrash Rabbah* anthology, producing comprehensive volumes of notes and glosses on 'each *midrash* of the *Rabbot* on the Pentateuch and the Megillot'.[2] Others promised books of homiletic commentaries 'containing an explanation of the *midrashim* expounded by our rabbis (of blessed memory) in the *Rabbah* of the Pentateuch and the Five Megillot'.[3]

Although this new scholarly enterprise was inspired by the ingathering and consolidation of the ten '*Rabbah*' *midrashim* into a single printed anthology, commentators were also critical of the new books of *Midrash Rabbah*. They bewailed the

---

[1] Jacob Elbaum, '*Yalqut Shim'oni* and the Medieval Midrashic Anthology', in David Stern (ed.), *The Anthology in Jewish Literature* (Oxford, 2004), 171 n. 1; on the application of this term to *Midrash Rabbah*, see Marc Bregman, 'Midrash Rabbah and the Medieval Collector Mentality', in Stern, 200.

[2] See the rhymed preface to Naphtali Hertz, *Perush lemidrash ḥamesh megilot rabah* (Kraków, 1569), fo. 2*a*.   [3] Abraham b. Asher, *Or hasekhel* (Venice, 1567), fo. 1*a*.

many textual errors in these volumes, the obscure (and, in particular, non-Hebrew) vocabulary in the *midrashim* and the lack of appropriate expositions. Their commentaries attempted to remedy these deficiencies by influencing both the content and the presentation of books of *Midrash Rabbah*. This two-part story begins at the presses of Constantinople, where the status of this anthology of *midrashim* before and after its presentation as a printed text will be examined. I will then analyse the responses of sixteenth-century scholars to the printing of *Midrash Rabbah*, turning in particular to works by Meir Benveniste, Issachar Berman, and Abraham ben Asher. Using their commentaries, and taking examples from their expositions of selected *midrashim*, I will illustrate how these scholars attempted to transform the text and appearance of *Midrash Rabbah*.

The ten '*Rabbah*' *midrashim* only gradually assumed a group identity. In the earliest extant manuscripts, each appears on its own or in combination with a diverse selection of *midrashim*. The British Library manuscript Add. 27169 joins *Genesis Rabbah* and *Leviticus Rabbah*.[4] A manuscript in the Bibliothèque Nationale adds *Numbers Rabbah* to this combination.[5] Other manuscripts mix '*Rabbah*' *midrashim* with parts of *Midrash tanḥuma*, *Mekhilta derabi yishma'el*, *Sifra*, *Sifrei*, and other midrashic or aggadic works.[6] A fivefold '*Midrash Rabbah*' anthology on the Pentateuch, however, is represented by a small and close-knit group of manuscripts copied in late fifteenth-century Spain. A number of them seem to have emerged from the same location, some written on paper bearing the same watermark; two appear to have been copied by the same scribe.[7] We cannot argue from silence that *Midrash Rabbah* did not exist as a collection before this time, perhaps in other centres of Jewry as well. Nevertheless, by the eve of the expulsion, a '*Rabbah*' collection of *midrashim* on the Pentateuch had certainly emerged in Spain and was being copied into the sixteenth century.

The *midrashim* on the Five Megillot, however, were gathered together at an even later date. The only extant manuscript that contains all five was written in 1513, and is now in the Bodleian Library.[8] The designation '*Rabbah*' is not used

---

[4] Myron Lerner, 'The Works of Aggadic Midrash and the Esther Midrashim', in Shemuel Safrai (ed.), *The Literature of the Sages*, vol. ii (Assen, 2006), 167.

[5] MS Paris, Bibliothèque Nationale, 149. See Bregman, 'Midrash Rabbah', 197.

[6] For instance, the *Midrash ḥakhamim* (MS JTS 4937a) and MS Biblioteca Angelica 61.

[7] MS JNUL 24° 5977 and MS Bodleian Opp. Add., Fol. 3. The most complete of these manuscripts (including MS JNUL 24° 5977; MS Bodleian Opp. Add., Fol. 3; MS Bodleian Opp. Add., Fol. 51; and MS Sassoon 920) may be supplemented by a number of damaged manuscripts containing two or more '*Rabbah*' *midrashim* on the Pentateuch, but whose original extent is unknown, for instance, MS JTS 5014 and MS JNUL 8° 515. See Bregman, 'Midrash Rabbah', 205 n. 28. On the similarities between these manuscripts and their origination, see *Midrash Shemot Rabbah, Chapters I–XIV*, ed. Avigdor Shinan (Tel Aviv, 1984), 25–6; Bregman, 'Midrash Rabbah', 208 n. 28; Malachi Beit-Arié, *Catalogue of the Hebrew Manuscripts in the Bodleian Library: Supplement of Addenda and Corrigenda to Vol. 1 (A. Neubauer's Catalogue)* (Oxford, 1994), 454 on MS Bodleian Opp. Add., Fol. 51 (no. 2335).

[8] MS Bodleian Seld. A. Sup. 102, written in Sephardi script, was perhaps copied in the Ottoman empire. See Beit-Arié, *Catalogue of the Hebrew Manuscripts*, 22 (no. 164). See also Lerner, 'The Works of Aggadic Midrash', 168.

in this volume. Instead, its *midrashim* are entitled *Lamentations Rabbati, Midrash Ruth, Midrash Ecclesiastes, Song of Songs Rabbati*, and *Midrash Ahasuerus*. These diverse titles lend the volume the character of an *ad hoc* miscellany gathered for convenience rather than that of a heterogeneous companion to a fivefold '*Midrash Rabbah*' on the Pentateuch.

The development of these two apparently distinct anthologies of *midrashim* continued when they were printed at Constantinople shortly after the production of these manuscripts. In 1512, the *Sefer rabot* was published, comprising the five *midrashim* on the Pentateuch, each entitled '*Rabbah*'. The *Midrash ḥamesh megilot* was issued in 1514[9] and contained the five *midrashim* on the Megillot that had been gathered together only one year earlier in the Bodleian manuscript. The divergent titles of these two books suggest that the printers did not yet view them as companion volumes. Again, the constituent *midrashim* in the *Midrash ḥamesh megilot* were not accorded the title '*Rabbah*',[10] and it seems that they were not primarily identified by their relationship to the fivefold *Sefer rabot* on the Pentateuch.

The Constantinople printers of these volumes also seem to have enjoyed considerable freedom with regard to the texts they printed. Bregman notes that the only 'specifically Sephardic text-types' used in the production of these books were manuscripts of *Genesis Rabbah*. The printers' texts of other *midrashim* appear to stem from diverse locations, including Italy and southern France, while the textual tradition of *Deuteronomy Rabbah* is Ashkenazi.[11] Furthermore, despite the printers' assurance that 'the work of heaven was completed, refined and purified and distilled seven times over', they edited these texts with considerable flexibility, both adding and omitting passages. In the case of *Genesis Rabbah*, text was added from sources including various *midrashim*, the Jerusalem Talmud, and Pseudo-Rashi's commentary.[12]

The development of the Constantinople editions of the *Sefer rabot* and the *Midrash ḥamesh megilot*, therefore, was marked by a high degree of fluidity. This

---

[9] On the date of this edition, see Myron Lerner, 'The First Edition of Midrash on the Five Megillot' (Heb.), in Zvi Malachi (ed.), *The A. M. Haberman Memorial Volume* [Yad leheman: kovets meḥkarim lezekher a.m. haberman] (Lod, 1983), 289–311.

[10] *Shir hashirim rabati, Midrash rut, Midrash megilat ester, Eikhah rabati, Midrash kohelet*.

[11] Bregman, 'Midrash Rabbah', 199, 206 n. 32; see also Myron Lerner, 'New Light on the Spanish Recension of *Deuteronomy Rabbah* (1): The Evolution of Lieberman's Edition' (Heb.), *Te'udah*, 11 (1996), 107–45; id., 'New Light on the Spanish Recension of *Deuteronomy Rabbah* (2): On the Origin of Pericopes Va'etḥanan–Ekev' (Heb.), *Tarbiz*, 70 (2001), 417–27.

[12] Hanoch Albeck, *Introduction and Indices to Midrash Genesis Rabbah* (Heb.) (Berlin, 1931–6), 127–8. See also Lerner, 'The Works of Aggadic Midrash', 170–1. Thus, Jacob Elbaum suggests that the 'printers and proofreaders in the Hebrew printing houses did not regard the midrashim they worked with as closed texts' (Elbaum, '*Yalqut Shim'oni*', 169). The texts of the '*Rabbah*' *midrashim* printed in Constantinople have received individual attention in a number of studies: Albeck, *Introduction* (Heb.), 128; *Midrash Shemot Rabbah*, ed. Shinan, 27; *Midrash Wayyikra Rabbah*, ed. Mordecai Margulies, vol. v (Jerusalem, 1960), p. xxxvii; Lerner, 'The First Edition' (Heb.), 289–311; id., 'New Light (1)' (Heb.), 107–45; id., 'The Works of Aggadic Midrash', 133–229; Hananel Mack, 'The Reworking of a Midrash by Printers in Istanbul in 1512' (Heb.), *Pe'amim*, 52 (1992), 37–45.

extended from the text of their constituent *midrashim* to the tenuous precedent (particularly in the case of the Megillot) for collecting these individual works together at all. The nature of the relationship of these two volumes to each other is particularly uncertain, and it is only with hindsight that we can conceive of them as *editiones principes* of the later tenfold *Midrash Rabbah*.

The status of these volumes had changed, however, by the time they came to be reprinted in Venice. The two collections of *midrashim* on the Pentateuch and Megillot were issued together at the presses of Daniel Bomberg and Marco Antonio Giustiniani in 1545. The new title given to the Megillot *midrashim* (*Midrash ḥamesh megilot meharabot*) established their relationship with those on the Pentateuch (the '*rabot*') for the first time.[13] A short verse printed on the same title page, each line of which ends with the word *rabot*, leaves the reader in no doubt of this association. The book then continues, not with *Song of Songs Rabbati* as in the Constantinople edition, but with *Song of Songs Rabbah*.[14]

By the time this book reached the presses of Kraków in 1587, the tendency to associate the *midrashim* on the Megillot with those on the Pentateuch had become definitive. The Kraków edition is entitled *Sefer rabot*: 'midrashic explanations of the five books of the Pentateuch, shedding light like polished glass; and the Five Megillot, revealing (*megalot*) hidden things'.[15] The reader is left in no doubt that this book contains a unified collection of ten *midrashim* on both the Pentateuch and the Megillot.

The status of the text of the '*Rabbah*' *midrashim* also appears to have changed in these later editions. While the Constantinople printing endeavour, of necessity, involved the selection of manuscripts to compile a text to be printed, the Venetian printers were more reluctant to create new texts. According to Hanoch Albeck, the text of the Venice edition of *Genesis Rabbah* is that of the Constantinople *editiones principes*. However, he detects a number of changes, additions, and deletions, and concludes that the printers also had a manuscript at their disposal.[16] Avigdor Shinan suggests that *Exodus Rabbah* was subjected to even less editorial scrutiny.[17] The later Venice 1566 print of *Midrash Rabbah* issued by Giorgio di Cavalli was simply a line-by-line and page-by-page reprint of the 1545 edition. This trend towards reproducing the latest printed edition could not contrast more with the eclecticism of the Constantinople printers of the *editiones principes* of these *midrashim*.

In the course of the sixteenth century, therefore, a consolidated text of the *midrashim* on the Pentateuch and the Megillot was produced and these works were gathered to form a new tenfold anthology, the primary context in which they could be consulted in printed form. However, the publication of the successive editions

---

[13] Lerner, 'The Works of Aggadic Midrash', 168.
[14] Albeck, *Introduction* (Heb.), 192 n. 1.
[15] *Sefer rabot* (Kraków, 1587), fo. 1*a*.
[16] Albeck, *Introduction* (Heb.), 130–1.
[17] 'The later prints are only copies of the *editio princeps*, or copies with emendation or "improvement" according to the *Tanḥuma* or other *midrashim*', *Midrash Shemot Rabbah*, ed. Shinan, 27.

of *Midrash Rabbah* generated an unfortunate side-effect. The limited editing carried out by printers who relied heavily on recent editions led to the perpetuation of textual errors from print to print. In the eyes of the many sixteenth-century commentators on *Midrash Rabbah*, this added to the already overwhelming difficulties entailed in understanding rabbinic *midrashim*. The would-be reader of the new books of *Midrash Rabbah*, hindered by textual corruption, obscure vocabulary, and the lack of appropriate commentaries, was helpless as he faced the unfathomable riches contained in the words of the sages. In partial opposition to the ingathering and consolidation of printed editions of *Midrash Rabbah* that have been outlined thus far, many sixteenth-century commentators called for the revision of its text and the addition of suitable expositions.

Meir Benveniste of Salonica was the first scholar to respond to the new books of *Midrash Rabbah* by publishing a commentary. His *Ot emet*, first printed in 1565, contains long lists of annotations (*hagahot*) for several recently printed midrashic works.[18] To compile these, Meir turned to manuscript sources, the *Arukh*, the commentary of Pseudo-Rashi, and parallel texts in the *Yalkut shimoni*, Talmuds, and other aggadic and midrashic works. He also included the notes and glosses of expert scholars. For several works, including the *midrashim* of *Midrash Rabbah*, Benveniste chose to combine his own corrections with those of the contemporary scholar and learned annotator Judah Gedaliah.

In his preface to his *Ot emet*, Benveniste reveals his concern for the text of recently printed books of Midrash:

> I arrange these annotations according to the Venetian print of the *midrashim* since they have page numbers, even though I studied a few of them—the *Mekhilta* and the *Tanhuma*—as printed at Constantinople.... While I found the Venice print more correct when I compiled my annotations here, I also found a few errors in it which were correct in the Constantinople print. Therefore, if anyone finds any doubt[ful passage] in the Venetian prints of these two *midrashim*, he should look in the Constantinople print because he might find the correct [version] there.[19]

Benveniste's lists of annotations are labelled according to the pages and lines of printed editions, explaining his need to refer to editions of the *Mekhilta* and *Tanhuma* that have page numbers. In this quotation, Benveniste reveals his particular concern for identifying the correct reading and supplying this where it is lacking in a particular edition. The result is a handbook of annotations tailor-made for individual printed texts. In the case of *Midrash Rabbah*, it seems that Benveniste provided emendations and definitions that related to the obscure vocabulary and textual deficiencies of the Venice 1545 edition.

---

[18] The *Mekhilta derabi yishma'el, Sifra, Sifrei, Midrash tanhuma, Midrash shemu'el, Midrash tehilim, Midrash mishlei*, and the *Yalkut shimoni* (as well as the prayer-book, on which see Meir Benveniste, *Ot emet* (Salonica, 1565), fos. 3*a–b*, 173*b*).

[19] Benveniste, *Ot emet*, fo. 3*a*.

To illustrate Benveniste's method of emending and explaining the difficulties he encountered in this edition, we will turn to his comments on *Lamentations Rabbah*. The twelfth of the *petiḥtot* which begin this *midrash* contains a number of uncertainties and textual errors which Benveniste sought to resolve by means of his annotations.

This *petiḥta* begins by expounding Proverbs 25: 20, '[Like] taking off a garment on a cold day [and like] vinegar on soda [is one who] sings songs to a bad heart.' The *midrash* explores the meaning of this obscure proverb,[20] first by means of a *mashal* (parable) and then by explicating each element of the verse in turn. Like other *petiḥtot* of *Lamentations Rabbah*, this *petiḥta* focuses on key events associated with the Ninth of Av, expounding the exile and the destruction of the first and second temples as one. The *midrash* presents exile and destruction as the inevitable consequences of idolatry and failing to heed prophetic warnings. We will focus in particular on the first part of this *petiḥta* and on Benveniste's annotations.[21]

Rabbi Hanina ben Papa began [a discourse with the following verse], '[Like] taking off a garment on a cold day [and like] vinegar on soda [is one who] sings songs to a bad heart.'[22] Rabbi Hanina and Rabbi Jonathan both say, 'To what might one compare the ten tribes and the tribe of Judah and Benjamin? Two people were wrapped in a new cloak during the rainy season. One would [tug] [Venice 1545: *boged*][23] one way and one would [tug] the other until they tore it. Thus the ten tribes went on worshipping idols in Samaria, and the tribe of Judah and Benjamin [went on] worshipping idols in Jerusalem until they caused Jerusalem to be destroyed.' Another interpretation [of] '[like] taking off a garment on a cold day'. Rabbi Hanina ben Papa and Rabbi Shimon [had a discussion]. Rabbi Hanina ben Papa said, 'When Nebuchadnezzar attacked Israel, he divested them of two garments: the garments of the [priesthood] [Venice 1545: שהונה][24] and the garments of the monarchy.' 'On a cold day', because they called the calf, 'This is your [God] [Venice 1545: כלהיך][25], O Israel.'[26] '[Like] vinegar on soda': Rabbi Joshua said, 'It is like a person who had a wine cellar. He tested the first barrel and found it was vinegar, the second, and found it was vinegar, the third, and found it was [vinegar] [Venice 1545: 'wine'].[27] He said, "This is enough [to show] that all [has gone] bad."' '[One who] sings songs to a bad heart': Rabbi Berekhiah said, 'Whatever the singer sings, it does not enter into the ear [of the dancer] [Venice 1545: דדקרא].[28] Whatever the singer sings, the foolish son does not hear.'

The *petiḥta* begins with a *mashal* that likens the ten tribes and Judah and Benjamin to people tugging (*boged*) a new cloak in opposite directions, eventually tearing it. The word *boged*, whose meaning can only be judged from the context, is a play on

[20] This proverb attracts particular attention because of its terse formulation and unfamiliar use of the words *ma'adeh* ('taking off') and *neter* ('soda'). The root *ayin-dalet-heh* more usually means 'to decorate', and the term *neter* is used only once elsewhere in the Bible (Jer. 2: 22).
[21] Translation based on the text of *Midrash rabot* (Venice, 1545), fo. 48*b* (second pagination).
[22] Prov. 25: 20.　　　　　　　　　　　　　　　　[23] The translation 'tug' is conjectural.
[24] The translation 'priesthood' is based on a correction of the text to *kehunah*.
[25] The translation 'your God' is based on a correction of the text to *eloheikha*.
[26] Exod. 32: 4.　　　[27] The translation 'wine' is based on a correction of *ḥomets*, 'vinegar', to *yayin*.
[28] The translation 'of the dancer' is based on a correction of the text to *derakada*.

the word *beged*, 'clothing', in Proverbs 25: 20. Yet because this verb usually means 'to be unfaithful', it serves to introduce the theme of idolatry into the exposition of the proverb. According to this *mashal*, the new cloak may be likened to Jerusalem, located between the northern tribes and Judah and Benjamin. Because the Israelites continuously pulled away towards idolatry, Jerusalem was destroyed.

The *petiḥta* proceeds to expound each element of Proverbs 25: 20 in turn. '[Like] one taking off [*ma'adeh*] a garment' is explained with reference to the destruction of the First Temple and the Babylonian exile: Nebuchadnezzar 'divested' (*he'edah*) Israel of the priesthood and monarchy. 'On a cold day [*beyom karah*]' is expounded by means of a play on the word *karah* (קרה). It is taken to suggest the verb 'to call' (*kara*, קרא), thereby invoking the idolatry at Sinai: 'they called [*karu*, קראו] the calf, "This is your God, O Israel."'

The expositions of the phrases '[like] vinegar on soda' and '[one who] sings songs to a bad heart' are particularly obscure, partly due to textual difficulties. Rabbi Joshua's simile of the wine cellar should perhaps be understood to describe a wholesale condemnation of Israel—just as an entire batch of wine would be rejected if three barrels were tested and found to be vinegar, so individual instances of unfaithfulness and idolatry indict Israel as a whole. However, as the Venice 1545 text suggests that the owner found not vinegar but wine in the third barrel, the meaning of the conclusion 'this is enough [to show] that all [has gone] bad' and the implications of the simile are unclear.

With regard to Rabbi Berekhiah's adage, we are left to speculate as to why the dancer and the foolish son did not hear the singer. Later in the *petiḥta*, '[one who] sings songs to a bad heart' in Proverbs 25: 20 is explained with reference to the warnings of the prophets which hard-hearted 'scoffers' choose to ignore. Rabbi Berekhiah's adage may similarly indicate foolish disregard for prophetic warning. However, the meaning of his exposition is obscured by the incomprehensible text of the Venice 1545 edition: 'Whatever the singer sings, it does not enter into the ear דדקרא.'

Meir Benveniste was the first to publish corrections and interpretations of this text. As expected, he has labelled these in the *Ot emet* according to the page and line numbers of the Venice 1545 edition. Benveniste writes:

Line 27	*Boged* should read *oḥez* (also at the end of the line).
Beginning of line 33	It should read *kehunah*.
Beginning of line 34	It should read *eloheikha*.
Line 36	'And he found it was wine'. It should read 'and he found it was vinegar'.
	'This is enough [to show] that all [has gone] bad.' ° This means that, having tested three barrels that were found to be vinegar, he has tested enough.
Line 38	דדקרא ° This means someone stabbed by the stroke of a sword.[29]

---

[29] Benveniste, *Ot emet*, fo. 103*b*.

Benveniste suggests a number of corrections to the Venice 1545 text. Because the word *boged* is not attested elsewhere with the expected meaning of 'tug', he suggests emending it to *oḥez*, 'hold, seize'.[30] Benveniste briefly corrects the erroneous spellings שהונה and כלהיך to the expected כהונה (*kehunah*, 'priesthood') and אלהיך (*eloheikha*, 'your God'). He also takes issue with the simile of the wine cellar. While the 1545 text suggests that the owner finds wine in the third of the barrels he checks, Benveniste corrects this to 'vinegar'.

Benveniste also provides interpretations of the expositions attributed to Rabbi Joshua and Rabbi Berekhiah. As indicated in the *Ot emet* by a circle, and as explained in the preface,[31] these have been taken from the annotations of Judah Gedaliah. Both interpretations help the reader to understand the vocabulary and the syntax of the text. Benveniste does not explain the significance of these expositions in a *midrash* orientated around exile and the destruction of the first and second temples. Instead, the first of his comments offers a Hebrew paraphrase to amplify the Aramaic conclusion of the simile of the wine cellar. The *Ot emet* explains that, having found three barrels to be vinegar, the owner can conclude that all have gone bad. Turning to Rabbi Berekhiah's adage, Benveniste does not emend the obscure דדקרא. Rather, he suggests deriving this form from the root *dalet-kof-resh*, yielding the perplexing statement, 'Whatever the singer sings, it does not enter into the ear of the one who has been stabbed. Whatever the singer sings, the foolish son does not hear.'

What did Benveniste envisage his readers would do with these notes on the twelfth *petiḥta* of *Lamentations Rabbah*? In the preface to *Ot emet*, he provides a number of clues about the purpose and intended use of his glosses. He describes the process by which owners of books of *midrashim* would copy the handwritten marginalia of already annotated books into their own. Testifying to the earlier circulation of his own annotations in this form, he writes,

Do not rely or depend on the few annotated *midrashim* found in this city that were copied from books of my annotations. It was some time since they were copied and, without a doubt, they do not even contain half of the annotation[s].[32]

The process of copying *hagahot* from the margins of one book to another added particular value to the books annotated by expert scholars. For instance, the Salonica 1597 edition of the *Zohar ḥadash*, prepared for publication by Rabbi Naphtali ben Joseph Ashkenazi, advertises the presence of annotations from the book 'found in the house of . . . Judah Gedaliah (of blessed memory)'.[33] This intriguing information is fleshed out in the preface, where Rabbi Naphtali writes of his meeting with

---

[30] In proposing this emendation, Benveniste perhaps has in mind the opening of Mishnah *BM* 1: 1: 'Two people take hold [*oḥazin*] of one cloak. One says, "I found it." The other says, "I found it"', Hanoch Albeck (ed.), *Shishah sidrei mishnah: seder nezikin* (Jerusalem, 1953), 65.

[31] See Benveniste, *Ot emet*, fo. 2a.   [32] Ibid.

[33] *Zohar ḥadash* (Salonica, 1597), fo. 1a (the title page of the Megillot).

Moses, son of the late Judah Gedaliah:

> He brought us... to the lodgings... [of] the great luminary, the erudite, the pious, the humble, who labours at the doors of the Torah: our honoured Rabbi Judah Gedaliah (of blessed memory, may his soul be bound up in the bond of everlasting life). All his life he laboured at the work of heaven, studying and teaching and annotating his books, building a wall[34] around them with beautiful precision. I found... his son... Rabbi Moses Gedaliah (may the All Merciful protect him and bless him) and he showed me all the house of his treasures[35] and we copied from them as much as possible.[36]

It seems that Judah Gedaliah's annotated books were so valuable to Rabbi Naphtali ben Joseph Ashkenazi that he and Judah's son Moses rifled through the late scholar's possessions in search of his notes.

In *Ot emet*, the annotations of both Meir Benveniste and Judah Gedaliah have been divorced from their original location on the pages of printed books. Instead, they have been distilled into long lists of glosses, a concentrated format in which they could be published in printed form. By labelling these annotations and emendations according to the page and line to which they belonged, Benveniste allowed the reader to transfer them into the margins of a copy of a particular printed edition. As he describes:

> All these annotations are necessary for whomsoever might wish to write them down in the margin of the *midrashim*, each at its place. A unit of text is often incomprehensible without my annotation at the beginning of it. Therefore, anyone who finds the point of the text difficult [to understand] does not need to set out in search of the annotation, but only needs to look in the place where the difficulty arose.[37]

By gathering together the emendations and definitions of Meir Benveniste and Judah Gedaliah in one long list, therefore, *Ot emet* eliminated the need for readers to seek out a prominent scholar's copy of *Midrash Rabbah*. As these notes were copied into the pages of the Venice 1545 edition of *Midrash Rabbah*, the deficiencies perceived by these scholars were corrected by readers themselves.

It is not known whether Benveniste's book was widely used according to his instructions. Yet among the notes copied into one of the Venice 1545 editions of the *Midrash Rabbah* in the Bodleian Library[38] appear a selection of Benveniste's annotations written in Sephardi semi-cursive and cursive scripts of the late sixteenth century.[39] For instance, the text of the twelfth *petiḥta* of *Lamentations Rabbah* has

---

[34] On the translation of *dy"k*, see Ya'akov Spiegel, *Chapters in the History of the Jewish Book: Scholars and their Annotations* [Amudim betoledot hasefer ha'ivri: hagahot umegihim] (Ramat Gan, 1996), 357 n. 112.

[35] Isa. 39: 2.

[36] *Zohar ḥadash*, fos. 3b–4a. Quoted in Joseph Hacker, 'Towards a Historical Account of the Study and Dissemination of Kabbalah in Salonica in the Sixteenth Century' (Heb.), in Rachel Elior and Peter Schäfer (eds.), *Creation and Re-creation in Jewish Thought: Festschrift in Honor of Joseph Dan* (Tübingen, 2005), 169.   [37] Benveniste, *Ot emet*, fo. 3a.

[38] *Midrash rabot* (Venice: Bomberg, 1545), shelfmark N. 1. 15. Jur.

[39] I am indebted to Professor Malachi Beit-Arié for kindly agreeing to examine the annotations of this book.

been obediently corrected in accordance with Benveniste's instructions. The annotator has struck out the word *boged* and inserted *oḥez* above the printed text. The misprints of *kehunah* and *eloheikha* have been corrected. Rabbi Joshua's simile of the wine cellar has been emended so that the third barrel contains not 'wine' (which has been struck out) but 'vinegar'. Although the annotator has not noted the first of the two comments of Judah Gedaliah that appear in *Ot emet*, he has written the second as a note in the margin.

We cannot be sure of the identity of this annotator. However, on the inside cover of the book is the name Aaron ben Solomon Hasson, possibly the scholar of this name active in Salonica in the late sixteenth century.[40] While we cannot be sure that he was responsible for the notes contained in the book, it remains a possibility that *Ot emet* stimulated contemporary scholars to read and to study *Midrash Rabbah* by emending and annotating its text according to Meir Benveniste's instructions.

Ot emet, therefore, was an innovative response to new printed editions of *midrashim*, including the Venice 1545 edition of *Midrash Rabbah*. In contrast to the printers of this edition, who had tended to rely on the Constantinople edition rather than create a new text from manuscript sources, Benveniste provided his readers with the tools to annotate and emend their books. As a result, the errors he had identified in the Venice 1545 edition of *Midrash Rabbah* could be corrected, and individual copies could acquire the character that this edition lacked—that of a text thoroughly revised according to various readings of the *midrashim* and parallel texts.

Later commentators on *Midrash Rabbah* wished to take this process a step further by having their corrections and glosses incorporated into future printed editions. To demonstrate this, we must turn to the Polish press of Isaac ben Aaron Prostitz, where the Venetian text of *Midrash Rabbah* was reprinted in 1587.[41] The distinctive feature of this new edition, however, was the addition of a commentary: the *Matenot kehunah* of Issachar Berman ben Naphtali Hakohen of Szczebrzeszyn.

In the preface to this work, Issachar lamented the state of the text of *Midrash Rabbah*:

The copyists' errors and mistakes are myriad in number. If I were to count them, they would be more in number than the sand.[42] They are innumerable, too many for someone to straighten what has been made crooked.[43] The sins [of the copyists] are many. They have wronged us, and who can comprehend the errors?[44]

A significant part of Issachar's project was correcting the textual errors of the Venetian edition. In this regard, his project resembled that of Benveniste.[45] Unlike

---

[40] David Conforte, *Kore hadorot*, ed. David Cassel (Berlin, 1846), fos. 37b, 43a, 45a, 46a–b, 47a, 49a; *Encyclopaedia Judaica*, s.v. 'Ibn Ezra, Joseph ben Isaac'; Joseph Nehama, *Histoire des Israélites de Salonique*, vol. v (Salonica, 1935–78), 205. According to Nehama, Aaron died in 1614.

[41] Albeck, *Introduction* (Heb.), 134.   [42] Ps. 139: 18.

[43] Eccles. 7: 3.   [44] Ps. 19: 13. *Sefer rabot*, fo. 2a.

[45] Whose work is cited in the *Matenot kehunah*. See Jacob Reifmann, *Ohel yisakhar*, with annotations by Nehemiah Brüll (Przemyslu, 1887), 3.

Ot emet, however, Issachar's comments were not destined for publication as a separate handbook to *Midrash Rabbah* from which readers might correct their copies by hand. Instead, in Isaac Prostitz's reprint of the Venetian text of *Midrash Rabbah*, the reader could look at the foot of the page to see Issachar's comments. Thus the printers began to publish the Venetian text—complete with 'errors and mistakes'—at the top of the page, and the corrections at the bottom.

The absurdity of this plan did not go unnoticed by Issachar. A short description of the publishing process portrays him confronting the printers, who had already reached *Exodus Rabbah*, saying, 'You are not doing the right thing by publishing something that has not been corrected at our hand.'[46] His words at the conclusion of the book record that he 'ordered those in charge of the printing work not to repeat the former mistaken readings in the book, in order that they might exchange the bad for good'.[47]

This edition most clearly illustrates the enduring influence of the consolidated Venetian text of *Midrash Rabbah* on the one hand, and the role of commentaries in its continuing evolution on the other. The Kraków printers began by reprinting the Venetian text but, following Issachar's warnings, they emended it according to his commentary.[48] Thus, not only was the appearance of the printed text of *Midrash Rabbah* transformed through the addition of the *Matenot kehunah* at the foot of its pages, but the text of the *midrashim* themselves was changed through the direct influence of Issachar Berman and his commentary.[49]

This can be illustrated by turning back to the twelfth *petiḥta* of *Lamentations Rabbah* as it appeared in the Kraków 1587 edition. At the foot of the text is Issachar's commentary, which reads:

During the rainy season. It is a chilly time of the year and they need to cover themselves.
One would tug. Pulling and tugging the cloak over him to cover [himself] with it.

---

[46] *Sefer rabot*, second pagination, fo. 130*b*.   [47] Ibid.

[48] Although the text from *Exodus Rabbah* onwards is corrected according to the instructions of the *Matenot kehunah*, Issachar's now redundant textual emendations remain at the foot of the page. See the words of the printers in *Sefer rabot*, second pagination, fo. 130*b*; Albeck, *Introduction* (Heb.), 134.

[49] This text as corrected by Issachar exerted an extraordinary influence over future printed editions. For instance, the Salonica 1593–6 edition of *Midrash Rabbah* was intended to contain Judah Gedaliah's *hagahot* ('annotations') alongside a version of the Venice 1545 text. However, part way through the production process, the printers acquired the Kraków 1587 edition of *Midrash Rabbah* and adopted both its text and its commentary. Thus, at the end of *Genesis Rabbah* (fo. 85*b*) is written, 'we began to print it with the annotations of the expert scholar mentioned above [i.e. Judah Gedaliah]. But now the Lord has brought into our possession the annotations of our master and teacher R. Issachar Baer b. Naphtali Hakohen of Szczebrzeszyn entitled *Matenot kehunah*. We agreed to print it too, so that the building might be supported by two pillars and so that the desire of all readers might be fulfilled.' Despite the two promised pillars—the *hagahot* of Judah Gedaliah and the *Matenot kehunah* of Issachar Berman—from *Exodus Rabbah* onwards, the *Matenot kehunah* all but displaces Judah Gedaliah's work. A Salonica edition of *Genesis Rabbah* with Issachar Berman's comments alone was issued separately in 1595. See Albeck, *Introduction* (Heb.), 136.

Taking off. This means 'to remove', as Targum Onkelos translates *vayasar* as *ve'a'adi*.

Because they called ... This interprets *karah* as *kara* by exchanging the letters.

The third, and found it was vinegar. He said is the correct reading.

This is enough, etc. This is the proof and confirmation that all of them are vinegar, and it is not necessary to check further.

Whatever the singer sings. This is to say that he reproves and reproves again a foolish and stupid son. Despite this, [the son] does not listen or agree—so Rashi interprets in [his commentary on] the book of Proverbs. The reading in the *Arukh*, under the entry *resh-kof-dalet* is 'in the ears of the dancer (*derakada*)'. This means, 'in the ears of the fool dancing in the pub'.[50]

As Issachar's starting point was the Venice 1545 text, he discusses many of the textual problems that Benveniste also noted. Yet Issachar's distinct and creative approach to this *midrash* can be seen particularly in those comments that guide the reader to a clear understanding of the *petiḥta*, amplify its meaning with short paraphrases, and explain midrashic modes of interpretation. Thus Issachar begins by elaborating on the descriptive details of the *mashal*, depicting the extreme cold and damp that led each character to 'pull and tug' the cloak over himself.[51] These descriptions explain the significance of the word *boged* by means of a passing paraphrase, and Issachar silently ignores Benveniste's suggestion that the word be emended.

Issachar's interest in explaining midrashic modes of interpretation is evident in his fourth comment. He carefully describes the exposition of 'on a cold day [*beyom karah*]' by means of the statement 'because they called [*karu*] the calf, "This is your God, O Israel"'. Issachar puts the word *karah* (קרה) alongside the triliteral root *kara* (קרא), demonstrating as clearly as possible that the *midrash* has exchanged the letter *heh* of *karah* for the *alef* of the verb *kara*.

The textual errors in the *petiḥta* are also addressed in Issachar's comments. For instance, he emends the simile of the wine cellar to indicate that the owner found vinegar in each of the three barrels that he tested. In the following comment he then explains the meaning of this simile by paraphrasing its conclusion in Hebrew: having found that three barrels contain vinegar, the owner has no need to examine them all.

Issachar's desire to explain this *petiḥta* led him to study it with reference to Targum Onkelos, Rashi's commentary on Proverbs, and the *Arukh* of Nathan ben Yehiel. For instance, he discusses the unusual meaning of the root *ayin-dalet-heh* in Proverbs 25: 20 and in the Midrash.[52] This appears elsewhere in the Hebrew Bible as a verb with the meaning 'to decorate'. Issachar, however, suggests that its

---

[50] *Sefer rabot*, second pagination, fo. 52*a*.

[51] In particular, Issachar's first comment suggests that the phrase *yemot hageshamim* specifically indicates a 'rainy season' and describes it as 'chilly' to link it to the 'on a cold day' of Proverbs 25: 20.

[52] '[Like] taking off [*ma'adeh*] a garment on a cold day' and 'Nebuchadnezzar divested [*he'edah*] Israel of the priesthood and monarchy'.

significance in these passages might lie in the Aramaic meaning of the root. Perhaps alluding to Rashi's commentary on Proverbs 25: 20,[53] he notes that Targum Onkelos uses it to render the Hebrew verb 'to remove'.[54] This latter is proposed as a synonym.

In Issachar's final comment, he explains Rabbi Berekhiah's simile of the singer, the dancer, and the foolish son by referring explicitly to Rashi's comment on Proverbs 25: 20 and then to the *Arukh*. Rashi explains '[one who] sings songs to a bad heart' as 'one who teaches Torah to a bad student who, in his heart, does not intend to carry it out'. Issachar paraphrases Rashi's words to relate them to a 'son' rather than a 'student' and implies that the singer is a parent whose reproofs are not heeded by the child. The *Matenot kehunah* also corrects the text of this passage by turning to the *Arukh*. Ignoring *Ot emet*'s perplexing definition of the obscure word דדקרא, Issachar suggests that the similar letters *dalet* and *resh* have been transposed and that we should read דרקדא (*derakada*), 'of the dancer'. He defends this emendation by claiming the support of the *Arukh*, which, under the entry *resh-kof-dalet*, quotes this very midrashic passage.[55] Issachar also attempts to explain why the song might not be heard by this 'dancer'. Perhaps inspired by the preceding simile of the wine cellar,[56] he depicts a fool in the pub who is too drunk to pay attention to the music to which he is dancing.

While Issachar's comments on this *petiḥta* are printed beneath it in full, the Kraków printers also incorporated his emendations into the midrashic text itself. In place of the mistakes in the Venice 1545 edition, the similes of the wine cellar and of the dancer have been corrected according to the *Matenot kehunah*.[57] By means of his commentary, therefore, Issachar has shaped both the presentation and the text of this *midrash*. He has provided the reader with a carefully edited text and supplied a commentary to clarify the *midrash*, to elaborate on its details, and to explain the modes of interpretation it employs. While the reader of the Venice 1545 edition was able to add emendations and glosses by copying Meir Benveniste's notes by hand, Issachar's *Matenot kehunah* exerted a direct influence on the text of the Kraków edition and formed an integral part of its layout.

The most distinctive transformation of the appearance of *Midrash Rabbah*, however, was accomplished by the commentators Abraham ben Asher of Safed and Samuel Yafeh of Constantinople.[58] As explained above, the Venice 1545 and Kraków

---

[53] Rashi interprets *ma'adeh* with reference to the Aramaic of Exod. 8: 4 saying, 'The Targum translates *vayaser* as *veyadei*' (*Mikraot gedolot* (Venice, 1547), fo. 776a).

[54] e.g. Gen. 8: 13, 30: 35, 41: 42. (See Alexander Sperber (ed.), *The Bible in Aramaic*, vol. i: *The Pentateuch According to Targum Onkelos* (Leiden, 1959), 12, 48, 70.)

[55] For instance, the Venice 1531 edition: Nathan b. Yehiel, *Sefer he'arukh*, fo. 221b.

[56] And with allusion to BT *BK* 86a and *Pes.* 49a.

[57] Although not addressed by Issachar, the spelling of *kehunah* and *eloheikha* has been corrected in the Kraków 1587 edition.

[58] On Samuel Yafeh's commentary, see Meir Benayahu, 'Rabbi Samuel Yafeh Ashkenazi and Other Commentators of *Midrash Rabbah*: Some Biographical and Bibliographical Details' (Heb.), *Tarbiz*, 42 (1972/3), 419–60.

1587 editions gathered the ten '*Rabbah*' *midrashim* into a single volume. Abraham ben Asher and Samuel Yafeh, however, conceived of *Midrash Rabbah* as a multi-volume series, with *midrashim* contained in separate books.[59] The reason for this was the extraordinarily verbose expositions they wished to add to the midrashic text. Their commentaries increased the size of *Midrash Rabbah* to such an extent that it could no longer be contained in a single volume. For instance, the Venice 1545 edition contains the ten *midrashim* of *Midrash Rabbah* in approximately 300 folios; the Kraków 1587 edition, with the addition of Issachar Berman's commentary, amounts to 430 folios. These are dwarfed by the first volumes of Abraham ben Asher's *Or hasekhel* and Samuel Yafeh's *Yefeh to'ar*, which contain text and commentaries on *Genesis Rabbah* alone in 192 and 540 folios respectively. The expense associated with the publication of such enormous tomes hindered the printing of these works.[60] Only the first volume of *Yefeh to'ar* was printed during the sixteenth century; no further volumes of *Or hasekhel* were ever published.[61]

Although Abraham ben Asher and Samuel Yafeh provide occasional emendations and definitions of difficult words in *Midrash Rabbah*, this was not their primary focus. Instead, they aimed to guide readers towards correct and harmonious understandings of each *midrash* by means of extended, discursive comments. At times, these stretch to lengthy discourses that employ modes of interpretation prominent in contemporary Sephardi homiletic expositions of Scripture.[62] For instance,

---

[59] Thus, Abraham b. Asher's *Or hasekhel* on *Genesis Rabbah* alone was printed in Venice in 1567. Samuel Yafeh's *Yefeh to'ar* on Genesis (Venice, 1597), Exodus (Venice, 1657), Leviticus (Constantinople, 1648), and Song of Songs (Izmir, 1739) were printed separately. Some of Yafeh's commentaries on the Megillot, however, were collected together under the title *Sefer yefeh anaf* and printed in Frankfurt an der Oder in 1695/6.

[60] See Samuel Yafeh, *Yefeh to'ar* (Venice, 1597), fo. 1b.

[61] Note also that the first volume of the *Or hasekhel* was a victim of the burning of Hebrew books in Venice in 1568, after which its printer, Giovanni Griffio, issued no further Hebrew works. See Paul Grendler, 'The Destruction of Hebrew Books in Venice, 1568', *Proceedings of the American Academy for Jewish Research*, 45 (1978), 114–15; Marvin Heller, *The Sixteenth Century Hebrew Book: An Abridged Thesaurus* (Leiden, 2004), 609.

[62] See Joseph Hacker, 'The Intellectual Activity of the Jews of the Ottoman Empire During the Sixteenth and Seventeenth Centuries', in Isadore Twersky and Bernard Septimus (eds.), *Jewish Thought in the Seventeenth Century* (Cambridge, Mass., 1987), 110–16; Hava Tirosh-Samuelson, 'The Ultimate End of Human Life in Postexpulsion Philosophic Literature', in Benjamin Gampel (ed.), *Crisis and Creativity in the Sephardic World 1391–1648* (New York, 1997), 223–54; Mordechai Pachter, 'Homiletic and Ethical Literature of Safed in the Sixteenth Century' [Sifrut haderush vehamusar shel ḥakhmei tsefat bame'ah ha-16 uma'arekhet ra'ayonoteiha ha'ikariyim], Ph.D. diss., Hebrew University of Jerusalem, 1976.

A number of studies detail the exposition of individual scholars. On Joseph Taitazak, see Bracha Sack, 'R. Joseph Taitazak's Commentaries' (Heb.), *Jerusalem Studies in Jewish Thought*, 7 (1988), 341–55; Joseph Sermoneta, 'Scholastic Philosophic Literature in Rabbi Joseph Taitazak's *Porat yosef*' (Heb.), *Sefunot*, 11 (1971–7), 135–85; Shimon Shalem, 'The Exegetic Method of R. Joseph Taitazak and his Circle: Its Nature and its Form of Inquiry' (Heb.), ibid. 115–34.

On Moses Almosnino, see Naphtali Ben-Menahem, 'The Writings of Rabbi Moses Almosnino' (Heb.), *Sinai*, 10 (1946/7), 268–85; Marc Saperstein, *Jewish Preaching, 1200–1800: An Anthology* (London, 1989), 217–39.

Abraham ben Asher and Samuel Yafeh often structure their comments around the enumeration and subsequent resolution of *sefekot* or *kushiyot*, the 'difficulties' that arise in a passage under discussion. This mode of exposition, perhaps related to the scholastic method of *quaestiones et dubitationes*, had been employed by Sephardi commentators from the early fourteenth century onwards and is most famous for its use in the works of Isaac Abravanel (1437–1508) and Isaac Arama (c.1420–94). In commentaries on biblical books and in written collections of homilies, sixteenth-century commentators often subjected whole groups of verses to this expository cross-examination in an endeavour to reveal the thematic unity of extended passages.[63]

Despite the glut of homiletic commentaries on biblical books written and published in the sixteenth century, Abraham ben Asher and Samuel Yafeh were almost unique in their endeavours to interpret *midrashim* in this way. They envisaged the text of *Midrash Rabbah* surrounded by their extensive discursive interpretations, expounding the minutiae of rabbinic discussions, questioning their consistency, and reconciling any apparent discrepancies by means of multiple expositions.

In order to illustrate elements of this discursive approach to expounding Midrash, we will turn to Abraham ben Asher's interpretation of *Genesis Rabbah* 18: 4 in *Or hasekhel*. On this occasion, Abraham does not expound the *midrash* by listing *kushiyot* and supplying resolutions in the manner of a homily. Instead, his desire to demonstrate the coherent and consistent nature of this *midrash* led him to provide two harmonizing interpretations.

Genesis Rabbah 18: 4 contains an exposition of Adam's declaration, 'This one, this time [*zot hapa'am*] is bone of my bones and flesh of my flesh. This one will be called woman, for she was taken out of man' (Gen. 2: 23). We will focus on the first part of this *midrash*, translated below according to the text printed in *Or hasekhel*.

On Moses Alsheikh, see Shimon Shalem, 'The Exegetical and Homiletical Method of R. Moses Alsheikh's Commentaries on the Bible' (Heb.), *Sefunot*, 5 (1961), 151–206; id., 'Thought and Morals in the Commentaries of R. Moses Alsheikh' (Heb.), *Sefunot*, 6 (1962), 197–258; id., 'The Life and Works of Rabbi Moses Alsheikh' (Heb.), *Sefunot*, 7 (1963), 179–97; id., *Rabbi Moses Alsheikh* (Heb.) (Jerusalem, 1966); Louis Jacobs, *Jewish Biblical Exegesis* (New York, 1973), 144–52; Kalman Bland, 'Issues in Sixteenth-Century Jewish Exegesis', in David Steinmetz (ed.), *The Bible in the Sixteenth Century* (Durham, NC, 1990), 50–67.

On Isaac Arollia, see Alan Cooper, 'The Message of Lamentations', *Journal of the Ancient Near Eastern Society*, 28 (2001), 1–18; id., 'Elements of Popular Piety in Late Medieval and Early Modern Jewish Psalms Commentary', in Shawna Dolansky (ed.), *Sacred History, Sacred Literature* (Winona Lake, Ind., 2008), 275–91.

On Eliezer Ashkenazi, see Alan Cooper, 'An Extraordinary Sixteenth-Century Biblical Commentary: Eliezer Ashkenazi on the Song of Moses', in Barry Walfish (ed.), *The Frank Talmage Memorial Volume* (Haifa, 1993), 129–50.

[63] See Marc Saperstein, 'The Method of Doubts', in Jane Dammen McAuliffe, Barry Walfish, and Joseph Ward Goering (eds.), *With Reverence for the Word* (Oxford, 2010), 139–43, 146; Saperstein, *Jewish Preaching*, 74–5; Eric Lawee, 'Isaac Abarbanel: From Medieval to Renaissance Jewish Biblical

'And the man said, "This one, this time [*zot hapa'am*] [is bone of my bones and flesh of my flesh.]"'[64] Rabbi Judah ben Rabbi said, 'When [God] first created her for him, he saw her full of guts and gore. So [God] removed her from him and created her a second time [*pa'am sheniyah*], as it is written, "This one, this time [*zot hapa'am*]".

This is she of that [first] time [*otah hapa'am*]. This is she who is going to strike against me like a bell, as it says, "a bell [*pa'amon*] of gold and a pomegranate".[65]

This is she who used to beat me [*shehayetah mefa'amtani*] all night long.'[66]

The exact significance of the word *pa'am* in Genesis 2: 23, meaning 'occasion', 'footstep', or '(rhythmic) beat', is unclear. Its demonstrative use suggests the interpretation that Adam distinguished the present 'bone of my bones and flesh of my flesh' from some former creation.

The *midrash* under discussion is one of the references in *Genesis Rabbah* to a tradition that Adam had two wives.[67] Although Adam's first wife later became associated with the night-demon Lilith, this identification is not in evidence in this *midrash*. Rather, the text seems to depict Adam as the unfortunate witness of the act of creation by which God, having removed his rib, 'built' it into Eve.[68] In this *midrash*, when Adam saw Eve 'full of guts and gore', God removed her to 'create her a second time'. The recreated Eve was accepted by Adam with the declaration, 'This one, this time [*zot hapa'am*] is bone of my bones and flesh of my flesh.'

The *midrash*, however, does not leave Adam and Eve happily united. The second part of the text suddenly introduces previously unmentioned defiant character traits in Eve. First, the word *pa'am* is expounded by means of the related word *pa'amon* in Exodus 28: 34 to suggest that Eve will strike against Adam like a bell.[69] Second, using a verbal form of *pa'am* meaning 'beat' or 'disturb', Adam also says, 'This is she who used to beat me [*shehayetah mefa'amtani*] all night long.'[70] According to these additional interpretations, therefore, Adam recognized Eve by her defiant character as a mere recreation of his first, undesirable wife and he rejected her.

Abraham ben Asher approaches this *midrash* by highlighting four ambiguities. Foremost among these is Adam's attitude to his recreated wife and whether he

---

Scholarship', in Magne Sæbø (ed.), *Hebrew Bible/Old Testament: The History of Its Interpretation*, vol. ii (Göttingen, 1996), 195–6, 198.

[64] Gen. 2: 23. For this translation of *zot hapa'am*, see Hermann Gunkel, *Genesis*, trans. Mark Biddle (Macon, Ga., 1997), 13—'"this one this time" = "this one, finally"'. See also Claus Westermann, *Genesis 1–11*, trans. John Scullion (Minneapolis, Minn., 1984), 231. [65] Exod. 28: 34.

[66] Abraham b. Asher, *Or hasekhel*, fo. 47a.

[67] See the parallel *midrash* in *Gen. Rabbah* 17: 7 and also 22: 7. On these *midrashim*, see Daniel Boyarin, *Carnal Israel: Reading Sex in Talmudic Culture* (Berkeley, Calif., 1993), 76–106.

[68] Gen. 2: 21–2.

[69] See below for Abraham b. Asher's discussion of this in terms of Genesis 3: 17, 'For you listened to the voice [or 'the sound', *lekol*] of your wife.'

[70] See also BT *Sot. 9b*, where the verbal form *lepa'amo* in Judges 13: 25 ('to move him', i.e. Samson) is similarly expounded with reference to *pa'amon* ('bell'), and Exod. 28: 34.

accepted her (as in the first part of the *midrash*) or rejected her (as in the second). Abraham attempts to harmonize the two sections of this *midrash* so that they convey the same attitude. A second ambiguity arises from the phrases 'this is she who is going to strike against me' and 'this is she who used to beat me all night long'. We might expect both of these parallel clauses to be in the same tense, referring either to Adam's past experience of Eve's undesirable traits or to his fear that he will again suffer at her hands in the future. As will be shown below, Abraham emends these for the sake of a consistent interpretation. He also examines the second of these phrases to determine the precise meaning of the word *mefa'amtani* and the chronological implications of 'all night long' in the context of the Genesis Creation accounts. He comments,

'This is she who is going to strike against me like a bell' means 'quarrelling with me with words'. And according to the interpretation of Rashi, this means that the First Eve used to dispute with [Adam] and hit him at the time of sexual intercourse, and she did not want to be subdued beneath him. And when [Adam] saw this [second] one, he knew and recognized that she was not like the first, and he said in amazement, 'Is this she who is going to strike against me like a bell? Is this she who used to beat me [*shehaytah mefa'amtani*] all night long?' This means that 'she used to strike against me'. The Targum renders 'and his spirit was agitated' [*vatipa'em ruḥo*][71] in Aramaic as *umitarpa ruḥei*. The meaning is similar to 'he knocked at the door' [*teraf abava*].[72] And where it says 'all night long', it is not specified that there had not yet been a night since Adam had been created. Rather, the meaning is about the time of sexual intercourse.

And it is also possible to interpret and to say 'this is she of that [first] time'. This means that, even though [God] created her again for [Adam], adorned and very beautiful,[73] [Adam] recognized that she was the [same] as at that [first] time when she was created from his bone and his flesh. 'This is she who is going to strike me' means that the holy spirit shone upon him, and hinted in his words that she was going to 'cry aloud at him',[74] as Scripture says, 'For you listened to the voice of your wife'.[75] 'This is she who used to beat me'— it should be 'who will beat me'. And he said this about nightfall at the conclusion of the sabbath as he was afraid and saying 'Woe is me!', as he said below. And Rashi (of blessed memory) reads *shemefa'amtani*. And this reading fits with this interpretation. This is also the reading of the *Yalkut*.[76]

In order to harmonize the whole *midrash* with the view that Adam accepted the second Eve, Abraham ben Asher begins by introducing two subtle changes to its meaning. First, he suggests that Adam's negative assessments of Eve's character ('this is she who is going to strike against me like a bell . . . this is she who used to beat me all night long') were, in fact, spoken 'in amazement'. He finds this indication in the text of some manuscript versions[77] of the *midrash* and also in Pseudo-Rashi's

---

[71] Gen. 41: 8.   [72] BT *Eruv.* 104*a*, *Ber.* 28*a*, *Ḥul.* 95*b*.

[73] Abraham b. Asher uses the word *mekushetet* ('adorned'), perhaps taking his cue from 'this is she who is going to strike [*lehakish*] against me like a bell'. On the adorning of Eve, see *Gen. Rabbah* 18: 1.

[74] See *Gen. Rabbah* 20: 8 (also 19: 5).   [75] Gen. 3: 17.   [76] Abraham b. Asher, *Or hasekhel*, fo. 47*a*.

[77] See *Midrash Bereshit Rabba*, ed. Judah Theodor and Chanock Albeck (Berlin, 1903–29), 164.

commentary on *Genesis Rabbah*.⁷⁸ Abraham also responds to the divergent tenses of these two clauses. Asserting that both should be understood in the past tense, he suggests that Adam's pessimistic estimation of his wife's character related only to the first Eve and not to the second. By means of these two interpretations, the meaning of Adam's words is reversed and they are transformed into incredulous questions expecting a negative response: 'Is this she who used to strike against me like a bell? Is this she who used to beat me all night long?' Rather than recognizing in his second wife the same undesirable characteristics of the first, therefore, Adam remarked with astonishment that the traits of the old Eve did not appear in the new, and he accepted her.

Abraham's first comment also clarifies the meaning and implications of Adam's statement 'This is she who used to beat me [*shehaytah mefa'amtani*] all night long.' First, he defines the word *mefa'amtani* by suggesting an Aramaic equivalent. In Genesis 41: 8, the same Hebrew verb is rendered in Targum Onkelos by the Aramaic root *tet-resh-peh*. Abraham identifies instances in which this means 'to knock, strike', and suggests that the Hebrew word *mefa'amtani* also contains this shade of meaning. He also explains the phrase 'all night long'. The *midrash* takes it for granted that Eve was created from Adam, even suggesting that this process extended over a period of days and nights. In the first Genesis Creation account, however, man and woman were both created on the sixth day, with no intervening night. Abraham removes any discrepancy by suggesting that the midrashic designation 'all night long' is not a chronological indication, but a euphemism for 'the time of sexual intercourse'.⁷⁹

---

⁷⁸ Abraham b. Asher's allusions to 'Rashi' in this comment relate to a medieval commentary on *Midrash Rabbah* that circulated in the Ottoman empire in the 16th cent. Abraham b. Asher compiled a text of this commentary from two divergent manuscripts and published this in *Or hasekhel* alongside his own expositions. He begins his exposition of this *midrash* by following Pseudo-Rashi closely. On the nature of Pseudo-Rashi's commentary, see Israel Ta-Shma, 'Ashkenazi Jewry in the Eleventh Century', in id., *Creativity and Tradition: Studies in Medieval Rabbinic Scholarship, Literature and Thought* (Cambridge, Mass., 2006), 4–5; id., *Keneset meḥkarim: Studies in Medieval Rabbinic Literature* [Keneset meḥkarim : iyunim basifrut harabanit biyemei habeinayim], vol. i: *Ashkenaz* (Jerusalem, 2004), 96–114; Ronald Brown, 'An Antedate to Rashi's Commentary to *Genesis Rabbah*' (Heb.), *Tarbiz*, 53 (1983), 478; Judah Theodor, 'The Commentary on *Genesis Rabbah*' (Heb.), in M. Brann (ed.), *Festschrift zu Israel Lewy* (Breslau, 1911), 132–54; Abraham Epstein, 'R. Joseph Kara and the Commentary on *Genesis Rabbah* attributed to Rashi' (Heb.), *Haḥoker*, 1/2 (1891), 29–35; id., 'Der sogenannte Raschi-Commentar zu Bereschit-Rabba', *Magazin für die Wissenschaft des Judentums*, 14 (1887), 1–17; D. Schorr, 'The Commentary on *Genesis Rabbah* and the Commentary on *Masekhet nedarim* attributed to Rashi' (Heb.), *Heḥaluts*, 10 (1878), 111–21.

⁷⁹ Abraham b. Asher explains this at the beginning of his comment, attributing to Rashi the interpretation that Eve 'hit [Adam] at the time of sexual intercourse, and she did not want to be subdued beneath him'. While Pseudo-Rashi's commentary does indeed state that 'all night long' means 'at the time of sexual intercourse', Abraham b. Asher has amplified this comment by suggesting that Eve 'did not want to be subdued beneath' Adam. This detail is comparable to the account in the *Alphabet of Ben Sira*:

When the Holy One, blessed be He, created Adam alone, He said, 'It is not good for the man to be on

While Abraham has so far harmonized the two parts of the *midrash* to suggest that Adam accepted the recreated Eve, he proceeds to introduce a second, divergent exposition with the words 'and it is also possible to interpret'. In this additional interpretation, he suggests that Adam rejected Eve because he recognized that she was merely a recreation of his first wife, complete with undesirable traits. Adam came to this realization when he said, 'This is she who is going to strike against me like a bell.' According to Abraham, 'the holy spirit shone upon him and hinted in his words that [Eve] was going to "cry aloud at him"'. The 'illumination of the holy spirit' is used elsewhere in *Genesis Rabbah* itself[80] to indicate 'an omen contained in a chance uttering', Saul Lieberman's definition of the related concepts of 'consulting the holy spirit' or 'consulting the *bat kol*'.[81] Thus, through a level of divine inspiration, Adam became aware that his recreated wife would defy him, and he rejected her.[82]

In order to support this new interpretation, Abraham must contradict a number of the tenets he previously established. Earlier in this comment, he emended the second part of the *midrash*, placing it in the past tense to convey that Adam was amazed that the newly recreated Eve had been divested of her unfortunate traits. He now wishes to stress the opposite—that Eve's newfound beauty belied her enduring violent character. He suggests, therefore, that the second part of the *midrash* should be in the future tense, and emends the perfect *shehayetah mefa'amtani* to the imperfect *sheteheh mefa'amtani*. Abraham draws attention to an alternative reading to support his interpretation. He observes that Pseudo-Rashi's commentary on *Genesis Rabbah* cites this passage without the word *hayetah*, a

---

his own' [Gen. 2: 18]. He created a woman for him, also from the ground, and He called her Lilith. They immediately began fighting [*mitgarin*] one another. She said, 'I'm not lying underneath' [*shokhevet lematah*] and he said, 'I'm not lying underneath but only on top, since you are fit for the lower position and I for the upper.' She said to him, 'We are both equal because we are both from [the] ground.' When Lilith saw, she pronounced the Ineffable Name and flew into the atmosphere. Adam stood in prayer before his Creator and said, 'Sovereign of the Universe, the woman you gave me has fled from me!' (trans. from *Sefer alfa beita deven sira* (Venice, 1544), fo. 23a).

By suggesting that Eve not only beat Adam at the time of sexual intercourse, but also that she refused to adopt a subordinate sexual position, Abraham b. Asher has perhaps drawn on this source in addition to Pseudo-Rashi's comment. (On the printing of the *Alphabet of Ben Sira* in Constantinople in 1519, see Joseph Hacker, 'Introduction', in *The Alphabet of Ben Sira: Facsimile of the 1519 Edition from the Valmadonna Trust Library* (Verona, 1997), 16–37.)

[80] For instance, in the exposition of Genesis 37: 33 in *Gen. Rabbah* 84: 19, Jacob recognizes Joseph's coat and says, 'It is my son's coat. A wild animal has eaten him [Gen. 37: 33].' R. Huna expounds, 'The holy spirit shone upon him. "A wild animal has eaten him"—this is Potiphar's wife.' (Abraham b. Asher, *Or hasekhel*, fo. 166a; see also *Gen. Rabbah* 85: 9.)

[81] Saul Lieberman, *Hellenism in Jewish Palestine* (New York, 1950), 195 n. 11.

[82] For Abraham b. Asher, Adam's words 'this is she who is going to strike against me like a bell' are a premonition of Gen. 3: 17, 'For you listened to the voice [*lekol*] of your wife.' This verse is expounded in *Gen. Rabbah* 20: 8 (Abraham b. Asher, *Or hasekhel*, fo. 53b) to suggest that Eve was speaking with Adam in a raised voice. Abraham b. Asher suggests that Adam's words intimate that the newly created Eve is going to 'sound against him like a bell'.

reading he also observes in the *Yalkut shimoni*.[83] As a result of this interpretation, Adam's words come to mean, 'This is she who is going to strike against me like a bell . . . this is she who will beat me all night long.'

Abraham had previously interpreted 'all night long' as sexual intercourse. However, he now resorts to a more literal interpretation: '[Adam] said this about the evening of the conclusion of the sabbath as he was afraid and said "Woe is me!", as he said below.' It seems that he is referring to a legend in *Genesis Rabbah* 11: 2 and 12: 6 in which the primordial Adam is deprived of his magnificent attributes and, as the sun sets at the conclusion of the sabbath, becomes afraid of being attacked under cover of darkness. Genesis 3: 15, 'he will bruise your head and you will bruise his heel', is cited to suggest a prophecy of violence against Adam.[84] By invoking this *midrash* in the context of the creation of Eve, Abraham suggests that 'This is she who will beat me all night long' refers to Adam's fear that the second Eve will attack him as darkness approaches. His anticipation of this violent behaviour led him to reject his recreated wife.

With the words 'and it is also possible to interpret', Abraham has joined two conflicting expositions. In the first, Adam accepted the second Eve; in the second, he rejected her. In the first, 'all night long' refers to sexual intercourse; in the second it refers to the darkness concluding the first sabbath. As Abraham attempts to reconcile the tenses of 'This is she who is going to strike against me like a bell' and 'This is she who used to beat me', he first interprets both as if in the past tense and then as if in the future.

In each of his divergent expositions, Abraham's primary goal is to demonstrate the possibility of drawing harmonious meaning from an ambiguous text. He has found two possible ways of doing so. Following the contrasting approaches in the *midrash* itself, he first interprets that Adam accepted the new Eve, supporting this exposition by emending and defining elements of the text. He then expounds the opposite understanding in a similar way, aligning the details of the text to reveal another internally consistent interpretation. The discrepancies between these two expositions are not relevant to Abraham. Rather, they constitute independent demonstrations that the words of the sages are replete with harmonious and consistent interpretations.

Abraham does not state explicitly why he chose to apply this discursive and harmonizing mode of exposition to *Genesis Rabbah*, nor does he suggest how his interpretations should be used. However, in the preface to *Or hasekhel* he details his motivation for writing his commentary and suggests his intended audience. Here Abraham contrasts his desire to compose *Or hasekhel* to his study of halakhah among the scholars of Safed. His education under Joseph Karo and his work as a communal rabbi active in Safed, Damascus, and Aleppo (where he served as *rosh beit din*) is

---

[83] Cf. *Yalkut shimoni* (Salonica, 1521), fo. 9b.

[84] On this midrash, see Peter Schäfer, *The Jewish Jesus: How Judaism and Christianity Shaped Each Other* (Princeton, NJ, 2012), 201.

recorded in a number of responsa.[85] Abraham describes his halakhic studies, saying, 'The Lord has given me a pathway between the wells [of salvation], sons that excel in halakhah, with whom we took sweet counsel together in the deep matters of halakhah.'[86] He then reveals that he undertook a distinct area of investigation:

Now when I saw my brothers and companions . . . I said to myself, 'Come now, I will test you with pleasure,'[87] to feed in the gardens and to gather lilies.[88] Let us go forth into the field[89] to gather the lights of the sayings of the rabbis, pure sayings.[90] . . . So [I] applied my heart[91] to expound and to investigate the sayings of the fathers of wisdom, the sages of blessed memory.[92]

In order to understand Abraham's words, we must turn to the work of a contemporary scholar of Safed, Moses Alsheikh (1508–93). In the preface to his commentary on the Pentateuch, *Torat mosheh*, Alsheikh describes his weekly schedule of study as dominated almost entirely by halakhic investigation, including speculative study through the methods of *iyun*,[93] study of the Talmud and the *posekim* (halakhic decisors), and the composition of responsa. Alsheikh complains that he was forced to limit his study of 'midrashic and plain explanations' of scripture to Fridays by way of last-minute preparation for his sabbath sermon.[94]

For Abraham ben Asher and Moses Alsheikh, it seems that the exposition of Midrash was a felicitous side-track in a curriculum otherwise devoted to halakhic enquiry. Eloquently advocating the value of studying the exposition of the sages,

---

[85] See Meir Benayahu, *Yosef beḥiri: maran rabi yosef karo* (Heb.) (Jerusalem, 1991), 312–13; see also Abraham b. Asher, *Or hasekhel*, fo. 1*b*.

[86] Zech. 3: 7; Ps. 55: 15. Abraham b. Asher, *Or hasekhel*, fo. 1*b*.   [87] Eccles. 2: 1.

[88] S. of S. 6: 2.   [89] Ibid. 7: 12.   [90] Ps. 12: 7.

[91] Cf. Eccles. 1: 17.   [92] Abraham b. Asher, *Or hasekhel*, fo. 1*b*.

[93] On the nature of *iyun*, see Daniel Boyarin, 'Moslem, Christian, and Jewish Cultural Interaction in Sefardic Talmudic Interpretation', *Review of Rabbinic Judaism*, 5 (2002), 1–33; Aviram Ravitsky, 'Talmudic Methodology and Aristotelian Logic: David ibn Bilia's Commentary on the Thirteen Hermeneutic Principles', *Jewish Quarterly Review*, 99 (2009), 184–99; id., 'Talmudic Methodology and Scholastic Logic: The Commentary of R. Abraham Elijah Cohen on the Thirteen Principles' (Heb.), *Da'at*, 63 (2008), 87–102; id., *Aristotelian Logic and Talmudic Methodology: The Application of Aristotelian Logic to the Interpretation of the Thirteen Hermeneutic Principles* [Logikah aristotelit umetodologiyah talmudit: yisumah shel halogikah ha'aristotelit baperushim lamidot shehatorah nidreshet bahen] (Jerusalem, 2009); Shlomo Toledano, 'The Talmudic Methodology of Rabbi Betsalel Ashkenazi' (Heb.), *Tarbiz*, 78 (2009), 479–520; Haim Dimitrovsky, 'An Unknown Chapter in the Relations between the Nagid Isaac Sholal and Rabbi Jacob Berab' (Heb.), *Shalem*, 6 (1992) 83–163; Haim Bentov, 'Methods of Study of Talmud in the Yeshivot of Salonica and Turkey after the Expulsion from Spain' (Heb.), *Sefunot*, 13 (1971–8), 5–102.

[94] 'From my childhood the extensive study of the Talmud in the yeshiva nurtured me like a father [Job 31: 18], thrusting and parrying in the disputes of Abbaye and Rava as far as "Hoba" [Gen. 14: 15], speculative analysis [*iyun*] by night and [talmudic] halakhah by day, with the voice of the archers [Judg. 5: 11], arrows of victory [2 Kgs. 13: 17], understand[ing] the tradition every morning [Isa. 28: 19], thereafter [turning] to the *posekim* until sunset, replying according to the halakhah to those who ask what is relevant [Mishnah *Avot* 5: 7]. I only appointed a fixed time for [the exposition of] midrashic and plain explanations when the Lord sent me good fortune [Gen. 27: 20] and lightened me with time to find rest [Ps. 32: 6] from halakhah on the sixth day. For every sabbath the people would come to me to expound to

and commending the implicit worth of rabbinic Midrash, Abraham desired to 'test' his fellow scholars with the delights of the Midrash. To this end, he undertook to provide a new edition of *Midrash Rabbah* in which the text was surrounded by commentary. He thereby sought to promote and facilitate the detailed study of the Midrash and to uphold *Midrash Rabbah* as a weighty and authoritative work requiring thorough investigation with the guidance of learned commentators.

While Abraham related his commentary on *Midrash Rabbah* to the halakhic investigation that dominated his studies, Samuel Yafeh described his motivation for composing *Yefeh to'ar* by focusing on his distinctive homiletic mode of interpretation. In the first volume, he contrasted his own exposition of *Midrash Rabbah* to what he perceived as two extreme tendencies in the work of his contemporaries:

> When I came to the threshold of the gates of *Midrash Rabbah* on the Torah, the father of all collections of aggadic Midrash, I found the door locked, as I found no interpretation except for the briefest pamphlet of difficult words derived from the *Arukh*. And even though some writers adduced some section of this *midrash* in their homilies, such as Abraham Bibago and Isaac Arama, not even one out of sixty aggadot was cited. As for those which were mentioned, they were not careful to explain the true meaning of the text, but rather explained its general sense according to the lesson they wanted to get across, even if it were for rhetorical use.[95]

On the one hand, Samuel Yafeh objects to the mode of exposition he finds in a commentary that goes no further than to provide definitions of difficult words.[96] On the other hand, he invokes the celebrated Spanish expositors and philosophers Abraham Bibago and Isaac Arama as epitomizing a selective use of Midrash and aggadah, unfaithfulness to its 'true meaning', and biased interpretation according to their own agenda. Scholars who followed in the footsteps of Arama and Bibago, Joseph Hacker suggests, included Solomon Leveit Halevi, Abraham Shalom, Meir Arama, and Joseph Taitazak.[97] In the published sermons and homiletic commentaries of these and other scholars, philosophical ideas are intertwined with biblical exposition and rabbinic aggadah, even becoming a 'vehicle' for philosophical expression.[98] Samuel Yafeh's commentary offers an alternative mode of homiletic exegesis. No longer is the elucidation of rabbinic Midrash limited to the citation of 'one out of sixty'

them according to the Torah, the Holy Scriptures, which they would read, each *parashah* at the appointed time.' (Moses Alsheikh, *Torat mosheh* (Venice, 1601), fo. 1*b*).

[95] From Samuel Yafeh, *Yefeh to'ar*, fo. 1*b*; final section as translated in Hacker, 'The Intellectual Activity of the Jews', 115.

[96] If Samuel Yafeh is referring to a printed book, this is most likely to be a derogatory reference to *Ot emet*.   [97] Hacker, 'The Intellectual Activity of the Jews', 116.

[98] 'The most favored mode of Jewish self-expression for postexpulsion philosophically trained scholars, and the major vehicle for the dissemination of postexpulsion philosophy, was not the digest or the commentary but traditional Jewish hermeneutics, the genre of scriptural exegesis and homily, both oral and written. Philosophers wrote many biblical commentaries and homilies and creatively interwove philosophy with rabbinic aggadah and Kabbalah. The shift from exposition of philosophic texts, more prevalent before the expulsion, to philosophic exegesis of sacred texts, more prevalent after the expulsion,

passages explained 'according to the lesson the expositor wanted to get across' in a philosophical exposition of Scripture. Instead, the rabbinic interpretation of the Bible takes centre stage, with the commentator's attention directed towards expounding its full meaning without relying on philosophical ideas.

Or hasekhel of Abraham ben Asher and *Yefeh to'ar* of Samuel Yafeh represent the most extreme transformations of the content and appearance of books of *Midrash Rabbah* in the sixteenth century. According to these scholars, their endeavours were stimulated by the curriculum of study in Safed and by a desire to focus homiletic exposition not on the interweaving of scripture with aggadah and philosophical discussion, but on the biblical interpretation of the rabbis of the Midrash. In publishing their commentaries as part of new editions of the text of *Midrash Rabbah* itself, their concerns intersected with a wider desire to add to books of *Midrash Rabbah* every resource needed by the reader to understand the *midrashim* correctly. Abraham ben Asher and Samuel Yafeh joined their contemporary commentators Meir Benveniste, Judah Gedaliah, and Issachar Berman in striving to facilitate the study of Midrash by enhancing the content and appearance of new books of *Midrash Rabbah*.

The innovative and creative works of these scholars were wholly dependent on the recent ingathering, consolidation, and printing of *Midrash Rabbah* as a single tenfold anthology of *midrashim*. Thus each of the commentators intended to compose a commentary on all ten of the *midrashim* newly gathered together in these editions, and their commentaries are intended for use alongside specific printed editions of *Midrash Rabbah*.[99] Nevertheless, the enterprise of these scholars was also founded on a certain dissatisfaction with the shape and content of these very books. Thus, Meir Benveniste and Judah Gedaliah provided their readers with the means to correct and annotate their own copies of the Venice 1545 edition. Issachar Berman's *Matenot kehunah* transformed the text and appearance of successive editions of *Midrash Rabbah*, as printers emended their texts in conformity with his corrections and printed his commentary alongside the midrashic text. Abraham ben Asher and Samuel Yafeh added extensive homiletic expositions to *Midrash Rabbah* to elucidate the correct understanding of the Midrash and to promote the comprehensive study of the sages' expositions of Scripture.

The sixteenth-century production of *Midrash Rabbah*, therefore, is marked by two partly opposing trends. On the one hand, the complete flexibility of the

---

reflected this conscious theological position: revealed religion perfects natural human reason and the divinely revealed Torah contains all human reason because it is identical with the infinite wisdom of God.' Tirosh-Samuelson, 'The Ultimate End of Human Life', 233.

[99] *Ot emet* contains the comments of Meir Benveniste and Judah Gedaliah arranged for use with the Venice 1545 edition; Naphtali Hertz refers to the Venice 1545 edition; Abraham b. Asher and Samuel Yafeh's comments are printed alongside the Venetian text; Issachar Berman commented on the Venetian text and his comments are printed alongside the Kraków 1587 edition.

Constantinople printers of the *editiones principes* in compiling a text from different manuscripts and different books was short-lived. It was replaced by a disinclination to generate new texts of *midrashim* and a preference for relying on recent editions rather than starting afresh from manuscripts. In partial opposition to this trend are the voices of commentators calling for the transformation of the text and the appearance of books of *Midrash Rabbah*, which they studied so meticulously. The innovative work of these scholars in providing annotations, textual corrections, and discursive expositions ensured that the consolidated text of the *Midrash Rabbah* anthology of *midrashim* continued to be transformed through the creativity of commentators.

SEVENTEEN

MIDRASH IN MEDIEVAL AND EARLY MODERN SERMONS

MARC SAPERSTEIN

IN THE FOLLOWING STUDY I will be using the word 'Midrash' loosely to refer not just to statements in collections known as Midrash, but to the full corpus of aggadic statements from rabbinic literature, including the Talmud, hooked to a biblical verse. I will not be dealing with the evidence for preaching in the rabbinic period and in the late midrashic literature. The nature of the rabbinic sources removes us at some distance from the sermon as I understand it: an oral communication, for which written texts provide at best an imperfect record.

Despite the impressive work of scholars who have continued to mine this literature for evidence of the sermons delivered during the classical rabbinic period, I doubt that the classical rabbinic texts have preserved a single direct and complete record of a sermon actually delivered. This is in stark contrast with the texts of hundreds of sermons delivered by Christian contemporaries of the Jewish sages: Augustine, Chrysostom, and many other Church Fathers, whose sermons, stenographically transcribed during delivery, are replete with references to the specific situation and convey the personal voice of the preacher. Indeed, we have few such Jewish texts from before the latter part of the fourteenth century.[1]

My topic will therefore not be the sermon in Midrash, but Midrash in the sermon. I will be focusing on specific examples of sermons by three medieval or early modern preachers: Jacob Anatoli, from thirteenth-century southern France, Shem Tov ibn Shem Tov, from late fifteenth-century Spain, and Saul Levi Morteira, from seventeenth-century Amsterdam. Since, unlike technical treatises on philosophy or rabbinic law, the sermon is intended for the entire community of Jews, who would hear it in their vernacular language within the context of public worship, it provided an important medium for disseminating the non-legal component of rabbinic literature to those who would rarely have encountered it in formal Jewish study.

---

[1] On this new type of sermon text, intended primarily not as a model for other preachers but as a record of what was said, see Marc Saperstein, *Jewish Preaching 1200–1800* (New Haven, Conn., 1989), 18–21.

I

Jacob Anatoli was one of the earliest Jewish preachers in Christian Europe who has left a written record of sermonic texts.[2] Son-in-law of Samuel ibn Tibbon, the translator of Maimonides' *Guide of the Perplexed*, he was deeply influenced by the philosophical tradition. He translated several technical Aristotelian works from Arabic into Hebrew, claiming that a sound knowledge of logic was necessary for Jews to be able to withstand 'the clever scholars of the other nations who polemicize against us'.[3] Strongly influenced by Maimonides, he began to apply the philosophical insights of his master in sermons delivered at weddings and then at sabbath services. Before very long, however, resistance from some of the listeners compelled him to desist, and he turned to writing Hebrew texts on the weekly Torah portion that could be used as models for other preachers.[4]

Anatoli's use of rabbinic aggadot is rarely integral to the structure or substance of his sermons. Discussion of a midrashic passage is often introduced as a component that could be eliminated without seriously compromising the integrity of the text. Yet many passages are interesting as illustrations of a philosophical approach to rabbinic aggadah that is chronologically intermediate between the programmatic statements and interpretations scattered by Maimonides in his *Guide* and the more systematic commentaries beginning in the middle of the thirteenth century.[5]

Characteristic of his approach is the following general formulation from a sermon on the portion 'Ki tavo':

> We would say that one of the things every intellectual [*ḥakham lev*] should know in reviewing and delving into words of aggadah, and finding that according to their simple, surface meaning they are inconsistent with reality or in the category of the impossible, is that these words were said to inspire him and those like him, regarding a matter concealed from the masses. The person who said them intended to inspire the elite in an esoteric manner, as the Bible says, 'The secret of the Eternal is for those who fear him' [Ps. 25: 14]. (171*a*)[6]

Here he is addressing a long-standing intellectual challenge for Jews committed both to the rabbinic tradition and to philosophical truth, who found the familiar

---

[2] For the relationship of these Hebrew texts to sermons actually delivered by Anatoli, see Saperstein, *Jewish Preaching*, 15–16.   [3] For the source, see ibid. 111 n. 2.

[4] On Anatoli, see ibid. 111–23, including the annotated translation of a homily on the weekly Torah portion 'Shemot', and 'Christians and Christianity in the Sermons of Jacob Anatoli', in Marc Saperstein, *'Your Voice Like a Ram's Horn': Themes and Texts in Traditional Jewish Preaching* (Cincinnati, Ohio, 1996), 55–74.

[5] Philosophical interpretation of aggadah was the subject of my first book, Marc Saperstein, *Decoding the Rabbis: A Thirteenth-Century Commentary on the Aggadah* (Cambridge, Mass., 1980); for background, see ibid. 1–20.

[6] Page references in parentheses are to Jacob Anatoli, *Malmad hatalmidim* (Lyck, 1866). A critical edition of this text remains a desideratum.

texts of Talmud and Midrash filled with rabbinic dicta that fitted into one of the categories mentioned: either they were inconsistent with reality as every ordinary person knows it, or they were philosophically impossible.[7] The specific statement that evokes this general comment is a midrashic comment on Hosea 11: 9 pertaining to Jerusalem: 'Said the Holy One, blessed be He, "I will not enter the supernal Jerusalem until I enter the earthly Jerusalem" [BT *Ta'anit* 5a]'. The idea that there could be an actual city in the heavens constructed from wood and stones is inconsistent with the reality that is known to all, and the statement must therefore be understood metaphorically (171a).

Another example of this approach is in the sermon on 'Nitsavim', which is read shortly before Rosh Hashanah. The well-known aggadah begins: 'Three books are opened on Rosh Hashanah'. That Anatoli feels the need to make it clear that this and other references to heavenly books are all to be understood figuratively, as metaphorical expressions for the fullness of divine memory, using the image of royal chronicles that record the deeds of the loyal servant and the deeds of the rebel, indicates that this approach to rabbinic discourse was not obvious or beyond question in his time (175a).

This was a relatively trivial assertion, however. The major problem addressed was not the literal meaning of the three books, but rather the destiny decreed for three categories of human beings. What does it mean to be inscribed for life or death, based on whether one is determined to be righteous or wicked? If one interprets the statement to mean that

> whoever lives out the year following Rosh Hashanah is shown not to have been wicked during the previous year, for if he had been wicked he would have been judged to death and died, and similarly whoever dies during the year is shown to have been wicked: this is a total lie, for it is refuted by reality [*hametsiut*]. (175a)

Anatoli then proceeds to provide an interpretation of the rabbinic text based on a different understanding of 'inscribed for life'.[8] The firm insistence that human experience of reality is a test that must determine the meaning of rabbinic aggadic discourse is a fine example of a position that must have been somewhat contentious among contemporaries in his environment.

In a sermon on the portion 'Yitro', Anatoli is led from the discussion of the sabbath commandment to the theme of Creation. In this context he cites the opening of *Genesis Rabbah*, with its climactic assertion that God 'looked into the Torah and created the world'. Immediately upon concluding the quotation, he overturns the simple meaning by insisting that 'Torah' in this context does not refer to the familiar five books with a narrative of events and genealogical tables and laws:

---

[7] Cf. the discussion of reasons for repudiation of the simple meaning of aggadic statements, with examples, in Saperstein, *Decoding the Rabbis*, 35–46. Similar criteria had long been applied to Jewish biblical exegesis.

[8] For other examples of Jewish scholars troubled by the apparently simple meaning of this text, see Saperstein, 'Inscribed for Life or Death?', in id., *'Your Voice'*, 37–44.

There is no doubt that 'Torah' is etymologically linked with 'teaching' [*hora'ah*] and study, and in this context it is used as a synonym for wisdom. We call the commandments 'Torah' because of the wisdom within them, but here it is used to refer to absolute Wisdom. (63*a*)

This Wisdom is what the philosophers called the realm of the intellects, and they called the last of these the Active Intellect. We may wonder at words of the sages who used this very language: *amon* ['nursling' or 'apprentice', Prov. 8: 30] and *uman* ['craftsman']. How excellent was their explanation that follows this, stating that the Torah said 'I was the working tool [*keli umanuto*] of the Holy One, blessed be He', so that no one would think that the Active Intellect was itself a totally independent craftsman, like those other craftsmen who work for an earthly king and have the capacity to proceed on their own initiative. That is not the case here; it [the Active Intellect] is no more than a working tool, and no work is completed except through the power of that which makes it move. . . .

Similarly the rabbis said, 'The Holy One, blessed be He, looked into the Torah and created the world': this is exactly what the philosophers said, namely, that God looked into the realm of intellects and from it caused reality to emanate. (63*b*)

In Anatoli's reading, the purpose of the beginning of *Genesis Rabbah* is to repudiate the idea that the Active Intellect functioned as an independent demiurge in the creation of the material world, and his claim—something of a stretch to be sure, in that he appears to pass over the distinction between creation and emanation—is that this midrashic teaching is identical to a respectable philosophical doctrine.

Another example relating to the opening chapters of Genesis is triggered by the common philosophical interpretation of clothing as an allegorical representation of the moral qualities, as in Zechariah 3: 4. This deeper meaning of clothing, he continues,

comes at the beginning of Creation, in a true story: God made them garments of skin [*kotnot or*, written with *ayin*: עוֹר] and clothed them [Gen. 3: 21]. It may be that this is in the way we have mentioned: the good qualities for the soul, especially wisdom, are like leather to the body, which is why the allegory of leather is used. Now it is known that in our language, *kotnot* is used for clothing of honour, and garments of leather are white and smooth. And in the Torah of Rabbi Meir they found it was written, 'garments of light' [*or* written with *alef*: אוֹר: *Gen. Rabbah* 20: 21]. This appears to mean that Rabbi Meir would correct the allegories to make them express their deeper meaning. (133*b*)[9]

After providing several other examples of Rabbi Meir's apparent emendations, Anatoli continues:

At the beginning of Creation, the man and his wife were naked, and they felt no shame walking in front of the creatures, for this is the pattern of human behaviour: people

---

[9] For other philosophical-allegorical interpretations of this verse citing the apparently divergent textual tradition in the Torah of R. Meir, dating from a generation or two after Anatoli, see Bahya b. Asher on Gen. 3: 21, and Levi b. Abraham, cited in *Ma'aseh nisim: perush latorah lerabi nisim ben rabi mosheh mimarseilles*, ed. Howard Kreisel (Jerusalem, 1960), 268 n. 384.

sin at first without feeling shame. Afterwards they felt ashamed, and hid ... and they covered only their nakedness with belts made of fig leaves [*aleh te'enah*, Gen. 3: 7]. This means that they sought pretexts and excuses [*to'anot ve'ilot*] for following their desire. And that is what the sages said: 'fig leaf: a leaf because he brought an excuse into the world' [*Gen. Rabbah* 19: 6].

At this point Anatoli raises a fundamental issue of philosophical interpretation: does the allegorical meaning supplement or substitute for the simple meaning of the words?[10] In this case, did they actually cover themselves with fig leaves or not? Here both possibilities are said to be legitimate readings:

Now it may be that this statement of theirs refers to an actual leaf, as in the word that the Torah uses for it [*aleh*]. For the leaf covers the fruit; because it is not intended for itself but to protect the fruit, it is called *aleh*.[11] Therefore whatever is intended to cover up something may be allegorically represented by a leaf. Or it is possible that it refers [only] to an *ilah*, meaning a reason, just as the fig [*te'enah*] refers to the excuse [*to'anah*]. Similarly with the allusion in the word *ḥagurot*, belts or loincloths, as in the verse, 'She makes cloth and sells it, and offers a loincloth [*ḥagur*] to the Canaanite' [Prov. 31: 24]. We have already explained that 'Canaanite' alludes to the evil impulse. And in *Genesis Rabbah* the cloth is mentioned as alluding to loincloths, and there also the evil impulse is mentioned. (134*a*)

This passage could almost be a commentary on the Midrash, an intricate weaving of allegorical interpretations of the Bible and rabbinic aggadah in a manner that seems rather far removed from the portion 'Beha'alotekha', on which the sermon is supposed to be based.

I would like to analyse in more detail the discussion of an aggadic *midrash* in Anatoli's sermon for the intermediate sabbath between Rosh Hashanah and Yom Kippur (Sabbath of Repentance, Shabat Shuvah), traditionally one of the most important preaching occasions in the Jewish calendar. Following the tradition of the midrashic *petiḥta*, the verse cited at the beginning of the sermon is usually from the Writings, especially Proverbs, but in this case it is Isaiah 55: 6, 'Seek the Eternal when/where He is to be found, call upon Him when He is nearby.' Immediately we are led to the rabbinic unpacking of the verse: 'when He is near' means that there is a special time in the year that is uniquely propitious for prayers that beseech mercy (BT *RH* 18*a*). And immediately there is a problem. The verse cited by the Talmud in this context, Deuteronomy 4: 7 ('For what great nation is there that has a god so close at hand as is the Eternal our God whenever we call upon

---

[10] On this often critically important distinction, see Isaac Heinemann's discussion of *Umdeutung* and *Mehrdeutung* in his classic study, 'Die Wissenschaftliche Allegoristik des Judischen Mittelalters', *Hebrew Union College Annual*, 23 (1950/1), 611–43, and my comment on this article in Saperstein, *Decoding the Rabbis*, 229 n. 94.

[11] Here he seems to be suggesting that the Hebrew word for leaf, *aleh*, is derived from the word *al*, meaning 'on', and thus suggests covering or protecting something.

Him?'—especially the beginning of the verse, which is *not* cited in the talmudic text),[12] indicates that the people of Israel is unique in having God close and accessible to them *whenever* they call out to Him, implying that there is no time that is especially favourable.

Thus at the very beginning of the sermon, the preacher raises an apparent conflict between one biblical verse and a different verse, as used in a rabbinic statement, that appears to assert that God is not always directly accessible to the sincere worshipper. Anatoli's response is that the rabbinic statement was made homiletically (*bederekh derash*) in order to support and strengthen the tradition. The rabbis apparently say that God's nearness at special times precedes our calling and provides the occasion for it; their true meaning, however, is the opposite: genuine calling out to God is the reason for the divine nearness, as shown in Psalm 145: 18. But this does not imply that God actually moves closer or becomes more distant, for place does not pertain to God; 'near' is human language to express God's hearing and responding to the one who calls him (181*a*). Nor is 'calling' to God to be taken literally, 'for the true calling does not apply to the mouth but rather to the understanding of the heart'—true belief and proper behaviour.

In this context, Anatoli invokes the *haftarah* of the day, 'Return, O Israel, to the Eternal' (Hosea 14: 2), which is appropriate at any time during the year; the singling out of a time especially designated for repentance is a concession to human weakness and the tendency towards procrastination and denial. This biblical and rabbinic designation of a special period is chosen in connection with a 'widely accepted traditional view' (*da'at mekubal umefursam*) that Rosh Hashanah is associated with the repentance of Adam and the binding of Isaac (181*b*).

Even in this introductory portion of his sermon, Anatoli demonstrates an engagement with midrashic material naturally linked with biblical verses, including a willingness to distance himself from what seems to be the obvious meaning of a rabbinic assertion that there are times when God is more accessible than others. I will skip over part of what follows to focus on an aggadic statement relating to Yom Kippur, to which the preacher devotes a considerable amount of attention.

The passage is introduced with an assertion about two kinds of atonement required on Yom Kippur. The first, like the other kinds of atonement specified in the Torah, pertains to action and behaviour, while 'The second type pertains to transgressions of thought, the basis of everything else: if such transgressions are present, all is present, while if they have been annulled, all evil is annulled.' At this point, the preacher cites a passage from *Pirkei derabi eli'ezer* 46: 1 (identified only as a statement of 'our rabbis'), which has no obvious connection with the primacy of intellectual transgressions:

---

[12] Anatoli remarks as an *obiter dictum* that 'it is characteristic of the sages to abbreviate in some places by citing part [of a verse] and omitting part, even when their point is based on the part of the verse not cited' (181*a*).

Samael[13] said before the Holy One, blessed be He: 'Sovereign of all the universe! You have given me authority [*reshut*] over all the nations of the world, but over Israel You have not given me authority.' God responded, 'Behold, you have authority over them on the Day of Atonement if they have sinned, but if not, you have no authority over them.' Therefore they give him a bribe [*shoḥad*] on the Day of Atonement so that he will not annul their sacrifice, as it is said, 'One lot for the Lord, and one lot for Azazel' [Lev. 16: 8]. (182*b*)

Having cited the rabbinic passage, Anatoli continues with a statement that must have captured the attention of any alert listener or reader: 'Now this statement is one of the strangest in rabbinic literature. According to its apparently simple meaning it justifies mocking whoever said it.' That kind of seemingly radical assertion may explain the opposition that eventually led Anatoli to discontinue his preaching.[14] But characteristically, he immediately continues in a manner that distances himself from such a strong repudiation of rabbinic wisdom: 'with true understanding, it [the passage from *Pirkei derabi eli'ezer*] inspires eternal joy, for it reveals to us one of the mysteries of the Torah: the purpose of the great and awesome day' (182*b*).

This reassurance to his listeners does not last for long. Continuing this introduction to his discussion, Anatoli again expresses himself in a manner that is overtly controversial, polemical, and potentially offensive in its dismissive ridicule for beliefs that may well have been held by some in the congregation (if the text was actually delivered on the Sabbath of Repentance), or by some of his readers:

Few understand this true meaning; most people invert the intention according to their limited understanding, thereby making darkness light and light darkness. In this manner the words of the sages become the basis for evil beliefs; in this manner the belief in the existence of demons—Samael and his cohort—has spread.

Here we have moved from a misunderstanding of a statement in a rabbinic *midrash*, to 'evil beliefs' in general purportedly based on the sages, to the widespread specific belief in the existence of demons. In the middle of this attack against the views of unspecified Jews, Anatoli turns to the Christian environment and—in a passage that has been erased in the British Library manuscript of the *Malmad* (Add. MS 26,898, fo. 148*b*)—he invokes a central doctrine of Christian theology:

Indeed, some of the nations hold the belief in this foolishness, asserting that the highest cohort of angels, superior to all others, fell from heaven because of their pride and were transformed into a cohort of demons, which entice human beings and cause all evil, and they are the ones who rule over hell [*gehinom*] until their redeemer comes. This is the

---

[13] A malevolent figure in the panoply of Jewish angelology, sometimes identified with Satan, sometimes thought to be distinct: see Rachel Adelman, *The Return of the Repressed: Pirqe de-Rabbi Eliezer and the Pseudepigrapha* (Leiden, 2009), 124–8 and *passim*, along with the articles cited in n. 15 and the source cited in n. 16 below.

[14] On this confrontation, see Marc Saperstein, 'Attempts to Control the Pulpit: Medieval Judaism and Beyond', in Katherine L. Jansen and Miri Rubin (eds.), *Charisma and Religious Authority: Jewish, Christian, and Muslim Preaching, 1200–1500* (Turnhout, 2010), 93–4.

foundation of their faith, and on this basis they interpreted the biblical passage about Sennacherib, claiming that Samael is called there *heilel ben shaḥar* [cf. Isa. 14: 12]. This matter is so irrational that no one should even think about it, let alone write about it, except that this delusion has spread among the nations to the point that many of our own people believe in demons. (183*b*)

After this polemical presentation of a widespread belief about Samael among Jews and Christians, relevant to the occasion of the sermon because of a rabbinic aggadah, and expressed in both the popular belief in the existence of demons and the Christian theological doctrine concerning the fall of Lucifer and his current role as ruler of hell, Anatoli feels the need to protect the sages: 'I have no doubt that this view is the result of a misunderstanding of early rabbinic statements' (182*b*). But then he proceeds to explain—perhaps somewhat surprisingly—which rabbinic statements could have served to engender the 'evil beliefs'.

Again he turns to the homiletical Midrash, this time in a discussion of the Eden story:

Thus the claim of the nations that the supreme cohort of angels fell from heaven to earth and became the group of demons results from the popular understanding of a rabbinic statement in *Pirkei derabi eli'ezer*, where it states that [God] cast Samael and his cohort [*kat*] from a holy place in heaven [PdRE 14], and it also says, 'The ministering angels said, "If we do not take counsel against this first man [*adam harishon*] [so that he sins], we will not be able to prevail against him." Samael was the great prince in heaven . . . What did he do? He took his cohort and descended and saw all the creatures that the Holy One, blessed be He, had created, and found none so adept at evil as the serpent, which had an appearance like that of a camel, so he mounted and rode upon it. The Torah cried out, saying, "O Samael, etc. [now that the world has been created, is it time to rebel against the Omnipresent?"]' [PdRE 13].

There does indeed seem to be a plausibility in the argument that a rabbinic statement about Samael descending to earth with a group of fellow angels in order to induce the first man to sin might have served as the source of the Christian doctrine of Lucifer as fallen angel—although Anatoli pays little attention to the chronology of the relevant texts.[15]

At this point, having planted some rather stimulating thoughts about what he has characterized as a misunderstanding of the Midrash, the preacher must return

---

[15] On Satan as responsible for inducing the sin and fall of the first man and woman, see most recently Henry Ansgar Kelly, *Satan: A Biography* (Cambridge, 2006), 176–9; he identifies the first Christian writer to make this connection as Justin Martyr in the 2nd cent. CE, which long predates *Pirkei derabi eli'ezer*, or any other Jewish source attributing this role to Samael. Cf. Günter Stemberger, 'Samael und Uzza: zur Rolle der Dämonen im späten Midrasch', in A. Lange et al. (eds.), *Die Dämonen* (Tübingen, 2003), 637–41; Sylvie-Anne Goldberg, 'Satan et Samaël: le double visage de la mort juive', in Marie-France Baron (ed.), *La Mort et ses représentations dans judaïsme* (Paris, 2000), 114–15. For possible Christian sources of the *Pirkei derabi eli'ezer* passage, see Helen Spurling and Emmanouela Grypeou, 'Pirkei de-Rabbi Eliezer and Eastern Christian Exegesis', *Collectanea Christiana Orientalia*, 4 (2007), 220–4.

to the text and present his own understanding of what the rabbis really meant. He begins this task with a generalization concerning rabbinic discourse on this matter: 'Now it is known that in rabbinic literature, Samael is a name for Satan.' This association becomes the basis for a transition from a metaphysical to a psychological interpretation of the rabbinic statements, based on Maimonides' *Guide of the Perplexed*: Maimonides, citing one of the statements in *Pirkei derabi eli'ezer*, showed the way in which a Jew committed to philosophical analysis should understand the intentions of the sages. Thus Anatoli informs his listeners/readers that Maimonides himself 'taught us all that Samael is a name for Satan' (*Guide* ii. 30).[16] Maimonides also stated that '"Satan" is the inclination to evil' (*Guide* iii. 22, citing Resh Lakish in BT *BB* 16a), an assertion that potentially demythologizes the meaning of 'Satan'.[17]

From these two statements, Anatoli draws a conclusion as if from a syllogism: thus 'the inclination to evil and its powers are referred to by the rabbis as Samael and his cohort. For all these powers [contained in the human propensity for evil] come under the governance of heaven.' To believe that God created a group (of demon-angels) to rule over man and cause him to sin and bring about evil and destruction is 'total heresy'. It is 'just like the position of the dualists, who say that there are two gods, one good, one evil' (183a, cf. 173b). This of course alludes not only to a heresy that, according to Anatoli, has plagued Jews from antiquity, but undoubtedly also to the Catharist dualistic heresy that had by no means been extinguished in southern France, despite the Albigensian Crusade and the establishment of the Papal Inquisition in Anatoli's own lifetime.

Having shifted the grounds from metaphysics to psychology, Anatoli returns to the original *midrash* about Samael's authority on Yom Kippur that triggered the entire discussion. The assertion in the *midrash* that Samael is given authority over Israel on Yom Kippur if there is sin among them is explained to mean that 'this day is appointed for them to sanctify themselves, afflict themselves, make confession, and proclaim the ineffable Divine Name in their confession. If there is among them a sin in their faith, then Samael—the inclination to evil—has authority over them.' Everything depends on thought; repentance from bad acts must include abandoning bad beliefs (*de'ot*) caused by ignorance of God's ways and God's knowledge, because Israel think of their ways as similar to God's and their knowledge to God's. This is the cause of bad things and the essence of evil (184b).

This is clearly a text in which a midrashic passage plays a significant role, inspiring some of the strongest language in the text and taking up perhaps a quarter of the sermon. Nevertheless, while the discussion certainly enriches the discourse and takes up a significant proportion of it, it is not an integral component of the sermon's

---

[16] Trans. Michael Friedländer (New York, 1946), pt. 2, 154–5; previously Anatoli had written simply 'it is known', but here he provides a source.

[17] Friedländer, pt. 3, 98. For other contemporary applications of this psychological allegorization of Satan as the inclination to evil, see Saperstein, *Decoding the Rabbis*, 68–70.

structure or its major theme; it would be possible to remove the entire discussion of the Samael passages without losing the central argument of the text about God's accessibility. This would change by the latter part of the fifteenth century.

II

Shem Tov ibn Shem Tov flourished in the generation of the expulsion from Spain. Author of several technical philosophical works and commentaries on Mishnah *Avot* and Maimonides' *Guide*, his collection of sermons on the weekly and holiday portions, completed in 1489, was printed three times in the sixteenth century (Salonica, 1525; Venice, 1547; Padua, 1567), a rather extraordinary indication of their popularity.

During the period between Anatoli and Shem Tov—more specifically, in the middle of the fifteenth century—a significant change occurred in the structure of the Sephardi Jewish sermon that elevated the rabbinic text to the role of a formal component. As I have shown in some detail,[18] by the late fifteenth century, the standard practice for beginning a sermon is no longer to cite and discuss a verse from the Ketuvim, as in the classical *petiḥta* of homiletical Midrash, but rather to begin with a verse chosen from the weekly Torah portion, known as the *nose* or 'theme-verse', and to follow immediately with a statement from rabbinic literature, almost always aggadic in content, called the *ma'amar* or 'dictum'. This rabbinic text may be directly and obviously connected with the theme-verse, but it may have no apparent connection at all. At some point in the sermon, the preacher will turn to the rabbinic text cited at the beginning and establish its relevance to the subject being discussed. Each sermon therefore has to engage at least one rabbinic text in a significant manner, as it is an integral component of the sermon structure. This remained the classical structure for Sephardi preaching well into the nineteenth century.[19]

Shem Tov's sermon on the portion 'Vayeḥi' is devoted to an explication of the Jewish understanding of salvation, triggered by the use of the word *yeshuah* in his theme-verse: 'For your salvation [*lishuatekha*] I wait, O Eternal' (Gen. 49: 18).[20] This selection of a specific topic for the sermon, unusual in the thirteenth or fourteenth century, was one of the homiletical options in this generation, as can be seen in the conclusion of a brief *Treatise for the Guidance of Preachers* written in the first half of the fifteenth century:

---

[18] Saperstein, *Jewish Preaching*, 63–5.

[19] See e.g. Benjamin Artom, *Sermons* (London, 1876); he does not always begin with a verse from the Torah portion, sometimes using a verse from Psalms or the Prophets, but he always follows the opening biblical verse with a passage from rabbinic literature.

[20] A fully annotated translation of this sermon, with an introduction, can be found in Saperstein, *Jewish Preaching*, 180–98.

The types of sermons are three. The first is compound, such as a sermon the divisions of which are based on the divisions in the opening verse. The second is simple, such as one that takes a single theme, and brings many proofs from verses and aggadot and other rabbinic statements to explore the topic. The third is neither simple nor compound, but composed of questions and answers, simple interpretations of verses and [discussion of] topics.[21]

The sermon on 'Vayeḥi' is a good example of the second, thematic type, although it is divided into sections, and includes some questions and answers as well.

Following the opening—a rabbinic *ma'amar* from Babylonian Talmud *Pesaḥim* 56a about Jacob's intention on his deathbed to disclose 'the secret of the messianic advent', which is triggered by another eschatological term from Genesis 49: 1, 'the end of days' (*aḥarit hayamim*)—the preacher begins the introduction to the body of his sermon with a clear statement of its substance and structure: 'There are three modes of salvation that we anticipate; they are the foundation of our faith and the essential meaning of the Torah.' The three modes are the advent of the messiah in history, the spiritual life in the world to come, and the resurrection of the dead. All three, according to the preacher, are mentioned in the portion 'Vayeḥi'. The discussion of each concept will be based less on biblical verses than on an appropriate passage from aggadic Midrash.

First is the examination of the messianic advent, based on the *ma'amar*. Since the preacher has just cited this text to his listeners, he does not need to repeat its content, but rather begins by raising a series of conceptual problems, or *sefekot*, 'doubts', about it. This method of analysis was in wide vogue among Jews at the time, famously used in Isaac Abravanel's biblical commentaries, but also applied to biblical and rabbinic passages in commentaries and sermons by many other writers.[22] Having raised the questions, the preacher proceeds to explicate the aggadic passage, which asserts that, according to Genesis 49: 1, Jacob had intended to disclose to his children exactly when the messiah would come—but at that critical moment, the divine presence disappeared from him, and he was left in confusion.

Shem Tov uses this midrashic statement to expound an aspect of the psychology of messianic belief. All Jews believe that the messiah will come to bring physical salvation. However, 'If the ignorant masses knew that the messiah would not come during their lifetime, few of them would remain Jews; they would instead become assimilated among the non-Jews.' Since the actual advent would be centuries, even millennia after Jacob's death, he was prevented by God from disclosing this truth. The implication is that it is only the hope that the messiah will come during their own lifetime that explains the continued loyalty of ordinary Jews throughout the centuries.

[21] See Saperstein, *'Your Voice'*, 174 (Hebrew text on p. 178).

[22] For examples from this generation and background in late medieval Jewish literature, see Saperstein, 'The Method of Doubts: Problematizing the Bible in Late Medieval Jewish Exegesis', in Jane Dammen McAuliffe, Barry D. Walfish, and Joseph W. Goering (eds.), *With Reverence for the Word: Medieval Scriptural Exegesis in Judaism, Christianity, and Islam* (Oxford, 2003), 133–56.

The preacher proceeds to provide two different interpretations, one according to the manifest public meaning, the other a secret hidden meaning for the continuation of the *ma'amar* about Jacob's statement, 'Blessed is the name of His sovereign glory forever and ever' and its proper use in public prayer. He then turns away from the *ma'amar* for a discussion of the 'conditions of the messiah', based largely on Isaiah 11 (a section that was eliminated from the printed editions but preserved in manuscript).[23] But the critical point about the nature of this messianic mode of salvation is our uncertainty about when it will occur, and the reason for this uncertainty is clarified through the preacher's explication of the aggadic *ma'amar*.

The second mode of salvation is purely spiritual: the life of the world to come. In this context, the preacher introduces a second midrashic statement:

When Rabbi Abbahu was dying, the Holy One, blessed be He, showed him thirteen streams of balsam. Amazed, he said, 'All these for Abbahu?' He applied to himself the verse, 'Yet I had thought, I have laboured for nothing' [Isa. 49: 4].[24]

Once again, the preacher begins immediately with a 'great problem' raised by the statement: how could Abbahu have had doubts about his reward in the world to come? In addition, why rivers, why thirteen, and why balsam? The sermon continues with an explication of the passage, including three different explanations of the reason for Abbahu's citation of Isaiah 49: 4, before turning to an exegesis of Psalm 16 in connection with the reward of the world to come, the essence of which we cannot know, because it is entirely remote from human experience.

The third mode of salvation, combining the physical and the spiritual elements, is resurrection of the dead. Here the preacher introduces a third midrashic passage, directly relevant to the Torah portion:

Why were the patriarchs so demanding of burial in the Land [of Israel]? Rabbi Eleazar said, 'There is a hidden reason for this.' What did he mean by 'There is a hidden reason for this'? Said Rabbi Joshua ben Levi, 'I shall walk before the Lord in the lands of the living' [Ps. 116: 9].

As in the other two cases, this discussion addresses the midrashic statement by exposing its apparent problems. Especially challenging is the question, 'Why does it make any difference where a body is buried, since it eventually disintegrates and is absorbed by the earth?' The answer is a reference to the well-known chronological dimensions of the resurrection: the dead in the Land of Israel will be raised to life first; those buried outside the Land of Israel will roll through underground

---

[23] Abravanel also discusses the attributes of the messiah in his commentary on Isaiah 11, but I see no sign of direct dependence between the two texts. For the theme of *conditiones messie* in Christian literature, see Beryl Smalley, 'John Baconthorpe's Postill on St Matthew', in ead., *Studies in Medieval Thought and Learning from Abelard to Wyclif* (London, 1981), 294–314: twenty-seven conditions prove that Jesus fulfilled Old Testament prophecy. The full text is in Cambridge University MS Dd.10.466, fos. 53^v–54^r.

[24] *Gen. Rabbah* 62: 3; *Tanḥuma*, 'Vayeḥi' 4; BT *AZ* 42a.

caverns until they reach the Land, to be resurrected there.²⁵ That explains the yearning of the righteous to be buried in the Land.

But what about the continuation of the passage, which he then proceeds to cite? Two sages saw the coffin of a Jew who had lived and died in the diaspora being brought to be buried within the Land; they react to this incident in radically different ways:

Rabbi [Judah] said to Rabbi Eliezer, 'What has this man availed by coming to be buried in the Land when he expired outside the Land? I apply to him the verse, "You made My heritage an abomination"—during your lifetime you did not immigrate here—and in your death, "you defile My land"' [Jer. 2: 7].

It seems clear from this statement by Rabbi Judah that being buried in the Land of Israel brings no benefit to the person who lived and died outside it, and is even considered a sin by defiling the Land. Here the preacher indulges in something of a tirade, which may have had resonance for his listeners, attacking death-bed conversions by those whose lives were devoted to the vanities of the world. With their last breaths, they command their children to give money to charity, and to bury them in a proper tallit with tefillin—'as if the commandments could be performed by the dead!'²⁶ These are the people to whom Rabbi Judah refers in his scathing remark.²⁷

However, those worthy through their lives of observing the Torah properly and going to the Land of Israel are worthy of being buried there, so that they will receive the reward of resurrection without the anguish of rolling under the earth. The sermon concludes with a brief discussion of the belief in resurrection: it is beyond our capacity to understand, yet not beyond God's capacity to perform. Unlike the spiritual reward in the world to come, it is not something that comes naturally to the perfected soul, but a divine miracle, bestowed only upon the righteous and limited to the Jewish people. Its purpose is to allow those resurrected to perform great deeds they could not accomplish in their first existence, and thereby merit greater reward, whether for the reunited body and soul, or for the soul itself in the world to come.

---

²⁵ This rather bizarre doctrine is presented in BT *Ket.* 111*a* as a compromise between the extreme anti-diaspora statement of R. Eleazar—'The dead [buried] outside the land [of Israel] will not be resurrected'—and the unwillingness to deprive those who had been born, lived, and died outside the land of inclusion in the resurrection. The solution is that those buried in the Land of Israel will be resurrected first, while those buried outside the land will roll through subterranean tunnels to arrive in the land where they too will eventually be resurrected: a process that might serve as an inducement for diaspora Jews to come and live, or at least be buried, in the Land of Israel.

²⁶ For the halakhic issues regarding burial in tallit and tefillin, see Saperstein, *Jewish Preaching*, 195–6 nn. 41, 46.

²⁷ For other medieval expressions of opposition to the practice of bringing bodies for burial in the Land of Israel based on this rabbinic passage, see Marc Saperstein, 'Selected Passages from Yedaiah Bedersi's Commentary on the Midrashim', in Isadore Twersky (ed.), *Studies in Medieval Jewish History and Literature*, 3 vols. (Cambridge, Mass., 1979–2000) ii. 428–9, esp. n. 13.

This is a fine example of the sermon as an instrument of education, what we might call life-long Jewish learning, for the listeners. The preacher chooses a central doctrine for his message—Jewish eschatology. It is suggested not so much by the biblical narrative at the end of Genesis, which has no explicitly eschatological content, but rather by a passage of rabbinic aggadah rooted in the weekly portion. The sermon is clearly structured in three main sections, each discussing a separate rabbinic passage, relevant to the three components of Jewish eschatological doctrine: the messianic age, the world to come, and resurrection.[28] Especially noteworthy in the use of the aggadic statements is that each one is introduced with several problems or doubts, which the preacher articulates, discusses, and appears to resolve.

The deeper problems of Jewish eschatology, pertaining to the interrelationship among these three components, are not discussed. Does resurrection come at the beginning or the end of the messianic era? Does the eternal reward in the world to come begin immediately after death? If so, why should a soul in the presence of God be brought back to earth for resurrection? Can Jews attain their eternal reward in pre-messianic times? If so, what is the value of the messiah for them? Such questions are not raised in the sermon, as they might have been too unsettling for a general audience in the midst of a worship service. But the presentation of ideas and their integration with traditional sources suggest that listeners might well have come away with a fuller understanding of the teachings of their tradition.

III

My third example is a sermon by Saul Levi Morteira, who preached throughout the year on sabbath mornings to the Portuguese community of Amsterdam, from 1619 until shortly before his death in 1660. His sermons, like those of Shem Tov, are structured in the classical Sephardi style, beginning with a verse from the weekly portion (*nose*), followed by a rabbinic dictum, usually aggadic (*ma'amar*), an introduction defining the conceptual problem that will be addressed (*derush*), the body of the sermon exploring various aspects of that conceptual problem, and a conclusion.[29] In most cases, the *ma'amar* is left until the end of the sermon, and indeed I have argued that the autograph manuscripts written by Morteira indicate that in some cases he

---

[28] It is possible that this reveals the existence of 'preaching aids' or commonplace books, which collected statements from classical Jewish literature and organized them according to topic arranged alphabetically, as was common among contemporary Christian preachers, but this remains unclear. For later examples of such books, see Saperstein, *Jewish Preaching*, 286 (on *Yalkut ḥadash* by Israel of Belzyce), and 302 (on *Midrash talpiyot* by Elijah Hakohen of Izmir). Bahya b. Asher's *Kad hakemaḥ* may be viewed as a rudimentary preaching aid: see Saperstein, *Jewish Preaching*, 17, with n. 28 on Christian aids.

[29] For a more detailed discussion of structure based on the 1645 volume of Morteira's sermons called *Givat sha'ul*, see Saperstein, 'Your Voice', 107–26.

did not choose the *ma'amar* until he had finished writing most of the sermon text.[30] Occasionally, however, the *ma'amar* becomes the basis for the structure of the sermon following the introduction.

For example, in an early sermon on the opening verse of 'Mishpatim' (Exod. 21: 1), Morteira cites the statement from *Exodus Rabbah* (30: 4), 'Moses devoted himself fully to three things, and they were called by his name: the people of Israel, Torah, and the laws.' The body of the sermon explores in turn each one of these areas of Moses' activities during his career, through which he attained the permanence of immortality here on earth, each one antithetical to the methods used by the pagans in antiquity in their efforts to attain permanence. Pagan rulers built statues of themselves, while Moses devoted himself to his people; pagans constructed lofty buildings bearing their names, while Moses built the foundations of Torah education; pagans named months in their honour (July, August), while Moses exemplified the ethical standards he wanted his people to emulate.[31] The aggadic statement, rather than the biblical verse, provides the tripartite framework on which the content of the sermon is developed.

A more complex example of a *midrash* providing not only the structure but the content and substance of the sermon is in the text I have published in translation called 'Dust of the Earth', on 'Vayetse'.[32] The title is drawn from the theme-verse 'Your descendants shall be as the dust of the earth' (Gen. 28: 14). The *ma'amar*, from *Genesis Rabbah* 41: 9, is directly connected with this verse, providing four explanations of the unlikely comparison between Jacob's descendants—the people of Israel—and dust:[33]

> Just as the dust of the earth is found from one end of the world to the other, so shall your children be scattered from one end of the world to the other.
> Just as the dust of the earth can be blessed only through water, so will Israel be blessed only for the sake of Torah, which is likened to water.
> Just as the dust of the earth wears out even metal utensils yet itself endures forever, so will Israel exist while the nations of the world will cease to be.
> Just as the dust is downtrodden, so will your children be downtrodden under the heel of foreign kingdoms.

Beginning the body of his sermon, Morteira gives his own rather ingenious reading of the verse in response to the obvious problem: why God conveys a message about Abraham's descendants that would appear to be a source of distress. He connects the phrase *afar ha'arets* ('dust of the earth') with the preceding verse:

---

[30] See Marc Saperstein, *Exile in Amsterdam: Saul Levi Morteira's Sermons to a Congregation of 'New Jews'* (Cincinnati, Ohio, 2003), 45, 73.

[31] This sermon was published in *Givat sha'ul* (Amsterdam, 1645); cf. Saperstein, 'Your Voice', 113, 116.

[32] See Saperstein, *Exile in Amsterdam*, 377–92.

[33] Morteira actually uses the *midrash* on Gen. 13: 16, a similar promise made earlier to Abraham, which is a fuller version of the rabbinic dictum.

'The land [ha'arets] on which you are lying I will assign to you and your offspring' (Gen. 28: 13). Just as this refers to the land of Canaan, which would become the 'Land of Israel', so in the following verse, 'Your offspring shall be as the dust of the land [of Canaan!], even when you shall spread out to the west and to the east, the north and the south.' Thus even in the period of Jewish exile, just as the dust will never depart from the Land, so it will never be without the Jewish people, for some will always remain in it to establish their claim.

The main part of the sermon, however, is not about the continued Jewish presence in the Land of Israel, but rather about Jewish experience in exile. Morteira notes that the sages, as reflected in the midrashic passage, interpreted the verse very differently from the way he did. Their message is that while God will indeed punish the Jewish people for their transgressions, one aspect of the exile and dispersion will work not for their destruction but for their benefit. This is indeed a message that fits the context of reassuring good news to Jacob.

The first midrashic statement expounding the relevance of the comparison between Jews and dust is that both are scattered throughout the world. Morteira then proceeds to identify and discuss four benefits of a world-wide diaspora as opposed to an exile (like that of Babylonia) where all Jews were in one place. First, a massive Jewish population in any one country would arouse hostility and envy among the native population; it is therefore better that Jews be scattered 'a few here and a few there, so that our large population would not be apparent'. Second, the duty of the Jewish people is to bear witness to God's greatness before all the nations on earth, rather than before only one nation, thereby achieving greater merit and atonement for their sins. Third, the Jews would be more vulnerable if concentrated in one nation in which a hostile ruler happened to arise, as in the time of Ahasuerus; scattered, they cannot annihilate us, 'for when one abandons us, another takes us in'. And fourth, in one country, the economic competition among Jews would be lethal, while scattered among many countries, all Jews can earn enough to survive.

But this is only one of the four analogies between Jews and dust proposed by the *midrash*. The next one is that dust is blessed through water, as the Jews are blessed by Torah, likened to water—meaning that when the world is deserving of destruction for its evil deeds, the presence of Jews everywhere studying Torah is a protection of the world from the threat of destruction. Furthermore, dust wears out metal yet endures; thus, when Jews are scattered throughout the world, when one nation declines and Jews need to find homes elsewhere, they will find a community in every country to facilitate their adjustment to a new home.

Finally, Jews, like the dust, are downtrodden. This is perhaps the most challenging midrashic statement of all: how can it be interpreted to communicate a message of reassurance to Jacob about his descendants in their dispersion? The answer: if Jews were in one exilic country, their massive numbers and the length of their exile might lead them 'to select a leader and rise up against the people in whose midst we lived, thereby seeking to speed up the end'. Remaining downtrodden ensures that the Jews 'will not anticipate being saved through their own initiative', but will quietistically await redemption that comes from God: 'The Eternal will battle for you; you hold your peace' (Exod. 14: 14).[34]

There are three levels to the exposition of this discourse on the advantages of dispersion in exile. The first is the biblical text, which is continuously cited as a *leitmotif*. The second is the *midrash*, which provides the structure for the body of the sermon through four statements about the similarities between the Jewish people and dust. And the third is the preacher, who unpacks the *midrash* in a manner that allows him to articulate a coherent theory of Jewish existence at the time he is preaching.

There is a noticeable difference in the treatment of aggadic Midrash as compared with the earlier preachers. Anatoli felt the need to interpret the discourse about Samael and the cohort of angels that descended from heaven in a manner that explicitly repudiated its apparent simple meaning, drawing from Maimonides an approach consistent with the philosophical view that demons simply did not exist. Shem Tov similarly identified problems, difficulties, and doubts in each of the aggadot he cited pertaining to Jewish eschatology, and resolved the problems in his discussion. In both cases, the approach to Midrash is exegetical, unpacking a meaning that is consistent with the preacher's world-view.

Morteira's approach to the midrashic interpretation of God's statement that Jacob's seed would be 'like the dust of the earth' is not essentially exegetical but rather homiletical. The passage is mined to provide support for the argument being made by the preacher about the nature of Jewish exile. This shift from exegetical to homiletical exposition of classical texts—Bible and Midrash—would become a major characteristic of modern Jewish preaching.[35]

Returning to Amsterdam: since a passage of rabbinic aggadah had become an integral component of the sermon, which in turn was an integral part of the weekly sabbath worship service, all members of the community who listened to the sermon delivered by the rabbi in their vernacular language would be exposed to at least one aggadic text, applied to the central subject of the sermon, on a regular basis, ideally

---

[34] On Morteira's characteristically quietistic approach to messianism, see Saperstein, *Exile in Amsterdam*, 373–4.

[35] See on this Marc Saperstein, *Jewish Preaching in Times of War: 1800–2001* (Oxford, 2008), 2–4. For one example of the homiletical approach, see the use by the following preachers of the *midrash* stating that the Israelites divided into four disparate groups at the sea, each with a different policy for facing the current crisis (JT *Ta'an.* 2: 5; *Mekhilta*, 'Beshalaḥ' 2): Isaac Nissenbaum, *Festivals: Selected Sermons* [Mo'adim: derashot nivḥarot] (Jerusalem, 1980), 41 (before 1906); Joseph H. Hertz, *Sermons* (London, 1938), 221 (1923); Morris Feuerlicht, in *A Set of Holiday Sermons* (Cincinnati, Ohio, 1933), 6 (1933); Harris Swift, *Because I Believe* (New York, 1954), 156 (1935); Harold I. Saperstein, *Witness from the Pulpit* (Lanham, Md., 2000), 72–3 (1939); Israel Goldstein, *Toward a Solution* (New York, 1940), 144–7 (1940). In each case the preacher applies the four responses to divisions among the Jewish people facing a contemporary crisis without devoting much thought to the original text. The shift from exegetical to homiletical use of Midrash is complete.

every week. For women, who were not part of the organized institutions of formal Jewish education, and for men, whose educational curriculum focused primarily on halakhic rather than aggadic texts, the sermon provided an opportunity to become gradually more familiar with this major component of rabbinic literature.

EIGHTEEN

RABBI JUDAH LOEW OF PRAGUE AND HIS ATTITUDE TO THE AGGADAH

JACOB ELBAUM

I

The history of the exposition of the aggadah may be seen, essentially, as the attempt to reconcile an ever-changing religious situation with a traditional and authoritative text, since the Torah, which here includes the dicta of the sages of the Talmud, had of necessity to remain a living entity. 'The injunctions of scribes are more precious than those of the Written Torah' (*S. of S. Rabbah* 1) and have equal binding force, at least in the eyes of the later rabbinic authorities.

If the verses of the Torah are to be explicated by the methods of *pardes*—*peshat* (the plain sense of the text), *remez* (conveying hidden allusions), *derash* (midrashic interpretation), and *sod* (imparting mystic teachings)—so, too, do the rabbinic dicta contain all these various connotations.[1] Nor is this all: just like the Bible itself, so rabbinic expositions eventually came to be looked upon as foundations from which philosophical and kabbalistic systems could be evolved.

Thus exposition of the aggadot (like biblical exposition) fulfilled two distinct needs which were at times complementary and at times in conflict: (1) the pressure of apologetics (not in a negative sense), emanating from the urge to relate the new and the novel to fixed and immutable traditions, and (2) the search for authoritative support, since tradition implies authority, and every innovator accordingly must attempt to derive from it support for his ideas.

At first sight, it seems most astonishing that only every rarely is the aggadah treated in the expository literature as poetic imagery ('poetical conceit', in Maimonides' formulation), to be interpreted in accordance with the canons of 'the craft of poetry'. Yet further reflections show this attitude to be quite understandable,

---

An earlier version of this chapter was published as 'Rabbi Judah Loew of Prague and his Attitude to the Aggadah', in J. Heinemann and D. Noy (eds.), *Studies in Aggadah and Folk-Literature*, Scripta Hierosolymitana 22 (Jerusalem: Magnes Press, 1971), 28–47.

[1] For the origin of the term *pardes* see Isaiah Tishby, *Mishnat hazohar*, vol. ii (Jerusalem, 1961), 376. See also Judah L. Zlotnik, *Ma'amarim misefer midrash hameliṭsah ha'ivrit* (Jerusalem, 1939), 31 n. 2.

since authoritative classics, by their very nature, are regarded with a most solemn veneration in a system based on tradition.

One of the most common and enlightening features of this literature is that even expositors who ascribed a meaning far removed from the plain sense to the aggadah honestly believed themselves to be presenting the true meaning originally intended by the author.

If what I have stated above holds true for the expositors of the aggadah in general, it is certainly applicable to interpreters employing the method of *derash*. There is no doubt that their explanations reveal more about the views of the expositor than the original intention of the text, although some manifestations do have validity in respect of the aggadah itself.

II

The literary works of Rabbi Judah Loew of Prague (1512–1609), known as Maharal of Prague, include books which, *ab initio*, are defined as 'expositions of the aggadot' (or *ḥidushei agadot*), where the author dealt with aggadot in the order of their appearance in the Talmud;[2] and also works which were devoted to specific topics. An examination of both types, however, reveals that the approach to the aggadot and the method employed are essentially identical in both classes of works, the order of the source material alone being different in each instance. In the thematic works, the sources are presented in conformity with specific topics, as the subject requires; while in the books of *ḥidushim* (novel interpretations), Rabbi Loew takes up the aggadot in order of their appearance in the Talmud.[3] Even though the aggadot he deals with (in his *ḥidushim*) vary considerably in their nature, there can be no doubt that he devotes his attention to those which, as a whole or in their individual details, lend support to his principal concepts.

In this study, we shall mainly concentrate our attention on his works *Ḥidushei agadot* and *Be'er hagolah*, the latter having as its purpose the defence of the Torah, in the sense of the *midrashim* and the halakhic and aggadic dicta of the rabbis of the Talmud.

III

According to Rabbi Loew, the sayings of the earlier authorities may be likened to Mount Sinai: 'Whoever touches [tampers with] them shall surely be stoned or shot through',[4] and whoever misreads them shall have to 'offer his soul restitution'.[5]

---

[2] A. Neubauer, *Catalogue of Hebrew Manuscripts in the Bodleian Library* (Oxford 1886–1906), nos. 917, 918 (MSS Opp. 101 and Opp. 102). The work has now appeared in two printed editions: *Sefer ḥidushei agadot maharal miprag*, 4 vols., ed. L. Honig (London, 1960), and *Sefer perushei maharal miprag . . . le'agadot hashas*, 4 vols., ed. Mosheh Shelomoh Kasher and Ya'akov Yehoshua Blecherowitz (Jerusalem, 1958–67). There are variants in the manuscripts, but these are not reflected in the printed editions.

[3] The commentary is not complete. Tractate *Berakhot* is missing, and there are only tractates *Shabat* and *Rosh hashanah* in the Order of *Mo'ed* (and this only in MS Opp. 101).

[4] According to Exod. 19: 13.   [5] *Be'er hagolah* (London, 1964), introd., 15.

The implication is that seemingly far-fetched utterances of the earlier authorities are not deficient on their own account. What seems strange in them is the result of their being imperfectly understood by the reader. The ancient sages were the repositories of true wisdom, as Rabbi Yohanan had stated long ago:

> The hearts of the ancients were like the door of the *ulam* [the hall leading to the interior of the Temple, which was twenty cubits wide]; but the hearts of the later generations were like the door of the *heikhal* [the outer sanctuary, which was ten cubits wide]; while our minds are as wide open as the eye of a fine needle. Rabbi Akiva is classed among the ancients; Rabbi Eleazar ben Shamua, among the later generations. Others say: Rabbi Eleazar ben Shamua is classed among the ancients and Rabbi Oshaiah Berebi among the later generations. [BT *Eruv*. 53*a*]

Following this line of logic, Rabbi Loew argued:

> If the flow of waters of wisdom had diminished during the period separating the generation of Rabbi Eleazar ben Shamua from that of Rabbi Yohanan, a span of only two or three generations at the most . . . what must have happened by now, when the earth as a whole has dried, and no moisture of wisdom at all is to be found? Nor has Rabbi Yohanan left anything of value or importance for us to accomplish in our generation. And this, the paucity of our intelligence, is the reason for the words of the earlier sages appearing as a closed book to us.[6]

Accordingly, the earlier sages were superior to those who came later. The generations have been continually becoming weaker. Human intelligence has become progressively more enfeebled, in inverse proportion to the increase in man's corporeality. It is due to the fact that the later generations are devoid of knowledge and intelligence that the words of the earlier generations are a closed book to them.

This assumption, that the capacity of the recipient has diminished, is perhaps inherent in every traditional approach (although the idea and its application have been variously adapted to accord with the conceptions of the exponent). Rabbi Loew, however, develops another aspect in this theory: the profundity of the ideas themselves. The words of the sages are 'secret fare' and therefore, 'appropriately expressed in order to conceal esoteric ideas'.[7]

The conclusion inevitably follows that:

> if anything in their remarks seems far-fetched by ordinary human standards, it is because deep wisdom lies hidden beneath them, their words being 'parable and figure' expressed in the manner of the wise, as the wisest of all—i.e. King Solomon—has averred [Prov. 1: 6]: 'to understand a proverb and a figure, the words of the wise and their dark sayings'. Now, if we are unable to determine what the sages had in mind, shall we therefore think ill of them? Furthermore, it is no wonder that we fail to grasp the secret implications of their remarks. Just as our times are far removed from theirs—a vast distance separating them from us—so is there a vast difference between their wisdom and ours, correspon-

---

[6] Ibid. 13.   [7] Ibid. *Be'er* 4, 49*b*.

ding to the interval in time. Everyone acknowledges the fact that wisdom belonged to the ancients rather than to the present generations. The vast difference between the earlier and later sages, in respect of wisdom, has been described by the sages of Israel in the terms mentioned above. We are therefore justified in asserting that we are incapable of understanding the hidden implications of their utterances. Had they been our contemporaries, it would be appropriate for us to appraise their words critically, but the difference between their times and ours accounts for the difference between their wisdom and ours.[8]

This basic conception leads Rabbi Loew to reject outright any adverse criticism of the sages of the Talmud, and this negative attitude in turn produces his positive effort to uncover the hidden, to reveal what lies 'beneath the proverb and figure' (something wholly other than the poetic metaphor we have referred to above).

In the light of what has been stated so far, Rabbi Loew's trenchant criticism of the views of Rabbi Azariah de' Rossi in the latter's *Me'or einayim* becomes intelligible:

How is he not afraid to speak out against the sages and to speak of them as if they were his colleagues and contemporaries? This has never happened in Israel until the present generation. And now 'remember the days of old, consider the years of many generations' [Deut. 32: 7]—each generation having its own sages [BT *San.* 38b]. Has anything like this ever taken place? When you reflect upon the *amora'im* [talmudic sages], you find that they would not disagree with their predecessors, the *tana'im* [mishnaic sages], and those who came after the *amora'im* would not differ with them, since the later generations realized that they could not bear comparison with the former who were closer [in time and spirit] to the prophets. And now, in this generation, so inferior and bereft of all wisdom, shall someone arise and raise his voice against the holy ones who preceded us by more than one thousand years, and say: 'Consider my ways and be wise?'[9]

Wisdom has its well-springs in the past. The further one is removed from those times, the further is he removed from the source of living waters. The thousand years intervening between the period of the earlier sages and the present generation are of themselves sufficient proof that the present generation is, by nature, 'inferior and bereft of all wisdom'.

Rabbi Loew had no doubt that every single rabbinic dictum contains absolute truth. No distinction is to be drawn between the halakhah and the aggadah. Nor is the rule that the *amora'im* were not to take issue with the statements of the *tana'im* any less applicable to the aggadah than to the halakhah. Furthermore, the 'high seriousness'[10] he ascribes to the sages of the Talmud leads him to accord authority to their remarks, even where these have no halakhic implications. And he applies the same rules employed in understanding the Torah to the explication of rabbinic literature. It is no accident, then, that Rabbi Loew applied to rabbinic dicta what

---

[8] *Be'er hagolah*, Be'er 4, 51.   [9] Ibid., Be'er 6, 127a.
[10] The term used by Isaac Heinemann. Cf. his *The Methods of the Aggadah* [Darkhei ha'agadah] (Jerusalem, 1954), ch. 16, 187 ff., for the entire subject.

Maimonides had laid down in connection with the use of parables and figures by the Bible itself.

In his introduction to the *Guide*, Maimonides explained the verse 'A word fitly spoken is like golden apples in vessels of silver' (Prov. 25: 11) as indicating that 'there are two aspects to prophecy, an external and an internal one—the external meaning ought to be valuable as silver and the internal meaning still more precious; the former being in comparison to the latter as gold is to silver.' He continues:

> The parables of the prophets, peace be upon them, are similar. Their external meaning contains wisdom that is useful in many respects, among which is the welfare of human societies, as is shown by the external meaning of proverbs and of similar sayings, while their internal meaning, on the other hand, contains wisdom that is useful for beliefs concerned with the truth as it is.[11]

Rabbi Loew chose the same parable, declaring that 'the words of the sages follow the words of the Torah and those of the prophets in that they possess a literal and a hidden meaning. They [the words of the Torah and the prophets] may be compared to golden apples in vessels of silver, where the inner content is comparable to gold and the outer to silver. Both are precious. So, too, *are the words of the sages which possess both a literal and a hidden meaning; and the hidden meaning is the more valuable wisdom, although the revealed is nevertheless desirable and "good to behold"*' (emphasis mine).[12]

In adopting the same analogy, Rabbi Loew also distinguishes between the relative values of gold and silver. Yet, while Maimonides emphasizes, Rabbi Loew seeks to reduce the difference between the two, as if he wished to demonstrate his displeasure with the distinction drawn by the allegorists between the value of the hidden and the revealed. This, however, is not the essential novelty in his conception (he does not, after all, deny the difference in value altogether). His innovation is the extension of Maimonides' rule to the realm of rabbinic wisdom, since these rabbinic dicta are elaborations of the words of the Torah and the prophets. Accordingly, one must distinguish between the revealed and the hidden here too; and, in his view, the critics of the sages of the Talmud had made no effort to penetrate beyond the outer meaning.

The extension of Maimonides' rule in biblical exegesis to the realm of rabbinic literature does not agree with Maimonides' own outlook as expressed in his *Guide* (iii. 43 and elsewhere). He contended there that the *midrashim* 'have the character of poetical conceits whose meaning is not obscure for someone endowed with understanding. At that time this method was generally known and used by everybody just as the poets use poetical expressions.'

According to Maimonides, then, the midrashic interpretations of the sages correspond more closely to the usages of the poets than to the Bible, and he accordingly made no effort to explain the various expressions used in rabbinic dicta. All he

---

[11] Maimonides, *Guide of the Perplexed*, trans. S. Pines (Chicago, Ill.: University of Chicago Press, 1963), introd., p. 12.   [12] *Be'er hagolah*, *Be'er* 5, 88a.

did was to attempt to grasp their essential meaning. This is by no means the way in which Maimonides approached the Bible. He was not concerned with the manner in which the sages made use of their figures. Rabbi Loew, on the other hand, refused to ascribe anything in the words of the rabbis to poetic embellishment. Such an approach was as inadmissible to him as it was in respect of the Torah itself.

At the beginning of the third section (*be'er*) of his *Be'er hagolah*, Rabbi Loew takes issue with 'those who evince astonishment at their [the rabbis'] comments, which seem far-fetched, as if they were uttered in the manner of ordinary mortals engaged in conversation and using stylistic elaboration—as if these comments were not themselves words of the Torah. But this is not so. These [hermeneutic interpretations] convey the essential meaning of the Torah.' Rabbi Loew may here be expressing his direct retort to Maimonides' observation. In expounding the verse, 'And thou shalt have a paddle among your weapons' (Deut. 23: 14), Bar Kappara remarked: 'Do not read *azenekha* [your weapons], but *oznekha* [your ear]' (BT *Ket.* 5a). Maimonides considered this 'a most witty poetical conceit'; Rabbi Loew uses precisely the same passage in his denial that the sages were using poetic metaphors and stresses that there is no mere poetic effect here, but 'a statement that is true and correct'.[13]

While Rabbi Loew's criticism against Maimonides is veiled, his anger is openly vented against Rabbi Azariah de' Rossi, who gave broad extension to Maimonides' reference to poetic figures in the words of the rabbis, and thus insinuated that they had used many figures 'wherewith to persuade the masses':

You see him [Azariah de' Rossi] saying that these were inventions, a plot whereby to entice the masses. Now these are words of mockery and the liability [for such allegations] is well known.[14]

Upon hearing the remarks uttered by this individual against the Law of Moses and the rabbis, alleging that the aggadic passages are mere devices to catch the attention of people by illegitimate means, the heart of every believer will be torn [with grief].[15]

The reference here is directly aimed at de' Rossi's argument in his *Imrei binah* (ch. 15) that

these usages [the methods of the aggadah] are termed metaphor, symbol, and allegory by the gentile sages;[16] such devices were most popular among gentile sages in ancient times.

. . . they, however, based their lessons on fables involving animals and human affairs,[17] while our sages, believing that everything is contained in the Torah, derived

---

[13] *Be'er hagolah*, *Be'er* 3, 41b.

[14] Ibid., *Be'er* 6, 134a. The words 'And the punishment is well known' refers to the talmudic statement: 'Whoever mocks the words of the sages is punished with boiling excrement' (BT *Eruv.* 21b).

[15] *Be'er hagolah*, *Be'er* 6, 134b–135a.

[16] Azariah de' Rossi, *Me'or einayim*, ed. D. Cassel (Vilna, 1866), 208. Cf. ibid. for the entire topic.

[17] The non-Jewish sages also used to 'invent fables of the sons of gods or of men or of diverse beasts' (ibid., ch. 40, 339).

their lessons from the biblical narratives, though they were fully aware that their remarks did not convey the plain sense of the words.[18]

This was the method of poetic invention. They followed the path of the poets, though the subject matter of their 'poetry' was not the same as that of the non-Jewish sages, but referred to the Torah.[19]

As has been stated, Rabbi Loew dismissed any thought that the rabbinic dicta might use poetic metaphor. He categorically denied that 'any of their utterances were in the manner of those who speak with linguistic embellishment', and maintained that hidden meanings underlay each of the rabbis' many sayings. To provide support for his contention that the methods of the rabbis followed the example of the Torah itself,[20] he adduced many examples of rabbinic dicta which gave

---

[18] Ibid. 213.

[19] On this topic too, see ibid., ch. 16. There the author deals with the account of Titus and the gnat. Azariah de' Rossi's views merit separate treatment and are not our concern here. Yet it deserves to be emphasized here that his views on the aggadah follow logically from his general attitude to the sages of the Talmud. De' Rossi held, following Maimonides and others, that the non-legal opinions of the sages are merely human and are not above dispute. Although 'the fingernails of the earlier generations are superior to the bellies of the later generations' (BT *Yoma* 9b), the later generations, by virtue of having mastered the views of the earlier sages, are comparable to dwarfs riding on giants (so in *Shibolei haleket*). See *Me'or einayim*, ch. 14, 196, and also the excerpt quoted from Maimonides. The absolute superiority of the earlier sages pertained to matters derived from prophecy, to which they were closer. By this line of demarcation, de' Rossi distinguished clearly between the area of law, halakhah, which had been handed down by tradition from Mount Sinai and through the prophets in whose presence 'every knee must bow' before any reflection or study could be engaged in (ibid., ch. 11, 154) on the one hand, and opinions expressed on other matters, which pertained to the aggadah, on the other hand. See in addition to the above-mentioned chapters ibid., ch. 28 (and also the quotation from Maimonides, *Guide of the Perplexed*, pt. 2, ch. 8; pt. 3, ch. 14; *Me'or einayim*, ch. 11, 156). The midrashic interpretations and aggadic accounts are to him the inventions of poets, and he strives to uncover what lies behind their figures, metaphors, symbols, and allegories—the lessons that these interpretations impart, which come 'either to acknowledge the goodness of God's ways, or His mighty deeds, or else to praise a virtue and condemn a vice, or else to impart knowledge and weed out folly, etc.—comments which, though correct in themselves, do not convey the meanings of the biblical passages to which they have been appended only to attract attention and to aid the memory' (ibid., ch. 15, 206).

The same applies to the Titus story: 'You are permitted to hold,' he argues,

> that the account is pure fiction—a mode of imparting edification which obtained among the pure in thought, for the purpose of imbuing the hearts of the masses with the idea that our God is great, mighty in power, capable of meting out retribution to all that rise up against Him, especially the arrogant foreigner, even through the agency of the minutest of His creatures. With great perspicuity, they applied their invention to the utterly wicked Titus. (ibid., ch. 16, 217)

See R. Loew's rejoinder to these very assertions, *Be'er hagolah*, *Be'er* 6, 137a. See also de' Rossi's quotation from the *Letter* of R. Sherira Gaon that

> the aggadot in some part are similar to the angels created from *nehar dinur* ['river of fire'], mentioned by the sages in several instances [BT *Ḥag.* 14a; *Gen. Rabbah* 78, etc.], who, having rendered their song, depart, never to return. Once the expositor has achieved his purpose in using them, they are not to be referred to or cited as evidence that the events portrayed therein really occurred. (ibid., ch. 15, 208)

See R. Loew's rebuttal, *Be'er hagolah*, *Be'er* 6, 133b ff.   [20] Ibid., *Be'er* 3, 40a.

conspicuous and conclusive evidence, in his opinion, that the rabbis did use the same kind of metaphors; and he accordingly laid down methodological rules for penetrating to the true meanings of the various dicta and aggadot.

IV

To Rabbi Loew it was indisputably certain that the sages were the repositories of profound wisdom and were acquainted with all branches of science. This basic assumption, however, does not seem to be borne out by the facts. The details of their various remarks seem to contradict the assertion that they were superior human beings. Hence, Rabbi Loew is constrained to explain many of their statements as 'parables' containing deep, hidden meanings.

The fact is, Rabbi Loew argues further, that

> the greater the wisdom of the sage, the more profound are his utterances; the less the wisdom one possesses, the more superficial will his remarks be . . . The extent to which ideas are hidden is commensurate with the wisdom of each person.[21]

Rabbi Loew finds his assumption reinforced by the very assertions of the sages themselves. Where the sages had no intention of imparting recondite wisdom, they themselves used to state that their accounts were to be taken literally. It follows, then, that where the possibility of a 'parable' has not been explicitly excluded, we must accept the remarks as being indeed expressed metaphorically.[22]

He adds that the talmudic sages scrupulously shunned all falsehood. They admonished against lying, going so far as to aver that 'whoever dissembles in his speech is as though he had engaged in idolatry' (BT *San.* 92a). Certainly, it is preposterous to attribute to them statements which are patently false, accounts of events that never took place, 'inventions'—and even more so 'that they should have had in mind, God forbid, to make any statements that ran counter to the faith in Him, may He be blessed'.[23]

The very strangeness of the remarks themselves is the proof that the authors were speaking metaphorically. It is impossible to conceive that the sages of the Talmud should have said things which even the 'small-minded, the intellectually

---

[21] *Be'er hagolah*, *Be'er* 3, 40a. See also the beginning of *Be'er* 5, 87b (this will be dealt with below) and his remarks in *Be'er* 6, 137b. In his view, the words of the rabbis of the Talmud are termed 'the words of the wise' because they are eminently rational. The depth of their remarks may be discerned by clarifying the 'obscure by reference to the explicit'. The profundity of the rabbinic wisdom in the aggadah may be proved, by analogy, from their penetrating conceptions and judgments in the realm of halakhah. In this connection see *Be'er* 4, 50b.

[22] His proof is drawn from the account of the disciple of R. Eliezer. The pupil rendered a halakhic decision in the presence of the master (BT *Eruv.* 63a), whereupon R. Eliezer informed his wife, Imma Shalom, that the pupil would not live out the year. Now the name of the pupil and his father are explicitly mentioned. These details were inserted to preclude anyone dismissing the story as a mere parable. See *Be'er hagolah*, *Be'er* 4, and esp. 51b, s.v. *ve'atah*.

[23] Ibid. 50b, s.v. *vekha asher*. Here he alluded to one of the areas that involve the use of parable; see also beginning of *Be'er* 6, 105a.

weak, would not utter'. Instead, the words of the sages must obviously be understood as 'proverb and figure, the words of the wise and their dark sayings' (Prov. 1: 6):

The very nature of wisdom postulates that words of wisdom should only be expressed by means of proverb, figure, and allusion, since all wisdom is esoteric and undisclosed; and so it should be, to prevent wisdom becoming something to be trodden underfoot by every ignoramus, for that would be the opposite of wisdom.[24]

It is the inherent nature of wisdom to be hidden, and even the gentile sages conduct themselves similarly.[25]

In his opinion, it is axiomatic that 'hatred works in them [the critics], making them look upon the path leading to the house of the Lord as being perverted; love, on the other hand, reduces hills to plains.'[26] According to his assumption, the greater the apparent exaggeration in the rabbinic dicta, the better the vessel for containing the profundity of rabbinic wisdom that the words constitute.[27]

This last premise, however, seems to be in direct contradiction to the very assertions of the sages themselves. They themselves have admitted to using 'exaggerations' on several occasions;[28] yet even this open admission is accounted for by Rabbi Loew in the context of his views. He argues:

Yet I do not maintain that in those instances in which the rabbis exaggerated they were giving vent to mere idle words, such as ordinary persons do; it is instead very profound wisdom.[29]

He strives to uncover the idea alluded to in the exaggeration, and asserts, 'Indeed, I maintain, and this is true, that the sages were not at all given to hyperbole, for the manner of the wise is only to utter the essentials.'[30]

V

So far, I have indicated one of the areas where Rabbi Loew saw fit to delineate planes of varying elevation in understanding what the sages of the Talmud had to say, i.e. in respect of hyperbole and exaggeration.[31] I shall designate others further on.

[24] Ibid., *Be'er* 5, 87*b*, s.v. *uvedavar zeh*. See also his *Ḥidushei agadot* (London, 1960; henceforth this edition will be referred to as L), iv. 95*a* (on BT *Ḥul*. 57*b*).

[25] The rabbinic dicta, however, are superior, since even their outer aspects are of value. This does not apply to non-Jewish wisdom. There, if one fails to understand what the figure conveys, he has gained nothing. Furthermore, 'no matter how wise the non-Jewish sages might have been, their wisdom was merely human. As for the rabbis, their wisdom is the inner core of secret knowledge, that which they received from their master, and he from his, all the way back to Moses, our teacher, of blessed memory' (*Be'er hagolah*, *Be'er* 5, 95*b*). [26] Ibid. 87*b*.

[27] In reply to the adverse criticism of the stories of Rabbah bar bar Hana, R. Loew wrote: 'To the very extent that these stories have been regarded as mere fantasies they are profound' (ibid. 88*b*).

[28] On this see Heinemann, *Methods of the Aggadah* (Heb.), 205 nn. 45a–48.

[29] *Ḥidushei agadot* (L), iii. 172*b* (on BT *San*. 82*b*), s.v. *mai dikhetiv*: 'That wicked man engaged in intercourse 424 times that day.' [30] Ibid. 173*b*.

[31] And so too on many occasions in reference to the numbers and measures enumerated by the sages.

Another important area where Rabbi Loew strives to find the hidden essence underlying the externals is in reference to statements that seem to attribute corporeality and anthropomorphism to God, ascribing to him human actions and attributes. He solves this problem by using the rule that none of these modes of expression describe the objective reality of the Godhead, but rather the reaction of the human beings experiencing the effects of God's deeds, of man who conceives divine action in terms of his own understanding.[32]

Other dicta in which Rabbi Loew seeks to uncover the abstract that lies beyond the concrete sense of the words include expressions which seem to contradict the laws of nature as these are comprehended by mankind, by means of sense impressions,[33] logic,[34] and the *consensus omnium*.[35] In all these instances, he attempts to find a solution that commends itself to reason.

In fine, the strange episodes, the far-fetched statements, and the details and stylistic usage that appear as no more than ornamentation are all intended to convey deeper meanings.[36] Nothing, not even the seemingly most trivial detail, is mentioned in vain.[37]

Cf. his above-mentioned explanations of the aggadot of Rabbah bar bar Hana, *Be'er hagolah*, Be'er 5, 88b ff. See also *Ḥidushei agadot* (L), iii. 85 ff. In his discussion there, the principles he adopted to explain the aggadot are clearly set down. I shall deal with several aspects of this topic later. See also his remarks on the evidence given by Abba Sha'ul (BT *Nid*. 24b), ibid. iv. 155a ff.

[32] See Aharon F[ritz] Kleinberger, *Educational Theory of the Maharal of Prague* [Hamaḥashavah hapedagogit shel maharal miprag] (Jerusalem, 1962), 68–71. In this connection see also the many hyperbolic expressions in *Be'er hagolah*, Be'er 4.

[33] See e.g. his discussion of the earthquakes, ibid. 63a, s.v. *beferek haro'eh*. See ibid., Be'er 6, 126a, 156a, as well as his other observations. See also *Ḥidushei agadot* (L), iii. 116a (on BT *BB* 84a), and ibid. iv. 95a ff. (on BT *Ḥul*. 57b).

[34] See *Gevurot hashem*, ch. 47 (Pardes edn., Tel Aviv, 1955), 58b, concerning the hymn uttered by the embryos in their mothers' wombs as they emerged from the Red Sea, and *Ḥidushei agadot* (L), ii. 66a–b. See similarly his remarks on demons, *Ḥidushei agadot* (L), i. 124b ff. (on BT *Git*. 68a).

On this topic, see too the stories of King Solomon and Asmedai (king of the demons), ibid. 128a ff.; also on the seven-headed dragon in BT *Kid*. 29b. R. Loew accounts for every single detail in the story, e.g. the significance of the number seven. As far as the story itself is concerned, he confessed that he was not certain whether 'this appeared so to him, i.e. in a dream, for the implication is that it appeared so to him, or whether he saw it in his imagination during the day—yet it is all the same'. Here, R. Loew probably relied on Maimonides' remarks in the *Guide* (pt. 2, ch. 42) about seeing angels. Yet it is doubtful whether he accepted Maimonides' views in this matter. In regard to the revelation of Elijah, R. Loew adopted a rationalistic approach (illuminated by his special insight)—see *Ḥidushei agadot* (L), iii. 41a (on BT *BM* 85b), also *Netsaḥ yisra'el*, ch. 28, and the corresponding section in *Ḥidushei agadot* (L), iii. 216a–b (on BT *San*. 98a), concerning Elijah and R. Joshua b. Levi. Here, too, he repeatedly emphasizes that all is incorporeal.

[35] This rule also applies to what has been accepted as the halakhic decision. See ibid. i. 136a, s.v. *melamed sheba*. The matter is correspondingly dealt with in *Be'er hagolah*, Be'er 5, 95b ff. His views on marital relations there are interesting but do not come within the purview of the discussion here.

[36] See e.g. ibid. 56a–b; also ibid., Be'er 6, 107a, s.v. *omnam*; ibid. 111a, s.v. *od*. See below his observation on the semantics of the sages of the Talmud.

[37] In this connection, see e.g. his discussion of the assertion in BT *RH* 23a: 'There are four species of

VI

The principal rules guiding Rabbi Loew in his commentaries are:

1. All descriptions of the divine, as already indicated, are given from the point of view of human experience:

for the view of the sages, which coincides with the view of the Torah, is that all these statements are expressed from the point of view of the person affected, since He, may He be blessed, is conceived by those affected in accordance with their own capacities. God appears to them in the manner fitting them, without it really being so . . . And this is a most fundamental principle, revealed by the sages in their esoteric and concealed *midrashim*.[38]

cedar trees . . . In the school of Rav, it was said: There are ten species of cedar trees' (*Ḥidushei agadot* (L), i. 123*b*). R. Loew contends there, inter alia, that the intention here is not to impart knowledge on the actual number of species of cedar trees, 'but to allude to the mystic wisdom pertaining to cedar trees'. The sages of the Talmud did not engage in classifying cedar trees in accordance with their respective species, but here intimated the hidden wisdom connected with the cedar, and the secret wisdom here laid bare is one of the secret disciplines of kabbalah. (In his manuscript he erased his exposition of that wisdom. He apparently had no wish to make it public.) The general idea expressed here is: cedar is a generic term. The various types of cedar trees belong to certain species. The view that there are ten such species holds that the totality is comprised of ten specific items, viz. the ten spheres (*sefirot*) (See Zohar i. 35*a*: 'We have been taught that the saplings are like the proboscids of locusts'; see also R. Bahya's commentary on the Pentateuch, Gen. 11: 9; and so too Menahem ben Benjamin Recanati, in his Pentateuch commentary ad loc.) Those who spoke about four species hinted at the four heads of the river which went out of Eden. Apparently the reference here is to *Tikunei hazohar*, §55: '"And a river went out from Eden"—this is Eden which no eye has looked on, except God . . . hidden and concealed, since it is the supreme crown. "And from there it divided and became four heads"—these are the letters of the Tetragrammaton, which stand for: father and mother, son and daughter [i.e. Hokhmah—'wisdom'; Binah—'intelligence'; Tiferet—'beauty'; Malkhut—'kingdom'].' These are the four cedars 'emanating from the place whence comes the oil [i.e. from the Aged One—the 'crown']' (see Zohar iii. 30*b*). R. Loew here engages in the analysis of mystical concepts, and reconciles the conflicting and contradictory opinions of the sages (although his reluctance to expose mystical discussions to public gaze is quite enlightening; apparently he rested content with merely alluding to his ideas).

Kabbalistic expositions of rabbinic dicta are frequently found in *Ḥidushei agadot*. We shall illustrate this aspect by one single reference. In *Ḥidushei agadot* (L), iii. 3*b*–4*a* on BT *Bava Kama* 17*a*, where it is stated that 36,000 men with shoulders bared marched in the funeral procession of King Hezekiah, R. Loew confessed that 'I know of no reason for this number.' Nevertheless, he attempted to solve the problem in two ways: (*a*) 'The earthly kingdom is similar to the celestial.' In the celestial kingdom there are thirty-six saints (BT *Suk.* 45*b*), and similarly on earth as well. On earth, however, the number has been multiplied by 1,000, since a saint is equal to 1,000 ordinary men ('One man among a thousand have I found [Eccl. 7: 28]'). (*b*) A mystical explanation: thirty-six refers to one shoulder, for both the numbers would be seventy-two. Here the allusion is, with some variation, to the attributes of 'Mercy' (right) and 'Power' (left) in the divine names, traditionally 72 in number (see Zohar ii. 51*b*).

His exhaustive treatment of even the minutest details is most strikingly illustrated in his discussion of the tales of Rabbah bar bar Hana. See *Ḥidushei agadot* (L), iii. 85*a* ff. (on BT *BB*).

[38] *Be'er hagolah*, *Be'er* 4, 64*a*, and many others. See e.g. ibid. 56*a*, 57*b*, 66*a*, 68*b*–69*a*, 81*b*, and many other similar instances throughout all his writings.

2. The sages did not study nature so as to ascertain its order, but to discover the cause producing that order,³⁹ to discover, not the natural order, but the intelligent ordering;⁴⁰ not the natural cause, but the cause underlying the natural causes: 'Everything has a natural cause which determines it, but for every natural cause there is a divine cause—the cause of the cause, the first cause, and it is of this latter cause that the sages spoke.'⁴¹

Rabbi Loew endeavours to expose this 'cause of causes', expressed by the sages, in their recondite manner, in terms of things hidden and concealed.

3. As for the historical accounts given by the rabbis of the Talmud, Rabbi Loew categorically asserts, 'I maintain that the remarks of the sages are not in the manner of history books, where the authors chronicle past events.'⁴²

4. These guidelines are undoubtedly derived from one general principle: 'The sages did not speak of the material, but of that which is divested of the material.' The incidents do not constitute the subject matter for the rabbis to study; only the essences do:

This is the way of the sages. They speak of the essences only, the substance of the substance of the thing.⁴³ They are sages, and have no truck with sense experience.⁴⁴

---

³⁹ See *Be'er hagolah*, *Be'er* 4, 63*b*. 'He, may He be blessed, does all, and does it through the agency of nature.' ⁴⁰ Ibid., *Be'er* 5, 98*a*.
⁴¹ Ibid., *Be'er* 6, 106*a*. See the evidence of this approach throughout the *Be'er* referred to. There is no need to go into details. See especially his observation on 118*b*: 'The words of the Torah are altogether different from their [the gentile geometers'] wisdom.' For his attitude towards the geometers, see also ibid. 123*a* ff.
⁴² Ibid. 133*a*. R. Loew's attitude to *Josippon*, as revealed in this section, is most interesting. He accepts the accounts as authentic, but claims that *Josippon* only recorded the concrete, outer manifestations of the events, while the sages of the Talmud, the 'authentic sages', also penetrated to the inner events and concealed thoughts (see ibid. 138*a*). On this same subject, see also how, in his *Netsah yisra'el* (chs. 5–9), he deals with the accounts of the destruction of the Temple and also in his *Hidushei agadot* (L), ii. 97*b*, 118*b* ff. (on BT *Gitin*). There he also repeats his rule, that 'what the sages related as having occurred at the destruction of the Land of Israel is not to be regarded as having occurred by pure chance'. Among other things, he also dealt with the number given for the slain of Betar, etc. See also ibid. 117*b*, s.v. *sheharag*. He felt impelled to interpret many 'historical aggadot' in his other writings. His basic conception referred to here is manifested throughout his works.
⁴³ See *Be'er hagolah*, *Be'er* 4, 75*a*; also ibid. 65*a*, 78*a*, 101*a*, 128*a*, etc. See also his formulation in *Hidushei agadot* (L), ii. 114*b* (on BT *Gitin*), where he lays down that 'this is an important principle in the dicta of the sages of the Talmud. They sought the particular essence. We have explained this many times in our works *Be'er hagolah* and *Gevurot hashem*.' See also his handling of the tales of the *shamir* (a legendary worm (or stone) created on the eve of the first sabbath, capable of cutting stone; see Mishnah *Avot* 5: 9), *Hidushei agadot* (L), ii. 127*b* ff. (on BT *Git.* 68*b*).
In *Hidushei agadot* (L), iii. 31*a–b* (on BT *BM* 83*b*), R. Loew refers the reader to his *Be'er hagolah*, *Be'er* 4 in connection with the rule stated above. It reappears frequently in his discussions of various topics. See e.g. *Hidushei agadot* (L), iii. 27*b*, 35*b*, 40*a*, 47*a*. The view is stressed time and again, also in the course of his expositions of the tales of Rabbah bar bar Hana in BT *BB*. See ibid. 55 ff.
⁴⁴ *Hidushei agadot* (L), iv. 35*a* ff. (on BT *AZ* 10*a*).

The sages of the Talmud did not, then, occupy themselves with trivialities, with isolated events, but with the rules governing the order of nature and with the nature of those rules. Their concrete formulations refer to the abstract, 'the intellectual', as he sometimes puts it.[45] The intention is to isolate the essences. It is the essential (as he understands it, obviously) that he endeavours to reveal.[46]

His attitude to the quantitative enumerations of the rabbis is also an important feature of his approach. According to him, the rule applies here, too, that the 'essence distilled from the material of the number'[47] is what should be sought after, since 'the sages were not dealing with material quantities, which were of no concern to them'.[48] '*All* the observations of the sages are intellectual',[49] and the numbers used by them indicate the 'true essence'.[50] Indeed, he devotes much attention to the hidden meanings of the various quantities and numbers, for in using these numbers, the sages intended to indicate certain essential features.[51]

An illuminating example of his approach is his attitude towards the talmudic and midrashic statements on the centrality of the Land of Israel (BT *Yoma* 54*b*). In his conception, the reference here is not to any geographical location. The world, after all, is spherical, and so the dicta regarding centrality can only be valid in respect of value. The Land of Israel is characterized as the 'centre' on account of its

---

[45] See *Be'er hagolah*, Be'er 4, 78*b*.

[46] The most commonly used terms for 'essence' in his interpretation of the aggadot are *mahut* and *etsem*. They seem to occur in practically every exposition of rabbinic dicta and aggadot.

[47] *Be'er hagolah*, Be'er 6, 112*b*.   [48] Ibid. 113*b*; see also 125*a*.   [49] Ibid. 115*b*.

[50] Ibid. 114*a*; see also 126*a*. R. Loew explains that the measurements ascribed to Adam teach of his natural excellence. The measurements ascribed to Pharaoh, on the other hand, signify the depths of depravity of this 'lowest of men', and so the redemption of Israel from the depths of degradation thereby becomes symbolized. See *Be'er hagolah*, Be'er 6, 99*b* ff. Measurements impart, then, information on the essential nature of the person involved. Whatever is stated in this manner concerning any individual indicates his essential nature. Of Moses it has been said that he was ten cubits tall. Now 'this does not refer to his material height, but signifies that he was fit for perfection. His soul had attained a level comparable to ten cubits in height' (*Ḥidushei agadot* (L), iii. 33*b*). See also his remarks on the rabbinic exposition of Deut. 34: 1: '"And Moses went up from the plain of Moab unto Mount Nebo"—The *baraita* teaches: there were twelve steps there and Moses ascended all in a single stride' (BT *Sot.* 13*b*). R. Loew takes this comment to convey Moses' spiritual greatness, that he was a person who had achieved perfection. The twelve steps correspond to the sum of the numerical values of the letters in the word *zeh* (twelve), 'as it is said: "for this [*zeh*] man Moses" [Exod. 32: 1]. Describing Moses thus signifies that he had attained perfection', since *zeh* is also used to designate 'the perfect, real existence', and also 'complete, real existence' in respect of 'form'. This perfection of Moses, alluded to by the number 12, is also revealed in his age, 120 years, which is twelve in abbreviated numbers [*bemispar katan*: using only numbers from 1 to 9]. The numerical values of the letters of Moses' name, if only the integers are added up, also equal twelve (*mem*=40; *shin*=300, *heh*=5). (See also *Gur aryeh* on Deut. 32; *Ḥidushei agadot* (L), ii. 55*a* (on BT *Sot.*).

[51] This topic is dealt with extensively in all his works. We shall point out a few more details. The number 6 indicates the 'essential completion'. See *Be'er hagolah*, Be'er 6, 112*b*, 113*a*. The number 60 also indicates a 'complete, full amount'—see ibid., Be'er 5, 89*b*. See also *Netsaḥ yisra'el*, ch. 6, for a lengthy discussion of the significance of 60 and 3 (and so too in *Ḥidushei agadot* (L), iii. 38*a* (on BT *Git.* 57*b*); also ibid. iv. 121*a*, 128*a* (on BT *Bekh.*).

holiness. What the rabbis intended to convey was that, in so far as the essence of the world is concerned, the Land of Israel is the focal point.[52]

5. Maharal's conception imposed a twofold task. He was 'obliged', on the one hand, to plumb the depths of rabbinic thought, and, on the other, he was not freed of the duty (as were the allegorists) of defending the use of the modes of expression in the referents. The wording of the allusion is not incidental; no more and no less is mentioned than is absolutely necessary. The consequence, then, is inevitable, though to some extent paradoxical: every interpretation has two facets. It must indicate the wisdom contained in the referent and also the profound idea locked up in the essence. What characterizes his approach, however, in the interpretation of the aggadot is that, after the essence, the ideal core of the dictum, has been analysed, he reverts to the verbal formulation in all its details, large and small, and shows how the essence is alluded to in these details and how the specific formulation indicates the essence.[53]

---

[52] *Be'er hagolah*, Be'er 6, 130*b*–132*a*. (The 'middle', or 'equal', or 'straight', in his terminology, is basic to his whole conception.)

For his conception of the Land of Israel and its position in the world see *Gevurot hashem*, ch. 8; *Derekh hayim*, on Mishnah *Avot* 5: 2; *Netivot olam*, vol. i: 'Netiv ha'avodah', ch. 18, 139*a*–*b*; *Tiferet yisra'el*, ch. 64; *Netsah yisra'el*, ch. 6; and the beginning of *Derush al hatorah*. See also *Hidushei agadot* (L), ii. 147*b* (on BT *Kid*. 69*a*); his comments on BT *Ket*. 113*a* ff., ibid. 166*b* ff.; on *Sot*. 34*b*, ibid. 68*b*–69*a*; as well as his comments on *Kid*. 49*b*, ibid. 145*b*. On this entire topic see A. Gottesdiener, 'The Lion Among the Sages of Prague' (Heb.), in Yehudah Leib Hakohen Fishman (ed.), *Rabbi Kook Memorial Volume* (Heb.) (Jerusalem, 1937), pt. 4, pp. 431–43.

[53] This approach is not restricted to certain specific topics; it is basic to all his thinking. There is no need to go into detail. We shall, however, touch on one or two items. In his discussion of the remarks of the sages that Moses was suspected of adultery and Jeremiah of consorting with a harlot, R. Loew first takes up Moses' personality, that he was to Israel as 'form' is to 'matter'. Hence he was the equal of all of them together. 'Now if a person reflects on this matter many gates of the Torah which are now firmly locked will be opened for him.' R. Loew attempts to comprehend all the details related about Moses in Scripture and rabbinic literature in the light of his assumption and the statement mentioned above. It then becomes clear to him that man being to woman as 'form' is to 'matter', so Moses, who was the 'form' of Israel, was also the 'form', as it were, of their women. Their error lay in their failure to grasp that Moses stood on an especially elevated level and hence he did not impose his 'form' on their 'matter'. He became one of the 'separated forms' or 'intelligences'. Jeremiah, in turn, was similar to Moses (he prophesied to Judah and Israel, while the other prophets only delivered their prophecies to one or the other kingdom). But Jeremiah only constituted their 'form' in some respects. Hence they stated of him that he had attached himself to a harlot, meaning that the combination was imperfect. An additional interpretation (based on the same principle), and 'this is the proper interpretation', is that Moses wished to gain dominion over the people, to make them utterly dependent upon him, intending apparently to make himself the 'husband [master] of Israel' without forging a direct relationship between the people and God (who is referred to as the 'Master' of Israel throughout Scripture). This is the meaning of his being suspected of adultery. (Jeremiah lived at the time when the Shekhinah had removed itself from Israel. The people were less dependent on him, and so in regard to him, the imperfect relationship is referred to as immorality.) In respect of Moses, the people erred in failing to realize that his was a separated quality—he was neither attached to nor combined with them. (This makes his argument, 'I have not taken a single ass from them, neither have I hurt one of them', intelligible. He had had no actual contact with them.)

An investigation of this type entails the minutest examination of the rabbinic utterances. Rabbi Loew accordingly believes that the modes of expression require special attention, since we are liable to be led astray by our own language usage. In his opinion the critics of the sages of the Talmud fail to see that the rabbis had their own particular modes of expression, which, in turn, possessed their own particular semantic relations. It is the function of the expositor to reveal the true meaning of the words in terms of the authors' individual linguistic patterns. The linguistic analysis of their expressions is the tool that will ensure that the rabbinic dicta will be properly understood. Once this is accomplished, then what may seem strange and alien in the remarks of the sages will suddenly become clear and intelligible.[54]

For the further elaboration of this topic see *Gevurot hashem*, ch. 19. There, apparently, we have the first draft of his treatment of the subject dealt with later in *Be'er hagolah*, Be'er 5, 96a ff. In the former work, only the first explanation is given, and this is, after all, not the 'proper interpretation', according to his remark in *Be'er hagolah*. (Characteristically, however, he notes in his *Gevurot hashem* that he had explained the dictum in question in *Be'er hagolah*, which was published sixteen years later.) On the other hand, the wording of *Be'er hagolah* seems to be a preliminary draft of what he was to set down later in his *Ḥidushei agadot* (L), iii. 2b–3b (on BT BK 16b). See also *Netivot olam*, 'Netiv ha'anavah', end of ch. 4.

His treatment of the account of the gnat entering Titus' head (BT Git. 56b) follows the same line of thought. See *Be'er hagolah*, Be'er 6, 137a–139b, s.v. *od asaf*. See also *Netsah yisra'el*, ch. 5; *Ḥidushei agadot* (L), ii. 107b ff. (on BT Git. 56b).

Using the same criteria, R. Loew took up the tales of Solomon and Asmedai. In his view, the narratives were intended to disclose the high level attained by Solomon and the holiness of the kingdom from which he was deposed (ibid. 128b ff.).

See also his exposition of the account of the encounter of R. Kahana and R. Yohanan, BT BK 114a; *Ḥidushei agadot* (L), iii. 15b ff. So, too, on the expedition of Alexander the Great to Africa (BT Tam. 31b), *Ḥidushei agadot* (L), iv. 148a ff. The details are not pertinent to our discussion.

[54] See for instance his observations on BT Ber. 7a: 'R. Yohanan said in the name of R. Yose b. Zimra: From where is it deduced that the Holy One, blessed be He, prays? It is said: "And I shall bring them to My holy mountain and make them rejoice in My house of prayer."' R. Loew argues that criticism of the sages of the Talmud for having, as it were, impaired the unity of God, is unfounded. The error of the critics derives from their inability to understand the rabbis' meanings and modes of expression. The sages of the Talmud knew 'the hidden recesses of wisdom and prayer, and what constituted the essential nature and language of prayer'. He proceeds to clarify the true denotation of the verb *palel*, which indicates the true nature of prayer. Further on, he continues to clarify the various other expressions appearing in this statement (*Be'er hagolah*, Be'er 4, 51b ff.).

He similarly explains such terms as *kaparah* ('atonement'), and thereby the statement: 'Atone for me for having reduced the size of the moon' (ibid. 54b, s.v. *beferek kama dishevuot*); *nitsuah* ('victory'), in *nitshuni banai*—'my children have defeated Me' (ibid. 56b, s.v. *vehashem*); *tsehok* ('laughter' or 'mockery'), in 'The Holy One, blessed be He, sports with the Leviathan' (ibid. 70b, s.v. *ve'omnam*, where he distinguishes between laughter of mockery and laughter of joy). (His views are most interesting but cannot be elaborated on here.) The meaning of *mahol* ('dance'), too, is elucidated in his exposition of the dictum (BT Ta'an. 31b): 'The Holy One, blessed be He, will hold a dance for the righteous in the Garden of Eden.' There he explains the essential nature of dancing and deduces from its use in this context that dance is 'an expression of profound wisdom' (see *Be'er hagolah*, Be'er 4, 75 ff.). So, too, is the term *giluah* ('shaving') explained in the verse: 'In that day shall God shave with a razor the one that is hired', which refers to Sennacherib, 'and this shaving has an altogether spiritual connotation' (ibid. 78 ff.). Similarly, he discusses 'blessing' in connection with God's saying: 'My son, Ishmael, bless me' (BT Ber. 7b; *Be'er hagolah*, Be'er 4, 79b).

6. One of the means adopted by Rabbi Loew in his efforts to penetrate to the recesses of rabbinic thought is the method of comparison: what is said in one context is illuminated by a statement in another. Indeed, he is accustomed to interpret the particular passage he deals with by adducing references culled from the entire range of rabbinic literature, and he emphasizes this principle at the beginning of the fifth part of *Be'er hagolah*. He argues:[55]

> The critics should have noticed that the rabbis' observations seem to contain matters far removed from reason, that are obscure when considered in isolation, yet the meaning hidden in one context is revealed in another.[56] So it is in respect of the *midrash* of the *Sefer Hazohar* and the *Midrash bahir* of Rabbi Nehuniah ben Hakanah and other wisdom literature, which are hidden away in the treasure stores of the sages; they reveal to us the hidden thoughts of the Torah to which the rabbis have alluded.[57]

7. His approach, however, engenders a somewhat ambivalent attitude towards such dicta as can be explained in their plain sense. Any expositor bent on uncovering the deeper layers of rabbinic thought runs the risk of discriminating against interpretations which follow the plain sense, even where such explanations are eminently reasonable and acceptable. This seems to be true of Rabbi Loew. At times he gives a literal interpretation of a passage, and yet a certain dissatisfaction on his part can be detected, since the plain sense does not express the deep rabbinic thought that he would expect it to. As a result, he refuses to rest content with the literal exposition, but goes on to indicate what, in his opinion, also lies hidden beneath the surface.[58]

Similarly, the connotation of *akhilah* ('eating') interests him. He sets down the rule: 'You must know that when the sages attempted to explain the nature of the good that is held in store for the righteous they did so in terms of eating and this is of great significance to those who know the truth' (*Be'er hagolah*, Be'er 5, 91b, s.v. *beferek hasefinah*). See also in this connection his comments on BT *BB* 70b in *Ḥidushei agadot* (L), iii. 104b, s.v. *kol*, and also 109b ff.).

See, further, his observations on the sin of Ham in *Be'er hagolah* (Be'er 5, 102b ff., s.v. *beferek ben sorer*) in regard to the 'seeing' of Ham. Also his treatment of the meaning of *kol* (Be'er 6, 115b ff., s.v. *beferek kama diyoma*, and especially 117b), where he establishes the rule that '*kol* refers to the potential becoming actual'. In this connection, see also his treatment of the significance of the *shofar* (*Ḥidushei agadot* (L), i. 105a ff.).

[55] *Be'er hagolah*, Be'er 5 86b; see also 87b, s.v. *uvedavar zeh*.

[56] This is a well-known rule of the sages (*Tanḥuma*, 'Ḥukat' 23; *Num. Rabbah* 19: 27): 'The statements of the Torah are interdependent; what one conceals, the other reveals.' So too, 'the words of the Torah are poor in one context and rich in another' (JT *RH* 3: 5; see also Tosafot on BT *Ker.* 14a, s.v. *ela*).

[57] Although scholars have noted R. Loew's attitude to kabbalistic doctrines in their writings, the topic has not been treated adequately. New allusions appearing in his *Ḥidushei agadot* point to a much closer connection than has been assumed hitherto.

[58] The oven of Akhnai is a case in point. It may be taken in its literal sense, 'concretely' as R. Loew would say, 'since certainly R. Eliezer the Great was worthy of having a tangible miracle performed on his behalf', but such an explanation did not satisfy him completely. He therefore offered a spiritual exposition of the episode in *Ḥidushei agadot* (L), iii. 26b and esp. 27b (on BT *BM* 59b). See also *Be'er hagolah*, Be'er 4, 55b, s.v. *beferek hazahav*, where he explains the passage from other aspects. See also *Netivot olam*, 'Netiv ahavat re'a', ch. 2, where he deals at length with this passage. (Possibly, his comments here are

This does not imply, of course, that he was not expert in elucidating passages in their literal sense.[59]

His evaluation of the midrashic method of exposition, employed by the sages, as such, is a topic that lies beyond the scope of this study. From what has been stated generally, two conclusions may, however, be drawn: (*a*) the same approach he adopts in elucidating the dicta and aggadot of the Talmud is also followed in his study of the midrashic interpretations of scriptural passages; (*b*) his premises regarding the exposition of the Bible by the sages of the Talmud, which he derived from analysis of their midrashic interpretations of the Scriptures, served him as his main tool in elucidating the rabbinic dicta themselves.

VII

I have dealt broadly with Maharal's attitude towards the dicta and midrashic interpretations of the sages of the Talmud, yet I have cited very few of his actual interpretations, and even those referred to were by way of allusion only. Even there, however, my intention was only to use the individual instance as an illustration of the rule.

What is manifest in Rabbi Loew's interpretations certainly bears his individual stamp, and the details and generalizations combine together in one coherent system. Yet his whole system, which is to a great extent original, goes beyond the limits of my discussion here. Let it, however, be said that, in his attitude towards rabbinic dicta, Rabbi Loew clearly reflects the traditional attitude of the German rabbis of his generation, and he is one of the most interesting exponents of the prevailing attitude. His firm belief in the inherent truth of rabbinic dicta never

---

preliminary to his exhaustive treatment in *Ḥidushei agadot*, though the question of the relation between the two works is somewhat complicated.)

See also his comments on the corpses revived by Ezekiel in *Ḥidushei agadot* (L), iii. 186*a* (on BT *San.*). R. Loew argues that even R. Eliezer b. R. Yose Hagalili, who said that the corpses brought back to life subsequently immigrated to the Land of Israel, did not assert that this occurred in the flesh.

The same method is adopted in elucidating the story of David and Ishbi (BT *San. 95a*). R. Loew argues: 'The whole passage may be explained literally, that the episode actually took place concretely, but it is better to explain it all spiritually.' He proceeds to account for all the details mentioned about Ishbi (the son of Orpah) losing his powers through David (who was descended from Ruth), and David's nephew, Abishai. See also *Ḥidushei agadot* (L), iii. 194*b* ff.

So too, does R. Loew explain the encounters between Rabbi Judah the Prince and Antoninus recounted in BT *AZ* 10*a*. After explaining the execution of the slaves by Antoninus corporeally, he argues: 'But I say that the words of the sages do not refer to concrete events.' He even went further and asserted that the sages had no truck with the material world. In this, they were different from the prophets, who did refer to tangible things. See *Ḥidushei agadot* (L), iv. 35*b*, and *Netsaḥ yisra'el*, ch. 7.

[59] One example among many is his interpretation of the passage referring to 'And Jacob remained alone' in BT *Ḥul.* 91*a*: 'R. Eliezer said: He remained behind to attend to his small utensils.' R. Loew maintains that Jacob certainly would not have forgotten something of great significance (*Ḥidushei agadot* (L), iv. 105*b*).

falters, as it did not among his colleagues in Germany (for instance, Rabbi Joseph Ashkenazi, the 'Tanna of Safed', his contemporary). But Rabbi Loew endeavours to illuminate that truth by his own individual outlook.

Furthermore, even in his detaching of the sages' remarks from their concrete, plain sense, he remains unique. His approach, at first sight, seems to use the allegorical method that takes the actual formulations figuratively and considers them as lacking any essential correspondence with the 'inner meaning'. Rabbi Loew's indefatigable efforts to relate the inner meaning to the outer mode of expression establish a relationship between the symbol and what it stands for. The concrete image is by no means incidental, and this is most fundamental in his conception. Here he does, however, join the company of the mystic expositors, as some of his 'deep-hidden' explanations make evident. That these explanations do follow along those lines is indisputable. Yet it may, perhaps, be said that his remarks nevertheless preserve their own distinct colouring: in exoteric matters his terminology is philosophical; for the esoteric, mystical. As noted above, I do not intend to subject his ideas and the fundamental aspects of his conception to critical scrutiny.

At all events, we have before us a conception which manifests an extreme, conservative attitude to the aggadah, yet which of itself and in its method contains undoubtedly fresh and original thinking. Rabbi Loew infused his own lively spirit into the aggadah and added to its vividness. Both its own light and his shine forth from his expositions of the aggadah.

NINETEEN

THE DESTRUCTION OF THE TEMPLE
A Yiddish Booklet for the Ninth of Av

JACOB ELBAUM and CHAVA TURNIANSKY

THE MIDRASH AND YIDDISH BEFORE THE SEVENTEENTH CENTURY

Although no list of Yiddish translations of *midrashim* through the ages is available, we know that full translations of the most comprehensive and popular ones (*Midrash tanḥuma* and *Midrash Rabbah*) began to appear only in the last two decades of the nineteenth century.[1] On the other hand, to this day, no Yiddish translation of the Talmud, or any separate tractate thereof, is known. However, the wealth of midrashic material that had accumulated by the fourteenth century was an inexhaustible source of elements of all kinds which were incorporated, in diverse forms of translation, reworking, and adaptation, into most genres of Old Yiddish literature from its very beginnings.

In the oldest known literary document of Yiddish literature—the Cambridge Codex T—S 10 K 22, dated 1382[2]—an abundant use of midrashic sources may be observed. Four poems in this anthology, one about 'paradise' and three about the biblical figures of Abraham, Aaron, and Joseph, rely almost entirely on the Midrash.[3] These four relatively short poems from the fourteenth century constitute the

---

[1] The earliest translation seems to be that of *Tanḥuma*, Warsaw (1884), which was reprinted there in 1886 and 1896, and appeared in photocopied editions in Williamsburg (1963) and Israel (1964). A full translation of *Midrash Rabbah* appeared for the first time in Warsaw (1893–5), where it was reprinted several times (1898, 1913). Another full translation appeared in St Louis in 1919, and the well-known translation of the *Midrash Rabbah* (the Five Scrolls only) by Shimshon Dunsky was published in Montreal between 1957 and 1973.

[2] See Lajb Fuks, *The Oldest Known Literary Documents of Yiddish Literature (c.1382)*, 2 vols. (Leiden, 1957).

[3] See Walter Roll, 'Zu den ersten drei Texten der Cambridger Handschrift von 1382', *Zeitschrift für deutsches Altertum*, 104 (1975), 54–68; Dov Sadan, 'The Midrashic Background of "The Paradise" and its Implications for the Evaluation of the Cambridge Yiddish Codex (1382)', *The Field of Yiddish*, 2 (1965), 253–62; Wulf-Otto Dreessen, 'Midraschepik und Bibelepik: Biblische Stoffe in der volkssprachlichen Literatur der Juden und Christen des Mittelalters im deutschen Sprachgebiet', *Zeitschrift für deutsche Philologie*, 100 (1981), 78–97.

cornerstone of Old Yiddish epic poetry on biblical themes. They were followed, probably in the fifteenth century, by a more extensive poem on *akedat yitshak* (the binding of Isaac),[4] and later by the first confrontation of the genre with an entire biblical book, the book of Esther, which produced at least eleven versions.[5] In both cases a great variety of midrashic sources played a vital, but no longer exclusive, role. Other elements—mainly translations and interpretations of biblical passages—are interwoven in the narrative. The expansion of the genre towards the books of the Former Prophets in the second half of the fifteenth and the beginning of the sixteenth centuries brought about a decisive change in the thematic scope and narrative confines of the works, which resulted in a significant extension of the number of sources of elements used in these poems. The authors of these comprehensive epics, particularly the *Shmuel-bukh* (on the books of Samuel) and the *Melokhim-bukh* (on the books of Kings), the crowns of the genre, did not satisfy themselves with joining one midrashic element to another. They wove a strikingly rich mosaic-like fabric in which elements from the Bible and numerous midrashic and exegetical sources are organically integrated. The variety of their sources attests to the fact that these authors strove to make exhaustive use of every single story, commentary, or *midrash* that had ever been created on the pertinent biblical verses or on their subject matter.[6] The beginning of the seventeenth century marked the onset of the genre's gradual decline. In 1644 David ben Menahem, the author of a series of poems on the first seventeen portions of the Pentateuch and on four of the Five Megillot, which were collected in a single book *Mizmor letodah*, criticizes the use of midrashic sources and declares himself in favour of rhymed literal Yiddish translations of the biblical text.[7]

During the sixteenth century the genre of the *mayse*—mainly a religious or quasi-religious story in prose, at times comparable in scope to the Latin medieval *exemplum* and at others to the Italian *novella*—appeared and developed in Yiddish,

---

[4] See Percy Matenko and Samuel Sloan, 'The Aqedath Jishaq: A Sixteenth Century Yiddish Epic', in Percy Matenko, *Two Studies in Yiddish Culture* (Leiden, 1968), 3–70; Wulf-Otto Dreessen, *Akedass Jizhak: Ein Altjiddisches Gedicht über die Opferung Isaaks: Mit Einleitung und Kommentar kritisch herausgegeben* (Hamburg, 1971); id., 'Midraschepik und Bibelepik', 78–97.

[5] See Chone Shmeruk, 'Yiddish Long Poems on the Book of Esther to the Eighteenth Century' (Heb.), in id. (ed.), *Yiddish Biblical Plays 1697–1750, Edited from Manuscripts and Printed Versions with an Introduction by Chone Shmeruk* [Mahazot mikra'iyim beyidish, 1697–1750: hehedir lefi kitvei yad udefusim vehosif mavo hone shmeruk] (Jerusalem, 1979), 131–8; Wulf-Otto Dreessen, 'Die altjiddischen Estherdichtungen: Überlegungen zur Rekonstruktion der Geschichte der älteren jiddischen Literatur', *Daphnis*, 6 (1977), 218–33; Jutta Baum-Sheridan, *Studien zu den westjiddischen Estherdichtungen* (Hamburg, 1996).

[6] On the sources of the *Shmuel-bukh* see Felix Falk and Lajb Fuks (eds.), *Das Schemuelbuch des Mosche Esrim Wearba: Ein biblisches Epos aus dem 15. Jahrhundert*, vol. ii (Assen, 1961), 107–13. On those of the *Melokhim-bukh* see Lajb Fuks (ed.), *Das altjiddische Epos Melokim-buk*, vol. ii (Assen, 1965), 6–52.

[7] For a survey of the genre, see Chava Turniansky, 'On Old-Yiddish Biblical Epics', *International Folklore Review*, 8 (1991), 26–33; ead., 'The Research of the Yiddish Epic Poems on the Bible' (Heb.), *Newsletter of the World Union of Jewish Studies*, 27 (1987), 27–40; Chone Shmeruk, *Yiddish Literature: Aspects of Its History* [Sifrut yidish: perakim letoledoteiha] (Tel Aviv, 1978), 117–36.

drawing from several sources, but most intensely from the Talmud and Midrash.[8] It was the Ashkenazim in sixteenth-century northern Italy who initiated the genre and brought it to its peak.[9] They were the first to gather *mayses* into small collections; the oldest—sixteen *mayses* from *Lamentations Rabbah*—follows a fairly free translation of the festival prayer-book (*maḥzor*) preserved in a manuscript dated 1504. These *mayses* are intended for the Ninth of Av, and offer the oldest evidence that *mayses* first appeared as additions to, or insertions into, suitable contexts.[10] In a somewhat later manuscript (1510), four *mayses* from talmudic–midrashic sources precede a Yiddish translation of the Psalms, followed by two epic poems, one on the book of Joshua and the other on the book of Judges.[11] In a much more comprehensive and variegated miscellanea manuscript, completed in 1561, seven *mayses* appear, most of them of midrashic origin.[12] Another miscellanea manuscript, dated 1579, presents a free homiletic translation of Mishnah *Pirkei avot* (Chapters of the Fathers) into Yiddish, in which 45 *mayses* pertaining to the relevant *tana'im* (mishnaic sages) are interspersed. The translation is followed by 28 additional *mayses* of the same sort and of similar origin.[13] In an extensive anthology, dated 1580 and concerned exclusively with narrative prose of various kinds, there are 22 *mayses* taken from the Talmud or from the *Midrash aseret hadibrot* (Midrash on the Ten Commandments).[14]

The last two decades of the sixteenth century witnessed the transformation of the small, or relatively small, collections of *mayses* into large comprehensive compilations. About 130 *mayses*, most of them from the Talmud and the Midrash, appear in a manuscript written in an unknown place called 'Rovere' (northern Italy) around 1585–90 by Moshe Vaysvaser of Prague.[15] A similar collection of about 120 *mayses*

---

[8] On these and other sources of the *mayses* see Sara Zfatman, 'The *Mayse-Bukh*: An Old Yiddish Literary Genre' (Heb.), *Hasifrut*, 28 (1979), 126–52.

[9] See Chone Shmeruk, 'The Beginnings of Yiddish Narrative Prose and its Centre in Italy' (Heb.), in Daniel Carpi, Attilio Milano, and Alexander Rofé (eds.), *Scritti in memoria di Leone Carpi* [Sefer zikaron le'aryeh le'one karpi: kovets meḥkarim letoledot hayehudim be'italiyah] (Jerusalem, 1967), 119–40; Zfatman, 'The *Mayse-Bukh*' (Heb.).

[10] See Chava Turniansky and Erika Timm, *Yiddish in Italia: Yiddish Manuscripts and Printed Books from the 15th to the 17th Century* (Milan, 2003), no. 12, p. 20; Sarah Zfatman, *Yiddish Narrative Prose from Its Beginnings to* Shivḥei habesht *(1504–1814): An Annotated Bibliography* [Hasiporet beyidish mereshitah ad 'Shivḥei habesht' (1504–1814): bibliografiyah mu'eret] (Jerusalem, 1985), 11, item *alef*.

[11] See Turniansky and Timm, *Yiddish in Italia*, no. 10, p. 16; Zfatman, *Yiddish Narrative Prose*, 11, item *bet*.

[12] See Turniansky and Timm, *Yiddish in Italia*, no. 47, pp. 96–7; Zfatman, *Yiddish Narrative Prose*, 13, item *dalet*.

[13] For the critical edition of the entire manuscript see Anshel Levi, *An Old Yiddish Midrash on the 'Chapters of the Fathers'* [Midrash lefirkei avot beyidish kama'it], ed. Ya'akov Maitlis (Jerusalem, 1978). For brief information see Turniansky and Timm, *Yiddish in Italia*, no. 48, p. 100; Zfatman, *Yiddish Narrative Prose*, 14, item *heh*.

[14] Ibid. 15–18, item *vav*. For single *mayses* of talmudic–midrashic origin preserved in manuscripts of this period see Zfatman, *Yiddish Narrative Prose*, 18–19, item *heh*; 22–3, item *yod-alef*.

[15] 'Rovere' is probably either Rovereto or Rovere della Luna, both near Trento. See Turniansky and Timm, *Yiddish in Italia*, no. 64, p. 126; Erika Timm, 'Zur Frühgeschichte der jiddischen Erzählprosa:

was written by Shmuel Bak of the same 'Rovere' for his aunt in Innsbruck during a visit to her in 1596.[16] These two kindred manuscript collections were the precursors of *Eyn shoyn Mayse-bukh* (A Beautiful Book of Stories), which was printed in Basel in 1602 and reprinted many times during the seventeenth and eighteenth centuries and even later.[17] The *Mayse-bukh* comprises 257 stories,[18] more than half of them (at least 150) from various talmudic and midrashic sources.[19] Many of these *mayses*—although bearing various linguistic and stylistic differences—appear in the earlier manuscript collections.[20]

This brief survey clearly attests to the development and flourishing of the *mayse* genre within one century. It also demonstrates the transitions involved, first from the individual story to small and growing clusters of stories among literary items of other kinds, and then to comprehensive compilations of stories alone. The permanent function of the Talmud and the Midrash as main sources becomes obvious, whether the stories are derived directly from them or via intermediaries, such as *Ein ya'akov*[21]—Jacob ibn Habib's extensive collection of nearly all the aggadic passages of the Talmud in the original language, which was printed several times in the sixteenth century—or other Hebrew sources and compilations.

While the ample and extensive use of aggadic–talmudic and midrashic material for the sake of the above-mentioned Yiddish genres—the biblical epic and the narrative prose—is conspicuous, the use of these sources in many other kinds of Yiddish works is less noticeable and needs to be revealed by detailed research. Thus, for example, Targum Sheni, the Talmud tractate *Megilah*, and *Esther Rabbah* are the sources for the long poem on Purim (1128 lines) written in Venice around 1553–4 by a *melamed* (children's teacher) from Poland;[22] and many midrashic elements appear in *Targum ḥamesh megilot*, Jacob ben Samuel Bunem's poetic adaptation into Yiddish of the Aramaic translation of the Five Megillot (Freiburg, 1584). The presence of aggadah and Midrash in Yiddish homiletic prose—and especially in the most popular *Tsene-rene*,[23] as well as in the paraphrastic translations of the Bible into

---

Eine neuaufgefundene Maise-Handschrift', *Beiträge zur Geschichte der deutschen Sprache und Literatur*, 117 (1995), 243–80. The last pages of the manuscript contain a Yiddish translation of the *midrash Eleh ezkerah*.

[16] See Turniansky and Timm, *Yiddish in Italia*, no. 65, p. 128; Zfatman, 'The *Mayse-Bukh*' (Heb.).

[17] See Zfatman, *Yiddish Narrative Prose*, 36–9, no. 17.

[18] The title page promises 'more than 300 *mayses*'. On this number see Timm, 'Zur Frühgeschichte der jiddischen Erzählprosa', 270–2.   [19] See Zfatman, *Yiddish Narrative Prose*, 38.

[20] See Timm, 'Zur Frühgeschichte der jiddischen Erzählprosa', 273–6.

[21] Ibid. 262–3.   [22] See Turniansky and Timm, *Yiddish in Italia*, no. 60, p. 120.

[23] We do not know when the *Tsene-rene* was written nor when it was first printed. It consists of a rendering in Yiddish of the Pentateuch, the Megillot, and the *haftarot* (prophetic readings), making use of numerous sources, including Midrash, Talmud, Rashi (1040–1105), and other exegetes, particularly Bahya ben Asher (d. 1340). The earliest extant edition appeared in 1622 (apparently in Hanau and not in Basle as is stated on the title page) in two parts, one on the Torah and the other on the Five Scrolls and the *haftarot*. According to the title page of the section on the Torah, which mentions three earlier editions, one in Lublin followed by two in Kraków, this is the fourth edition. See Jacob Elbaum and

Yiddish—has not yet been researched, and the same applies to other genres, whether the use of Midrash in them is an a priori conjecture or not.

KHURBN BEYS HAMIKDESH — THE DESTRUCTION OF THE TEMPLE

The case study for our contribution to this volume is a hitherto unresearched Yiddish collection of aggadot on the destruction of the Temple in a booklet of twelve pages (4to) with no title page, no title, and no mention of the author, the year, or the place of publication. This booklet, probably a unicum, was discovered by Sara Zfatman in the Stadt- und Universitätsbibliothek in Frankfurt am Main. Opposite the first page, a librarian's annotation in Roman characters reads: 'Chorban ha-Bait [Krakau 1583]'.[24] Although there is no doubt that the booklet was printed in the printing house of Isaac ben Aaron of Prostits in Kraków (1569–1612), the precise date of printing is not known. An item called *Khurbn habayis be-loshn Ashkenaz* (The Destruction of the Temple in Yiddish), which appears in the lists of books submitted by the Jews of Mantua for Church censorship in 1595,[25] may point to our booklet and assist us in establishing the *terminus ad quem* of its printing.

The significance of this booklet lies in two main factors: (1) it includes the fullest collection of sequences of talmudic narrative in Yiddish that we know of up to its time; (2) it coincides entirely—except for a few small differences in vocabulary and style—with the distinct cluster of stories entitled *Khurbn* or *Khurbn beys hamikdesh* that appears in the *Tsene-rene* after the discussion of the book of Lamentations. If this collection is an original component of the *Tsene-rene*, and perhaps even if not, there is much to be learned from it about the manner in which this foundational text of Yiddish literature was consolidated.

1. The Characteristics of the Collection

At first glance it would seem that the author of *Khurbn beys hamikdesh* carried out an act of pure compilation. From Babylonian Talmud *Gitin* 52*b*–58*a* he translated into

---

Chava Turniansky, 'Tsene-rene', *The YIVO Encyclopedia of Jews in Eastern Europe*, 2. vols. (New Haven, Conn., 2008), ii. 1912–3.

[24] For this and further information on the booklet see Sara Zfatman, '"Khurbn habayis", Kraków before 1595: One More Yiddish Print from Poland in the 16th Century' (Heb.), *Kiryat sefer*, 54 (1979), 201–2; Chone Shmeruk, *Yiddish Literature in Poland: Historical Studies and Perspectives* [Sifrut yidish bepolin: meḥkarim ve'iyunim historiyim] (Jerusalem, 1981), nos. 61, 114; Shifra Baruchson-Arbib, *Books and Readers: The Reading Interests of Italian Jews at the Close of the Renaissance* [Sefarim vekorim: tarbut hakeriah shel yehudei italiyah beshilhei harenesans] (Ramat Gan, 1993), 157. A later, most accurate edition of the booklet, following a paraphrastic rendering into Yiddish of the book of Lamentations, appeared in *Khurbn beys hamikdesh mit megilles eykho* (Pest, 1862) (digital photograph provided by the Stadt- und Universitätsbibliothek in Frankfurt am Main).

[25] See Agnes Romer-Segal, 'Yiddish Literature and its Readers in the 16th Century: Books in the Censor's Lists, Mantua 1595' (Heb.), *Kiryat sefer*, 53 (1978), 779–88.

Yiddish a collection of stories on the destruction of the Temple, incorporated a story from tractate *Ta'anit* for completion,[26] and added to it most of Petiḥta 24 from *Lamentations Rabbah*.[27] Yet even a superficial comparison shows that the text is not in any way identical to the sources—neither in its sequence nor in its details. The author does not use the entire talmudic text from *Gitin* but deletes certain units;[28] in addition, he occasionally alters the order of the content, creates his own links between the elements of the narrative, and adds supplementary material from other sources. But this is not the most important trait. What is more fundamental is the author's assumption of the authority to add to and detract from the details of the stories, as a result of which some of them undergo changes that affect their very nature. Indeed, an examination of the stories themselves, sentence by sentence, in close comparison with their sources, reveals that there is not one story in the entire collection that is a precise reflection of the original text. Although it is well known that any translation made according to the considerations of the target language automatically results in changes of presentation—in terms of idioms, syntax, and the like—it is still possible to distinguish between a modification necessitated by the act of translation and a change made by a translator who allows himself the freedom of translating the text as he desires—a factor which creates a distance between his translation and its source.

A thorough examination of these phenomena requires a detailed comparison of each and every story of the source text against its Yiddish version, followed by a detailed discussion of the results. Since this task is impossible in the framework of this study, we shall merely mention a few of the phenomena.

The author opens his collection in the same manner as the source in *Gitin*—with the words of Rabbi Yohanan, which constitute a sort of exposition of the first story: 'What is meant by the verse, "Happy is the man that feareth always, but he that hardeneth his heart shall fall into mischief"? The destruction of Jerusalem came through a Kamza and a Bar Kamza.' There is no doubt that the verse quoted here (Prov. 28: 14) is quite difficult to translate literally in the manner of the *taytsh*—the traditional word-for-word translation of the Bible into Yiddish. The writer thus chose to interpret it, which he does following the commentary of Ralbag (Rabbi Levi ben Gershom, 1288–1344), available in the editions of *Mikraot gedolot* printed in the sixteenth century. Ralbag's interpretation, 'It was the hardening of the heart

---

[26] See below, section 3.

[27] Translations have been taken from: Jacob Neusner, *Lamentations Rabbah: An Analytical Translation* (Atlanta, Ga., 1989); *Hebrew-English Edition of the Babylonian Talmud: Tractate Gittin*, trans. Maurice Simon, ed. Isidore Epstein (London, 1977). In some instances alterations were made for the sake of greater accuracy.

[28] For example, compare BT *Git.* 57a on the verse: 'The Lord hath swallowed up all the habitations of Jacob and hath not pitied' (Lam. 2: 2) and *Khurbn*, 6a. As usual, even the brief talmudic text quoted is not provided with an attribution. So also regarding the matter which immediately follows: 'Once when R. Manyumi b. Helkiah and R. Helkiah b. Tobiah and R. Huna b. Hiya were sitting together they said: if anyone knows anything about Kefar Sekania of Egypt, let him say', translated as 'Three scholars were sitting together. They spoke thus: anyone who can say something about the city of Kefar Sekania, speak.' There are many other similar cases.

that destroyed the First and the Second Temples', also connects with the subject of the first story, about the shaming of Bar Kamza that led to his denunciation of the Jews to the Roman emperor. Indeed, the integration of materials derived from other sources into the talmudic text for the purpose of expounding the narrative has far-reaching consequences in several instances. These may clearly be observed in relation to the following two matters in our collection. The first is the supplement added to the mention of Nakdimon ben Gorion and the rising of the sun. The author, unsatisfied with the mere hint at this matter in *Gitin*, retells the entire story from the Babylonian Talmud, *Ta'anit* 19b–20a (with some changes in style, which will be commented on shortly). The second example is the integration of details from the 'tale of a woman and her seven sons' (*Lam. Rabbah* 1: 50) into the similar story in *Gitin*, while retaining the outline and style of the talmudic source.

The order of the contents of the collection in *Gitin* was largely preserved. However, the author of *Khurbn beys hamikdesh* departs from this order when he transfers the story about Martha, daughter of Boethius, 'the wealthiest woman of Jerusalem', from its original location (in *Gitin* 56b), after the mention of the three rich Jerusalemites and before the story about Abba Sikra, to after the story about Abba Sikra and the meeting of Rabbi Yohanan ben Zakkai with Vespasian, who was to become emperor. The differences in sequence are summarized in this table:

Gitin	*Khurbn*
Kamza and bar Kamza	Kamza and bar Kamza
Emperor Nero	Emperor Nero
Emperor Aspasian	Emperor Aspasian
Three rich Jerusalemites	Three rich Jerusalemites
Nakdimon	Nakdimon
	Nakdimon and the Bishop (from *Ta'anit*)
Kalba Sabua, Ben Tsitsit Hakeset	Kalba Sabua, Ben Tsitsit Hakeset
Martha daughter of Boethius	Abba Sikra
Abba Sikra	Yohanan ben Zakkai and Vespasian
Yohanan ben Zakkai and Vespasian	Martha daughter of Boethius
Titus	Titus
Onkelos	Onkelos
The destruction of Tur Malka	The destruction of Tur Malka
Three sages about Kefar Sekania	Three sages about Kefar Sekania
The man who wished to divorce his wife	The man who wished to divorce his wife
The destruction of Beitar	The destruction of Beitar
The blood of Zechariah	The blood of Zechariah
The four hundred children	The four hundred children
The woman and her seven children	The woman and her seven children
The synagogues of Beitar	The synagogues of Beitar
Joshua ben Hananiah in Rome	Joshua ben Hananiah in Rome
The son and daughter of Ishmael ben Elisha	The son and daughter of Ishmael ben Elisha
The carpenter's apprentice	The carpenter's apprentice
	Petiḥta 24 from *Lamentations Rabbah*

We cannot satisfactorily explain the displacement of this story from its natural location in the collection in *Gitin*, although it may have been moved in order to emphasize the degree of despair felt by Rabbi Yohanan ben Zakkai, which motivated his request for some minor favours of Vespasian. In any case, the removal of the story from its natural place seems to have induced the author to elaborate at the end of it the reason for Rabbi Zadok's 'illness'—which is explained in the story about Martha, daughter of Boethius, and is easily understood by anyone reading our collection consecutively—and to return to the subject within the story about the rich woman approximately as it appears in the talmudic source. Despite the twice-repeated mention of Rabbi Zadok's fast, there is no mention of the treatment of his illness, which in the Talmud is attached to the story about Rabbi Yohanan and Vespasian.

2. Verses and their Translations

As noted earlier, it is impossible to discuss fully the changes which occurred in the stories as a result of their translation. However, one striking point must be addressed, and this is the issue of the biblical verses.[29] Verses used in a translated story often needed clarification on three levels: (a) quotation; (b) literal translation; and (c) explanation. For example, the segment of the anecdote about Nero in the second story in *Gitin* (56*b*): 'He said to a certain boy: Repeat to me [the last] verse of Scripture you have learnt. He said: "And I will lay my vengeance upon Edom by the hand of my people Israel"[30] [Ezek. 25: 14]', reads in *Khurbn beys hamikdesh* as follows:

Later on he found a young child and said to him: Tell me a verse—for he wanted to try his luck and see which verse the child would tell him. The child then told him the verse "And I will lay my vengeance upon Edom by the hand of my people Israel." This means: Our Lord God said: I will have vengeance on Edom because of [or: on behalf of] My people Israel. That is: when Edom will destroy the Temple, and send My people into exile, after that I will have vengeance on him.

It seems obvious that, since the author had decided to include this story, he could not avoid citing the verse which stands at its centre. At the same time it is evident that when the explicit verse was not absolutely necessary, the author preferred to circumvent it, as he does in the story of Titus, the source of which opens with: 'Vespasian sent to Titus, who said, "Where is their God, the rock in whom they trusted" [Deut. 32: 37]. This was the wicked Titus, who blasphemed and insulted

---

[29] On the use of biblical verses by the sages see Jonah Fraenkel, *The Aggadic Narrative: Harmony of Form and Content* [Sipur ha'agadah: aḥdut shel tokhen vetsurah] (Tel Aviv, 2001), 198–219. For an earlier version, see id., 'Bible Verses Quoted in Tales of the Sages', in Joseph Heinemann and Dov Noy (eds.), *Studies in Aggadah and Folk Literature* (Jerusalem, 1971), 80–99.

[30] Most of the following translations of biblical verses into English are taken from the Jewish Publication Society 1917 version, but at times we used those that appear in English versions of the Talmud and *Lamentations Rabbah* (see above, n. 27). All translations from *Khurbn beys hamikdesh* are ours.

Heaven. What did he do? He took a harlot by the hand and entered the Holy of Holies.' The author begins his translation as follows:

So the emperor went to Rome and sent the evil Titus to Jerusalem. When he came, he conquered the city and said: Where is the God of Israel in whom they trust and hope, why does he not come and save them? What did he do? He took a prostitute and went in with her into the Temple, into the Holy of Holies itself, where no one was allowed to enter during the whole year except for the High Priest on Yom Kippur.

In this case the author has chosen to paraphrase the verse in order to make matters easier for his readers, and for that purpose he has also explained the significance of entering the Holy of Holies. Here again, the author avoids quoting verses wherever he is able to do so. Any comparison of the translation with the source in *Gitin* shows that all the contextual midrashic elaborations of verses that are not essential to the substance of the stories, but rather additions intended to teach a moral lesson, or to serve as links between issues or components of the narrative, are not reproduced by the author of *Khurbn beys hamikdesh*. An instance in which the original link was exchanged for another, because the author disconnected the story from the verse that preceded it in the source, will be discussed later on when dealing with the tale of the woman and her seven sons.

An illuminating example of the 'translator's' role with regard to the use of verses may be observed in the story about Rabbi Yohanan ben Zakkai and Vespasian. The story is replete with verses, the most important of which is, 'And Lebanon shall fall by a mighty one' (Isa. 10: 34).[31] A comparison of the source with the 'translation' demonstrates that the author of *Khurbn beys hamikdesh* attempted to avoid the complex midrashic explanation in the original and preferred to present only what follows from it. One of the results of this omission is that the claim that the Temple will only be destroyed at the hands of a king lacks substantiation, for it is not corroborated by a verse citation. The reader may wonder what verse Rabbi Yohanan used in his conversation with Vespasian, which apparently motivated his actions (or at least justified his appraisals) concerning the current events, created an opportunity to reveal what was expected to happen in the future, and granted him the necessary confidence to persuade Vespasian that the royal crown was already waiting for him in distant Rome. The source reads:

He [Vespasian] said: Your life is forfeit on two accounts, one because I am not a king and you call me a king, and again, if I am a king, why did you not come to me before now? He replied: As for your saying that you are not a king, in truth you are a king, since if you were not a king Jerusalem would not be delivered into your hand, as it is written, 'And Lebanon shall fall by a mighty one' [Isa. 10: 34]. 'Mighty one' [is an epithet] applied only to a king, as it is written, 'And their mighty one shall be of themselves, etc.' [Jer. 30: 21]; and Lebanon refers to the Sanctuary, as it says, 'This goodly mountain and Lebanon' [Deut. 3: 25].

---

[31] See the observation of Fraenkel, *The Aggadic Narrative* (Heb.), 212–18, who hints at additional discussions of this well-known story.

In contrast, the Yiddish version reads:[32]

Then said the emperor to Rabbi Yohanan: You are twice guilty: once, you call me king [but] I am not a king, so you are mocking me. Secondly, if I am a king, why did you not come out to [see] me until now? Then said Rabbi Yohanan: You say that you are not a king, but you are indeed a king, because I know that Jerusalem and the temple will be delivered into your hand, and we learn that from the verse that [says] the Temple will not be delivered except into the hand of a king. If you were not a king, Jerusalem could not be delivered into your hand.

Notwithstanding this tendency, the author of *Khurbn beys hamikdesh* does not delete all verses. Several sentences later he quotes the verse '[God] turneth wise men backward, and maketh their knowledge foolish' (Isa. 44: 25), which he places in the mouth of Rabbi Akiva (according to the method he uses wherever there are several attributions), instead of pointing out, as does the source, that 'some say' it was Rabbi Akiva. Shortly thereafter he also quotes the verse 'And good tidings make the bone fat' (Prov. 15: 30). In this case the author was able to adhere to the source and simply introduce these verses of wisdom, since they do not require an explanation that would interfere with the flow of the text.[33]

3. The Stories

As mentioned earlier, the author of *Khurbn beys hamikdesh* expanded on the story about Nakdimon ben Gorion found in tractate *Ta'anit* of the Babylonian Talmud (19b–20a). He reproduced the opening sentence from *Gitin* 56a: 'There were in it [Jerusalem] three men of great wealth, Nakdimon ben Gorion, Ben Kalba Sabua, and Ben Tsitsit Hakeset', but transformed the sequel, 'Nakdimon ben Gorion was so called because the sun continued shining for his sake', into a sort of introduction that includes information not found in his source. He also added clarification of the source's condensed wording: 'And these names were not their real names. The first one was called Nakdimon because a miracle happened to him, in that the sun shone on his behalf longer than was usual for it to shine at any other time.'[34] With this sentence providing a transition device, he moves to the story from *Ta'anit*.

---

[32] The cursive script points to the author's independent additions.

[33] Following this, the author of *Khurbn beys hamikdesh* changes the continuation of the story—incidentally this change omits the quotation of the verse: 'But a broken spirit drieth the bones' (Prov. 17: 22)—and introduces only the explanation appropriate to his subject matter: 'When one sees an enemy before him, his bone turns thin.' There are similar examples: one at the close of the story in BT *Gitin* about the son and daughter of Rabbi Ishmael, which concludes with the words '"For them Jeremiah utters lamentation [Lam. 1: 15]"—*For these I am weeping, mine eye, mine eye drops water*' (Git. 58a), translated in *Khurbn* as 'For these *Jeremiah the prophet* lamented my eyes drip down water.'

[34] See *Khurbn*, 2a. These words of introduction are built upon the tradition found in BT *Ta'an.* 20a: 'His name was not Nakdimon ben Boni and he was called Nakdimon because the sun had broken through [*nikdera*] on his behalf,' translated in *Khurbn*: 'for this reason was he called Nakdimon—it is translated as "shine", because of him the sun shone; alternatively his real name was Boni'.

His decision to insert it here is not obvious. Inasmuch as this story is a clear digression from the main issue of the collection—the destruction of the Temple—the compiler presumably weighed up the digression against the irresistible appeal of this classic story, and deliberately chose to incorporate it into his text.[35]

The story itself follows the framework of the source, but the Yiddish author, as is his wont, introduces explanations wherever he deems these necessary for his readers, or because he wishes to instruct them in the manner of all those who wrote for readers whose acquaintance with the Hebrew sources came only through Yiddish. It is for this reason that he adds to his citation from the source ('It once happened that the Israelites came to Jerusalem for the festivals, and there was not enough water [in the city] for drinking purposes' (*Ta'anit* 19*b*)) this explanatory rewording: 'Once all [the people of] Israel came to Jerusalem for the festival because at Passover, at Shavuot, and at Sukkot all Israel had to come to Jerusalem. Once all Israel went [there] and they had no water to drink.' In the following sentences, as in many similar instances when he seems unsatisfied with the impersonal marker 'he said to him', the author specifies the names of the speakers (for example, *da shprakh der tsadik tsu dem hegmon*, that is: 'the pious man said to the bishop'). At the same time he exchanges a nickname (Nakdimon ben Gorion) for the real name (Boni ben Gorion), and expands short sentences. Thus, instead of simply translating the source 'And he fixed with him a time', our translator writes: 'And he fixed with him a time when he could deliver the wells or the money to him', and goes on to explain what Nakdimon means by 'I have still time' by expanding the phrase: 'a lot of rain can come, so that your wells will be full again'. When confronted with idiomatic phrases and expressions, the author sometimes omits them (as he does with 'the Holy One caused the world to storm only on thy account') or remodels them (as, for instance, when instead of Nakdimon's invocation to the Creator, 'Announce to the world that Thou hast favourites here on earth!', he has him say, 'Show the world that we are the beloved ones on this earth [*Vayz der velt daz mir zayn di gilibtn in oylem*]'.[36] It is also characteristic of this author that, having concretized the abstract subject of the sentence in the source, he further elaborates: 'and just as you performed a miracle for me with the rain, perform a miracle for me with the sun'.

*

The author of *Khurbn beys hamikdesh* diversifies the opening formulae of the stories he brings into his compilation (*es gishakh ayn mayse, ayn mayse iz gishehn, ayn mayse gishakh*, meaning 'it once happened', 'an event occurred') and even begins the tale of the woman and her seven sons in quite a different manner from that of his main

---

[35] On this story see Jacob Elbaum, 'Nakdimon ben Gorion and the Bishop: On the Nature of One Jerusalemite Story' (Heb.), *Gilyonot lamoreh*, 5–6 (1977), 28–34.

[36] It is worthwhile to compare the 'translation' of these passages (and of the story as a whole) in *Khurbn beys hamikdesh* with an apparently earlier translation; see Levi, *An Old Yiddish Midrash*, 131–2. Without going into details we may note that Levi's 'translation' is rather more accurate.

source in *Gitin* 57*b*. While there the story is brought as an additional illustration to the verse 'Yea, for Thy sake we are killed all the day long' (Ps. 44: 23), in *Khurbn beys hamikdesh* it is introduced directly as an independent tale with no mention of the verse. However, in this case the modification is not a result of the author's conception alone, but is already found in the text of *Lamentations Rabbah* 1: 50, from which he draws details to complete his version of the story. Yet it is perfectly clear that he does not replace one source with the other; nor does he adapt all the details found in the second source, but rather integrates them and builds up a new, compound version. Here too, as throughout his compilation, he modifies or omits details from his sources on one hand, but on the other hand adds elements of his own when he feels that the brevity of the source may hinder understanding. Thus, for example, the story in *Lamentations Rabbah* opens: 'There was a case of Miriam, daughter of Tanhum, who was taken captive with her seven sons.' It is from this source that the detail about the children being taken captive—which does not appear in the talmudic source—was added to the version of the story in *Khurbn beys hamikdesh*, but the name of the mother, as well as the fact that she was also taken captive, is not mentioned ('there was a case of a woman that had seven sons who were taken captive').

As a rule, matters that seem unclear in the source story are explained. For example, 'the first' [son] (in *Git.* and in *Lam. Rabbah*) is translated as 'the eldest'. From there on the boys are listed in the same manner as in *Lamentations Rabbah* (the second, the third, the fourth, and so on). The overall influence of *Lamentations Rabbah* is quite obvious throughout, and it seems that the Yiddish author superimposed this version on that from *Gitin*, adding his own supplements according to the subject matter. Thus, the emperor's command in the Yiddish version, 'Bow down to the *avodah zarah* [idol]', is assembled from 'Worship the *avodah zarah*' (*Git.* 57*b*) and 'Bow down to the *tselem* [image]' (*Lam. Rabbah*). There are various other examples of this kind.

The most obvious element 'imported' from *Lamentations Rabbah* is that of the biblical verses employed by the seven sons as arguments for their refusal to obey the emperor. There is no doubt that the writer preferred the verses quoted in *Lamentations Rabbah* to those cited in *Gitin*. Similarly, he specifically favoured the more lengthy style of the discussion between the seventh son and the emperor as it appears in this midrashic source. In his usual manner he also made some additions, including a slightly strange one added to the translation of the sentence: 'Your brothers have had their fill of years and life and have had happiness,' which in *Khurbn beys hamikdesh* reads, 'Look, your brothers lived long and indulged in a lot of good living [*fil guts ginet*], it is [therefore] no wonder that they let themselves be killed.'

According to his overall method of shaping the stories in his collection, the author indicates who speaks whenever the source reads 'he said' (which appears in both his sources and is the common designation of the speaker in the Talmud as well as in the Midrash). For purposes of clarification he also adds his own explicit comments to the verses used to justify the refusal to worship idols, for example: 'I will not bow down to that [piece of] wood' (says the first son), 'therefore I will not worship your god' (says the second), and 'therefore I will not have your god' (says the sixth).

All this notwithstanding, it would seem that the most essential feature our author introduces into the mechanism of this rabbinic story is that of variation. In contrast to the repeated attempts of all stories of this kind to retain a uniform style and language—as is illustrated by the care taken to use the same expressions throughout the rabbinic narrative—the author of *Khurbn beys hamikdesh* chooses to highlight variations of one kind or another. Such concern for diversity brings about notable change with respect to the question, 'Is there a divinity in the world?' In *Lamentations Rabbah* the question is followed by a description of the Creator in human form, which is built entirely on Psalms 115: 2–8. The adaptation of the details of this biblical sequence by the emperor (in the *Lam. Rabbah* version) clearly indicates that the storyteller presents the ruler as searching for a divinity with human attributes. Yet the young child repeatedly instructs him that God only has the *qualities* of the human organs and their power, and that this—and not their corporeal constitution—is the intention of the personification employed in these biblical expressions. The transformation of the extended dialogue in *Khurbn beys hamikdesh* into a long (but condensed) monologue by the young child appears to betray the writer's distaste for repetition. The result is to focus attention on the meaning of the 'attributes' to which the emperor referred, finding climactic expression at the close of the discourse: 'If your God is that strong, why doesn't He save you from my hands as Hananiah, Mishael, and Azariah were saved from Nebuchadnezzar, who had them thrown into the lime oven?'

This instance illustrates another characteristic of our author's adaptation of the sources. Even while adding certain explanations (for example, what Hananiah, Mishael, and Azariah were saved from), he also removes phrases intended only to embellish or intensify the content. Thus whereas *Lamentations Rabbah* reads, 'If you do not kill us, the Holy One, blessed be He, has many killers, many bears, many wolves, and lions, and snakes, and leopards, and scorpions who can harm us and kill us. But the Holy One, blessed be He, will exact from you vengeance for our blood in the future,' the translation reads, 'And if you would not kill us, our God has many agents who could have killed us. But our God [Himself] will take vengeance on you for our blood.' Similar reasons, as well as changing concepts of female modesty, may have induced the author to remove a feature from the description of the mother's actions towards her son: 'They gave her [her son], and she took out her breasts and nursed him.' Another omission occurs at the end of the story, where the author of *Khurbn beys hamikdesh* returns to the version of the story in *Gitin*. He merely mentions that a voice came forth, and said, 'The mother of the children rejoices' (Ps. 113: 9), and omits the entire conclusion of the *derashah* in *Lamentations Rabbah* with its three scriptural passages: 'To fulfil what is said [in the Scriptures], "She who has borne seven sons languished" [Jer. 15: 9]'; 'and a voice came forth saying,

"The mother of the children rejoices" [Ps. 113: 9]', 'and the Holy Spirit screaming, "For these things I weep" [Lam. 1: 16]'.

*

We will now give a synoptic presentation of the tale of a man who developed a desire for his master's wife, which is narrated at the conclusion of the cycle of stories both in *Gitin* and *Khurbn beys hamikdesh*:[37]

BT *Gitin 19a*	*Khurbn beys hamikdesh*
R. Judah said in the name of Rav: What is signified by the verse 'And they oppress a man and his house, even a man and his heritage?' [Micah 2: 2]	
A certain man once conceived a desire for the wife of his master, he being a carpenter's apprentice.	Once upon a time there was a man who developed a liking for the wife of his master, who had taught him a trade, and he didn't know how to get her.
Once his master needed to borrow [money].	Once his master needed money and he asked him to lend it to him.
He said to him: Send your wife to me and I will lend her the money. So he sent his wife to him, And she stayed for three days with him. He then went to him and asked Where is my wife whom I sent to you? He replied: I sent her away at once, but I heard that some youngsters abused her on the road. He said to him: What shall I do? He said to him: If you listen to my advice, divorce her. He said to him: She has a large *ketubah* [marriage settlement]. He said to him: I will lend you (the money), and give her her *ketubah*.	So he said to him: Send your wife to me, and I will send it with her. So he sent his wife and he kept her with him for three days. Then his master came and asked him: Where is my wife that I sent to you? So he said: I had her go home immediately but I was told that on the road she frolicked a lot. He said: What shall I do with her? He said: Will you obey me? Divorce her. Then he said: She has a large *ketubah*. I do not have [enough] to pay her. He said: I will lend you (the money).
So he went and divorced her and the other went and married her.	So he took the money and divorced her and gave her [her] *ketubah*. As soon as the master divorced her, he married her.

---

[37] *Khurbn*, 9a. Before this story and after the tale of R. Ishmael b. Elisha's son and daughter is the story of Resh Lakish about Zofnat bat Paniel (BT *Git. 58a*), which is not included in *Khurbn beys hamikdesh*.

When the time for payment arrived	Then came the time to pay back the money he had lent him for the *ketubah*,
and he was not able to pay him,	and he did not have [the money] to pay.
	Then he said to him: Pay me back my money. So he said: I have none.
He said to him:	He said to him: Since you have no money,
Come and work off your debt with me.	be my servant and work off the money for me.
So they used to sit and eat and drink while he waited on them,	So he had to be his servant, [and] when he with his wife ate and drank he had to stand by the table and pour [their wine] for them.
and tears used to fall from his eyes and drop into their cups.	And his tears fell into the cup.
From that hour the doom was sealed;	At that time it was sealed that Jerusalem would be destroyed.
some however say that it was for two wicks in one light.	
	May God let us merit to build it again soon in our days. Amen.

In *Gitin* the story is reported by Rabbi Judah in the name of Rav (as is the preceding story about the son and daughter of Rabbi Ishmael ben Elisha), whereas the author of *Khurbn beys hamikdesh* edits out the names of the speakers and the quotation from Micah, and moves directly to the story. As in the earlier stories adapted from the *Gitin* cycle, here, too, the basic structure of the narrative is retained, along with changes in the details—many of which alter the very nature of the story. For example, the author tends to add explanatory sentences, specifically those which either reveal—at the content level—the motivations behind the characters' actions (while in the rabbinic story these motives are usually uncovered only through the actions themselves), or complete—at the narrative level—partial or fragmentary sentences, both of which are characteristic features of the rabbinic story in general. To the 'factual' sentence in the exposition of the story, that the man 'conceived a desire for the wife of his master', the author of *Khurbn beys hamikdesh* added: 'and did not know how to get her'. This change transforms the apprentice (who is not referred to as a carpenter's apprentice in the Yiddish version, since it was already explained that the 'master' taught him a trade),[38] into someone obsessed with thoughts bearing on the fulfilment of his desire. This sharpening of the base

---

[38] It is almost certain that the author of *Khurbn beys hamikdesh* used Rashi's commentary when he converted the sentence 'he being a carpenter's apprentice' into 'who taught him a trade'.

qualities of the apprentice is also evident from the transformation of the sentence: 'but I heard that some youngsters abused her on the road' into 'but I was told that on the road she frolicked a lot'. This revision transforms the woman from the victim of abuse to the initiator of an act of immorality. The translation of the sentence 'So he went and divorced her and the other went and married her' by '*As soon as* the master had divorced her, he married her' also gives more emphasis to the apprentice's tenacity than appears in the source.

Other changes follow: the bluntness of the Yiddish rendering of the sentence 'Come and work off your debt with me' is much stronger than the phrase used in the source.[39] The additional conclusion, 'so he had to be his servant', which recurs in the summarizing scene: 'And he had to stand by the table and pour [their wine] for them', provides the Yiddish reader with information that the Hebrew reader arrives at independently; moreover, it serves to emphasize the cruelty of the apprentice. Thus, overall, the 'translator' chooses to reinforce what is said in the source by means of various additions (including dialogue), and also explicates what the reader of the talmudic source would need to infer.[40] At the conclusion of the story, the author of *Khurbn beys hamikdesh* chose not to translate the alternative reason for the destruction of the Temple quoted in his source: 'some however say that it was for two wicks in one light'. It is not clear whether this choice was due to the difficulty of translating the metaphor, or simply because of the problematic formulation noted by several commentators.[41]

*

The section in *Khurbn beys hamikdesh* that comprises the selection of stories from tractate *Gitin* concludes with the wish (absent in the source): 'May God let us merit to rebuild [Jerusalem] soon in our days, Amen.' What follows is a rendering of most of Petiḥta 24 of *Lamentations Rabbah* (according to the printed edition). The 'translator' skips over the whole section in which Isaiah 22: 1–12 is expounded verse by verse, and begins with the midrashic elaboration of Psalms 42: 5: 'These things I remember and pour out my soul within me', which is linked to the last-mentioned verse, Isaiah 22: 12 ('My Lord God of Hosts summoned on that day to weeping and lamenting, to tonsuring and girding with sackcloth').[42] Our Yiddish author deals with his selection of subjects from Petiḥta 24 according to the methods and principles already discussed: he omits the 'demonstrative' verses that often impede the

---

[39] The sentence 'Come and work off your debt with me' is translated as 'Be my servant and work off the money for me.' It is unnecessary to say that this is not a literal translation of the Hebrew text. As was already mentioned, this sentence follows a long dialogue (not found in the source), which leads gradually to the choice (or lack thereof) expressed in the sentence 'so he had to be his servant' (also not found in the source).

[40] Similarly, it is possible to say that this was also the method of a number of Hebrew writers adapting tales of the sages during the Middle Ages.

[41] The phrase seems to have sexual connotations. See e.g. Rashi on BT *Git.* 58a, and R. Samuel Edels (Maharsha), *Ḥidushei agadot*, ad loc.

[42] Although the translator does quote the verse, it is only as an introduction to the matter following.

narrative flow, essential verses are paraphrased,[43] and he shortens extended passages or adds further explanations where necessary. Idiomatic expressions are converted.[44] Although a detailed discussion of all the changes introduced into the text requires more extensive consideration, we will focus here on one central matter—the author's decision to highlight Petiḥta 24 of *Lamentations Rabbah*. This choice is proof of his intention to present his readers with a well-structured literary unit, and not simply a string of midrashic explications as separate stories. The material he uses from this *petiḥta* includes three complementary units: (1) Israel's confession of its sins; (2) the Creator's response to the destruction of the Temple—a literary unit[45] that concludes in the original source with the bold remark, 'Woe to the king who prospered in his youth but did not prosper in his old age,' placed in the mouth of God; and (3), a long story,[46] which concludes with the promise of future consolation due to the great merit of Rachel rather than that of Moses and the patriarchs. Rachel reminds God of what happened when her father replaced her with her sister before her wedding to Jacob: 'I gave my sister all the signs that I had given to my husband, so that he would think that she was Rachel,' and even spoke to Jacob from her place 'under the bed',

so that he would not discern the voice of my sister. I paid my sister only kindness, and I was not jealous of her nor allowed her to be shamed, although I am a mere mortal, dust and ashes. I had no envy of my rival, and did not place her at risk for shame and humiliation. But you are the King, living and enduring and merciful. How is it then that you are jealous of idolatry, which is worthless, and have sent my children into exile on its account, allowing them to be killed by the sword, and permitting the enemy to do whatever they wanted to them?[47]

This impassioned claim in the manner of *kal vaḥomer* (*a minori ad maius*) brings about the Creator's promise, 'For Rachel I am going to bring Israel back to their land.'

The corresponding passage in *Khurbn beys hamikdesh* reads:

And the word-signs on which I agreed with Jacob I taught to my sister so that he would not notice that it was her. And I lay down under the bed and I spoke for her so that he would not recognize my sister by her voice. Thus I did and I was not jealous of her. Lord of the world [*riboyn shel oylem*], look, *I* am a human being of flesh and blood, dust and ashes, and *I* did not envy my sister and *You* are a merciful king. Why were You jealous of

---

[43] For example, the expository details (the basis of which is to be found in Petiḥta 24) of Isa. 33: 8: 'Highways are desolate, wayfarers have ceased.'

[44] For example, 'deceitful prophets who were in my midst misled me from the way of life to the way of death' is rendered by 'deceitful prophets who were in our midst led me from the good path to the evil path'; the sentence 'I shall [. . .] take an oath that I shall not become engaged with it until the time of the end' is translated as 'I will swear that I will not pay attention to it until it is entirely destroyed'; 'God above, creator of heavens and earth' is briefly designated 'the Creator'; there are many other examples.

[45] The story is entitled 'The Holy One Weeping', in Hayim Nahman Bialik and Yehoshua Hana Ravnitsky (eds.), *The Book of Legends: Sefer Ha-Aggadah: Legends from the Talmud and Midrash*, trans. William Braude (New York, 1992), 145–7.   [46] Entitled 'Mourning by the Fathers', ibid. 146–8.

[47] From Neusner's translation of Petiḥta 24 (Jacob Neusner, *Lamentations Rabbah*, 78–9).

the idols [*avodah zarah*] which Israel worshipped? Why did your Holy Name mind so much the image [*tselem*] which does not mean a thing and for that reason You expelled my children and the enemies did with them whatever they wanted? At once God took pity and said: Rachel, because of you I will bring Israel back to their land. *Amen selah*.[48]

The rendering of this *petiḥta* constitutes an obvious completion to the first unit of *Khurbn beys hamikdesh*. The long stories from Petiḥta 24 are used by the author in directing his readers' attention away from those narratives that lie at the core of the *Gitin* cycle and attest to the moral failings of the people of Jerusalem (insulting and shaming others, behaving with extreme strictness, 'oppressing a man and his house', etc.) that brought about the destruction of the Holy City (and of the city of Beitar). Instead the depiction of God's sorrow is crucial; he appears to be surprised by what happened after he had said, 'I will close my eyes to it and will swear that I will not pay attention to it until they have entirely destroyed it.' All that remains for him is to weep. The author adds stories that deal with the sorrow of the fathers of the nation, whose pleas for divine mercy are disregarded, and concludes with the poignant narrative about Rachel's virtues. Having herself overcome human feelings of envy, it is she who teaches God to overcome his envy of the idol worshipped by the people of Israel. For her merits, redemption is promised.

4. *Khurbn beys hamikdesh* in the *Tsene-rene*

The second volume of the oldest extant edition of the *Tsene-rene* (1622)[49] begins with the Five Megillot, continues with the *haftarot* (prophetic readings) for the weekly readings, and concludes with the *haftarot* for special sabbaths and festivals (the last being Simhat Torah). Appearing as a running header on the pages of the Five Megillot is the word *midrashim*.[50] And indeed, in the discussion of the Megillot, the translation and explanation of the verses are combined with a selection of *midrashim*. Exceptional in this cycle is Lamentations, in which there are two distinct sections. The first is a translation of the book intertwined with explanations (usually from Rashi's commentary), ending with the closing note 'End of the book of Lamentations' (*selik megilat eikhah*).[51] The following relatively lengthy section,[52] with the header *khurbn* ('destruction'), and referred to in the title page of the

---

[48] See *Khurbn*, 12b. Here, too, the verses of justification (Jer. 3: 14–16) found in the source have been omitted. These complex stories, of which only certain aspects have been discussed, are worthy of a wider discussion; see Galit Hasan-Rokem, 'The Voice is the Voice of my Sister: Feminine Images and Feminine Symbols in Lamentations Rabbah' (Heb.), in Yael Azmon (ed.), *A View into the Lives of Women in Jewish Societies* [Eshnav leḥayeihen shel nashim beḥevrot yehudiyot] (Jerusalem, 1995), 95–111; ead., *Web of Life: Folklore and Midrash in Rabbinic Literature*, trans. Batya Stein (Stanford, Calif., 2000).

[49] See above, n. 23. From the wording of the title page of the second part it seems that this was composed later than the first. In most of the following editions both parts of the *Tsene-rene* appear in one volume.

[50] The header *midrashim* appears at the top of the left-hand column of the page, which is printed in two columns. At the top of the right-hand column appears the name of the Megillah in question.

[51] *Tsene-rene* (1622), 15b.   [52] Ibid. 15c–20c.

volume as *khurbn in loshn ashkenaz*, is entirely different; it is, in fact, none other than the very collection of stories under discussion in this chapter. Since the text of the booklet printed in Kraków and the text that appears in the *Tsene-rene* are virtually identical,[53] an explanation for the relationship between the two must be sought.

First, the question of authorship of our text must be considered. Was its author Rabbi Jacob ben Isaac Ashkenazi of Janów, the renowned author of the *Tsene-rene*, whose name appears on the title pages of both volumes of the book?[54] In a meticulously systematic analysis of the language of the *Tsene-rene* Simon Neuberg has demonstrated that the vocabulary of each of the three sections (Torah, Megillot, *haftarot*) differs clearly from that of the other two, a phenomenon that becomes particularly prominent in the section *khurbn in loshn ashkenaz*, which, together with Ruth, differs in its linguistic features most conspicuously from that of the other four Megillot in the *Tsene-rene*.[55] The conclusions of the linguistic analysis seem to indicate quite clearly that Rabbi Jacob, the author of the first volume of the *Tsene-rene* (on the Torah), was not the author of the various components of the second volume of this book (Megillot and *haftarot*). The discussion of the questions about the integration of the two volumes into one opus is beyond the framework of this article.[56] It is, however, relevant that an earlier printed Yiddish booklet on the destruction of the Temple has been inserted directly after the Yiddish translation and explanation of Lamentations. The difference between the *Tsene-Rene*'s treatment of Lamentations and that of the other four Megillot leads to the conclusion that whoever included the booklet in the second volume of the *Tsene-rene* wished to differentiate Lamentations from the other Megillot. Since the *khurbn* booklet consisted of *midrashim*, the preceding rendition of Lamentations required no more than a Yiddish translation and explanation of the text, as had been done in the section of the *haftarot*. Indeed, there is a great similarity between the manner of rendition of the *haftarot* and the methods used in the rendition of Lamentations.

[53] There are a few differences in the orthography (as is usual when there are two printings of a Yiddish book within a short space of time), and several lexical differences, where one of two words with the same meaning appears at times in one text and at times in the other.   [54] See above, n. 23.

[55] See Simon Neuberg, *Pragmatische Aspekte der jiddischen Sprachgeschichte am Beispiel der 'Zenerene'*, Jidische Schtudies, Beiträge zur Geschichte der Sprache und Literatur der aschkenasischen Juden 7, ed. Walter Roll and Erika Timm (Hamburg, 1999), 109–15.

[56] Since the three first editions are not extant, we do not know if they (or any one of them) consisted of two volumes, which is the case of the fourth and oldest extant edition (1622). In order to solve the puzzle of the second volume of the *Tsene-rene* further research into the language, style, and, most importantly, the methods of adapting the literary materials is needed. It is also necessary to analyse meticulously and compare the wording of the title pages of both volumes, paying special attention to what is said in that of the second volume: 'Behold, this is a new thing, the like of which there never was, the Five Scrolls as well as the *haftarot*, and in addition the *khurbn* in *loshn ashkenaz* which he pondered, and sought out, and set in order, the pious great Rabbi Jacob ben Rabbi Isaac of blessed memory [...] who pitched his tent to dwell in the holy community of Janow.' Sara Zfatman, "Khurbn habayis", 202 n. 6, considered that 'it is possible to find in the language of the title page [of the second volume] a hint that the *Khurbn* is an appendix to the original work of R. Jacob ben Isaac of Janow'.

The translation and explanation of Lamentations together with the legends of the destruction of the Temple (either adjacent to the explanation[57] or as an independent text) created a unique framework which probably served a practical purpose: providing appropriate reading matter for mourners on the Ninth of Av, a day when regular learning is forbidden.[58]

Most enlightening on this matter are, for example, the words of Rabbi Mordechai Yaffe (1530–1612) that on the Ninth of Av

> it is forbidden to read the Torah, Prophets, and Writings, and to learn Mishnah or Midrash or Gemara or halakhah or aggadah that rejoice the heart, but one should read the book of Job and the [prophecies of] evil in Jeremiah, which break the heart [...], and it is permitted to learn Midrash Lamentations in order to remember the destruction of the Temple, and likewise the aggadot of the destruction in Chapter 'Hanizakin' and in Chapter 'Ḥelek' and to read the destruction described in Josippon [...], and also the commentary on Lamentations and Job is permitted.[59]

This Yiddish booklet was not the first text to provide materials permitted for reading or learning on the Ninth of Av. It was preceded by the Hebrew collection *Zikhron ḥurban habayit* ('Memory of the Destruction of the Temple', Cremona, 1565), at the core of which are the stories of destruction from *Gitin*.[60] However, as has already been noted,[61] there is no discernible influence from this collection on the Yiddish booklet.

This Yiddish compilation came to be an integral part of the *Tsene-rene*, appearing in all known editions,[62] while at the same time it continued to appear in print as an independent booklet.[63] The longevity that the compilation enjoyed was not due to its appearance as an independent booklet, but because of its place in the *Tsene-rene*. Indeed, in one of the later printed editions of *Khurbn beys hamikdesh*

---

[57] As it appears in the booklets mentioned above, end of n. 24, and below, n. 63.

[58] 'Matters of Torah rejoice the heart [...]; therefore on the ninth day of Ab it is forbidden to study the Torah, excepting such subjects that sadden the heart', see Solomon Ganzfried, *Code of Jewish Law (Kitzur Schulchan Aruch): A Compilation of Jewish Laws and Customs*, trans. Hyman E. Goldin, 4 vols. in 1 (New York, 1928), iii. 62.

[59] Our translation (of Yaffe's *Levush* on the *Tur*, 'Oraḥ ḥayim', §554, no. a–b) and our emphasis; see also the corresponding section in *Mishnah berurah*, and the quotation above, n. 58.

[60] See Meir Benayahu, *Hebrew Printing in Cremona* [Hadefus ha'ivri bikrimona] (Jerusalem, 1971), 225.   [61] See Zfatman, '"Khurbn habayis"' (Heb.), 201 n. 2.

[62] The changes within the text are no different from the changes which the text of the *Tsene-rene* in general underwent and is still undergoing.

[63] We recently identified two editions of our booklet in the National Library of Israel, in Jerusalem; they were printed in the 19th cent. in eastern Europe. These two booklets, one of thirteen folios (JNUL R 8ᵛᵒ 54A1231), and the other of sixteen folios (including a translation into Yiddish of the 'Will of Eliezer Hagadol' (R 8ᵛᵒ JNUL 2006A5379)) lack title pages and the text has undergone lexical and orthographic changes. The *Khurbn beys hamikdesh* was also included in another book, published in Brooklyn, New York (c.1990; JNUL S90A4045). The title page reads: '*Seder kinot letishah be'av* [Order of Lamentations for the Ninth of Av] [...] with explanations in Yiddish and good, nice parables. We have also added *Khurbn beis hamikdesh* and the order of service for evening, morning, and afternoon prayers.'

(1862),⁶⁴ the sequential explanation of the verses of Lamentations from the *Tsene-rene* is printed before the cycle of stories. This was explicitly noted in the German translation of both units that appeared in the twentieth century.⁶⁵

Further research on the use of Midrash in the rest of the *Tsene-rene*, as well as in the other genres of Yiddish literature of the early modern period, will no doubt reveal additional methods of adaptation used by the authors for the sake of their readers, allow for a fuller differentiation between conventional and innovative techniques, and explain how considerable portions of the Midrash became a living, integral part of the spiritual assets of the Yiddish-reading public who did not understand the original sources.

---

⁶⁴ See above, n. 24.

⁶⁵ See *Die Zerstörung Jerusalems aus dem Buche Zeena Ureena*, trans. into German by Alexander Eliasberg (Berlin, 1921).

TWENTY

MIDRASH IN HABAD HASIDISM

NAFTALI LOEWENTHAL

T HIS CHAPTER attempts to examine the continuum joining Midrash, ethos, and spirituality in the Habad school of hasidism, both in terms of the development of theoretical structures linking the midrashic process with personal spiritual quest, and the use of Midrash to impart traditionalist, hasidic, and sometimes eschatological ideas. This relates to the striking interplay of esoteric and exoteric elements in hasidic teaching. For though there are overtly esoteric themes, discussing *sefirot* (divine emanations), spiritual 'worlds', and other aspects of the corpus of Jewish mystical thought, a long tradition in Judaism reserves such teachings for a spiritual elite.[1] Midrash, by contrast, is ostensibly accessible to all, whether as a written text for study or as an oral and popular exposition. Hence it is notable that hasidic teachers in general, and those of the Habad school in particular, use Midrash in order to communicate spiritual teachings in the society at large. Moreover, the particular mode of instruction that hasidism evolved, the hasidic *derush* (exposition),[2] sometimes called *torah* (teaching) or *ma'amar* (discourse), can itself be seen as an extended form of latter-day Midrash. While all the above is relevant to varying degrees in many hasidic groups, this study generally limits its scope to the use of Midrash in the Habad school. Nevertheless, in order to consider this topic in context, we shall begin with a brief overview of the use of Midrash in the broader hasidic movement.

ON MIDRASH IN HASIDISM

Midrash and aggadah have had a prominent role in hasidism from the very beginning of the movement in the middle of the eighteenth century. Many of the sayings

---

Thanks are due to several of my friends and colleagues for assistance in this project, most particularly Dr Joanna Weinberg and Professors Michael Fishbane and Eve Tavor Bannet. Of course the errors remain my own.

[1] See Mishnah *Ḥag.* 2: 1.
[2] The term *derush* is being used here to described a hasidic exposition or discourse. This term can also be used to describe the entire genre of homiletical teaching, quite apart from the hasidic movement. I am using the term *derash* to mean a single instance of homiletical thought, interpreting Scripture (or sometimes other texts, as I discuss here), which might be found in virtually any Jewish literary context, hasidic or not.

of Rabbi Israel Ba'al Shem Tov (1698–1760), collected in the writings of his disciples, quote talmudic aggadah and phrases from the Midrash as well as sayings from the Zohar.³ The main collections of teachings of his disciple Rabbi Dov Ber, the Maggid of Mezhirech (d. 1772), who was the central focus of the hasidic movement in its second generation,⁴ liberally quote from the talmudic aggadah, *Midrash Rabbah*, and to some extent other *midrashim* such as *Tanḥuma*, and also the Zohar. The first great publicist of the hasidic movement, Rabbi Jacob Joseph of Polonnoye (d. c.1784) in his erudite *Toledot ya'akov yosef*, the first printed hasidic work (Korets, 1780), weaves together themes from a very broad range of Jewish literature, including the Zohar and the Lurianic writings, as well as Maimonides' *Mishneh torah* and later halakhic works. In his work, citations from the talmudic aggadah, *Midrash Rabbah*, *Tanḥuma*, halakhic *midrashim*, and later collections of Midrash are abundant. The work *Me'or einayim* (Slavita, 1798), the collection of teachings by Rabbi Menahem Nahum of Tchernobil (d. 1798), who studied with both the Ba'al Shem Tov and the Maggid of Mezhirech, refers to a more limited range of literature than does the *Toledot ya'akov yosef*. However, citations from the talmudic aggadah, *Midrash Rabbah*, and *Tanḥuma* are still prominent.⁵

The significance of Midrash for hasidic teachers continued into the later generations of the movement. An outstanding example is seen in the *Sefat emet al hatorah* by Rabbi Judah Leib Alter (1847–1905), grandson of Rabbi Isaac Meir Rothenberg (1799–1866), the founder of the dynasty of the Ger hasidim, centred in Gora Kalwaria near Warsaw. His work *Sefat emet* ('Speech of Truth', cf. Prov. 12: 19), published posthumously,⁶ provides a record of the inspired Torah teachings he delivered at his *tisch* (table, signifying a gathering with a hasidic leader) on Friday nights or perhaps at the Third Meal (*se'udah shelishit*) on sabbath afternoons, listed

---

³ An early collection of sayings and teachings ascribed to the Ba'al Shem Tov is *Keter shem tov* (Zolkiev, 1794/5), culling fragments from five previously published books. In 1938 *Sefer ba'al shem tov* was printed in Lodz in two volumes, collecting passages from 210 printed works. Menachem Kallus translated and annotated a section of this work in *Pillar of Prayer: Guidance in Contemplative Prayer, Sacred Study, and the Spiritual Life, from the Baal Shem Tov and his Circle* (Louisville, Ky., 2011).

⁴ See Ada Rapoport-Albert, 'Hasidism after 1772: Structural Continuity and Change', in ead. (ed.), *Hasidism Reappraised* (London, 1996), 76–140. The main collection of R. Dov Ber's teachings is *Magid devarav leya'akov*, first printed in Koretz, 1781; annotated, critical edn. by Rivka Schatz-Uffenheimer (Jerusalem, 1976).

⁵ See *Menahem Nahum of Chernobyl: Upright Practices, The Light of the Eyes*, trans. and ed. Arthur Green (New York, 1982), 8. Arthur Green suggests that many hasidic teachers (Habad and Bratslav excluded) would restrict themselves to citing works familiar to the members of their intended audience in order that the ethical and spiritual force of the homily would carry more weight. The familiar works he lists include popular talmudic tractates, *Midrash Rabbah* and *Tanḥuma*, and Rashi's commentary on the Torah.

⁶ *Sefat emet al hatorah* (Piotrkov, 1905–8). See Arthur Green, *The Language of Truth: The Torah Commentary of the Sefat Emet, Rabbi Yehudah Leib Alter of Ger* (Philadelphia, Pa., 1998) and Yoram Jacobson, 'From Youth to Leadership and from Kabbalah to Hasidism: Stages in the Spiritual Development of the Author of *Sefat emet*' (Heb.), in Rachel Elior and Joseph Dan (eds.), *Rivka Schatz-Uffenheimer Memorial Volume* [Sefer hazikaron lerivkah shats-ufenheimer], vol. ii (Jerusalem, 1996), 429–46.

year by year, from late 1870 until December 1904. Each teaching begins with a key text and combines a number of such texts in a chain developing a theme. Very often the key text is a brief quotation from *Midrash Rabbah* on the weekly Torah portion, or from *Tanḥuma*, though it is sometimes taken from other midrashic collections. Other key texts might include a verse from Scripture, a phrase from Rashi's commentary on the Torah, a line from Mishnah *Pirkei avot*, or a teaching that he had heard from his grandfather, Rabbi Isaac Meir. Significantly, on virtually every page, there are several quotations and discussions from the Midrash.

The emergence of this unusual focus on Midrash in the *Sefat emet* relates to the interplay of esoteric versus exoteric teachings in the hasidic movement as a whole, and Kotsk and Ger hasidism in particular. While some branches of hasidism, in particular the Habad school and also their some-time opponent Rabbi Tsevi Hirsch of Zhidachow (d. 1831),[7] overtly discussed themes from the kabbalah, the direction taken by the great Rabbi Menahem Mendel of Kotsk (d. 1859) was to ridicule such study. There is a story that a Habad hasid came to Rabbi Menahem Mendel of Kotsk, who asked him what *kavanah* (kabbalistic 'intention') he employed while reciting the Shema and Amidah prayers. The hasid told him. The anecdote does not recount exactly what he said—but presumably it was not a *kavanah* in the Lurianic sense,[8] but rather a Habad teaching about the flow of spiritual life-force from the Ein Sof (Infinite), giving existence to all the worlds, and the way all is 'really' subsumed in the Oneness of the Ein Sof, as described in Rabbi Shneur Zalman of Lyady's *Likutei amarim—Tanya* (1797) in connection with recitation of the Shema,[9] or some similar Habad teaching. Hearing this, the Kotsker cried out with a loud voice 'Un vi iz der pipik?'—and what about the *pipik* (lit., stomach), the guts, the coarse and genuine reality of man?[10]

Thus Rabbi Isaac Meir avoided overt esotericism, and his collected writings, called *Ḥidushei harim*,[11] are devoted to talmudic and halakhic analysis. It seems that his grandson and successor,[12] Rabbi Judah Leib, felt that in addition to Talmud and

---

[7] See Zevi Hirsch Eichenstein, *Turn Aside from Evil and Do Good: An Introduction and a Way to the Tree of Life*, trans. and ed. Louis Jacobs (London, 1995).

[8] R. Isaac Luria's prescriptions for the conceptualization of specific kabbalistic themes (*kavanot*) while reciting the various sections of the daily prayers were presented in works such as R. Shabbatai of Rashkov's Lurianic prayer-book, *Kavanat halimud* (Korets, 1794/5). Although this edition of this work was published by the hasidim, there was a trend to abandon the specific Lurianic *kavanot* in favour of hasidic interpretations and approaches to prayer. See Joseph G. Weiss, 'The Kavanoth of Prayer in Early Hasidism' in id., *Studies in Eastern European Jewish Mysticism*, ed. D. Goldstein (Oxford, 1985), 95–125, and Louis Jacobs, *Hasidic Prayer* (London, 1972).

[9] *Tanya*, pt. 2, *Sha'ar hayiḥud veha'emunah*. See ch. 1.

[10] Yisrael Ya'akov Artan, *Emet ve'emunah* (Jerusalem, 1940), p. 14, §91. The editor adds the following: 'As a hasid of Kotsk said to a hasid of another *rebbe*, "your *rebbe* speaks unto Heaven and our *rebbe* says Torah which goes into the *pipik*."'

[11] The first publication of the several volumes of this work were in Józefów 1867, Warsaw 1870–80.

[12] When R. Isaac Meir died in 1866, Judah Leib was only 18 years old, and he refused to accept the position of *rebbe*. R. Hanokh Heynekh Hakohen Levin of Aleksandrow became *rebbe* instead. When

halakhah there must be some further level of communication by a *rebbe* to his hasidim. His use of Midrash in the *Sefat emet* and, indeed, the entire project of this work express his goal of revealing an inner, spiritual dimension of the Torah. His writings show that he was conversant with Habad teachings,[13] and he sometimes cites the Zohar as well. However, far more frequently and consistently, it is the Midrash that provides him with the means to develop his spiritual themes.

HASIDIC TEACHINGS *AS* MIDRASH

I turn now to a further aspect of the relationship between hasidic *derush* and Midrash. Not only does the hasidic teaching *use* Midrash but, in some cases, *in itself* it can be seen as a form of latter-day Midrash. Indeed, it is a revival of the midrashic mode, in which a text acts as the germinator of an inspired outpouring of visionary narrative, perceptions, and ideas. This characterization applies to the teachings in the *Sefat emet*, with the rider that the 'text' is often a phrase of Midrash or a comment by Rashi, rather than simply a verse from Scripture (as will be discussed below). Another important earlier example of this kind is evident in the teachings of the great-grandson of the Ba'al Shem Tov, Rabbi Nahman of Bratslav (d. 1810). He was a prominent figure in the third generation of hasidism, whose influence extends strongly to the present day. Shaul Magid, in the context of discussing the teachings of Rabbi Nahman collected in his *Likutei moharan* (Ostraha, 1808) in relation to the Midrash mode, suggests various ways of extending the boundaries of the definition of Midrash in order to include Rabbi Nahman's fascinating *torot* (teachings).

Are Rabbi Nahman's teachings to be considered 'associative' or even 'poetic Midrash'?[14] Magid tries to draw a distinction between what he sees as the exegeti-

---

the latter passed away in 1870, R. Judah Leib accepted the position of leader of the Gerer dynasty. At the same time he was, like his grandfather R. Isaac Meir, the rabbi and *av beit din* of Gora Kalwaria.

[13] See Arthur Green, *The Language of Truth*, introd., p. xxxvii.

[14] See Shaul Magid 'Associative Midrash: Reflections on a Hermeneutical Theory in *Likutei MoHaRan*', in id. (ed.), *God's Voice from the Void: Old and New Studies in Bratslav Hasidism* (New York, 2002), 15–66. As presented by Magid, citing Daniel Boyarin's *Intertextuality and the Reading of Midrash* (Bloomington, Ind., 1994), classical 'Midrash' expounds the scriptural text often by means of an intertextual process, i.e. citing a passage from elsewhere in the biblical corpus in order to illuminate the text it is expounding. For Boyarin, the passage cited by the Midrash is not a proof-text (i.e. a passage presented in order to support previously determined conclusions) but rather is '*the generating force*' behind the midrashic exposition (*Intertextuality*, 22; italics in the original). By contrast, states Magid, 'associative Midrash' refers to R. Nahman's broadening of this process through his use of the term *beḥinah*, which enables him to establish associative relationships between concepts, one being a *beḥinah* ('aspect') of the other. The term 'poetic Midrash' expresses a further claim, that R. Nahman is writing in his 'own' voice, not that of the text he is expounding, and his teachings in *Likutei moharan* can therefore be considered poetry, unlike midrashic exegesis, which remains bound to the scriptural text it is expounding. However, says Magid, R. Nahman's poetry is 'couched in a proemic (i.e. midrashic) form' ('Associative Midrash', 21), and in that sense is 'poetic Midrash'.

cal goal of Midrash and the personal spiritual praxis of Rabbi Nahman's hasidic texts. Whereas classical Midrash draws on a 'far verse' (i.e. distant in Scripture from the verse being expounded) in order to generate an exegetical discourse that will lead back to a novel explication of the initial verse, Rabbi Nahman typically moves from his opening text to some 'transtextual' hasidic praxis, perspective, or ideal.[15] In addition to this feature, his use of the term *beḥinah* (aspect) to create intertextual links (A is the *beḥinah* of B; i.e. A = B) vastly broadens his ability[16] to weave a tapestry that extends far beyond the more controlled links between texts delineated in classical Midrash—links effected by such technical artifices as *al tikra* ('do not read [the text as written, but rather in a modified form]'), *kiveyakhol* ('so to speak') or even *ke'ilu* ('as if').[17] As described by Magid, these differences notwithstanding, the midrashic form is essentially preserved in Rabbi Nahman's teachings. Moreover, one could argue that even the apparent differences do not carry us very far from the classical midrashic approach, since it too seeks to convey ideals and achieve emotional-spiritual edification through various forms of creative association and identification. And further: just as the classical Midrash believes that its theological exegesis is a genuine reading of the inner depth of the text, at the level of *derush*, the hasidic teachers correspondingly believe that their theosophy is genuinely embodied in the 'text', whether on the level of *derush*, *remez* (hint), or *sod* (the esoteric level).[18]

MIDRASH AND THE ESOTERIC TRADITION

Our discussion raises the more general question of the relationship of Midrash to the esoteric or kabbalistic tradition of Jewish thought. In an interesting passage in his *Major Trends in Jewish Mysticism*, Gershom Scholem discusses the difference in attitude expressed by Jewish philosophers and kabbalists to both halakhah and Midrash/aggadah. He regards the philosophers as seemingly uncomfortable with both, in contrast with the kabbalists, who turn to these subjects more enthusiastically.[19] In his view, their great attraction to the aggadah is because 'the whole of the Aggada can in a way be regarded as a popular mythology of the Jewish universe'.[20] He adds that the kabbalists broaden the scope of that 'mythology' so as to include the cosmic dimension. Scholem goes on to state that what is missing from the old aggadah is man's direct effect on the divine. Michael Fishbane critically discusses

---

[15] Magid, 'Associative Midrash', 28–31, 38–40.   [16] Ibid. 20, 43–9.
[17] See Michael Fishbane, *The Garments of Torah: Essays in Biblical Hermeneutics* (Bloomington, Ind., 1989), 22–32, and more extensively in id., *Biblical Myth and Rabbinic Mythmaking* (Oxford, 2003), appendix 1.
[18] The traditional four levels of interpretation (*pardes*) are *peshat* (the literal), *remez* ('hints' to further teachings), *derush* (deeper exposition), and *sod* (the esoteric level). See the recent discussion of ways of interpreting these four levels in Michael Fishbane, *Sacred Attunement: A Jewish Theology* (Chicago, 2008), 64–107. See also R. Menachem M. Schneerson, *On the Essence of Chassidus*, trans. Susan Handelman (and Y. Greenberg) (Brooklyn, NY, 1998).
[19] Gershom Scholem, *Major Trends in Jewish Mysticism* (New York, paperback edn., 1961), 29.
[20] Ibid. 31.

this idea and successfully demonstrates that there are some midrashic passages where a direct human effect on the divine is depicted in a manner very similar to that described by the kabbalists, for whom the theurgical aspect of both halakhah and *kavanah* (the 'intention' behind the performance of halakhah or of prayer) is central.[21] Fishbane shows how the *Pesikta derav kahana* moves in its interpretation of the phrase 'But the righteous one holds fast to his way, and the pure of hands will increase strength' (Job 17: 9), from first depicting God's effect upon the righteous ('"the pure of hands" refers to the Holy One . . . [who] "will increase strength"—give power to the righteous to fulfil His Will'), to expressing the effect of the righteous upon the divine: 'Whenever the righteous do the will of the Holy One, blessed be He, they increase strength in the *dynamis*' (*mosifin ko'aḥ bagevurah*).[22] Fishbane gives further attention to this theme in his *Biblical Myth and Rabbinic Mythmaking*, where he explores midrashic depictions of the divine's dependence on human repentance, the effect of Jewish obedience to the Law on the erotic coupling of the cherubs in the Holy of Holies in the Temple, and examples of human action that arouse divine mercy and power.[23]

In general, as David Flusser puts it, one could say that both rabbinic mysticism and aggadah are the product of the same *Weltanschauung*, although he also sounds a note of caution regarding such an approach, stating that in order to understand their reciprocal relationship more serious research is needed into the field of aggadah.[24] Fishbane draws attention to Flusser's comment and, it could be said, in part sets himself the task of revealing that dimension of thought in which mysticism and Midrash, kabbalistic theosophy, and aggadic images and narrative can be found together.[25] This paper attempts in a very limited way to follow his example, focusing on the Habad hasidic school, providing just a glimpse of a very broad and varied topic.

---

[21] Michael Fishbane, *The Garments of Torah*, 24.

[22] Ibid. See *Pesikta derav kahana, According to an Oxford Manuscript, with Variants from All Known Manuscripts and Genizoth Fragments and Parallel Passages*, ed. Dov (Bernard) Mandelbaum, 2 vols. (New York, 1962), ii. 379–81 (*piska* 25); *Pesikta vehi agadat erets yisra'el meyuḥeset lerav kahana*, ed. S. Buber (Lyck, 1868, repr. New York, 1949), 166a–b (*piska* 26). See by contrast Moshe Idel, *Kabbalah: New Perspectives* (New Haven, Conn., 1988), 173–81, exploring the difference between midrashic and kabbalistic explanations of Ps. 121: 5, in which the divine is described as 'a shadow' of man.

[23] Michael Fishbane, *Biblical Myth and Rabbinic Mythmaking*, 172–82.

[24] David Flusser, 'Scholem's Recent Book on Merkabah Literature', *Journal of Jewish Studies*, 11 (1960), 68, reviewing Gershom Scholem, *Jewish Gnosticism, Merkabah Mysticism and the Talmudic Tradition: Based on the Israel Goldstein Lectures, delivered at the Jewish Theological Seminary of America, New York* (New York, 1960).

[25] See Michael Fishbane, *The Exegetical Imagination: On Jewish Thought and Theology* (Cambridge, Mass., 1998), 197 n. 1. A differing view on the relationship between aggadic Midrash and mysticism is expressed by Joseph Dan and Shaul Magid. See Joseph Dan, 'Jewish Mysticism in Late Antiquity: An Introduction', in id., *Jewish Mysticism: Late Antiquity* (Northvale, NJ, 1998), p. xxii, and Shaul Magid, 'Associative Midrash', 17 and 50 n. 12, quoting Joseph Dan's depiction of the writing of the Heikhalot mystics as 'a negation of Midrash' because it transcends textual exegesis.

THE CHAIN OF TEXTUAL SANCTITY

In order to engage with this material, we have to cross a certain barrier—for our general understanding is that Midrash is an interpretation of the biblical text. As Moshe Idel puts it: 'There are two main components in the interpretative experience: the text and the interpreter. The text is the canonized Hebrew Bible whose precise borders are delineated and whose sacrosanct status is sealed.'[26] However, as Joseph Dan has pointed out, 'to the Jew of the Middle Ages, all of Talmudic–midrashic literature, as well as the Bible, was considered holy' and could therefore function as the starting point of a sermon or *derash* (a homiletic insight) whose goal was to reveal some further dimension of the text with which it began.[27] This is apparent in the writings of the Maharal of Prague (Rabbi Judah Loew, c.1520–1609), and can be seen most clearly in the *Eight Gates* (*Shemoneh she'arim*) of his contemporary Rabbi Hayim Vital (1543–1620), who transmitted the teachings of his master Rabbi Isaac Luria (1534–72). One of the 'Gates' is called *sha'ar hapesukim*, 'the Gate of [Scriptural] Verses', and expounds the kabbalistic meanings of passages in Scripture; another is called *sha'ar ma'amarei rashbi*, '[the] Gate of the Teachings of Rabbi Shimon bar Yohai', and expounds the Zohar. And a third is called *sha'ar ma'amarei ḥazal* '[the] Gate of the Teachings of our Sages, of Blessed Memory', and expounds passages from the Talmud, the Midrash, and Mishnah *Pirkei avot*.[28] Throughout, the mode of 'exposition' is quite other than a scholarly elucidation or exegesis. Rather, successive levels of textual meaning are disclosed to reveal a broad spiritual landscape. This overall concern was central to the work of the kabbalists. The text at hand, sometimes especially processed by such complex methods as *gematriyah* (calculating the numerical values of words), became a window through which the student could perceive intimations of the divine.

In this way Scripture, the Written Torah, becomes the head of a chain of sacred texts extending through the generations. In the hasidic *derush* literature, the 'sacred text' being exposited might even be from the very recent past, as we will see.

VARIETIES OF 'TEXT' IN HASIDISM

As is the case for the Maharal or Rabbi Hayim Vital, so too for the hasidim the sacred phrase that triggers hasidic interpretative responses may be from Scripture, Mishnah, Talmud, Midrash, Rashi's commentary on the Torah, or from a passage in the daily prayers.[29] There are even instances where the phrasing of Rabbi Joseph

---

[26] Moshe Idel, 'Infinities of Torah in Kabbalah', in Geoffrey H. Hartman and Sanford Budick (eds.), *Midrash and Literature* (New Haven, Conn., 1986), 141.

[27] See Joseph Dan, 'Homiletic Literature', in *Encyclopaedia Judaica* (Jerusalem, 1972), viii, col. 948.

[28] It is intriguing that *sha'ar hapesukim*—focusing on the verses of Scripture—is the fourth gate, *after* those of *ma'amrei rashbi* and *ḥazal*, which are second and third respectively.

[29] This is true also of some of the *derush* literature which preceded hasidism proper. Mendel Piekarz discusses this in his *The Beginning of Hasidism: Ideological Trends in Derush and Musar Literature* [Bimei tsemiḥat haḥasidut: megamot ra'ayoniyot besifrei derush umusar] (Jerusalem, 1978) 35–95.

Karo's code of law, the *Shulḥan arukh*, is used as the target 'text'. And not only this, but, in some cases, one master's hasidic teaching may also become the 'text' that a later master expounds.

Let us return to Rabbi Nahman of Bratslav's *Likutei moharan*, which, as will be recalled, expounds new teachings on the basis of a biblical verse, an aggadah from the Talmud, or a quotation from the Zohar. In the next generation, Rabbi Nahman's disciple, Rabbi Nathan Sternhartz (1780–1845), in his *Likutei halakhot* (Zolkiev, 1847–8), juxtaposes his master's teaching from *Likutei moharan* and a halakhic statement from the *Shulḥan arukh*. The statement of the halakhah, sometimes only a brief phrase, becomes the 'text' for exposition, and Rabbi Nathan's own interpretation, based on a specific teaching of Rabbi Nahman, opens it up as a spiritual pathway—providing the illumination of Bratslav thought. Similar processes are seen in the *derush* literature of other hasidic groups, including Rabbi Judah Leib Alter's *Sefat emet*, discussed above, where a line from the Midrash, *Pirkei avot*, or even Rashi's commentary on the Torah becomes the 'text' which is expounded in terms of the transtextual themes of Gerer hasidism—including, in particular, teachings in the name of Rabbi Judah Leib's grandfather, Rabbi Isaac Meir, founder of this school.

MIDRASH IN HABAD

These preliminary remarks set the stage for us to consider the role of Midrash in the Habad–Lubavitch school. Here we find that Midrash becomes an important medium in its goal of transmitting to the widest reaches of its hasidic following the ideals of inwardness and of a spiritualized conception of life. The quest to communicate spirituality using esoteric teachings distinguished Habad from earlier hasidic paths.[30] Midrash *per se*, and the creation of a literary genre which can be seen as a latter-day form of spiritual Midrash, are important tools in this task.

A letter by Rabbi Joseph Isaac Schneersohn (1880–1950), written in 1921 in the early years of his leadership as the sixth Lubavitcher Rebbe, ascribes an exalted spiritual power to intimate and personalized study of the *Midrash Rabbah*, which, he claims, may sometimes even achieve that which hasidic teachings alone might fail to accomplish. He writes:

Avodah [service] is demanded from us, literally, a term relating to the curing of skins [*orot me'ubadim*],[31] that one takes a thick hide and puts it in a special vessel, and by means of a number of additives the hide becomes soft and fit for its intended purpose: so too is *avodah*. In our case, we have everything in plenty. The hide is thick, and we are put in the vessel, in the saucepan, and we also have the right ingredients, they are the waters of revealed Torah and hasidic teachings. Nonetheless, the hide does not get soft. So we have to ask many questions: whose fault is it? Is it on account of the hide or because of the

---

[30] See Naftali Loewenthal, *Communicating the Infinite: the Emergence of the Habad School* (Chicago, 1990). [31] The Hebrew word for 'curing' (of leather) has the same root as that for 'service'.

broth? It is anyway clear that there is a problem, and we have to root out and eradicate that problem. Sometimes good counsel is to have a session studying *Midrash Rabbah*, with understanding, applying it to oneself, so that it arouses the heart, as my sacred great-grandfather [Rabbi Menahem Mendel] the Tsemah Tsedek [1789–1866], said: 'Zohar exalts the soul, the Midrash arouses the heart, and Tehilim [Psalms] with tears wash out the vessel.' Thus I heard from Rabbi Hanokh Hendel of blessed memory, who was told this in *yeḥidut* [private audience, with Rabbi Menahem Mendel]. Ultimately, one has to make the effort, and plead with the Divine that He help us and shine His countenance upon us with kindness and mercy.[32]

Here study of a traditional midrashic collection such as *Midrash Rabbah* is presented as helping a person attain a state of inner purity and wholesomeness which, claims Rabbi Joseph Isaac, is an important adjunct to study of the Habad hasidic teachings. In Habad thought, as we might expect, the Habad teachings are generally seen as paramount in their power to open spiritual doors. But in this context we note a most unusual and even surprising affirmation of the importance and power of studying Midrash in its classical collections. In addition, Habad teachings often employed midrashic passages and themes in order to create their own genre of spiritual communication, *ḥasidut* (hasidic teachings), also called *dakh*, an acronym of the liturgical phrase *divrei elokim ḥayim* 'words of the living God'.[33]

To begin our exploration of this process, let us turn back to the beginning of Habad at the end of the eighteenth century and, in particular, the tract *Likutei amarim—Tanya* by Rabbi Shneur Zalman of Lyady (1745–1812). This work is a manual on spiritual service of the divine, creating a structured system which, the author felt, imparted the path of his teachers in the hasidic movement.

The author set as his task the intensive communication of spiritual teachings, which he saw as a necessary task both for the wellbeing of the Jewish people and for the eventual coming of the messiah. In this he was responding to a theme in a letter by the Ba'al Shem Tov, which reports that he was told by the messiah in a mystical 'ascent of the soul' that the redemption would come 'when your teachings burst outward'.[34] This idea itself is consistent with the teaching of the kabbalist Rabbi Hayim Vital, who similarly stated in the introduction to his *Ets ḥayim* ('Tree of Life') that study of the kabbalah would both preserve the Jewish people and bring the messiah.[35]

---

[32] R. Joseph Isaac Schneersohn, *Igerot kodesh admor yosef yitsḥak*, vol. xiv (Brooklyn, NY, 1998), 30–1; see also vol. x (Brooklyn, NY, 1984), 390. The phrase concerning the Zohar, Midrash, and Psalms is quoted in R. Menahem Mendel Schneerson's anthology of hasidic sayings arranged as a diary, *Hayom yom* (Brooklyn, NY, 1943 and frequently reprinted); see the entry for 16 Tevet.

[33] The talmudic use of this phrase is to suggest the spiritual transcendence of opposites: although two sages may maintain opposing views, on a higher level both opinions are true (cf. BT *Eruv.* 13*b*, *Git.* 6*b*), and this is an apt way of defining the process of hasidic discourse. See R. Shneur Zalman's *Likutei torah* (Brooklyn, NY, 1999), 'Aḥarei', 27*b*.

[34] Prov. 5: 16. See Immanuel Etkes, *The Besht: Magician, Mystic, and Leader*, trans. Saadya Sternberg (Waltham, Mass., 2005), 79–87.

[35] See R. Hayim Vital, *Tree of Life* [Sefer ets ḥayim], 2 vols. (Tel Aviv, 1960), i. 5–21. Cf. Rachel Elior's

The opening up of the corpus of sacred wisdom to wider circles than before brought criticism of Rabbi Shneur Zalman both from kabbalists who were opposed to hasidism, such as Rabbi Elijah, the Gaon of Vilna (1720–97), and from some other hasidic leaders, colleagues of Rabbi Shneur Zalman, who were against too much revelation of spiritual or mystical thought. As Rabbi Abraham of Kalisk (1741–1810) put it: 'Too much oil can extinguish the lamp.'[36] Nonetheless, Rabbi Shneur Zalman made communication of spirituality his central endeavour, and created a form of Midrash that presents esoteric, cosmic perceptions in the apparently exoteric, accessible medium of the Habad hasidic discourse.

TANYA: FINDING ONE'S PLACE IN THE TORAH

A theoretical underpinning of this process is seen in Rabbi Shneur Zalman's *Tanya*. In his introduction to this work, the author discusses different forms of spiritual guidance.[37] Direct face-to-face communication is paramount; then follow different kinds of written text. Of these, the most important are those based on the midrashic expositions of the sages, 'in whom the spirit of God spoke and His word was on their tongue'.[38]

Rabbi Shneur Zalman goes on to say that all the myriads of the Jewish people cleave to the Torah, and the Torah connects them to God. On the one hand, this expresses the mystic power of the Torah, 'as is known from the sacred Zohar'. This might refer to the idea that 'there are three levels [*dargin*] which are interconnected: the Holy One, the Torah, and [the people] Israel'.[39] All this pertains to the Jewish people as a whole. However, asks Rabbi Shneur Zalman, what about the individual? He answers that each person is individually bonded to the Torah and thus to God because *of the possibility of the multiple interpretation of the Torah*:

because the Torah is given to be interpreted [both] in general and in particular, even down to the most minute detail, to [apply to] each and every individual soul of Israel, which is rooted in it.[40]

The interpretation of the Torah, the *derash*, provides the link between the individual and the Torah. However, states Rabbi Shneur Zalman, the problem is that 'Not every person is able to recognize his own individual place in the Torah.' That

---

discussion of this introduction, which stands as an independent essay by R. Hayim Vital, in her 'Messianic Expectations and Spiritualization of Religious Life in the Sixteenth Century', *Revue des études juives*, 145 (1986), 35–49; repr. in David B. Ruderman (ed.), *Essential Papers on Jewish Culture in Renaissance and Baroque Italy* (New York, 1992), 283–98.

[36] See R. Abraham's letter expressing his disapproval of R. Shneur Zalman's imparting of mystical teachings, in Jacob Barnai, *Hasidic Letters from Erets Yisra'el* [Igerot ḥasidim me'erets yisra'el] (Jerusalem, 1980), 240.

[37] R. Shneur Zalman of Lyady, *Likutei amarim—Tanya* (Slavuta, 1796; Vilna, 1900; bilingual edn, trans. N. Mindel et al., London, 1973), introd., fo. 3*b*.

[38] Cf. 2 Sam. 23: 2.   [39] Zohar iii. 73*a*.   [40] *Tanya*, introd., 3*b*.

is, many individuals cannot find their personal interpretative route to their particular place in the Torah, bonding them as an individual to God. Rabbi Shneur Zalman explains that there are many different pathways, as for example the different routes of Hillel and Shammai. He then announces that he has written this tract for his followers, with whom he feels a close bond. The unspoken implication is that he claims to have found a way, through his book, to help them find their individual place in the Torah—their own path of *derash* which leads to their bond with the Torah and with God. Viewed in this way, he conceived his book, which he saw as based on the teachings of his forebears, the Ba'al Shem Tov and the Maggid,[41] as helping forge a personal route in *derash*, one which leads to the divine.

EXPOUNDING AN AGGADAH

The *Tanya* starts with a quotation of an aggadah from the Babylonian Talmud, tractate *Nidah*, concerning the way the soul is made to take an oath before it comes into the world. According to this, the soul is adjured: 'Be a *tsadik* [righteous person], and not a *rasha* [evildoer], and even if the whole world considers you a *tsadik*, consider yourself as a *rasha*.'[42]

For the first fourteen chapters Rabbi Shneur Zalman's tract expounds the meaning of that aggadah in terms of what it means spiritually to be a *tsadik* or a *rasha*, drawing on kabbalistic teachings of the Zohar, Rabbi Hayim Vital, and other sources. Subsequent chapters, and subsequent sections of the work, either introduce a new 'text'—often a scriptural verse, or a quotation from Talmud or Zohar—or simply continue to explain the author's system of inner spiritual psychology as it relates to contemplation, inspiration, repentance, and action.

The *Tanya* can thus be seen as a work which initially expounds a specific aggadah from the Talmud. This exposition, together with the opening of other 'texts', is the vehicle which, in the view of the author, will help readers find their individual 'path' in the Torah.

THE RIVER OF TORAH

It is interesting that near the beginning of *Tanya* we find an image depicting the chain of sacred texts that includes Midrash and aggadah as part of the flow of divine revelation, authentically expressing the divine essence of the scriptural text, seemingly on a par with the halakhic dimension of Torah teaching.

Although God is termed Ein Sof [Infinite] . . . 'and thought does not grasp Him at all'[43] . . . [nonetheless] 'in the place where you find the greatness of the Holy One, there you find His humility',[44] and He contracted His will and wisdom in the 613 commandments

---

[41] R. Dov Ber, the Maggid of Mezeritch.
[42] BT *Nid.* 30b. In fact in this place in the Talmud this passage starts *darash r. simlai*, although in BT *Yev.* 71b it is referred to by the word *vehatanya*.
[43] *Tikunei zohar* (Jerusalem, 1965), beginning of 2nd introd., fo. 30a.
[44] BT *Meg.* 31a.

of the Torah, and their *halakhot*, and in the combinations of letters of the Bible, and their explanations which are in the aggadot and *midrashim* of our Sages—so that every soul ... in a human body will be able to grasp them in his mind and uphold them as much as possible in action, speech, and thought. Hence the Torah is compared to water [in a talmudic aggadah[45]], because just as water flows from a high place to a low place, so the Torah descends from the place of its glory, the divine will and wisdom, [where] Torah and the Holy One are one, and thought cannot grasp Him at all—and from there it descended ... level after level in the down-chaining of the worlds, until it was garbed in physical things and worldly matters.[46]

Thus not only the verse of Scripture, but the halakhah, and indeed the Midrash or aggadah, are all sacred. The descending movement starts with the Written Torah, the biblical verse, or rather the supernal form of that sacred text, beyond thought. Then comes the text itself and all further levels of explanation, each of which may itself be explained further, bringing the flow of the water of Torah closer to the individual person; with the flow of Torah also comes the sense of contact with the divine. For Rabbi Shneur Zalman, the lower 'exoteric' reaches of the river are joined with and even carry something of the very mystical origins of Torah, the point where Torah and the Holy One are joined, beyond thought and beyond the many levels of our world.

RABBI SHNEUR ZALMAN'S DISCOURSES

Apart from his written tract *Tanya*, Rabbi Shneur Zalman also taught oral discourses that were transcribed after the sabbath by his closest disciples and have been published in about two dozen volumes.[47] These contain *derushim*, most of which start by expounding a verse of Scripture, generally from the Pentateuch, sometimes from the *haftarah*, and quite frequently on verses from Song of Songs. However there is also a volume collecting a substantial number of *derushim* that begin by expounding passages from Talmud, Zohar, and the text of the prayers.[48] The teachings in another volume take as their 'text' a theme in the kabbalah or an idea from hasidic teaching.[49] The typical form of these discourses starts with the 'text', then launches into a topic of hasidic 'philosophy', based on ideas about the soul, Godliness, the spiritual nature of existence, one's relationship with the divine through Torah study, prayer, and performance of the commandments—and then returns to the original 'text'.

As suggested above, when discussing Shaul Magid's treatment of Bratslav teachings, the foregoing techniques could be seen to parallel the way in which a *midrash* like *Leviticus Rabbah* uses the initial text from the Pentateuch to open up a theolog-

---

[45] BT *Ta'an.* 7a.   [46] *Tanya*, pt. 1, ch. 4, fo. 8b.

[47] The first publications, edited by R. Menahem Mendel (the Tsemah Tsedek), third leader of Habad–Lubavitch, were *Torah or* (Kopyst, 1837) and *Likutei torah* (Zhitomir, 1848). In the second half of the 20th cent. the Kehot Publication Society published over twenty volumes of R. Shneur Zalman's teachings from manuscript transcriptions with the generic title *Maamorei admur hazoken*.

[48] *Maamorei admur hazoken al maamorei razal (shas, zohar, usefiloh)* (Brooklyn, NY, 1984).

[49] *Maamorei admur hazoken al inyonim* (Brooklyn, NY, 1983).

ical discourse through associated texts drawn from such 'wisdom' sources as the books of Proverbs and Ecclesiastes.

Looking at the work of Rabbi Shneur Zalman, we therefore see the creation of a large literature in which a form of kabbalistic midrashic exegesis became the vehicle to convey to his followers hasidic mystical ideas about *bitul*, hasidic selflessness, love of the divine, the significance of the commandments, and inspired perceptions of the nature of existence. Many of these ideas were also taught by his colleagues in the leadership of the hasidic movement at the turn of the nineteenth century. However, together with the midrashic element in his exposition of these concepts there was also a 'philosophical' dimension, which provides a sense of a rational, discursive development of a theme.[50] These elements together created the distinctively cerebral 'Habad' genre of hasidic teachings,[51] which was continued by Rabbi Shneur Zalman's successors in the leadership of that school.

STUDY OF THE AGGADAH

Rabbi Shneur Zalman was a noted halakhist who compiled a new edition of the *Shulḥan arukh*.[52] It is interesting that in his halakhic writings he strongly encouraged the study of the aggadah. His first published work, a halakhic tract on the laws of Torah study, in a passage giving advice to the seasoned scholar who has thorough knowledge of the entire Written and Oral Torah recommends regular study of the aggadah, quoting *Sifrei Deuteronomy*: 'If you want to know He who spoke and the world came into being—learn the words of aggadah, for through them you will know the Holy One, blessed be He, and will cleave to His ways.'[53] He also declares that 'most secrets of the Torah, the wisdom of the kabbalah, and knowledge of the divine are concealed in the aggadah', an idea based on the Lurianic writings.[54] This idea is also cited in a letter by Rabbi Shneur Zalman to the communities of his followers, instituting daily study of the *Ein ya'akov* anthology of talmudic aggadah compiled by Rabbi Jacob ibn Habib (1460–1526) in the synagogue 'between the afternoon and the evening prayer', adding that according to the Lurianic writings

---

[50] See Naftali Loewenthal, '"Reason" and "Beyond Reason" in Habad Hasidism', in Moshe Hallamish (ed.), *Alei shefer: Studies in the Literature of Jewish Thought Presented to Rabbi Dr Alexandre Safran* (Ramat Gan, 1990), 109–26.

[51] Note that the word Habad is an acronym of Hokhmah, Binah, and Da'at—wisdom, understanding, and knowledge—the 'cerebral' *sefirot*, contrasting with Hesed (kindness), Gevurah (severity), and so on, the *sefirot* depicting 'emotion'.

[52] For a full bibliographical account of R. Shneur Zalman's halakhic writings, see Y. Mondshine, *The Halakhic Works of Rabbi Shneur Zalman of Liadi* [Sifrei hahalakhah shel admor hazaken (ba'al hatanya vehashulḥan arukh): bibliografiyah] (Kfar Chabad, 1984).

[53] R. Shneur Zalman, *Hilkhot talmud torah* (first published anonymously Shklov, 1794; Brooklyn, NY, 1968), 2: 2, fo. 13*a*, citing *Sifrei Deuteronomy* on 'Ekev', end of §13 (on Deut. 11: 22). See also ibid. 2: 9, fo. 15*b*.

[54] Ibid. 2: 2, fo. 13*a*; cf. the Lurianic prayer book, *Kavanat halimud*, ed. R. Shabbatai of Rashkov (Korets, 1794/5; modern repr. Israel, no place, no date), fo. 130*a*.

study of the aggadah achieves atonement for the individual.[55] He saw this study as approximating to the study of overtly mystical teachings, and perhaps even more important.

Hence we see Rabbi Shneur Zalman at the turn of the nineteenth century as a figure who encouraged the study of aggadah in the hasidic community, and who, like his contemporaries Rabbi Menahem Nahum of Chernobyl, Rabbi Nahman of Bratslav, and later figures like Rabbi Judah Leib Alter, created in his own teachings a midrashic literature for his own time—namely, a hasidic *derush* literature, which became the substance of the communication of hasidic spirituality among his followers.

We will now consider some aspects of this focus on Midrash and midrashic modes of exposition in Habad during the subsequent two centuries.

MIDRASH AND TWENTIETH-CENTURY HABAD

In subsequent generations, each Habad leader—sometimes there was more than one at the same time—would produce teachings broadly of the style of Rabbi Shneur Zalman's oral discourses and often modelled on his original themes. These are published in many Hebrew volumes—about a score by Rabbi Shneur Zalman's son and successor Rabbi Dov Ber (1773–1827), and more than twice as many by his successor Rabbi Menahem Mendel, the Tsemah Tsedek (d. 1866).

Fluency of knowledge of Midrash as well as of other aspects of Torah was an important element in the repertoire of these hasidic leaders. It is said that the fifth Lubavitcher Rebbe, Rabbi Shalom Dovber (d. 1920) would study the whole *Midrash Rabbah* every year, week by week—'"borrowing in the long *sidrot*"[56] and "paying back" in the shorter ones'.[57] He would also study the Torah, Prophets, and Writings daily, learning chapters by heart, as well as studying the Mishnah, the two Talmuds, and halakhic writings.[58] These ingredients helped him weave his fascinating lengthy tracts of kabbalistic–hasidic philosophy, which he would teach week by week, each one interleaved with a comment on the weekly Torah portion.[59] It is noteworthy that *Midrash Rabbah* is included in this list of 'revealed Torah' that he would study

---

[55] See *Tanya*, pt. 4, ch. 23, fo. 137a, and the passage in the Lurianic prayer-book about the study of aggadah cited in the previous note.

[56] *Seder*, *sedra*, *sidra*, and *parashah* are terms for one of the fifty-three portions into which the Pentateuch is divided for communal recitation in the synagogue each week. *Midrash Rabbah* and several other midrashic collections are divided in the same way, except that some portions are much longer than others. The passage quoted suggests R. Shalom Dovber would study *Midrash Rabbah* week by week approximately following the current Torah portion, balancing the longer portions in the Midrash against those which are shorter.

[57] See R. Menachem Schneerson, *Hayom yom*, entry for 3 Nisan.   [58] Ibid.

[59] For a brief discussion of the hasidic discourses of R. Shalom Dovber, see Naftali Loewenthal, 'Joining Worlds: The Revealed and Hidden Torah, Study and Action—The Yeshivah of the Last Rebbe of Lubavitch' (Heb.), in Immanuel Etkes (ed.), *Yeshivot and Batei Midrash* [Yeshivot uvatei midrash] (Jerusalem, 2006), 385–6.

regularly, apart from kabbalistic and hasidic works, which provided the main themes for his published writings.[60]

One can suggest that in the traditional community in eastern Europe, *Midrash Rabbah* was seen as a central canon of basic Midrash. Indeed, the complete 'set' of *Midrash Rabbah*, on the Pentateuch and the Five Megillot, had been printed as a unit as early as 1545 in Venice, by Bomberg, in 'square letters', thus enhancing its status as a sacred text.[61] This sense of 'canonization' of course did not exclude from study the other important collections of *midrashim*, such as *Tanḥuma*, but it did mean that complete editions of *Midrash Rabbah* were frequently published, including the splendid 1878 Vilna edition 'with fifteen commentaries' (the 1887 edition added even more). The composition of these commentaries, such as the *Matanot kehunah* by R. Issachar Ber Katz in the sixteenth century (first printed in Kraków, in 1597), and their inclusion on the printed pages of such grand editions added to the general sense of significance of *Midrash Rabbah*.

There is no evidence at all that the students of the Lubavitch yeshiva founded in 1897 spent much time specifically studying passages from the Midrash. However, they did assiduously study the Habad hasidic teachings that incorporate them. In the case of the sixth *rebbe*, Rabbi Joseph Isaac, during the 1930s when his main yeshiva was in Otwock, near Warsaw, some yeshiva students were privileged to hear his discourses directly. On Friday evening, when he would recite the discourse in public, a group of just ten yeshiva students was permitted to join the senior hasidic followers who were present. After this one hearing they would be expected to know it by heart, and during the sabbath they would each repeat it so that other members of the yeshiva and the community could hear it. A student who could not memorize the entire discourse in one hearing would not be permitted to be a member of the chosen ten the next time.[62] After being rescued from the Warsaw ghetto, and

---

[60] The story is related that R. Shalom Dovber asked his prominent follower, R. Asher of Nikolayev (editor of the 1900 Vilna edn. of *Tanya*)—'Do you have a *Midrash Rabbah* at home?' R. Asher replied in the negative. The Rebbe continued: 'If you have Rabbenu Tam tefillin, you also have to have a *Midrash Rabbah*' (heard from Yisroel Kozminsky, July 2009). The association of *Midrash Rabbah* with the second pair of tefillin worn by hasidim, which have an exalted spiritual status, is striking. Regarding Rabbenu Tam tefillin in Habad, see N. Loewenthal, '"From the Source of *Raḥamim*": Graveside Prayer of Habad Hasidism', in Robert H. Hayward and Brad Embry (eds.), *Studies in Jewish Prayer* (Oxford, 2005), 207–23, esp. 211–12.

[61] When Hebrew printing began, 'square' or 'block' Hebrew letters, that is, a simplified form of the script employed in Torah scrolls or in formal documents, were used for printing biblical texts, and also for Mishnah and Talmud. Commentaries on the Bible and Talmud, and other works of lesser sanctity, were printed in a form of cursive script. This became known as 'Rashi' lettering since it was used for Rashi's commentaries on the Bible and Talmud. Printing *Midrash Rabbah* in square letters rather than 'Rashi' lettering helped to emphasize its significance as a major Jewish text. It is interesting that the first edition of *Tanya* (as well as all subsequent editions) was also printed in 'square letters', distinguishing it from many rabbinic works of the period which were printed in 'Rashi' typeface.

[62] Oral communication in 2003 from the late R. Zev Greenglass (d. 2011), for many years *rosh yeshivah* of the Lubavitch yeshiva in Montreal, who had been a student in Otwock.

reaching the United States in 1940,[63] Rabbi Joseph Isaac founded the Lubavitch yeshiva at 770 Eastern Parkway in Brooklyn, where he also resided. The rules for hearing the discourses were relaxed,[64] and he would also write them down. Later his successor, Rabbi Menachem Mendel Schneerson, the seventh Lubavitcher Rebbe (1902–94), would deliver discourses at large hasidic gatherings. A special melody would precede the discourse and everyone would stand while it was delivered. A group of *ḥozerim*, 'repeaters', led by Rabbi Yoel Kahn, would memorize the discourse during that one hearing and later transcribe it. As in the previous generation, the yeshiva students were expected to be able to repeat by heart the various discourses they had studied.[65]

I thus see the twentieth-century discourses of Habad as combining an intense, esoteric quality, exemplified by the restricted permission to hear them and the special melody, with the quest to communicate. This duality is also expressed in their content, combining esoteric kabbalistic terminology and ideas, blended with exoteric midrashic themes. (And to a varying extent, as mentioned above, these elements have an overlay of a philosophical, discursive style.)

Apart from the more formal, and more mystical, discourses, both the sixth and seventh Lubavitch leaders would give *siḥot* (talks). The edited *siḥot* of the seventh *rebbe* fill over forty volumes and are wide-ranging discussions of the Torah readings and the festivals, in which there is constant quotation and interpretation of midrashic and aggadic material. This became a vehicle for presentation of the seventh *rebbe*'s ideas and world-view. Illustrative is a teaching on the concept of Midrash itself, which presents the idea that Midrash and other 'oral' aspects of Torah are the result of a mass repentance on the part of the Jewish people. This act spiritually empowered them to the extent that they could *add* to the Torah.

THE SECOND TABLETS OF THE LAW

According to *Exodus Rabbah*, Moses was very upset about the breaking of the first Tablets of the Law. However,

> God said to him: Do not be upset about the First Tablets, which only contained the Ten Commandments. For on the Second Tablets I am giving you there will be *halakhot*, Midrash, and aggadot, as it says 'He shall tell you the secrets of wisdom, for there is double [what you imagine] in [divine] knowledge.' [Job 11: 6][66]

---

[63] See Bryan Mark Rigg, *Rescued from the Reich: How One of Hitler's Soldiers Saved the Lubavitcher Rebbe* (New Haven, Conn., 2004).

[64] Due to accelerating multiple sclerosis his speech was slurred and it was hard to understand what he was saying.

[65] This demand is initiated at bar mitzvah, when the 13-year-old boy is expected to recite by heart a discourse on the meaning of tefillin.

[66] *Exod. Rabbah* 46: 1. In the scriptural verse, Zophar the Naamathite is rebuking Job, expressing the wish that God would reveal more of his wisdom to him, so that he would realize he had been dealt with leniently. See also BT *Ned.* 22b.

Rabbi Menachem Schneerson discussed this idea in a number of talks. At the time of the original giving of the Torah, the Israelites should have been *tsadikim* (righteous). But in fact they were not: they served the Golden Calf—hence the Tablets of the Law were broken. Had the people been righteous, they would have received only the Law in the brief form of the Decalogue. Why? Because the chief characteristic of a *tsadik* is that he keeps the Law, following its instructions fully and without deviation. He is wholly guided by it; that is, he 'receives from' and wholeheartedly accepts the Torah (*mekabel fun torah*) as God's direct word of instruction. But this, in fact, limits him.

By contrast, when the Israelites received the Second Tablets they were not on the level of the righteous, but rather of the *ba'al teshuvah*, or penitent—for they had sinned with the Golden Calf, and had subsequently repented. Now the power of repentance is such that 'it arouses and reveals the source of the soul ... which is higher than the Torah'. And since those who received the Second Tablets had repented, they reached a spiritual level higher than that they had attained at the original revelation. Instead of merely *receiving* instruction from the Torah (being *mekabel fun torah*), like *tsadikim*, the righteous, these ancestors of the Jews were actually empowered to *add* something to the Torah—*zeynen yidden mashpia in torah*.

As a result the Second Tablets are not just a series of brief divine statements of the Law but now somehow incorporate all future human discussions of *halakhot*, Midrash, and aggadot. The spiritual power of repentance thus remarkably enabled them *leḥadesh*, to extrapolate new Torah teachings themselves.[67] This statement was made notwithstanding another favourite theme for Rabbi Schneerson, which stressed that all future Torah teachings were communicated to Moses himself at Sinai.[68]

Another, complementary explanation by Rabbi Menachem Schneerson is that through the process of the breaking of the First Tablets and the recognition of sin, the Jewish people achieved the quality of *shiflut*, humility. This enabled them to open their hearts to the infinity of Torah as expressed in the breadth of '*halakhot*, Midrash, and aggadot'—in contrast to the specific and defined text of Scripture. This is indicated in the liturgical phrase (found in the private meditation at the conclusion of the Amidah): 'Let my soul be as dust to everything; open my heart to Your Torah.'[69] That is, if one is as humble as the dust, the breadth of Torah is accessible to the heart. For Rabbi Schneerson, this bounty of Midrash includes the mystical dimensions of Torah and hasidic teaching, which he regarded as included in the 'secrets of wisdom' mentioned in the above-quoted passage from *Exodus Rabbah*.[70] What is of special significance is that this perspective also views Midrash and mysticism as on a theological and exegetical continuum. If there is a difference, this

---

[67] R. Menachem Schneerson, *Likutei siḥot*, vol. ix (Brooklyn, NY, 1978), 242.
[68] See JT *Pe'ah* 2: 4; *Tanḥuma* (Buber), 'Ki tisa' 17.
[69] *Likutei siḥot*, vol. xxvi (Brooklyn, NY, 1988), 249–52.
[70] See *Likutei siḥot*, vol. xxix (Brooklyn, NY, 1991), 258.

might be due to the fact that within the normative cultural milieu, Midrash *can* be openly expressed, whereas mysticism needs to be concealed. However, when the borders between the exoteric and esoteric are to some extent dissolved, and mysticism is more openly revealed—as in Habad hasidism—then *all* Torah teachings take on a mystical hue. For the devotee of esoteric mysticism, of course, this has, in fact, always been the case.

It is interesting to compare these interpretations by Rabbi Menachem Schneerson on the difference between the First and Second Tablets with that of Rabbi Judah Leib Alter. The late twentieth-century Habad explanation just noted sees the addition of '*halakhot*, Midrash, and aggadot' to the original statements of the Ten Commandments as something positive. In contrast Rabbi Judah Leib Alter, in his *Sefat emet*, depicts this change as the very opposite—namely, as an expression of the concealment of the divine. In his view, before the sin of the Golden Calf Godliness was revealed to an extraordinary degree. Citing the famous *midrash*: '"Engraved on the Tablets" [Exod. 32: 16]—Do not read *ḥarut* "engraved", but [rather] *ḥerut* "freedom"',[71] he taught that at Sinai the Jewish people were spiritually 'free' to ascend to higher worlds and descend to this material world without hindrance, like Adam before he sinned, or like Elijah. Correspondingly, the Torah was similarly 'free', and the ultimate revelation of the divine could be expressed in the Ten Commandments heard at Sinai. The transgression of the Golden Calf changed all this fundamentally: the sacred letters of the Ten Commandments could no longer dwell freely in this world on the physical tablets and 'flew away'.[72] From that time on Torah was not free—and even after the repentance of Israel and the giving of the Second Tablets, the Torah had to be concealed, even 'imprisoned', in the vessels of halakhah, Midrash, and aggadah. Only in this form could it enter our physical world. But despite this situation, on the sacred sabbath some aspect of the prior freedom returns and the Torah text again reveals the divine. It is for this reason that there is a public reading of the Torah on the sabbath.[73]

For the *Sefat emet* the Midrash and halakhah thus conceal (even 'imprison') the divine, yet this teaching also emphasizes the sense of contact with divine holiness through the chanting of the Torah on the sabbath. By contrast, the Lubavitcher Rebbe's interpretation depicts the halakhah, Midrash, and aggadah as expressing the infinite boundlessness of the Torah, for the effect of repentance empowered the people of Israel to add this dimension and to receive it within their hearts. The differences in interpretation can be understood as relating to the Habad emphasis on the great spiritual power of mystical texts, as against their dismissal in Kotsk–Ger, as noted earlier. For the author of the *Sefat emet*, the goal is not to authenticate the chain of Oral Torah texts but to heighten one's experience of the pure Written Torah on the sabbath.[74] Another point for consideration in evaluating the two contrasting

---

[71] Mishnah *Avot* 6: 2.   [72] See *Pesikta zutarta* (also known as *Midrash lekaḥ tov*), 'Ekev'.
[73] *Sefat emet* (Piotrkov, 1905), *Exodus*, 'Ki tisa' 5756 [1896], fo. 106a, p. 211.
[74] See Yoram Jacobson's article on the theme of the sabbath in Ger hasidism: 'The Sanctification of

interpretations of this *midrash* is the virtual apotheosis of the power of repentance in contemporary Lubavitch thought, which leads to its particular form of religious activism. As seen, the foregoing interpretation of *Exodus Rabbah* given by Rabbi Menachem Schneerson presents the idea that repentance fuels the highest attainments—including the ability to add to the Torah.

BATI LEGANI: A *MIDRASH* AS THE BASIS OF A WORLD-VIEW

I shall now investigate how specific midrashic texts were used to generate certain varieties of spiritual consciousness. In doing so, I go back in time to the sixth *rebbe*, Rabbi Joseph Isaac, who became a hasidic leader after the death of his father in 1920. At that time the centre of 'Lubavitch' hasidism had moved to Rostov-Don, in southern Russia, and the religious life of the Jewish community throughout the USSR was severely curtailed by the Bolsheviks and, more particularly, by the Yevsektzia, the Jewish arm of the Communist party. David Fishman has described this period of struggle, in which Rabbi Joseph Isaac fought to maintain traditional Jewish practice, including running secret *ḥadarim* where children were taught about Judaism.[75] He sent his leading followers to the various regions of the USSR in order to strengthen Jewish life. Some of these were arrested, and a number were tortured and killed.

In January 1923 Rabbi Joseph Isaac gave two lengthy discourses on two successive sabbaths (of the portions 'Bo' and 'Beshalaḥ', Exod. chs. 10–17). These discourses developed a unified theme, although the second had opening and concluding sections linked to the Torah reading for the second sabbath. In the opening paragraph, the first discourse quotes from the Song of Songs: 'You that dwell in the gardens, the companions hearken for your voice, let me hear it,'[76] and gives Rashi's commentary, which is loosely related to a passage in *Midrash Rabbah*, which Rabbi Joseph Isaac also cites:

Rashi says 'You who sit in the gardens'—[meaning] God says to the Jewish people, 'You who are scattered in exile, grazing in the gardens of other people, dwelling in synagogues and study houses, the *ḥaverim* are listening—the ministering angels who are your friends ... come to hear your voice in the synagogues'; and this is from *Midrash Rabbah*[77] [which states] that 'When [the people of] Israel sits in the synagogues and study houses and says

---

the Profane in Gur Hasidism: Reflections on the Concept of the Sabbath in the Teachings of the "Sefat Emet"' (Heb.), in Rachel Elior et al. (eds.), *Hasidism in Poland* [Ḥasidim ve'anshei ma'aseh: meḥkarim beḥasidut polin] (Jerusalem, 1994), 241–77, and Michael Fishbane, 'Transcendental Consciousness and Stillness in the Mystical Theology of R. Yehudah Arieh Leib of Gur', in Gerald J. Blidstein (ed.), *Sabbath: Idea, History, Reality* (Be'er Sheva, 2004), 119–29.

[75] See David E. Fishman, 'Preserving Tradition in the Land of Revolution: The Religious Leadership of Soviet Jewry, 1917–1930', in Jack Wertheimer (ed.), *The Uses of Tradition: Jewish Continuity in the Modern Era* (New York, 1992), 85–118.

[76] S. of S. 8: 13.

[77] See S. of S. *Rabbah* 8: 15.

the Shema and studies Torah, the *ḥaverim* listen, I [God] and My *pamaliyah* [group of ministering angels] come to hear your voice.'[78]

The goal of this discourse, of course, is to encourage the beleaguered traditional Jews of the USSR, especially his own hasidic followers, to continue to pray, attend the synagogue, and to study Torah, despite the risks involved. The midrashic depiction of the angels is used to promote normative Jewish practice in a time of struggle—an interpretation quite close to the original intent of the midrashic text. But although this passage is a recurrent theme of the discourse, Rabbi Joseph Isaac then turns to another topic, which would eventually captivate the imagination of the Habad movement for half a century.

'To explain this matter', says Rabbi Joseph Isaac, 'note that it is written "I have come into My garden [*bati legani*], My sister, [My] bride" [S. of S. 5: 1].' He then quotes *Midrash Rabbah* (that is, *S. of S. Rabbah*) on that verse:

It does not say to [a or the] garden but *gani*, meaning *liginuni*, to My bridal chamber, to the place of My root [or 'essence', *ikari*] at the beginning. For the essence of the Shekhinah was in the lower world [*bataḥtonim*], but because of the sin of the Tree of Knowledge the Shekhinah departed from the earth to the [lowest heavenly] firmament; and because of the sin[s] of Cain and Enosh the Shekhinah departed from the first firmament to the second and the third; and after that, in the generation of the Flood, it departed from the third firmament to the fourth.[79]

This description of the original presence of the Shekhinah in the world, in the Garden of Eden, and its subsequent departure to ever more distant firmaments because of human sin is found in several midrashic sources: in *Song of Songs Rabbah* (5: 1), cited by Rabbi Joseph Isaac, and also in *Genesis Rabbah* (19: 13), *Pesikta rabati* (5: 7), *Tanḥuma* ('Pekudei', 6; 'Naso' 16); *Tanḥuma* (Buber) ('Naso' 24); and *Numbers Rabbah* ('Naso' 13: 4). It also appears in the first section of the fascinating *Pesikta derav kahana*, a *midrash* known to Rashi, then lost, but rediscovered in the early nineteenth century.[80]

---

[78] R. Joseph Isaac Schneersohn, *Sefer hama'amarim 5682–5683* [1921–3] (Brooklyn, NY, 1986), 168.
[79] Ibid.
[80] Leopold Zunz suggested the existence of the *Pesikta derav kahana* in his *Die gottesdienstlichen Vortraege der Juden historisch entwickelt* (1832). Over the next decades several manuscripts came to light. In 1868 Solomon Buber published it for the first time, and in 1962 a new critical edition edited by Dov (Bernard) Mandelbaum appeared (see above, n. 22). Both in the Buber edition and in that of Mandelbaum, the explanation of Song 5: 1 is the first *piska* in the collection. Solomon Buber based his edition, and the order of the sections, on a manuscript from Safed, copied in Egypt in 1565 (now in the Alliance Française library in Paris), comparing it with three other manuscripts. One of the latter was a manuscript in the Bodleian Library (MS Marshall Or. 24), dating from 1291. Mandelbaum based his edition of the text on this Oxford manuscript of the *Pesikta derav kahana*. Leopold Zunz intuited the existence of *Pesikta derav kahana* on the evidence of references to it by medieval scholars. According to his listing, the *midrash* began with the *piska* for Rosh Hashanah. This suggested order is seen in another Oxford manuscript (Opp. Add. 4to, 128; Neubauer no. 2339/11), which was only relatively recently discovered to be a text of *Pesikta derav kahana*. In this text the first *piska* is for Rosh Hashanah (*baḥodesh hashevi'i*) and the collection continues in

As we might expect, the precise wording of this account of the departure of the Shekhinah differs from one version to another. It is interesting that Rabbi Joseph Isaac's phrasing, which states that the Shekhinah ascended 'from the third firmament to the fourth' (that is, mentioning both the lower firmament that is abandoned and then the one above it), is not the one found in the *Song of Songs Rabbah* version that he cites, but rather occurs in *Tanḥuma* (Buber) and *Pesikta derav kahana* versions.[81]

Pesikta derav kahana was first published by Solomon Buber (Lyck, 1868) who also published his edition of the *Tanḥuma* (Vilna, 1885). Rabbi Joseph Isaac possessed an extensive library, now housed at the Lubavitch headquarters in Brooklyn. The catalogue of this collection is available and shows that the library contains Buber's editions of *Pesikta derav kahana* and of *Tanḥuma*.[82] I have not, however, been able to ascertain whether these had been acquired by 1923, when these discourses were composed. Later, after Rabbi Joseph Isaac's death in 1950, the Lubavitch Library, under the leadership of his successor Rabbi Menachem Mendel, also obtained Bernard Mandelbaum's edition of *Pesikta derav kahana*.[83]

Although he might be partly quoting one or other of these texts, Rabbi Joseph Isaac does not mention either *Pesikta derav kahana* or *Tanḥuma*, but only the *Midrash Rabbah*. This is due to the above-mentioned 'canonization' of the *Midrash Rabbah* among eastern European Jewry—as mentioned above, partly as a result of printers' promotion of the work and also of the fact that significant commentaries on it had been written.[84] Since Buber's editions of *Pesikta derav kahana* and *Tanḥuma* were probably rare volumes in Rostov, it was natural for Rabbi Joseph Isaac to cite the popular and accessible *Song of Songs Rabbah*. (Notably, the catalogue of his library lists 179 entries for *Midrash Rabbah*—from the earliest printings until those of the twentieth century.)

In the next part of his discourse, where the Shekhinah is far away from the world, the different midrashic versions present slightly varying accounts of its

---

the order of the Jewish calendar. Evidence in favour of this order comes from Nathan ben Yehiel of Rome's *Arukh* (entries for מסקיד, מסאסא) which mentions the Rosh Hashanah *piska* as *rosh piskaot*, i.e. 'the beginning of the *piskaot*', a term understood to be a reference to *Pesikta derav kahana*. (On this see Mandelbaum's introduction to his edition of *Pesikta derav kahana*, i. 7–9, 12–13).

[81] See Buber edn., 1b; Mandelbaum edn., vol. i, p. 2. See also Buber's edition of *Midrash Tanḥuma* (Vilna, 1885), ii, 'Naso', §24, fos. 19a–b.

[82] The catalogue is available on the 'Chabad Library CD-ROM' and also online at <www.chabadlibrary.org>.

[83] The interest in midrashic texts among the Habad–Lubavitch leadership is indicated by the following anecdote. At the time when Bernard Mandelbaum began working on his edition of *Pesikta derav kahana* he went to visit R. Menachem Schneerson, the Lubavitcher Rebbe. The Rebbe asked him which manuscripts he was using, and he gave the information. The Rebbe then said 'But there are two more manuscripts!', of which Mandelbaum was ignorant. (This was related by Mandelbaum's father-in-law, Murray Werber, to Professor Arnold Enker, who related it to me in July 2004.)

[84] See above, and Zeev Gries, 'The Book as a Cultural Agent from the Beginning of Printing to the Modern Period' (Heb.), in Howard Kreisel, *Study and Knowledge in Jewish Thought* [Limud veda'at bemaḥshavah yehudit], vol. ii (Be'er Sheva, 2004), 237–58.

retreat, and Rabbi Joseph Isaac provides only a general outline. Thereupon, he depicts the return of the Shekhinah to the world:

And after that there arose seven *tsadikim* who brought the Shekhinah below. Abraham had the merit to draw it from the seventh firmament to the sixth, Isaac from the sixth to the fifth, until Moses who is the seventh (and all sevenths are precious) brought it down to the world.[85]

Song of Songs Rabbah, *Pesikta derav kahana*, and *Tanḥuma* (Buber) all provide a full list of the seven *tsadikim*, unlike Rabbi Joseph Isaac. However, none of them mention that 'all sevenths are precious'. But a fully developed exposition of this idea does occur elsewhere (in *Pesikta derav kahana* and *Lev. Rabbah*)—namely, that all sevenths are precious, whether in terms of firmaments, lands, generations, leader-figures, or kings, and so on.[86] We shall return to this theme.

After having described the fact that Moses brought the divine presence back into the world, Rabbi Joseph Isaac's discourse continues: 'And the main revelation of Godliness was in the Temple, as it says "And they should make for Me a Sanctuary and I will dwell in them" [Exod. 25: 8].' There follows a striking idea, based on the writings of several sixteenth-century kabbalists: 'Scripture does not say "in it", that the Divine Presence will dwell "in it", in the Sanctuary, but "in them"—in each individual.'[87]

This interpretation expresses the idea that the Sanctuary is a personal indwelling of the divine. By contrast, the midrashic sources on which this discourse is based speak of the dwelling of the divine itself in the Sanctuary. In *Pesikta derav kahana*, especially, the whole *pesikta* becomes a hymn to the greatness of the Sanctuary, portrayed through a variety of images. Among these are: the (secluded) Tent of Meeting, where the king and his nubile daughter (Israel) can meet;[88] a place filled with divine radiance, much as a cave by the sea is filled with water;[89] and a structure made of red, green, black, and white fire— the Lower Sanctuary reflecting the Upper.[90]

Rabbi Joseph Isaac's discourse does not contain any of this imagery. However, in its first half (recited on the first sabbath) it presents a variety of ways in which to understand the task of the individual Jew who is carrying out the service in the inner Sanctuary. Thus, the animal offerings brought to the flames of the altar in the Sanctuary express the attempt to infuse one's animal soul with divine fire, and

---

[85] *Sefer hama'amarim 5682–5683*, 168.
[86] *Pesikta derav kahana*, *piska* for Rosh Hashanah (Mandelbaum edn., vol. ii, pp. 343–4; Buber edn., 154*b* (para. 75)). See also *Lev. Rabbah* 29: 11.
[87] Moses Alsheikh, *Torat mosheh*, on the verse; Elijah b. Moses Vidas, *Reshit ḥokhmah*, vol. i (Jerusalem, 1984), 'Gate of Love', ch. 6, #19, 463; R. Isaiah Halevi Horowitz, *Shenei luḥot haberit*, vol. ii (New York, 1960), *Masekhet ta'anit: derush lehesped mitat hatsadikim uleḥurban*, 134*b*.
[88] *Pesikta derav kahana*, Buber edn., 2*a*; Mandelbaum edn., vol. i, §3, pp. 3–4.
[89] *Pesikta derav kahana*, Buber edn., 2*b*; Mandelbaum edn., vol. i, §2, p. 4.
[90] *Pesikta derav kahana*, Buber edn., 4*b*–5*a*; Mandelbaum edn., vol. i, §3, pp. 7–8.

thereby transform it. The planks of the Sanctuary, on the other hand, are made of *atsei shitim* (variously translated as cedar or acacia wood), and these are explained as hinting at the word *shetut* (folly)—an exegetical link already found in the Talmud and *Tanḥuma* (with reference to Num. 25: 1).[91] Rabbi Joseph Isaac goes on to describe two kinds of 'folly'—a negative folly, descending below the level of reason, which leads to sin, and a 'sacred folly', which expresses a relationship with the divine and transcends reason. As an example of the latter, Rabbi Joseph Isaac then quotes an aggadah from the Talmud (*Ket.* 17*a*) describing the wild dancing of Rabbi Samuel bar Rabbi Isaac on the occasion of a wedding. It is reported that he would juggle with three sticks of myrtle, to the scorn of the other sages, such as Rabbi Zeira. However, when he died a pillar of light revealed his greatness. Rabbi Joseph Isaac links this with the famous teaching of Rabbi Akiva (BT *Sot.* 17*a*), which points out one of the divine names (Y-H) shares letters found in the words *ish* (*alef-yod-shin*, man) and *ishah* (*alef-shin-heh*, woman); that is, if a man and woman join together in loving matrimony their relationship connotes the very presence of the Shekhinah. According to Rabbi Joseph Isaac, Rabbi Samuel was most sensitive to the revelation of the Shekhinah at a wedding and therefore danced in a manner beyond reason, with a 'sacred folly'.[92]

After this, the discourse goes on to speak of the great value of spiritual dedication, or *mesirat nefesh* (self-surrender), for the divine, as well as the power to transform the negative into positive. This point is also made with respect to the Sanctuary. Thus Exodus 26: 15 speaks of using planks for building the Sanctuary. Since a plank is called *keresh*, and this can be understood (midrashically) as an anagram of the word *sheker*, or falsehood, one may find here a hint of the spiritual goal of transforming the falsehood of the negative form of folly into the positive holiness of being like a plank that comprises the holy Sanctuary.[93] The discourse concludes by reverting to a discussion of the Jews in their synagogues and study houses, being overheard by the admiring *ḥaverim*, or angels (see the previous discussion).

The second discourse,[94] delivered a week later, focuses on the divine quality of *netsaḥ* (literally, 'eternity', but the Hebrew root also means 'victory'), which represents both the divine *sefirah* of that name and a specific quality in a person (the will to victory). The high goal of a spiritually developed person is to develop this quality, this will to victory, so that it may reach to the most exalted levels of Ein Sof (the Infinite) and draw down heavenly qualities into this world below. In this manner, the divine may be revealed in the inner sanctuary of the individual. The thrust of this teaching can also be understood in the context of Rabbi Joseph Isaac's defiant stance in the USSR in 1923, as an exhortation to a total dedication to Judaism at all costs.

[91] *Sefer hama'amarim 5682–5683*, 172; see BT *San.* 106*a*, *Tanḥuma*, 'Balak' 16.
[92] *Sefer hama'amarim 5682–5683*, 175. R. Joseph Isaac does not cite the negative possibility in R. Akiva's *derush*, that if their marriage is not successful (morally or spiritually) then they would be destroyed by the *esh* ('fire') which is present in both the words *ish* and *ishah*.
[93] Ibid. 182.
[94] Ibid. 183–96.

In 1927 Rabbi Joseph Isaac was arrested for his work in strengthening Judaism, and it seems that only international protest saved him from the death sentence. Instead, he was expelled from the USSR and eventually took up residence in Otwock, Poland, where he had established a Lubavitch yeshiva. In the spring of 1939, perhaps with a sense of impending doom, he wrote a précis of the first half of the discourse described above and gave it to his followers to study.[95] In it, the order at the beginning has been changed. It starts with 'I have come into my garden' (S. of S. 5: 1) and therefore begins with a history of Creation, defining the divine goal as the wish for a dwelling of holiness in this world, which is achieved in the inner sanctuary. The next time we encounter this discourse is in Brooklyn in 1950, when a transcript of the full 1923 version[96] was prepared for printing, subdivided into twenty chapters.[97] Rabbi Joseph Isaac's son-in-law, Rabbi Menachem Mendel, who was responsible for the Lubavitch publications, added (as he often did) some source references as footnotes to the work. The discourse was printed in order to be studied on 10 Shevat, the *yahrzeit* of Rabbi Joseph Isaac's grandmother Rivkah (1833–1914), wife of the fourth Lubavitcher Rebbe, Rabbi Samuel Schneersohn (1834–82). However, on this day Rabbi Joseph Isaac himself passed away, and thus this discourse, with its comprehensive view of the purpose of Creation, was regarded as his last will and testament. Whereas in its original setting, in 1923, it could be seen as expressing a stance against Communist oppression, in 1950 it expressed a different challenge: the materialism and comfort of American life. The idea of the synagogue and the Torah study circle as the place where the angels, the *ḥaverim*, listen to the voices of the Jewish people (now a passage introducing the sixth chapter of the discourse) had new significance in a very different context.

Before we approach this new topic, let us review what has been discussed so far. Beginning with Rabbi Shneur Zalman, and extending into the twentieth century, Midrash served, both in its own right and as a generator of new forms, as a medium which could translate intense and recondite spiritual perspectives into more broadly accessible, relatively 'exoteric' modes. One effect of this was the evolution of an unusual, even unique, contemporary expression of eschatological processes.

ESCHATOLOGY AND MIDRASH

On 10 Shevat 1951 Rabbi Menachem Mendel formally accepted the role of *rebbe*, thus becoming the seventh Lubavitcher Rebbe. He gave a discourse of his own, based on the last discourse of his father-in-law and beginning with the same *midrash* on the phrase *bati legani* (S. of S. 5: 1, see above). In the course of his lengthy dis-

---

[95] R. Joseph Isaac Schneersohn, *Sefer hama'amarim: kuntresim*, vol. ii (Brooklyn, NY, 1986), 828–34.

[96] The transcript was written by R. Elijah Nahum Skolier. See *Yemei bereshit: yoman mitekufat 'kabalat hanesiut'* (Brooklyn, NY, 1993), 98.

[97] Brief summaries were appended to each chapter, as in the case of other discourses by R. Joseph Isaac.

course, he focused on the phrase interpolated by Rabbi Joseph Isaac: 'all sevenths are precious', which in its context explained why Moses, the seventh *tsadik*, was able to draw the Shekhinah back to the world. This theme of the power of the 'seventh' was used to highlight what one might regard as an incidental feature of the Habad–Lubavitch movement: namely, that Rabbi Menachem Mendel represented the seventh generation of Habad–Lubavitch leadership.[98] But now, in his first discourse as *rebbe*, he emphasized the theme of the special empowerment and responsibility of the seventh generation to bring the divine presence into the world.[99] The theme of the 'seventh' fuelled his outreach work and sense of the implicit holiness of *this* world: the Shekhinah can indeed be revealed here on earth, for, despite all appearances to the contrary, the world is a 'garden'. Each year on 10 Shevat he would deliver another discourse, always based on the original *midrash* on the phrase *bati legani*, and expound the original discourse chapter by chapter, year by year. Thus in 1951 the focus was on the first chapter, in 1952 on the second, and so on.

These discourses, collected in two volumes, represent a further stage of the ongoing interpretative process. They expound not only the scriptural verse and the midrashic text, but Rabbi Joseph Isaac's exposition and elaboration of the *midrash* as well. Their theme is set by the midrashic approach to the text 'I have come into my garden' as meaning that the goal of Creation is that the divine presence should have a dwelling-place in our physical world, in the Temple itself, and in the temple in the heart of each individual.

To take just one example, we saw above the logical progression from the verse 'I have come into my garden' to the symbolism of the Sanctuary, its walls made of acacia wood, representing folly, and ultimately sacred folly, as illustrated by the description of Rabbi Samuel dancing wildly at a wedding (because of the revelation of the Shekhinah expressed in the union of bride and groom). In his discourse of 10 Shevat, 1955, Rabbi Menachem Mendel elaborates on the theme of bride and groom, and expounds on the liturgical text of the wedding blessings. Citing an earlier discourse of Rabbi Dov Ber, the second Lubavitcher Rebbe, the Rebbe remarked:

[on the] fact that one says in the wedding blessings, 'Make the beloved companions rejoice, as You made Your creation rejoice in Gan Eden long ago [*mikedem*]'. [Rabbi Dov Ber] explains that *mikedem* means before the down-chaining of the worlds. For in the realm of the down-chaining of the worlds, the male is above and the female below ... but [originally, and ultimately] not only are they equal, but ... the bride is above the groom and he receives from her ... [Moreover], at the conclusion of the wedding blessings one says

---

[98] Beginning with R. Shneur Zalman, the list comprises his son R. Dov Ber, his son-in-law (a grandson of R. Shneur Zalman), R. Menahem Mendel (the Tsemah Tsedek), his son R. Samuel, his son R. Shalom Dov Ber, and finally his son, R. Joseph Isaac. This list traces a line through the generations, ignoring various rivals in each generation from the second onwards who were 'Habad' but not 'Lubavitch'. R. Menachem Mendel, the seventh leader, was a descendant of the Tsemah Tsedek and son-in-law of his predecessor R. Joseph Isaac.

[99] See R. Menachem Mendel Schneerson, *Bati legani*, vol. i (Brooklyn, NY, 1977), 31.

'Make the groom rejoice with the bride,' so that the groom may rejoice with that which is higher than him... This explains the connection of dancing to a wedding. For in order to draw down an aspect that is higher than the down-chaining of the worlds, there must be a worship that transcends reason—and that is why [the sages] would dance.[100]

If we follow the logic of this discourse, the theme of the indwelling of the divine in this world is linked to an emphasis on the spiritual power of the feminine. It is admitted that this is not the current mode in the 'down-chaining of worlds', which here means not only the realm of the *sefirot* but also, more generally, the pre-messianic world order, yet it is the ultimate mode to which one should aspire. For in the time of the messiah, the Essence of the Divine, beyond the 'down-chaining' of the *sefirot*, will be revealed. In social-historical terms this theoretical passage joins to a process that slowly unfolded during Rabbi Menachem Mendel's leadership, unusually empowering women in the context of strictly Orthodox (*ḥaredi*) society.[101]

A more general feature of the *Bati legani* discourses relates to the messianic thrust in Habad. The war years of the 1940s had been a period of intense messianism for the small Lubavitch circle around Rabbi Joseph Isaac. His slogan had been *le'alter liteshuvah, le'alter lige'ulah*: 'immediate repentance, immediate redemption'. Whereas this was muted in the late 1940s after the end of the war, it came to the fore once again as the annual cycle of commentary on the twenty chapters of *Bati legani* drew towards completion in 1970. In his discourse of 10 Shevat that year Rabbi Menachem Mendel linked the outreach work of Habad with the theme of the 'bursting [spreading] outward of the wellsprings', which, as expressed in the letter of the Ba'al Shem Tov cited earlier, would lead to the advent of the messiah.[102] In 1970 the messianic fervour was still contained within the Lubavitch movement, in contrast to the much more intense and overt messianic tension that emerged at the close of the second cycle of discourses in 1990. At the source of both phenomena, however, was the interpretation of the Midrash which declared that the 'seventh' has the power to draw the Shekhinah back down into the world.[103]

---

[100] Schneerson, *Bati legani*, i. 65. See R. Dov Ber, *Seder tefilot mikol hashanah* (Brooklyn, NY, 1971), 'Derushim laḥatunah', 134*a*, 136*b*.

[101] See Bonnie J. Morris, *Lubavitcher Women in America: the Post War Era* (Albany, NY, 1998); N. Loewenthal, 'Women and the Dialectic of Spirituality in Hasidism', in I. Etkes et al. (eds.), *Within Hasidic Circles: Studies in Hasidism in Memory of Mordecai Wilensky* (Jerusalem, 1999), *7-*65; and concerning an earlier period, Ada Rapoport-Albert, 'The Emergence of a Female Constituency in Twentieth Century Habad Hasidism', in David Assaf and Ada Rapoport-Albert (eds.), *Let the Old Make Way for the New: Studies in the Social and Cultural History of Eastern European Jewry Presented to Immanuel Etkes* [Yashan mipenei ḥadash: meḥkarim betoledot yehudei mizraḥ eiropah uvetarbutam. Shai le'imanu'el etkes], 2 vols. (Jerusalem 2009), i: *Hasidism and the Musar Movement* [Ḥasidim uva'alei musar], English section, 7*-68*.

[102] *Bati legani*, i. 232.

[103] See Yitzchak Kraus, *The Seventh: Messianism in the Last Generation of Habad* [Hashevi'i: meshiḥiyut bador hashevi'i shel ḥabad] (Tel Aviv, 2007).

FROM THE MOUNTAIN TO THE PEOPLE

My delineation of Habad's use of a specific *midrash* in different situations over the past ninety years underlines the ability of latter-day hasidic masters to expound a chain of texts, from Scripture to Midrash, and from Midrash to a hasidic text, which then itself becomes the 'text' for further exposition—all with the belief that the sanctity of the divine continues to be transmitted through every link of the chain of transmission. For the Habad movement, this process became a central feature of the endeavour to communicate spirituality to ever wider circles of society.

It is interesting to note the relationship of the *Bati legani* chain of discourses we have discussed to its main midrashic sources in the exposition found in *Pesikta derav kahana*.[104] In this first *piska* in the Buber and Mandelbaum editions,[105] compiled for Hanukah, there is a strong restorative and redemptive theme. The *Pesikta* begins with the classic formulation in rabbinic texts of the state of exile and redemption. After quoting Numbers 7: 1 ('And it was on the day that Moses completed the erection of the Sanctuary', which according to the post-talmudic tractate *Soferim*[106] begins the Torah reading for Hanukah) and Song of Songs 5: 1 ('I have come into My garden'), 'Rabbi Azaria said in the name of Rabbi Simon: [This can be compared] to a king who became angry with the queen and drove her away, sending her out of his palace. After a time, he wished to bring her back.' This forceful metaphor of exile and redemption is transformed into a depiction of the redemptive state as the very goal of Creation, described in the account of Adam and Eve in the Garden of Eden, outlined above.

Both for the fifth-century *Pesikta* and for twentieth-century Habad, the idea of the future restoration of the Temple was prominent. This continuity of theme is striking. Despite the passage of time, and the very different social and historical contexts of the early Midrash and later hasidic discourses, both concern divine immanence, expressed through the erection of the Sanctuary (whether in physical or inner psychological and spiritual terms) and redemption. Indeed, both communicate an inspiring perspective on existence of epic proportions. Thus classical Midrash and latter-day hasidic discourses, based on this *midrash* but also becoming a form of Midrash in themselves, continue to transmit the river of Torah from the esoteric heights of the mountain to the human realities of the everyday world.

---

[104] I am grateful to Michael Fishbane for drawing this to my attention.

[105] The Oxford manuscript which is the basis of the Mandelbaum edition is the earliest known (1291). However, see n. 80 above.

[106] *Soferim* 20: 10. In many communities today this passage is recited only on the first day of Hanukah; on Shabat Hanukah, the passage from Numbers 7 for the corresponding day of Hanukah (beginning Num. 7: 18 'On the second day', Num. 7: 24 'On the third day', and so on) is recited.

INDEX

A

Aaron ben Jose(ph) Hakohen 273, 280
Abba ben Judah 256
Abbahu 17–18, 19–21, 164, 382
Abel, dispute with Cain, Syriac traditions of 88–90
Abraham 121, 229, 272
   circumcision 28–9
   food offered to angels 272–4
   gifts to children of his concubines 293–9
   and Moriah 91
Abrams, Daniel 322–3, 324 n. 17
Abramson, Shraga 216 n. 15, 282–3 n. 47, 287–8 n. 64
Abravanel, Isaac 361, 381, 382 n. 23
Abulafia, Abraham 330
Abun ben Judah 263
Adam, in Tosafist commentary 307, 361–7
aggadah/aggadic Midrash 162, 167, 182–5, 189–90, 191, 192, 328 n. 31, 389–90
   hasidic study of 441–2
   Jerome's use of 64–5, 68, 79 n. 77
   medieval 87, 160, 171–2, 174–95, 224, 229
   and mysticism 433–5
   in Yiddish 411–27
Aibo 110, 118–19
Akedah, location of 90–1
Akhnai's oven, story of 404 n. 58
Akiva 13, 22, 23, 24, 91, 106, 107, 156, 253, 391, 416, 451
   death of 201, 202, 209
Albeck, Hanoch 286 nn. 58 & 59, 350
Albert of Aachen 204 n. 21
Aleinu (prayer) 205
Alexander, Philip 28 n. 12, 42–3 n. 6, 156 n. 38
Alexander of Macedon, stories about 188–95
Alexandria, synagogue in 228
Alphabet of Ben-Sira 177, 364–5 n. 79
Alsheikh, Moses 367
Alter, Judah Leib 430–1, 432, 436, 446
Amalek:
   arrival of 314–16
   attack on the Jews by 316
   destruction/defeat of 30–6, 37, 38, 39

Amidah (prayer) 103, 104
Ammi 182–3, 224
Amnon of Mainz 206
Anatoli, Jacob 371, 372–80, 387
ancient Midrash, *see* classical Midrash
angels:
   descriptions of 28–9, 226, 341, 448
   and humans 151–2, 272–4
anthologies of Midrash 5, 8, 251
   medieval 176–82, 347
   in Yiddish 409–10
   see also *Midrash Rabbah*
anti-Christian polemics 160, 162, 228
   by Anatoli 377–8
   by Rashi 239–40, 242, 246, 247
anti-Jewish violence:
   in France 205, 206–7, 208
   in Germany 198–9, 205, 207–8
   in Spain 208
   in Ukraine 209
Antiquities of the Jews (Josephus) 176, 190
Aphrahat 73 n. 57, 86, 87, 90
apocrypha of New Testament 159
Apollinaris of Laodicea 64
Arama, Isaac 361, 368
Aramaic:
   dialects 83
   poetry 87 n. 21
   translations of Scripture into, *see* Targum/Targumim
Artapanos 176
Arukh (Nathan ben Yehiel) 5–6, 184, 214–15, 220–1, 449 n. 80
   manuscripts of 221–2
   midrashic material in 217–18, 222–9
   non-Jewish context of 218–20
   poetry in 215, 220
   sources of 215–18
   use of 230–1, 359
asceticism 144, 154–5
Aseret harugei malkhut (The Ten Martyrs) 185–8
Ashkenazi, Jacob ben Isaac 425
Ashkenazi, Naphtali ben Joseph 354–5

Ashkenazi Jews/Jewry, medieval martyrdom of 198–201, 202–3, 205, 207, 208
atonement:
 Christian doctrines of 139–40
 Maharal (Judah Loew) on 403 n. 54
 substitutionary 150–1, 152, 153
 on Yom Kippur 376

B

Ba'al Shem Tov, Israel 430, 437
Babylonian Talmud:
 on Abraham's gifts to his concubines' children 293–4
 aggadah in 182–3
 on Esau's sins 306–7
 Gitin cycle stories in 416–22
 on God offering Torah to the nations 241
 on Gog and Magog 166–7
 on honouring one's father and mother 49
 on Jesus 163, 165
 on literal meaning of verses 237
 on names of devil 73
 on Nebuchadnezzar 75
 on Passover 122
 on Rabbi Akiva's death 202
 on Rebecca's age at marriage 300–1, 302
 on revelation of the Law at Sinai 74
 on Solomon's Temple 116
 on synagogue in Alexandria 228
 Tosafot on 269, 271–2
 on Zephaniah 70–1
Bar Kamza 413
Bar Kappara 394
Bar Kokhba revolt 31
Baraita derabi pinḥas ben ya'ir, see *Midrash tadshe*
Baranina 64
Bardy, Gustave 62, 66
Barth, Lewis M. 157 n. 42
Barukh ben Isaac 273, 277
basilica, meaning of word 228
Bati legani discourses 454, 455
Bede 218
Be'er hagolah (Maharal, Judah Loew) 390, 394, 400 nn. 41 & 43, 403 n. 53, 404
beḥinah (aspect) 432 n. 14, 433
Beit-Arié, Malachi 130 n. 74, 222
Bekhor Shor (Joseph ben Isaac) 267–8, 277, 278–9, 288, 308–9, 317 n. 147
Ben Asher, Abraham 359–68, 369
Ben Azzai 22

Ben Gershon, Levi, *see* Ralbag
benedictions, in liturgy 103
Benjamin ben Samuel 118, 122–3
Benjamin of Tudela 154, 214
Benveniste, Meir 351–2, 353–4, 355, 369
Ber Katz, Issachar 443
Berekhiah 22–3, 255, 352, 353, 354, 359
Bereshit rabati 94, 172, 173, 285–6
Berman, Issachar 356–9, 369
Berukhim, Abraham ben Eliezer Halevi 322
Bet ha-Midrash (Jellinek) 160, 173
Bethlehem, messiah being born in 74
Bibago, Abraham 368
Bible, *see* Scripture
Biblical Myth and Rabbinic Mythmaking (Fishbane) 434
Billerbeck, Paul 41
biographies:
 of Alexander of Macedon 189
 of Moses 174–6
Blair, Ann 230–1
Bloch, Renée 62, 63
Blois (France), medieval Jewish martyrs at 205, 206
Boer, Pieter A. H. de 129 n. 74
Bomberg, Daniel 350
Bonfil, Robert 170 nn. 3 & 5
Book of Persecutions (Habermann) 203
books:
 annotations in 354–5
 burning of 360 n. 61
 preaching aids 384 n. 28
Braude, William 18 n. 13, 137 n. 1, 140 n. 10, 141, 143, 149 n. 24
Bregman, Marc 349
Buber, Solomon 218, 223, 257, 448 n. 80, 449

C

Cain, dispute with Abel, Syriac traditions of 88–90
Cairo Genizah, *see* Genizah fragments
cantors, see *ḥazanim*
Carmel, Mt. 127, 128, 129, 130
Catharism 379
Cavallera, Ferdinand 66
'child and the book of Genesis' story 179–82
Christianity:
 on atonement/penal substitution 139–40
 exegetical methods of 245–6
 influence on Midrash of 4, 138–40, 167

Jewish influence on 61–2
Jewish polemics against 160, 162, 228,
  377–8; by Rashi 239–40, 242, 246, 247
messiah in 138 n. 4, 140 n. 8
midrashic influence on 3–4, 41–2, 48–9, 50,
  55, 86–95
post-biblical rabbinic teachings rejected by
  239, 244
Rashi's Bible commentaries criticized by
  243–5
Torah rejected by 241
violence against Jews 198–9
see also Syriac Christianity
Christian writings, early:
  Apology against Rufinus (Jerome) 67, 80, 81
  Commentary on Amos (Jerome) 68–9, 76–7
  Commentary on Genesis (Ephrem) 87, 92, 93
  Commentary on Habakkuk (Jerome) 72–6
  Commentary on the Minor Prophets (Jerome) 67, 68
  Commentary on Zechariah (Jerome) 66
  Commentary on Zephaniah (Jerome) 70–2
  Demonstrations (Aphrahat) 87
  Dialogue with Trypho (Justin Martyr) 155
  Hebrew Questions on Genesis (Jerome) 57, 66
chronicles, midrashic 5, 161
Church Fathers, Jewish influence on 61–2, 63
circumcision 337
  of Abraham 28–9
  of Alexander 193, 194
classical Midrash 2, 172–4, 177–8, 328
clothing:
  as allegorical representation of moral
    qualities 374–5
  of Esau 308–9
  of high priesthood 57–8
  of Nimrod 305–6, 307–8
Cohen, Gerson D. 198 n. 3
collections of Midrash, *see* anthologies of
  Midrash
Commandments:
  to honour one's parents 46, 48–51, 55,
    178–82
  Midrash on 48, 177–82
  revelation of 13–14, 15 n. 6, 24
  transgressions of 52–3
Community Rule, *see* Qumran
'contest between mountains' story 125,
  126–30

covenants, punishments for violations of
  313–14 n. 139
creation 17
  of Eve 361–7
  hasidism on 453
  kabbalists on 335 n. 67
  Midrash on 17–19, 20, 173–4, 373–4
  Rashi on 243
  sermons on 373–5
Crusades, anti-Jewish violence related to
  198–9, 205
Cuomo, Luisa 218 n. 25, 228

D

Da'at zekenim 274 n. 23, 283–93, 295–6,
  300–1, 301–2, 303, 304–6, 308, 309–10,
  313, 316–17, 318
Dan, Joseph 160, 171 nn. 5 & 7, 434 n. 25, 435
dancing at weddings 451, 453, 454
Danzig, Neil 222
Darkhei ha'agadah (Heinemann) 169
David ben Menahem 408
Day of Judgement 145–6
death:
  resurrection and 382–3
  spiritual salvation and 382
Decalogue, *see* Commandments
defilement, Jesus on 43–4
demons:
  adjuration of 294, 295–6
  belief in 377–8, 387
  see also devil
derash exegesis 250–1, 390
  versus *peshat* 6–7, 249–66
Derashot ufiskei halakhot (Hayim ben Isaac) 318
derush (exposition) hasidic teaching 429, 432,
  433
  literature 435–6, 441–2
description poems 254, 256
Deuteronomy:
  Midrash on 13, 14, 107, 202, 315 n. 141
  Rashi's commentaries on 241
  Tosafist commentaries on 284–5, 287
deuterosis 239
devil:
  names of 72–3
  Samael as 377–9, 387
diachrony 332
dialogue:
  midrashic use of 89, 123–30, 164–5
  poetry 88

diaspora 386–7
dictionaries:
  Arabic 213
  of Hai Gaon 213, 214
  medieval 220
  of Nathan ben Yehiel, see *Arukh*
  of Papias 219–20
Didache, vices listed in 53
Didymus the Blind 64
Dionisotti, Carlotta 218
disciples of Jesus:
  eating without washing hands 44
dispute poems, Syriac 89
diversity, of Midrash 327–8
divine name 36, 38
  Abraham's transmission of 293–4, 295–9
  letters of used to create the world 19, 20–1
  Targumim on 36—7, 38
divine oaths 33, 34, 38
Divrei hayamim shel mosheh 174–6
Dov Ber, Maggid of Mezhirech 430, 439 n. 41

E
Eastern Christianity, midrashic influences on 4
Ecclesiastes 22, 339–40
Ein ya'akov (Ibn Habib) 410, 441
Eisenstein, J. D. 159–60
Elazar ben Killir 108–9, 111–12, 117 n. 46, 118–20, 133–5
Eleazar, Rabbi 18, 19, 20, 21, 22 n. 22, 31–3, 34, 35, 38, 39, 335–6, 382, 383 n. 25
Eleazar ben Shamua 391
Eleazar of Worms 205
An Elegant Composition Concerning Relief After Adversity (Nissim ben Jacob of Kairouan) 181 n. 41
Eliezer, Rabbi 35–6, 37, 50, 268 n. 6, 396 n. 22, 404 nn. 58 & 59
Elifaz 314–15
Elitzur, Shulamit 115 n. 43, 116 n. 44, 121 nn. 56 & 58
Ephraim of Bonn 205
Ephraim ben Samson 295
Ephrem 86, 87, 88, 90, 91, 92–3, 94–5
epics 174–6, 408
epithets (*kinuyim*) 117 n. 49
Esau 242, 305–10, 314, 315–16
eschatology, Jewish 384, 387
esotericism:
  in hasidism 431

Jewish 329, 331, 429
  and Midrash 433–5
Esther Rabbah 75
Ets ḥayim (Hayim Vital) 437
Eve:
  clothing of 307
  creation/re-creation of 361–7
  sin of 119, 123 n. 61
Evreux, tosafist academy at 311, 311 n. 133
exegesis:
  Christian versus Jewish 245–6
  by Jerome 61, 64, 66, 67–8, 69, 76–7, 79–80
  Karaite 288 n. 64
  Maimonides on 393
  methods of 42, 48, 49
  peshat versus *derash* 6—7, 249–66
  of rabbinic aggadah 390–406
  by Rashi 235, 237, 238, 246
  Syriac Christian 83, 88–90, 91, 92–3, 94–5
  tosafist 267–8, 275–83, 294–9, 300–19
  zoharic 328–31, 333–4, 338–43
exegetical uses of Midrash 1, 3, 6, 7, 16–17, 21–4, 95, 432–3
  on Balaam's end 162–3
  on Commandments 48, 177–8
  on Deuteronomy 13, 14, 107, 202
  on Exodus 25, 30–4, 35–6, 37–8, 39, 40, 48, 55, 112–14, 124–6
  on Genesis 17–21, 57–8, 88–9, 91, 173, 226
  and homiletical uses 387
  on messiah/Mourners for Zion 142–53
  on Numbers 162, 164
  on Passover 120–1
  on Psalms 105–6, 124, 166–7
  on red heifer ritual 109–11, 118–20, 134
  on Zechariah 140, 143, 145
Exodus (biblical book):
  Hebrew base text of 29–30, 38
  Midrash on 25, 30–4, 35–6, 37–8, 39, 40, 48, 55, 112–15, 121 n. 58
  Rashi's commentaries on 242, 312, 316
  Targumim on 25, 33, 34–5, 36–7, 38–9
Exodus Rabbah:
  hasidic use of 444–5, 447
  printed editions of 350
  used for sermons 385
Extractiones de Talmud 244–5
Eyn shoyn Mayse-bukh (A Beautiful Book of Stories) 410
Ezra (biblical book) 198

Ezra (biblical figure) 17
Ezra da Fano 223 n. 48

F
'fall of the watchers' 144
fire, God's words emerging from 13, 22
firstborn rights 57–8
Fishbane, Michael 25, 30, 38, 39, 40, 138, 197, 329, 433–4
Fishman, Talya 221, 230
Flusser, David 434
folktales, midrashic use of 180, 183, 224, 229
Foucault, Michel 99
'Fountain of Life', story of Alexander's discovery of 193–4
framework story genre 176–7, 186

G
Gamliel, Rabbi 121
Gedaliah, Judah 351, 354–5, 357 n. 49, 369
Gedaliah, Moses 355
Geertz, Clifford 171
Geiger, Abraham 164 n. 22
gematriyah, Tosafist use of 294, 296 n. 89
gender, kabbalistic interpretations of 334–5
Genesis 17
   Jerome on 57
   Judah and Tamar episode in 94–5
   and Leviticus 180–1
   on man's domination over woman 283–9
   Midrash on 17–21, 57–8, 88–9, 91, 92, 94, 125, 173–4
   Rashi's commentaries on 243, 272 n. 17, 288, 293, 300, 301, 305, 306, 308, 312, 315–16
   Syriac exegesis of 88–90, 91, 92
   Targumim on 28–9
   tosafist exegesis of 278–9, 293–9, 300–12
Genesis Rabbah:
   on Cain's dispute with Abel 89
   commentaries on 270 n. 11, 360, 361–7
   editing of 19, 21
   printed editions of 349, 350
   stories in: on contest of the mountains 125, 127–8; on creation 17–18, 20; on Moriah site 91
   use of: by Nathan ben Yehiel 222, 224–5, 226, 227–8, 229; by Rashi 305; in sermons 373–4, 375, 385; by Tosafists 269–71, 273, 280, 283–4, 285, 288, 289–92, 293, 305, 306–7, 308, 311, 317

Genizah fragments:
   of Midrash 222
   of *Toledot yeshu* 163 n. 18
geonim, influences on Nathan ben Yehiel 217
Germany:
   Jewish martyrs/martyrdom in 198–201, 202–3, 205
   medieval anti-Jewish violence in 198–9, 205, 207–8
Gershom ben Judah 200 n. 7, 216
Gersonides, *see* Ralbag
Gevurot hashem (Maharal, Judah Loew) 403 n. 53
gezerah shavah rule of exegesis 48
Ginzberg, Louis 61–2, 164 n. 22, 217
Gitin cycle stories in Yiddish 416–22
Glossarium ansileubi 219
God:
   anthropomorphic descriptions of 92–3, 398, 399, 419
   controversy with the righteous 145–6
   divine name 30, 33, 39
   human relationship with 225–6
   kabbalist/zoharic conceptions of 330, 340–2
   love of 202
   omnipresence and local presence of 113–14, 115–16, 126
   and people of Israel 241–3, 253, 315
   suffering of 147–8
   see also divine name; Shekhinah
Golden Calf, sin of 24, 446
Gospel of Mark:
   on ritual purity 43–4, 45–7, 51–2, 54
   on vices 52, 53
Gospel of Matthew:
   on honouring one's parents 50–1, 55
   midrashic influences on 48–9, 50
   on ritual purity 43, 44–7, 48, 52, 54
Gospels, as Midrash 42
grammatical languages 228
Graves, Michael 60 n. 10, 62 n. 18, 64–5, 67 n. 41, 68 n. 45, 76 n. 66, 80 n. 84
Greek language:
   Nathan ben Yehiel's knowledge of 228
   oral transmission of Midrash in 65
   see also Hellenization
Grossman, Avraham 216–17 n. 17, 234 n. 3, 240, 242, 243
Guide of the Perplexed (Maimonides) 379, 393, 398 n. 34

H

Habad hasidism, *see* hasidism
Hacker, Joseph 368
Hadar zekenim 283, 297–8, 300, 301, 302, 303, 304–5, 306–9, 309–10, 310–11, 312–13, 314–15, 316, 318
Ḥagigah, in Jerusalem Talmud 19, 20–1
Hai Gaon 213, 214, 216, 218–19
Hamnuna the Elder 339–40
Hananel ben Hushiel of Kairouan 216
Hanina ben Papa 352
Harkavy, Abraham E. 217
hasidism:
  derush literature in 435–6, 441–2
  Midrash in 8–9, 429–33, 436–55
Hasson, Aaron ben Solomon 356
Hayim ben Isaac 318
Hayim ben Makhir 207–8
ḥazanim (cantors):
  as creators of tradition 131–2, 134–5
  midrashic texts sung by 4
  piyutim performed by 103–4, 121, 123
Hebraei, Jerome on 78–9
Hebraica veritas (Jerome) 58, 64 n. 28, 72
Hebrew language 15–16
  grammar of 17
  as holy language 72
  Jerome's knowledge of 58–61, 62 n. 18
  rabbinic 156 n. 37
  reading traditions of biblical Hebrew 61
  vocalization 61
  writing 61
Hebrew Questions on Genesis (Jerome) 57, 66
heh (letter of alphabet), story of creation through 17, 18–19, 20, 243
Heikhalot literature 156
Heinemann, Isaac 169, 170, 250
Hellenization, of Syriac literature 83
hermeneutics:
  and time 325–8
  and walking 333, 334, 335–8
Hexapla (Origen) 59
Hezekiah ben Jacob of Magdeburg 298
Hezekiah ben Manoah 277, 282 n. 47
Ḥidushei agadot (Maharal, Judah Loew) 390, 399 n. 37, 400 nn. 42 & 43, 404–5 nn. 57 & 58
Ḥidushei harim (Isaac Meir Rothenberg) 431

Hirsch, Tsevi 431
historical narratives:
  literary embellishments of 198
  of medieval Jewish martyrdom 202–3, 205–6, 207–8
  see also chronicles
historical propaganda 161, 167
History of Alexander, see *Toledot alexandros*
Hiya 337
Ḥizekuni (Hezekiah ben Manoah) 282 n. 47, 283 n. 48, 293–4, 295, 300 n. 101, 316
holy language, Hebrew as 72
homilies:
  medieval 328
  midrashic 87, 118, 137–8, 141–2, 251, 255–63, 387
  piyutim as 130
  zoharic 329–30
honouring one's parents 46, 48–51, 55, 178–82
Hugh of St Victor 245
humanity, messiah as representative of 151–2
humility, virtue of 128, 130

I

Ibn Ezra, Abraham 242, 262 n. 43, 263 n. 48, 279 n. 33, 288 n. 64, 293 n. 79, 299, 302 n. 104, 313 n. 136
Ibn Habib, Jacob 410, 441
Ibn Shem Tov, Shem Tov 371, 380–4, 387
Ibn Shu'eib, Joshua 284 n. 51, 288 n. 64
Ibn Tibbon, Moses 263–4
Ibn Tibbon, Samuel 372
Ibn Yahya, Gedaliah 215
Idel, Moshe 138 n. 4, 325 n. 18, 435
imitatio Dei 148
impurity 43–4
  and the divine name 295
  of women 123 n. 61
  see also purity
interpretative narrative (Ricoeur) 171 n. 7
intertextuality, of Midrash 432 n. 14, 433
Isaac, Rabbi 338
Isaac ben Abraham, Rabbi (Rizba/Riba of Dampierre) 289–90, 292 n. 74, 311 n. 133
Isaac ben Joseph of Corbeil 318 n. 149
Isaac ben Judah 277, 282 n. 44
Isaac ben Rabbi Shalom 205
Isaac ben Samuel of Dampierre (Ri Hazaken), Rabbi 284–5, 286, 304 n. 112
Isaac of Evreux, Rabbi 311–12

Isaiah:
  in Gospels of Mark and Matthew 46, 47–9, 53
  and messiah 138, 149–50, 166
  Midrash on 140–1, 142–3
  used for sermons 375–6
Isaiah di Trani the Elder (Rid) 230, 262, 275–6, 277 n. 30, 304, 305 n. 112
Isaiah di Trani the Younger 276 n. 26
Ishmael, Rabbi 23, 106, 107, 156, 186, 416 n. 33
Isho'barnun 91
Isho'dad of Merv 91
Isidore of Seville 219
Israel, Land of:
  Alexander reaches 194–5
  burial in 382–3
  centrality of 401–2
  Esau's leaving of 315–16
Israel (people of), and God 241–3, 253, 315
Italian language, in *Arukh* (Nathan ben Yehiel) 218
Italy 219
  study of Midrash in 5–6

J
Jacob ben Meir (Rabbenu Tam) 238, 273 n. 18, 276 n. 26, 302, 303
Jacob ben Nahman 295, 297–8
Jacob of Corbeil 273 n. 18
Jacob of Monteux 297, 298
Jacob of Orléans 273 n. 18, 275, 277
Jacob of Serugh 87, 91, 94
Jacob Joseph of Polonnoye 430
Japhet, Sara 282 n. 47, 283 n. 48, 294, 309 n. 127, 311 n. 130
Jay, Pierre 78 n. 75, 80 n. 81
Jellinek, Adolph 160, 162, 173
Jeremiah (prophet) 22, 402 n. 53, 416 n. 33
Jeremiah, Rabbi 49
Jerome:
  commentaries on Genesis 57
  criticism on 80–1
  exegesis by 61, 64, 66, 67–8, 69, 76–7, 79–80
  Iuxta Hebraeos 79
  knowledge: of Hebrew 58–61, 62 n. 18; of Jewish traditions 61–3, 66
  midrashic influences on 4, 58, 63–80, 79 n. 77, 81
  Prologue of the Commentary on Jeremiah 66

Jerusalem, Alexander's visit to 190–2
Jerusalem Talmud 165
  on Balaam's end 162
  Ḥagigah 19, 20–1
  on honouring one's parents 49–50
  on Passover 121
  on Rabbi Akiva's death 202
Jesus:
  aerial flight of 162
  Midrash on 159–67
  polemics with Pharisees 45, 46, 47–9
  on ritual purity 43, 44–7
Jewish traditions:
  ḥazanim as creators of 131–2, 134–5
  Jerome's knowledge of 61–3, 66
  midrashic 102
  and *piyutim* 103–4, 134
  Scripture as reflection of 99–100, 131
Jonathan, Rabbi 49–50, 352
Jose, Rabbi 37
Joseph (biblical figure):
  dreams of 92
  kidnapping and sale of 186, 187, 277–80
  messiah as son of 151
  and Potiphar's wife 310–12
Joseph ibn Zaddik of Arevalo 215 n. 10
Joseph Isaac, *see* Schneersohn, Joseph Isaac
Josephus, Flavius 176, 190, 191, 201 n. 11
Joshua (biblical book) 197–8
Joshua, Rabbi 22 n. 22, 352, 353
Joshua ben Hananiah 31, 32, 33–4, 37, 38
Joshua ben Levi 382
Joshua of Sikhnin 109, 111
Josippon 161, 191, 199, 200, 400 n. 42
Judah seduced by Tamar, Syriac treatment of 94–5
Judah, Rabbi 333, 334, 362, 383, 421
Judah bar Simon 14, 113 n. 35
Judah ben Eliezer 311 n. 133
Judah Hanasi 107
Judah Hehasid 275, 277, 279, 293, 295–7, 299–300, 303
Judaism:
  political messiah in 138 n. 4
  scriptural foundations of 14
  suffering messiah doctrine in 138–9, 149–53, 155
  see also Rabbinic Judaism
Judgement, Day of 145–6
Julian of Eclanum 80

Justin Martyr 155, 167, 378 n. 15

K

kabbalah/kabbalists 323, 329–32, 431 n. 8
   on God and Torah 339–41
   and hasidism 437–8, 441, 444
   Maharal's use of 399 n. 37, 404 n. 57
   and Midrash 433–5
   see also Zohar
Kahana 252
Kalonymus ben Judah 203–4, 207
Kamesar, Adam 66, 79 n. 77, 80, 87
Kamin, Sarah 237, 245, 249–50
Kara, Joseph 269 n. 9, 270, 276 n. 27, 313 n. 136
Karaites:
   biblical exegesis by 288 n. 64
   Mourners for Zion 153–4
Kasher, M. M. 280 n. 36, 311 n. 133
Katz, Avigdor ben Elijah 317
Katz, Jacob 202, 241–2, 243
Kavanat halimud (Shabbatai of Rashkov) 431 n. 8
Keter shem tov (Ba'al Shem Tov) 430 n. 3
Khurbn habayis be-loshn Ashkenaz (The Destruction of the Temple in Yiddish) 411, 425
Killir, *see* Elazar ben Killir
Kimhi, David (Radak) 167, 272 n. 17, 279 n. 33
kinot (laments) 203–4, 207 n. 29
kinuyim, *see* epithets 117 n. 49
Kitab al-hawi (Hai Gaon) 213, 214
Kohut, Alexander 215 n. 8, 216, 221–2
Kol bo (Shemaryah ben Simhah) 318
korban 50–1

L

Lamentations Rabbah 70, 148, 157, 222–3
   commentaries on 352–4
   Yiddish translations/adaptations of 409, 418, 419–20, 422–4
laments, see *kinot*
Lamirande, Emilien 62–3
langue–parole 104–5, 132
Latin:
   Bible in (Vulgate) 58
   midrashic texts in 4
   Talmud passages in 244
law, Jewish:
   and active martyrdom 199
   revelation of 13–14, 15 n. 6, 24, 74, 105–7

legends, midrashic adaptations of 5
Legends of the Jews (Ginzberg) 61–2
León, Moses ben Shem Tov de 321, 331 n. 45
Levi, Rabbi 30, 39, 167
Levi ben Gershon, *see* Ralbag
Levinas, Emmanuel 332
Leviticus:
   and Genesis 180–1
Leviticus Rabbah 117 n. 48, 222, 226, 227–8, 229
   commentaries on 270 n. 11
lexicography 213
   Jewish 213–14
   medieval non-Jewish 219
Likutei amarim—Tanya (Shneur Zalman of Lyady) 437, 438–40
Likutei halakhot (Sternhartz) 436
Likutei moharan (Nahman of Bratslav) 432, 436
Lilith 362
linguistics/linguistic analysis:
   of biblical texts 15, 17, 132, 133
   langue–parole in 104–5, 132
   of Midrash 132–3
   of *piyutim* 133
   signifier–signified in 132–3
Lipschuetz, Eliezer 234
literal exegesis:
   and anti-Christian polemics 245–6
   Maharal on 404–5 n. 58
   and Zohar/kabbalah 340, 341, 343
   see also *peshat*
literature, Jewish/Hebrew:
   hasidic 435–6, 441–2
   medieval 177, 188
   and Midrash 3, 171–2
   Yiddish 407–10
literature, Syriac 83
liturgy, Jewish 103–4, 120
   Midrash used in 2, 4–5, 8–9
   yearly cycle of 157
Lockshin, Martin 278 n. 31, 313 n. 136
Loew, Judah (Maharal) 8, 390–406, 435
Lubavitcher hasidism, *see* hasidism
Lucifer 378
Luria, Isaac 431 n. 8, 435

M

Ma'aseh yeshu, see *Toledot yeshu*
mahzor (festival prayer-book) 122
   of Yannai 112, 114–17

Index

Maimonides, Moses 379, 393, 398 n. 34
  on *Midrash* 393–4
Mainz, martyrs of 202, 203
Major Trends in Jewish Mysticism (Gershom Scholem) 433
Mandelbaum, Dov (Bernhard) 448 n. 80, 449 n. 83
Mann, Jacob 139 n. 7
manuscripts:
  of *Arukh* (Nathan ben Yehiel) 221–2
  of *Midrash Rabbah* 348
  of Rashi's Bible commentaries 238–9
  of Zohar 324, 354
Margaliot, Reuven 322 n. 5
Margulies, Mordechai 222
Martha (daughter of Boethius), story about 414
Martini, Raymund 163 n. 18, 165–6
martyrs/martyrdom:
  medieval Jewish 198–208
  midrashic stories about 5, 185–8, 199–200, 201
  piyutim alluding to 119–20
  and Shema Yisra'el (prayer) 201–5
  theology of 140 n. 8
Masada, deaths at 199, 200
Matenot kehunah 359, 369, 443
Matsliah, Rabbi 216
Matt, Daniel C. 321 n. 3, 322 n. 5, 331 n. 45
mayse genre 408–10
Megilat setarim (Nissim ben Jacob of Kairouan) 216
Meir, Rabbi 374
Meir of Rothenburg 207
Meir ben Shene'ur 313
Mekhilta derabi shimon bar yoḥai 31, 34
Mekhilta derabi yishma'el 31, 32, 33, 34, 35, 36 n. 28, 37–8, 39, 48, 51, 55, 121
  on revelation of the law at Sinai 105–7
  on trembling of Sinai 124
Melokhim-bukh (Yiddish epic) 408
memory chains, Midrash as 21
memra (verse homily) genre 87
Menahem Mendel (Tsemah Tsedek) 440 n. 47, 442
Menahem Mendel of Kotsk 431
Menahem ben Rabbi Jacob 207 n. 29
Menahem the Scribe 194–5
Me'or einayim (Azariah de' Rossi) 392

Me'or einayim (Menahem Nahum of Tchernobil) 430
merit:
  attributed 151
  of messiah 152
Meroz, Ronit 323–4
meshalim (parables) 224–5
Meshulam ben Kalonymus 216–17, 221, 229
messiah:
  Christian conceptions of 138 n. 4, 140 n. 8
  coming of 153, 166, 381
  Midrash on 138, 139–43, 145, 153
  Simon bar Kokhba as 32
  suffering of 138–9, 149–53, 155
messianism 144
  in hasidism 454
  rabbinic 146, 148, 156–7
metaphors:
  midrashic texts/words of sages as 372–3, 396–7
  in Song of Songs 261
methodologies, exegetical 42, 48, 49
  Christian versus Jewish 245–6
  comparison 404
  peshat versus *derash* 6–7, 249–66
  of Rashi 235, 237, 238, 246
  of Sephardi scholars 361
meturgeman 25, 27
Midrash aseret hadibrot (Midrash of the Ten Commandments) 177, 178–82
Midrash eleh ezkerah, see *Aseret harugei malkhut*
Midrash hagadol 91 n. 34, 92
Midrash Rabbah 165, 348–9
  commentaries on 347–8, 351–70
  copying of annotations to 355–6
  hasidic use/study of 436–7, 442–3, 447, 448, 449
  printed editions of 8, 347, 349–51, 356–7, 360, 369–70, 443
  translations of 407 n. 1
Midrash of Rabbi Isaac 323
Midrash tadshe 173–4
Midrash tanḥuma, see *Tanḥuma*
Midrash tehilim 218
Midrash yelamedenu, see *Yelamedenu*
midrashic influences:
  on Christianity 4, 41–2, 48–9, 50, 55, 86–95
  on Jerome 4, 58, 63–80, 79 n. 77, 81
  on New Testament 3–4, 41–2, 48–9, 50, 55
Minḥat yehudah 286 n. 59, 311–12 n. 133, 318

Mishnah:
    on love of God 202
    on Passover 121
    on purity/impurity 43, 109, 123 n. 61, 226
    on sacrifices 118
    on Targum use in liturgy 27
    on vows 50
modern scholarship:
    on Jewish influences on Church Fathers 61–2
    peshat exegesis applied by 266
Moriah, identification of 90–1
Morteira, Saul Levi 371, 384–7
Moses 385
    altar/Tabernacle built by 37–8, 112–14
    book/Torah of 15, 17
    as high priest 110
    Midrash on 174–6, 444–5
    perfection of 401 n. 50
    and Simeon bar Yohai 338
    suspected adultery of 402 n. 53
    as Teacher of Tradition 100
Moses of Coucy 275
Moses of Evreux 311, 311 n. 133, 313 n. 139
Moses Hadarshan 217, 286, 311 n. 130
Moses ben Nahman (Nahmanides) 299
Moses ben Shene'ur 280
Moses Solomon bar Abraham 301
Moses Zal(t)man 275, 279, 294, 295, 297 n. 92
Moshav zekenim 270 n. 10, 274 n. 21, 277 n. 30, 279 nn. 33 & 34, 285 n. 57, 287 n. 63, 292–3, 304–5 n. 112, 316 n. 145, 317–18 n. 147
mountains:
    contest of 125, 126–30
    quaking of 124–7
'Mountains of Darkness', story of Alexander's crossing of 192–3
Mourners for Zion 140–1 n. 1, 153–5
    Midrash on 137–8, 141, 142–3, 144–5, 147–9, 153
Musafia, Benjamin 215 n. 8
mystic itinerants 334
mysticism, Jewish 263 n. 49, 429
    in hasidism 431, 437–8, 440, 444, 445–6
    Maharal's (Judah Loew) use of 399 n. 37, 406
    and Midrash 7, 328, 433–5, 445–6
    see also kabbalah/kabbalists

N

Nahman of Bratslav 432–3, 436
Nahmanides (Moses ben Nahman) 299
Nakdimon ben Gorion story 416–17
narrative Midrash 87
    medieval 160, 171–2, 174–82
    see also aggadah/aggadic Midrash; historical narratives
narrative poetry, as Midrash 87
Narsai 87, 91
Nathan, Rabbi 128, 129, 163 n. 17
Nathan of Hannover 209
Nathan ben Yehiel 5–6, 184, 214, 215, 449 n. 80
    see also Arukh
Nebuchadnezzar 74–5
Netivot olam (Maharal, Judah Loew) 404–5 n. 58
Netsaḥ yisra'el (Maharal, Judah Loew) 400 n. 42
Neuberg, Simon 425
New Testament:
    apocrypha of 159
    exegesis of 42
    on honouring one's parents 50–1, 55
    midrashic influences on 3–4, 41–2, 48–9, 50
    on Psalms 1 and 2 167
    on ritual purity 43–9, 51–2
Nimrod 305–6, 307–8, 309
Nimukei ḥumash (Isaiah di Trani) 275–6
Ninth of Av 157, 426
    homilies associated with 137–8
    mayses for 409
Nissim ben Jacob of Kairouan 181 n. 41, 216, 221
Noah, age of 289–91, 292
Numbers (biblical book), Midrash on 162, 164

O

oaths, divine 33, 34, 38
    see also vows
Onkelos, *see under* Targum
Or hasekhel (Abraham ben Asher) 360, 361–7, 369
oral transmission:
    combined with written tradition 220–1
    of Midrash 3, 64–5, 77
organic thinking 169
Origen 59, 67
Osaiah Berebi 391
Ot emet (Benveniste) 351, 353–4, 355–6, 369 n. 99

P

Pa'ane'aḥ raza (Isaac ben Judah) 277, 287, 286–7, 296–7
Palestinian Talmud, *see* Jerusalem Talmud
Paltiel, Rabbi Hayim ben Jacob 281, 284–5
Papias 219–20
Pappus, Rabbi 24
parables (*meshalim*) 224–5
'parallelomania' 63 n. 26
parents, commandment to honour 46, 48–51, 55, 178–82
pashteh dikera (simple meaning of the verse) 268
Passover rituals 120–3
patriarchs 121, 152
pedagogic uses:
  of biblical texts 93
  of Midrash 2, 4, 6
  of *piyutim* 118, 121–3, 132, 134
  of Targumim 27
performative Midrash 5, 197, 198
  active martyrdom as 200–1
  Shema Yisra'el (prayer) as 204–5, 209
Perushim ufesakim (Avigdor ben Elijah Katz) 317
Pesakim (Isaiah di Trani the Elder) 230
peshat (plain) exegesis 6–7, 249–50, 251–2, 266
  decline of 263–5, 266
  modern revival of 266
  and Rashi's Bible commentaries 253–4, 258–9, 312
  of Song of Songs 253–4, 255, 257, 260–3, 265
  Tosafist use of 310–11, 317
  zoharic views of 342, 343
Peshitta (Syriac Bible translation) 84, 86
Pesikta derav kahana 113 n. 37, 223, 226, 434
  on Exodus 25, 30–1, 32–3, 37, 38, 39, 40
  hasidic use of 448, 449, 450, 455
  on red heifer ritual 109, 110, 118, 134
Pesikta rabati 137–53, 155, 157, 315
  classification of 156
  dating of 154
  on Ten Commandments 177–8
Pharisees:
  on honouring one's parents 50, 53, 55
  polemics of Jesus with 45, 46, 47–9
Philo 14, 86
Pinhas Hakohen ben Jacob 118, 120–1
Pirkei derabi eli'ezer 156, 157, 306, 376–7, 378

piska (midrashic genre) 137–8
'pit and weasel' story 182–5, 224, 229
piyutim (liturgical poetry) 99
  Ashkenazi 200 n. 7, 205, 206, 207
  and Jewish culture 102–4
  linguistic analysis of 133
  and *memra* 87 n. 21
  Midrash used in 4, 99, 103, 107–8, 111–12, 114–17, 118–23, 126–30, 133–5
  poetic theology, *piyutim* as 104, 119, 127
poetry 330–1
  description poems 254, 256
  liturgical, see *piyutim*
  midrashic 87–8, 254–7, 407–8, 432 n. 14
  by Nathan ben Yehiel 215, 220
  penitential, see *seliḥot*
  Syriac 87–8, 89–90
  Yiddish 407–8
polemics:
  anti-Christian 160, 162, 228, 377–8
  of Jesus and the Pharisees 45, 46, 47–9
  midrashic 160, 167
  of Rashi 239–40, 242, 246, 247
  and romance 160
Poznański, Samuel 282
praise poems 254, 255
prayer books:
  festival (*maḥzorim*) 122
  of Sa'adyah Gaon 130
  of Yannai 112, 114–17
prayers:
  Aleinu 205
  Amidah 103, 104
  cycles of 103
  and *piyutim* 104
  Shema Yisra'el 201–9, 273 n. 18
present, relation with future and past 326, 330
printing:
  of medieval dictionaries 220
  of Midrash anthologies 8, 347, 349–51, 355–7, 360, 369–70, 443
prokope, Nathan ben Yehiel on meaning of 227–8
propaganda, historical 161, 167
prophets:
  false 166
  wisdom of 393
Prostitz, Isaac ben Aaron 356, 357
Proverbs (biblical book) 16–17, 48, 49
  Midrash on 177, 352–4, 357–9, 416 n. 33

Psalms:
   of David 22
   on God's words emerging from fire 13
   Midrash on 105–6, 124, 141, 143, 166–7, 422
   piyutim's allusions to 117
   Rashi's commentaries on 242, 243
Pseudo-Rashi on *Genesis Rabbah* 364 n. 78, 365
puns, multilingual, in Midrash 19
purity:
   moral 43, 52–3
   ritual: Gospels on 43–9, 51–2, 54; and red heifer ritual 109; and uttering divine name 295

Q

Qumran:
   Community Rule document 52–3
   Florilegium 166
   scrolls on Mourners for Zion 154 n. 31
   Targumim found at 27

R

Rabbenu Tam, *see* Jacob ben Meir
Rabbinic Judaism:
   centrality of Torah study in 146, 148
   influence of Mourners for Zion on 157
   shared heritage with Syriac Christianity 84–5
rabbinic Midrash 5–6, 85, 156
   exegesis of 390–406
Rachel (biblical figure) 423–4
Radak, *see* Kimhi, David
Ralbag (Levi ben Gershon) 264–5, 412–13
Rashbam, *see* Samuel ben Meir
Rashi (Solomon Yitzhaki) 6, 163, 183, 185, 217, 229 n. 66, 233
   biblical commentaries 233–6, 237–8, 246, 319; and Christian Bible interpretations 239–40; Christian perceptions of 243–5, 246–7; influences of 236–7, 238, 241–2, 243, 294, 359, 447; as Midrash (rewritten) 236, 238–9, 240–3, 245, 246; and *peshat* Bible exegesis 253–4, 258–9, 312; Tosafist use of 269 n. 9, 272 n. 17, 278 n. 31, 288–9, 299, 300–1, 301–2, 304–7, 308–9, 309–10, 312, 316
   midrashic materials used by 234–5, 270–1, 315–16, 421 n. 38
   repetition, his use of 242–3

Rebecca (biblical figure), age of at marriage 300–5
red heifer ritual 109–11, 112, 118–20, 133–5
redemption:
   in hasidism 437
   suffering as means to 147, 149
repentance, power of 445, 447
Resheph, as name for devil 72–3
resurrection of the dead 382–3
revelation of the law 13–14, 15 n. 6, 24, 74, 105–7
righteous, the 291
   God's controversy with 145–6
   hasidism on 439, 445
   Mourners for Zion as 145
   sins of 152–3
Rigord (French chronicler) 206–7
ritual killing 204, 207, 208
ritual purity:
   and divine name 295
   Gospels on 43–9, 51–2, 54
   and red heifer ritual 109
   see also impurity
rituals:
   active martyrdom as 200
   of Passover 120–3
   red heifer sacrifice 109–11, 112, 118–20, 133–5
Rizba, *see* Isaac ben Abraham, Rabbi
romance:
   and historical propaganda 161
   as Midrash 188–95
   and polemics 160
Rome:
   Jewish community in 215
   Jewish revolts against 31–2
Rosh Hashanah 376
Rossi, Azariah de' 392, 394, 395 n. 19
Rufinus 67, 78 n. 75

S

sacrifices 118
   active martyrdom as 200
   see also red heifer ritual
Safed, curriculum of studies at 367–8, 369
sages:
   meanings of words of 393–406
   non-Jewish 394
   wisdom of 391–2, 396
Samael, as Satan 377–9, 387

Samely, Alexander 25–6
Samuel, Rabbi 20, 21, 123
Samuel Hehasid 303–4
Samuel ben Meir (Rashbam) 230
   Bible exegesis by 250, 259–63, 278
   Rashi's influence on 236–8, 246
   as Tosafist 267, 276 n. 27, 285, 293 n. 79,
     299, 303 n. 105, 308–9, 309 n. 128, 312
     n. 134, 313 n. 136, 317 n. 147
Samuel bar Nahman 50
Samuel bar Rabbi Isaac 451
Samuel ben Shene'ur of Evreux 311, 311
   n. 133
Sanctuary, discourse on 450–1
Satan, *see* devil
Saussure, Ferdinand de 104, 132 n. 79
Schäfer, Peter 138 n. 3, 164 n. 21
Schmelzer, Menahem 135 n. 84
Schneersohn, Joseph Isaac 436–7, 448, 452,
   453
Schneerson, Menachem Mendel 444, 445–6,
   452–4
Scholem, Gershom 138, 321, 324, 325, 328,
   342, 433
Scripture 2, 15–16, 99–100, 131
   allusions to: in Midrash 143, 149–50; in
     piyutim 116–17, 127, 134
   closure of 3, 14–15, 16, 100–1
   and Midrash 2, 16, 21, 26, 85, 169–70,
     173–4, 326–8, 435; in Yiddish translations
     414–15, 422–3
   polyvalency of 85–6
   and Zohar/kabbalah 329, 339–40
   see also translations of Scripture
sects 143
Seder eliyahu rabah 272
Seder olam 300, 302, 303, 304, 304 n. 112
Sefat emet al hatorah (Alter) 430–1, 432, 436,
   446
Sefer bilad 295–6
Sefer hagan 273, 277, 279–80, 288, 290–2, 305
   n. 112, 308–9, 311–12 n. 133, 313, 313–14
   n. 139, 316 n. 145, 318
Sefer hayashar 91, 315 n. 141
Sefer he'arukh, see *Arukh*
Sefer toledot yeshu, see *Toledot yeshu*
Sefer yosipon, see *Josippon*
Sefer zekhirah (Ephraim of Bonn) 205
selihot (penitential poems) 207–8

Sephardi Jews:
   sermons of 380, 384
sermons 371, 387
   'dust of the earth' 385–7
   Jewish experience of exile 386
   midrashic texts used for 5, 8–9, 371–87
   piyutim as 109–12
serpent:
   as devil 73
   Eve seduced by 119
seven (number), power/perfection of 289–90,
   291–2, 453, 454
   'seven-headed dragon' story 398 n. 34
   'woman and seven sons' story 417–20
Shalom Dovber 442
Shalshelet hakabalah (Chain of Tradition;
   Gedaliah ibn Yahya) 215
Shekhinah 91 n. 34, 116, 128, 129
   departure and return of 448–9, 450, 453,
     454
   Zohar on 333–4
Shema Yisra'el (prayer):
   powers engendered by recitation of 273
     n. 18
   recitation by martyrs/at ritual killings 201–9
Shemaryah ben Simhah 318
Shemayah 239
Shimon Hagadol 107–8
Shinan, Avigdor 350
Shmuel-bukh (Yiddish epic) 408
Shneur Zalman of Lyady 431, 437–42
siddurim (prayer books) 130
Sifrei debei rav 116
Sifrei Deuteronomy 13, 14, 107, 116–17, 202,
   241, 300, 302, 303, 441
Simeon/Shimon bar Yohai 243, 335–6, 337
   n. 80, 338, 341
Simlai 164–5, 229
Simon bar Kokhba 31–2
sin/sins:
   atonement for 119
   of Esau 306–7, 308
   of Eve 119, 123 n. 61
   of forefathers 187
   of Golden Calf 24, 446
   of the righteous 152–3
   sexual intercourse as 144
   source of 378
Sinai:
   God's choice of 126, 128–30

Sinai (*cont.*):
    revelation of the law in 13–14, 15 n. 6, 24, 105–7
    trembling of 124–5, 126–7
Soferim 455
Solomon (biblical figure) 22
    and Asmedai tales 398 n. 34, 403 n. 53
    proverbs of 16–17
    Temple of 113, 116
Solomon ben Judah of Dreux 289–90, 292 n. 74, 313 n. 139
Solomon Suleiman al-Sanjari 126–30
Song of the Sea, interpretation of 312
Song of Songs 115–16
    commentaries on 262–3; of Gersonides 264–5; of Ibn Ezra 262 n. 43; of Ibn Tibbon 263–4; of Rashbam 259–62; of Rashi 237, 242, 243, 253–4, 258–9
    Midrash on 146–7, 148 n. 21, 253–7, 258, 260, 263, 264, 265–6
    Zohar on 338–9
Song of Songs Rabbah 13 n. 2, 14, 22 n. 22, 117 n. 48, 255, 256, 257, 449
sorcery, red heifer ritual as 109–10
Soviet Union, hasidism in 447–8, 452
Spain, anti-Jewish violence in 208
spiritual uses of Midrash 432–3, 436–8, 446
spirituality, hasidism on 450–2
Sternhartz, Nathan 436
storytelling, midrashic 5, 171–2
    see also aggadah/aggadic Midrash
Strack, Herman L. 41, 164 n. 22
suffering:
    of God 147–8
    of Israel 153
    of messiah 138–9, 149–53, 155
    of Mourners for Zion 147
Symmachus 61, 80
Syriac Christianity:
    exegesis of 83, 88–90, 91, 92–3, 94–5
    Midrash in 4, 86–95
    shared heritage with Rabbinic Judaism 84–5
Syriac language/dialect 73, 83
    Bible translations in 83–4, 86, 90

T
Ta-Shma, Israel 219, 230 n. 68
Tabernacle 112–13, 116
Tabor, Mt. 127, 128, 129, 130
Tabula Smaragdina 341
Tales of Ben-Sira 176–7

Talmud:
    Christian perceptions of 239 n. 20, 244
    Maharal's (Judah Loew) commentaries on 392–406
    and Midrash 184, 225–6, 412–14, 416–22
    Tosafist orientation on 267, 318–19
    transmission of 221
    see also Babylonian Talmud; Jerusalem Talmud
Tamar, interpretation of by Jacob of Serugh 94–5
Tanḥuma 57–8, 72, 223, 225 n. 56, 243, 256–7, 258, 260, 263, 265, 431, 449
    Yiddish translation of 407 n. 1
Tanya, see Likutei amarim—Tanya
Targum:
    Jonathan 27–8, 61 n. 13, 68, 69, 72
    of Lamentations 157
    Neofiti 28–9, 36, 84
    Onkelos 27–8, 36, 37, 39, 84, 312, 358, 359
    of Psalms 85 n. 7
    Pseudo-Jonathan 28–9, 35, 36, 163
    of Song of Songs 146–7, 148 n. 21
    Yerushalmi 19 n. 18
Targum/Targumim 3, 25–6, 28
    didactic purposes of 27
    God's name in 36–7, 38
    Jerome and 65 n. 29, 68, 69
    midrashic elements in 28–9, 33
    origins of 26–7
    and Syriac tradition 84—5, 88, 89, 91
    Tosafist use of 286–8
Temple:
    aggadot on destruction of 411–27
    God's dwelling in 126
    mourning for loss of 144, 426; *see also* Ninth of Av
    of Solomon 113, 116
temporality:
    in Midrash 325–8
    and walking in the visionary landscape image 331–9
    in Western philosophy 332
    in Zohar 329–31, 332–3
Ten Commandments, *see* Commandments
Ten Tribes, story of confrontation with Alexander 194–5
Tertullian 139
Theodor, Judah 222
Theodore of Mopsuestia 80

theology:
    of martyrdom 140 n. 8
    and Midrash 5
    poetic/oral 104, 119, 127, 132
    of redemption 147
throne, of God 30, 33, 39
thunder, seeing 106
time, *see* temporality
Tishby, Isaiah 321
Toledot alexandros (History of Alexander of Macedon) 188–95
Toledot ya'akov yosef (Jacob Joseph) 430
Toledot yeshu 163–7
    as Midrash 159–62, 167
Torah:
    Christianity's and Islam's rejection of 241
    dangers of teaching to non-Jews 187
    hasidic conceptions of 438–40, 446
    meaning of term 15–16, 374
    study of 146, 148
    Zohar on 340–2
    see also Scripture
Torat mosheh (Alsheikh) 367
Tosafists 7, 183–4, 230, 267
    Bible exegesis by 267–8, 275–83, 293–5, 300–19
    midrashic materials/approaches used by 269–75, 278, 279–81, 283–93, 303, 305–7, 308, 309–310, 311–12, 314–16, 316–19
Tosafot Evreux 311, 311 n. 133
Tosafot hashalem 276–7 n. 28, 287 n. 63, 317 n. 146
Tosefta 202
translations of Midrash:
    Latin 4
    Yiddish 8, 407–27
translations of Scripture:
    Aramaic, *see* Targum/Targumim
    Greek 90
    Latin 58, 79
    Syriac 83–4, 86, 90
translations of Talmud 244
Treatise for the Guidance of Preachers 380–1
tsadik, *see* righteous
Tsemah bar Paltoi Gaon 214 n. 4
Tsene-rene 410 n. 23, 411, 424–7
Twersky, Isadore 230

U
Urbach, E. E. 267, 290 n. 70, 311 n. 133

V
Vayvaser, Moshe 409
Venice:
    Midrash Rabbah editions printed in 350, 351, 355, 369
Vital, Hayim 435, 437
vocalization of Hebrew 61
vows 50
    see also oaths

W
wasf poetic genre 254
    see also description poems
'weasel and pit' story 182–5, 224, 229
weddings:
    blessings at 453–4
    dancing at 451, 453, 454
Weitzman, Michael 83–4
Williams, Megan Hale 64 n. 28, 78 n. 75, 79
wisdom:
    non-Jewish 397 n. 25
    of prophets 393
    of sages 391–2, 396
    Torah as 374
woman:
    creation of 361–7
    desirable conduct for 333–5
    in hasidism 454
    impurity of 123 n. 61
    man's domination over 283–9
'woman and her seven sons' story 417–20

Y
Yafeh, Samuel 359–61, 368–9
Yaffe, Mordechai 416
Yalkut shimoni 163, 366
Yannai 49–50, 112, 114–17, 122, 141, 142, 156 n. 37
Yefeh to'ar (Samuel Yafeh) 360, 368–9
Yehudah ben Elazar 273 n. 18
Yeisa the Elder 337
Yelamedenu 163, 223, 225 n. 56, 227, 263
Yesod (Moses of Narbonne/Hadarshan) 217
Yesod shirim (*Tapuhei zahav*, Berukhim) 322
Yevein metsulah (Nathan of Hannover) 209
Yiddish translations of Midrash 8, 407–10
    aggadot on destruction of the Temple 411–27
    Gitin (cycle stories in Yiddish) 416–22

Yohanan ben Zakkai 109–10, 122, 252, 391,
    403 n. 54, 412, 414
  and Vespasian story 415–16
Yom Kippur 376–7, 379
Yom Tov of Joigny 275, 277
Yose, Rabbi 333–4, 337
Yosi ben Haninah 110, 134, 135, 156 n. 37
Yosi/Yose Hagelili 125, 128 n. 71, 284, 286
    n. 58
Yosipon, see *Josippon*
Yudan Neshiya 17–18, 19, 20

Z
Zadok, Rabbi 414
Zechariah, Midrash on 140, 143, 145, 149, 152
Zephaniah, Midrash on 141
Zfatman, Sara 411, 415 n. 56
Zikhron ḥurban habayit (Memory of the
    Destruction of the Temple) 416
Zohar:
  authorship of 321–3, 324–5
  manuscripts/editions of 324, 354
  midrashic character of 7, 324, 325 n. 21,
    328–9, 337, 338–43
  temporality in 330–1, 332–3
  and walking in the visionary landscape/the
    hermeneutical path 331–2, 335–8
Zohar ḥadash 322
Zunz, Leopold 173 n. 11, 223, 282, 448 n. 80

www.ingramcontent.com/pod-product-compliance
Lightning Source LLC
Chambersburg PA
CBHW052137300426
44115CB00011B/1411